Biological Distance Analysis

Biological Distance Analysis
Forensic and Bioarchaeological Perspectives

Edited by
Marin A. Pilloud
Joseph T. Hefner

ELSEVIER

AMSTERDAM • BOSTON • HEIDELBERG • LONDON • NEW YORK • OXFORD
PARIS • SAN DIEGO • SAN FRANCISCO • SINGAPORE • SYDNEY • TOKYO
Academic Press is an imprint of Elsevier

AP

Academic Press is an imprint of Elsevier
125 London Wall, London EC2Y 5AS, United Kingdom
525 B Street, Suite 1800, San Diego, CA 92101-4495, United States
50 Hampshire Street, 5th Floor, Cambridge, MA 02139, United States
The Boulevard, Langford Lane, Kidlington, Oxford OX5 1GB, United Kingdom

Library of Congress Cataloging-in-Publication Data
A catalog record for this book is available from the Library of Congress

British Library Cataloguing-in-Publication Data
A catalogue record for this book is available from the British Library

ISBN: 978-0-12-801966-5

For information on all Academic Press publications
visit our website at https://www.elsevier.com/

Publisher: Sara Tenney
Acquisition Editor: Elizabeth Brown
Editorial Project Manager: Joslyn Chaiprasert-Paguio
Production Project Manager: Lisa Jones
Designer: Maria Ines Cruz

Typeset by TNQ Books and Journals

Contents

Contributors xvii
Foreword xxi
Preface xxiii
Acknowledgments xxix

SECTION 1 BIODISTANCE DATA, DATASETS, AND ANALYTICAL METHODS

CHAPTER 1 **A Brief History of Biological Distance Analysis** 3
J.T. Hefner, M.A. Pilloud, J.E. Buikstra, C.C.M. Vogelsberg
Introduction 3
Natural Philosophy and Anatomy 4
Craniometric Analysis 4
Nonmetric Trait Analysis 6
Dental Morphology 8
Dental Metrics 9
Changes in Statistical Approaches 10
Scales of Analysis and Kinship 11
Ancient DNA and Biodistance 12
Forensic Anthropology, Race, and Human Variation 12
Conclusions 13
Endnotes 13
References 14

CHAPTER 2 **Biological Distances and Population Genetics in Bioarchaeology** 23
J.H. Relethford
Introduction 23
Euclidean Distance 24
Mahalanobis's Distance 25
R-Matrix Theory and Biological Distance 25
R-Matrix Theory and Quantitative Traits 26
Assessing the Impact of Genetic Drift 29
Examining Differential Long-Range Gene Flow 29
Closing Thoughts 30
References 31

CHAPTER 3 **Craniometric Data Analysis and Estimation of Biodistance** 35
B. Dudzik, A. Kolatorowicz
History of Craniometric Data Collection and Analysis 36
Data Collection Protocols 37
Types of Measurements 37
Selecting Measurements 40
Instrumentation 41
Options for Recording Measurements 46
Error in Craniometry 46
Procedures 48
Heritability 49
Bioarchaeological and Forensic Approaches to Craniometric Data 52
Common Statistical Methods in Forensic Anthropology and Bioarchaeology 53
Conclusions 55
References 55

CHAPTER 4 **Advanced Methods in 3-D Craniofacial Morphological Analysis** 61
P. Urbanová, A.H. Ross
Introduction 61
Reference Data Sets on Craniofacial Variation 65
Computer-Aided Landmark Processing for Sex and Ancestry Assessment 66
Material 68
3D-ID Database 68
European Data Sets 69
Brazilian Data Sets 71
Methods 72
Results 72
Validation of 3D-ID Database on European Samples 74
The Forensic 3-D Database—European Data Sets 76
Morphological Variation Among Brazilian Groups 76
Morphological Affinity of Brazilian Groups to 3D-ID Data Sets 79
European Brazilians and Iberian Populations 79
Japanese Brazilians, Asians, Mesoamericans, and South Americans 80
African Brazilians, African Americans, and Native Africans 80
Discussion 81
Conclusion 85
References 86

CHAPTER 5 **Cranial Nonmetric and Morphoscopic Data Sets** 91
C.M. Pink, C. Maier, M.A. Pilloud, J.T. Hefner
Introduction 91
Nomenclature 92
Cranial Nonmetric Data Sets 93
Data Collection Protocols 94
Heritability and Cranial Nonmetric Traits 95
Morphoscopic Data 97
Data Collection Protocols 97
Heritability of Morphoscopic Traits 98
Measures of Biological Distance 98
Bioarchaeology 99
Forensic Anthropology 101
Conclusions 102
References 102

CHAPTER 6 **Dental Morphology in Biodistance Analysis** 109
M.A. Pilloud, H.J.H. Edgar, R. George, G.R. Scott
Dental Morphology 111
Dental Terminology 111
Heritability 113
Dental Development 114
Threshold Traits 115
Data Collection and Treatment 116
Population Variation 118
Sinodont/Sundadont 118
Afridont 119
Eurodont 120
Forensic Application 120
Bioarchaeological Application 122
Intracemetery 123
Population Level 123
Evolution and Dental Morphology 123
Hominins 124
Anatomically Modern Humans 124
Conclusions 125
Endnotes 125
References 126

CHAPTER 7 **Dental Metrics in Biodistance Analysis** 135
M.A. Pilloud, M.W. Kenyhercz
Dental Development 136
Dental Metrics: The Data 136
Mesiodistal Diameter 137
Buccolingual Diameter 137
Crown Height 137
Alternative Measurements 139
Heritability 140
Biological Considerations 141
Sex 141
Age 142
Biological Stress 143
Statistical Analysis 143
Observer Error 143
Sexual Dimorphism 144
Methods to Negate Multicollinearity 144
Population Variation and Evolution 146
Forensic Applications 147
Bioarchaeological Applications 148
Conclusions 149
Endnote 149
References 149

CHAPTER 8 **Do Biological Distances Reflect Genetic Distances? A Comparison of Craniometric and Genetic Distances at Local and Global Scales** 157
H.F. Smith, B.I. Hulsey, F.L. (Pack) West, G.S. Cabana
Background 158
Methods 161
Samples 161
Data Collection: Morphological 161
Data Collection: Genetic 165
Analytical Methods 167
Results 169
Local Interindividual Analyses: Norris Farms #36 Individuals 169
Discussion 173
Acknowledgments 176
References 176

CHAPTER 9 **Missing Data Imputation Methods and Their Performance With Biodistance Analyses** 181
M.W. Kenyhercz, N.V. Passalacqua
Materials 182
Methods 183
Imputation Methods 183
Results 186
Missing Data at 25% 186
Missing Data at 50% 189
Discussion 192
Conclusions 193
Acknowledgments 194
References 194

SECTION 2 BIODISTANCE IN A FORENSIC SETTING

CHAPTER 10 **Forensic Classification and Biodistance in the 21st Century: The Rise of Learning Machines** 197
S.D. Ousley
Introduction 197
Estimating Classification Accuracy 198
Overfitting 199
Finding the Best Measurements 200
Other Traditional Classification Methods 201
Resampling 202
Machine Learning 204
Materials and Methods 206
Results and Discussion 206
Summary 210
Acknowledgments 211
References 211

CHAPTER 11 **Forensic Ancestry Assessment Using Cranial Nonmetric Traits Traditionally Applied to Biological Distance Studies** 213
C.M. Pink
Introduction 213
Materials and Methods 215
Variable Selection 215
Statistical Models 215
Machine Learning 215

Decision Tree ... 218
Random Forest ... 218
Support Vector Machines ... 219
Results ... 219
Discussion ... 221
SVM Models ... 223
The Nature of Phenotypic Variation in Cranial Nonmetric Traits ... 223
Biological Distance and Cranial Nonmetric Trait Data ... 225
Conclusions ... 226
Acknowledgments ... 226
References ... 226

CHAPTER 12 **Biological Distance, Migrants, and Reference Group Selection in Forensic Anthropology** ... 231
K. Spradley
Background ... 233
Materials and Methods ... 234
Population Groups ... 234
Analyses ... 236
Results ... 236
Discussion ... 241
References ... 243

CHAPTER 13 **The Craniometric Implications of a Complex Population History in South Africa** ... 245
K.E. Stull, M.W. Kenyhercz, M.L. Tise, E.N. L'Abbé, P. Tuamsuk
Introduction ... 245
Population History of South Africa ... 246
Genetic Composition of Modern South African Populations ... 248
Materials ... 248
Methods ... 251
Results ... 252
All Groups Pooled Sexes ... 252
Females ... 253
Males ... 253
Discussion and Conclusions ... 255
Acknowledgments ... 260
References ... 260

CHAPTER 14 **Complexity of Assessing Migrant Death Place of Origin** ... 265
A.H. Ross, C.A. Juarez, P. Urbanová
The Unidentified Decedents in the United States ... 266
Demographic Profiles of the Foreign-Born Latinos ... 266
Deceased Undocumented Latinos in the United States ... 267
Medical Examiner and Coroner's Offices' Casework Issues ... 268
Arizona Unidentified Decedents Versus North Carolina Unidentified Decedents ... 268
Sample ... 269
Methods ... 269
Geometric Morphometrics ... 269
Results ... 271
The Two-Pronged Approach to Provenance: Geometric Morphometrics and Isotopes ... 274
A Case Example Using the Two-Pronged Approach ... 275
Isotope Methods ... 277
Results ... 277
Conclusion ... 279
References ... 279

CHAPTER 15 **Estimating Ancestry of Fragmentary Remains Via Multiple Classifier Systems: A Study of the Mississippi State Asylum Skeletal Assemblage** ... 285
N.P. Herrmann, A. Plemons, E.F. Harris
Introduction ... 285
Mississippi State Asylum History ... 286
Materials and Methods ... 287
Reference Datasets ... 287
Data Collection and Analysis ... 288
Results ... 289
Discussion ... 297
Conclusions ... 297
References ... 298

CHAPTER 16 **Biological Distance Analysis, Cranial Morphoscopic Traits, and Ancestry Assessment in Forensic Anthropology** ... 301
J.T. Hefner
Introduction ... 301
Materials and Methods ... 302
Sample Descriptions ... 303
Canonical Analysis of the Principal Coordinates ... 304
Results ... 306

Discussion.......313
Acknowledgments.......314
References.......314

CHAPTER 17 **Dominance in Dental Morphological Traits: Implications for Biological Distance Studies**.......317
H.J.H. Edgar, S.D. Ousley
Background.......318
Developmental Influences on Dental Morphology.......319
Genes Influencing Dental Morphology.......319
Quantitative Analyses of Genetic Effects.......320
Statistical Issues.......321
Materials.......322
Methods.......323
Results.......324
Discussion.......326
Conclusions.......329
Acknowledgments.......329
References.......329

SECTION 3 BIODISTANCE AND POPULATION STUDIES

CHAPTER 18 **Postmarital Residence Analysis**.......335
L.W. Konigsberg, S.R. Frankenberg
Introduction.......335
The Assessment of Quantitative Trait Phenotypic Variability in Males and in Females.......337
Analysis of Postmarital Residence in Prehistoric West Central Illinois.......338
Analyzing Male and Female Within-Site Haplotypic Diversity.......338
Analyzing Male and Female Within-Site Phenotypic Diversity for Dichotomous Traits.......339
Discussion.......344
References.......345

CHAPTER 19 **Population Structure During the Collapse of the Moche (AD 200–850): A Comparison of Results Derived From Deciduous and Permanent Tooth Trait Data From San José de Moro, Jequetepeque Valley, Perú**.......349
R.C. Sutter, T. Chhatiawala
Introduction.......349
Background.......351

Materials and Methods 352
Biodistance and Population Structure Analyses 353
Results 356
Biodistances and Population Structure 356
Discussion and Conclusions 358
References 359

CHAPTER 20 **Alternate Methods to Assess Phenetic Affinities and Genetic Structure Among Seven South African "Bantu" Groups Based on Dental Nonmetric Data** 363
J.D. Irish
Materials 364
A Brief History 365
Samples and Context 365
Methods 366
Dental Trait Recording 366
Model-Free Quantitative Analyses 367
Model-Bound Quantitative Analyses 368
Population Hypotheses/Expectations 370
Results 370
Model-Free Quantitative Analyses 374
Model-Bound Quantitative Analyses 375
Discussion 379
Summary and Conclusions 385
Acknowledgments 386
References 386

CHAPTER 21 **Crossroads of the Old World: Dental Morphological Data and the Evidence for a Eurasian Cline** 391
K. Heim, C. Maier, M.A. Pilloud, G.R. Scott
Materials 392
Methods 393
Results 396
Discussion 399
Conclusions 407
Acknowledgments 407
Endnote 407
References 407

CHAPTER 22 **A Baffling Convergence: Tooth Crown and Root Traits in Europe and New Guinea** ... 411
G.R. Scott, R. Schomberg
Introduction ... 411
A Closer Look at the Baffling Convergence ... 412
Traits ... 412
Methods ... 412
Results ... 415
Analysis of Variance ... 415
Correspondence Between Distance Values ... 416
Distance Values ... 417
Dendrograms ... 417
Discussion ... 421
Conclusions ... 422
Acknowledgments ... 423
Endnote ... 423
References ... 423

CHAPTER 23 **Population Biodistance in Global Perspective: Assessing the Influence of Population History and Environmental Effects on Patterns of Craniomandibular Variation** ... 425
N. von Cramon-Taubadel
Introduction ... 425
Case Study 1: Do Global Patterns of Cranial Shape Variation Conform to the Predictions of a Neutral Model of Microevolutionary Expectation? ... 428
Materials ... 429
Methods ... 429
Results ... 432
Discussion ... 435
Case Study 2: To What Extent Can Global Patterns of Craniomandibular Variation Be Explained by Variation in Subsistence Strategy? ... 436
Materials ... 437
Methods ... 437
Results ... 437
Discussion ... 440
Conclusions ... 441
References ... 442

CHAPTER 24 **A Biodistance Analysis of Mandibles From Taiwan, Asia, and the Pacific: A Search for Polynesian Origins** ... 447
M. Pietrusewsky, A. Lauer, C.-H. Tsang, K.-T. Li, M.T. Douglas
Introduction ... 447
Biological Distance Studies ... 448
Material and Methods ... 449
The Nankuanli East (南關里東) Site: Early Neolithic ... 449
Shihsanhang Site, Northwestern Taiwan: Iron Age ... 449
Comparative Skeletal Assemblages ... 449
Mandible Measurements and Multivariate Statistics ... 449
Results ... 453
Stepwise Discriminant Function Analysis ... 453
Mahalanobis' Generalized Distance ... 454
Discussion ... 456
Conclusions ... 458
Acknowledgments ... 459
Endnotes ... 459
References ... 459

CHAPTER 25 **The Biocultural Evolution in the Osmore Valley: Morphological Dental Traits in Pre-Inca Populations** ... 463
A. Cucina, C. Arganini, A. Coppa, F. Candilio
Introduction ... 463
Materials and Methods ... 464
Results ... 466
Discussion ... 473
Acknowledgments ... 475
References ... 475

Appendix: Biodistance Resources 479
Index 483

Contributors

C. Arganini
Council for Agricultural Research and Economics, Research Center on Food and Nutrition (CRA-NUT), Rome, Italy

J.E. Buikstra
Arizona State University, Tempe, AZ, United States

G.S. Cabana
University of Tennessee, Knoxville, TN, United States

F. Candilio
"Sapienza" University of Rome, Rome, Italy; University of Pennsylvania Museum of Archaeology and Anthropology, Philadelphia, PA, United States

T. Chhatiawala
Indiana University-Purdue University Fort Wayne, Fort Wayne, IN, United States

A. Coppa
"Sapienza" University of Rome, Rome, Italy; MNHN, Paris, France

A. Cucina
Universidad Autónoma de Yucatán, Mérida, Yucatán, Mexico; UC-MEXUS, University of California Riverside, Riverside, CA, United States

M.T. Douglas
University of Hawaii at Manoa, Honolulu, HI, United States

B. Dudzik
Lincoln Memorial University, Harrogate, TN, United States

H.J.H. Edgar
University of New Mexico, Albuquerque, NM, United States

S.R. Frankenberg
University of Illinois at Urbana-Champaign, Urbana, IL, United States

R. George
University of Nevada, Reno, Reno, NV, United States

E.F. Harris
The University of Tennessee Health Science Center, Memphis, TN, United States

J.T. Hefner
Michigan State University, East Lansing, MI, United States

K. Heim
University of Nevada, Reno, Reno, NV, United States

N.P. Herrmann
Texas State University, San Marcos, TX, United States

B.I. Hulsey
University of Tennessee, Knoxville, TN, United States

J.D. Irish
Liverpool John Moores University, Liverpool, United Kingdom

C.A. Juarez
North Carolina State University, Raleigh, NC, United States

M.W. Kenyhercz
University of Tennessee, Knoxville, TN, United States; University of Pretoria, Pretoria, South Africa

A. Kolatorowicz
Lincoln Memorial University, Harrogate, TN, United States

L.W. Konigsberg
University of Illinois at Urbana-Champaign, Urbana, IL, United States

E.N. L'Abbé
University of Pretoria, Pretoria, South Africa

A. Lauer
International Archaeological Research Institute, Inc., Honolulu, HI, United States

K.-T. Li
Academia Sinica, Taipei, Taiwan, Republic of China

C. Maier
University of Nevada, Reno, Reno, NV, United States

S.D. Ousley
Mercyhurst University, Erie, PA, United States

N.V. Passalacqua
Western Carolina University, Cullowhee, NC, United States

M. Pietrusewsky
University of Hawaii at Manoa, Honolulu, HI, United States

M.A. Pilloud
University of Nevada, Reno, Reno, NV, United States

C.M. Pink
Metropolitan State University of Denver, Denver, CO, United States

A. Plemons
Mississippi State University, Mississippi State, MS, United States

J.H. Relethford
State University of New York College at Oneonta, Oneonta, NY, United States

A.H. Ross
North Carolina State University, Raleigh, NC, United States

R. Schomberg
University of Nevada, Reno, Reno, NV, United States

G.R. Scott
University of Nevada, Reno, Reno, NV, United States

H.F. Smith
Midwestern University, Glendale, AZ, United States; Arizona State University, Tempe, AZ, United States

K. Spradley
Texas State University, San Marcos, TX, United States

K.E. Stull
University of Nevada, Reno, Reno, NV, United States; University of Pretoria, Pretoria, South Africa

R.C. Sutter
Indiana University-Purdue University Fort Wayne, Fort Wayne, IN, United States

M.L. Tise
History Flight, Inc., Marathon, FL, United States

C.-H. Tsang
Academia Sinica, Taipei, Taiwan, Republic of China

P. Tuamsuk
Khon Kaen University, Khon Kaen, Thailand

P. Urbanová
Masaryk University Brno, Brno, Czech Republic

C.C.M. Vogelsberg
Michigan State University, East Lansing, MI, United States

N. von Cramon-Taubadel
University at Buffalo, Buffalo, NY, United States

F.L. (Pack) West
University of Tennessee, Knoxville, TN, United States

Foreword

Historically, and to the present day, one of the core questions anthropologists have asked about people inhabiting the planet, today and for all time, is *Who is related to whom?* Often this question pertains to relatedness between two individuals, but given their general focus on populations, biological anthropologists are more often interested in how a specific population or society relates to another population or society in both spatial and temporal contexts. The topic is an especially prominent one for biological anthropologists interested in addressing questions about relatedness, both among the living and the dead. As this book and all of its contributors make so clear, human remains—bones and teeth—provide a rich source for documenting biological variation via the powerful analytical tools offered by multivariate statistics.

Biodistance research, as defined and presented in this book, addresses mostly phenotypic (morphological) variation in the cranium and dentition. The study of phenotypic variation has deep historical roots, but much of this history has focused on developing typologies, which ignored underlying causes of variation and evolutionary context. Biodistance research has dramatically changed owing to widespread understanding of the biology of hard tissues; increased sophistication of analytical methods for the study of complex processes and factors that influence variation in bones and teeth; and the increasing appreciation for cultural, behavioral, and environmental context. These attributes provide a base for the development of powerful approaches to study biodistance at a number of levels, from continents containing numerous populations, to regional settings with fewer populations, and to local settings that focus on intrapopulation variation.

Biodistance research as it pertains to past populations is motivated by three key themes, including (1) investigating evolutionary history, (2) developing an understanding of archaeological and biohistorical issues dealing with biological and cultural transformations and the degree to which these transformations are influenced by external or internal circumstances, and (3) assessing biodistance in relation to population structure and its influence on health and nutrition (Buikstra, 1990). As a bioarchaeologist, I am most familiar with key issues relating to past populations. However, this book will appeal to anyone interested in population history, past and present. It successfully provides a comprehensive overview with chapters written by leading figures in biodistance analysis. These authorities address various fundamental issues surrounding biodistance analysis, including archaeological context; interpretative frameworks informed by the archaeological record and population history; and appropriate statistical tools developed by anthropological statisticians who are well informed about context, theory, and method. Most importantly, however, the book reminds us that bioarchaeologists and forensic anthropologists are asking many of the same kinds of questions for understanding biological relatedness. Now is the time for the two fields to recognize common interests in developing future approaches to this study.

In the opening chapter to the book, Hefner, Pilloud, Buikstra, and Vogelsberg make clear that bioarchaeology and forensic anthropology are complementary, especially in regard to understanding ancestry, analytical methods, and pressing questions and hypotheses to be addressed. Indeed, both fields inform the other—it is through the living and recently living that we begin to understand the biology underlying the variation we see in past populations. Moreover, practitioners in both fields start with individuals, and collections of individuals, in order to develop the composite picture of variation. Namely, they focus on individuals in data collection, analyze the data using common statistical methods, understand potential limitations of data sets comprised of multiple individuals, and develop larger conclusions about relatedness of the populations from which these individuals are drawn. Underscoring both disciplines is the focus on understanding human variation, the central tenet of biological anthropology in general. The chapters provide the reader with a wonderful overview of the latest developments in methods and analysis, including a range of applications of new statistical tools, new methods, and fundamental case studies drawn from both forensic and bioarchaeological contexts. For example, the analysis of three-dimensional data is an emerging trend that has considerable potential for transforming the manner in which anthropologists collect data. Calipers will always be useful, and the tool of choice for many. But, three-dimensional data collection for documenting and interpreting complex morphology—such as in a human skull—is rapidly becoming part of the biodistance tool kit. Urbanová and Ross provide an impressive overview of ways in which these data are transforming our ability to understand diversity that is both statistically and biologically sophisticated.

The book is a required and much-needed source for illustrating the diverse range of methods and circumstances employed by bioarchaeologists and forensic anthropologists in understanding the biology of bones and teeth, characterizing variation, and analyzing population relationships. The insights gained from the discussions in this book are sure to provide a platform for future researchers and to inspire others to undertake similar kinds of studies. The following pages motivate us to continue to develop models and approaches for understanding the richness of human population history.

Clark Spencer Larsen

REFERENCE

Buikstra, J.E., 1990. Skeletal biological distance studies in American physical anthropology: recent trends. American Journal of Physical Anthropology 82, 1–7.

Preface

There has been an explosion in the development of methodological approaches for analyzing skeletal data that began as early as the late 1800s and continues well into the present. Human variation is the common thread these methodologies share. The historical development of biodistance analysis has roots in the research paradigm of Franz Boas, which focused on human variation, quantitative analysis, and empirical research. His approach, fortified in many ways through the efforts of Aleš Hrdlička, established the importance of human variation in biological anthropology and the necessity of quantification in the study of that variation. Certainly many scholars throughout the 20th century focused on skeletal variation within and between groups, for both modern populations and archaeological samples (eg, Earnest Hooton, T. Dale Stewart, Jane Buikstra, Lyle Konigsberg, John Relethford). Over time these studies incorporated a significant statistical component, thereby laying the bedrock for the quantification of biological relationships within the framework of biological distance, or biodistance, analysis.

In the 21st century, the popularity of biodistance studies continues to grow. The sheer volume of manuscripts, theses, and dissertations making use of these analytical methods attest to their growing popularity. Despite the rise in ancient DNA studies, biodistance analysis remains a popular (although at times misunderstood) analytical tool, in large part because the approach can be used to calculate biological/genetic relationships using data readily available (and often singularly of interest) to biological anthropologists.

Additionally, the dramatic rise in the number of statistical programs and methods, coupled with the meteoritic rise of computing power available to researchers, changed the manner in which biodistance studies were conducted. The analytical complexity of research foci resulting from these factors, coupled to new genetic models to explain the relationship between individuals or groups, provides an exciting and seemingly endless number of diagnostic options. In our own research programs focusing on population variation, we recognized that a comprehensive volume dedicated to the study of biodistance was missing. This volume represents our attempt to fill that gap in the literature by exploring advances in statistical methods and analytical techniques, providing the necessary historical context through which the development of biodistance analysis passed, and outlining skeletal datasets predominately used by biological anthropologists.

We realized in developing this volume it would be critical to include (and in a sense juxtapose) both bioarchaeological and forensic approaches to biodistance analysis. Although these two areas of research are often presented as diametrically opposed sides of the same coin, in reality they are not only similar, but quite complementary, sharing parallel research questions, methodological approaches, as well as analogous methods of statistical analysis. We cannot understand the individual (the primary subject in forensic anthropology) without understanding the population (the primary subject in bioarchaeology), and vice versa.

In compiling this volume, we sought experts who are currently employing biodistance techniques from both of these fields to present their novel research in a compendium readily accessible to graduate students, researchers, and professionals (not necessarily mutually exclusive groups). We initially asked many of the contributors to this volume to participate in a symposium presented at the 84th annual meeting of the American Association of Physical Anthropologists in St. Louis, Missouri in 2015. That symposium and subsequent discussions concerning the proceedings proved an invaluable source of feedback from the many attendees, jurors, and participants. This volume is the result of that feedback and those worthwhile discussions.

As this volume developed, it naturally divided into three sections. The first section provides the historical context of biodistance analysis, while also addressing datasets and analytical methods used by bioarchaeologists and forensic anthropologists. The second section explores forensic anthropological applications and case studies utilizing traditional and novel methodological approaches to the identification questions so inherent in forensic research. The final section presents population-level analyses and methodological approaches from a predominantly bioarchaeological perspective. We conclude with an appendix compiling some of the more referenced statistical programs and biological anthropological datasets used in biodistance analyses. While not exhaustive, we hope that many of those interested in the study of biodistance will find it useful for their own research.

BIODISTANCE DATA, DATASETS, AND ANALYTICAL METHODS

To place the current state of biodistance analysis in proper context, we open this volume with an exploration into the history of biodistance study (Chapter 1). While likely well known to many scholars in anthropology, our intent in (re)producing an historical perspective is to provide the present state of biodistance analysis a context so intimately enmeshed with the development of statistical methods and datasets that they cannot be easily separated.

After setting the historical background for biodistance analysis, several chapters are dedicated to describing datasets commonly used in biodistance studies. Chapters 2 through 7 comprise works on heritability, data collection techniques, protocols and procedures, biological considerations, and statistical applications. Dudzik and Kolatorowicz (Chapter 3) outline craniometric analysis and datasets, exploring issues that may arise during data collection. The following chapter (4, by Urbanová and Ross) outlines recent advances in craniometric studies that now include three-dimensional landmark data and geometric morphometric analytical techniques. Chapter 5 (Pink and colleagues) explores nonmetric and morphoscopic datasets, traditional analytical options, and differences between these data types.

Chapters 6 and 7 focus exclusively on dental data. In Chapter 6, Pilloud and colleagues describe dental morphology in deciduous and permanent dentition to document how those data can be used in forensic and bioarchaeological analyses. This chapter highlights dental variation among anatomically modern humans, but also reflects on the evolution of these traits. Chapter 7 (Pilloud and Kenyhercz) details dental metric analysis and includes comprehensive discussions on data collection methods and statistical treatment. The authors also highlight various effects on tooth size from factors like the genome, sex, age, biological stress, and development.

The remaining chapters in this section address fundamental concepts to the study of biodistance. Relethford (Chapter 2) explores the application of population genetics within biodistance studies (particularly bioarchaeology), focusing significantly on the use of the R matrix with skeletal data. Smith and colleagues (Chapter 8) explore the similarities and differences between genetic distances and the phenotype (in this case, craniometric data). Finally, Kenyhercz and Passalacqua (Chapter 9) discuss the issue of missing data and provide several novel solutions for missing data imputation.

BIODISTANCE IN A FORENSIC SETTING

This section is a compilation of studies confronting the issue of biological distance in a forensic setting, focusing specifically on forensic anthropological analyses. These chapters vary in scope, but all address fundamental issues surrounding the use of biodistance studies in forensic anthropology with a focus on estimating ancestry. Forensic anthropology has moved well beyond the typological views of the past; gone are the days of estimating race using typological trait lists and antiquated terms like Mongoloid, Caucasoid, and Negroid. Forensic anthropologists now exercise a more nuanced view of population histories to inform their estimations of ancestry. The field recognizes population variation as a product of evolutionary forces, while acknowledging the nonzero correlation between biology, skeletal morphology, and geographic origin.

Several chapters address ancestry estimations involving Hispanic populations. This term can be ambiguous since it largely refers to a group aligned only by language; disparate groups are the norm, not the exception. Spradley (Chapter 12) and Ross, Juarez, and Urbanová (Chapter 14) address issues concerning ancestry estimation of groups traditionally placed under the umbrella-term Hispanic. In addition, Edgar and Ousley (Chapter 17) explore the issue of dental trait dominance with a focus on Hispanic populations to investigate the difficulties encountered when discriminating between various Hispanic groups using dental morphology. The authors compare genetic and dental data and determine that dominance in certain dental morphological traits may explain discrepancies between the datasets.

In Chapter 14, Stull and colleagues summarize the complex population history of South Africa and discuss how that history influences and informs estimations of ancestry in that region. Herrmann, Plemons, and Harris (Chapter 15) embark on ancestry estimation for a fragmentary historic cemetery sample using multiple analytical methods and employ novel approaches and impressive graphics in their analysis to provide a convincing argument for their assessments.

The remaining chapters in this section address methodological issues. Ousley (Chapter 10) explores classification statistics, eloquently explaining methods ranging from Fisher's linear discriminant analysis to state-of-the-art machine learning methods. Pink (Chapter 11) and Hefner (Chapter 16) explore cranial morphology and the forensic assessment of ancestry. Pink tests whether traditional cranial nonmetric trait data can be used to accurately estimate an individual's population affiliation, while Hefner utilizes cranial macromorphoscopic traits to explore population relatedness, individual classifications, and biological distance.

BIODISTANCE AND POPULATION STUDIES

In the final section of this volume, biodistance studies at the population level, most generally in a bioarchaeological framework, are explored. This research highlights various methodological approaches and their use with different data types. These studies present novel and traditional methods and explore archaeological and methodological issues.

The section begins with a look at postmarital residence patterns using cranial nonmetric traits (Chapter 18, Konigsberg and Frankenberg). These data are compared to genetic data to identify postmarital residence shifts in connection to maize agriculture in West Central Illinois. The authors also highlight fundamental issues in the study of sex-based skeletal differences to explore residence patterns.

Several chapters in this section address the use of dental morphology to answer anthropological questions. Irish (Chapter 20) explores group affiliation in the Raymond ADart collection applying the mean measure of divergence and Mahalanobis D^2 to dental morphological data. Heim et al. (Chapter 21) postulate the existence of a dental morphological cline throughout Eurasia with a focus on Central Asia. Data are explored through time to identify the origins of this cline. Scott and Schomberg (Chapter 22) investigate dental morphology in a large global sample to address similarities in New Guinea and European populations. Finally, Sutter and Chhatiawala (Chapter 19) and Cucina et al. (Chapter 25) explore archaeological questions in Perú. Sutter and Chhatiawala focus on population structure in San José de Moro, Jequetepeque Valley. Of particular interest is their use of deciduous teeth to test hypotheses. Cucina et al. then use permanent dentition to study population dynamics in the pre-Inca Osmore Valley.

Two chapters in this section utilize metric data. Pietrusewsky and colleagues (Chapter 24) apply biodistance statistics to mandibular measurements in an effort to study the population history of Taiwan and the origin of Polynesians. They use a temporal series to identify movement throughout the region. In Chapter 23, von Cramon-Taubadel compares craniometric and mandibular geometric morphometric data to assess how evolutionary forces relate to climate and diet in shaping global variation in the cranium and mandible. This study represents a comprehensive survey of the factors shaping population variation using innovative methods.

FINAL THOUGHTS

The primary purpose of this volume is to highlight the complexity involved in biodistance analysis, whether at the individual or population level, while also providing analytical and methodological options to researchers. There is no short, easy, or simple solution to the calculation of a biological distance—many concerns should be considered before an analysis can begin. The skeleton is a dynamic tissue affected by multiple factors throughout life. Consideration must be given to the influence of stress, age, activity levels, diet, and disease, and when possible controlled. Other factors relating to heredity, epigenetics, and development, which can also alter the skeletal data used in biodistance analysis, require careful consideration at the outset. Finally, researchers must be aware of the population histories and evolutionary forces responsible for shaping modern human variation.

Forensic anthropologists will continue to explore evolutionary and biological relationships, particularly as they relate to modern population variability. Understanding the mechanisms behind human variation is critical when interpreting or using that variation to estimate ancestry in a forensic setting. Advances in biodistance studies can vastly improve ancestry assessment methodologies, while refining their accuracy, reifying their application, and justifying their use in court with theoretical underpinnings and known error rates.

Bioarchaeologists will continue to advance and improve biodistance methods at the population level. In addition, these researchers are now employing those same methods at smaller, regional scales, addressing questions heretofore only remotely considered, like small-scale migration, kinship, social structure, temporal variation, and postmarital residence.

The continued interaction between bioarchaeologists and forensic anthropologists is necessary. The two fields are inextricably linked, and for good reason—they greatly complement one another. Research within forensic anthropology has improved our understanding of areas like taphonomy, degenerative changes, and trauma. Likewise, studies in bioarchaeology exploring a variety of biological processes and archaeological queries improve our understanding of past population histories and inform our current understanding of human variation. Although they often work with disparate datasets, within the context of biodistance analysis, the two fields can improve the quality and power of statistical approaches used to explore human variation at any scale.

While we underscore that biodistance studies are complex and require thoughtful implementation, we see great promise in their future. As statistical methods advance and our knowledge base into the genetic influence on skeletal morphology grows, there is great potential to answer many meaningful questions. Our youthful optimism permits one final thought: we hope this volume motivates future research and encourages advances in biological distance analysis.

Marin A. Pilloud
University of Nevada, Reno, Reno, NV, United States
Joseph T. Hefner
Michigan State University, East Lansing, MI, United States

Acknowledgments

At the outset the editors wish to thank the contributors to this volume for their dedication, tireless effort, and superb manuscripts. It has been a pleasure to work with every one of you. Second, we would like to thank the peer reviewers: Christian Crowder (Harris County Institute of Forensic Sciences), Amelia Hubbard (Wright State University), Kristina Kilgrove (University of West Florida), Christopher Maier (University of Nevada, Reno), Efthymia Nikita (British School of Athens), Kathleen Paul (Arizona State University), Vincent H. Stefan (Lehman College—CUNY), Jaime Ullinger (Quinnipiac University), Jennifer Vollner (Michigan State University), Timothy Weaver (University of California, Davis), and Katie Zejdlik (Western Carolina University). Each of you provided valuable insights into and thoughtful criticisms of these chapters, making the entire volume significantly better. Finally, we are grateful to our editors at Academic Press, Joslyn T. Chaiprasert-Paguio and Elizabeth Brown, for their patience and guidance.

SECTION

1

Biodistance Data, Datasets, and Analytical Methods

CHAPTER

A Brief History of Biological Distance Analysis

1

J.T. Hefner[1], M.A. Pilloud[2], J.E. Buikstra[3], C.C.M. Vogelsberg[1]

Michigan State University, East Lansing, MI, United States[1]; University of Nevada, Reno, NV, United States[2]; Arizona State University, Tempe, AZ, United States[3]

CHAPTER OUTLINE HEAD

Introduction 3
Natural Philosophy and Anatomy 4
Craniometric Analysis 4
Nonmetric Trait Analysis 6
Dental Morphology 8
Dental Metrics 9
Changes in Statistical Approaches 10
Scales of Analysis and Kinship 11
Ancient DNA and Biodistance 12
Forensic Anthropology, Race, and Human Variation 12
Conclusions 13
Endnotes 13
References 14

INTRODUCTION

Biological distance, or biodistance,[1] analysis employs data derived from skeletal remains to reflect population relatedness (similarity/dissimilarity) through the application of multivariate statistical methods. The approaches used in biodistance studies have changed markedly over recent centuries, exploring phenotypic expressions assumed to be informative. Variations include measured attributes and those characterized by degrees of expression (nonmetric or morphological). Most frequently grounded in cranial and dental variation in shape and size, such morphological variation has frequently been assumed to carry phylogenetic information. Researchers working with biodistance data have assumed either simple or more complex polygenic inheritance, the latter frequently invoking quasi-continuous models, with thresholds for expression. Most recently, biodistance researchers have been "ground-truthing" more complex models that include epigenetic effects (Hunter et al., 2010).

While understanding the nature of genetic relationships, usually at a predefined level of analysis (eg, inter- or intrasite specific, global variation, regional continuity), has a long and varied history in physical anthropology, the unifying assumption has changed very little from the early days of anthropology: people

Biological Distance Analysis. http://dx.doi.org/10.1016/B978-0-12-801966-5.00001-9

sharing similar morphological features share a common ancestry when compared to groups with fewer shared features. Especially prominent during the latter part of the 20th century and ongoing during the 21st are studies of the relationship between complex skeletal and dental structures and the genome, along with the development of increasingly robust analytical methods.

The following is a brief historical overview of biodistance analysis research, focusing on *meta*-themes in the field, shifts in thinking among researchers in biological anthropology, and several outside influences that impact biodistance analysis. The target data sources include morphological and metric variants of the cranium and dentition. The infracranial skeleton is not addressed here, due to less historical and contemporary emphasis in biodistance study as a result of the historic focus on the skull and the less—genetically controlled variability between groups in postcranial morphology (Wescott, 2005). Data categories and how they are variously employed in biodistance analysis are outlined in detail later in this volume.

NATURAL PHILOSOPHY AND ANATOMY

Modern biological anthropology was largely founded on the efforts of 18th- and 19th-century European and North American scholars and naturalists. These natural philosophers used soft tissue (eg, skin color, hair, and eye form) and skeletal form (eg, facial angle, limb proportions) to classify humans into biological packages. One of the more well-known efforts was by the creator of modern taxonomy, Linnaeus (1707—78), who distinguished four subspecies of humans primarily based on shared anatomical characteristics. His encompassing goal was to organize the natural world into a single, hierarchical system whose sole purpose was the absolute, comprehensive knowledge of God's design. The system he proposed and the methods he outlined to classify organisms effectively established the modern taxonomic approach to classification (Armelagos et al., 1982; McGee and Warms, 2012).

Not everyone agreed with the Linnaean model of race, an early indication of the unfixed nature of racial taxonomy, which was never a static classification system. Blumenbach (1752—1840), for example, influenced by Kant and Buffon before him (Larson, 1994), believed differences between the "varieties" of humans resulted from differing climates, nutrition, and modes of life, which had an effect on the *nisus formativus*, or vital force, of an individual. Blumenbach did not view humans as fixed entities at the time of biblical "creation". Rather he saw the various groups of humans as degenerations (from Latin: *degeneris* [removed from one's origin]) from an original, perfect form. To Blumenbach and other like-minded contemporaries, differences among humans could be attributed to population migrations and environmental shifts causing soft tissue and skeletal changes, which after a period of time become heritable (Brace, 2005). At the turn of the 19th century, scholars were gradually becoming aware of humankind's remarkable diversity and variation, but they continued to focus on a small number of phenotypic traits with little or no regard for within-species variation (Armelagos et al., 1982, p. 306).

CRANIOMETRIC ANALYSIS

Early anatomists and natural philosophers studying human variation believed many of the observed differences within and between "races" could be measured. While postcranial metric differences were investigated (eg, Verneau, 1875), most early studies focused on the skull. Many of the early practitioners of craniometry (ie, the measurement of skulls) were typologists attempting to create types of look-alike species or races. Camper (1722—89), the father of craniometry, focused on facial prognathism using the angulation between the cranial base and the vertical portion of the midface to measure distinction from apes (Camper, 1791).[2]

Blumenbach (1752–1840) approached typology geographically, characterizing human variation in terms of environmental influence and migration. In *De Generis Humani Varietate Nativa Liber*, Blumenbach (1775) initially outlined racial classifications based on cranial observations. Although he considered the Caucasoid race archetypical and the other four (Mongoloids, Ethiopians, Americans, and Malays) races as degenerations, he viewed humans as one species; the major and minor racial categories were useful only as descriptors of observed gradients. He also inferred that some populations were more similar because they lived near each other (Wolpoff and Caspari, 1997).

Morton (1799–1851) developed a series of measurements to better quantify the differences between and within the races that he defined while building on the work of Blumenbach. Focusing initially upon American Indians, Morton (1839) considered cranial variation innate and fixed, not the result of environmental factors (*contra* Blumenbach). Notwithstanding some of the more recent controversies surrounding his science (eg, Gould, 1996; Lewis et al., 2011), Morton recognized the link between skeletal morphology and ancestry in explaining the history of humankind. Broca (1824–80) amplified and standardized the statistical analysis of craniometric data. Following the tradition of Lacassagne,[3] Broca developed the French school of physical anthropology, a greatly admired and emulated institution. Most of Broca's work focused on the size of various regions of the brain in order to show that racial types were in fact different species (Broca, 1863).

Unlike most of his contemporaries, whose efforts focused on abnormal variants, Hrdlička (1869–1943) explored the history of humankind based on phenotypic variation in "normal" representatives of human groups. Building on the earlier work of Morton, Matthews, and others (Buikstra, 2006), he developed a distinctive American school of physical anthropology. Using then-standard cranial measurements, Hrdlička (eg, Hrdlička, 1927b) grouped individuals by locality and provided descriptive statistics for each group (means and ranges). Unwilling to draw inferences explicitly based upon statistical comparisons, he merely described distributions of craniometric data.

Hooton (1887–1954), by contrast, was considerably more comfortable with statistics. He used a variety of methods to assess regional variation among Native American populations, beginning with the visual grouping of similar crania, which he then assigned to types that were seemingly confirmed by statistical assessments. As one of the first nonmedical physical anthropologists, Hooton explored a variety of archaeological questions using analyses of population variation. His explorations of variation in cranial morphology over space and time represent pioneering efforts in both biodistance and bioarchaeological studies (Buikstra, 2006).

Neumann (1907–71) is often considered one of the last typologists, but in fact he was also one of the first anthropologists to fully incorporate archaeological data into his taxonomic classifications, which were developed using cranial morphology and descriptive statistics. Using craniometric data from over 10,000 North American indigenous people, Neumann (1952) identified eight varieties that reflected broad geographical and temporal contexts across the continent. Neumann's approach departed from standard typological studies in that intrapopulation variation could be inferred and human history prior to the arrival of Europeans defined (Armelagos et al., 1982, p. 311).

Martin's (1914) *Lehrbuch der Anthropologie in systematischer Darstellung mit besonderer Berücksichtigung der anthropologischen Methoden für Studierende Ärtze und Forschungsreisende* (Textbook of anthropology in a systematic manner with special regard to anthropological methods for students, physicians, and explorers) was the author's attempt to standardize and thus legitimize physical anthropology, reflecting the rising

German school and largely ignoring the French, English, and Italian efforts of Broca, the Pearson Biometric Laboratory, and Lombroso, respectively. Martin's was a remarkable effort. At 1181 pages, the *Lehrbuch* covered all aspects of anthropology—from somatology and osteology to the nuances of physiogeny, and of course included a treatise on craniology. Martin outlined craniometric instrumentation, detailed definitions of each bony landmark, individual measurements (interlandmark distances), and finally geometric descriptors of the cranial measurements. Notably, the *Lehrbuch* was not the first attempt at standardization; rather, Martin was building upon Morton's and Broca's earlier attempts to standardize data collection. The *Lehrbuch* is notable for its continued impact. Despite the time between its initial publication and today, the *Lehrbuch* remains an important reference for anyone involved in craniometric data collection and analysis.

Hrdlička's *Practical Anthropometry* (1939) is another important foundation for modern-day biological anthropologists. While Hrdlička utilized aspects of the *Lehrbuch* in the later editions of *Anthropometry* (1920), subsequently reprinted through numerous editions as *Practical Anthropometry* (Hrdlička, 1952), in which he outlined craniometric data collection and analysis, his methodological and theoretical considerations more closely followed Broca's French school. Hooton, a proponent of nonmetric variation with a keen eye for morphological variation and shape (Brues, 1990; Hefner, 2009), was more influenced by the German and Italian schools, elements of which can be easily found in the Harvard Blanks, the data collection sheet he developed which is still largely used in laboratories around the United States (Brues, 1990). As illustrated by Stojanowski and Euber (2011), few of the measurements recorded by Hrdlička and by Hooton are directly comparable.

Howells (1973) slightly refined both Pearson's and Martin's treatments of craniometric data, but relied heavily on the latter's definitions of bony landmarks. Since Martin's coding system could not be easily incorporated into workable computer code, Howells's remedy, which remains in use today, was the establishment of a three-letter system to designate cranial measurements. For example, maximum cranial length, measured from glabella to opisthocranion, is identified by Howells (1973) as "GOL" (glabella-occipital length), equivalent to Martin's (1914, p. 584) definition of the same which he identified as "1."

Today, craniometric analysis has shifted from simple caliper measurements to more complex data collection techniques (eg, 3-D digitizers) and analysis (eg, geometric morphometrics). However, these studies, which rely so heavily on technology and computing power, still use the cranial landmark definitions standardized by Martin. These landmarks and measurements are well summarized and defined by Moore-Jansen et al. (1994), and further outlined by Jantz and Ousley (2005) for *Fordisc 3.0*, a computer program utilized by forensic anthropologists for the analysis of craniometric data.

NONMETRIC TRAIT ANALYSIS

Human anatomical research during the 18th and 19th centuries included discussions of cranial nonmetric traits,[4] which were first designated as skeletal "anomalies." Described in great detail, these traits were rarely used to draw inferences about degree of relatedness, migration, or typology; instead they were simply described as novel, but anomalous, variants. Kerckring (1640–93), an anatomist and naturalist, described several of these anomalies in his text *Anatomical Gleanings* (Kerckring, 1670), including the first description of Kerckring's ossicle, an accessory center of ossification in the occipital bone just posterior to the foramen magnum. By the late 1880s, descriptions of nonmetric skeletal variants were quite common

(Blumenbach, 1775; Virchow, 1875). Chambellan's (1883) dissertation on wormian bones (*Étude anatomique et anthropologique sur les os wormiens*) was the first scholarly attempt to link skeletal anomalies to anthropological research.[5] Dorsey (1897), citing Chambellan's dissertation, answered an unambiguously anthropological question, correlating cranial deformation among the Kwakiutl with the presence of wormian bones. Although this study was limited to descriptions of 10 crania, future directions were suggested. For example, Dorsey used the last two paragraphs of his manuscript to hypothesize the causes of these wormian bones and to provide some relative data on their frequency distribution among males and females.

In 1900, Russell produced *Studies in Cranial Variation*, which was a study "almost wholly statistical" (Russell, 1900, p. 737) carried out using nearly 2000 skulls from the Peabody Museum at Harvard University. Russell defined and documented the frequency of 10 morphological variants among Amerindian groups. In the end, however, Russell did not consider these anything other than interesting observations, seeing no reason to "expect them to establish firmly any hypotheses regarding the origin or affinities of the Amerinds" (Russell, 1900, p. 743). Similarly, LeDouble (1903, 1906, 1912) described variations in trait manifestations on the cranium and spine, but did very little beyond individual trait descriptions, with the exception of his prescient inferences about intertrait correlations and development. In the 1930s, Wood-Jones (1931a,b,c, 1933) investigated morphological and nonmetric variation as criteria for race identification. Acknowledging inter- and intraobserver error issues in both craniometric and nonmetric analyses, Wood-Jones had two main objectives: (1) clearly define morphological criteria for nonmetric variations (first in mammals very generally, then within human groups), and (2) call attention to the diagnostic value of these traits in racial classifications. The approach Wood-Jones advocated represented an important shift in thinking from emphasizing variation within an individual to variation within and between groups.

Throughout the 1930s and 1940s, biological anthropology remained predominantly typological, emphasizing individuals and not populations. Nonmetric traits were considered idiosyncratic anomalies rather than expressions of human variation. Typological thinking, however, would soon suffer from the impact of Washburn's "The New Physical Anthropology" (Washburn, 1951) and his emphasis on hypothesis testing, biochemical mechanisms in human evolution, and other processual explorations into human origins. Washburn effectively laid the foundation for future studies that linked developmental and historical aspects of human variation and human evolution. As Saunders and Rainey state: "Washburn's theoretical foreshadowing helped prepare the way for interest…in the genetic studies of mice in the 1950 and 1960s" (Saunders and Rainey, 2008, p. 542) using quasi-continuous (cranial nonmetric) traits.

This influence can be seen in the work of Grünberg (1952, 1955, 1963), who explored genetic variants among mice, which would eventually lead to studies of human samples. For example, Laughlin and Jorgenson (1956) examined frequency distributions of eight cranial nonmetric traits to elucidate regional variation in a sample of Eskimo crania from Greenland. Employing historical migration data, the authors hypothesized that the greatest differences in trait expression, and therefore the most divergent groups, would be the polar (terminal) populations. Their analysis of nonmetric data not only supported their hypothesis, but also effectively established cranial nonmetric traits as viable proxies for genetic data in biodistance analysis.

Following work by Laughlin and Jorgenson (1956), a number of studies highlighted the advantages and disadvantages of nonmetric trait analysis in human osteology (Anderson, 1968; Berry, 1975; Saunders, 1989), including explicit comparisons of metric and nonmetric methods. Important among these studies was the work of Berry and Berry (1971, 1972), who focused on 30 cranial nonmetric traits. They argued analyses employing nonmetric traits were superior to metric studies because nonmetric features were easy to collect, were not subjected to environmental effects and were relatively free of age and sex effects (Berry and Berry, 1967). Although such assertions have been critiqued and the methods refined (Cheverud and Buikstra, 1981, 1982; Dodo, 1974; Richtsmeier et al., 1984; Rightmire, 1972; Self and Leamy, 1978), Berry and Berry's contributions to biodistance studies remain well cited and influential (Saunders and Rainey, 2008).

Ossenberg (1969), building on the genetics research from mice studies, collected data on 37 "discontinuous" traits from nearly 1300 human crania. Her intent was to synthesize the use of these variants beyond mere description and to explore patterns in age, sex, side incidence, inter- and intratrait correlations, effects on trait expression from cranial deformation, and importantly, temporal trends. Using these data, Ossenberg (1969) identified regional and temporal trends among the Dakota Sioux and selective factors influencing trait frequencies (ie, convergence/divergence, gene flow, and drift). Her data remain important, and, following the tradition of Howells (http://web.utk.edu/~auerbach/HOWL.htm), Ossenberg made all of her data freely available (http://hdl.handle.net/1974/7870).

Expanding on the Berry and Berry (1967) trait list, Hauser and De Stefano (1989) published a seminal survey of morphological variants of the human skull. Their list of 84 variants served to define, standardize, and explore heritability and function. This treatment stands as essential reading on the topic of cranial nonmetric traits. A modern summary of these traits, often used in bioarchaeology, is provided by Buikstra and Ubelaker (1994).

DENTAL MORPHOLOGY

Dental morphological variation, like skeletal nonmetric traits, was first described by dental anatomists documenting abnormal "variants" (Scott and Turner, 1997). These scholars include von Carabelli (1842), Tomes (1914), and Owen (1845). Owen's *Odontography* (1845) is one of the earliest monographs on the comparative dental anatomy of fish, reptiles, and mammals. These early 19th-century studies were prevalent based on their ability to address phylogenetic and taxonomic questions (Alt et al., 1998).

Thompson (1903) provided an early study on dental variation among modern human populations, describing the morphological variants of the "Inca Peruvians." Complete with illustrations, Thompson's monograph included general dental observations—eg, staining of the teeth from coca leaves—calculus, and carious lesions, as well as a prescient discussion of dental morphological variation by tooth type. Subsequently, the role of populations in dental morphological studies shifted from establishing taxonomy to the recognition of population variability (Alt et al., 1998). This shift in focus to the population level is obvious in the research of Campbell (1925), Shaw (1931), and Krogman (1927). Hrdlička also became a prominent figure in the analysis of dental morphology during the early 1900s (Alt et al., 1998), producing influential publications that included definitions of incisor shoveling (Hrdlička, 1911, 1920a,b, 1921, 1924).

Emerging from these earlier works, interest in dental morphology grew. Starting in the 1940s and extending well into the 1970s, two prominent scholars, Dahlberg and Pedersen (Scott and Turner, 1997), formalized the field of dental anthropology by producing works that remain important today. In the 1950s, contributions from Moorrees (1957), Hanihara (1954, 1955), Kraus (1951, 1959), and Lasker (Lasker, 1945, 1950; Lasker and Lee, 1957) lent further credence to this growing discipline.

In the decade that followed, Brothwell (1963) edited the volume *Dental Anthropology*, which covered a range of topics, including several chapters dedicated to dental morphological variation. Shortly thereafter, in 1965, the first International Symposium on Tooth Morphology was held in Denmark. Eventually, in 1986, the Dental Anthropology Association was founded (Alt et al., 1998).

Like Martin's work with craniometric data, the Arizona State University Dental Anthropology System (ASUDAS) described in Turner et al. (1991) firmly standardized dental morphology as a field of study. The ASUDAS provided much-needed standardization within the field and allowed researchers to collect and compare large amounts of data. Finally, Scott and Turner's (1997) classic volume on dental morphology described the study of dental morphology, encouraging future scholarship.

DENTAL METRICS

The history of the study of tooth size is less-well-documented than that of the measurement of other parts of the skeleton (Tobias, 1990). Muhlreiter is credited with the first human odontometric study on a skeletal sample from Salzburg dating to 1874 (Kieser, 1990). This work was followed by that of Flower (1885), who evaluated differences in tooth size among various populations.

This early work on dental metrics established definitions of crown measurements. Muhlreiter described the measurement taken in the mesiodistal dimension as the distance between contact points measured from the buccal surface (Kieser, 1990). Various critiques of this measurement later emerged, largely relating to issues arising when measuring different tooth classes (Nelson, 1938) and measuring contact points on the buccal surface (Selmer-Olsen, 1949). Hrdlička (1952) and Goose (1963) later defined the mesiodistal measurement following Muhlreiter's contact points; however, each of their measurements was defined by points on the occlusal surface rather than on the buccal and lingual surfaces.

Moorrees and Reed (1954) provided an alternate definition for tooth crown measurements: the maximum dimensions. Within their definition, the mesiodistal diameter was taken at the greatest expansion of the crown parallel to the occlusal and labial surfaces, regardless of location of the contact facets. The maximum buccolingal diameter was measured parallel to the mesiodistal measurement at the greatest expansion between the buccal and lingual surfaces. This definition by Moorrees and Reed (1954) continues to be the one most commonly used in studies of odontometrics. Tobias (1967) provides a fuller definition of these crown dimensions that may be of more use to the practitioner. Likewise, Kieser (1990) gives a detailed overview of crown measurements and their use in anthropological studies.

Within the field of odontometrics, alternative measurements of the teeth have also been proposed, beyond the traditional dimensions of the tooth crown. Azouley and Regnault (1893) first defined cervical measurements of teeth, followed by Black (1902) and Goose (1956). These measurements were rediscovered and popularized by Hillson et al. (2005), who not only provided further description of cervical measurements, but also developed calipers specifically designed to take these measurements (Hillson—Fitzgerald calipers are available at www.paleo-tech.com). Cervical measurements have also been defined for deciduous teeth (Pilloud and Hillson, 2012). Hillson et al. (2005) describe molar measurements of the crown taken on the diagonal in an attempt to remove subjectivity from recording maximum dimensions of molars in odontometric studies.

CHANGES IN STATISTICAL APPROACHES

Observational studies of skeletal morphology during the early 20th century laid the foundation for future analyses of population relationships. Early investigations of tooth crown morphology, odontometrics, and metric and nonmetric variation of the cranial and postcranial skeleton (Campbell, 1925; Hrdlička, 1920a,b; 1921, 1927a; Krogman, 1927; Shaw, 1931) hinted at a potential for distinguishing between groups. Pearson (1926) devised the coefficient of racial likeness (CRL), a statistical constant providing a measure of the degree of similarity/dissimilarity between two populations using craniometric, anthropometric, or odontometric data. The coefficients derived from the CRL start at zero and go upward. The resulting values (coefficients) provide the measure of similarity. A coefficient less than 1 indicates "intimate association, a coefficient between 1 and 4 close association, 4 to 7 moderate association, 7 to 10 slight association, 10 to 13 doubtful association" (Seltzer, 1937, p. 102). Scores above 13 indicate divergence between the two groups. This method was first used in a paper on Burmese skulls by Tildesley (1921) and in subsequent papers by Morant (1923, 1924, 1925).

The CRL was critiqued because (1) it could not account for intermeasurement correlations, (2) only a single standard deviation was used for all groups, and (3) the variable number has an effect on the calculation of the coefficient (Seltzer, 1937). Fisher (1936a) critiqued the CRL as an unreliable test of significance that could not account for correlation or covariation, and instead offered an alternative measure useful in comparisons of two populations (Fisher, 1936b). Mahalanobis also reacted to these criticisms, creating a measure of group distance that was not merely a test of the divergence between groups. After a period of professional differences with Pearson on the proper solutions to problems identified in the CRL (Mahalanobis, 1948), Mahalanobis (1936) published his seminal paper on the "generalized distance," now termed the Mahalanobis distance statistic or D^2.

During the 1940s, Rao (1948) introduced Penrose's (1952) "size and shape" as an alternative to the CRL. A relatively simple statistic comparing distances in mean values of measurements between populations, this calculation uses "shape" as a measure of variance and "size" as the square of the mean differences between groups. Penrose's size and shape was adopted by many anthropologists (eg, Brothwell, 1959; Laughlin and Jorgensen, 1956). The following year, Sanghvi (1953) published a distance statistic for frequency data utilizing the chi-square statistic to calculate a measure of dissimilarity.

During the following decade, Giles and Elliot (1962) published a set of discriminant function equations for the forensic estimation of "race," which discriminated among "Blacks," "Whites," and a sample of pre- and protohistoric Native Americans from Indian Knoll, Kentucky. Although the concept of discriminant function in estimating group affiliation was previously discussed by Rao (1948), this publication provided easily applied equations for forensic practitioners.

The 1970s were witness to several advances in biological distance studies. Smith (1972) introduced the "mean measure of divergence," a more complicated calculation measuring differences of trait incidence in populations against the variance found within each population. This method was first used by Grewal (1962) in mice studies, but was popularized among anthropologists when Berry and Berry (1967) used the technique with human samples.

The application of statistics to answer biological distance questions was continuously explored, taking advantage of computing power introduced in the 1960s and 1970s (Campbell, 1978; Corruccini, 1975). Sjøvold (1973) modified the mean measure of divergence, as did Green and Suchey (1976) and Souza and Houghton (1977) a few years later. Penrose's "size and shape" and the D^2 were also adjusted (Van Vark, 1970). Studies also began to focus on methodological concerns such as intertrait correlation (Garn et al.,

1966) and the effects of environment, development, age, and sex on trait expression (Dahlberg, 1971; Garn et al., 1964, 1979; Hanihara, 1978; Moss, 1978). Corruccini spent considerable effort determining the significance of the different types of data in population studies and how each data type affected the expression of population differences (Corruccini, 1974).

Population genetic theory also gained visibility within biological distance studies at this time. Harpending and Jenkins (1973) focused on a method to measure population divergence using genetic frequencies that incorporated the effects of evolution on trait frequencies, the R matrix, and the inbreeding coefficient. For an excellent review of the R matrix, see Konigsberg (2006). Almost two decades later, Relethford and Blangero (1990) extended this method to include quantitative traits, a method commonly used in bioarchaeological research; however, see , Chapter 2 (this volume) for a discussion of the use of the R matrix with skeletal data. Additionally, Relethford and Lees (1982) explicitly distinguished between model-free and model-bound analyses for studying quantitative trait patterns within groups. Model-free approaches use population history to describe patterns in the data, whereas model-bound approaches employ a population-genetics and evolutionary framework (Relethford and Harpending, 1994).

SCALES OF ANALYSIS AND KINSHIP

During the 19th century, skeletal series around the world were collected, observed, and measured primarily to answer global- and continental-scale questions, including the polygenic vs. monogenic debates about the origins of humankind (Stanton, 1960). Morton studied diversity across the Americas (Morton, 1839) and also made inferences about ancient Egyptians (Morton, 1844). A nonmetric feature, the Inca bone, was invoked by Matthews et al. (1893) to relate archaeological samples from the Salt River valley of Arizona to peoples of Perú. Continental-scale questions and biodistance answers continued into the early 20th century, as exemplified by Neumann's (1952) decades-long study of Native American crania published at mid-century.

In concert with the mid-20th-century "new" physical anthropology and the attendant scorn levied at those who measured and observed archaeological bone (eg, Buettner-Janusch, 1969), the development of radiocarbon dating (Libby, 1952) freed archaeologists from their preoccupation with temporal sequences. They turned to questions of subsistence and settlement systems, venturing to address sociotechnic and even ideotechnic aspects of the human condition as part of the "new" archaeology (Binford, 1962, 1964). Bioarchaeologists responded with increased emphasis on studies of diet and health, resulting in a temporary hiatus from biodistance analysis (Buikstra et al., 1990).

Resurgence in biodistance studies at the end of the 20th century expanded the scales of inquiry to include small-scale relationships. Lane and Sublett (1972) pioneered this effort in their studies of residence among ancestral Allegany Seneca. Scholars "drilled down" to focus on regions and even single sites, making inferences about local community structure and relationships (eg, Bentley, 1986; Bondioli et al., 1986; Owsley et al., 1982; Rösing 1986; Soafer et al., 1986). Stojanowski and Schillaci (2006) reviewed biodistance studies on small-scale cemetery groups, which offered new ways to explore social structure, variation, and evolution and serve as a comparison with other archaeological methods of exploring societies.

Most studies conducted at the cemetery or regional levels have made assumptions that equate kinship with biological similarities as if genetic heritage and kin relations are isomorphic. Recent developments in sociocultural anthropology concerning the social construction of kinship have been reviewed by Johnson and Paul (2015), who highlight the need for a more nuanced approach to biodistance studies. By incorporating social constructs into investigations of past kin relationships, bioarchaeologists have opportunities to refine investigations of ancient group relatedness, whatever the scale (eg, Gregoricka, 2013; Paul et al., 2013; Pilloud and Larsen, 2011).

ANCIENT DNA AND BIODISTANCE

The introduction of molecular anthropology and the extraction of ancient DNA (aDNA) greatly influence modern biodistance analysis. In fact, studies incorporating aDNA with morphological measurements of biological affinity (see Adachi et al., 2006; Corruccini et al., 2002; Shinoda et al., 1998) have shown great promise.

The first use of aDNA was the extraction and sequencing of DNA from a 150-year-old museum specimen (Higuchi et al., 1984). Pääbo (1985a,b; 1986) went on to confirm aDNA extraction from even older specimens (>1000 years). An encouraging result directing further research, analysis, and important methodological refinements like polymerase chain reaction (PCR) (Mullis and Faloona, 1987) and nested PCR to address resulting-skewing sequence artifacts introduced during bacterial amplification (Saiki et al., 1988). Brotherton et al. (2007) addressed postmortem aDNA modification damage in ancient specimens using a single primer extension, or SPEX, amplification. SPEX generates more accurate sequence data (and identifies areas of postmortem modification) by targeting specific strands of DNA at defined loci, which are then, through redundancy of measures, used to distinguish authentic DNA from first-generation copied sequences (postmortem damage/noise) (Brotherton et al., 2007, p. 5719).

Although PCR and SPEX have reduced contamination issues in aDNA studies, such errors remain an issue (eg, Cooper and Poinar, 2000; Handt et al., 1994; Richards et al., 1995; Stoneking, 1995), but have not attenuated this line of research. Today, studies of aDNA center on pathogen and microorganism identifications (Bos et al., 2014; Harkins et al., 2015; Klaus et al., 2010; Stone et al., 2009; Wilbur et al., 2009), and of particular import to this volume, population-based studies on relatedness and distance (Bamshad et al., 2003; Cabana et al., 2014; Lanfear et al., 2012; Monsalve et al., 2002; Raff et al., 2010; Raghavan et al., 2014; Stone and Stoneking, 1996, 1998, 1999; Torres et al., 2013). These studies are proving extremely valuable for addressing long-standing debates like the peopling of the Americas (Lanfear et al., 2012; Raff et al., 2010; Raghavan et al., 2014; Tackney et al., 2015), debunking traditional views of race and typology (Goodman et al., 2003; Wolpoff and Caspari, 1997), and identifying individuals from forensic contexts (Irwin et al., 2007; Morild et al., 2015; Mundorff et al., 2009).

FORENSIC ANTHROPOLOGY, RACE, AND HUMAN VARIATION

Here we find it necessary to address one final aspect somewhat related to biodistance analysis, since the topic relates to the often debated concept of race/racial designations and the assessment of ancestry by forensic anthropologists. Ancestry assessment in United States is the assignment of an *individual* to a *group*—usually some geographic designation, like African, American Black, European, etc.—based on a combination of metric and nonmetric variables collected from unknown skeletal remains. Researchers have demonstrated that these measurements and observations are useful for estimating ancestry of an unknown decedent (Hefner, 2009; Hefner and Ousley, 2014; Jantz and Ousley, 2005; Sauer, 1992). Other researchers outside of the forensic arena, however, see this aspect of forensic anthropology as an acceptance of the classic biological race concept, heavily criticizing forensic practitioners for embracing an outdated concept (Armelagos and Goodman, 1998; Belcher and Armelagos, 2005; Goodman, 1997; Goodman and Armelagos, 1996). Sauer (1992) and Ousley et al. (2009) demonstrate that forensic anthropologists do not embrace the old paradigm; however, they also very effectively demonstrate why and how forensic anthropologists can estimate ancestry. Namely, there is a demonstrable correlation between social race, skeletal morphology, and ancestry. This concordance is likely due to genetic drift, assortative mating, institutional racism, and geographic patterning among US populations (Ousley et al., 2009).

CONCLUSIONS

Biodistance analysis began as the study of anomalous variants in the human skull and has transformed over the centuries into the computationally expensive analysis of the genome, all in an effort to understand the complex relationships between and within populations. While research on old questions still abound, for instance the modern research into nonmetric trait correlations (Edgar and Lease, 2007; Harris, 2007; Reid et al., 1991; Williams and Corruccini, 2007), a new generation of scholars seeks the incorporation of skeletal morphology for the interpretation of genetic affinity (Kuba, 2006), the genetics governing trait expression (Hughes et al., 2000; Lauc, 2003), robust statistical methods for the analysis of biological data (Bedrick et al., 2000; Dutilleul et al., 2000; Krzanowski, 2003; Petersen, 2000, 2007; Stojanowski, 2003), and the role of developmental biology on the expression of morphological variants (Jernvall and Jung, 2000). As methodologies have improved, so has the application of these analytical approaches. Studies of biological distance have moved away from mere typology and have shifted to embrace biological and anthropological theory to start answering broad social questions.

Endnotes

1. The term "biological distance analysis" has been used in population biology (Balakrishan and Sanghvi, 1968; Morton, 1975) and anthropology (Constandse-Westermann, 1972; Laughlin, 1960) since the early 1960s and 1970s. The origins of the abbreviated "biodistance" are not as clear, but the earliest published example we found was Brown (1977).
2. Camper's son, Adriaan G. Camper, published a book posthumously in 1791 that outlined his father's work.
3. Alexandre Lacassagne, the founder of the Lacassagne School of Criminology in Lyon, France (a rival of Lombroso's Italian school), played a major role in the development of forensic pathology (he was responsible for the standardization of the postmortem examination still used today), but he also influenced the development of forensic anthropology. His students were actively encouraged to pursue data collection from skeletal remains as a means of identification. For example, his student Ètienne Rollet developed stature equations from long bone measurements (Stewart and Kerley, 1979, p. 194).
4. Cranial nonmetric traits, sometimes wrongly referred to as epigenetic or quasi-continuous, include slight variations in bony morphology. These are generally in one of four forms: (1) ossicles within sutures, (2) abnormal proliferations (eg, bony spurs, bony bridges), (3) ossification failures (eg, septal aperture), or (4) foramina variations (eg, zygomatico-facial foramina) (Buikstra and Ubelaker, 1994, p. 85).
5. Although Chambellan's dissertation appears to be the first instance, Ole Worm (1588–1654), for whom wormian bones are named, had a decidedly anthropological slant to his natural collections.

References

Adachi, N., Suzuki, T., Sakaue, K., Takigawa, W., Ohshima, N., Dodo, Y., 2006. Kinship analysis of the Jomon skeletons unearthed from a double burial at the Usu-Moshiri site, Hokkaido, Japan. Anthropological Science 114, 29–34.

Alt, K.W., Brace, C.L., Turp, J.C., 1998. The history of dental anthropology. In: Alt, K.W., Rösing, F.W., Teschler-Nicola, M. (Eds.), Dental Anthropology: Fundamentals, Limits, and Prospects. Springer, New York, pp. 15–39.

Anderson, J.E., 1968. Skeletal "anomalies" as genetic indicators. In: Brothwell, D.R. (Ed.), The Skeletal Biology of Earlier Human Populations. Pergamon Press, Oxford, pp. 135–147.

Armelagos, G., Goodman, A.H., 1998. Race, racism, and anthropology. In: Goodman, A.F., Leatherman, T.L. (Eds.), Building a New Biocultural Synthesis: Political-economic Perspectives on Human Biology. University of Michigan Press, Ann Arbor, pp. 359–378.

Armelagos, G.J., Carlson, D.S., Van Gerven, D.P., 1982. The theoretical foundations and development of skeletal biology. In: Spencer, F. (Ed.), A History of American Physical Anthropology, 1930–1980. Academic Press, New York, pp. 305–328.

Azouley, O., Regnault, O., 1893. Variation in the form of the teeth. Bulletins and Memoirs of the Anthropological Society of Paris 4, 266.

Balakrishan, V., Sanghvi, L.D., 1968. Distance between populations on the basis of attribute data. Biometrics 24, 859–865.

Bamshad, M.J., Wooding, S., Watkins, W.S., Ostler, C.T., Batzer, M.A., Jorde, L.B., 2003. Human population genetic structure and inference of group membership. The American Journal of Human Genetics 72 (3), 578–589.

Bedrick, E.J., Lapidus, J., Powell, J.F., 2000. Estimating the Mahalanobis distance from mixed continuous and discrete data. Biometrics 56 (2), 394–401.

Belcher, R.L., Armelagos, G.J., 2005. Forensic misclassification of ancient Nubian crania: implications for assumptions about human variation. Current Anthropology 46 (2), 340–346.

Bentley, G.R., 1986. Dental morphology and social reconstruction at early bronze age Bab edh-Dhra', Jordan. American Journal of Physical Anthropology 69, 175 (abstract).

Berry, A., 1975. Factors affecting the incidence of non-metrical skeletal variants. Journal of Anatomy 120 (Pt 3), 519–535.

Berry, A.C., Berry, R.J., 1971. In: Chiarelli, A.B. (Ed.), Epigenetic Polymorphism in the Primate Skeleton. Academic Press, London, pp. 12–42.

Berry, A.C., Berry, R.J., 1972. Origins and relationships of the ancient Egyptians. Based on a study of non-metrical variations in the skull. Journal of Human Evolution 1, 199–208.

Berry, R.J., Berry, A.C., 1967. Epigenetic variation in the human cranium. Journal of Anatomy 101, 361–379.

Binford, L.R., 1962. Archaeology as anthropology. American Antiquity 217–225.

Binford, L.R., 1964. A consideration of archaeological research design. American Antiquity 425–441.

Black, G.V., 1902. Descriptive Anatomy of the Human Teeth. The Wilmington Dental Manufacturing Co., Philadelphia.

Blumenbach, J.F., 1775. De Generis Humani Varietate Nativa Liber [On the Natural Variety of Mankind]. Vandenhoek et Ruprecht, Goettingae.

Bondioli, L., Corruccini, R., Macchiarelli, R., 1986. Familial segregation in the iron age community of Alfedena, Abruzzo, Italy, based on osteodental trait analysis. American Journal of Physical Anthropology 71, 393–400.

Bos, K.I., Harkins, K.M., Herbig, A., Coscolla, M., Weber, N., Comas, I., Forrest, S.A., Bryant, J.M., Harris, S.R., Schuenemann, V.J., Campbell, T.J., Majander, K., Wilbur, A.K., Guichon, R.A., Wolfe Steadman, D.L., Cook, D.C., Niemann, S., Behr, M.A., Zumarraga, M., Bastida, R., Huson, D., Nieselt, K., Young, D., Parkhill, J., Buikstra, J.E., Gagneux, S., Stone, A.C., Krause, J., 2014. Pre-Columbian mycobacterial genomes reveal seals as a source of New World human tuberculosis. Nature 514 (7523), 494–497.

Brace, C.L., 2005. "Race" Is a Four-letter Word: The Genesis of the Concept. Oxford University Press, New York.

Broca, M.P., 1863. Review of the proceedings of the anthropological society of Paris. Anthropological Review 1 (2), 274–310.

Brotherton, P., Endicott, P., Sanchez, J.J., Beaumont, M., Barnett, R., Austin, J., Cooper, A., 2007. Novel high-resolution characterization of ancient DNA reveals C > U-type base modification events as the sole cause of post mortem miscoding lesions. Nucleic Acids Research 35 (17), 5717–5728.

Brothwell, D.R., 1959. The use of non-metrical characters of the skull differentiation populations. Deutsch Gesellshaft Anthropologie Bericht Uber Tagung 6, 103–109.

Brothwell, D.R. (Ed.), 1963. Dental Anthropology. Pergamon, New York.

Brown, J.A., 1977. Current directions in Midwestern archaeology. Annual Review of Anthropology 6, 161–179.

Brues, A.M., 1990. The once and future diagnosis of race. In: Gill, G.W., Rhine, S. (Eds.), Skeletal Attribution of Race: Methods for Forensic Anthropology Maxwell Museum of Anthropology, Albuquerque, pp. 1–9.

Buettner-Janusch, J., 1969. Division of anthropology: the nature and future of physical anthropology. Transactions of the New York Academy of Sciences 31 (2 Series II), 128–138.

Buikstra, J.E., 2006. An historical introduction. In: Buikstra, J.E., Beck, L.A. (Eds.), Bioarchaeology: The Contextual Analysis of Human Remains. Academic Press, San Diego, CA, pp. 7–25.

Buikstra, J.E., Frankenberg, S.R., Konigsberg, L.W., 1990. Skeletal biological distance studies in american physical anthropology: recent trends. American Journal of Physical Anthropology 82, 1–7.

Buikstra, J.E., Ubelaker, D.H. (Eds.), 1994. Standards for data collection from human skeletal remains. Arkansas Archeological Survey Research Series No. 44, Fayetteville, Arkansas.

Cabana, G.S., Cecil, M., Lewis, J., Tito, R.Y., Covey, R.A., Angela, M.C., Cruz, A.F.D.L., Durand, D., Housman, G., Hulsey, B.I., Iannacone, G.C., Paul, W., Lopez, Martinez, A., Medina, A., Ortega Davila, O., Pinto, K.P.O., Santillan, S.I.P., Rojas Dominguez, P., Rubel, M., Smith, H.F., Smith, S.E., Rubin de Celis Massa, V., Lizarraga, B.R., Stone, A.C., 2014. Population genetic structure of traditional populations in the Peruvian Central Andes and implications for South American population history. Human Biology 86 (3), 147–165.

Campbell, N.A., 1978. Multivariate analysis in biological anthropology: some further considerations. Journal of Human Evolution 7, 197–203.

Campbell, T.D., 1925. The Dentition and Palate of the Australian Aboriginal. Hassell Press, Adelaide.

Camper, P., 1791. In: Over het natuurlijk verschil der wezenstrekken in menschen van onderscheiden landaart en ouderdom; over het schoon in antyke beelden en gesneedene stenen, Utrecht.

Chambellan, V., 1883. Etude anatomique et anthropologique sur les os wormiens. A. Delahaye et E. Lecrosnier.

Cheverud, J.M., Buikstra, J.E., 1981. Quantitative genetics of skeletal nonmetric traits in the rhesus macaques on Cayo Santiago. II. Phenotypic, genetic, and environmental correlations between traits. American Journal of Physical Anthropology 54 (1), 51–58.

Cheverud, J.M., Buikstra, J.E., 1982. Quantitative genetics of skeletal nonmetric traits in the Rhesus Macaques of Cayo Santiago. III. Relative heritability of skeletal nonmetric and metric traits. American Journal of Physical Anthropology 59, 151–155.

Constandse-Westermann, T.S., 1972. Coefficients of Biological Distance; an Introduction to the Various Methods of Assessment of Biological Distances between Populations, with Special Reference to Human Biological Problems. Anthropological Publications, Oosterhout, Netherlands.

Cooper, A., Poinar, H., 2000. Ancient DNA: do it right or not at all. Science 289, 1139.

Corruccini, R.S., 1974. An examination of the meaning of cranial discrete traits for human skeletal biological studies. American Journal of Physical Anthropology 40, 425–446.

Corruccini, R.S., 1975. Multivariate analysis in biological anthropology: some considerations. Journal of Human Evolution 4, 1–19.

Corruccini, R.S., Shimada, I., Shinoda, K.-I., 2002. Dental and mtDNA relatedness among thousand-year-old remains from Huaca Loro, Peru. Dental Anthropology 16, 9–14.

Dahlberg, A.A., 1971. Penetrance and expressivity of dental traits. In: Dahlberg, A.A. (Ed.), Dental Morphology and Evolution. University of Chicago Press, Chicago, pp. 257–262.
Dodo, Y., 1974. Non-metrical cranial traits in the Hokkaido Ainu and the northern Japanese of recent times. Journal of the Anthropological Society of Nippon 82, 31–51.
Dorsey, G.A., 1897. Wormian bones in artificially deformed Kwakiutl crania. American Anthropologist 10 (6), 169–173.
Dutilleul, P., Stockwell, J.D., Frigon, D., Legendre, P., 2000. The Mantel test versus Pearson's correlation analysis: assessment of the differences for biological and environmental studies. Journal of Agricultural, Biological, and Environmental Statistics 5 (2), 131–150.
Edgar, H.J.H., Lease, L.R., 2007. Correlations between deciduous and permanent tooth morphology in a European American sample. American Journal of Physical Anthropology 133 (1), 726–734.
Fisher, R.A., 1936a. "The coefficient of racial likeness" and the ruture of craniometry. The Journal of the Royal Anthropological Institute of Great Britain and Ireland 66, 57–63.
Fisher, R.A., 1936b. The use of multiple measurements in taxonomic problems. Annals of Eugenics 7 (2), 179–188.
Flower, W.H., 1885. On the size of the teeth as a character of race. Journal of the Anthropological Institute of Great Britain and Ireland 14, 183–187.
Garn, S.M., Lewis, A.B., Dahlberg, A.A., Kerewsky, R.S., 1966. Interaction between relative molar size and relative number of cusps. Journal of Dental Research 45, 1240.
Garn, S.M., Lewis, A.B., Kerewsky, R.S., 1964. Sex difference in tooth size. Journal of Dental Research 43, 306.
Garn, S.M., Osborne, R., McCabe, K., 1979. The effects of prenatal factors on crown dimesions. American Journal of Physical Anthropology 51, 665–678.
Giles, E., Elliot, O., 1962. Race identification from cranial measurements. Journal of Forensic Sciences 7, 147–157.
Goodman, A.H., 1997. Bred in the bone? The Sciences 37 (2), 20–25.
Goodman, A.H., Armelagos, G.J., 1996. The resurrection of race: the concept of race in physical anthropology in the 1990s. In: Reynolds, L., Lieberman, L. (Eds.), Race and Other Misadventures: Essays in Honor of Ashley Montagu in His Ninetieth Year. General Hall, Dix Hills, New York, pp. 174–186.
Goodman, A.H., Heath, D., Lindee, M.S., 2003. Genetic Nature/Culture: Anthropology and Science beyond the Two-culture Divide. University of California Press, Berkeley, California.
Goose, D.H., 1956. Variability in the form of maxillary permanent incisors. Journal of Dental Research 35, 902–908.
Goose, D.H., 1963. Dental measurement: an assessment of its value in anthropological studies. In: Brothwell, D.R. (Ed.), Dental Anthropology. Pergamon, New York, pp. 125–148.
Gould, S.J., 1996. The Mismeasure of Man. WI Norton, New York.
Greene, R., Suchey, J., 1976. The use of inverse sine transformation in the analysis of non-metrical data. American Journal of Physical Anthropology 45, 61–68.
Gregoricka, L.A., 2013. Geographic origins and dietary transitions during the bronze age in the oman peninsula. American Journal of Physical Anthropology 152 (3), 353–369.
Grewal, M., 1962. The rate of divergence in the C57BL strain of mice. Genetical Research 3, 226–237.
Grünberg, H., 1952. Genetical studies on the skeleton of the mouse. IV. Quasi-continuous variations. Journal of Genetics 51, 95–114.
Grüneberg, H., 1955. Genetical studies on the skeleton of the mouse xv. Relations between major and minor variants. Journal of Genetics 53 (3), 515–533.
Grüneberg, H., 1963. The Pathology of Development. John Wiley and Sons, Inc., New York.
Handt, O., Richards, M., Trommsdorff, M., Kilger, C., Simanainen, J., Georgiev, O., Bauer, K., Stone, A., Hedges, R., Schaffner, W., et al., 1994. Molecular genetic analyses of the Tyrolean Ice Man. Science 264 (5166), 1775–1778.
Hanihara, K., 1954. Studies on the deciduous dentition of the Japanese and the Japanese-American hybrids: I. Deciduous incisors. Journal of the Anthropological Society of Nippon 63 (5), 168–185.
Hanihara, K., 1955. Studies on the deciduous dentition of the Japanese and the Japanese-American hybrids: II. Deciduous canines. Journal of the Anthropological Society of Nippon 64 (2), 63–82.

Hanihara, K., 1978. Differences in sexual dimorphism in dental morphology among several human populations. In: Bulter, P.M., Joysey, K.A. (Eds.), Development, Function and Evolution of Teeth. Academic Press, London, pp. 127–134.

Harkins, K.M., Buikstra, J.E., Campbell, T., Bos, K.I., Johnson, E.D., Krause, J., Stone, A.C., 2015. Screening ancient tuberculosis with qPCR: challenges and opportunities. Philosophical Transactions of the Royal Society of London B: Biological Sciences 370 (1660), 20130622.

Harpending, H.C., Jenkins, T., 1973. Genetic distance among southern African populations. In: Crawford, M.H., Workman, P. (Eds.), Methods and Theories of Anthropological Genetics. University of New Mexico Press, Albuquerque, pp. 177–199.

Harris, E.F., 2007. Carabelli's trait and tooth size of human maxillary first molars. American Journal of Physical Anthropology 132 (2), 238–246.

Hauser, G., De Stefano, G., 1989. Epigenetic Variants of the Human Skull. Schweizerbart, Stuttgart.

Hefner, J.T., 2009. Cranial non-metric variation and estimating ancestry. Journal of Forensic Sciences 54 (5), 985–995.

Hefner, J.T., Ousley, S.D., 2014. Statistical classification methods for estimating ancestry using morphoscopic traits. Journal of Forensic Sciences 59 (4), 883–890.

Higuchi, R.G., Bowman, B., Freiberger, M., Ryder, A.O., Wilson, A.C., 1984. DNA sequence from the quagga, an extinct member of the horse family. Nature 312, 282–284.

Hillson, S., FitzGerald, C., Flinn, H., 2005. Alternative dental measurements: proposals and relationships with other measurements. American Journal of Physical Anthropology 126, 413–426.

Howells, W.W., 1973. Cranial variation in man. A study by multivariate analysis of patterns of difference. Among recent human populations. Papers of the Peabody Museum of Archaeology and Ethnology 67, 1–259.

Hrdlička, A., 1911. Human dentition and teeth from the evolutionary and racial standpoint. Dominion Dental Journal 23, 403–421.

Hrdlička, A., 1920a. Anthropometry. Wistar Iinstitute, Philadelphia.

Hrdlička, A., 1920b. Shovel shaped teeth. American Journal of Physical Anthropology 3, 429–465.

Hrdlička, A., 1921. Further studies of tooth morphology. American Journal of Physical Anthropology 4, 141–176.

Hrdlička, A., 1924. New data on the teeth of early man and certain fossil European apes. American Journal of Physical Anthropology 7, 109–132.

Hrdlička, A., 1927a. Anthropology of the American negro. Historical notes. American Journal of Physical Anthropology 10 (2), 205–233.

Hrdlička, A., 1927b. Catalogue of human crania in the United States National Museum collection. In: Proceedings of the United States Museum. Washington Smithsonian Institution Press, pp. 1–127.

Hrdlička, A, 1939. Practical Anthropometry. Wistar Institute of Anatomy and Biology, Philadelphia.

Hrdlička, A., 1952. Practical Anthropometry, fourth ed. Wistar Inst, Philadelphia.

Hughes, T., Dempsey, P., Richards, L., Townsend, G.C., 2000. Genetic analysis of deciduous tooth size in Australian twins. Archives of Oral Biology 45 (11), 997–1004.

Hunter, J.P., Guatelli-Steinberg, D., Weston, T.C., Durner, R., Betsinger, T.K., 2010. Model of tooth morphogenesis predicts Carabelli cusp expression, size, and symmetry in humans. PLoS One 5 (7), e11844.

Irwin, J.A., Leney, M.D., Loreille, O., Barritt, S.M., Christensen, A.F., Holland, T.D., Smith, B.C., Parsons, T.J., 2007. Application of low copy number STR typing to the identification of aged, degraded skeletal remains. Journal of forensic Sciences 52 (6), 1322–1327.

Jantz, R.L., Ousley, S., 2005. FORDISC 3: Computerized Forensic Discriminant Functions. The University of Tennessee, Knoxville.

Jernvall, J., Jung, H.-S., 2000. Genotype, phenotype, and developmental biology of molar tooth characters. Yearbook of Physical Anthropology 43, 171–190.

Johnson, K., Paul, K., 2015. Bioarchaeology and kinship: integrating theory, social relatedness, and biology in ancient family research. Journal of Archaeological Research 1–49.

Kerckring, T., 1670. Spicilegium Anatomicum Continens Osteogeniam Foetuum (Amstelodami).
Kieser, J.A., 1990. Human Adult Odontometrics: The Study of Variation in Adult Tooth Size. Cambridge University Press, Cambridge.
Klaus, H.D., Wilbur, A.K., Temple, D.H., Buikstra, J.E., Stone, A.C., Fernandez, M., Wester, C., Tam, M.E., 2010. Tuberculosis on the north coast of Peru: skeletal and molecular paleopathology of late pre-Hispanic and post-contact mycobacterial disease. Journal of Archaeological Science 37 (10), 2587–2597.
Konigsberg, L., 2006. A post-Neumann history of biological and genetic distance studies in bioarchaeology. In: Buikstra, J.E., Beck, L.A. (Eds.), Bioarchaeology: The Contextual Analysis of Human Remians. Academic Press, Amsterdam, pp. 263–280.
Kraus, B.S., 1951. Carabelli's anomaly of the maxillary molar teeth. American Journal of Human Genetics 3, 348–355.
Kraus, B.S., 1959. Occurrence of the Carabelli trait in Southwest ethnic groups. American Journal of Physical Anthropology 17, 117–123.
Krogman, W.M., 1927. Anthropological aspects of the human teeth and dentition. Journal of Dental Research 7, 1–108.
Krzanowski, W., 2003. Non-parametric estimation of distance between groups. Journal of Applied Statistics 30 (7), 743–750.
Kuba, C.L., 2006. Nonmetric Traits and the Detection of Family Groups in Archaeological Remains. Department of Anthropology: Arizona State University.
Lane, R.A., Sublett, A., 1972. Osteology of social organization: residence pattern. American Antiquity 37 (2), 186–201.
Lanfear, R., Calcott, B., Ho, S.Y., Guindon, S., 2012. PartitionFinder: combined selection of partitioning schemes and substitution models for phylogenetic analyses. Molecular Biology and Evolution 29 (6), 1695–1701.
Larson, J.L., 1994. Interpreting Nature: The Science of Living Form from Linnaeus to Kant. Johns Hopkins University Press.
Lasker, G.W., 1945. Observations on the teeth of Chinese born and reared in China and America. American Journal of Physical Anthropology 3 (2), 129–150.
Lasker, G.W., 1950. Genetic Analysis of Racial Traits of the Teeth. Cold Spring Harbor Symposia on Quantitative Biology, 15, 191–203. Cold Spring Harbor Laboratory Press.
Lasker, G.W., Lee, M.M., 1957. Racial traits in the human teeth. Journal of Forensic Sciences 2, 401–419.
Lauc, T., 2003. Influence of inbreeding on the Carabelli trait in a human isolate. Dental Anthropology 16 (3), 65–72.
Laughlin, W.S., 1960. Aspects of current physical anthropology: method and theory. Southwestern Journal of Anthropology 16 (1), 75–92.
Laughlin, W.S., Jorgensen, J.B., 1956. Isolate variation in Greenlandic Eskimo crania. Acta Genetica et Statistica Medica 6, 3–12.
Le Double, A.-F., 1903. Traité des variations des os du crâne de l'homme et de leur signification au point de vue de l'anthropologie zoologique. Vigot, Paris.
Le Double, A.-F., 1906. Traité des variations des os de la face de l'homme: et de leur signification au point de vue de l'anthropologie zoologique. Vigot frères, Paris.
Le Double, A.-F., 1912. Variations de la Colonne Vertebrate de l'Homme. Vigot, Paris.
Lewis, J.E., DeGusta, D., Meyer, M.R., Monge, J.M., Mann, A.E., Holloway, R.L., 2011. The mismeasure of science: Stephen Jay Gould versus Samuel George Morton on skulls and bias. PLoS Biology 9 (6), e1001071.
Libby, W.F., 1952. Radiocarbon Dating. University of Chicago Press, Chicago.
Mahalanobis, P.C., 1936. On the generalized distance in statistics. In: National Historic Institute of Science, India, 2, pp. 49–55.
Mahalanobis, P.C., 1948. Appendix 1. Historical note on the D2-statistic. Sankhya 9, 237–239.
Martin, R., 1914. Lehrbuch der Anthropologie in systematischer Darstellung mit besonderer Berücksichtigung der anthropologischen Methoden. Gustav Fischer, Jena.

Matthews, W., Wortman, J.L., Billings, J.S., 1893. Human bones of the Hemenway collection in the United States Army Medical Museum. Memoirs of the National Academy of Sciences 6 (Memoir 7), 141–186.

McGee, R., Warms, R.L., 2012. Anthropological Theory: An Introductory History, fifth ed. McGraw-Hill, New York.

Monsalve, M.V., Stone, A.C., Lewis, C.M., Rempel, A., Richards, M., Straathof, D., Devine, D.V., 2002. Brief communication: molecular analysis of the Kwaday Dan Ts'finchi ancient remains found in a glacier in Canada. American Journal of Physical Anthropology 119 (3), 288–291.

Moore-Jansen, P.H., Ousley, S.D., Jantz, R.L., 1994. Data Collection Procedures for Forensic Skeletal Material. The University of Tennessee Forensic Anthropology Series, Knoxville, Tennessee.

Moorrees, C.F.A., 1957. The Aleut Dentition. Harvard University Press, Cambridge, Massachusetts.

Moorrees, C.F.A., Reed, R.B., 1954. Correlations among crown diameters of human teeth. Archives of Oral Biology 9, 685–697.

Morant, G.M., 1923. A first study of the Tibetan skull. Biometrika 14 (3/4), 193–260.

Morant, G.M., 1924. A study of certain oriental series of crania including the Nepalese and Tibetan series in the British Museum (natural history). Biometrika 16 (1/2), 1–105.

Morant, G.M., 1925. A study of Egyptian craniology from prehistoric to Roman times. Biometrika 17 (1/2), 1–52.

Morild, I., Hamre, S.S., Huel, R., Parsons, T.J., 2015. Identification of missing Norwegian world war II soldiers, in Karelia Russia. Journal of Forensic Sciences 60, 1104–1110.

Morton, N., 1975. Kinship, information and biological distance. Theoretical Population Biology 7 (2), 246–255.

Morton, S.G., 1839. Crania Americana. J. Dobson, Philadelphia.

Morton, S.G., 1844. Crania Aegyptica. John Penington, Philadelphia.

Moss, M.L., 1978. Analysis of developmental processes possible related to human dental sexual dimorphism. In: Bulter, P.M., Joysey, K.A. (Eds.), Development, Function and Evolution of Teeth. Academic Press, London, pp. 135–144.

Mullis, K.B., Faloona, F.A., 1987. Specific synthesis of DNA in vitro via a polymerase catalyzed chain reaction. Methods of Enzymology 155, 335–350.

Mundorff, A.Z., Bartelink, E.J., Mar-Cash, E., 2009. DNA preservation in skeletal elements from the World Trade Center disaster: recommendations for mass fatality management. Journal of Forensic Sciences 54 (4), 739–745.

Nelson, C.T., 1938. The teeth of the Indians of Pecos Pueblo. American Journal of Physical Anthropology 23 (3), 261–293.

Neumann, G.K., 1952. Archaeology and race in the American Indian. In: Griffen, J.B. (Ed.), Archeology of the Eastern United States. University of Chicago Press, Chicago, pp. 13–34.

Ossenberg, N.S., 1969. Discontinuous Morphological Variation in the Human Cranium. University of Toronto.

Ousley, S., Jantz, R.L., Fried, D., 2009. Understanding race and human variation: why forensic anthropologists are good at identifying race. American Journal of Physical Anthropology 139, 68–76.

Owen, R., 1845. Odontography, or, a Treatise on the Comparative Anatomy of the Teeth, their Physiological Relations, Mode of Developement, and Microscipic Structure, in the Vertebrate Animals: Text. Bailliere.

Owsley, D.W., Bennett, S.M., Jantz, R.L., 1982. Intercemetery morphological variation in Arikara crania from the mobridge site. American Journal of Physical Anthropology 58, 179–185.

Pääbo, S., 1985a. Molecular cloning of ancient Egyptian mummy DNA. Nature 314, 644–645.

Pääbo, S., 1985b. Preservation of DNA in ancient Egyptian mummies. Journal of Archaeological Science 12 (6), 411–417.

Pääbo, S., 1986. Molecular genetic investigations of ancient human remains. Cold Spring Harbor Symposia on Quantitative Biology 51, 441–446.

Paul, K.S., Stojanowski, C.M., Butler, M.M., 2013. Biological and spatial structure of an early classic period cemetery at Charco Redondo, Oaxaca. American Journal of Physical Anthropology 152 (2), 217–229.

Pearson, K., 1926. On the coefficient of racial likeness. Biometrika 18 (1/2), 105–117.

Penrose, L.S., 1952. Distance, size, and shape. Annals of Eugenics 18, 337–343.

Petersen, H., 2000. On statistical methods for comparison of intrasample morphometric variability: Zalavar revisited. American Journal of Physical Anthropology 113 (1), 79–84.
Petersen, H., 2007. Mahalanobis distance, missing values, and the end of the Mesolithic. American Journal of Physical Anthropology 44, 188.
Pilloud, M.A., Hillson, S., 2012. Brief communication: the use of alternative dental measurements on deciduous teeth. American Journal of Physical Anthropology 149, 299–306.
Pilloud, M.A., Larsen, C.S., 2011. "Official" and "practical" kin: inferring social community structure from dental phenotype at Neolithic Çatalhöyük, Turkey. American Journal of Physical Anthropology 145, 519–530.
Raff, J., Tackney, J., O'Rourke, D.H., 2010. South from Alaska: a pilot aDNA study of genetic history on the Alaska Peninsula and the Eastern Aleutians. Human Biology 82 (5–6), 677–693.
Raghavan, M., DeGiorgio, M., Albrechtsen, A., Moltke, I., Skoglund, P., Korneliussen, T.S., Grønnow, B., Appelt, M., Gulløv, H.C., Friesen, T.M., 2014. The genetic prehistory of the New World Arctic. Science 345 (6200), 1255832.
Rao, C.R., 1948. The utilization of multiple measurements in problems of biological classification. Journal of the Royal Statistical Society. Series B (Methodological) 10 (2), 159–203.
Reid, C., Van Reenan, J.F., Groeneveld, H.T., 1991. Tooth size and the Carabelli trait. American Journal of Physical Anthropology 84 (4), 427–432.
Relethford, J.H., Blangero, J., 1990. Detection of differential gene flow from patterns of quantitative variation. Human Biology 62 (1), 5–25.
Relethford, J.H., Harpending, H.C., 1994. Craniometric variation, genetic theory, and modern human origins. American Journal of Physical Anthropology 95, 249–270.
Relethford, J.H., Lees, F., 1982. The use of quantitative traits in the study of human population structure. Yearbook of Physical Anthropology 25, 113–132.
Richards, M.B., Sykes, B.C., Hedges, R.E., 1995. Authenticating DNA extracted from ancient skeletal remains. Journal of Archaeological Science 22 (2), 291–299.
Richtsmeier, J.T., Cheverud, J.M., Buikstra, J.E., 1984. The relationship between cranial metric and nonmetric traits in the rhesus macaques from Cayo Santiago. American Journal of Physical Anthropology 64 (3), 213–222.
Rightmire, G.P., 1972. Cranial measurements and discrete traits compared in distance studies of African Negro skulls. Human Biology 44, 263–276.
Russell, F., 1900. Studies in cranial variation. The American Naturalist 34 (405), 737–745.
Rösing, F.W., 1986. Kith or kin? On the feasability of kinship reconstructions in skeletons. In: David, R.A. (Ed.), Science in Egyptology. Manchester University Press, Manchester, pp. 223–237.
Saiki, R.K., Gelfand, D.H., Stoffel, S., Scharf, S.J., Higuchi, R., Horn, G.T., Mullis, K.B., Erlich, H.A., 1988. Primer-directed enzymatic amplification of DNA with a thermostable DNA polymerase. Science 239 (4839), 487–491.
Sanghvi, L.D., 1953. Comparison of genetical and morphological methods for a study of biological differences. American Journal of Physical Anthropology 11 (3), 385–404.
Sauer, N.J., 1992. Forensic anthropology and the concept of race: if races don't exist, why are forensic anthropologists so good at identifying them? Social Science and Medicine 34, 107–111.
Saunders, S.R., 1989. Nonmetric skeletal variation. In: Iscan, M.Y., Kennedy, K.A.R. (Eds.), Reconstruction of Life from the Skeleton. Alan R. Liss, Inc., New York, pp. 95–108.
Saunders, S.R., Rainey, D.L., 2008. In: Katzenberg, M.A., Saunders, S.R. (Eds.), Nonmetric Trait Variation in the Skeleton: Abnormalities, Anomalies, and Atavisms. John Wiley & Sons, Inc., Hoboken, pp. 533–559.
Scott, G.R., Turner, C.G., 1997. The Anthropology of Modern Human Teeth. Cambridge University Press, Cambridge.
Self, S.G., Leamy, L., 1978. Heritability of quasi-continuous skeletal traits in a randombred population of house mice. Genetics 88, 109–120.
Selmer-Olsen, R., 1949. An odontological study of the Norwegian Lapps. Skrift Norske Vidensk-Akademi 3, 1–167.

Seltzer, C.C., 1937. A critique of the coefficient of racial likeness. American Journal of Physical Anthropology 23 (1), 101–109.

Shaw, J.C.M., 1931. The Teeth, the Bony Palate, and the Mandible in the Bantu Races of South Africa. Bale and Danielsson, London.

Shinoda, K., Matzumura, H., Nishimoto, T., 1998. Genetical and morphological analysis on kinship of the Nakazuma Jomon people using mitochondrial DNA and tooth crown measurements. Zoo-archaeology 11, 1–21.

Sjøvold, T., 1973. The occurrence of minor non-metrical variants in the skeleton and their quantitative treatment for population comparisons. Homo 24, 204–233.

Smith, C., 1972. Coefficients of biological distance. Annals of Human Genetics 36, 241–245.

Soafer, J.A., Smith, P., Kaye, E., 1986. Affinities between contemporary and skeletal Jewish and non-Jewish groups based on tooth morphology. American Journal of Physical Anthropology 70, 265–275.

de Souza, P., Houghton, P., 1977. The mean measure of divergence and the use of non-metric data in the estimation of biological distances. Journal of Archaeological Science 4, 163–169.

Stanton, W., 1960. The Leopard's Spots: Scientifie Attitudes towards Race in American, 1815–59. University of Chicago Press, Chicago.

Stewart, T.D., Kerley, E.R., 1979. Essentials of Forensic Anthropology: Especially as Developed in the United States. Charles C. Thomas, Springfield.

Stojanowski, C., 2003. Matrix decomposition model for investigating prehistoric intracemetery biological variation. American Journal of Physical Anthropology 122, 216–231.

Stojanowski, C.M., Euber, J.K., 2011. Technical note: comparability of Hrdlička's Catalog of crania data based on measurement landmark definitions. American Journal of Physical Anthropology 146 (1), 143–149.

Stojanowski, C.M., Schillaci, M.A., 2006. Phenotypic approaches for understanding patterns of intracemetery biological variation. Yearbook of Physical Anthropology 49, 49–88.

Stone, A.C., Stoneking, M., 1996. Genetic analyses of an 8000 year-old Native American skeleton. Ancient Biomolecules 1 (1), 83–87.

Stone, A.C., Stoneking, M., 1998. mtDNA analysis of a prehistoric Oneota population: implications for the peopling of the New World. American Journal of Human Genetics 62, 1153–1170.

Stone, A.C., Stoneking, M., 1999. Analysis of ancient DNA from a prehistoric Amerindian cemetery. Philosophical Transactions of the Royal Society B: Biological Sciences 354 (1379), 153–159.

Stone, A.C., Wilbur, A.K., Buikstra, J.E., Roberts, C.A., 2009. Tuberculosis and leprosy in perspective. Yearbook of Physical Anthropology 140 (Suppl 49), 66–94.

Stoneking, M., 1995. Ancient DNA: how do you know when you have it and what can you do with it? American Journal of Human Genetics 57, 1259–1262.

Tackney, J., Potter, B., Raff, J., Powers, M., Watkins, S., Warner, D., Reuther, J., Irish, J., O'Rourke, D., 2015. Two contemporaneous mitogenomes from terminal Pleistocene burials in eastern Beringia. Proceedings of the National Academy of Sciences 112 (45), 13833–13838.

Thompson, A., 1903. Ethnographic Odontology: The Inca Peruvians. Gilcrease Museum Press, Tulsa.

Tildesley, M.L., 1921. A first study of the Burmese skull. Biometrika 13 (2/3), 176–262.

Tobias, P.V., 1967. Olduvai Gorge: The Cranium of Australopithecus (Zinjanthropus) Boisei. Cambridge University Press, Cambridge.

Tobias, P.V., 1990. Preface. In: Kieser, J.A. (Ed.), Human Adult Odontometrics: The Study of Variation in Adult Tooth Size. Cambridge University Press, Cambridge, pp. ix–x.

Tomes, C.S., 1914. A Manual of Dental Anatomy: Human and Comparative. P. Blakiston's Son, Philadelphia.

Torres, J.B., Stone, A.C., Kittles, R., 2013. An anthropological genetic perspective on Creolization in the Anglophone Caribbean. American Journal of Physical Anthropology 151 (1), 135–143.

Turner, C.G., Nichol, C.R., Scott, G.R., 1991. Scoring procedures for key morphological traits of the permanent dentition. The Arizona State University Dental Anthropology System. In: Kelley, M.A., Larsen, C.S. (Eds.), Advances in Dental Anthropology. Wiley-Liss, New York, pp. 13–31.

Van Vark, G.N., 1970. Some Statistical Procedures for the Investigation of Prehistoric Human Skeletal Material. V.R.B. Offsetdrukkerij, Groningen.

Verneau, R., 1875. Le bassin dans les sexes et dans les races. J.B. Bailliere, Paris.

Virchow, R., 1875. Über einige Merkmale niederer Menschenrassen am Schädel. Abhandi. der Berliner Akademie.

von Carabelli, G., 1842. Anatomie des Mundes. Braumuller und Seidel, Wien.

Washburn, S.L., 1951. The new physical anthropology. Transactions of the New York Academy of Sciences 13, 258–304.

Wescott, D.J., 2005. Population variation in femur subtrochanteric shape. Journal of Forensic Sciences 50 (2), 286–293.

Wilbur, A.K., Bouwman, A.S., Stone, A.C., Roberts, C.A., Pfister, L.-A., Buikstra, J.E., Brown, T.A., 2009. Deficiencies and challenges in the study of ancient tuberculosis DNA. Journal of Archaeological Science 36 (9), 1990–1997.

Williams, B.A., Corruccini, R.S., 2007. The relationship between crown size and complexity in two collections. Dental Anthropology 20 (2–3), 29–32.

Wolpoff, M.H., Caspari, R., 1997. Race and Human Evolution. Simon and Schuster, New York.

Wood-Jones, F., 1931a. The Non-metrical morphological characters of the skull as criteria for racial diagnosis: part I: general discussion of the morphological characters employed in racial diagnosis. Journal of Anatomy 65 (Pt 2), 179–195.

Wood-Jones, F., 1931b. The non-metrical morphological characters of the skull as criteria for racial diagnosis: part II: the non-metrical morphological characters of the Hawaiian skull. Journal of Anatomy 65 (Pt 3), 368–378.

Wood-Jones, F., 1931c. The non-metrical morphological characters of the skull as criteria for racial diagnosis: part III: the non-metrical morphological characters of the skulls of prehistoric inhabitants of Guam. Journal of Anatomy 65 (Pt 4), 438–445.

Wood-Jones, F., 1933. The non-metrical morphological characters of the skull as criteria for racial diagnosis: part IV. The non-metrical morphological characters of the Northern Chinese skull. Journal of Anatomy 68 (Pt 1), 96–108.

CHAPTER 2

Biological Distances and Population Genetics in Bioarchaeology

J.H. Relethford
State University of New York College at Oneonta, Oneonta, NY, United States

CHAPTER OUTLINE HEAD

Introduction 23
Euclidean Distance 24
Mahalanobis's Distance 25
R-Matrix Theory and Biological Distance 25
R-Matrix Theory and Quantitative Traits 26
Assessing the Impact of Genetic Drift 29
Examining Differential Long-Range Gene Flow 29
Closing Thoughts 30
References 31

INTRODUCTION

Distance analysis is a common tool in population biology, where a number of distance measures have been proposed to examine genetic and/or phenotypic dissimilarity between pairs of populations (Sneath and Sokal, 1973). Examination of distances between all pairs of populations in an analysis can provide insight into population structure and history, with applications ranging from basic description to formal hypothesis testing. Some distance measures are purely genetic, based on the frequency of different alleles or haplotypes in populations. Other distance measures are phenotypic in nature; in bioarchaeology, such distance measures are typically referred to as biological distances (or "biodistances") and are derived using both metric and nonmetric traits.

When we use phenotypic biological distances to address questions of population structure, origin, and history, we are taking the phenotype as a proxy for underlying patterns of genetic affinity. If, for example, we find that populations A and B are more phenotypically similar (less distant) to one another than they are to population C, we infer that populations A and B are more genetically similar to each other than either is to population C. The cause of this similarity might be common ancestry, gene flow, or some other factor (or combination of factors) that would require further analysis to reveal. Howells (1973) saw the relationship between phenotypic distance and underlying genetic affinity as being either model-free or model-bound, in terms of whether the distance measure is defined in reference to a specific theoretical model of population genetics and whether actual model parameters are estimated (see also

Biological Distance Analysis. http://dx.doi.org/10.1016/B978-0-12-801966-5.00002-0

Relethford and Lees, 1982). However, as noted by Konigsberg (2006) and Relethford (2007), the difference between these categories is not always clear, as some model-free methods are based on population-genetic models but do not involve formal estimation of model parameters. For example, the commonly expected positive relationship between genetic/biological distance and geographic distance is based on the theoretical isolation-by-distance model of population genetics, meaning that the expectation is model-bound. However, this expected relationship could be tested with different methods ranging from a simple correlation or a formal fit to the isolation-by-distance model. Although the latter would involve the actual estimation of model parameters (eg, Relethford, 2004), the former approach would also be model-bound to some extent, as the expected direction of relationship between biological distance and geographic distance is derived from population-genetic theory. For the current chapter, my focus will be on the more explicit link of population genetics and biodistances that involves not only underlying models of population and quantitative genetics, but also estimation of specific parameters, such as F_{ST}.

The purpose of this chapter is to review the relationship between population-genetic models and two measures of biological distance that are used with quantitative traits (metric traits). In bioarchaeology, such data typically consist of measurements of cranial, skeletal, and dental traits, such as maximum head length or buccolingual breadth. Another source of data in biodistance studies is nonmetric traits, defined as the presence or absence of various cranial and dental traits (such as Carabelli's cusp). Only quantitative metric traits will be discussed in the current chapter. The relationship between population-genetic models and nonmetric traits involves a different quantitative-genetic model (the threshold model), which is outside the scope of this paper and discussed elsewhere (see Konigsberg, 2006 for treatment of nonmetric traits). The current chapter does not consider all possible extensions of population genetics to biodistances studies, but deals exclusively with the more specific application of what is known as R-matrix theory, which has been the focus of my own research. Konigsberg (2006) provides a more complete review of population genetics in bioarchaeology, including an informative history of such efforts.

EUCLIDEAN DISTANCE

For quantitative traits, the simplest and most intuitive measure is the Euclidean distance between populations. The squared distance (D^2) between populations i and j is

$$D_{ij}^2 = \sum (\overline{X}_{ik} - \overline{X}_{jk})^2 \tag{2.1}$$

where $\overline{X}_{ik}$ and $\overline{X}_{jk}$ are the means of trait k for populations i and j, respectively, and summation is over all traits. In order to avoid the problem of having traits with larger values having disproportionate impact (such as head length relative to a smaller measure such as nose breadth), the means that are used must be standardized values (Z scores) (Sneath and Sokal, 1973). Although squared-distance values have direct merit in some types of analyses, such as isolation-by-distance analysis (Relethford, 2004), the square root of the squared distance $(D = \sqrt{D^2})$ would be used in other contexts, such as input to a cluster analysis program. Eq. (2.1) is dependent on the number of traits, t, and for comparative purposes, it might be preferable to use an average squared-distance value of D^2/t and a distance value of $\sqrt{D^2/t}$ (Sneath and Sokal, 1973).

MAHALANOBIS'S DISTANCE

A major drawback of Euclidean distance as defined above is that correlated traits can contribute disproportionately to the overall distance. For example, if a craniometric analysis relied on three measures—say, upper facial height, nasal height, and head length—the first two measures would be highly correlated and therefore facial length would have more impact on overall distance than head length would. What is needed is a multivariate distance measure that takes the intercorrelation of traits into account. The typical solution has been Mahalanobis's (1936) generalized distance, which has been used for decades by biological anthropologists. The squared Mahalanobis distance between populations *i* and *j* is computed as

$$D_{ij}^2 = (X_i - X_j)' W^{-1} (X_i - X_j) \tag{2.2}$$

Here, X_i and X_j refer to the vector of *t* traits for populations *i* and *j*, respectively, *W* is the *t*-by-*t* variance–covariance matrix pooled over all groups in the analysis (not just *i* and *j*), and the prime symbol (′) indicates transposition (Sneath and Sokal, 1973). Note that I am using the same symbol for squared distance, D^2, as was used for Euclidean distance to show similarity in form, as Mahalanobis's D^2 is a squared Euclidean distance in a transformed multidimensional space (Sneath and Sokal, 1973). As with Euclidean distance, the value of the Mahalanobis distance will increase with the number of traits, meaning that one could not compare directly a distance value from one study with 10 traits with another analysis using 20 traits.

Some obvious restrictions on data analysis are of particular importance in bioarchaeological studies where the condition of skeletal remains often means missing data and/or small sample sizes. Multivariate methods such as Mahalanobis's distance require complete cases (no missing data), and depending on the condition of the remains, one often winds up playing a balancing act between deleting traits and deleting cases. If the number of missing values for a given trait is relatively small, missing data can be estimated using data imputation methods (see Chapter 9, this volume). Sample size is also important and should be kept as large as possible. Distance measures can be biased by small sample size, so Mahalanobis's squared distance should be corrected by subtracting the quantity $t(n_i + n_j)/(n_i n_j)$ from the value of D_{ij}^2 from Eq. (2.2), where n_i and n_j are the sample sizes for populations *i* and *j*, respectively, and *t* is the number of traits (Rightmire, 1970). If the resulting bias-corrected D^2 is negative, it must be truncated at zero value. Bias correction is useful, but cannot compensate when sample sizes are too small.

Mahalanobis distances have been used in numerous studies in biology (including biological anthropology) over the past 50 years as a relative measure of population dissimilarity. Using Howells's (1973) definition, we would consider the Mahalanobis distance to be a model-free distance, because its derivation is based on statistical concerns, not any specific model of population genetics. However, it turns out that distance measures derived from model-bound methods are very closely related to Mahalanobis distances. This relationship is explored in the next section, which deals with biological distances derived from R-matrix theory.

R-MATRIX THEORY AND BIOLOGICAL DISTANCE

For allele frequency data, one of the many genetic distance measures that have been developed is based on R-matrix theory. An R matrix provides information on genetic similarity within and between populations based on standardized allele/haplotype frequency differences. Much of the development of R-matrix theory can be found in Harpending and Jenkins (1973) and Workman et al. (1973). For an analysis of g populations, the R matrix consists of g rows and g columns. For any given allele, the element of the R matrix for populations *i* and *j* is

$$r_{ij} = \frac{(p_i - \bar{p})(p_j - \bar{p})}{\bar{p}\,(1 - \bar{p})} \tag{2.3}$$

where p_i and p_j are the allele frequencies in populations *i* and *j*, respectively, and $\bar{p}$ is the mean allele frequency over all populations in the analysis (not just *i* and *j*). The overall R matrix is obtained by averaging Eq. (2.3) over all alleles. The R matrix is a variance—covariance matrix of standardized allele frequencies. The mean allele frequency $\bar{p}$ is derived by weighting each population's allele frequency by its corresponding *population* size (not sample size). This weighting is used in order to obtain the expected mean allele frequency under random mating (no population subdivision), as this value is dependent on the total number of a given allele in the total population.

The elements of the R matrix can be used to estimate other useful population-genetic measures. One of these is the average diagonal element of the R matrix ($i = j$), weighted by population size, which gives an estimate of Wright's F_{ST} as

$$F_{ST} = \sum w_i r_{ii} \tag{2.4}$$

where w_i is the relative population size of population *i* ($=N_i/N_T$, where N_T is the total population size summed over all groups). F_{ST} is a measure of genetic differentiation among groups relative to the total amount of genetic variation expected under no subdivision. F_{ST} can be difficult to interpret and compare across studies because it is affected by population size, rates of local and long-range gene flow, and time depth, among other influences.

The R matrix can also be used to derive the genetic distance between pairs of populations. The squared genetic distance between populations *i* and *j* is (Harpending and Jenkins, 1973; Morton, 1975)

$$D_{ij}^2 = r_{ii} + r_{jj} - 2r_{ij}. \tag{2.5}$$

Further extensions to R-matrix theory include adjustments for sampling bias, as described by Workman et al. (1973).

R-MATRIX THEORY AND QUANTITATIVE TRAITS

An advantage of R-matrix theory is that it has been possible to extend the basic concepts to data other than allele/haplotype frequencies, allowing comparison of different results across different types of data (eg, Relethford, 2004). In addition to use with allele/haplotype frequencies, methods have been developed to estimate the R matrix from migration data (Rogers and Harpending, 1986) and surname frequencies (Relethford, 1988). For the purposes of this chapter, the most important extension has been incorporating R-matrix theory into the derivation of biological distances from quantitative traits. The bulk of the work on this extension is covered in three papers (Relethford and Blangero, 1990; Relethford et al., 1997; Williams-Blangero and Blangero, 1989). This extension of R-matrix theory to quantitative traits is based on the equal-and-additive-effects model of quantitative genetics, where multiple loci contribute equally to the phenotype.

Williams-Blangero and Blangero (1989) showed that the Mahalanobis distance is similar to the *minimum* genetic distance expected under the equal-and-additive-effects model if the heritability (h^2) of all traits is equal to 1. When h^2 is less than 1, the actual genetic distance will be higher. They also derived a method with which to compute the *minimum* possible value of F_{ST}, which has some rough comparative value across studies as a measure of phenotypic differentiation. Relethford and Blangero (1990) extended these findings and presented a multivariate model for estimating the R matrix, as well as F_{ST} and genetic distances, from quantitative traits. For g groups, the R matrix is derived from a g-by-g codivergence matrix (C) defined as

$$C = \Delta G^{-1}\Delta' \tag{2.6}$$

where Δ is a g-by-t matrix consisting of deviations of group means from the total grand mean pooled over all populations, and G is the pooled within-group additive genetic matrix. Both the grand mean and the within-group additive genetic matrix are obtained by weighting by *population* size (rather than by sample size as for the Mahalanobis distance). If population size is not known (as might often be the case in bioarchaeological studies), the researcher may wish to assume equal population size and weigh all populations equally ($w_i = 1/g$).

F_{ST} is then computed from the diagonal elements of the C matrix as

$$F_{ST} = \frac{\sum w_i c_{ii}}{2t + \sum w_i c_{ii}} \tag{2.7}$$

summed over all g populations. The R matrix is then computed as (Relethford and Blangero, 1990)

$$R = \frac{C(1 - F_{ST})}{2t}. \tag{2.8}$$

This matrix can be used to derive genetic distances using Eq. (2.5). Methods for computing bias correction for sample size and standard errors for elements of the R matrix, genetic distances, and F_{ST} are presented in Relethford et al. (1997).

These R-matrix methods require information on the pooled within-group additive genetic covariance matrix. In cases where heritabilities are known, or at least inferred from other studies, the pooled within-groups additive genetic covariance matrix, as well as the genetic distances and F_{ST}, can be estimated. The most common method has been to use a single average heritability, as we seldom have trait-specific heritabilities for a specific population, even for present-day populations. In the case of bioarchaeological studies, we would need to use an average heritability derived across traits and samples as a rough approximation (eg, Relethford, 1994). Here, the additive genetic covariance matrix in Eq. (2.6) would be estimated as $G = h^2P$, where P is the pooled within-group variance—covariance matrix (weighted by population size).

When heritabilities are not known, the elements of the R matrix, the derived distances, and F_{ST} are all *minimum* values. For example, if F_{ST} is estimated from the pooled within-group *phenotypic* covariance matrix as 0.05, this means that the actual value of F_{ST} cannot be less than 0.05, but with lower (and more realistic) heritabilities, the actual F_{ST} could be higher. The relationship between F_{ST} and minimum F_{ST} depends on the specific heritabilities of each trait, but for an average value across all traits it would be

$$F_{ST} = \frac{\text{Min}F_{ST}}{\text{Min}F_{ST} + h^2(1 - \text{Min}F_{ST})} \tag{2.9}$$

where h^2 is the average heritability (Relethford, 2007). Given a minimum F_{ST} of 0.05, the actual F_{ST} would be 0.055 for $h^2 = 0.9$, 0.070 for $h^2 = 0.7$, and 0.095 for $h^2 = 0.5$.

Both F_{ST} and minimum F_{ST} are useful comparative statistics within certain limits. We need to remember that F_{ST} is based on a population-genetic model that might not always fit any particular case (eg, Long and Kittles, 2003). Comparing F_{ST} values does allow us to make a *rough* statement about relative differentiation across studies, allowing for comparison of different population structures (eg, Jorde, 1980). However, there are certain caveats and restrictions that must be kept in mind when examining local population structure using F_{ST}. First, minimum F_{ST} values should not be compared if there is any suggestion that average heritability is likely to vary much from one population to the next, because the relationship between F_{ST} and minimum F_{ST} [Eq. (2.9)] would be affected. This is not likely to be a huge problem in many bioarchaeological studies that focus on geographically and environmentally local analyses, such as a set of villages in a local area. Second, comparison of F_{ST} values must be done across populations of similar scale. Comparing differentiation via F_{ST} among a group of small villages in a local valley with F_{ST} values obtained among regional or continental groups would not be useful, as these different studies use different units of analysis, encompass different geographic ranges, and have different population sizes. In other words, avoid mixing apples and oranges.

A third concern is that F_{ST} should not be used if it is computed from samples taken from a wide temporal range. An advantage of bioarchaeological studies is that different periods can be sampled for diachronic analysis, but sometimes data from different time intervals will need to be pooled in order to achieve reasonable sample sizes (eg, Byrd, 2014). Care must be taken when applying population-genetic methods to pooled data, because F_{ST} is a measure that assumes gene flow and genetic drift among a set of interbreeding populations at a single point in time. It is a synchronic, not diachronic, measure of genetic variation. If F_{ST} is derived using samples across periods in a single analysis, the researcher must assume that there is no significant genetic change over time. For example, in order to mix populations A and B from one period with populations C, D, and E from a different period, we must assume that none of these five populations have changed genetically over time in order to pool them all in the same analysis. In some cases, it may be desirable to remove temporal trends prior to pooling data (eg, Konigsberg, 1990; Stojanowski, 2004).

Another way to use F_{ST} in a temporal analysis is to compute F_{ST} separately for several periods. This approach has been used with data from present-day populations where a large age distribution allows separating the total sample into several generations, and then F_{ST} can be derived within each generation (eg, Jorde et al., 1982; Relethford et al., 1997). This approach could be extended to bioarchaeological studies where F_{ST} is computed on more than one period. Again, sample size determines whether this would be possible. If so, comparison of F_{ST} values over time could ideally be used to make inferences regarding demographic change. For example, an increase in gene flow or population size should result in a reduction in F_{ST}. In reality, however, using F_{ST} to track demographic change can be difficult because of the complex interplay between population size, rates of gene flow, and previous levels of F_{ST} and their proximity to an equilibrium state. Depending on specific conditions, any changes in F_{ST} could actually be counterintuitive, and shifts in F_{ST} might not tell us anything (Relethford, 1991; Relethford et al., 1997).

ASSESSING THE IMPACT OF GENETIC DRIFT

R-matrix distance analysis offers additional insight into population structure and history when the data are suitable. One potential avenue of investigation is the analysis of the differential impact of genetic drift. When there is a great deal of variation in population size in an analysis, and where these differences have persisted over time, it is likely that smaller populations have become more dissimilar because of genetic drift. Because there might be other factors affecting population dissimilarity, such as geographic distance and migration patterns, it would be useful to determine to what extent genetic drift obscures population history. If approximate population size is known for all populations in an analysis (at least in relative terms), then the R matrix (and corresponding genetic distances) can be scaled to account for differential drift, given that certain assumptions are met (Relethford, 1996). This scaling will show the greatest impact where there is a wide range in population size (eg, Relethford and Crawford, 2013). The elements of the scaled R matrix are

$$g\sqrt{w_i}\sqrt{w_j}r_{ij} \quad (2.10)$$

where w_i and w_j are the relative population sizes of populations *i* and *j*. The scaled R matrix can then be used to derive a scaled genetic distance matrix by substituting the scaled values for the elements of the R matrix in Eq. (2.5).

Population sizes are best known for present-day and historical populations where census data are readily available. In cases where population sizes have changed significantly over time, a harmonic mean can be used to estimate the average effective population size. In bioarchaeological studies, estimates of population size may be available in some cases based on a number of observations, including site size, cemetery size, the number and size of housing structures, and ethnohistoric data (eg, Nystrom, 2006; Scherer, 2007; Schillaci and Stojanowski, 2005; Steadman, 2001; Stojanowski, 2004). As the primary impact of genetic drift will be for cases where populations vary significantly in size, rough estimates (if archaeologically supported) should suffice in most cases. Analyses can also be rerun using different combinations of weights that relate to different demographic hypotheses (eg, Stojanowski, 2005).

EXAMINING DIFFERENTIAL LONG-RANGE GENE FLOW

Any interpretation of local population structure and history should consider external forces, such as the genetic impact of gene flow outside the area of local analysis (eg, migrants from another region moving into a river valley). Harpending and Ward (1982) developed a model for examining the effects of external gene flow from an "outside world" on genetic variation (heterozygosity) within a set of local populations. This model uses data on allele frequencies to compute an R matrix [Eq. (2.3)], the level of heterozygosity within each local population (H_i), and the heterozygosity of the total region of analysis (H_T). For local population *i*, the level of heterozygosity *expected* under the assumption of uniform external gene flow across all populations is computed as

$$E[H_i] = H_T(1 - r_{ii}). \quad (2.11)$$

This expected value is then compared to the *observed* level of heterozygosity in each population as $(H_i - E[H_i])$. If this residual value is positive, such that observed heterozygosity is greater than that expected, we can infer that population *i* has received more external gene flow than expected on average, whereas if the residual value is negative, then the opposite is inferred. The Harpending–Ward model is therefore useful for making inferences about differences in the level of external gene flow into a set of *local* populations from the unobserved "outside world." The Harpending–Ward model has been used in a number of studies of present-day human populations as a useful tool for unraveling population structure and history. However, we still lack precise knowledge concerning statistical power and standard errors for this method.

Relethford and Blangero (1990) used the equal-and-additive-effects model of quantitative genetics to extend the Harpending–Ward model for use with quantitative (metric) traits. The R matrix is computed as described above [Eqs. (2.6)–(2.8)] and used to estimate the *expected* level of phenotypic variation in population *i* (V_i) as

$$E[V_i] = \frac{V_w(1 - r_{ii})}{1 - F_{ST}} \tag{2.12}$$

where V_w is the observed pooled within-group variance weighted by population size. As with the Harpending–Ward model, the expected value is compared with the *observed* value of V_i. For the multivariate case, both V_i and V_w are average variances over all *t* traits after standardizing all raw data (Z scores).

Relethford and Blangero (1990) found that in this type of analysis, choice of heritability for estimating the R matrix was not critical, as the quantity $(1 - r_{ii})/(1 - F_{ST})$ in Eq. (2.12) was not affected greatly by choice of average heritability. Sample size and location did appear to have an impact. In their analysis of 19th-century Irish anthropometrics, Relethford and Blangero (1990) found that it was difficult to interpret residual phenotypic variation until several geographically proximate local populations were pooled, at which point the patterns of residual variation made more sense. It is not clear whether these results reflect sample size or subtle patterns of localized gene flow swamping long-range effects. As with the Harpending–Ward model for allele frequencies, we still lack information on the statistical properties of the Relethford–Blangero model (as it has become known). However, jackknifing residual variances over traits has allowed for some statistical inference (eg, Steadman, 2001).

As with R matrix distances and F_{ST}, care must be taken when applying the Relethford–Blangero model to data that have been pooled over a wide temporal range, as the underlying population-genetic model is synchronic. Temporal trends in the data should be assessed and controlled for in some cases. Stojanowski (2004) provides an example of how temporal trends can affect interpretation of residual phenotypic variation.

CLOSING THOUGHTS

When my colleague John Blangero and I were exploring population-genetic models for quantitative traits in the late 1980s, we were not working on bioarchaeological data (neither of us is a bioarchaeologist), but were looking at anthropometric variation from historical (19th century) Ireland and dermatoglyphics from present-day Nepal. Although others have applied our methods to both historical and present-day populations (see examples in Relethford, 2007), it seems to me that our work may have had the greatest impact on skeletal biology and bioarchaeology. In recent years, a number of studies have used cranial and dental metric data to address questions of prehistoric population structure and history using R-matrix methods, including estimation of F_{ST} and application of the Relethford–Blangero method to examine differential external gene flow. Some examples include a number of studies published in the *American Journal of Physical Anthropology* in the past 15 years (Byrd, 2014; Nystrom, 2006; Scherer, 2007; Schillaci and Stojanowski, 2005; Steadman, 2001; Stojanowski, 2004, 2005; Tatarek and Sciulli, 2000; Varela and Cocilovo, 2002). This is not meant to be an exhaustive list, and is given only to provide examples of the application of our methods to bioarchaeological investigation; these studies provide examples of how researchers have dealt with issues of sample size, missing data, population size estimates, and temporal trends, among others.

The classic distance measure used with quantitative traits has been Mahalanobis's generalized distance. This distance is intuitively appealing, as it extends the concept of Euclidean distance to a case where intercorrelation of metric traits is taken into account. For many applications in bioarchaeology, particularly those that focus primarily on an overall assessment of the pattern of relationship among populations, Mahalanobis's distance is sufficient. A matrix of Mahalanobis distances can be used with a wide range of classic methods. Graphic methods, such as cluster analysis and multidimensional scaling, can be used to produce distance "maps" that visually show the relationship of populations to each other. Often, such simple pictures can answer a number of questions regarding population structure and history. Mahalanobis distances can also be used for more formal hypothesis testing by examining the correlation between phenotypic distance and other distances such as geographic distance.

The use of R-matrix methods may provide greater insight in certain cases. Although somewhat crude, F_{ST} and minimum F_{ST} do provide a rough comparative measure of differentiation. Using an R matrix based on population sizes gives a more accurate reflection of underlying genetic distances and can allow for assessment of the effects of genetic drift. The Relethford–Blangero method can provide information on variation in external gene flow. Although all R-matrix methods of analysis have potential as model-bound approaches, they do make additional assumptions that must always be taken into account, including the mode of inheritance, heritability estimation, data from a single period, and others discussed in this chapter. More research is needed on addressing problems resulting from violation of these assumptions in order to determine how robust the methods are, particularly in a bioarchaeological context.

References

Byrd, R.M., 2014. Phenotypic variation of transitional forager-farmers in the Sonoran Desert. The American Journal of Physical Anthropology 155, 579–590.

Harpending, H., Jenkins, T., 1973. Genetic distance among southern African populations. In: Crawford, M.H., Workman, P.L. (Eds.), Methods and Theories of Anthropological Genetics. University of New Mexico Press, Albuquerque, pp. 177–200.

Harpending, H., Ward, R., 1982. Chemical systematics and human evolution. In: Nitecki, M. (Ed.), Biochemical Aspects of Evolutionary Biology. University of Chicago Press, Chicago, pp. 213–256.

Howells, W.W., 1973. Measures of population distances. In: Crawford, M.H., Workman, P.L. (Eds.), Methods and Theories of Anthropological Genetics. University of New Mexico, Albuquerque, pp. 159–176.

Jorde, L.B., 1980. The genetic structure of subdivided human populations: a review. In: Mielke, J.H., Crawford, M.H. (Eds.), Current Developments in Anthropological Genetics, vol. 1: Theory and Methods. Plenum Press, New York, pp. 135–208.

Jorde, L.B., Workman, P.L., Eriksson, A.W., 1982. Genetic microevolution in the Åland Islands, Finland. In: Crawford, M.H., Mielke, J.H. (Eds.), Current Developments in Anthropological Genetics, vol. 2: Ecology and Population Structure. Plenum Press, New York, pp. 333–365.

Konigsberg, L.W., 1990. Analysis of prehistoric biological variation under a model of isolation by geographic and temporal distance. Human Biology 62, 49–70.

Konigsberg, L.W., 2006. A post-neumann history of biological and genetic distance studies in bioarchaeology. In: Buikstra, J.E., Beck, L.A. (Eds.), Bioarchaeology: The Contextual Analysis of Human Remains. Academic Press, Amsterdam, pp. 263–280.

Long, J.C., Kittles, R.A., 2003. Human genetic diversity and the nonexistence of biological races. Human Biology 75, 449–471.

Mahalanobis, P.C., 1936. On the generalized distance in statistics. National Historic Institute of Science, India 2, 49–55.

Morton, N., 1975. Kinship, information and biological distance. Theoretical Population Biology 7, 246–255.

Nystrom, K.C., 2006. Late Chachapoya population structure prior to Inka conquest. American Journal of Physical Anthropology 131, 334–342.

Relethford, J.H., 1988. Estimation of kinship and genetic distance from surnames. Human Biology 60, 475–492.

Relethford, J.H., 1991. Effect of changes in population size on genetic microdifferentiation. Human Biology 63, 629–641.

Relethford, J.H., 1994. Craniometric variation among modern human populations. American Journal of Physical Anthropology 95, 53–62.

Relethford, J.H., 1996. Genetic drift can obscure population history: problem and solution. Human Biology 68, 29–44.

Relethford, J.H., 2004. Global patterns of isolation by distance based on genetic and morphological data. Human Biology 76, 499–513.

Relethford, J.H., 2007. The use of quantitative traits in anthropological genetic studies of population structure and history. In: Crawford, M.H. (Ed.), Anthropological Genetics Theory, Methods and Applications. The Cambridge University Press, Cambridge, pp. 187–209.

Relethford, J.H., Blangero, J., 1990. Detection of differential gene flow from patterns of quantitative variation. Human Biology 62, 5–25.

Relethford, J.H., Crawford, M., Blangero, J., 1997. Genetic drift and gene flow in post-famine Ireland. Human Biology 69, 443–465.

Relethford, J.H., Crawford, M.H., 2013. Genetic drift and the population history of the irish travellers. American Journal of Physical Anthropology 150, 184–189.

Relethford, J.H., Lees, F., 1982. The use of quantitative traits in the study of human population structure. Yearbook of Physical Anthropology 25, 113–132.

Rightmire, G., 1970. Bushman, Hottentot and South African Negro crania studied by distance and discrimination. American Journal of Physical Anthropology 33, 169–195.

Rogers, A.R., Harpending, H.C., 1986. Migration and genetic drift in human populations. Evolution 1312–1327.

Scherer, A.K., 2007. Population structure of the classic period Maya. American Journal of Physical Anthropology 132, 367–380.

Schillaci, M.A., Stojanowski, C., 2005. Craniometric variation and population history of the prehistoric Tewa. American Journal of Physical Anthropology 126, 404–412.

Sneath, P.H.A., Sokal, R.R., 1973. Numerical Taxonomy. W.H. Freeman, San Francisco.

Steadman, D.W., 2001. Mississippians in motion? A population genetic analysis of interregional gene flow in West-Central Illinois. American Journal of Physical Anthropology 114, 61–73.

Stojanowski, C., 2004. Population history of native groups in pre- and postcontact Spanish Florida: aggregation, gene flow, and genetic drift on the Southeastern U.S. Atlantic coast. American Journal of Physical Anthropology 123, 316–332.

Stojanowski, C., 2005. Spanish colonial effects on Native American mating structure and genetic variability in northern and central Florida: evidence from Apaplachee and western Timucua. American Journal of Physical Anthropology 128, 273–286.
Tatarek, N.E., Sciulli, P.W., 2000. Comparison of population structure in Ohio's late archaic and late prehistoric periods. American Journal of Physical Anthropology 112, 363–376.
Varela, H.H., Cocilovo, J.A., 2002. Genetic drift and gene flow in a prehistoric population of the Azapa Valley and coast, Chile. American Journal of Physical Anthropology 118, 259–267.
Williams-Blangero, S., Blangero, J., 1989. Anthropometric variation and the genetic structure of the Jirels of Nepal. Human Biology 61, 1–12.
Workman, P.L., Harpending, H., Lalouel, J.M., Lynch, C., Niswander, J.D., Singleton, R., 1973. Population studies on Southwestern Indian tribes. VI. Papago population structure: a comparison of genetic and migration analyses. In: Morton, N.E. (Ed.), Genetic Structure of Populations. University of Hawaii Press, Honolulu, pp. 166–194.

CHAPTER

Craniometric Data Analysis and Estimation of Biodistance

3

B. Dudzik, A. Kolatorowicz
Lincoln Memorial University, Harrogate, TN, United States

CHAPTER OUTLINE HEAD

History of Craniometric Data Collection and Analysis 36
Data Collection Protocols 37
  Types of Measurements 37
  Selecting Measurements 40
  Instrumentation 41
  Options for Recording Measurements 46
  Error in Craniometry 46
  Procedures 48
Heritability 49
Bioarchaeological and Forensic Approaches to Craniometric Data 52
  Common Statistical Methods in Forensic Anthropology and Bioarchaeology 53
Conclusions 55
References 55

Many of the current methods used to estimate biological distance are built upon foundational research using metric data from the human skull. In particular, estimations of population affinity via analysis of bony components of the human head traditionally have been a central focus of anatomists and anthropologists, perhaps most notably in paleoanthropology, bioarchaeology, and forensic anthropology. The last 50 years have provided some of the most fundamental sources of knowledge with respect to cranial variation in extant and extinct populations. Identification and allocation of skeletal metric variables into groups representative of ancestral affiliation has been a cornerstone of anthropological research. In particular, craniometric analyses using multivariate statistical approaches provide evidence for evolutionary histories of anatomically modern human and hominin populations. In analyses of biodistance, the quantification of morphological similarity (and/or dissimilarity) is an integral part of elucidating an evolutionary history. The estimation of biological relationships takes on specific terminologies in different contexts (ie, forensic versus archaeological), but overall, the common aim of such an analysis is to explore biological relationships among individuals and/or group samples.

Biological Distance Analysis. http://dx.doi.org/10.1016/B978-0-12-801966-5.00003-2

HISTORY OF CRANIOMETRIC DATA COLLECTION AND ANALYSIS

Craniometric analyses have a long and troubled past in physical anthropology. In portions of the 18th century and more recently during the 19th and early 20th centuries, cranial shape or size was incorrectly correlated with cognitive ability and social traits, for example (see Blumenbach, 1775; Linnaeus, 1735). These associations began with Linneaus, who through his attempts to classify large amounts of human cranial diversity, developed associated racial descriptions. However, Blumenbach observed correlations between human variation, geography, and subsistence, but maintained that diversity was reflective of change from an ideal form. Blumenbach established five broad races (Caucasian, Mongolian, Ethiopian, American, and Malayan) based on skull morphology and soft tissue characteristics. These categories illustrated morphological variability with degrees of facial prognathism and facial flatness, and were depicted in a later version of his original *De generis humani varietate nativa* (1775). While perhaps one of the first proponents of establishing world races, Blumenbach's contributions did not encompass collection or analysis of metric data and do not represent the role of current day anthropological research.

Early contributions by those who laid the foundation for biological research in anthropology most notably occurred in the early 20th century with the pioneering work of Aleš Hrdlička, Earnest Hooton, and Franz Boas. Their work shaped the burgeoning field of physical anthropology in the United States and provided much of the basis for future investigations of human skeletal variation. Collectively, these researchers introduced novel approaches to studying the human form by employing statistical analyses that used large-scale data sets to answer evolutionary questions at both global and individual levels (Caspari, 2009; Jantz and Spencer, 1997). The scientific focus of these forefathers ranged from the justification of eugenics with the typology-focused work of Hrdlička (1911, 1918) and Hooton (1930), to the influence of culture and environment on biological diversity with the works of Boas (1910, 1911, 1912).

The dawn of the 20th century brought a wave of quantitative work in which craniometric data were central. Contributions of a number of major anthropological players were at work establishing data procurement techniques, statistical approaches, and data sets that have provided much of the impetus behind current research in a number of disciplines. Although the political direction and validation of the use of racial forms to institute detestable acts such as genetic cleansing occurred, the early proponents of scientific analysis of diversity ultimately gave way to a new wave of anthropological endeavors. W.W. Howells was a Hooton student and went on to redefine racial constructs as geographic populations. In an incredible feat, Howells single-handedly collected the largest global craniometric data set (Howells, 1996), which has been used in some seminal biodistance works (eg, Relethford, 2002; Relethford and Harpending, 1994).

In addition to producing a (now) publicly available data set (see Appendix A—this volume), Howells also produced a refined version of definitions of cranial landmarks and measurements, colloquially referred to as "Howells's Definitions." A subset of these landmarks and measurements is typically collected in the majority of basic skeletal analyses based on Martin's (1914) publication (or sometimes revised versions), which added to the previously outlined body of work from Morton and Broca (Martin, 1914).

Other large-scale craniometric data sets available in the literature include those collected by Hanihara and Ishida (Hanihara, 2008). Modern, forensically relevant data banks include the Forensic Data Bank (FDB) available through the University of Tennessee and the Maxwell Museum Documented Skeletal Collection curated at the University of New Mexico. As more body donation programs that permanently curate skeletal material are established throughout the United Stares, the opportunity to study variation in modern Americans will grow immensely. Skeletal collections that are constantly adding individuals representing the population are important for documenting secular change. Recent historic studies have identified morphological change over time in American citizens, with the results of Jantz and Jantz (2000) showing that American skulls have increased in height and length over the last 150 years.

DATA COLLECTION PROTOCOLS

Data collection must be systematic in nature and follow standard protocols established by the discipline and/or by the laboratory where the work is being performed. Such practices ensure that data can be replicated and validated by other observers as well as compared or combined with other studies. One needs to consider which measurements will be necessary to answer the research question. Lesser known, nonstandard measurements and instrumentation may be required. The types of measurement, and the landmarks that define them, will determine the instrumentation required. At the same time, the specific instruments available to a researcher may limit the measurements a researcher can use. Other considerations, like form of recording (electronic versus paper), ease of measurement, and measurement error must be accounted for.

Types of Measurements

Traditional cranial measurements are classified into one of three categories: (1) box, (2) sutural, or (3) extreme curvature (Hursh, 1976). Box measurements are those that take into account extreme ends of the skull and are instrumentally defined. *Maxillo-alveolar breadth*, the "maximum breadth across the alveolar borders of the maxilla measured on the lateral surfaces at the location of the second maxillary molars" (Buikstra and Ubelaker, 1994, p. 75), is an example of a box measurement. Sutural measurements are distances between points, one of which is defined by a suture or similar feature. An example of a sutural measurement is *interorbital breadth*, the "direct distance between left and right dacryon" (Buikstra and Ubelaker, 1994, p. 76). Extreme curvature measurements are those based on regions of maximum change in the curve of a surface. The *frontal subtense*, "the maximum subtense, at the highest point on the convexity of the frontal bone in the midplane, to the nasion—bregma chord" (Howells, 1973, p. 181), is one example of an extreme curvature measure.

Hurst's classification scheme relates closely to the types of landmarks found on the skull: Type I, Type II, and Type III (Bookstein, 1991). Type I, also known as anatomical landmarks, are discrete juxtapositions of tissues in which homology is found locally (O'Higgins, 2000). Intersections such as *nasion*, "the point of intersection of the Naso-Frontal suture and the midsagittal plane" (Moore-Jansen et al., 1994, p. 46), is an example. Type II, or mathematical, landmarks locate the maxima of curvatures such as the tips of bony processes or the deepest point in a fossa. The landmark *jugale*, "the point in the notch between the temporal and frontal processes of the zygomatic bone" exemplifies mathematical landmarks. Homology is found via geometric evidence (O'Higgins, 2000). Type III, or extremal, landmarks are found opposite of other landmarks and are deficient in one coordinate (O'Higgins, 2000). The "instrumentally determined most posterior point of the skull not on the external occipital protuberance" (Buikstra and Ubelaker, 1994, p. 72), *opisthocranion*, is an example of a Type III landmark. A fourth type of landmark known as a semilandmark may be an arbitrarily chosen point along an arc to quantify a curve. Landmarks of this type are not real landmarks as defined above, yet they still provide information about form. Semilandmarks are not typically used in traditional craniometrics and will not be discussed further. Type I landmarks are the most easily identifiable, Type II less so, and Type III landmarks are the most difficult to consistently locate. The location of Type III landmarks allows an observer to define the ends of a measurement and quantify the interlandmark distance.

Cranial measurements, and the landmarks from which they are defined, may be divided into one of two categories based on popularity: standard and nonstandard measurements. Complete lists of cranial landmarks and measurements, their definitions, and special notes can be found in *Lehrbruch der Anthropologie* (Martin, 1914), *Practical Anthropometry* (Hrdlička, 1952), *Practical Anthropology* (Olivier, 1969), *Human Osteology: A Laboratory and Field Manual of the Human Skeleton* (Bass, 1971), *Data Collection Procedures for Forensic Skeletal Identification* (Moore-Jansen et al., 1994), and *Standards for Data Collection from Human Skeletal Remains* (Buikstra and Ubelaker, 1994). Here, "standard" measures are the 24 measurements found in the Buikstra and Ubelaker (1994) volume *Standards*, and require only spreading and sliding calipers (Table 3.1).

"Nonstandard" measurements are less commonly used and may require specialized instruments such as a coordinate caliper or a radiometer (Table 3.2). Because the measurements and instrumentation are uncommon, the price of such instrumentation is much greater than it is for standard instruments, making data collection costs prohibitive. Nonstandard instrumentation is more difficult to manipulate with more than three points to move, can take more time to record a measurement, and has a greater potential to damage specimens. Researchers have specifically discussed the benefits of using nonstandard instrumentation and the information that can be collected using it (Brues, 1990; Cunha and Van Vark, 1991; Gill et al., 1988; Howells, 1969, 1973; Pearson, 1934; Rightmire, 1970, 1976; Woo and Morant, 1934). The consensus is that unconventional measurements provide higher discriminatory power than provided by standard measurements (Jantz and Owsley, 1994). Previous versions of Fordisc (Jantz and Ousley, 1993;

Table 3.1 List of Standard Cranial Measurements

Maximum cranial length GOL^2	Nasal height NLH^1
Maximum cranial breadth XCB^2	Nasal breadth NLB^1
Bizygomatic diameter ZYB^2	Orbital breadth OBB^1
Basion–bregma height BBH^2	Orbital height OBH^1
Cranial base length BNL^2	Biorbital breadth EKB^1
Basion–prosthion length BPL^2	Interorbital breadth DKB^1
Maxillo–alveolar breadth MAB^2	Frontal chord FRC^1
Maxillo–alveolar length MAL^2	Parietal chord PAC^1
Biauricular breadth AUB^2	Occipital chord OCC^1
Upper facial height NPH^1	Foramen magnum length FOL^1
Minimum frontal breadth WFB^2	Foramen magnum breadth FOB^1
Upper facial breadth UFBR^2	Mastoid length MDH^1

Measurement abbreviation and superscript numerical indicator for type of instrument to be used. ^{1}sliding caliper, ^{2}spreading caliper, ^{3}coordinate caliper, ^{4}radiometer.
After Buikstra, J.E., Ubelaker, D.H., 1994. Standards for Data Collection From Human Skeletal Remains. Research Series 44. Arkansas Archeological Survey, Fayetteville, NC; Howells, W.W., 1973. Cranial variation in man: a study by multivariate analysis of patterns of difference among recent human populations. In: Papers of the Peabody Museum of Archaeology and Ethnology, pp. 1–259.

Table 3.2 List of Nonstandard Measurements

Mastoid width MDB[1]	Supraorbital projection SOS[3]
Nasio–occipital length NOL[2]	Glabella projection GLS[3]
Maximum frontal breadth XFB[2]	Simotic chord WNB[3]
Bistephanic breadth STB[1]	Frontal subtense SIS[3]
Minimum cranial breadth WCB[1]	Frontal fraction FRF[3]
Biasterionic breadth ASB[1]	Parietal subtense PAS[3]
Bijugal breadth JUB[1]	Parietal fraction PAF[3]
Malar length, inferior IML[1]	Vertex radius VRR[4]
Malar length, maximum XML[3]	Nasion radius NAR[4]
Malar subtense MLS[3]	Subspinale radius SSR[4]
Cheek height WMH[1]	Prosthion radius PRR[4]
Bimaxillary breadth ZMB[3]	Dacryon radius DKR[4]
Bimaxillary subtense SSS[3]	Zygoorbitale radius ZOR[4]
Bifrontal breadth FMB[3]	Frontomalare radius FMR[4]
Nasio–frontal subtense NAS[3]	Ectoconchion radius EKR[4]
Dacryon subtense DKS[3]	Zygomaxillare radius ZMR[4]
Naso–dacryl subtense NDS[3]	Molar alveolar radius AVR[4]

Three-letter abbreviations given. [1]sliding caliper, [2]spreading caliper, [3]coordinate caliper, [4]radiometer.
After Howells, W.W., 1973. Cranial variation in man: a study by multivariate analysis of patterns of difference among recent human populations. In: Papers of the Peabody Museum of Archaeology and Ethnology, pp. 1–259.

Ousley and Jantz, 1996) excluded such measurements; however, the latest version, 3.0 (Jantz and Ousley, 2005), has options to include the full set of Howells's (1973) measurements.

Measurements can also be described based on the exact aspect of form being measured. Length, width, height, breadth, diameter, circumference, thickness, arc, chord, fraction, subtense, projection, radius, and angle have been used by craniometricians. Lengths are taken from anterior to posterior, such as *cranial base length*, "the direct distance from nasion to basion" (Howells, 1973, p. 171). Breadths are taken from the left to right, crossing the median plane, between two mirrored landmarks such as *minimum cranial breadth*, "the breadth across the sphenoid at the base of the temporal fossa, at the infratemporal crests" (Howells, 1973, p. 173). Heights are taken from superior to inferior (eg, *basion–bregma height* or cranial height, "the direct distance from the lowest point on the anterior margin of the foramen magnum, basion (BA), to bregma" (Moore-Jansen et al., 1994, p. 50)). The one width measurement, *mastoid width*, is taken through the transverse axis of the base of the mastoid process, wherever it may lie. Chords are a measure of direct distance and almost always refer to measurements of the vault in which the shortest distance between two points on a curved surface is recorded. An example is the *occipital chord*, "the direct distance from lambda to opisthion" (Howells, 1973, p. 182).

Less common or obsolete measures include arc, projection, fraction, subtense, radius, circumference, and thickness. An arc is a curved line or segment of a circle as in the bones of the vault (eg, *frontal arc*, the distance from nasion to bregma along the curvature of the vault). A subtense is a perpendicular measurement from a chord to the outer surface of bone, describing how far the bone projects from a given plane (a magnitude of curvature). An example of a subtense measurement is the *parietal subtense*, "the

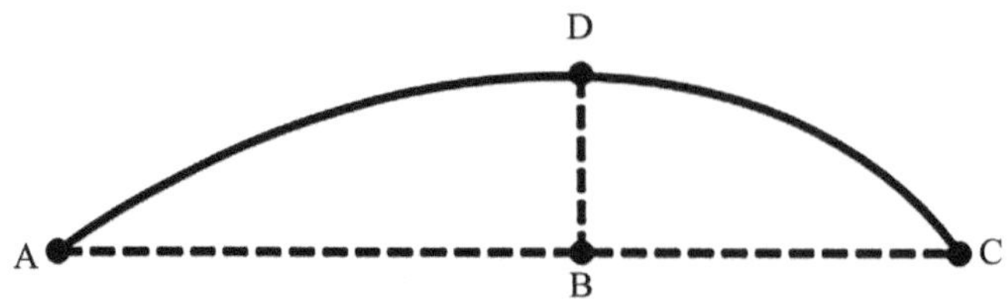

FIGURE 3.1 Measurements of a curved surface.

$\overline{AC}$ = chord, $\overline{BD}$ = subtense, $\overline{AB}$ = fraction, and $\overline{ADC}$ = arc.

maximum subtense, at the highest point on the convexity of the parietal bones in the midplane, to the bregma—lambda chord." A subtense may be referred to as a "projection" as in *supraorbital projection*, "the maximum projection of the left supraorbital arch between the midline, in the region of glabella or above, and the frontal bone just anterior to the temporal line in its forward part, measured as a subtense to the line defined" (Howells, 1973, p. 180). A fraction is a measure of how far along the chord the subtense lies; for example, the *frontal fraction*, "the distance along the nasion—bregma chord, recorded from nasion, at which the frontal subtense falls" (Howells, 1973, p. 181). Fig. 3.1 shows how chords, subtenses, fractions, and arcs are measured on a curved surface.

All radial measurements are taken from the transmeatal axis, a line that passes between the two external auditory meati. The perpendicular distance from the transmeatal axis to a specified landmark is recorded as in the *zygomaxillare radius*, "the perpendicular to the transmeatal axis from the left zygomaxillare anterior" (Howells, 1973, p. 184). Angles are not measurements taken directly from the skull; rather, they are calculated from two measurements that share a common landmark. For example, *nasion angle* is the angle at nasion whose sides are cranial base length and upper facial height. The only cranial circumferential measurement is *circumference of the vault*, described by Hrdliĉka (1952) as an obsolete measurement taken with an anthropometric tape that has been replaced by cranial length, width, and breadth measures. The term *diameter* has been replaced by *breadth*.

Familiarity with these abbreviations may save the observer time during data collection as well as space on recording forms. The first two letters in the three letter nomenclature tells the observer the bone or landmark being utilized (eg, frontal = FR, mastoid = MD, orbital = OB) and if it is a maximum (M) or minimum (W) measure. One measurement, inferior malar length (IML), uses a first letter that is not found in other measurements, "*I*," to indicate that it is the inferior length of the malar bone. The third letter describes aspects of the form being described: breadth (*B*), chord (*C*), fraction (*F*), height (*H*), length (*L*), radius (*R*), or subtense/projection (*S*). For maximum cranial length, the abbreviation is given as "GOL." The abbreviation tells the recorder that a length (*L*) is taken from glabella (G) to opisthocranion (O). For frontal fraction, FRF, "FR" indicates the frontal bone and "*F*" informs the observer that the measurement is a fraction.

Selecting Measurements

Craniometric studies fall into one of three categories regarding measurement selection. The first category is that no explanation is provided. Cunha and Van Vark (1991) examined a series of crania from turn-of-the-20th-century Portuguese crania. They took 61 measurements as defined by Howells (1973) and were able to correctly identify the sex of 80% of the individuals. In their study of Chinese crania, Song et al. (1992) chose a mixture of 38 standard and nonstandard measurements that produced 97% correct classification. Steyn and İşcan (1998) selected 12 "standard" measurements in their study of identifying the sex of South African individuals and were able to do so with a success rate of 86%. Although the accuracy rates of the aforementioned studies are high, the authors give no precise reasons why the variables they used were selected.

The second category of measurement selection is based on ease of recording. Giles and Elliot (1962, 1963) chose the eight standard variables to measure in developing their methodology because of "ease of recording." In similar fashion, Wright (1992) reduced Howells's set to 29 variables that were the easiest to measure.

The third category of craniometric studies is that in which measurements are selected to describe a certain region of the cranium. When Rightmire (1976) examined the skulls of Bantu-speaking African groups, he selected 37 measurements, some standard and others specifically designed to measure certain features of the midface, vault, and brow. In an assessment of craniometric relationships between Plains Indian groups within a cultural-evolutionary framework, Key (1983) recorded 65 measurements. Most of these came from Howells's (1973) set, but nine were created by the author "to more fully measure particular morphological complexes" (Key, 1983, p. 40). In his studies of cranial variation, Gill (1984) noticed that the greatest difference between Northwest Plains Indians and other groups existed in the nasal bridge. He took six unconventional measurements of the nasal region to develop a novel method. Ross and associates (2004) selected landmarks "that would reveal the overall cranial morphology of the crania" to help identify Cuban American skulls in forensic contexts.

Common measurements may not address specific research questions, so novel measurement can be derived. If a novel measurement is created, then it must be accompanied by (1) a definition, (2) specific landmarks associated with measurement (with reference to definitions), and (3) notes on proper execution of data collection (including position of skull and placement of caliper points).

Van Vark (1976) provided an algorithm for selecting variables that encapsulates the three primary considerations cited by researchers. First, make a list of variables that will best describe the area of interest. Second, order the variables from most to least important. Third, decide which ordered set should be included in data collection. Fiscal and time constraints may heavily influence one's final selection. No matter which variables are selected, they must be homologous or found in all individuals and groups within the sample so that comparison is possible (Bookstein, 1991).

Instrumentation

Sliding calipers and spreading calipers are the standard instruments found in most biological anthropology laboratories (Fig. 3.2). A flexible measuring tape was formerly used to document cranial circumference, but that measure is no longer in use, as the measurement is more accurate with spreading calipers. Special instruments are required to record nonstandard measurements such as subtenses, fractions, and radii. For subtenses and fractions, one uses a coordinate caliper or simometer (Figs. 3.3 and 3.4), which is a modified sliding caliper with an extra (third) arm. The simometer was first described in 1882 by de Mérejkowsky (Woo and Morant, 1934). The extra arm moves up and down in a plane perpendicular to the other arms and is used to measure subtenses. The third arm can also be moved anywhere horizontally between the two main arms. A fraction is taken from the fixed arm of the caliper to the third arm. Gill (1984) describes the

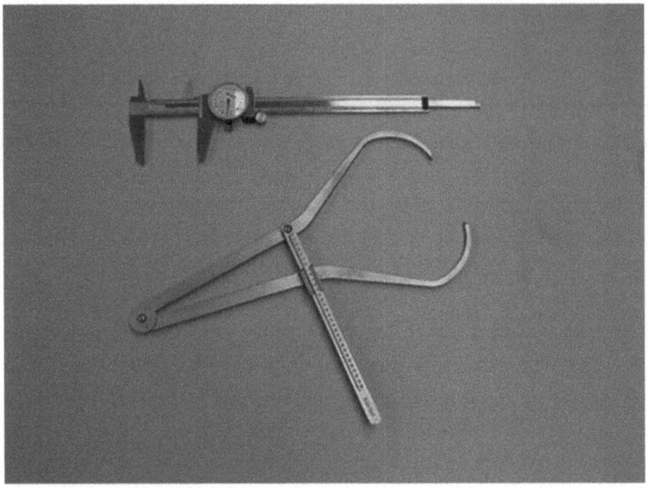

FIGURE 3.2

Dial-type sliding (top) and spreading (bottom) calipers.

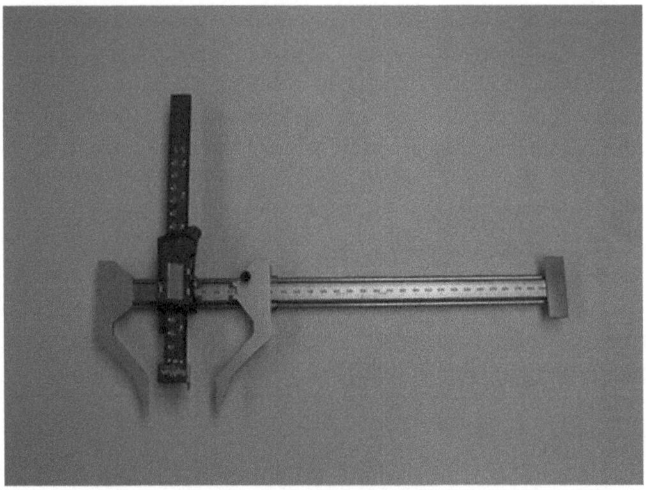

FIGURE 3.3

Coordinate caliper.

use of a simometer to take six additional measurements of the midface for ancestral assessment: maxillofrontal breadth, naso—maxillofrontal subtense, midorbital breadth, naso—zygoorbital subtense, alpha chord, and naso—alpha subtense. However, these measurements are rarely recorded or used in modern analyses.

An even more specialized instrument is used to record radii. The radiometer has three arms just like a coordinate caliper, but only the third, middle arm is used to record a distance (Figs. 3.5 and 3.6). Two of

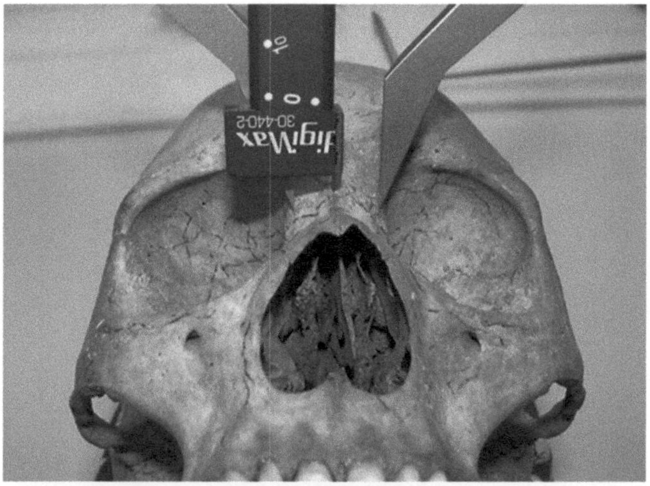

FIGURE 3.4

Coordinate caliper measuring naso–dacryl subtense, the projection of the nasal ridge.

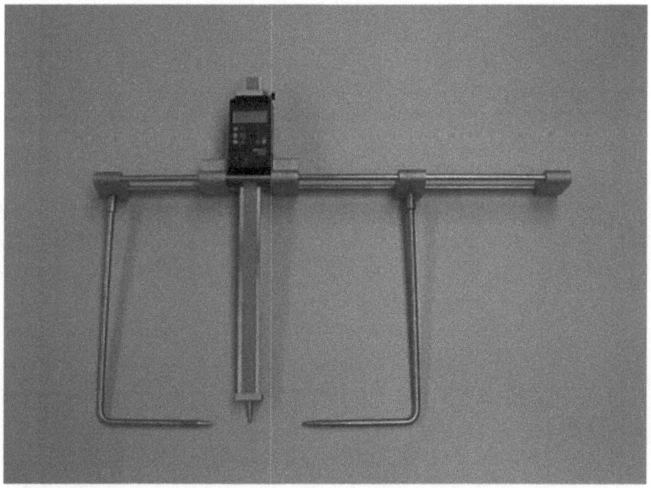

FIGURE 3.5

Radiometer.

the arms in the horizontal plane have points that face each other and are inserted into the external auditory meati to lock the radiometer in the transmeatal axis. Extreme care must be taken to avoid damage to the auditory meati. At this point, the device is free to rotate 360° about the axis while the third arm in the vertical plane moves inward to landmarks on the skull. This instrument measures radial distances from the transmeatal axis to a landmark. Howells (1973) describes 10 radial measurements, 5 of which are along the midsagittal plane.

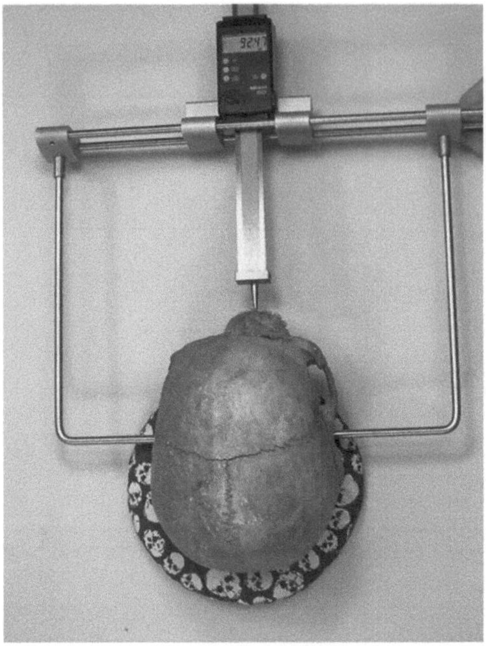

FIGURE 3.6

Radiometer measuring prosthion radius to quantify maxillary prognathism.

Instrumentation is available in analog and digital forms with two common scales of measure (Fig. 3.7). Most instruments include a straight scale for recording the distance between caliper points. The inside edge of the moveable caliper arm, or other line indicator, will directly specify the distance. In addition to a straight scale, some instruments include a smaller vernier scale attached to the moveable arm to allow for

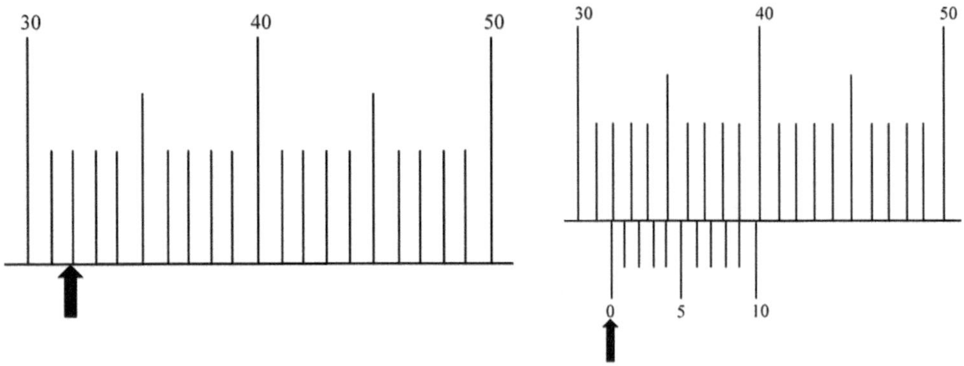

FIGURE 3.7

Straight scale (left) and vernier scale with 0.1 gradients (right). The *arrows* indicate the position of the movable arm on a caliper. The straight scale would be rounded up and read as "32." The vernier scale would be read as "31.9."

precision to the nearest tenth or hundredth of a unit. If an instrument utilizes a vernier scale, the straight scale is referred to as the "major scale," and the "0" on the smaller vernier scale is called the "pointer." To read a vernier scale, identify the location of the pointer in relation to the major scale. If the pointer aligns with a tick mark on the major scale, record that number. If the pointer does not line up with the major scale tick mark, look down the vernier scale and see which number, "1" through "10," aligns with a tick mark on the major scale. In Fig. 3.8, the pointer has passed the "31" and is very close to "32," so one looks further down the scale and sees that only the "9" lines up with a major scale tick mark. Outside of odontometrics, precision below 1.00 mm in osteometry is not common, and may be beyond the range of precision of most instrumentation. Howells (1973) instructs that simotic chord and simotic subtense be read to the nearest 0.1 mm.

Formal instrument calibration should be performed at regular intervals to ensure measurement integrity and prior to each measurement round following the manufacturer's instructions. Caliper tips may be worn down through years of use. The material used for manufacture will determine the degree of wear. Surgical grade steel will not wear appreciably over time; however, aluminum, which is lighter and more cost-effective, may wear more quickly. Instruments may become bent through mishandling, preventing components from lining up properly. Quality gauge blocks constructed from metal or ceramic should be used to ensure the instrument is reading correctly. If the instrument is not providing a measurement commensurate to the gauge block, ensure proper use of the instrument and contact the manufacturer. Digital scales may include a "tare" or "zero" button. Prior to measurement, close the caliper jaws and press this button so that the scale reads "0.00." Otherwise, systematic bias may be introduced to the measurements.

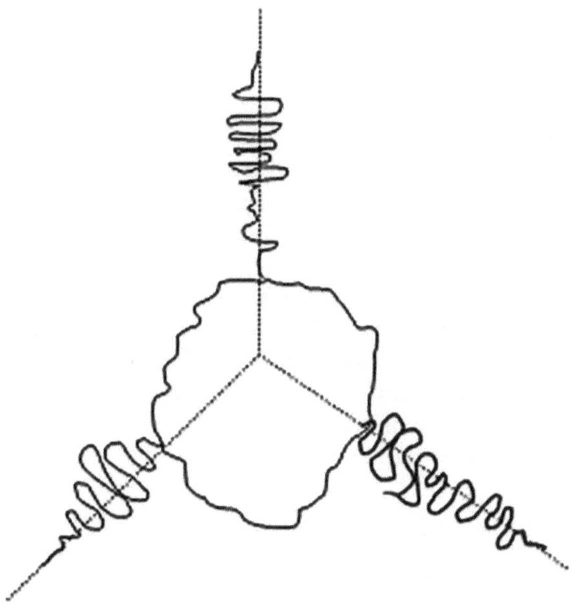

FIGURE 3.8

Approximation of Type I landmark when sutural bone is present. The intersection of the *dotted lines* represents where the landmark should be located.

Options for Recording Measurements

After the measurements and instrumentation have been chosen, one must contemplate the mode of data recording. Paper and electronic formats have their advantages and disadvantages and should be selected based on the needs of the researcher and the environment in which data collection will occur. Paper recording is low cost, requires simple technology (paper and writing utensil), and can be performed in the field if necessary in the case of repatriation of native individual remains or pressing medicolegal significance. (Note: Field recording of craniometric data is not advised. Attempt to bring material to a laboratory where it can be properly prepared and where conditions for data collection are ideal.) On the other hand, there is also an increased likelihood of incorrectly noting a value when initially recording the measurement on paper. A second transcription error can occur if the data on paper are entered into an electronic database or spreadsheet. At the same time, handwriting may be illegible or unfamiliar to those transcribing data. Decimal places can be missing or misplaced. Care must be taken to preserve the original paper documents through proper storage and electronic transcription. Copies of original recording sheets should be made and stored in a different location from the originals.

Electronic recording of traditional craniometric data mitigates transcription errors by providing direct input to a computer via a cable connection. The electronic scale instrument must have provisions for a digital output and then be connected directly to a computer or pass through a hub with different instruments and associated input tools. Options for sending the data to the computer include pressing a keyboard button, pressing a mouse button, depressing a foot switch, or pressing a switch directly on the instrument. This process decreases data collection time, as one does not have to put down the instrument to record the value, compared with paper recording.

Despite these advantages, consider that instruments that interface with computers and their input tools add additional expenses to one's research program. Moreover, data can be permanently lost through catastrophic hard drive failure if not stored in multiple locations such as through a file hosting service.

Electronic data are most commonly recorded on a spreadsheet in which individuals are represented by a column or row populated with observed measurements. All individuals are on the same sheet. Advanced sorting of spreadsheet data is required in order to find specific pieces of information. Conversely, a relational database allows one to run a query to search for pieces of data and individuals associated with search parameters. An example of such a search may be to identify all individuals in the database of African American ancestry who are male and edentulous. Spreadsheet recording requires no training in structured query language (SQL) in order to recall data. Examples of craniometric-specific programs for electronic recording include *Osteoware* (Dudar and Jones, 2011) and *ThreeSkull* (Ousley, 2004). Both are front-end graphical user interfaces supported by databasing freeware. *Osteoware* allows for direct input of interlandmark distances, whereas *ThreeSkull* allows for input of three-dimensional coordinate data that can be converted into traditional interlandmark distances. An SQL search can then be run with the supporting database to extract and export data for further analysis.

Error in Craniometry

Error in measurement can be found from multiple sources, including the measurement device, definition of the measure, quality of the measured material, the measurer, environment of the measurer, and measurement protocol (Claude, 2008). Error due to the measurement device is based on the accuracy and precision of the instrument. Instrument manufacturers provide precision and accuracy metrics for their devices as well as suggestions for calibrating the instrument. If a nonstandard instrument is used, one should report the precision and accuracy levels, if known. Error due to poor understanding of the definition (or the definition itself) arises from inadequately described measurements and vague landmark locations. Quality of the measured material is beyond the control of the observer and should be noted in the description of the sample and individual specimens on a case-by-case basis. The observer should decide whether a sample or specimen meets the standards for data collection as outlined in the protocol. An uncertainty of measurement may be due to taphonomic changes, traumatic injury, cultural modification, or preparation via chemical, mechanical, or entomological means. Preservation in non-climate-controlled facilities with excess or extremely low humidity may alter the original dimensions of individual bones (Utermohle et al., 1983). Error due to the measurer can result from lack of training, inexperience, hastily taking measurements because of time constraints, and fatigue. Review the measurements with an experienced craniometrician and consult related texts. Allow for more time than is thought necessary, and take regular breaks during data collection sessions.

The environment in which the measurer finds herself may not be controlled, especially if visiting a collection, but the effects of the environment on the measurer may be mitigated if preparations are made. The work surface should be level, and there should be adequate lighting. Hrdliĉka (1952) highlighted sources of possible error in reading an instrument's scale. Poor eyesight, reduced lighting in the work environment, difficulty in reading scale markings (due to wear of the instrument), and the measurer's inattentiveness all contribute to mistakes in data recording. Error due to measurement protocol relates to a nonstandardized, nonrepeatable procedure. Measurements may be in a nonlogical order, or the protocol may not have been practiced. Specific sources of error may be identified through a quantitative assessment of the repeatability of measurements within and between observers. A craniometrician should be aware of the accuracy and precision with which one measures distances and the specific measures that are prone to higher levels of error within and between observers. Error should be controlled for and reduced as much as possible through practice and training.

Formal observer error analyses should be performed when using new measurements. Intraobserver error informs the regularity by which the same measurements are recorded by the same observer. This may not capture systematic error such as reading instrumentation incorrectly or incorrectly placing caliper points, especially when true values are not known. Evaluating interobserver error guarantees that multiple observers are measuring the skull in the same way. This can identify systematic errors in individual observers or poor definition of measurement or landmark location. As mentioned previously, landmark type influences the degree of error. As an example, consider a scenario in which four observers take 30 measurements from 15 skulls and repeat their measurements four times. In this example, three of the observers have similar average values and variance for the repeated measures, while the fourth observer has average values that are systematically higher than all others. This observer may have been incorrectly reading the instrument. In a different scenario, values of 29 measurements are consistent except for one in which the variance is very high, with different average values for observers. Observers may have found that the measurement definition was poor or it was difficult to take.

Observer error should be assessed prior to formal data collection if resources and time allow. A separate sample should be used to practice taking the chosen measurements and refine the order of measurement collection. If a practice sample is not available, then one can assess observer error during formal data collection. Measure all individuals within the sample; at the end of data collection, randomly select a subsample of individuals already measured. Measure these individuals a second time. Repeated measures should take place in similar environments to mitigate effects due to changing surroundings. Repeated measures of the same specimens can be utilized for formal statistical data analysis to assess statistically significant differences in observations and the absolute amount of observer error in units of measure. Detailed discussions of analysis of error in measurement, including that in traditional anthropometry, are given by Jamison and Zegura (1974), Utermohle and Zegura (1982), Yezerinac et al. (1992), Palmeirim (1998), Perini et al. (2005), and Barnhart et al. (2007), all of which may be applied to craniometrics. Ultimately, the craniometrician must decide on an acceptable level of error.

Special attention should be paid to measurements that are defined by Type II or Type III landmarks such as mastoid length, mastoid height, maximum cranial breadth, maximum cranial length, bijugal breadth, orbital height, and palate length. Often, these measurements are more difficult to take because they are instrumentally defined, depending on the precise location of the first landmark in order to locate the second landmark. Subtenses/projections require the measurer to estimate landmark locations based on subjective evaluation of the maximum curvature of the bone surface. The longitudinal axis of the caliper must be parallel to the axis of the interlandmark distance, and the caliper scale must be viewed at a perpendicular angle. Off-axis scale readings or caliper placement may contribute to measurement error and inconsistency.

Procedures

The following is a generic protocol highlighting essential points to reflect on when collecting traditional cranial measurements using caliper-based instrumentation. This protocol can be modified to suit the needs of the individual researcher or study.

- Evaluate each specimen with what Hrdlička (1952) described as the "estimation of normalcy."
  - Ensure that the individual is free of pathological, genetic, or other conditions that may obscure bony landmarks and affect resulting dimensions.
- Stabilize the skull by placing it on a level surface with a supporting skull ring.
  - A measurement may require that the specimen be placed in a particular position and/or taken from a specific reference plane (eg, Frankfort horizontal).
- Select proper instrument(s) as described by measurement definition (confirm that instrument is calibrated) and ensure that instrument operates properly.
  - Caliper arms should move freely.
  - For electronic scale instruments, make sure the battery is functional, and have an extra, new battery available. (Remove battery between measurement rounds and for storage.)
- Identify landmark(s) required to measure distance and follow procedure for caliper placement.
  - Pay particular attention to the correct location of fixed and moveable caliper ends, if applicable.
  - If the suture of a Type I landmark is especially deep, do not place the caliper point within the depth of the suture; keep the caliper point on the surface.
  - If a sutural bone is present at the intersection of sutures, approximate the location of the landmark (Fig. 3.8).
- Tighten all locking screws after the caliper points are placed, then remove from specimen.
- Take the measurement to the nearest millimeter unless further precision is warranted.
  - Make certain that you are reading the scale properly by being familiar with the pointer location.
- Record left side for bilateral measurements, unless stated otherwise.
  - If the left side is unavailable, use the right side and indicate as such on the recording form.

- If a measurement cannot be recorded, make a note on the recording form with an explanation for why it is missing (eg, pathological condition, perimortem trauma, postmortem damage, resorption of alveoli).
- Finally, review the entered data to identify any errors made.

HERITABILITY

Understanding basic genetics and the heritability of traits is now imperative in studies of skull morphology, shape, and size. Anthropological studies utilizing craniometric data have moved far beyond simple descriptions of variation and require a working knowledge of the complex and interactive relationship between genetics and functional anatomy in the context of evolutionary biology.

Due to the nature of skeletal samples, few studies exist that have examined heritability of craniometric traits in a skeletal collection with documented genealogy. The first known study to perform this type of analysis is that of Sjøvold (1984), which examined skeletal samples from Hallstatt, Austria. This sample is considered extraordinary in anthropological terms, as it contains highly preserved skeletons from documented individuals spanning a temporal sequence of over 200 years, dating from roughly AD 1700–1900. Pedigrees were reconstructed with surnames and cultural artifacts associated with each individual, resulting in a unique collection of nearly 700 individuals. Sjøvold (1984) found instances of high heritability estimates in bizygomatic breadth and parietal chord subtense, but despite interesting correlations between parents and offspring, significant results were not reached.

More recent heritability studies using the Hallstatt sample come from Carson (2006) and Martínez-Abadías et al. (2009). The results of Carson (2006) generally support the heritability estimates identified previously, but found facial and cranial breadth measurements exhibit less heritability. The work of Martínez-Abadías et al. (2009) examined correlation among regions of the skull, partitioning developmental and functional modules into the neurocranium, viscerocranium, and basicranium. The high correlation among these three regions indicate evolvability occurs congruently, which suggests that no specific dimension is more heritable than another. Additionally, other publications found moderate heritability levels of craniometric variables using a range of samples and approaches (Carson, 2006; Sherwood et al., 2008, 2011; Sparks and Jantz, 2003).

The tenet that the cranium as a phenotype reflects underlying genotypic patterning is well supported in the literature, but the translation of genotype to phenotype is far from linear. The complexity of this association often exceeds the estimation methods available to adequately describe the relationship between genetics and morphology. Modern anthropological use of craniometric variation in conjunction with genetics appears extremely useful in reconstructing population histories (Howells, 1970, 1973, 1989; Howells and Crichton, 1966; Key, 1983; Ousley et al., 2009); yet, far fewer analyses have assessed morphological variation with a quantitative genetic approach.

As is likely extremely obvious, assessing heritability percentages of continuous variables, in this case metrics of the skull, can be complex (Konigsberg, 2000). A brief summary of a few key points will assist the reader in understanding this specific framework. First, quantitative variation in the context of inheritance of craniometric traits can be understood by describing a simple model that outlines the additive effects involved with polygenic traits. It is well known that a morphological feature (phenotype) that is considered polygenic will exhibit the effects of many loci upon a genotype. As the phenotype in this case is continuous, the additive effect of polygenic inheritance will ultimately exhibit a normal distribution of traits if enough individuals are observed. Examining the dispersion or variance of values expressed in a specific trait around an average value will allow for the estimation of variance resulting from inheritance versus environmental effects to ultimately parse out the potential heritability of a trait (Relethford, 2007). This process begins with the simple observations outlined by Hardy—Weinberg equilibrium. Namely, that genotypes will reflect gene frequencies, and disequilibrium of a population results from a number of perturbations that can affect levels of variance. As discussed in basic biology and genetics classes, this equilibrium does not exist in natural populations but rather serves as a null hypothesis. In terms of partitioning the effects of a perturbation on a phenotype, first the overall heritability of a trait must be estimated. Regression and maximum likelihood methods are employed to estimate a set of observed values based on unobserved values. These approaches can be applied in population studies to examine biological differences using foundational theories of population genetics (Relethford, 2007)

Although any measure of a skeletal element exhibits a continuous distribution, thresholds exist for minimum and maximum values. The use of craniometric variables to identify genetic relationships among populations requires an estimation of heritability for the dimensions included, but an average is typically employed (Relethford, 2007). In quantitative genetic studies using craniometric data, average narrow sense heritability measures are typically set at 0.55 based on the work of Devor (1986).

The relationship between heritability and continuous traits is far from completely understood, as the proportion of effects in an estimated inheritance model can vary for a number of important reasons. Some of the most influential research addressing the heritability of craniometric variability has been the work of Relethford et al. (Relethford, 2002, 2007, 2009, 2010; Relethford and Blangero, 1990; Relethford and Harpending, 1994; Relethford and Lees, 1982; Relethford et al., 1983). In the broadest sense, this work made it possible to empirically test whether cranial dimensions fit the expectations of neutral models of evolution. In other words, it is possible to elucidate whether observed morphologies are under selection or influenced by other evolutionary processes.

Specifically, Relethford (1994, 2001, 2007) has shown in a number of model-bound quantitative genetic approaches that selection pressures of interregional populations play a limited role in producing global patterns of cranial diversity. Relethford utilized metric data from the W. W. Howells worldwide data set (1996) and examined the relationship between global-scale craniometric variation and neutral genetic markers by implementing a model that could estimate equal and additive effects. That is, regional variation exhibited by cranial traits was compared with the percentages of variation observed in neutral gene frequencies (Relethford, 2001, 2007, 2002; Relethford and Blangero, 1990; Relethford and Harpending, 1994; Relethford and Lees, 1982). By comparing measures of F_{ST} (essentially differences between populations) among groups, within groups, and within a population following Wright (1950, 1965), Relethford examined degrees of diversity among global subgroups. In various iterations of regional partitioning of worldwide populations, F_{ST} estimates averaged just over 0.10, indicating low levels of variation among broad geographic groups. Furthermore, these studies showed that between-population variation was responsible for between 10% and 15% of worldwide diversity in terms of cranial morphology. These findings largely support the variation percentages identified in studies of neutral-genetic markers (Jorde et al., 2000; Jorde and Wooding, 2004; Watkins et al., 2001). Relethford concludes that these estimates support models that identify neutral evolutionary processes such as genetic drift coupled with variation introduced by gene flow. Such conclusions fuel arguments stating biological races do not exist (Lewontin, 1972; Stringer and Andrews, 1988). More recent work by Relethford (2010) illustrates the importance of population specific morphology from hyperadapted samples such as the Buryat and

Greenland Inuit, who inhabit an environment of extreme conditions and were shown to deviate from neutral expectations.

Relethford's body of work over the last several decades produced evidence that cranial dimensions of a population are correlated with geography and can thus be used to examine (in part) evolutionary events shaping modern human variation. However, as the author identified in a validation test of Howells's samples using discriminant function analysis (DFA), the number of defined groups does not necessarily affect classification accuracy, which remains high even if geographic samples are partitioned into six, eight, or nine categories (Relethford, 2009). This brings methodology and statistical approaches into question, and a number of interesting approaches, such as clustering algorithms and finite mixture analysis that allow for overlap among samples, are making their debut in the literature (Algee-Hewitt, 2011; Schmidt, 2012).

We have discussed a number of studies suggesting that craniometric data largely reflect patterns of genetic neutrality (Harvati and Weaver, 2006; Relethford and Harpending, 1994; Roseman and Weaver, 2004); an opposing school and a number of publications emphasize the role of selection pressures and argue that cranial traits are entirely too plastic to be used effectively for population history research. Evidence of environmental selection responses in the dimensions of the cranium, particularly in extreme climatic conditions, have been identified (Beals et al., 1984; Hubbe et al., 2009). Related works have also investigated morphological integration and modularity in the skull to better understand the combined effects of genetic and environmental factors on the cranium. For example, Gonzalez-Jose et al. (2004) proposed that morphological integration of the human cranium is mainly determined by effects of functional and developmental characteristics of traits. The authors showed that modern human populations exhibit a stable pattern of correlation and covariation among cranial modules, which supports previous studies demonstrating that morphological differences are highly concordant with genetic differences.

To further complicate matters, discourse exists regarding whether particular dimensions of the skull express varying degrees of heritability and how gene flow between distinct populations might affect these regions. Admixture has long been an interesting caveat for anthropologists to consider and deliciously complicates the discussion surrounding which areas of the cranium are more susceptible to environmental plasticity versus heritability. Gene frequencies of admixed populations will place a hybrid population intermediately between two parent populations, but the effects of admixture on phenotypic morphology have been less clear in the discipline of anthropology (Elston and Stewart, 1971). The effects of gene flow identifiable in cranial dimensions have been outlined with the work of Jantz (1973) and Key and Jantz (1981). These studies identified morphological overlap among European and Arikara populations, in addition to similarities with the neighboring Mandan group, suggesting genetic contribution from Europeans and the Mandan to the Arikara.

Several recent works have also examined admixture events in the context of cranial morphology. Holló et al. (2010) compared the neurocranium with the facial skeleton to ascertain whether predictions of population affinity varied with respect to different areas of the skull. Results suggest that the neurocranium contains more predictive power, as it matures faster than the facial skeleton and thus the developing viscerocranium is subjected to environmental variables for a longer period of time (Hallgrimsson et al., 2007). The cranial vault and base have also been identified by von Cramon-Taubadel (2011) to be better predictors of population affinity.

By isolating portions of the skull that are more resistant to perturbations, researchers can better identify anatomical regions to employ for specific analyses, thus eliminating nuisance parameters that can produce sometimes unintelligible results. For example, Martínez-Abadías et al. (2006) produced an interesting study that analyzed cranial dimensions of generations born soon after Spanish and Amerindian contact. Results of this study suggest that admixture between defined populations does not necessarily result in a linear relationship as is found in genetic models. Hybrid individuals are not as clearly intermediate between parental populations when the cranium is treated as a single entity. Rather, this analysis provides support for using the neurocranium as a more stable indicator of admixture. A more linear and intermediate relationship between distinct populations is identified with the cranial base and vault, whereas the facial skeleton does not provide such explicit evidence. These results suggest that phenotypic expression, at least in the bony structures that make up the face, is largely controlled by an additive polygenic system (Strauss and Hubbe, 2010). These results coincide with conclusions of a study by Harvati and Weaver (2006), who also found that different cranial regions preserved population histories in varying degrees. Neutral genetic distances were better correlated with the shape of the temporal bone, neurocranium, and overall cranial shape. Shape associated with the facial skeleton showed an association with climatic variables and did not preserve population history as effectively. Also relevant in this study was the inclusion of an arctic population, which is representative of an extreme morphology that can skew results, as was found by Relethford (2010).

Despite these highly complex concepts and sometimes confounding conclusions, the overarching consensus is that craniometric variation is geographically structured, and for the most part, coincides with patterns of variation found in studies of neutral DNA markers (Relethford, 2001). However, many caveats exist, and the opportunities for collaborative research between anthropologists and geneticists are vast.

BIOARCHAEOLOGICAL AND FORENSIC APPROACHES TO CRANIOMETRIC DATA

The measurement of life, or "biometry," is simply and eloquently defined by Sokal and Rohlf as "the application of statistical methods to the solution of biological problems" (2012, p. 1). Using a statistical framework to explore human diversity gained popularity in physical anthropology in the early 20th century with the aforementioned works of Hrdlička, Hooton, and Boas (among many others). With the advent of computers and automated computational power, statistical methods used to examine biological distance became a cornerstone of research in this discipline. Historically, one of the first published multivariate methods for estimating differences among human groups was the coefficient of racial likeness (Pearson, 1926), which quickly became obsolete due to the inability to compensate for correlation among variables (Fisher, 1936; Penrose, 1952; Howells, 1984). Penrose revamped Pearson's distance measure in 1954 to account for size and shape; however, many of the same correlation problems remained (Howells, 1984).

Estimation of population affinity can produce accurate results if contingencies such as available reference populations (to include temporal context and ancestral population) are available for statistical comparison (Ousley and Jantz, 2005; Konigsberg et al., 2009; Spradley et al., 2008). The statistical method, or model, employed will invariably depend on the data available and the goal of the research team.

In the forensic application of anthropological methods, often the goal of an analysis is to provide an estimate of group relatedness through statistical comparison of metric data in an effort to provide a quantified estimate of ancestry of an unknown individual. This is generally accomplished through classification of the unknown's osteometric data into a reference population based on overall similarity. In forensic anthropology, this approach has largely relied on linear DFA, since computer programs like Fordisc (Jantz and Ousley, 2005), CRANID (Wright, 1992), and 3D-ID (Slice and Ross, 2009) provide a user-friendly interface and built-in reference data for comparison.

In studies of biological distance in an archaeological context, broader questions are typically addressed, such as identifying whether a population exhibits evidence of gene flow, relatedness among socially stratified cultures, subsistence patterns, and migration. A number of publications have assessed craniofacial differences among hunter-gatherers and agriculturalists, for example (Paschetta et al., 2010; Gonzáles-José et al., 2005; Pinhasi et al., 2008). Results of these studies generally show size and robusticity differences, with hunter-gatherer populations exhibiting larger dimensions. Such findings are important, as they can be used to identify correlates and/or causes in the archaeological record for differences in morphologies. In sum, a range of statistical methods exists for the exploration of research questions using craniometrics of various temporal depths, and unsurprisingly, there is often overlap in methodologies.

Common Statistical Methods in Forensic Anthropology and Bioarchaeology

Linear discriminant function is a common statistical tool used by anthropologists, and was developed by Fisher (1936); a related statistic, the generalized distance measure (D^2) was published the same year by Mahalanobis (1936). DFA maximizes differences among groups included in an analysis by selecting variables that will be combined to produce a linear combination that produces the largest amount of between-group variance (Tatsuoka, 1970; Pietrusewsky, 2000). The linear combination of significant variables provides a discriminant function between each combination of samples. For example, a two-group analysis will produce one discriminant function, three groups will produce two functions, and so on. If an analysis examines more than two groups, this approach is referred to as canonical variate analysis, as the functions are now called canonical variates. With canonical variate analysis, prediction of group membership is reached by choosing the lowest D^2 between the unknown and the group average, termed the centroid. Observations in a sample are allotted a discriminant function score that can be plotted along axes for visual representation of single observations, group centroids, and the relationship between samples.

Giles and Elliot (1962) are credited with the first forensic employment of DFA for ancestry estimation and provided fill-in-the blank equations that practitioners used for roughly 30 years to easily calculate estimates of group affiliation. However, their reference samples included only early 20th-century blacks and whites and prehistoric Native American samples. The introduction of Fordisc 1.0 in 1992 rendered the Giles and Elliot approach somewhat obsolete, as automated computation with larger, more forensically relevant samples was then available.

The FDB was created under the direction of Richard Jantz and Peer Moore-Jansen, who had obtained funding from the National Institute of Justice. The FDB was novel, as it provided a large-scale, ever-growing and forensically relevant database of craniometric data of modern Americans. This gold mine of data allowed programmer-savvy individuals like Stephen Ousley (and Richard Jantz) to build a computerized program that would quickly compute DFA coefficients using FDB data. See Jantz and Ousley (2013) for a concise and straightforward review of the statistical capabilities of Fordisc, available reference samples, and interpretation of results. A similar program (DISPOP) written by Jantz (2000) uses the Howells data set, various Native American samples, and 20th-century American blacks and whites as a reference population to assess variation in a sample. DISPOP will also classify an unknown into a reference sample and produce a distance matrix, model performance statistics, and associated classification probabilities.

User discretion with these programs is strongly advised, as at least a cursory knowledge of multivariate statistics is necessary to (a) use the program to its full potential and (b) appropriately interpret results. Jantz and Ousley (2013) state that responsibility of a forensic case is ultimately up to the practitioner as "...Fordisc (does not) absolve the user of responsibility." With that disclaimer, Fordisc is absolutely a unique software package, as it encompasses not only osteometric data from the FDB, but also includes Howells's craniometric data set (1973, 1989, 1996), allowing the user to compare observations with worldwide populations as well as with 19th-century American blacks and whites.

A number of articles have been published in an effort to assess the validity of the Fordisc/DFA approach (eg, Belcher and Armelagos, 2005; Campbell and Armelagos, 2007), and the majority of them have been inherently flawed in research design and interpretation. However, Konigsberg et al. (2009) provide an interesting example that offers constructive criticism. The authors argue that using an informed, contextual prior when estimating ancestry in forensic cases could improve accuracy. The guidelines set forth by the authors bring up the interesting topic of Bayesian approaches in distance studies and the estimation of ancestry, which has been addressed in other publications (eg, Konigsberg et al., 2009).

DFA is not used in anthropology solely for individual classification in a forensic context. Moreover, Fordisc and the data sets encompassed in the program have been employed in a number of studies to examine biological questions of relatedness in an array of archaeological settings, including the forensic analysis of the skull recovered at the historical Georgian site of Fort King George and distinguishing between prehistoric and forensically relevant Native American remains in California (Hughes et al., 2012; Stojanowski and Duncan, 2009).

Specific measures of biological distances represented by metric data are typically associated with DFA and can be reported in different units. In a simplified way, one can think of distance measures as a transformation of biological information so that similarity among samples (and observations) can be compared. Typically, the most common measures include Euclidean and Mahalanobis distances. Euclidean distance is a linear measure that is derived from the Pythagorean theorem, which calculates the length of the hypotenuse of a right-angled triangle. You can likely recall the equation, $a^2 + b^2 = c^2$, from basic algebra courses (Fig. 3.9).

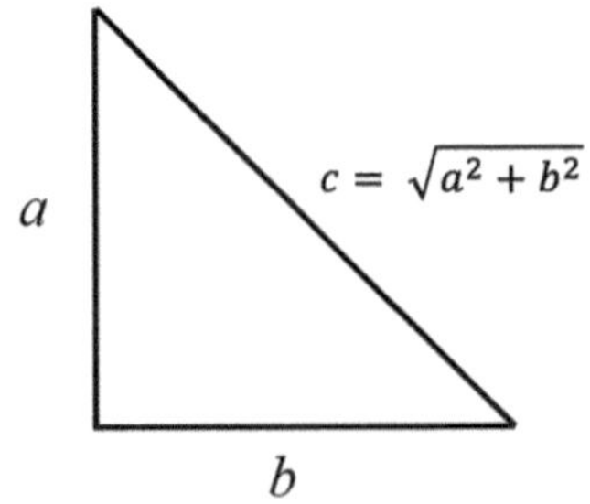

FIGURE 3.9

Finding the length of c using the Pythagorean theorem.

The Mahalanobis generalized distance is provided in Fordisc output and is one of the most common approaches for measuring biological distance using metric data. The variance of each variable and the covariance between variables is accounted for with this approach. The distance calculated between samples can be thought of as any standardized calculation, such as a z-score, that can measure distances among observations while accounting for variance.

Principal component analysis is often used to identify structure, patterns of variation, and outliers in a data set. As there is no prior group assignment, variance representative of the entire sample is used. Results of principal component analysis will result in axes (dimensions) that can be visualized to assess biological variation. Principal component analyses derive linear combinations of variables that are most representative of the variation expressed in a data set and thus can be used for variable reduction. Identifying which variables will provide dimensions with the greatest spread of variance will ultimately reduce the dimensionality of the group differences evident in the data into one or more dimensional spaces.

Clustering methods also provide options for estimation of group membership. For example, the K-nearest neighbor approach is the statistical method that the CRANID program employs for classification (Wright, 1992), and has been employed in a number of biodistance studies (Ousley et al., 2009; Hughes et al., 2013). Unlike DFA, K-nearest neighbor compares individuals with form clusters and does not assume an a priori structure to a sample, and has been used by others to exhibit classification accuracies (Ousley et al., 2009; Wagstaff et al., 2001). Finite mixture analysis is an additional clustering and classification method that does not assume mutually exclusive groups, rather operating on the tenet that mixture has occurred among two or more groups in the data being analyzed, and thus can be used in ancestry estimation (Algee-Hewitt, 2011; Konigsberg et al., 2009).

CONCLUSIONS

The use of cranial dimensions to glean meaningful biological information has evolved over the last several centuries into an interesting collaboration among a broad array of disciplines to include anatomy, physical anthropology, statistics, and genetics. While the research agenda of craniometric advocates over the course of history in physical anthropology has not always been objective or scientific, the utility of this type of data still flourishes. Traditional craniometric data recording is relatively cost-effective and less dependent on computer technology than other methods—eg, geometric morphometrics—making it a simpler and sometimes more practical alternative to the latest, more expensive options. Traditional craniometric analysis will continue to serve as a means to explore human variation and biological relationships within and among human populations. All osteologists, whether experienced or novice, should be familiar with all craniometric measurements and instrumentation, including standard and nonstandard as well as old and new. As novel evolutionary variables continue to influence the human population, we will continue to find meaning in studying the anatomy of our own skeletal system.

References

Algee-Hewitt, B.F.B., 2011. If and How Many 'Races'? the Application of Mixture Modeling to World-Wide Human Craniometric Variation. Department of Anthropology, University of Tennessee.

Barnhart, H.X., Haber, M.J., Lin, L.I., 2007. An overview on assessing agreement with continuous measurements. Journal of Biopharmaceutical Statistics 17 (4), 529–569.

Bass, W.M., 1971. Human Osteology: A Laboratory and Field Manual of the Human Skeleton. Missouri Archaeological Society, Columbia, Missouri.

Beals, K.L., Smith, C.L., Dodd, S.M., Angel, J.L., Armstrong, E., Blumenberg, B., Girgis, F.G., Turkel, S., Gibson, K.R., Henneberg, M., 1984. Brain size, cranial morphology, climate, and time machines (and comments and reply). Current Anthropology 301–330.

Belcher, R.L., Armelagos, G.J., 2005. Forensic misclassification of ancient Nubian crania: implications for assumptions about human variation. Current Anthropology 46 (2), 340–346.

Blumenbach, J.F., 1775. De Generis Humani Varietate Nativa Liber [On the Natural Variety of Mankind]. Vandenhoek et Ruprecht, Goettingae.

Boas, F., 1910. The real race problem. Crisis 7, 223–228.

Boas, F., 1911. The Mind of Primitive Man: A Course of Lectures Delivered Before the Lowell Institute, Boston, Mass, and the National University of Mexico, 1910–1911. Macmillan.

Boas, F., 1912. Changes in the bodily form of descendants of immigrants. American Anthropologist 14 (3), 530–562.

Bookstein, F.L., 1991. Morphological Tools for Landmark Data; Geometry and Biology. Cambridge University Press.

Brues, A.M., 1990. The once and future diagnosis of race. In: Gill, G.W., Rhine, S. (Eds.), Skeletal Attribution of Race: Methods for Forensic Anthropology Maxwell Museum of Anthropology, Albuquerque, pp. 1–9.

Buikstra, J.E., Ubelaker, D.H., 1994. Standards for Data Collection From Human Skeletal Remains. Research Series 44. Arkansas Archeological Survey, Fayetteville, NC.

Campbell, A., Armelagos, G., 2007. Assessment of FORDISC 3.0's accuracy in classifying individuals from WW Howell's populations and the forensic data bank. American Journal of Physical Anthropology. Wiley-Liss Div John Wiley & Sons Inc.

Carson, E., 2006. Maximum likelihood estimation of human craniometric heritabilities. American Journal of Physical Anthropology 131 (2), 169–180.

Caspari, R., 2009. 1918: Three perspectives on race and human variation. American Journal of Physical Anthropology 139 (1), 5–15.

Claude, J., 2008. Morphometrics With R. Springer, New York, USA.

Cunha, E., Van Vark, G., 1991. The construction of sex discriminant functions from a large collection of skulls of known sex. International Journal of Anthropology 6 (1), 53–66.

Devor, E.J., 1986. Transmission of human craniofacial dimensions. Journal of Craniofacial Genetics and Developmental Biology 7 (2), 95–106.

Dudar, J., Jones, E.B., 2011. Osteoware. Smithsonian Institution.

Elston, R.C., Stewart, J., 1971. A general model for the genetic analysis of pedigree data. Human Heredity 21 (6), 523–542.

Fisher, R.A., 1936. The use of multiple measurements in taxonomic problems. Annals of Eugenics 7 (2), 179–188.

Giles, E., Elliot, O., 1962. Race identification from cranial measurements. Journal of Forensic Sciences 7, 147–157.

Giles, E., Elliot, O., 1963. Sex determination by discriminant function analysis of crania. American Journal of Physical Anthropology 21 (1), 53–68.

Gill, G.W., Hughes, S.S., Bennett, S.M., Gilbert, B.M., 1988. Racial identification from the midfacial skeleton with special reference to American Indians and whites. Journal of Forensic Sciences 33 (1), 92–99.

Gill, G.W., 1984. A Forensic Test Case for a New Method of Geographical Race Determination. Human Identification: Case Studies in Forensic Anthropology. Charles C. Thomas, Springfield, Illinois, pp. 329–339.

González-José, R., Van der Molen, S., González-Pérez, E., Hernandez, M., 2004. Patterns of phenotypic covariation and correlation in modern humans as viewed from morphological integration. American Journal of Physical Anthropology 123 (1), 69–77.

Hallgrimsson, B., Lieberman, D.E., Young, N.M., Parsons, T., Wat, S., 2007. Evolution of covariance in the mammalian skull. In: Novartis Foundation Symposium. John Wiley, Chichester, New York, p. 164, 1999.

Hanihara, T., 2008. Hanihara Craniometric Dataset.

Harvati, K., Weaver, T.D., 2006. Human cranial anatomy and the differential preservation of population history and climate signatures. The Anatomical Record. Part A, Discoveries in Molecular, Cellular, and Evolutionary Biology 288 (12), 1225–1233.

Holló, G., Szathmáry, L., Marcsik, A., Barta, Z., 2010. Linear measurements of the neurocranium are better indicators of population differences than those of the facial skeleton: comparative study of 1961 skulls. Human Biology 82 (1), 29–46.

Hooton, E.A., 1930. Indians of Pecos Pueblo: A Study of Their Skeletal Remains. Papers of the Southwestern Expedition 4. New Haven.

Howells, W.W., Crichton, M., 1966. Craniometry and Multivariate Analysis. Part I. The Jomon Population of Japan, a Study by Discriminant Analysis of Japanese and Ainu Crania. Papers of the Peabody Museum of Archaeology and Ethnology, Cambridge, MA.

Howells, W., 1969. Criteria for selection of osteometric dimensions. American Journal of Physical Anthropology 30 (3), 451–457.

Howells, W.W., 1970. Multivariate analysis for the identification of race from crania. In: Personal Identification in Mass Disasters. National Museum of Natural History, Washington, DC, pp. 111–112.

Howells, W.W., 1973. Cranial variation in man: a study by multivariate analysis of patterns of difference among recent human populations. In: Papers of the Peabody Museum of Archaeology and Ethnology, pp. 1–259.

Howells, W.W., 1989. Skull Shapes and the Map: Craniometric Analyses in the Dispersion of Modern Homo. Harvard University Press, Cambridge, MA.

Howells, W.W., 1984. Introduction to multivariate statistical methods. In: Van Vark, G.N., Howells, W.W. (Eds.), Multivariate Statistical Methods in Physical Anthropology. D. Reidel Publishing Company, Dordrecht, pp. 1–12.

Howells, W., 1996. Howells' craniometric data on the internet. American Journal of Physical Anthropology 101 (3), 441–442.

Hrdlička, A., 1911. Human dentition and teeth from the evolutionary and racial standpoint. Dominion Dental Journal 23, 403–421.

Hrdlička, A., 1918. Physical anthropology: its scope and aims; its history and present status in America. American Journal of Physical Anthropology 1 (2), 133–182.

Hrdlička, A., 1952. Practical Anthropometry, fourth ed. Wistar Inst, Philadelphia.

Hubbe, M., Hanihara, T., Harvati, K., 2009. Climate signatures in the morphological differentiation of worldwide modern human populations. The Anatomical Record 292 (11), 1720–1733.

Hughes, C., Juarez, C., Zephro, L., Fowler, G., Chacon, S., 2012. Past or present? Differentiating California prehistoric native American remains from forensic cases: an empirical approach. International Journal of Osteoarchaeology 22 (1), 110–118.

Hughes, C.E., Tise, M.L., Trammell, L.H., Anderson, B.E., 2013. Cranial morphological variation among contemporary Mexicans: regional trends, ancestral affinities, and genetic comparisons. American Journal of Physical Anthropology 151 (4), 506–517.

Hursh, T., 1976. The study of cranial form: measurement techniques and analytical methods. In: Giles, E., Friedlander, J.S. (Eds.), The Measures of Man: Methodologies in Biological Anthropology. Peabody Museum Press, Cambridge, MA, pp. 465–491.

Jamison, P.L., Zegura, S.L., 1974. A univariate and multivariate examination of measurement error in anthropometry. American Journal of Physical Anthropology 40 (2), 197–203.

Jantz, R.L., Jantz, L.M., 2000. Secular change in craniofacial morphology. American Journal of Human Biology 12 (3), 327–338.

Jantz, R.L., Ousley, S.D., 1993. FORDISC 1.0: Computerized Forensic Discriminant Functions. University of Tennessee, Knoxville.

Jantz, R., Ousley, S., 2005. FORDISC 3.0: Computerized Forensic Discriminant Functions. Version 3.1. The University of Tennessee, Knoxville.

Jantz, R.L., Ousley, S.D., 2013. Introduction to Fordisc 3. In: Tersigni-Tarrant, M.A., Shirley, N.R. (Eds.), Forensic Anthropology: An Introduction. CRC Press, Boca Raton, FL, pp. 253–269.

Jantz, R.L., Owsley, D.W., 1994. White traders in the upper Missouri: evidence form the swan creek site. In: Jantz, R.L., Owsley, D.W. (Eds.), Skeletal Biology in the Great Plains: Migration, Warfare, Health, and Subsistence. Smithsonian Institute Press, Washington.

Jantz, R., Spencer, F., 1997. Franz Boas (1858–1942). In: Spencer, F. (Ed.), History of Physical Anthropology: An Encyclopedia. Garland Publishing, New York, NY, pp. 186–189.

Jantz, R.L., 1973. Microevolutionary change in Arikara crania: a multivariate analysis. American Journal of Physical Anthropology 38 (1), 15–26.

Jantz, R.L., 2000. DISPOP. University of Tennessee.

Jorde, L.B., Wooding, S.P., 2004. Genetic variation, classification and 'race'. Nature Genetics 36, S28–S33.

Jorde, L.B., Watkins, W., Bamshad, M., Dixon, M., Ricker, C., Seielstad, M., Batzer, M., 2000. The distribution of human genetic diversity: a comparison of mitochondrial, autosomal, and Y-chromosome data. The American Journal of Human Genetics 66 (3), 979–988.

Key, P., Jantz, R., 1981. A multivariate analysis of temporal change in Arikara craniometrics: a methodological approach. American Journal of Physical Anthropology 55 (2), 247–259.

Key, P.J., 1983. Craniometric Relationships Among Plains Indians: Culture-Historical and Evolutionary Implications. Report of Investigations. University of Tennessee.

Konigsberg, L.W., 2000. Quantitative variation and genetics. In: Stinson, S., Bogin, B., Huss-Ashmore, R., O'Rourke, D.H. (Eds.), Human Biology: An Evolutionary and Biocultural Perspective. Wiley-Liss, New York, pp. 135–162.

Konigsberg, L.W., Algee-Hewitt, B.F.B., Steadman, D.W., 2009. Estimation and evidence in forensic anthropology: sex and race. American Journal of Physical Anthropology 139, 77–90.

Lewontin, R.C., 1972. Testing the theory of natural selection. Nature 236, 181–182.

Linnaeus, C., 1735. Systema Naturae.

Mahalanobis, P.C., 1936. On the generalized distance in statistics. Proceedings of the National Institute of Sciences 2, 49–55.

Martin, R., 1914. Lehrbuch der Anthropologie in systematischer Darstellung mit besonderer Berücksichtigung der anthropologischen Methoden. Gustav Fischer, Jena.

Martínez-Abadías, N., González-José, R., González-Martín, A., Van der Molen, S., Talavera, A., Hernández, P., Hernández, M., 2006. Phenotypic evolution of human craniofacial morphology after admixture: a geometric morphometrics approach. American Journal of Physical Anthropology 129 (3), 387–398.

Martínez-Abadías, N., Esparza, M., Sjøvold, T., González-José, R., Santos, M., Hernández, M., 2009. Heritability of human cranial dimensions: comparing the evolvability of different cranial regions. Journal of Anatomy 214 (1), 19–35.

Moore-Jansen, P.H., Jantz, R.L., Ousley, S.D., 1994. Data Collection Procedures for Forensic Skeletal Material. Forensic Anthropology Center, Department of Anthropology, University of Tennessee.

O'Higgins, P., 2000. The study of morphological variation in the hominid fossil record: biology, landmarks and geometry. Journal of Anatomy 197 (01), 103–120.

Olivier, G., 1969. Practical Anthropology. CC Thomas Springfield, Illinois.

Ousley, S., Jantz, R., 1996. FORDISC 2.0. Personal Computer Forensic Discriminant Functions. University of Tennessee, Knoxville, TN.

Ousley, S., Jantz, R.L., 2005. FORDISC 3.0. Personal Computer Forensic Discriminant Functions. University of Tennessee, Knoxville, TN.

Ousley, S., Jantz, R., Freid, D., 2009. Understanding race and human variation: why forensic anthropologists are good at identifying race. American Journal of Physical Anthropology 139 (1), 68–76.

Ousley, S., 2004. 3Skull Computer Program. Version 2.

Palmeirim, J.M., 1998. Analysis of skull measurements and measurers: can we use data obtained by various observers? Journal of Mammalogy 79 (3), 1021–1028.

Paschetta, C., de Azevedo, S., Castillo, L., Martínez-Abadías, N., Hernández, M., Lieberman, D.E., González-José, R., 2010. The influence of masticatory loading on craniofacial morphology: a test case across technological transitions in the Ohio Valley. American Journal of Physical Anthropology 141 (2), 297–314.

Pearson, K., 1926. On the coefficient of racial likeness. Biometrika 18 (1/2), 105–117.

Pearson, K., 1934. On simometers and their handling. Biometrika 265–268.

Penrose, L.S., 1952. Distance, size and shape. Annals of Eugenics 17 (1), 337–343.

Perini, T.A., Oliveira, G.L.d., Ornellas, J.d.S., Oliveira, F.P.d., 2005. Technical error of measurement in anthropometry. Revista Brasileira de Medicina do Esporte 11 (1), 81–85.

Pietrusewsky, M., 2000. Metric analysis of skeletal remains: methods and applications. In: Katzenberg, M.A., Saunders, S.R. (Eds.), Biological Anthropology of the Human Skeleton. Wiley-Liss, New York, pp. 375–415.

Pinhasi, R., Eshed, V., Shaw, P., 2008. Evolutionary changes in the masticatory complex following the transition to farming in the southern Levant. American Journal of Physical Anthropology 135 (2), 136–148.

Relethford, J.H., Blangero, J., 1990. Detection of differential gene flow from patterns of quantitative variation. Human Biology 5–25.

Relethford, J.H., Harpending, H.C., 1994. Craniometric variation, genetic theory, and modern human origins. American Journal of Physical Anthropology 95 (3), 249–270.

Relethford, J.H., Lees, F., 1982. The use of quantitative traits in the study of human population structure. Yearbook of Physical Anthropology 25, 113–132.

Relethford, J.H., Stern, M.P., Gaskill, S.P., Hazuda, H.P., 1983. Social class, admixture, and skin color variation in Mexican-Americans and Anglo-Americans living in San Antonio, Texas. American Journal of Physical Anthropology 61 (1), 97–102.

Relethford, J.H., 1994. Craniometric variation among modern human populations. American Journal of Physical Anthropology 95 (1), 53–62.

Relethford, J.H., 2001. Global analysis of regional differences in craniometric diversity and population substructure. Human Biology 73 (5), 629–636.

Relethford, J.H., 2002. Apportionment of global human genetic diversity based on craniometrics and skin color. American Journal of Physical Anthropology 118 (4), 393–398.

Relethford, J.H., 2007. The use of quantitative traits in anthropological genetic studies of population structure and history. In: Crawford, M.H. (Ed.), Anthropological Genetics Theory, Methods and Applications. The Cambridge University Press, Cambridge, MA, pp. 187–209.

Relethford, J.H., 2009. Race and global patterns of phenotypic variation. American Journal of Physical Anthropology 139 (1), 16–22.

Relethford, J.H., 2010. Population-specific deviations of global human craniometric variation from a neutral model. American Journal of Physical Anthropology 142 (1), 105–111.

Rightmire, G., 1970. Bushman, Hottentot and South African Negro crania studied by distance and discrimination. American Journal of Physical Anthropology 33 (2), 169–195.

Rightmire, G., 1976. Metric versus discrete traits in African skulls. In: Giles, E., Friedlander, J.S. (Eds.), The Measures of Man: Methodologies in Biological Anthropology. Peabody Museum Press, Cambridge, pp. 209–220.

Roseman, C.C., Weaver, T.D., 2004. Multivariate apportionment of global human craniometric diversity. American Journal of Physical Anthropology 125 (3), 257–263.

Ross, A.H., Slice, D.E., Ubelaker, D.H., Falsetti, A.B., 2004. Population affinities of 19th century Cuban crania: implications for identification criteria in South Florida Cuban Americans. Journal of Forensic Sciences 49 (1), 11–16.

Schmidt, R., 2012. Unraveling the Population History of the Xiongnu to Explain Molecular and Archaeological Models of Prehistoric Mongolia. Department of Anthropology. University of Montana, Missoula, MT.

Sherwood, R.J., Duren, D.L., Demerath, E.W., Czerwinski, S.A., Siervogel, R.M., Towne, B., 2008. Quantitative genetics of modern human cranial variation. Journal of Human Evolution 54 (6), 909–914.

Sherwood, R.J., Duren, D.L., Mahaney, M.C., Blangero, J., Dyer, T.D., Cole, S.A., Czerwinski, S.A., Chumlea, W., Siervogel, R.M., Choh, A.C., 2011. A genome-wide linkage scan for quantitative trait loci influencing the craniofacial complex in humans (*Homo sapiens* sapiens). The Anatomical Record 294 (4), 664–675.

Sjøvold, T., 1984. A report on the heritability of some cranial measurements and non-metric traits. In: van Vark, G.N., Howells, W.W. (Eds.), Multivariate Statistical Methods in Physical Anthropology. D. Reidel Publishing Company, Holland, pp. 223–246.

Slice, D.E., Ross, A.H., 2009. 3D-ID: Geometric Morphometric Classification of Crania for Forensic Scientists.

Sokal, R., Rohlf, F., 2012. Biometry, fourth ed. WH Freeman and Company, New York.

Song, H.-W., Qing, L.Z., Tao, J.J., 1992. Sex diagnosis of Chinese skulls using multiple stepwise discriminant function analysis. Forensic Science International 54 (2), 135–140.

Sparks, C.S., Jantz, R.L., 2003. Changing times, changing faces: Franz Boas's immigrant study in modern perspective. American Anthropologist 105 (2), 333–337.

Spradley, M.K., Jantz, R.L., Robinson, A., Peccerelli, F., 2008. Demographic change and forensic identification: problems in metric identification of Hispanic skeletons. Journal of Forensic Sciences 53 (1), 21–28.

Steyn, M., Işcan, M.Y., 1998. Sexual dimorphism in the crania and mandibles of South African whites. Forensic Science International 98 (1), 9–16.

Stojanowski, C.M., Duncan, W.N., 2009. Historiography and forensic analysis of the Fort King George "skull": craniometric assessment using the specific population approach. American Journal of Physical Anthropology 140 (2), 275–289.

Strauss, A., Hubbe, M., 2010. Craniometric similarities within and between human populations in comparison with neutral genetic data. Human Biology 82 (3), 15–30.

Stringer, C.B., Andrews, P., 1988. Genetic and fossil evidence for the origin of modern humans. Science 239 (4845), 1263–1268.

Tatsuoka, M.M., 1970. Discriminant analysis: the study of group differences. Institute for personality and ability testing.

Utermohle, C.J., Zegura, S.L., 1982. Intra-and interobserver error in craniometry: a cautionary tale. American Journal of Physical Anthropology 57 (3), 303–310.

Utermohle, C.J., Zegura, S.L., Heathcote, G.M., 1983. Multiple observers, humidity, and choice of precision statistics: factors influencing craniometric data quality. American Journal of Physical Anthropology 61 (1), 85–95.

van Vark, G., 1976. A critical evaluation of the application of multivariate statistical methods to the study of human populations from their skeletal remains. Homo Gottingen 27 (2), 94–114.

von Cramon-Taubadel, N., 2011. The relative efficacy of functional and developmental cranial modules for reconstructing global human population history. American Journal of Physical Anthropology 146 (1), 83–93.

Wagstaff, K., Cardie, C., Rogers, S., Schrödl, S., 2001. Constrained k-means clustering with background knowledge. In: Proceedings of the Eighteenth International Conference on Machine Learning, 1, pp. 577–584.

Watkins, W., Ricker, C., Bamshad, M., Carroll, M., Nguyen, S., Batzer, M., Harpending, H., Rogers, A., Jorde, L., 2001. Patterns of ancestral human diversity: an analysis of Alu-insertion and restriction-site polymorphisms. The American Journal of Human Genetics 68 (3), 738–752.

Woo, T., Morant, G., 1934. A biometric study of the "flatness" of the facial skeleton in man. Biometrika 196–250.

Wright, S., 1950. Genetical structure of populations. Nature 166, 247–249.

Wright, S., 1965. The interpretation of population structure by F-statistics with special regard to systems of mating. Evolution 395–420.

Wright, R.V., 1992. Correlation between cranial form and geography in *Homo sapiens*: CRANID—a computer program for forensic and other applications. Archaeology in Oceania 27 (3), 128–134.

Yezerinac, S.M., Lougheed, S.C., Handford, P., 1992. Measurement error and morphometric studies: statistical power and observer experience. Systematic Biology 41 (4), 471–482.

CHAPTER

Advanced Methods in 3-D Craniofacial Morphological Analysis

4

P. Urbanová[1], A.H. Ross[2]
Masaryk University Brno, Brno, Czech Republic[1]; North Carolina State University, Raleigh, NC, United States[2]

CHAPTER OUTLINE HEAD

Introduction 61
Reference Data Sets on Craniofacial Variation 65
Computer-Aided Landmark Processing for Sex and Ancestry Assessment 66
Material 68
  3D-ID Database 68
  European Data Sets 69
  Brazilian Data Sets 71
  Methods 72
  Results 72
    Diachronic Changes in the Central European Data Sets 72
    Intrapopulation Variation for the Portuguese Sample 73
  Validation of 3D-ID Database on European Samples 74
    Sex Estimation 74
    Ancestry Assessment 75
  The Forensic 3-D Database—European Data Sets 76
  Morphological Variation Among Brazilian Groups 76
Morphological Affinity of Brazilian Groups to 3D-ID Data Sets 79
  European Brazilians and Iberian Populations 79
  Japanese Brazilians, Asians, Mesoamericans, and South Americans 80
  African Brazilians, African Americans, and Native Africans 80
Discussion 81
Conclusion 85
References 86

INTRODUCTION

This chapter presents a biodistance analysis as conducted on European and Hispanic populations using the human craniofacial region. The human skull, particularly the facial skeleton, is almost exclusively utilized to estimate ancestry of unknown skeletal remains. Due to worldwide geographic adaptations, this region

Biological Distance Analysis. http://dx.doi.org/10.1016/B978-0-12-801966-5.00004-4

has many advantages over postcranial elements such as numerous population and sex-specific traits that are more resistant to taphonomic factors (Lyman, 1994; Correia, 1997). In addition, a wide spectrum of methodological analyses can be applied.

Here, we outline 3-D advances in craniofacial morphological variation utilizing currently available 3-D descriptive and analytical techniques. The current state-of-the-art methods started as the work of a close-knit group of biostatisticians and biologists focused on biometrics and quantitative shape statistics (Rohlf, 1990; Ross et al., 1998; Adams et al., 2004) and further evolved into a set of exploratory and analytical tools that extend beyond simple quantifications of biological variation (Buchanan et al., 2007; Lycett and Chauhan, 2010). The parallel development in 3-D technologies has added additional layers of scientific knowledge. This led to the current situation where researchers not only must become familiar with various advanced statistical approaches, but also must acquire the additional skills necessary to pose as firsthand users to multiple computer vision and computer graphics techniques.

In studies of morphological variation, the pipeline of data processing includes two essential steps—feature extraction and feature classification. Outside the framework of forensic anthropology, the approach by which feature extraction has been adapted by anthropologists is customarily referred to as explicit encoding (Gleicher et al., 2011). Explicit encoding depicts similarities and differences among objects by extracting a number of essential properties. For example, in the human craniofacial complex, these properties are primarily represented by shape and size. Each of these components plays a different role in sex and ancestry estimation. Size is a property, which by multiple reports (Franklin et al., 2005b; Kimmerle et al., 2008; Urbanová, 2009) is a universal constant if studied across populations. It is also viewed as one of the main factors of sexual dimorphism in the human skeleton (Broca, 1875; Borovanský, 1936). Therefore, size operates as a useful variable in the estimation of biological sex. Shape, per contra, reflects various population-specific morphogenetic factors that interact in structural and functional adaptations (Roseman, 2004; Roseman and Weaver, 2004). For that reason, shape has been employed successfully as an indicator of an individual's ancestral origin.

A large number of strategies are capable of extracting group-specific (eg, sex and ancestry) features depicted in size and shape components. Traditional yet pertinent approaches include visual trait assessment (eg, morphoscopic traits) and osteometric analysis (eg, anthropometrics and craniometrics). With very few modifications, the traditional methods were utilized from the dawn of physical anthropology in the late 1800s until the early 1990s, when advanced methods that revolutionized the study of craniofacial variation emerged. This progress has been well documented throughout the years in a series of reviews by Rohlf (1990), Bookstein (1997), Pavlinov (2001), Richtsmeier et al. (2002), Adams et al. (2004), Slice (2007), and Mitteroecker and Gunz (2009). Two main aspects have had a significant impact on progress in the field: the ability to transfer physical skeletal remains in the three-dimensional digital workspace, and open access to computerized algorithms capable of data processing in a rapid and user-friendly fashion. This advancement was fueled by the fact that once digitized, 3-D data represent an unlimited source of quantitative as well as visual data, they can be easily transported and shared between experts or laboratories, and they can provide real-time access for reexamination of physical evidence.

A vast number of data acquisition modalities have been made available to forensic anthropologists. Mechanical devices such as MicroScribe, Polhemus, Faro, and other contact measurement systems (digitizers) facilitated the process by providing portable, easy-to-use, yet accurate systems to collect three-dimensional data sets. For these devices, transfer into the virtual workspace is restricted to points, curves, or outlines. The ability to acquire digital spatial data, however, has transformed the computational aspects of data processing. Cartesian coordinates collected with digitizers were shown to be easily transferable into interlandmark distances (Richtsmeier et al., 2002; Urbanová et al., 2014b) and could substitute caliper-based measurements collected on real bones. This started modifying the manner in which traditional osteometric analysis was executed (Franklin et al., 2005a; Spradley, 2014).

Further development in non-contact imaging technologies produced systems capable of generating high-resolution 3-D surface models. Acquisition units based on surface laser scanning (eg, NextEngine), structured light scanning (eg, ATOS), and close-range single-camera photogrammetry in conjunction with image processing software applications (123D Catch, PhotoModeller, PhotoScan, MeshLab, etc.) became widely popular among anthropologists (eg, Ege et al., 2004; Slizewski et al., 2010; Jurda and Urbanová, 2015) as well as other modern technology—inclined forensic specialists (Sansoni et al., 2009; Biwasaka et al., 2013; Errickson et al., 2014). Ultimately, less restricted access to medical imaging technologies (eg, clinical CT, cone beam CT units, μCT)—with their capacity to visualize both outer and inner body structures (ie, volumetric data)—have taken part in shaping the currently available methods (Luo et al., 2013; Brough et al., 2014; Abdel Fath et al., 2014; Musilová et al., 2015).

Digitized discrete points, curves, and outlines, as well as dense point clouds (or polygonal models) embodying surface and volumetric 3-D models can all be processed numerically in order to extract quantitative properties related to shape and size variation, while preserving complete information about the relative spatial arrangements of the data throughout the entire analysis. The set of quantitative techniques that allows processing of 3-D data is customarily subscribed under the rubric of geometric morphometrics. Geometric morphometrics has dominated studies of craniofacial variation for the last 25 years (eg, Inoue, 1990; Kohn et al., 1993; Ahlström, 1996; Bookstein et al., 1999; Chen et al., 2000; Franklin et al., 2005a; Bastir et al., 2006; Ross et al., 2004; Kimmerle et al., 2008). It offers an expert a set of guidelines on how to treat morphological data in order to acquire shape and size descriptors and how to minimize (or standardize) the presence of nonshape variance.

A configuration of 3-D points representing an object in geometric morphometrics is referred to as a landmark. Landmarks are commonly standardized by a Procrustes fit or analysis, a series of transformations for which a criterion to an optimal registration is given by a sum of squared landmark vectors at its minimum (Bookstein, 1982; Zelditch et al., 2004). The technique exists in numerous variants [eg, generalized Procrustes superimposition or analysis (GPA), ordinary Procrustes fit, and generalized resistant fit]. A Procrustes fit produces standardized coordinates invariant to size, location, and orientation, referred to as Procrustes coordinates, that represent the newly derived shape variables. In addition, an average set of points referred to as a consensus form, a unifying measure of size referred to as centroid size (a size variable), and a dissimilarity measure between shapes known as Procrustes distance are provided. In studies of biological diversity, Procrustes distance is taken as an equivalent of biodistance (Neustupa and Němcová, 2007). The variation within a processed data set can be further divided into two components, symmetrical and asymmetrical (Klingenberg et al., 2010). A symmetrical component is represented by averaged right and left bilateral landmarks with unilateral landmarks centered along the midline, whereas the asymmetrical component corresponds to a deviation of an original configuration from the ideally symmetrical component. The separation is primarily conducted in order to study multiple types of asymmetry in the morphometric data (Urbanová et al., 2014a). However, it may also be used to remove technical noise due to the subtle manual displacement of bilateral landmarks (Jurda et al., 2015).

Outlines (eg, curves, contours, or boundaries) are processed by outline-based approaches. Outlines, both closed and open, in contrast to landmarks, provide a more complex quasi-continuous representation of biological variation. The quasi-continuous character is induced by converting traced continuous data into a set of densely placed points. A set of variably spaced points can be treated as sliding semilandmarks

(Bookstein et al., 1999; Delson et al., 2001) or combined with regular landmarks (Bookstein et al., 1999; Monteiro et al., 2004). Closely spaced points along an outline can also be interpolated by mathematical functions. For that purpose, Fourier transformations have been a widely popular technique in studies of craniofacial variation (Lu, 1965; Lestrel and Brown, 1976; Lestrel and Huggare, 1997; Urbanová et al., 2006; Urbanová, 2011; Maxwell and Ross, 2014). The Fourier transformation is a core of Fourier (harmonic, spectral) analyses. Two essential forms of Fourier analysis are recognized: conventional Fourier analysis (Lestrel and Brown, 1976; Lestrel and Roche, 1986) and its upgraded variant named elliptical Fourier analysis or EFA (Kuhl and Giardina, 1982). In general, Fourier analysis is based on mathematical principles that decompose spatial information about an outline into an infinite series of sine and cosine functions, called harmonics, weighted by Fourier coefficients. Fourier coefficients represent shape variables, and they are further combinable into a biological dissimilarity measure named the harmonic distance coefficient (Kaesler, 1997). In order to quantify three-dimensional outlines, a 3-D extension to EFA has been proposed (Lestrel, 1997; Lestrel et al., 1997) and applied. For instance, to describe three-dimensional shape variations of the orbital rim (Urbanová, 2011).

The major drawback of a Fourier analysis is that it determines only the global aspect of shape changes, with minimum informative value regarding local irregularities. To overcome this inconvenience, the decomposition of outlines into a series of multiresolution wavelet functions has been proposed (Lestrel et al., 2004). The technique, otherwise known as wavelet analysis, possesses the capacity to specify both global and local shape variation through a set of dilatation and translation procedures of a selected basis or mother wavelet. Pinto et al. (2013, 2016) illustrated that the wavelet analysis applied to open curves, such as three-dimensional cross sections to the supraorbital margin, could increase the performance of a sex estimation method.

In recent years, studies quantifying morphological variations have reorientated to surface-based or volume-based 3-D image processing. Unlike landmark-based and outline-based data, processing of surface and volumetric data is a computationally demanding procedure. Although substantial progress has been achieved in regard to computational power and computer graphics, only recently have 3-D polygonal models been used in studies of craniofacial variation (Abdel Fath et al., 2014; Musilová et al., 2015; Jurda and Urbanová, 2015). Similar to discrete points or outlines, 3-D surface processing requires registration in order to minimize variance given by unequal location and rotation. This can be achieved by simple approaches such as three or more point registration, or in a more sophisticated manner by surface registration techniques (Spreeuwers, 2011). The most common procedures utilize either the iterative closest point (ICP) algorithm (Besl and McKay, 1992) or one of its numerous variants (eg, EM-ICP algorithm) (Granger and Pennec, 2002). For ICP the registration criterion is based on minimizing closest point-to-point distances between two models. This further establishes connectivity between points (vertices) of two and more meshes that is subsequently utilized to compute signed and absolute surface-to-surface deviations, of which various measures of dissimilarity can be retrieved. For instance, values of Hausdorff distances, minimum, maximum, and average deviations, and root mean square are frequently extracted (Urbanová et al., 2015).

For selected outline-based methods, extensions to surface data have been also proposed. For example, spherical harmonics can be viewed as the 3-D surface-quantifying modification to harmonic analysis. Alternatively, Gunz et al. (2005) introduced a 3-D extension to sliding semilandmarks.

In order to estimate a biological profile in the context of forensic anthropology, the extraction of craniofacial shape and size features is typically followed by a procedure aimed at classifying these features into an a priori defined group. Here, linear discriminant function analysis or principal components analysis combined with Mahalanobis and Euclidean distances has been widely used. In addition, machine-learning algorithms such as support vector machine, Bayesian models, *K*-nearest neighbor, or random forests have been applied.

In addition to explicit encoding, there are two other universal approaches to feature extraction—juxtaposition and superimposition (Gleicher et al., 2011). Although neither yields an explicit numerical or verbal expression of similarity or dissimilarity between biological objects per se, both methods are standardly employed in comparisons of digital visual data and applicable when interpreting numerical shape variables. Juxtaposition compares two or more visual objects side by side. In contrast, superimposition places one set of data on top of another. These simple yet intuitive methods are feasible and effective only with a limited number of 3-D data sets such as points, outlines, and surfaces. Although both approaches are nowadays linked to computer graphics, superimposition dates back to Francis Galton's (1883) superimposed negatives.

Currently, a wide spectrum of computer-aided visualization techniques is available to display, superimpose, or otherwise visualize 3-D morphological data. Generally, the applicability of these techniques is driven by data types. Hence, the most common manner to display landmark-based data is by drawing connecting lines between landmarks and creating wireframe graphs. Alternatively, lollipop graphs, transformation grids, or shaded wireframes can also be produced (Bookstein, 1989; Klingenberg, 2011; Klingenberg, 2013). Recently, Wiley and colleagues (2005) released Landmark software, which in addition to various data acquisition functionalities allows a user to warp a polygonal model marked with a set of points into a desired landmark configuration. Owing to their illustrative value and continuous characteristic, which enables the display of shape changes in its totality, graphic visualizations based on warped 3-D models have become vastly popular in studies of 3-D craniofacial variation (Klingenberg et al., 2010; Freidline et al., 2012; Klingenberg, 2013; Jurda et al., 2015). Furthermore, commercial software and freeware applications (eg, Fidentis Analyst, CloudCompare, Rhinoceros, MeshLab, Gom Inspect, RapidForm 2006, and Amira/Avizo), offer many other visualization options such as deviation color maps, heat plots, transparency, warping, sections, contour rendering, and fog simulations.

REFERENCE DATA SETS ON CRANIOFACIAL VARIATION

The theoretical concept of sex and ancestry assessment based on advanced 3-D methods dictates that shape features extracted from an unknown case must be interpreted within the context of other shapes. This comes from the fact that shape variables do not bear any significance unless described relative to the variance observed within a reference sample. This means that a sizable reference database must be included in every computation. The most important source of traditional craniometric data at the worldwide scale originates in the Howells database (Howells, 1973, 1989). The Howells database is composed of an amalgam of samples from various periods spanning from Ancient Egypt to the 1900s that are defined on the basis of geographical, linguistic, and cultural factors. Additional craniometric data on Australian Aborigines; Brits buried at Spitalfields, UK; and modern Southern and Northern Chinese and Japanese from the Tohoku modern collection (curated by the Department of Anatomy and Anthropology, Tohoku University School of Medicine, Sendai, Japan) had been made available at Peter Brown's personal website http://www.peterbrown-palaeoanthropology.net/resource.html.

Generally, population data on craniofacial variation can be extracted from published studies conducted on documented skeletal series. However, original data are scarcely incorporated. In the

North American region, the Robert J. Terry Anatomical Skeletal Collection, Hamann–Todd Osteological Collection, or J.C.B. Grant Collection (University of Toronto, Canada), together with the Forensic Anthropology Data Bank, have been abundantly exploited (Hunt and Albanese, 2005). In Europe, the Frassetto collection (University of Bologna, Italy), the Coimbra Collection of Identified Skeletons (University of Coimbra, Portugal), and the Cretan collection (University of Crete) have been studied in regard to craniofacial variation. African-documented series include the Raymond A. Dart Collection of Human Skeletons (the School of Anatomical Sciences, University of Witwatersrand, Johannesburg), the Pretoria Bone Collection (University of Pretoria, South Africa) (L'Abbé et al., 2005), and the Cape Town Documented Skeletal Collection (University of Cape Town, South Africa) (Ginter, 2005). The traditional cranial measurements, however, are not directly complementary to three-dimensional spatial data. Therefore, the use of the caliper-measured data sets for advanced methods is limited.

Several documented skeletal series have since been reexamined in order to collect geometric data. Three-dimensional data on crania of indigenous Southern African ethnic and linguistic groups (eg, Zulu, Sotho, Swazi) included in the R. A. Dart Collection have been collected by Daniel Franklin (2005). Three-dimensional data on Hispanic crania from Mexico and Arizona are available courtesy of Kate Spradley (Spradley, 2014; http://www.3d-id.org/forensic-3d-coordinates). Several European and North and South American collections have been digitized by the authors of this chapter (Urbanová, 2009; Urbanová et al., 2014b).

COMPUTER-AIDED LANDMARK PROCESSING FOR SEX AND ANCESTRY ASSESSMENT

The theoretical overview of current state-of the-art 3-D cranial data processing suggests that these procedures involve a large learning curve, particularly in areas requiring computer-assisted shape analysis algorithms and multivariate statistics. Therefore, integrating advanced methods into an everyday routine can be challenging, particularly for experts who have difficulty keeping up with current caseloads. In order to overcome these challenges and execute sex and ancestry assessments from human crania using methods of geometric morphometrics, the software programs 3D-ID (Slice and Ross, 2009) and COLIPR (Urbanová and Králík, 2008) were created. Both programs use a landmark-based approach combined with discriminant and canonical variates analysis (CVA) in order to provide the best sex and/or ancestry classification for an unknown case. COLIPR is a program that converts the spatial data for 22 landmarks into a set of interlandmark distances. It takes into account that some craniofacial measurements are captured tentatively by tracing the vicinity of endpoints until the maximum distance is reached and registered. The program adopts a mathematical solution by Valeri et al. (1998), who referred to a biological structure that occupies an area larger than a single point as fuzzy landmarks. The program was originally developed on three European-documented skeletal series. For an unknown cranium, the application calculates interlandmark distances and discriminant scores, and provides a sex diagnosis, based on Mahalanobis distances.

In comparison, 3D-ID takes full advantage of the 3-D character of input data. It employs up to 34 cranial landmarks (Fig. 4.1) that are processed by GPA in two optional variants—size-invariant and size-adjusted—and allocates sex based on Mahalanobis distances, together with providing posterior and typicality probabilities.

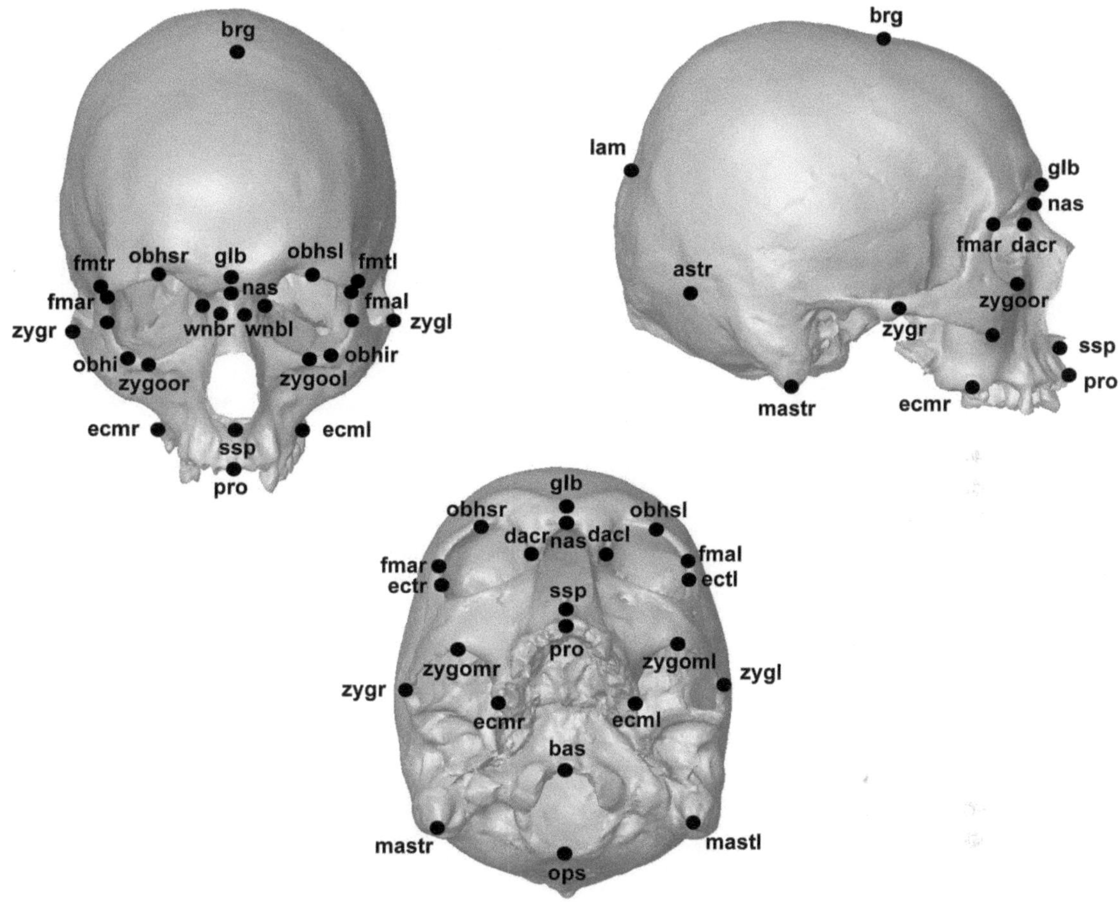

FIGURE 4.1
Landmarks included in 3D-ID software.

Urbanová et al. (2014b) showed that the performance of the algorithms and the broader applicability of the programs were mainly dependent upon the representativeness of the incorporated reference database. By 2013, the then-published version of 3D-ID included eight ancestral reference groups with minor coverage of European and South American populations. At the same time, the COLIPR-based reference database was extended in the extended COLIPR database by the incorporation of data sets from Central and Southern Europe and multi-ancestral documented series from São Paulo, Brazil. In 2014, another documented Brazilian skeletal collection was added to the database.

Through a collaborative project, a new reference database containing approximately 2300 specimens from 16 distinct groups has emerged (The Forensic 3-D database—http://www.3d-id.org/forensic-3d-coordinates). Prior to the merger, however, the two databases were tested for their compatibility (Fig. 4.2). A number of within-sample analyses including tests for diachronic changes, sampling, and

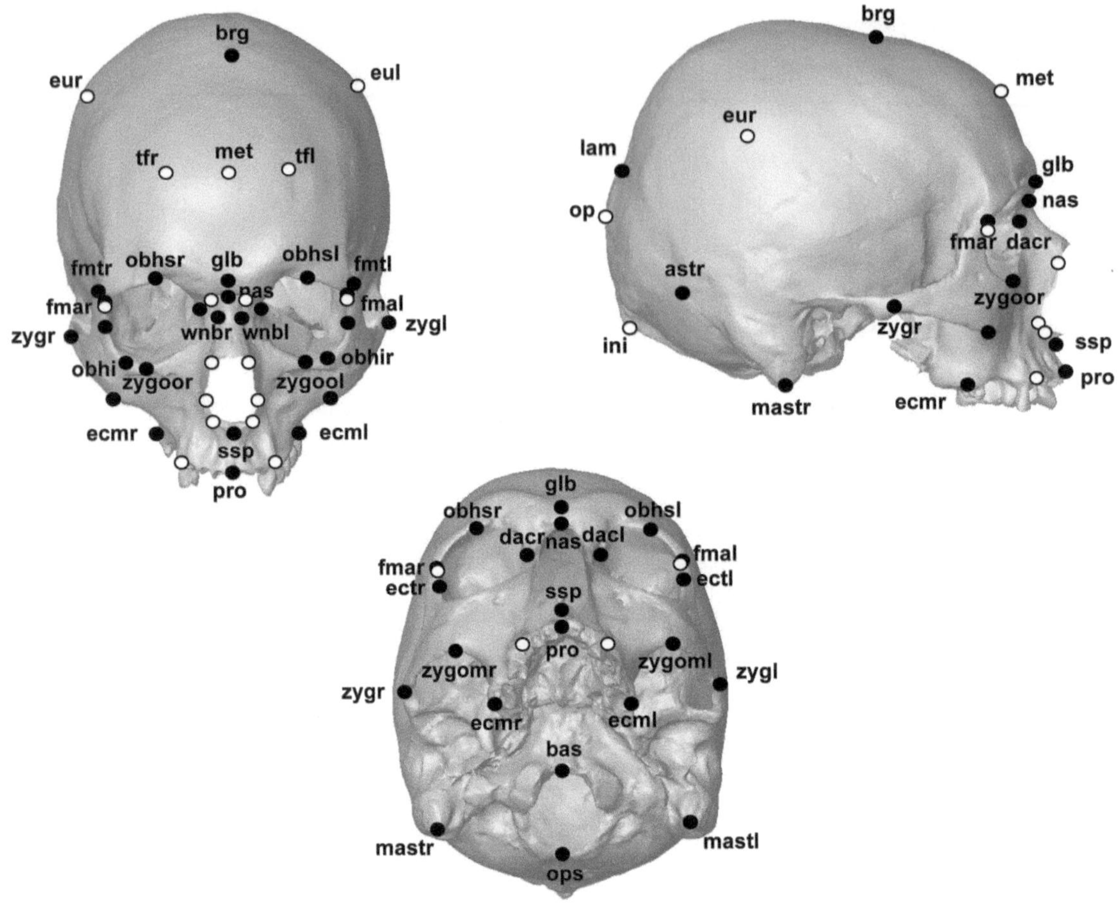

FIGURE 4.2

Landmarks collected for the original 3D-ID database (*black dots*) and additional landmarks for exclusively the in COLIPR database (*white dots*).

within-population differences were conducted to test database homogeneity. The following text presents the two-part analysis, which explored craniofacial variation within European and Brazilian data sets tested against those of ancestral groups included in the original 3D-ID database.

MATERIAL

3D-ID Database

For the original release of 3D-ID, data were collected from skeletal remains with known demographics (eg, ancestry, age, and sex) from national and international forensics laboratories and museums. In addition, ancestral classifications currently used to improve correct allocations of unknown individuals were reevaluated, and it was concluded that present-day classification systems (eg, tripartite classification of European, African, and Asian populations) do not adequately represent geographic realities, nor do they necessarily have biological meaning. For example, the term "Hispanic" includes all Spanish-speaking peoples, which does not adequately address distinct ethnohistorical origins and is a biologically meaningless term (Ross et al., 2004). Specifically, South American populations are very distinct from Central American populations and from Spaniards from Spain (Ocaña, 1913).

To address these shortcomings, reference samples were divided into geographic regions represented by closely related populations (Mesoamerican, Circum-Caribbean, South American, European American, European, etc.). Although there is still considerable variation within each region, these groupings better address the biological similarities and differences among these closely related groups.

European Americans are also an amalgamation of numerous European groups and thus should not be grouped together with European individuals from Europe. This holds true for individuals of African origin. The initial reference database before the merger totaled 1052 individuals (African = 27, African American = 272, Circum-Caribbean = 26, European = 220, European American = 372, South American = 80). The original reference sample was amassed from various national and international museum collections and laboratories and from many researchers kind enough to provide their data for this endeavor. Recent data sets for Guatemalans (provided by Kate Spradley, $N = 81$), Mexicans (provided by Bruce Anderson and Kate Spradley, $N = 326$), and Africans from Angola (collected by the second author, $N = 81$) have also been incorporated in the reference database.

European Data Sets

Altogether, six European-documented data sets are included in the extended COLIPR database. Three originated in Central Europe, two are composed of skeletal collections from Portugal, and one is of Greek origin. Central European data sets include the Pachner Collection of Identified Skulls, the Brno Anatomical Collection, and the Contemporary Czech Cranial Database. The Pachner Collection is housed in the Department of Anthropology and Human Genetics, Faculty of Science, Charles University in Prague, Czech Republic. The reference data set contains 3-D data from 137 crania of lower socioeconomic status. The sample also represents one of the original COLIPR data sets. The Brno Anatomical Collection originated from autopsied bodies at the Institute of Anatomy, Masaryk University, Brno. It represents a small sample of presumably German-speaking residents in South Moravia ($N = 21$). The Contemporary Czech Cranial Database contains specimens derived from a collection of 268 skulls (both crania and mandibles are available) embodying contemporary forensic cases curated by the Institute of Criminalistics Prague, Czech Police. All included specimens are of Czech or Central European origin (Slovak, Moravian, Silesian) and have been used in multiple studies as "present-day series" (Pachner, 1937; Novotný, 1986; Urbanová, 2009, 2011; Bigoni et al., 2010; Jurda et al., 2015), although the Pachner and Brno specimens are dated to the 1930s and 1940s, respectively.

The total number of Central European crania is 426, with a higher prevalence of male ($N = 311$) over female ($N = 115$). The dates of birth range from the 1830s to 1990s (Table 4.1) with an average age of 51.7 years (50.5 years for males, 53.5 years for females). If tested, the pooled sample exhibits heterogeneity in the documented age at death (Kruskal—Wallis ANOVA, $H = 28.46$, p-value $< .001$) due to younger age at death for the forensic cases.

Of the Portuguese skeletal series, the New Lisbon Collection (also known as the Luís Lopes Collection) and the Osteological Collection of Identified Skeletons have been added to the database (both as the

Table 4.1 Specimens Included in the Czech Cranial Data Sets Grouped by Dates of Birth

	N	%	Collection	N	%
<1850	5	1.2	Pachner collection	5	1.2
1850–1900	123	28.9	Pachner collection	123	28.9
1900–1950	185	43.4	Pachner collection	9	2.1
			Brno anatomical collection	16	3.8
			Contemporary database	160	37.6
>1950	113	26.5	Brno anatomical collection	4	0.9
			Contemporary database	109	25.6
Total	426	100.0		426	100.0

original COLIPR database). The majority of the individuals originate from Portuguese populations. The former is curated by the National Museum of Natural History, Department of Zoology and Anthropology, Bocage Museum, and the latter is housed in the Department of Anthropology, Faculty of Science and Technology, University of Coimbra, Portugal. Both data sets are documented to represent socioeconomically lower classes (Cardoso, 2006; Cunha and van Vark, 1991; Rocha, 1995). Altogether, 222 crania of Portuguese origin have been included in the database (Table 4.2). In total, the average age at death is 50.00 years (50.43 years for males, 49.31 years for females). Nevertheless, the average age at death differs between the data sets (M–W U test, $Z = -3.93$, p-value $= 0.001$). In the Coimbra dataset, the average age is 43.7 years (Cunha and Wasterlain, 2007), whereas in the Lisbon collection, it is 54.0 years. There is also an inconsistency in dates of birth between the collections. Individuals included in the Coimbra data set were born in the mid-1800s, whereas the Lisbon set contains individuals born in the early 1900s.

The Greek data set (WLH/ABH Collection) originated from the University of Athens Human Skeletal Reference Collection curated by the Department of Animal and Human Physiology, University of Athens, Greece. In total, the data set includes 177 individuals from a modern Greek population who died between 1960 and 1996. Documented skeletons were acquired from cemeteries in the Athens area. The early part of the collection was built between 1996 and 1997 by A. Lagia, of which 64 have been included in the cranial data set; the later part ($N = 113$) was accumulated between 2001 and 2003 by

Table 4.2 Structure of European Data Sets Included in the Extended COLIPR Database

	Male	Female	Total
Lisbon collection (Portugal)	68	64	132
Coimbra collection (Portugal)	47	43	90
Pachner collection (Prague, Czech Republic)	73	64	137
Brno anatomical collection (Brno, Czech Republic)	14	7	21
Contemporary Czech cranial database (Czech Republic)	224	44	268
WLH/ABH collection (Athens, Greece)	96	81	177
Total	522	303	825

C. Eliopoulos. Age at death averaged 61.07 years (61.42 years for males, 60.65 years for females). No statistically significant age related differences were observed between the two parts of the data set (M–W U test, $Z = 0.873$, p-value $= 0.402$). According to Eliopoulos et al. (2007), lower and middle socioeconomic classes are represented in the collection.

In total, the European data sets included in the extended COLIPR database consist of 825 crania of documented European origin. The data set contains 522 male and 303 female crania (Table 4.2). The average age (52.6 years) is relatively consistent across the studied data sets; on average, the youngest specimens were registered for the Coimbra sample, whereas the oldest were shown for the Greek sample.

Brazilian Data Sets

By 2014, two documented data sets had been included in the extended COLIPR database—the cranial collection of the Museum of Human Anatomy, University of São Paulo, São Paulo, Brazil (USP data set), and specimens curated by the Department of Anatomy, Federal University of São Paulo, São Paulo, Brazil (UNIFESP data set). In addition to geographical origin, age at death, and sex, these specimens are documented in regard to their ancestral group. In the database, ancestry is documented as African Brazilian, European Brazilian, Japanese Brazilian, and Admixed Brazilian (also as Brazilian of African descent, Brazilian of European descent, etc.). In total, 374 Brazilian individuals have been included in the extended COLIPR database (Table 4.3). The average age was 38.8 years (37.5 for the USP data set and 40.2 for the UNIFESP data set).

***Table 4.3** Structure of Brazilian Data Sets Included in the Extended COLIPR Database*

Data Set	Ancestral Group	Sex	N		
USP	African Brazilians	Female	19	48	188
		Male	29		
	European Brazilians	Female	21	82	
		Male	61		
	Japanese Brazilians	Female	9	22	
		Male	13		
	Admixed Brazilians	Female	17	36	
		Male	19		
UNIFESP	African Brazilians	Female	32	69	186
		Male	37		
	European Brazilians	Female	27	68	
		Male	41		
	Japanese Brazilians	Female	0	1	
		Male	1		
	Admixed Brazilians	Female	13	48	
		Male	35		
Total					374

Table 4.4 List of Studied Landmarks

N°	Abbreviation	Landmark
1/2	ecmr/ecml	Ectomolare right/left
3/4	zygomr/zygoml	Zygomaxillare right/left
5/6	zygoor/zygool	Zygoorbitale right/left
7/8	zygr/zygl	Zygion right/left
9/10	dacr/dacl	Dacryon right/left
11	nas	Nasion
12	glb	Glabella
13/14	fmtr/fmtl	Frontomalare temporale right/left
15/16	mastr/mastl	Mastoidale right/left
17/18	astr/astl	Asterion right/left
19	brg	Bregma
20	bas	Basion
21	lam	Lambda

Methods

Cranial morphology was described by a set of 21 landmark coordinates (Table 4.4, Fig. 4.3) collected using a MicroScribe portable digitizer. The variation in scale, rotation, and spatial position was removed by GPA. As asymmetry in cranial morphology was not the primary concern of the study, further analyses were carried out on the symmetrical component only. Shape variables (Procrustes coordinates) and size-adjusted shape variables (Procrustes coordinates multiplied by log values of centroid size) were processed. The differences among ancestral groups were explored through CVA. Distances (ie, biodistance) among groups were expressed in terms of Procrustes distances and tested by a permutation test using 10,000 permutations. In addition to group affiliation, sex was added as a determining factor, and the CVA was executed accordingly. A leave-one-out algorithm was used to calculate cross-validated classification rates. Dependencies of shape variables on continuous factors were tested by linear regression analysis. Multivariate analysis of covariance (MANCOVA) was employed when the influence of a categorical factor and a covariate on shape variables was explored.

All computations were executed using NTSYSpc version 2.21b and Statistica version 12. Graphic visualizations were prepared with Fidentis Analyst v. 1.27 (Chalás et al., 2014) and Landmark version 3.0 (Wiley et al., 2005).

Results

Diachronic Changes in the Central European Data Sets

Given the wide interval for dates of birth, the Central European data set was tested for the presence of temporal changes that could be interpreted as secular changes. The Procrustes coordinates of the symmetrical component regressed on specimens' dates of birth and ages revealed a statistically significant linear regression model (p-value < 0.05) that explained 4.63% of the total variance. The MANCOVA did not show any statistically significant interactions with sex (Wilk's $\lambda = 0.730$, p-value $= 0.926$).

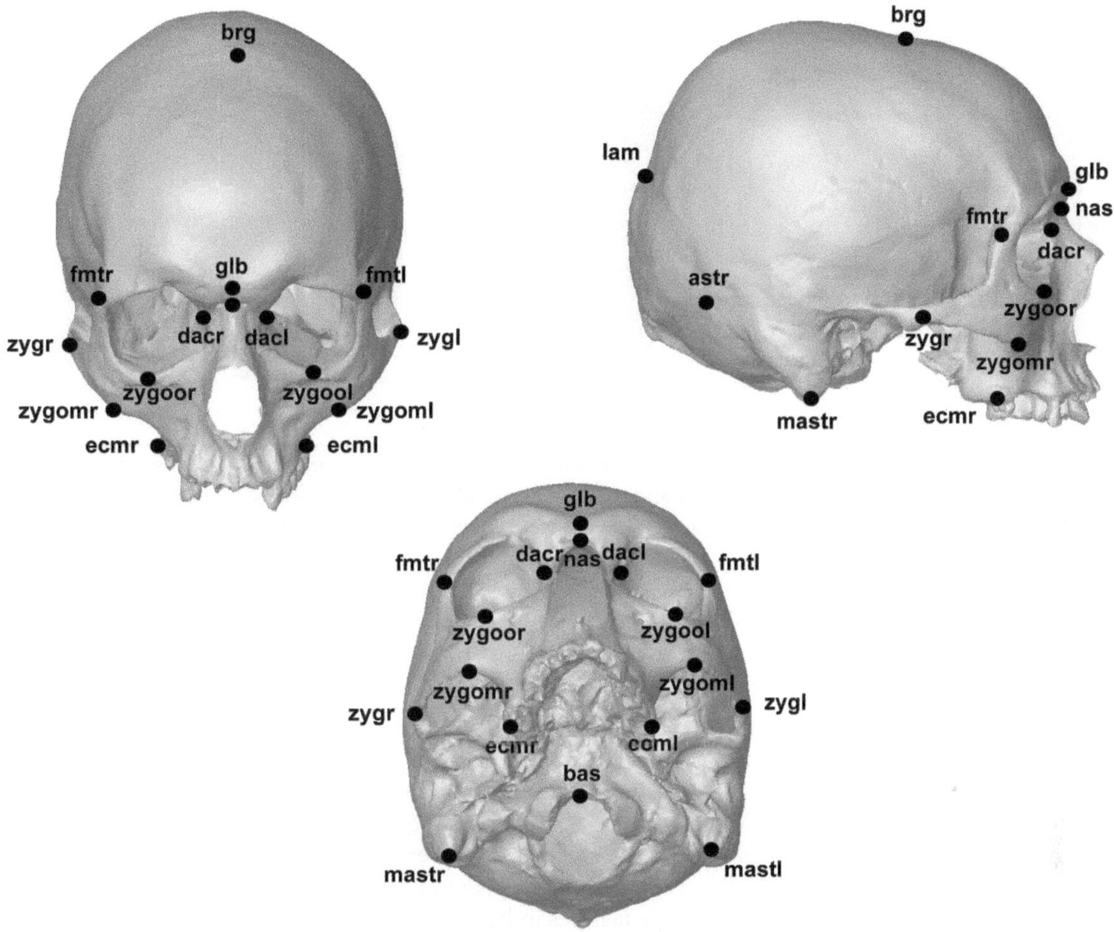

FIGURE 4.3

A configuration of 21 landmarks processed in the present study.

For the entire sample, the shape changes along the timeline included primarily a narrowing of the basicranium and expansion of the vault height by an inferior shift at basion. The face shows similar changes, with an elongation of the face on the alveolar process and zygomatic bones. In addition, a prominence of the glabellar and superciliary region gives the skulls a more masculine appearance (Fig. 4.4).

Intrapopulation Variation for the Portuguese Sample

The CVA of the two Portuguese data sets grouped by sex did not exhibit statistically significant differences in overall cranial morphology. Subtle differences were, however, registered on graphical visualizations and associated with the degree of prognathism and the shape of the frontal region. In the Coimbra sample, the slope of the frontal area is more pronounced and the alveolar process is more posteriorly placed than they are in the Lisbon subset.

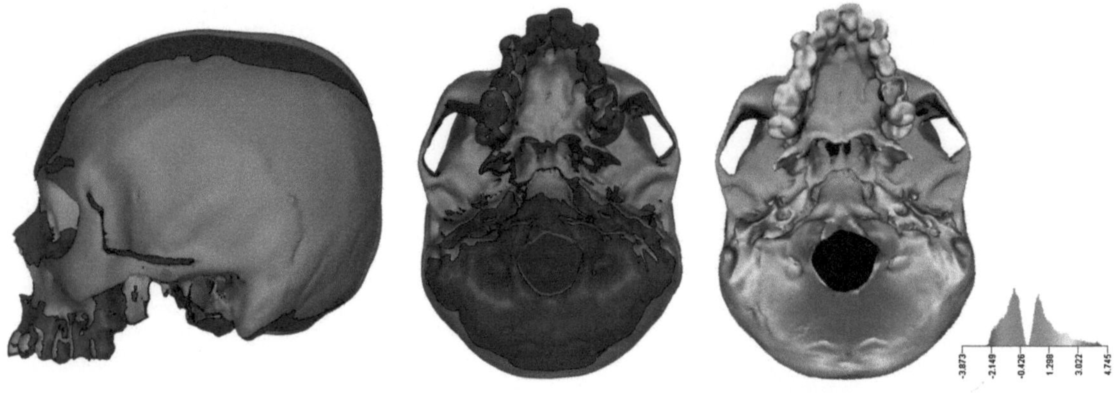

FIGURE 4.4

Demonstrating temporal changes within the Central European data set. A 3-D surface model was first warped based on 21 landmarks regressed on date of birth and age at death, the initial and warped models were superimposed, and the differences were displayed using fog simulation (left, middle) and color map (right) functionalities incorporated in Fidentis Analyst software.

Validation of 3D-ID Database on European Samples

Sex Estimation

The pooled reference data sets of documented European origin from the 3D-ID database provided a predictive model that correctly classified approximately 84% of specimens (cross-validated) if shape variables were processed, and over 87% if shape and size was combined into size-adjusted shape variables. When validated on the extended COLIPR database, the results showed a decrease in correct classification percentage for both shape and size/shape-related models. Moreover, the shape-based rates were extremely unbalanced, with more than half of the specimens misclassified (Table 4.5). Fig. 4.5 shows that there is a noticeable shift toward more masculine shape features in both sexes, which results in the misclassification of females. In addition, there is an observable change in the pattern of sexual dimorphism, where females of the extended COLIPR database tend toward masculinization. If size and shape variables are combined, these shifts are somewhat buffered and practically unnoticeable, at least when plotted (see Fig. 4.5).

***Table 4.5** Classification Rates (in %) for Sex Determination Derived From the Total 3D-ID Database and Rates Obtained After Validation on the Extended COLIPR Database*

	3D-ID Database			Extended COLIPR Database		
	Size	Shape	Size and Shape	Size	Shape	Size and Shape
Males	84.45	87.79	88.29	81.18	91.97	88.37
Females	67.55	76.78	85.22	80.62	46.37	74.05
Total	77.89	83.52	87.10	80.97	74.67	82.94

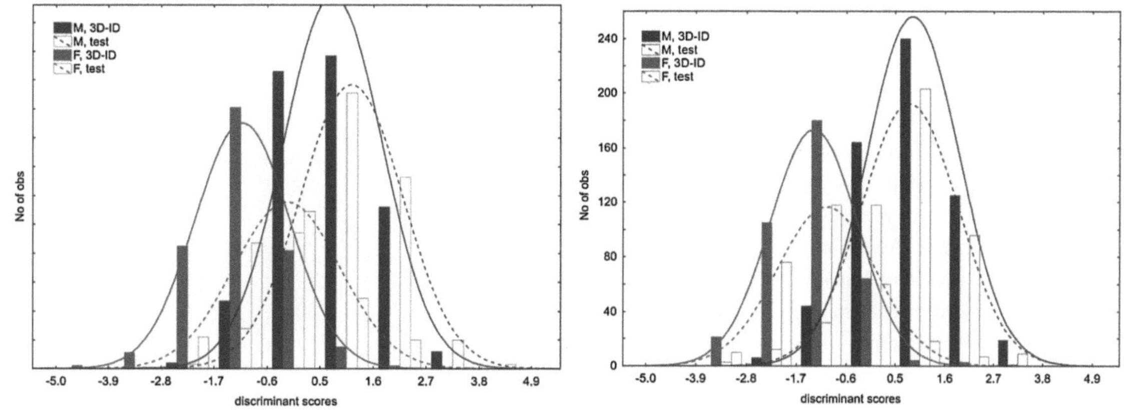

FIGURE 4.5

Distribution of discriminant scores for models based on shape variables (left) and shape-adjusted variables (right). Sex determination was conducted on specimens of the original 3D-ID database and validated on a sample derived from the COLIPR database.

Given the poor classification rates, the entire analysis was recomputed with specimens originating from the European data sets only. The predictive model offered cross-validated accuracy reaching nearly 89% of correctly classified cases for the shape component and over 90% if combined with the size parameter. If validated, however, the predictive model provided results less reliable than those of the pooled data set, averaging 78% for size-adjusted variables and only 39% of correctly classified females using shape variables (Table 4.6).

Ancestry Assessment

The performance in ancestry assessment was executed according to sex estimation. The original classification for the reference 3D-ID database ranged between 67% and 100% (65%–85% once cross-validated) of correctly classified cases if shape variables were processed. When the variables were adjusted for size, an improvement was registered only in several groups (Table 4.7). The validated rates provided very disappointing results, with over half the specimens misclassified as European Americans rather than European-born individuals (Table 4.8).

***Table 4.6** Classification Rates (in %) for Sex Determination Derived From the European Samples Included in the 3D-ID Database and Rates Obtained After Validation on the Extended COLIPR Database*

	3D-ID Database			Extended COLIPR Database		
	Size	Shape	Size and Shape	Size	Shape	Size and Shape
Males	83.88	90.00	91.82	87.74	91.33	90.27
Females	73.87	87.21	88.37	67.13	39.10	57.44
Total	79.96	88.78	90.31	79.92	71.52	77.82

Table 4.7 Classification Rates for Ancestry Assessment Derived From the Total 3D-ID Database

	N	Shape (%)	Size and Shape (%)
Southwestern Europeans	160	88	90
Southeastern Europeans	20	80	85
Southern Europeans	16	100	100
European Americans	330	88	88
African Americans	234	85	85
Hispanic Americans	8	75	88
Mesoamericans	86	74	78
Native Africans	11	91	91
Peruvians	90	86	87
Asians	4	100	100
Circum-Caribbeans	18	67	72
Total	**977**	**85**	**87**

Table 4.8 Results of Ancestry Assessment With Original 3D-ID Database as Reference and Extended COLIPR Database as Tested Data Set

	N	%
Southwestern Europeans	51	7
Southeastern Europeans	5	1
Southern Europeans	1	0
European Americans	413	54
African Americans	42	6
Hispanic Americans	33	4
Mesoamericans	49	6
Peruvians	10	1
Circum-Caribbeans	158	21

The Forensic 3-D Database—European Data Sets

Once the merged database was formed, the ancestry assessment for the European data sets that had been structured into four geographical European regions was recomputed (Table 4.9, Fig. 4.6). The results showed a significant improvement from those presented in Table 4.7. For Southwestern and Southern Europeans, however, new additions to the database resulted in a decrease in correct classification rates. This is expected, as the newly added specimens increase within-group variance.

Morphological Variation Among Brazilian Groups

In order to explore Brazilian morphological variation, the data set was subjected to CVA with ancestral groups as a four-level grouping factor. All pairwise comparisons were shown to be statistically significant at

Table 4.9 Classification Rates (in %) for European Data Sets as Structured in the Forensic 3-D Database				
	Shape	X-Validated	Shape and Size	X-Validated
Southwestern Europeans	81.17	69.9	79.05	69.8
Southeastern Europeans	100	52.6	100	61.9
Southern Europeans	89.89	72.7	95.21	79.3
Central Europeans	89.28	70	94.37	82.8

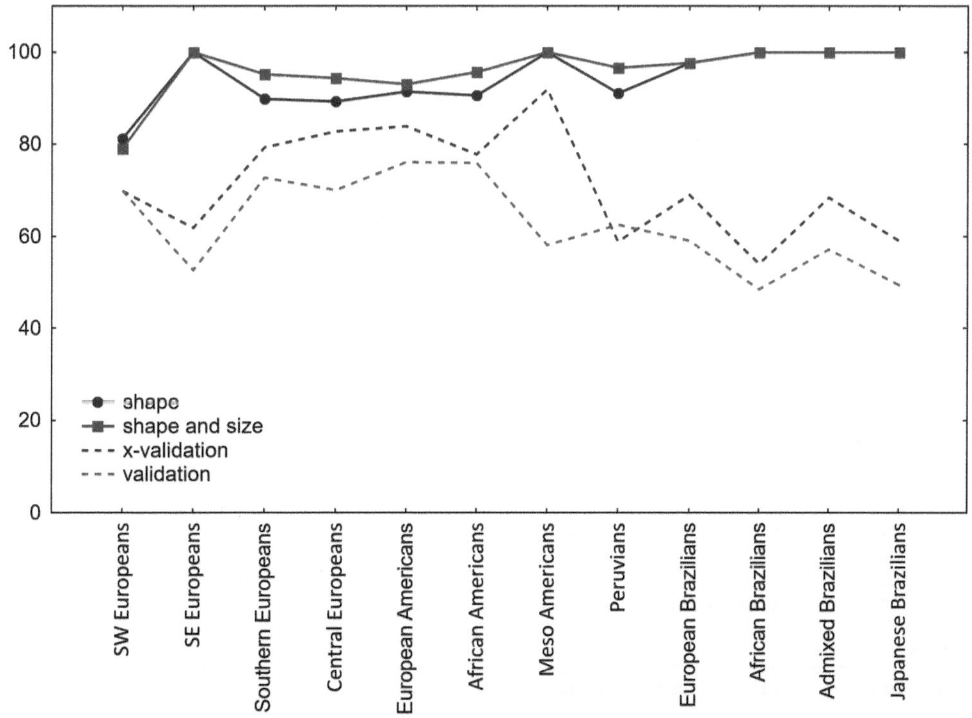

FIGURE 4.6

Classification rates for ancestry assessment featuring groups of the merged databases.

the 0.05 level. Japanese Brazilians were the most distinctive group, while African and Admixed Brazilians were the closest and most morphologically similar groups (Table 4.10).

CVA with ancestral group and sex as grouping factors showed no statistically significant sex-related differences between African Brazilians and European Brazilians. Within-sex pairwise comparisons demonstrated that similar to the pooled groups, Japanese Brazilian females and males were morphologically the most distinctive group of the same sex (Fig. 4.7). Numerically, Japanese Brazilian females were

Table 4.10 Procrustes Distances (Lower) and p-values (Upper) for Pairwise Comparisons Among Brazilian Ancestral Groups

	Japanese Brazilians	African Brazilians	European Brazilians	Admixed Brazilians
Japanese Brazilians		<0.0001	<0.0001	<0.0001
African Brazilians	0.0373		<0.0001	0.0329
European Brazilians	0.0337	0.0194		0.001
Admixed Brazilians	0.0306	0.0168	0.0192	

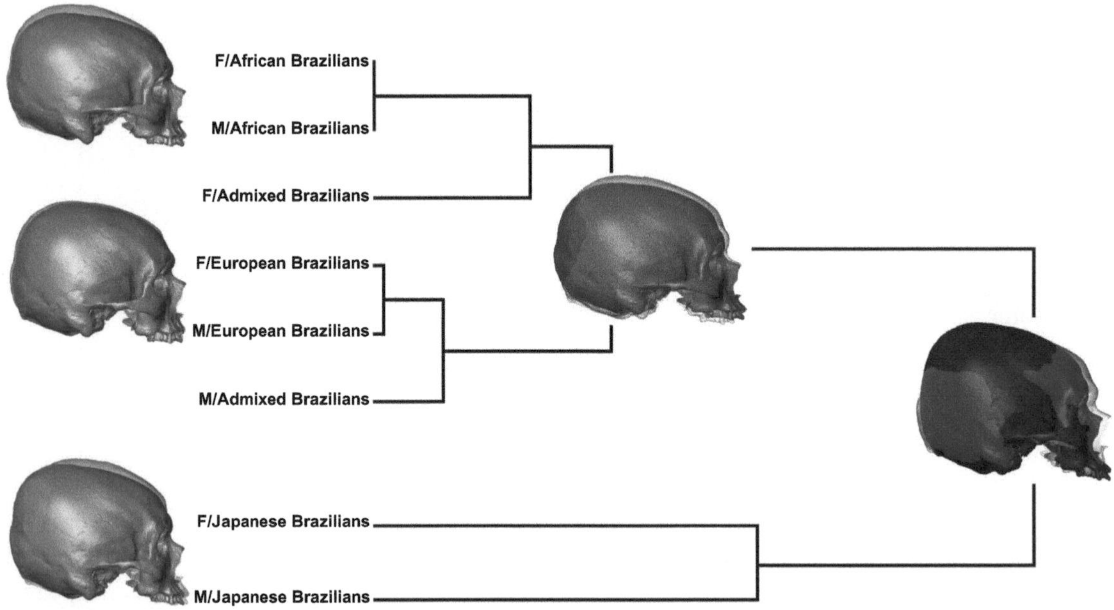

FIGURE 4.7

Morphological variation within the Brazilian data set.

closer to European descendants, while Japanese Brazilian males exhibited affinity to admixed crania. No statistically significant differences were evident between African Brazilian and European Brazilian females. Similarly, no differences were observed between European and Admixed Brazilian males.

In concordance with the morphological analysis, Japanese Brazilians were the group least likely to be misclassified in the context of other Brazilian groups (Table 4.11). As expected, the least morphologically distinctive were the admixed crania. Admixed males were most frequently misclassified as European Brazilian males. Admixed females were misclassified as either European or African Brazilians males. For the remaining groups, females of both European and African Brazilian ancestry were classified into their corresponding ancestral groups, albeit of the opposite sex. The same applied to male European Brazilians.

Table 4.11 Classification Rates for the Brazilian Ancestral and Sex Groups

	Shape		Shape and Size	
	Original (%)	X-Validated (%)	Original (%)	X-Validated (%)
African Brazilians/Males	70.6	41.2	72.5	41.2
African Brazilians/Females	45.2	29.0	51.6	19.4
European Brazilians/Males	70.7	58.7	73.3	62.7
European Brazilians/Females	53.6	32.1	57.1	42.9
Japanese Brazilians/Males	85.7	64.3	85.7	64.3
Japanese Brazilians/Females	100.0	55.6	100.0	44.4
Admixed Brazilians/Females	44.0	12.0	41.2	8.8
Admixed Brazilians/Males	47.1	11.8	48.0	12.0

Only male African Brazilian crania were correctly classified within the same sex, but in some cases were misclassified into the incorrect ancestral group.

MORPHOLOGICAL AFFINITY OF BRAZILIAN GROUPS TO 3D-ID DATA SETS

European Brazilians and Iberian Populations

The Brazilians of documented European descent were compared with data sets derived from Portuguese and Spanish populations and to the data set representing European Americans. All group-specific differences were shown to be statistically significant (Table 4.12). Brazilians of European descent demonstrated the closest similarities to the cranial collection from Coimbra, Portugal. The principal shape variation was associated with face breadth, demonstrating wider faces in Brazilian crania, which concurred with the narrowing of the biasterion breadth of the occipital. This shape change primarily distinguished European Brazilians from European Americans. The shape differences separating Brazilian Europeans from all three European collections were associated with the cranial length, as Brazilian skulls were characteristically short-headed.

***Table 4.12* Procrustes Distances (Lower) and p-values (Upper) for Pairwise Comparisons Among Selected Data Sets of European Descent**

	European Americans	European Brazilians	Portuguese (Coimbra)	Portuguese (Lisbon)	Spanish
European Americans		<0.0001	<0.0001	<0.0001	<0.0001
European Brazilians	0.0218		<0.0001	<0.0001	<0.0001
Portuguese (Coimbra)	0.0183	0.0180		<0.0001	<0.0001
Portuguese (Lisbon)	0.0188	0.0270	0.0184		<0.0001
Spanish	0.0282	0.0283	0.0235	0.0255	

Table 4.13 Procrustes Distances (Lower) and p-values (Upper) for Pairwise Comparisons Among Selected Data Sets of Asian and South American Descent

	Asians	Japanese Brazilians	Hispanic Americans	Mesoamericans	Peruvians
Asians		0.1048	0.001	<0.0001	<0.0001
Japanese Brazilians	0.0285		0.0029	<0.0001	<0.0001
Hispanic Americans	0.0449	0.0328		0.0021	<0.0001
Mesoamericans	0.0405	0.0313	0.0299		<0.0001
Peruvians	0.0512	0.0348	0.0346	0.0286	

Japanese Brazilians, Asians, Mesoamericans, and South Americans

Like European Brazilians, crania documented as Japanese Brazilians were compared with Asian, Hispanic American, Mesoamerican, and South American data sets. Results showed (Table 4.13, Fig. 4.8) that Japanese Brazilians shared similarities with Asian specimens (albeit this sample only has four specimens), and to a lesser extent Mesoamericans (comprising Mexican and Guatemalan samples) and American Hispanics (comprising unidentified North Carolina forensic cases). Morphologically, all groups have characteristically broad faces, yet Japanese Brazilian specimens exhibit a narrower cranial base and a higher vault resulting from an inferior shift in basion. They also show relatively higher zygomatic bones by an anterior displacement of zygoorbitale and superior displacement of zygomaxillare, suggesting that facial flatness is less pronounced than it is in Guatemalan and Panamanian crania. According to Procrustes distances, Peruvian crania were the most biologically distant group. They were associated with broader faces and smaller angled orbits with lower, shorter neurocrania than for Brazilian and Mesoamerican specimens.

African Brazilians, African Americans, and Native Africans

In order to explore morphological similarities/dissimilarities of African and Admixed Brazilians, these samples were compared with Native African and African American data sets. The among-group comparison showed that although African Brazilians exhibited affinity to African Americans, they formed a homogenous group with individuals of documented admixed origin. Morphologically, the major differences between African Americans and African Brazilians were related to cranial base breadth and vault height, with African American crania having a narrower cranial base and lower vault (Fig. 4.9). The lower cranial vault is related to the inferior displacement of bregma and superior displacement of basion. Both groups share similarities as far as the facial skeleton is concerned. Native African specimens are characteristically long-headed, while maintaining a relatively high cranial vault. The sex-specific analysis showed that African and Admixed Brazilians formed two homogenous groups separated more by sex than by group affinity, whereas African Americans of both sexes were morphologically distant (Fig. 4.10). It is noteworthy that Brazilian females of African and Admixed ancestry showed no statistical differences. On the contrary, Brazilian males of the African and Admixed ancestral groups differed at the 5% level of significance (p-value = 0.049) (Table 4.14).

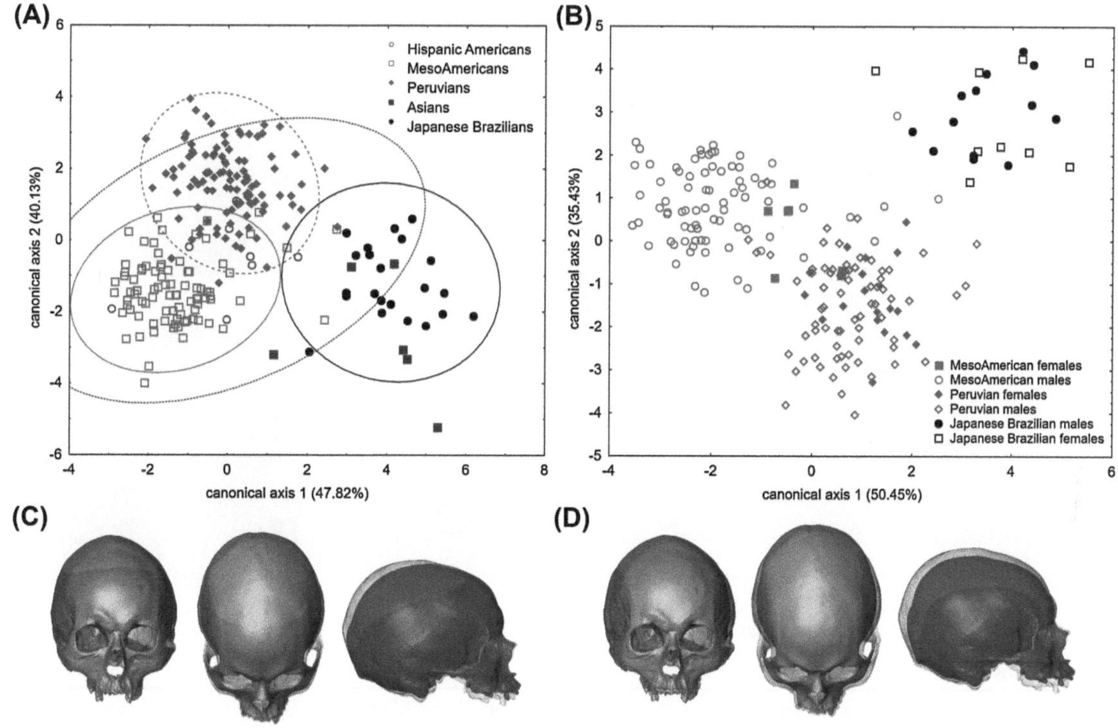

FIGURE 4.8

Comparison of crania documented as Japanese Brazilians to proxy groups of Asian, Mesoamerican, and South American descent, sex-independent (A) and sex-dependent (B). Variation illustrating shape changes along the CV1 (C) and CV2 (D) for the sex-independent test are also displayed as warped models.

DISCUSSION

Current state-of-the-art assessment of biological sex and ancestry in human skeletal remains places higher demands on an expert's operating and analytical skills, and technical lab equipment, compared with more traditional methods. Three-dimensional data acquisition hardware combined with methods of geometric morphometrics boosts diagnostic powers, particularly if based on craniofacial morphology (see Chapter 14; Ross et al., this volume). In order to simplify scientific knowledge, ease computational requirements, and reduce the need for a large reference database, several software tools were developed. However, these tools differ in every possible respect from skeletal features extracted and reference data composition, to the univariate and multivariate classification algorithms used to allocate an unknown individual. Combining multiple sources of morphological data and scientific knowledge to produce a universal diagnostic tool has the potential to become an integral part of routine forensic methodology.

The discriminative power of traditional craniometrics improves with an increase in the number of variables (Giles and Elliot, 1963; Urbanová et al., 2013). Analogously, the magnitude of sex- or population-specific differences increases with the complexity of shape descriptors (Urbanová, 2009).

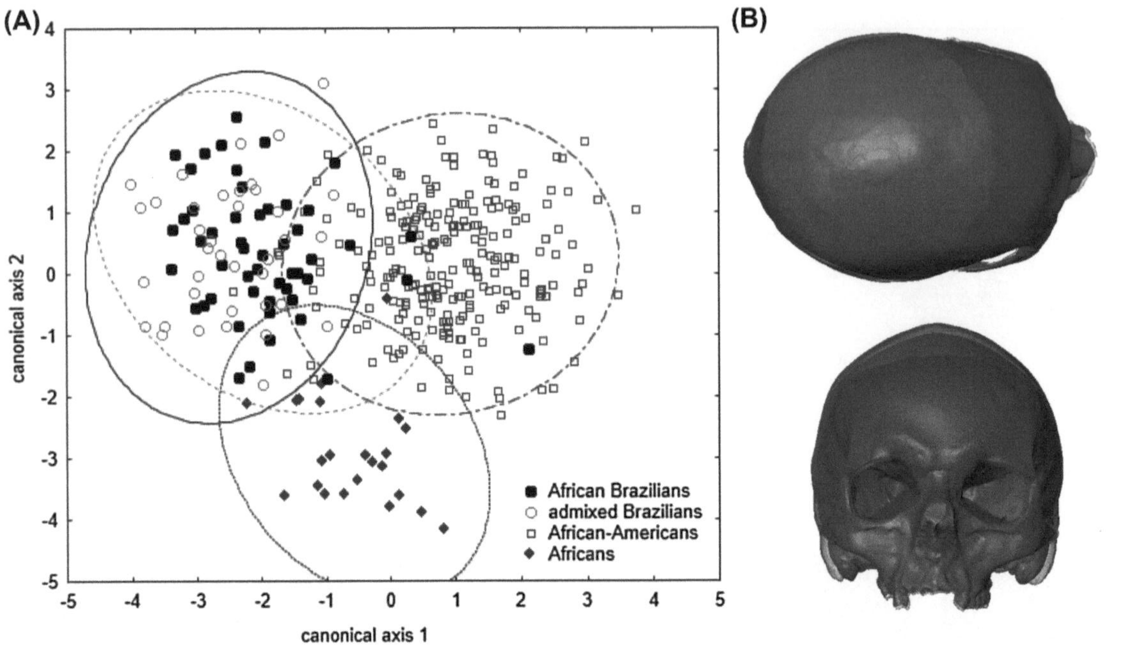

FIGURE 4.9

(A) Comparison of crania documented as African and Admixed Brazilians to proxy groups of African descent. Variation illustrating shape changes along the CV1 (B) is displayed as warped models.

Nevertheless, as far as geometric morphometric approaches are concerned, there are no standards or specific guidelines on how many landmarks should be collected to obtain the most accurate sex and ancestry assessments. For instance, Franklin (2005) recorded as many as 97 cranial landmarks for each cranium, of which 18 were believed necessary. While studying European-documented crania, Urbanová (2009) registered 53 landmarks. The software 3D-ID allows for processing of up to 34 landmarks while avoiding those points that are known to be prone to higher inter- or intraobserver error rates (eg, euryon, opisthocranion; cf. Ross and Williams, 2008).

The present study was conducted using a configuration of 21 landmarks. One advantage of geometric morphometrics is that the number of processed landmarks can vary among analyses. It cannot vary among specimens, however, unless missing data are treated, for instance, by replacing them with the univariate means or values estimated from the available data (Romaniuk and Desvignes, 2004; Strauss and Atanassov, 2006; see also Chapter 9; Kenyhercz and Passalacqua, this volume). Therefore, as is the case in the present study, the number of landmarks is generally driven by the state of preservation (ie, presence of missing data) and mutual compatibility of data sets (ie, landmarks and their definitions). Still, 21 landmarks correspond to 63 Cartesian coordinates that eventually translate into the same number of shape variables (ie, Procrustes coordinates). This number is almost twice the total of cranial measurements from the Forensic Anthropology Data Bank as offered by FORDISC 3.0 (cranial angles included).

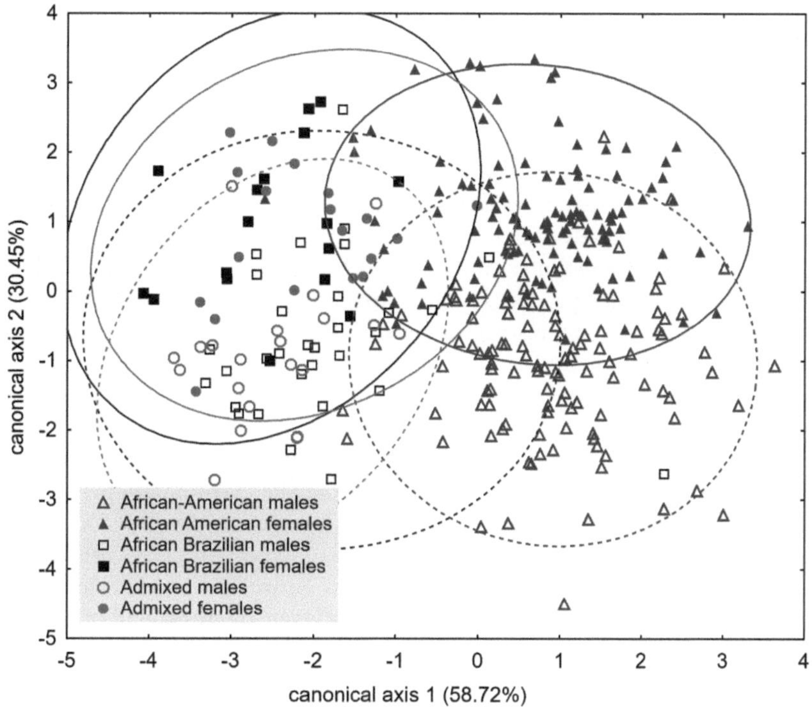

FIGURE 4.10

Sex-grouped morphological comparison of crania documented as African and Admixed Brazilians to proxy groups of African descent.

Table 4.14 ***Procrustes Distances (Lower) and p-values (Upper) for Pairwise Comparisons Among Selected Data Sets of African and Admixed Descent***

	African American/ Females	African American/ Males	African Brazilians/ Females	African Brazilians/ Males	Admixed Brazilians/ Females	Admixed Brazilians/ Males
African American/ Females		<0.0001	<0.0001	<0.0001	<0.0001	<0.0001
African American/ Males	0.0164		<0.0001	<0.0001	0.0319	<0.0001
African Brazilians/ Females	0.0270	0.0297		0.3015	0.5991	0.0226
African Brazilians/ Males	0.0250	0.0212	0.0170		0.0639	0.0490
Admixed Brazilians/ Females	0.0277	0.0319	0.0164	0.0206		0.0092
Admixed Brazilians/ Males	0.0339	0.0313	0.0241	0.0200	0.025	

The increment in the number of variables might also have a negative effect on the performance of a statistical model, as it might describe noise instead of the underlying relationship. Overfitting may particularly occur when the number of parameters is the same as or greater than the number of observations. Cross-validated rates are generally good indicators of model quality in such situations. For instance, 3D-ID provides cross-validated rates as well as a number of observations used as a reference sample.

The analysis of European data sets showed how unreliable it could be to employ unsuitably structured reference data sets to geographically different populations. These findings are in concordance with previous craniometric studies (Ramsthaler et al., 2007; Guyomarc'h and Bruzek, 2011). For assessment of biological sex, this inconsistency produces highly unbalanced classification rates, mostly due to shifts in patterns of sexual dimorphism. Interestingly, the shift was linked primarily to more sensitive shape variables than to relatively stable size-induced differences between male and female crania. Size has been claimed a constant across populations (Franklin et al., 2005b; Kimmerle et al., 2008). In the present study, size variation was expressed in terms of centroid size. According to Bookstein (1991), it is a single parameter in a statistical shape analysis that is not affected by shape variation. While the skull as a whole undergoes adaptive changes, elements that compose the cranium are prone to disproportional changes (ie, shape changes) due to various endogenous and exogenous factors. As both components co-form the total sexually dimorphic phenotype, it is logical to expect the size variable to act as a buffer mitigating population-dependent morphological variations between males and females.

For ancestry assessment, the original reference data misclassified almost half of the tested specimens. Again, this demonstrates that the composition of reference samples is paramount in quantitative ancestry assessment. It also shows that additional influencing agents besides ancestral origin, such as sampling bias and socioeconomic status, have to be taken into account when employing data sets from multiple sources. Specifically, the Central European sample was tested for temporal shifts within the data set. The appropriateness of the skeletal series that originated in the early and mid-1900s as the source of skeletal variation for current forensic cases has been questioned at multiple occasions (Cunha and van Vark, 1991).

The presence of secular trends has been cited as one of the sources of inconsistencies with contemporary populations. Secular changes are gradual diachronic changes documented across world populations that have taken place in the last two centuries commonly ascribed to the augmentation in food intake and the improvement in living conditions and public health (Bodzsár, 2000; Tanner, 1992). In studies of craniofacial morphology, the trend was associated with the increase in cranial height (Jantz and Meadows Jantz, 2000; Wescott and Jantz, 2005) and a relative narrowing of the facial skeleton (Weisensee and Jantz, 2011). This is in agreement with the observations made in the Central European data set. However, since this shift does not seem to follow a sex-specific trajectory and essentially extends morphological differences, secular change has little effect on the obtained classification rates in this study.

For the Brazilian data sets, the craniofacial analysis clarified results obtained previously by Urbanová et al. (2014b), who tested the applicability of available sex and ancestry techniques on Brazilian data sets with a relatively unsettling outcome. Specifically, the present study shed light on the pattern of morphological differences among Brazilian ancestral groups and enabled the identification of the source of the disappointing results from previous testing.

The contemporary Brazilian population has a very complex demographic composition, which varies for different Brazilian regions and/or states. For the State of São Paulo and particularly its capital, the City of São Paulo, four ancestral groups are generally recognized: European Brazilians, African Brazilians, Japanese (or Asian) Brazilians, and Admixed Brazilians. This composition is in agreement with other mixed populations whose geoethnical histories were shaped by intensive immigration waves and other socioeconomic events (eg, the slave trade). Unfortunately for the Brazilian forensic setting, the substantial lack of up-to-date methodological tools for sex and ancestry assessment complicates a routine assessment of skeletal remains.

Principally, the present study confirmed that Japanese Brazilians of either sex were the most distinctive of the Brazilian ancestral groups, mostly resulting from the prolonged cultural isolation of close-knit communities that persisted until recently, where admixture with other ethnic groups, albeit of neighborhood proximity, was seen as unwelcome and therefore was much less likely to occur (Lesser, 2013). According to recent statistics from the Brazilian Institute of Geography and Statistics, three-quarters of Japanese Brazilians are concentrated in the State of São Paulo, making up less than 2% of the population. This geographic demarcation certainly adds to their culturally induced separations. In the present analysis, the lack of extensive admixture was particularly evident from the comparisons with proxy groups of Asian and Mesoamerican/South American origin. Here, the Japanese Brazilian specimens clearly demonstrated affinity to the few indigenous Asian crania included in the analysis, although in general the Japanese Brazilian crania shared a similar phenotype with the South American and Mesoamerican samples, featuring broad flat faces and high zygomatic bones. These results are not surprising, as New World populations were originally settled by populations from Asia (Hrdlička, 1928).

Typically for the Brazilian data set, African Brazilians, together with Admixed and European Brazilians, compose morphologically highly complex groups where differences in sex-related rather than group-specific cranial features were identified as the primary source of the observed variation. This was particularly evident once Brazilians were put in context with specimens of other regions. For instance, African Brazilians were identified as a morphologically distinct group from African Americans as well as native Africans despite common assumptions about their similar ancestral origin. The differences were expressed by broader basicrania and shorter and higher vaults in Brazilians of African descent. Similarly, the Brazilians of European descent demonstrated the closest similarity to the cranial collection from Coimbra, Portugal. This does not seem surprising, as the European Brazilians descending from immigrants of Portuguese national origin predominate in most areas. In addition, the Portuguese have African admixture resulting from African colonies (Ross et al., 2011; Humphries and Ross, 2011), further complicating the already confusing demographic profile in Brazil and illustrating the diversity of Latin American populations. In terms of sex and ancestry assessment, the vague morphological demarcations among the three Brazilian groups translated into relatively low classification rates.

CONCLUSION

The results of this morphological study show that not all Hispanics/Latinos are the same and further demonstrate the importance of investigating regional or geographic morphological variation, while taking into account the unique ethnohistorical origins of Latin American (ie, "Hispanic") populations. The research also shows that the inclusion of geographically demarcated data sets in sex and ancestry assessment should be viewed as well justified. Specifically, this research underscores the need to use geographic areas rather than grouping Latin American populations into the biologically meaningless term "Hispanic," or lumping all Europeans into one sample for forensic casework to assess place of origin or ancestry. It further confirms previous results that software tools developed for US forensic contexts are not directly transferable into other regions of the world and vice versa.

References

Abdel Fatah, E.E., Shirley, N.R., Jantz, R.L., Mahfouz, M.R., 2014. Improving sex estimation from crania using a novel three-dimensional quantitative method. Journal of Forensic Sciences 59, 590–600.

Adams, D.C., Rohlf, F.J., Slice, D.E., 2004. Geometric morphometrics: ten years of progress following the 'revolution'. Italian Journal of Zoology 71, 5–16.

Ahlström, T., 1996. Sexual dimorphism in medieval human crania studied by three-dimensional thin-plate spline analysis. In: Marcus, L.F., et al. (Eds.), Advances in Morphometrics, NATO ASI Series. Plenum Press, New York and London, pp. 415–421.

Bastir, M., Rosas, A., O'Higgins, P., 2006. Craniofacial levels and the morphological maturation of the human skull. Journal of Anatomy 209, 637–654.

Besl, P.J., McKay, N.D., 1992. A method for registration of 3-D shapes. IEEE Transactions on Pattern Analysis and Machine Intelligence 14 (2), 239–256.

Bigoni, L., Velemínská, J., Brůžek, J., 2010. Three-dimensional geometric morphometric analysis of cranio-facial sexual dimorphism in a Central European sample of known sex. HOMO – Journal of Comparative Human Biology 61, 16–32.

Biwasaka, H., Sato, K., Aoki, Y., Kato, H., Maeno, Y., Tanijiri, T., Fujita, S., Dewa, K., 2013. Three dimensional surface analyses of pubic symphyseal faces of contemporary Japanese reconstructed with 3D digitized scanner. Legal Medicine 15 (5), 264–268.

Bodzsár, É.B., 2000. A review of Hungarian studies on growth and physique of children. Acta Biologica Szegediensis 44, 139–153.

Bookstein, F.L., 1982. Foundations of morphometrics. Annual Review of Ecology and Systematics 13, 451–470.

Bookstein, F.L., 1989. Principal warps: thin-plate splines and the decomposition of deformation. IEEE Transactions on Pattern Analysis and Machine Intelligence 11, 567–585.

Bookstein, F.L., 1991. Morphometric Tools for Landmark Data. Cambridge University Press, Cambridge.

Bookstein, F.L., 1997. Shape and the information in medical images: a decade of the morphometric synthesis. Computer Vision and Image Understanding 66 (2), 97–118.

Bookstein, F.L., Schaefer, K., Prossinger, H., Seidler, H., Fieder, M., Stringer, C., Weber, G., Arsuaga, J., Slice, D., Rohlf, F.J., Recheis, W., Mariam, A., Marcus, L., 1999. Comparing frontal cranial profiles in archaic and modern homo by morphometric analysis. The Anatomical Record (The New Anatomist) 257, 217–224.

Borovanský, L., 1936. Pohlavní Rozdíly Na Lebce Člověka [Sexual differences in human skull]. Česká akademie věd a umění, Praha.

Broca, P., 1875. Instructions craniologiques et craniométriques. Bulletin et mémoires de la Société d'Anthropologie de Paris (2nd Series) 2, 1–203.

Brough, A.L., Morgan, B., Robinson, C., Black, S., Cunningham, C., Adams, C., Rutty, G.N., 2014. A minimum data set approach to post-mortem computed tomography reporting for anthropological biological profiling. Forensic Science, Medicine, and Pathology 10 (4), 504–512.

Buchanan, B., Johnson, E., Strauss, R.E., Lewis, P.J., 2007. A morphometric approach to assessing late Paleoindian projectile point variability on the southern high plains. Plains Anthropologist 52 (203), 279–299.

Cardoso, H.F.V., 2006. Brief communication: the collection of identified human skeletons housed at the Bocage museum (National Museum of Natural History), Lisbon, Portugal. American Journal of Physical Anthropology 129 (2), 173–176.

Chalás, I., Urbanová, P., Kotulanová, Z., Jandová, M., Králík, M., Kozlíková, B., Sochor, J., 2014. Forensic 3D Facial Identication Software (FIDENTIS Analyst). Masaryk University. Available from: www.fidentis.cz.

Chen, S.Y.Y., Lestrel, P.E., Kerr, W.J.S., McColl, J.H., 2000. Describing shape changes in the human mandible using elliptical Fourier functions. European Journal of Orthodontics 22, 205–216.

Correia, P.M., 1997. Fire modification of bone: a review of the literature. In: Haglund, W.D., Sorg, M.H. (Eds.), Forensic Taphonomy. The Postmortem Fate of Human Remains. CRC Press, New York, pp. 275–293.

Cunha, E., Van Vark, G., 1991. The construction of sex discriminant functions from a large collection of skulls of known sex. International Journal of Anthropology 5, 53–66.

Cunha, E., Wasterlain, S., 2007. The Coimbra identified osteological collections. In: Grupe, G., Peters, J. (Eds.), Skeletal Series and Their Socio-Economic Context. Documenta Archaeobiologiae, vol. 5. Verlag Marie Leidorf GmbH, Rahden/Westf, pp. 23–33.

Delson, E., Harvati, K., Reddy, D., Marcus, L.F., Mowbray, K., Sawyer, G.J., Jacob, T., Márquez, S., 2001. The Sambungmacan 3 *Homo erectus* calvaria: a comparative morphometric and morphological analysis. The Anatomical Record 262, 360–377.

Ege, A., Seker, D.Z., Tuncay, I., Duran, Z., 2004. Photogrammetric analysis of the articular surface of the distal radius. Journal of International Medical Research 32 (4), 406–410.

Eliopoulos, C., Lagia, A., Manolis, S., 2007. A modern, documented human skeletal collection from Greece. HOMO – Journal of Comparative Human Biology 58, 221–228.

Errickson, D., Thompson, T.J.U., Rankin, B.W.J., 2014. The application of 3D visualization of osteological trauma for the courtroom: a critical review. Journal of Forensic Radiology and Imaging 2 (3), 132–137.

Franklin, D., 2005. Cranial Variation in Southern Africa. A Series of Inter-Landmark and Three-Dimensional Multivariate Morphometric Studies (Dissertation thesis). The University of Western Australia.

Franklin, D., Freedman, L., Milne, N., 2005a. Three-dimensional technology for linear morphological studies: a re-examination of cranial variation in four southern African indigenous populations. HOMO – Journal of Comparative Human Biology 56, 17–34.

Franklin, D., Freedman, L., Milne, N., 2005b. Sexual dimorphism and discriminant function sexing in indigenous South African crania. HOMO – Journal of Comparative Human Biology 55, 213–228.

Freidline, S.E., Gunz, P., Harvati, K., Hublin, J.J., 2012. Middle Pleistocene human facial morphology in an evolutionary and developmental context. Journal of Human Evolution 63 (5), 723–740.

Galton, F., 1883. Inquiries into Human Faculty and its Development. Macmillan.

Giles, E., Elliot, O., 1963. Sex determination by discriminant analysis of crania. American Journal of Physical Anthropology 21, 53–68.

Ginter, J.K., 2005. A test of the effectiveness of the revised maxillary suture obliteration method in estimating adult age at death. Journal of Forensic Sciences 50 (6), 1303–1309.

Gleicher, M., Albers, D., Walker, R., Jusufi, I., Hansen, C.D., Roberts, J.C., 2011. Visual comparison for information visualization. Information Visualization 10 (4), 289–309.

Granger, S., Pennec, X., 2002. Multi-scale EM-ICP: a fast and robust approach for surface registration. In: European Conference on Computer Vision (ECCV 2002), 2353 of LNCS, pp. 418–432.

Gunz, P., Mitteroecker, P., Bookstein, F.L., 2005. Semilandmarks in three dimensions. In: Slice, D. (Ed.), Modern Morphometrics in Physical Anthropology, Developments in Primatology: Progress and Prospects, vol. V. Kluwer Academic Press, New York, pp. 73–98.

Guyomarc'h, P., Bruzek, J., 2011. Accuracy and reliability in sex determination from skulls: a comparison of Fordisc® 3.0 and the discriminant function analysis. Forensic Science International 208, 180.e1-e180.e6.

Howells, W.W., 1973. Cranial variation in man. A study by multivariate analysis of patterns of differences among recent human populations. In: Papers of Peabody Museum for Archaeology and Ethnology, 67. Peabody Museum, Harvard University, Cambridge, MA.

Howells, W.W., 1989. Skull shapes and the map: craniometric analyses in the dispersion of modern Homo. In: Papers of Peabody Museum for Archaeology and Ethnology, 79. Peabody Museum, Harvard University, Cambridge, MA.

Hrdlička, A., 1928. The Origin and Antiquity of the American Indian. U.S. Government Printing Office, Washington.

Humphries, A., Ross, A.H., 2011. Sexual dimorphism in the Portuguese population. Anthropologie International Journal of the Science of Man 49, 13–20.

Hunt, D.R., Albanese, J., 2005. History and demographic composition of the Robert J. Terry anatomical collection. American Journal of Physical Anthropology 127, 406–417.
Inoue, M., 1990. Fourier analysis of the forehead shape of skull and sex determination by use of computer. Forensic Science International 47 (2), 101–112.
Jantz, R.L., Meadows Jantz, L., 2000. Secular change in craniofacial morphology. American Journal of Human Biology 12, 327–338.
Jurda, M., Urbanová, P., Králík, M., 2015. The post-mortem pressure distortion of human crania uncovered in an early medieval Pohansko (Czech Republic) Graveyard: post-mortem pressure distortion of human crania. International Journal of Osteoarchaeology 25 (4), 539–549.
Jurda, M., Urbanová, P., 2015. Sexual dimorphism in human crania from the perspective of 3D mesh-to-mesh comparison tools. In: 7th European Academy of Forensic Science Conference, Prague, September 6–11, 2015.
Kaesler, R.L., 1997. Phase angles, harmonic distance, and the analysis of form. In: Lestrel, P.E. (Ed.), Fourier Descriptors and Their Applications in Biology, pp. 106–125.
Kimmerle, E.H., Ross, A., Slice, D., 2008. Sexual dimorphism in America: geometric morphometric analysis of the craniofacial region. Journal of Forensic Sciences 53 (1), 54–57.
Klingenberg, C.P., Wetherill, L., Rogers, J., Moore, E., Ward, R., Autti-Rämö, I., Fagerlund, A., Jacobson, S.W., Robinson, L.K., Hoyme, H.E., Mattson, S.N., Li, T.K., Riley, E.P., Foroud, T., CIFASD Consortium, 2010. Prenatal alcohol exposure alters the patterns of facial asymmetry. Alcohol 44 (7–8), 649–657.
Klingenberg, C.P., 2011. MorphoJ: an integrated software package for geometric morphometrics. Molecular Ecology Resources 11, 353–357.
Klingenberg, C.P., 2013. Visualizations in geometric morphometrics: how to read and how to make graphs showing shape changes. Hystrix 24, 15–24.
Kohn, L.A.P., Leigh, S.R., Jacobs, S.C., Cheverud, J.M., 1993. Effects of annular cranial vault modifi cation on the cranial base and face. American Journal of Physical Anthropology 90, 147–168.
Kuhl, F.P., Giardina, C.R., 1982. Elliptic Fourier features of a closed contour. Computer Graphics and Image Processing 18, 236–258.
L'Abbé, E.N., Loots, M., Meiring, J.H., 2005. The Pretoria bone collection: a modern South African skeletal sample. HOMO – Journal of Comparative Human Biology 56 (2), 197–205.
Lesser, J., 2013. Immigration, Ethnicity, and National Identity in Brazil, 1808 to the Present. Cambridge University Press.
Lestrel, P.E., Brown, H.D., 1976. Fourier analysis of adolescent growth of the cranial vault: a longitudinal study. Human Biology 48 (3), 517–528.
Lestrel, P.E., Huggare, J.A., 1997. Cranial base changes in shunt-treated hydrocephalics: Fourier descriptior. In: Lestrel, P.E. (Ed.), Fourier Descriptors and Their Applications in Biology. Cambridge University Press, pp. 322–339.
Lestrel, P.E., 1997. Introduction and overview of Fourier descriptors. In: Lestrel, P.E. (Ed.), Fourier Descriptors and Their Applications in Biology, pp. 22–44.
Lestrel, P.E., Roche, A.F., 1986. Cranial base shape variation with age: a longitudinal study of shape using Fourier analysis. Human Biology 58, 527–540.
Lestrel, P.E., Read, D.W., Wolfe, C., 1997. Size and shape of the rabbit orbit: 3-D Fourier descriptors. In: Lestrel, P.E. (Ed.), Fourier Descriptors and Their Applications in Biology. Cambridge University Press, pp. 359–378.
Lestrel, P.E., Cesar Jr., R.M., Takahashi, O., Kanazawa, E., 2004. A Fourier-wavelet representation of 2D-shapes: sexual dimorphism in the Japanese cranial base. Anthropological Science 112 (1), 3–28.
Lu, K.H., 1965. Harmonic analysis of the human face. Biometrics 21 (2), 491–505.
Luo, L., Wang, M., Tian, Y., Duan, F., Wu, Z., Zhou, M., Rozenholc, Y., 2013. Automatic sex determination of skulls based on a statistical shape model. Computational and Mathematical Methods in Medicine 2013, 1–6.
Lycett, S.J., Chauhan, P.R., 2010. New perspectives on old stones. In: Analytical Approaches to Paleolithic Technologies. Springer Science+Business Media, LLC.

Lyman, R.L., 1994. Vertebrate Taphonomy. Cambridge University Press, Cambridge.
Maxwell, A.B., Ross, A.H., 2014. A radiographic study on the utility of cranial vault outlines for positive identifications. Journal of Forensic Sciences 59 (2), 314–318.
Mitteroecker, P., Gunz, P., 2009. Advances in geometric morphometrics. Evolutionary Biology 36, 235–247.
Monteiro, L.R., Guillermo, L.H., Rivera, L.A., Di Beneditto, A.P.M., 2004. Geometric methods combining contour and landmark information in the statistical analysis of biological shape. In: Mondaini, R. (Ed.), Proceedings of the Third Brazilian Symposium on Mathematical and Computational Biology, 2. E-Papers, Rio de Janeiro, pp. 336–355.
Musilová, B., Dupej, J., Chaumoitre, K., Bruzek, J., 2015. Sex estimation from skull using exocranial meshes. In: 7th European Academy of Forensic Science Conference, Prague, September 6–11, 2015.
Neustupa, J., Němcová, Y., 2007. A geometric morphometric study of the variation in scales of *Mallomonas striata* (Synurophyceae, Heterokontophyta). Phycologia 46, 123–130.
Novotný, V., 1986. Sex determination of the Pelvic bone: a systems approach. Anthropologie 24, 197–205.
Ocaña, J.G., 1913. Elogio de Don Federico Olóriz y Aguilera. Memorias de la Real Sociedad Española de Medicina Natural VII (5), 343–454.
Pachner, P., 1937. Pohlavní Rozdíly Na Lidské Pánvi [Sexual Differences in Human Pelvis]. Česká akademie věd a umění, Praha.
Pavlinov, I.Y., 2001. Geometric morphometrics, a new analytical approach to comparison of digitized images. In: Information Technologies in Biodiversity Research. St. Petersburg, pp. 40–64.
Pinto, D.S., Cesar Jr., R., Urbanová, P., 2013. Analysis of supraorbital margins in human skull for characterization of sexual dimorphism. In: SIBGRAPI (The Conference on Graphics, Patterns, WIP I 2013-W/, Editors. Arequipa Peru: SIBGRAPI.
Pinto, S., Urbanová, P., Cesar, R., 2016. Two-dimensional wavelet analysis of supraorbital margins of the human skull for characterizing sexual dimorphism. IEEE Transactions on Information Forensics and Security 11 (7), 1542–1548.
Ramsthaler, F., Kreutz, K., Verhoff, M.A., 2007. Accuracy of metric sex analysis of skeletal remains using Fordisc® based on a recent skull collection. International Journal of Legal Medicine 121 (6), 477–842.
Richtsmeier, J.T., Deleon, V.B., Lele, S.R., 2002. The promise of geometric morphometrics. Yearbook of Physical Anthropology 45, 63–91.
Rocha, M.A., 1995. Les collections ostéologiques humaines identifi ées du Musée Anthropologique de l'Université de Coimbra. Antropologia Portuguesa 13, 7–38.
Rohlf, F.J., 1990. Morphometrics. Annual Review of Ecology and Systematics 21, 299–316.
Romaniuk, B., Desvignes, M., 2004. Estimation of landmarks with occultation using statistical models. In: Advanced Concepts for Intelligent Vision Systems 2004, Brussels, Belgium.
Roseman, C.C., 2004. Detecting interregionally diversifying natural selection on modern human cranial form by using matched molecular and morphometric data. Proceedings of National Academy of Science 101, 12824–12829.
Roseman, C.C., Weaver, T.D., 2004. Multivariate apportionment of global human craniometric diversity. American Journal of Physical Anthropology 125, 257–263.
Ross, A.H., McKeown, A.H., Konigsberg, L.W., 1998. Allocation of Crania to Groups via the "New Morphology." American Academy of Forensic Sciences, San Francisco, CA (Published abstract).
Ross, A.H., Slice, D.E., Ubelaker, D.H., Falsetti, A.B., 2004. Population affinities of 19th century Cuban crania: implications for identification criteria in South Florida Cuban Americans. Journal of Forensic Sciences 49 (1), 11–16.
Ross, A.H., Ubelaker, D.H., Kimmerle, E.H., 2011. Implications of dimorphism, population variation, and secular change in estimating population affinity in the Iberian Peninsula. Forensic Science International 206, 214e1–214e5.
Ross, A.H., Williams, S., 2008. Testing repeatability and error of coordinate landmark data acquired from crania. Journal of Forensic Sciences 53 (4), 782–785.

Sansoni, G., Cattaneo, C., Trebeschi, M., Gibelli, D., Porta, D., Picozzi, M., 2009. Feasibility of contactless 3D optical measurement for the analysis of bone and soft tissue lesions: new technologies and perspectives in forensic sciences. Journal of Forensic Sciences 54 (3), 540–545.

Slice, D.E., 2007. Geometric morphometrics. Annual Review of Anthropology 36, 261–281.

Slice, D.E., Ross, A.H., 2009. 3D-ID: Geometric Morphometric Classification of Crania for Forensic Scientists. Version 1.0. Available from: http://www.3d-id.org.

Slizewski, A., Friess, M., Semal, P., 2010. Surface scanning of anthropological specimens: nominal-actual comparison with low cost laser scanner and high end fringe light projection surface scanning systems. Quartär 57, 179–187.

Spradley, K., 2014. Ancestry estimation in forensic anthropology: geometric morphometric derived data vs. traditional craniometric data with special reference to Hispanic crania. Proceedings to American academy of forensic sciences. In: 66th Annual Scientific Meeting, Seattle, WA, February 17–22, 2014.

Spreeuwers, L., 2011. Fast and accurate 3D face recognition. International Journal of Computer Vision 93, 389–414.

Strauss, R.E., Atanassov, M.N., 2006. Determining best complete subsets of specimens and characters for multivariate morphometric studies in the presence of large amounts of missing data. Biological Journal of the Linnean Society 88 (2), 309–328.

Tanner, J.M., 1992. Growth as a measure of the nutritional and hygienic status of a population. Hormone Research 38, 106–115.

Urbanová, P., Eliášová, H., Králík, M., 2006. Morphometric outline-based approaches in forensic anthropology. In: XX Congress of International Academy of Legal Medicine. Free Papers Proceedings. Budapest, Hungary, August 23–26, 2006. Budapest: Medimond S.r.l. International Proceedings.

Urbanová, P., Králík, M., 2008. COLIPR. Masaryk University, Brno. Available from: http://www.sci.muni.cz/lamorfa/wp-content/uploads/2015/03/Colipr_1.5.2.zip.

Urbanová, P., 2009. A Study of Human Craniofacial Variation by Using Geometric Morphometrics (Dissertation thesis). Masaryk University, Faculty of Science, Department of Anthropology.

Urbanová, P., 2011. Variation of the orbital rim by using the Elliptic Fourier analysis. In: Lestrel, P.E. (Ed.), Biological Shape Analysis Proceedings of the 1st International Symposium Tsukuba. World Scientific, Singapore, pp. 221–241.

Urbanová, P., Hejna, P., Zátopková, L., Šafr, M., 2013. What is the appropriate approach in sex determination of hyoid bones? Journal of Forensic and Legal Medicine 20 (8), 996–1003.

Urbanová, P., Hejna, P., Zátopková, L., Šafr, M., 2014a. The asymmetry and modularity of the hyoid bone. International Journal of Morphology 32 (1), 251–260.

Urbanová, P., Ross, A.H., Jurda, M., Nogueira, M.-I., 2014b. Testing the reliability of software tools in sex and ancestry estimation in a multi-ancestral Brazilian sample. Legal Medicine 16, 264–273.

Urbanová, P., Hejna, P., Jurda, M., 2015. Testing photogrammetry-based techniques for three-dimensional surface documentation in forensic pathology. Forensic Science International 250 (1), 77–86.

Valeri, C., Cole, T.I., Lele, S., Richtsmeier, J., 1998. Capturing data from surfaces using fuzzy landmarks. American Journal of Physical Anthropology 107, 113–124.

Weisensee, K.E., Jantz, R.L., 2011. Secular changes in craniofacial morphology of the Portuguese using geometric morphometrics. American Journal of Physical Anthropology 145, 548–559.

Wescott, D.J., Jantz, R.L., 2005. Assessing craniofacial secular change in American blacks and Whites using geometric Morphometry. In: Slice, D.E. (Ed.), Modern Morphometrics in Physical Anthropology. Kluwer Academic Publishers-Plenum Publishers, New York, pp. 231–245.

Wiley, D.F., Amenta, N., Alcantara, D.A., Ghosh, D., Kil Yong, J., Delson, E., Harcourt-Smith, W., Rohlf, F.J., St John, K., Hamann, B., 2005. Evolutionary morphing. In: Conference: 16th IEEE Visualization Conference (VIS 2005), October 23–28, 2005, Minneapolis, MN, USA.

Zelditch, M.L., Swiderski, D.L., Sheets, H.D., Fink, W.L., 2004. Geometric Morphometrics for Biologists: A Primer. Elsevier Academic Press, New York.

CHAPTER

5

Cranial Nonmetric and Morphoscopic Data Sets

C.M. Pink[1], C. Maier[2], M.A. Pilloud[2], J.T. Hefner[3]

Metropolitan State University of Denver, Denver, CO, United States[1]; University of Nevada, Reno, Reno, NV, United States[2]; Michigan State University, East Lansing, MI, United States[3]

CHAPTER OUTLINE HEAD

Introduction 91
  Nomenclature 92
Cranial Nonmetric Data Sets 93
  Data Collection Protocols 94
  Heritability and Cranial Nonmetric Traits 95
Morphoscopic Data 97
  Data Collection Protocols 97
  Heritability of Morphoscopic Traits 98
Measures of Biological Distance 98
  Bioarchaeology 99
  Forensic Anthropology 101
Conclusions 102
References 102

INTRODUCTION

Despite shared theoretical foundations, biological anthropologists and forensic anthropologists have different perspectives and pursue seemingly unrelated research questions when utilizing cranial nonmetric traits in their analyses. Biological anthropologists focus on population distances and heritability between groups using cranial nonmetric traits (generally discrete variants); conversely, forensic anthropologists use morphoscopic (or macromorphoscopic, morphological, etc.) traits to estimate the ancestry of an unidentified decedent. In fact, the traits (nonmetric and morphoscopic) used by each of these practitioners share a history (see Chapter 1, this volume), but confusion still exists between the two. In this chapter, we will explore both types of data and when possible provide information on currently available data sets. Of course, prior to any discussion of the use of these seemingly disparate types of data, we first attempt to sort out distinctions between nonmetric and morphoscopic traits.

Biological Distance Analysis. http://dx.doi.org/10.1016/B978-0-12-801966-5.00005-6

Nomenclature

In this volume, variants of the skull having multiple character states scored in a categorical (either ordinal or dichotomous) manner are referred to generally as cranial nonmetric traits. Hauser and DeStefano (1989), in their comprehensive volume on the topic, favored the term epigenetic because the authors felt it communicated both the genetic and the environmental influences on the expression of any particular character state. Waddington (1942, 1956) initially defined epigenetic as the original genetic instructions operating in a succession of environments from embryonic life through to adulthood that influence the progressive differentiation and determination of cells and tissues. Following the modern synthesis of DNA, several other definitions of *epigenetic* have been proffered in the literature. Holliday (1990) describes epigenetic as anything outside of DNA that influences the development of an organism or trait. Given variation in current definitions as they relate to the study of DNA, the term epigenetic is best left out of this discussion of cranial nonmetric trait variation.

Biological anthropologists using cranial nonmetric traits to explore population histories and relatedness have employed various terms in addition to epigenetic and nonmetric. Grüneberg (1952) discussed "quasi-continuous" variables to capture the multiple expressions of traits, where others preferred discontinuous (Ossenberg, 1969), discrete (Rightmire, 1972, 1976), or *discreta* (Rösing, 1982) to conceptualize traits with a binary expression (0,1 data). Berry and Searle (1963) used both epigenetic traits and minor variants to describe their data set, but later Berry and Berry (Berry and Berry, 1972; Berry, 1968) settled on nonmetric variants, avoiding any commitment to the exact contributions of genes and environment in the trait expression. This conservative approach is followed by the majority of biological anthropologists and is used throughout this volume when describing discrete cranial nonmetric traits.

Today, most practicing biological anthropologists accept the definition of nonmetric traits presented by Buikstra and Ubelaker (1994, p. 85): "dichotomous, discontinuous, epigenetic traits; nonpathological variations of skeletal tissues that can be better classified as present or absent (or as a point on a morphological gradient; e.g., small to large) rather than quantified by a measurement." The five major categories of nonmetric traits in the cranium are (1) extrasutural bone (eg, Inca bone); (2) proliferative ossifications (eg, pterygoalar bridging); (3) ossification failure (eg, septal aperture); (4) suture variation (eg, metopic suture); and (5) foramina variation (eg, zygomaticofacial foramen number) (Hauser and DeStefano, 1989; Buikstra and Ubelaker, 1994). Although the roles played by the genome and the environment in the inheritance of cranial nonmetric traits are poorly understood, these traits are routinely used by biological anthropologists in biological distance studies as a measure of relatedness within and between populations.

However, forensic anthropologists assess an individual's ancestry through the visual inspection of certain morphological, cranial nonmetric variants primarily comprising bony structures in the midfacial skeleton (Brues, 1990). Ousley and Hefner (2005) initially termed these particular traits "macromorphoscopic," identifying the distinction of the cranial nonmetric traits used in forensic anthropological research, which they felt differed significantly from the traits used in biological distance studies. Later, Hefner (2009) simplified Ousley and Hefner's (2005) term to *morphoscopic* traits while maintaining the original characterization of the variables. Morphoscopic traits, therefore, are quasi-continuous variables of the cranium essentially reflected as soft-tissue differences in the living. In a sense, these traits are similar to Brues's second class of traits, which "are apparent in both skeleton and living...due to the contour of bone in areas where it closely follows the surface" (Brues, 1958, p. 559). These traits are subdivided into five classes: (1) assessing bone shape (eg, nasal bone structure); (2) bony feature morphology (eg, inferior nasal aperture morphology); (3) suture shape (eg, zygomaticomaxillary suture); (4) presence/absence data (eg, postbregmatic depression); and (5) feature prominence/protrusion (eg, anterior nasal spine) (Hefner, 2009). Unlike the anthropological analyses based on cranial nonmetric traits mentioned in the preceding section, morphoscopic traits are used to assess (or predict, determine, estimate, etc.) the ancestry of a single individual for the purpose of identification. Although most introductory forensic anthropology textbooks provide lists (by ancestry) of these traits, Hefner (2009) has only recently standardized trait descriptions and analyzed trait distribution within large reference samples (Hefner, 2009).

The following two sections outline the application of cranial nonmetric data sets useful for (1) biodistance studies, and (2) the assessment of ancestry in forensic settings. Although some overlap and redundancy does occur, we make every effort to keep the two data types as distinct as possible.

CRANIAL NONMETRIC DATA SETS

Cranial nonmetric trait data are generally used to assess biological affinity within and between archaeological populations. This treatment of cranial nonmetric traits is usually referred to as biological distance, or biodistance, analysis. The historical development of these traits is thoroughly outlined by Hefner et al. (Chapter 1, this volume) and will only be summarized herein when necessary for capturing subtleties within the data.

Early in the 20th century, researchers examined cranial nonmetric trait frequencies to appreciate differences between populations (cf. Russell, 1900; Wood-Jones, 1931a,b). However, Lane and Sublett's (1972) exploration of postmarital residence patterns and Buikstra's (1980) extensive study of biological distance among groups in the Lower Illinois Valley were influential. These studies helped inspire the next generation of American biological anthropologists using cranial nonmetric traits. After the initial popularity of cranial nonmetric data for biological distance studies in the 1970s and 1980s, there was a period of relative stasis in the literature. Recently, cranial nonmetric trait studies have undergone a revitalization (Hallgrimsson et al., 2004; Hanihara et al., 2003; Irish, 2010; Nikita et al., 2012; Ossenberg et al., 2006; Sutter and Mertz, 2004; Torres-Rouff et al., 2013).

A recent indication in the rise of popularity for cranial nonmetric trait data is Ossenberg's (2013) publication of a massive cranial nonmetric trait database for public consumption (http://hdl.handle.net/1974/7870). Ossenberg's database is analogous to the Howells cranial measurement database; the Ossenberg data set is also representative of worldwide populations and is freely available to researchers. Furthermore, Konigsberg made available statistical code for calculating biological distance (http://www.anthro.illinois.edu/people/lylek/) with cranial nonmetric data. Their work demonstrates a renewed demand in the academic community for analytical tools tailored to address research questions based on cranial nonmetric trait data.

The advantages and disadvantages of cranial nonmetric traits (and similarly morphoscopic trait data) have been thoroughly outlined elsewhere and are summarized here only for continuity (Berry, 1975; Berry and Berry, 1967; Del Papa and Perez, 2007; Gualdi-Russo et al., 1999; Hallgrimsson et al., 2005; Konigsberg et al., 1993; Perizonius, 1979; Richtsmeier and McGrath, 1986). Cranial nonmetric traits can be obtained from fragmented assemblages, they are relatively easy to collect, and "best of all: *they work*" (Buikstra, 1974, p. 471, her emphasis). Multiple statistical methods (see below and elsewhere in this volume) are available for analysis; the choice of method is largely determined by the research question. However, there are drawbacks to cranial nonmetric trait data. Many traits are expressed bilaterally, and since asymmetry in trait expression is common, the researcher must determine a priori how to deal with those instances. Intertrait correlations are also frequent, as are associations with age and sex. Finally, the researcher should consider possible correlations between cultural body modification practices and nonmetric trait expression. Cranial modification is the most frequently cited example, although Konigsberg et al. (1993) do not ascribe much influence to trait expression and calculations of biological distance from modification.

Data Collection Protocols

Again, cranial nonmetric traits usually fall into one of a few categories—for example, variation in the form or number of foramina, ossicles within the cranial sutures, ossification failure, or excessive ossification (Buikstra and Ubelaker, 1994). More broadly, many nonmetric traits can also be described as *hyperostotic* (excess bone formation) or *hypostotic* (ossification failure) (Ossenberg, 1970). Although there is seemingly an endless number of cranial nonmetric traits used in biodistance studies, the majority are described fully in several seminal texts (Buikstra and Ubelaker, 1994; Hauser and De Stefano, 1989; Ossenberg, 1970). Table 5.1 presents commonly used cranial nonmetric traits and their categorizations (ie, foraminal/vascular, hyperostotic, hypostotic, or sutural).

A comprehensive data collection protocol to accommodate analytical considerations is a necessary requirement for cranial nonmetric trait analysis. Buikstra and Ubelaker (1994) suggest recording the character state in all observable specimens in addition to noting when a character state is unobservable for a particular specimen; observations of bilateral expression should be made for both sides, and traits that have more than two states (ie, present or absent) should be scored following a fully standardized and well-defined multistage system. Cranial nonmetric trait character states are often compressed into a dichotomous present/absent system for statistical analysis. However, it is clear that cranial nonmetric traits are complex, and their expression is the result of the additive effect of multiple genes (Grüneberg, 1963), so every care should be taken to capture as much variability in trait expression as possible. Minimally, analysts should follow the scoring rubric presented by Buikstra and Ubelaker (1994, Attachment 22) for 22 cranial nonmetric traits and make an effort to clearly define and record all character states for traits not on this rubric. The relationship between genetic variance and cranial nonmetric trait expression should be acknowledged before any statistical models are applied to relative frequency data within and between populations.

Several models have been proffered to explain how each character state is expressed. Falconer's (1965, 1967) threshold model may best explain the polygenic expression of cranial nonmetric traits and isolate some explanations for why trait compression (0, 1, 2, 3, 4 to 0, 1) may not truly capture the full range of trait variability. Falconer (1989) suggested converting trait incidences to mean liabilities that are assumed to be normally distributed. Thus the "unit of liability is [a trait's] standard deviation, $\boldsymbol{\sigma}$" (Falconer, 1989, p. 302). Trait liabilities can then be used in the calculation of biological distances, although they are not employed in all methods (Mahalanobis D^2 is the only method discussed in this chapter that uses trait liabilities). Fig. 5.1 illustrates this trait liability in two populations. In Population A, the trait incidence is 3%. In contrast, the trait incidence in Population B is much larger at 33%. Thus the liability for the trait in each of these populations is 1.88 (A) and 0.44 (B), with a difference of 1.22 standard deviations.

Cranial nonmetric traits are polygenic, and trait expression is the result of inheritance and environmental pressures (Cheverud and Buikstra, 1981a; Falconer, 1989). However, unlike many polygenic

Table 5.1 Commonly Observed Cranial Nonmetric Traits (cf. Buikstra and Ubelaker, 1994; Ossenberg, 2013)[a]

Trait	Category	Trait	Category
Metopic suture	Sutural	Foramen ovale incomplete	Hypostotic
Supraorbital foramen/notch	Vascular	Foramen spinosum incomplete	Hypostotic
Multiple infraorbital foramina	Vascular	Pterygospinous spur/bridge	Hyperostotic
Zygomaticofacial foramina	Vascular	Pterygoalar spur/bridge	Hyperostotic
Parietal (obelionic) foramen	Vascular	Tympanic dehiscence	Hypostotic
Epiteric bone	Sutural	Auditory exostosis	Hyperostotic
Coronal ossicle	Sutural	Mastoid foramen	Vascular
Bregmatic bone	Sutural	Multiple mental foramen	Vascular
Sagittal ossicle	Sutural	Palatine torus	Hyperostotic
Apical bone	Sutural	Mandibular torus	Hyperostotic
Lambdoid ossicle	Sutural	Mylohyoid bridge	Hyperostotic
Asterionic bone	Sutural	Paracondylar process	Hyperostotic
Ossicle in the occipitomastoid suture	Sutural	Os japonicum (transversozygomatic suture)	Sutural
Parietal notch bone	Sutural	Double condylar facet	Hypostotic
Inca bone	Sutural	Pharyngeal tubercle	Hyperostotic
Patent condylar canal	Vascular	Clinoid bridging	Hyperostotic
Divided hypoglossal canal	Vascular	Frontal groove	Vascular
Flexure for the superior sagittal sulcus	Vascular	Infraorbital suture	Sutural

[a]*Nonmetric traits of the infracranial skeleton are also frequently observed, but are not discussed in this chapter.*

traits expressing a continuous distribution, cranial nonmetric skeletal traits are categorical or quasi-continuous. Cheverud and Buikstra (1981a, p. 44) applied the threshold model using a continuously distributed liability to explain the expression of nonmetric traits, and note that only when the additive genetic and environmental effects surpass some threshold is the trait (or character state of that trait) expressed. The threshold model applies to within-individual variation in trait liabilities as well as population-level variation. Hallgrímsson et al. (2005) examination of disproportionate asymmetrical expression for rare bilateral traits found that the standard threshold model is a satisfactory explanatory model for the phenomenon. This has implications for the interpretation of biological distance results and perhaps more importantly for studies of fluctuating asymmetry, but that is beyond the scope of this chapter.

Heritability and Cranial Nonmetric Traits

Heritability (h^2) is the additive genetic variance divided by the phenotypic variance,

$$h^2 = \frac{\sigma_G^2}{\sigma_P^2}, \tag{5.1}$$

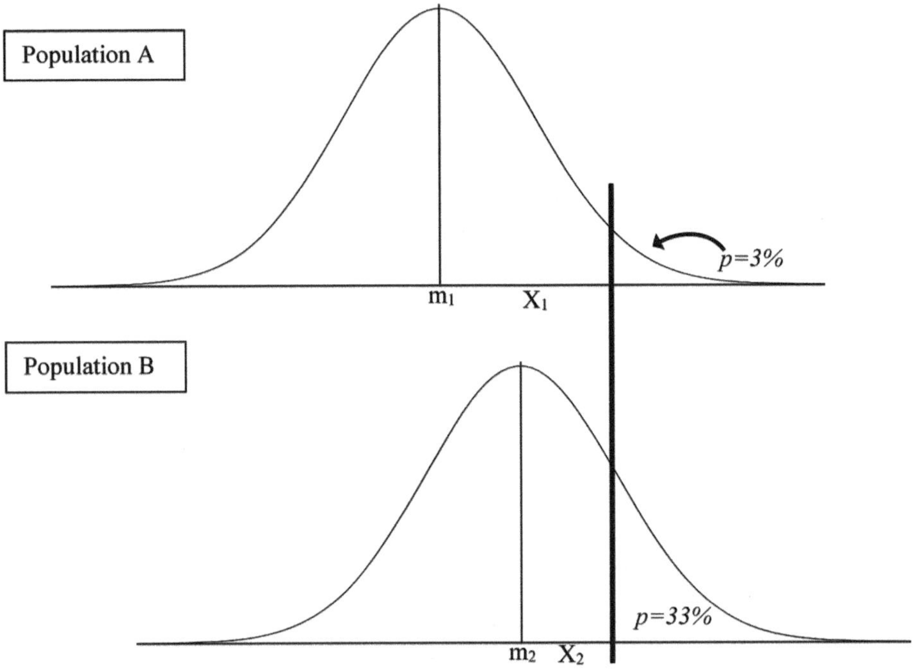

FIGURE 5.1

Threshold model for two populations.

After Falconer, D.S., 1989. Introduction to Quantitative Genetics, third ed. Longman, London, p. 301.

which essentially quantifies the genetic contribution to the expression of the trait. This is *narrow sense* heritability, only addressing the expression of a phenotype as determined by the genes (Falconer, 1989). Studies specifically addressing issues surrounding the heritability of these traits (*writ* large) are numerous (Berry, 1968, 1975; Berry et al., 1967; Cheverud and Buikstra, 1981a,b; Cheverud and Buikstra, 1982), although suitable samples have permitted only a few to address heritability in human samples (Carson, 2006; Lane, 1977; Sjøvold, 1984).

Sjøvold (1984) analyzed a pedigreed skeletal sample from Hallstatt, Austria, and found h^2 values ranging from 0.0 to 0.954. More recently, Carson (2006) reexamined the same population as Sjøvold (1984) and calculated heritabilities using a maximum-likelihood variance components analysis on traits scored both dichotomously and on a multilevel system. Using this approach, she found uniformly low h^2 values for the 36 traits considered. Of note, Carson (2006) also found that h^2 values were higher when the dichotomous scoring system was used. Clearly, the findings of Sjøvold (1984) and Carson (2006) are concerning for researchers attempting to address biological distance based on cranial nonmetric trait data, since many analytical methods assume high heritability. Following the influential research of Cheverud (1988), many biological distance studies assume the genotypic (**G**) and phenotypic (**P**) distance matrices are similar *and* proportional. However, Martínez-Abadías et al. (2009) analysis of the heritability of human cranial dimensions found correlated **G** and **P** matrices reflecting genetic patterns, but the matrices were neither identical nor necessarily proportional.

MORPHOSCOPIC DATA

As mentioned herein, morphoscopic data differ significantly from cranial nonmetric data. The historical development of morphoscopic data and the role played by Hooton have been presented elsewhere (eg, Brues, 1990; Hefner, 2003, 2007, 2009; Hefner and Ousley, 2014; Hefner et al., 2012) and will not be repeated here. Morphoscopic data are only now seeing treatment at the same level of scientific scrutiny that cranial nonmetric traits have been subjected to for a century. Interest in the levels of objectivity in forensic anthropological methods has directed recent research investigating the soundness of morphoscopic traits in the assessment of ancestry.

One part of this reinvigorated exploration into morphoscopic trait analysis is the adoption of new methods for data collection. In the past, so-called "trait lists" like those published by Rhine (1990) highlighted extreme trait values and were used by forensic anthropologists to *support* a craniometric analysis or to *predict* the ancestry of an unknown set of remains on the basis of majority voting (eg, the ancestry prediction is the result of a tally of observed traits). Many of the trait lists were derived from small or inadequate samples. Therefore, they did not fully account for human variation or trait frequencies within groups, and today are considered typological. Rhine (1990, p. 17) pointed out these limitations in his account of morphoscopic traits and stated that his lists, which have been heavily relied upon since their publication, should be treated more as a basis for preliminary analysis. The following sections do not review the old typology; instead, only traits and data collection protocols derived from the *new morphoscopics* are presented. This is not meant as a denigration of older methods; rather, we are providing standardization to forensic anthropology as we currently view the morphoscopic approach.

Importantly, morphoscopic data analysis requires the same treatment given cranial nonmetric traits: that is, researchers first should focus on the recordation of data for reference samples/populations of interest. Only then should those data be used to assess the ancestry of an unknown individual encountered during forensic casework. Doing otherwise puts the cart before the horse and leads to post hoc trait selection with an unreliable as well as unreplicable reliance on the experience of the analyst (Ousley and Hefner, 2005).

Until recently, there were no large data sets available that contained morphoscopic trait data from forensically significant populations. However, one of the authors (JTH), under a grant from the National Institute of Justice (NIJ, 2015-DN-BX-K012), developed The Macromorphoscopic Databank (MaMD), similar in scope and function to the craniometric data available from the Forensic Data Bank. Still in its infancy, the MaMD currently comprises over 2100 individuals from populations around the world. The entire database will be made freely available to interested researchers at the conclusion of the NIJ grant in 2017/2018. All of the data in the MaMD were collected using protocols developed at the Smithsonian Institution Repatriation Laboratory using software specifically developed to standardize data collection from human skeletal remains. That software and several alternatives are the focus of the following section.

Data Collection Protocols

As previously mentioned, morphoscopic traits are subdivided into five classes: (1) assessing bone shape (eg, nasal bone structure); (2) bony feature morphology (eg, inferior nasal aperture morphology); (3) suture shape (eg, zygomaticomaxillary suture); (4) presence/absence data (eg, postbregmatic depression); and (5) feature prominence/protrusion (eg, anterior nasal spine) (Hefner, 2009). A complete list of all morphoscopic trait data is beyond the scope of this chapter, however, Table 5.2 presents some commonly encountered and used morphoscopic traits. As with cranial nonmetric traits, morphoscopic data should be recorded in a systematic and repeatable manner.

Table 5.2 Commonly Observed Cranial Morphoscopic Traits

Trait	References
Anterior nasal spine	(Gill, 1998; Hefner, 2009; Rhine, 1990)
Inferior nasal aperture	(Gill, 1998; Hefner, 2009; Krogman and İşcan, 1986; Rhine, 1990)
Interorbital breadth	(Bass, 1987; Gill, 1998; Hefner, 2009; Rhine, 1990)
Malar tubercle	(Hauser and De Stefano, 1989; Hefner, 2009; Rhine, 1990)
Nasal aperture width	(Bass, 1987; Hefner, 2009; Rhine, 1990)
Nasal bone contour	(Gill, 1998; Hefner, 2009)
Nasal overgrowth	(Hefner, 2009; Rhine, 1990)
Postbregmatic depression	(Bass, 1987; Hefner, 2009; Krogman and İşcan, 1986; Rhine, 1990)
Supranasal suture	(Hauser and De Stefano, 1989; Hefner, 2009; Rhine, 1990)
Transverse palatine suture	(Gill, 1998; Hefner, 2009; Rhine, 1990)
Zygomaticomaxillary suture	(Gill, 1998; Hauser and De Stefano, 1989; Hefner, 2009; Rhine, 1990)
Nasion depression	Rhine (1990)
Palate shape	(Gill, 1971; Maier et al., 2015; Rhine, 1990)
Orbit form	(Gill, 1971; Rhine, 1990)
Mastoid form	Gill (1998)
Gonial angle	Rhine (1990)
Mandibular ramus form	(Angel and Kelley, 1990; Rhine, 1990)

Heritability of Morphoscopic Traits

Morphoscopic traits are primarily related to cranial form, not the presence or absence of specific osseous features such as foramina, ossicles, and bony proliferation. Therefore, the heritability of these traits can be difficult to discern, as cranial form is plastic and the environment may have a considerable effect (eg, Beals et al., 1983; Gill, 1998). Some traits (eg, sutural form and orbit shape) have a demonstrable genetic component, though in both of these instances the manifestation of adult morphology is reliant on the environment (Hauser and De Stefano, 1989; Oudhof, 1982; Szilvassy, 1986). Although these traits remain on traditional trait lists, they are not among the traits implemented in the *new morphoscopics*. For those traits currently employed in morphoscopic analysis of the skeleton, heritability has not been thoroughly investigated and remains unknown. The current understanding of morphoscopic trait data is that heredity and the environment are both important contributors to individual variation, though the relative contribution of each is unclear (Ta'ala, 2015).

MEASURES OF BIOLOGICAL DISTANCE

Hefner and colleagues (Chapter 1, this volume) provide the historical framework for the changing approaches of statistical analysis in biodistance studies. However, several methods—some used today, others no longer in favor—are briefly outlined below to provide the reader a basic understanding of their mechanisms. These statistical measurements of biological distance are treated as relevant to bioarchaeology (population and frequency based) and forensic anthropology (placing an unidentified individual).

Bioarchaeology

Smith's mean measure of divergence (MMD) converts nonmetric trait frequencies to a numerical value reflecting similarity, and was one of the first distance measures employed in bioarchaeology. The method is a popular distance measure still frequently used today. Smith's formula was initially developed for Grewal (1962) to explore biological divergence that developed over generations of laboratory mice. Smith's MMD, as described by Grewal (1962), and later clarified by Harris and Sjøvold (2004), is:

$$\mathrm{MMD} = \frac{\sum_{k=1}^{r} (\theta_{ik} - \theta_{jk})^2}{r} - \left(\frac{1}{n_i} + \frac{1}{n_j}\right), \tag{5.2}$$

where the difference between samples i and j for the arcsine-transformed frequencies of trait k is calculated and squared so that positive and negative values do not cancel one another. The sum of the differences is divided by the number of traits used in the equation, r, to generate the average difference between samples i and j. A correction term,

$$\left(\frac{1}{n_i} + \frac{1}{n_j}\right), \tag{5.3}$$

is then subtracted from the average to correct for sampling fluctuations. Since Grewal (1962), Smith's MMD has been used extensively on osteological and dental data to explore biological relationships within and among human populations (Berry, 1974; Berry and Berry, 1967, 1972; Buikstra, 1976; Donlon, 2000; Edgar, 2007; Greene, 1982; Hallgrimsson et al., 2004; Hanihara et al., 2003; Irish, 2010, 1997, 1998a,b; Irish and Turner, 1990; Ossenberg et al., 2006; Sutter and Verano, 2007). Sjøvold (1977) made a comprehensive study of the application of Smith's MMD in human populations, and when limitations were discovered in the following decades, he and Harris revised the formula. Harris and Sjøvold (2004) published the adjusted formula:

$$\mathrm{MMD} = \frac{\sum_{k=1}^{r} (\theta_{ik} - \theta_{jk})^2 - \left(\frac{1}{n_{ik}+\frac{1}{2}} + \frac{1}{n_{jk}+\frac{1}{2}}\right)}{r} \tag{5.4}$$

The correction term used in the original formula tended to result in an overestimate of the true variance between samples (Green and Suchey, 1976; Green et al., 1979). Essentially, very high (>0.95) and very low (<0.10) trait frequencies affect overall variance, and the new correction term (highlighted with a bracket in the formula above) was suggested (Freeman and Tukey, 1950). It is worth noting that others prefer the Anscombe (1948) transformation over Freeman and Tukey (cf., Irish, 2010, p. 379).

The statistical significance of MMD values can be determined by comparing the value with the standard deviation, calculated:

$$\sqrt{\frac{2\sum\left(\frac{1}{n_{ik}+\frac{1}{2}} + \frac{1}{n_{jk}+\frac{1}{2}}\right)^2}{r^2}} \tag{5.5}$$

If the MMD value is greater than two times the standard deviation, the two samples are significantly different (at $p = .05$); however, (Harris and Sjøvold, 2004) note that this is a statistical "rule of thumb" that may not be useful when sample sizes are disparate or very small. One may also standardize the MMD by dividing the original MMD by the standard deviation (Sjøvold, 1973). Using the corrected derivation of Smith's MMD, recent studies have generated biological distance matrices that correlate well with Mahalanobis D^2 matrices (Irish, 2010; Nikita et al., 2012; Schillaci et al., 2009). However, because MMD is not a Euclidean distance, it does not account for intertrait correlation.

Balakrishnan and Sanghvi's B^2 (1968; Sanghvi and Balakrishnan, 1972) was one of the first Euclidean distance measures for categorical data analysis and is considered analogous to the x^2 measure of distance. The distance between two populations P_m and P_n is calculated using sample variance with a dispersion matrix:

$$B_{mn}^2 = \sum_{j=1}^{r} \sum_{k=1}^{Sj} \sum_{l=1}^{Sj} \mathbf{C}_i^{-1} d_{jk} d_{jl}, \tag{5.6}$$

where

$$d_{jk} = p_{mjk} - p_{njk}, \tag{5.7}$$

The proportions are maximum likelihood estimates of the proportions of the kth class, of the jth character S_i, in the ith population, and $\mathbf{C}_i$ is the common weighted variance—covariance (dispersion) matrix (Balakrishan and Sanghvi, 1968). Unlike in MMD, the dispersion matrix used in the calculation of B^2 does account for intertrait correlations.

The Mahalanobis D^2 distance statistic is the preferred method for assessing biological distance today. The generalized D^2 statistic was first published by Mahalanobis (1936) as a measure of divergence between populations based on continuous data. The Mahalanobis D^2 was extended to cranial nonmetric traits by Williams-Blangero and Blangero (1989) and Konigsberg (1990). The categorical trait data are analyzed for biological distance using a tetrachoric correlation matrix rather than the dispersion matrix utilized in Balakrishnan and Sanghvi's B^2. Tetrachoric correlations are calculated within each group, then pooled using sample size to find the weighted average correlation (Konigsberg, 1990, p. 60). The formula provided by Konigsberg (1990) is:

$$D_{ij}^2 = (z_i - z_j)' \mathbf{T}^{-1} (z_i - z_j), \tag{5.8}$$

where z_i is the z-score for a trait in population i, and z_i is the z-score for the same trait in population j. $\mathbf{T}^{-1}$ is the inverse of the pooled within-group tetrachoric correlation matrix between all traits. Since this result represents the minimum possible distance between groups, it is considered a conservative estimate (Williams-Blangero, 1989). An advantage of Mahalanobis D^2 is that the tetrachoric correlation coefficient is more appropriate for traits with an underlying continuous distribution that are scored dichotomously such as cranial nonmetrics. Like all distance measures, D^2 is sensitive to small sample sizes, which affect the calculation of the tetrachoric correlations (Konigsberg et al., 1993). Similar to Smith's MMD, the significance of Mahalanobis D^2 distances can be tested with an F-test (Droessler, 1981; Konigsberg and Blangero, 1993). Balakrishnan and Sanghvi's B^2 and the Mahalanobis D^2 are not an exhaustive list of options for Euclidean distance measures. They are two of the more frequently used methods, however, which is why they are described here.

The F-statistic (F_{ST}) or inbreeding coefficient described by Sewall Wright (1951) is not a measure of biological distance, but the average inbreeding of a subpopulation relative to the whole population. If phenotypic and genetic variance—covariance matrices are considered proportional, the effective population sizes are equal across groups, and trait heritabilities are moderate to high, the minimum F_{ST} (phenotypic) is then proportional to the real F_{ST} (genetic) (Konigsberg and Ousley, 1995).

Relethford et al. (1997) provide a method for calculating F_{ST} based on phenotypic data following Rogers and Harpending (1986):

$$F_{ST} = \sum_{i=1}^{g} w_i r_{ii}, \tag{5.9}$$

where g is the number of populations, w_i is the relative population size of population i, and r_{ii} is the weighted average diagonal of the R matrix which estimates the amount of genetic microdifferentiation between populations. The F_{ST} calculation presented by Relethford and colleagues (1997) is based on metric data. Lyle Konigsberg provides code to derive an R matrix for cranial nonmetric data from the D^2 matrix (http://www.anthro.illinois.edu/people/lylek/).

A relatively small F_{ST} value indicates significant gene flow with increasing within-group heterogeneity, and decreasing between-group variation. This statistic can strengthen interpretations of population histories by giving quantitative estimates to the evolutionary processes of gene flow and genetic drift. One should take note that the calculation of F_{ST} is not robust for unequal and small sample sizes. Furthermore, the effects of genetic drift (isolation and founder's effect) and a small number of subpopulations can influence the F_{ST} value, making its interpretation problematic (Jorde, 1980). More recent studies have identified the effects of natural selection, which can also significantly alter patterns of between-population variation (Roseman, 2004; Roseman and Weaver, 2004). As with any statistic, F_{ST} must be interpreted with some caution.

These methodological considerations are by no means the only available approaches for cranial nonmetric traits, but represent those that are often used in the anthropological literature. If the reader is interested in applying the methods described above, the authors suggest a thorough review of the original sources. Many chapters in Section 3 of this volume present additional statistical analyses, as well as critiques, that one may find useful. The reader is encouraged to explore other avenues of analysis, particularly from other fields like numerical ecology and taxonomy, theoretical biology, data mining, and machine learning.

Forensic Anthropology

In contrast to the biodistance methods employed in bioarchaeological population-based studies, forensic anthropology centers on an unknown individual and the placement of that individual into a group based on the individual's peer-perceived ancestry. Morphoscopic data have not historically been treated to the same level of statistical rigor as their metric counterparts in forensic anthropology. This reluctance to explore statistical methods with these data is due in part to difficulties working with categorical data, but also because forensic anthropologists saw no need to validate the trait list approach. However, computer software packages are now available for the analysis of these data using robust classification statistics, and standardized data collection protocols for these traits (eg, Hefner, 2009) now allow the application of a more rigorous statistical framework.

Due to the assumptions required of parametric methods, nonparametric statistics may be more appropriate for the analysis of morphoscopic data. Some parametric methods such as discriminant function have been used and shown to accurately classify individuals in 70–77% of cases (Edgar, 2013; Hefner, 2015). However, the ordinal and binary scales on which morphoscopic data are recorded may violate the assumptions of parametric methods, and make any posterior probabilities associated with their results difficult to interpret (Feldesman, 2002; Hefner, 2015). Therefore, nonparametric methods may be more appropriate when working with these types of data. Such methods include *k*-nearest neighbor (Hefner et al., 2012), random forest modeling (Hefner et al., 2014), support vector machines (Hefner et al., 2015), and artificial neural networks (Hefner and Ousley, 2014). These methods can be readily applied in software packages such R (2015), SAS version 9.0 (2009), and SYSTAT for Windows version 11 (2012). Additionally, the MaMD is freely available to interested researchers and practitioners to serve as a reference database to use and test these methods.

A new method that has been developed to estimate ancestry within forensic anthropology is the optimized summed scored attribute (OSSA). Developed by Hefner and Ousley (2014), OSSA is a heuristic method to estimate group membership between two groups using the dichotomized scores of six morphoscopic traits. When comparing American Black and American White individuals, values more common in the American Black sample are recoded to "0" and those more common in the American White sample are recoded to "1" to *optimize* differences between these two groups. Once all traits are scored, the values are summed and compared with the expected distribution for the reference populations. This method correctly classified 86% of the sample cases (cross-validated).

Hefner and Ousley (2014) provide a suite of methods for the analysis of morphoscopic data in forensic anthropology. We have briefly summarized their results here, but readers are encouraged to see that manuscript for additional information on these classification statistics.

CONCLUSIONS

While more work may be needed to fully understand the heritability of these nonmetric and morphoscopic traits of the cranium, there is little doubt that they are reflective of population histories and individual ancestry. Therefore, they are relevant data sets in both bioarchaeology and forensic anthropology. These data are appealing to many researchers, as they are easy to collect, nondestructive, applicable to fragmentary remains, and can be taken rapidly on large data sets. The refinement of statistical methods, both in population-based analyses and in nonparametric methods, will make the use of these data more feasible for many scholars. Additionally, multiple statistical packages are readily available that can be used to easily analyze these data.

References

Angel, J.L., Kelley, J.O., 1990. Inversion of the posterior edge of the jaw ramus: new race trait. In: Gill, G.W., Rhine, S. (Eds.), Skeletal Attribution of Race: Methods for Forensic Anthropology. Maxwell Museum Anthropological Papers No. 4, Albuquerque, N.M., pp. 33–39.

Anscombe, F.J., 1948. The transformation of Poisson, binomial and negative-binomial data. Biometrika 35 (3/4), 246–254.

Balakrishan, V., Sanghvi, L.D., 1968. Distance between populations on the basis of attribute data. Biometrics 24, 859–865.

Bass, W.M., 1987. Human Osteology: A Laboratory and Field Manual, third ed. Missouri Archaeological Society, Columbia, Missouri.

Beals, K.L., Smith, C.L., Dodd, S.M., 1983. Climate and the evolution of brachycephalization. American Journal of Physical Anthropology 62, 425–437.

Berry, A., 1975. Factors affecting the incidence of non-metrical skeletal variants. Journal of Anatomy 120 (Pt 3), 519–535.

Berry, A.C., 1974. The use of non-metrical variation of the cranium in the study of Scandinavian population movements. American Journal of Physical Anthropology 40, 345–358.

Berry, A.C., Berry, R.J., 1972. Origins and relationships of the ancient Egyptians. Based on a study of non-metrical variations in the skull. Journal of Human Evolution 1, 199–208.

Berry, C.A., Berry, R., Ucko, P.J., 1967. Genetical change in ancient Egypt. Man 2 (4), 551–568.

Berry, R.J., 1968. Biology and non-metrical variation in mice and men. In: Brothwell, D.R. (Ed.), The Skeletal Biology of Earliear Human Populations. Pergamon Press, Oxford, pp. 101–133.

Berry, R.J., Berry, A.C., 1967. Epigenetic variation in the human cranium. Journal of Anatomy 101, 361–379.

Berry, R.J., Searle, A.G., 1963. Epigenetic polymorphism of the rodent skeleton. Proceedings of the Zoological Society of London 140 (4), 577–615.

Brues, A.M., 1958. Identification of skeletal remains. The Journal of Criminal Law, Criminology, and Police Science 48 (5), 551–563.

Brues, A.M., 1990. The once and future diagnosis of race. In: Gill, G.W., Rhine, S. (Eds.), Skeletal Attribution of Race: Methods for Forensic Anthropology Maxwell Museum of Anthropology, Albuquerque, pp. 1–9.

Buikstra, J.E., 1974. Non-metric traits – control of environmental noise. American Journal of Physical Anthropology 41 (3), 471.

Buikstra, J.E., 1976. Hopewell in the Lower Illinois Valley: A Regional Approach to the Study of Human Biological Variability and Prehsitoric Behavior. Northwestern University, Evanston.

Buikstra, J.E., 1980. Epigenetic distance: a study of biological variability in the lower Illinois River region. In: Browman, D.L. (Ed.), Early Native Americans: Prehistoric Deomgraphy, Economy, and Technology. Mouton, New York, pp. 271–300.

Buikstra, J.E., Ubelaker, D.H. (Eds.), 1994. Standards for Data Collection from Human Skeletal Remains. Arkansas Archeological Survey Research Series No. 44, Fayetteville, Arkansas.

Carson, E.A., 2006. Maximum-likelihood variance components analysis of heritabilities of cranial nonmetric traits. Human Biology 78 (4), 383–402.

Cheverud, J., 1988. A comparison of genetic and phenotypic correlations. Evolution 42, 958–968.

Cheverud, J.M., Buikstra, J.E., 1981a. Quantitative genetics of skeletal nonmetric traits in the rhesus macaques on Cayo Santiago. I. Single trait heritabilities. American Journal of Physical Anthropology 54 (1), 43–49.

Cheverud, J.M., Buikstra, J.E., 1981b. Quantitative genetics of skeletal nonmetric traits in the rhesus macaques on Cayo Santiago. II. Phenotypic, genetic, and environmental correlations between traits. American Journal of Physical Anthropology 54 (1), 51–58.

Cheverud, J.M., Buikstra, J.E., 1982. Quantitative genetics of skeletal nonmetric traits in the Rhesus Macaques of Cayo Santiago. III. Relative heritability of skeletal nonmetric and metric traits. American Journal of Physical Anthropology 59, 151–155.

Del Papa, M.C., Perez, S.I., 2007. The influence of artificial cranial vault deformation on the expression of cranial nonmetric traits: its importance in study of evolutionary relationships. American Journal of Physical Anthropology 134 (2), 251–262.

Donlon, D.A., 2000. The value of infracranial nonmetric variation in studies of modern *Homo sapiens*: an Australian focus. American Journal of Physical Anthropology 113 (3), 349–368.

Droessler, J., 1981. Craniometry and Biological Distance: Biocultural Continuity and Change at the Late-Woodland-Mississippian Interface. Center for American Archaeology, Evanston.

Edgar, H.J., 2007. Microevolution of African American dental morphology. American Journal of Physical Anthropology 132 (4), 535–544.

Edgar, H.J., 2013. Estimation of ancestry using dental morphological characteristics. Journal of Forensic Sciences 58 (s1), S3–S8.

Falconer, D.S., 1965. The inheritance of liability to certain diseases, estimated from the incidence among relatives. Annals of Human Genetics 29 (1), 51–76.

Falconer, D.S., 1967. The inheritance of liability to diseases with variable age of onset, with particular reference to diabetes mellitus. Annals of Human Genetics 31 (1), 1–20.

Falconer, D.S., 1989. Introduction to Quantitative Genetics, third ed. Longman, London.

Feldesman, M.R., 2002. Classification trees as an alternative to linear discriminant analysis. American Journal of Physical Anthropology 119 (3), 257–275.

Freeman, M.F., Tukey, J.W., 1950. The use of inverse sine transformations in the analysis of non-metric cranial data. American Journal of Physical Anthropology 45 (1), 61–68.

Gill, G.W., 1971. The Prehistoric Inhabitants of Northern Coastal Nayarit: Skeletal Analysis and Description of Burials. Department of Anthropology, University of Kansas, Lawrence, Kansas.

Gill, G.W., 1998. Craniofacial criteria in the skeletal attribution of race. In: Reichs, K.J. (Ed.), Forensic Osteology: Advances in the Identification of Human Remains. Charles C. Thomas, Springfield, pp. 293–317.

Green, R.F., Suchey, J.M., 1976. The use of the inverse sine transformation in the analysis of non-metric cranial data. American Journal of Physical Anthropology 45, 61–68.

Green, R.F., Suchey, J.M., Gokhale, D.V., 1979. The statistical treatment of correlated bilateral traits in the analysis of cranial material. American Journal of Physical Anthropology 50 (4), 629–634.

Greene, D.L., 1982. Discrete dental variations and biological distances of Nubian populations. American Journal of Physical Anthropology 58 (1), 75–79.

Grewal, M., 1962. The rate of divergence in the C57BL strain of mice. Genetical Research 3, 226–237.

Grüneberg, H., 1952. Genetical studies on the skeleton of the mouse. IV. Quasi-continuous variations. Journal of Genetics 51, 95–114.

Grüneberg, H., 1963. The Pathology of Development. John Wiley and Sons, Inc., New York.

Gualdi-Russo, E., Tasca, M.A., Brasili, P., 1999. Scoring of nonmetric cranial traits: a methodological approach. Journal of Anatomy 195 (4), 543–550.

Hallgrimsson, B., Donnabhain, B.O., Blom, D.E., Lozada, M.C., Willmore, K.T., 2005. Why are rare traits unilaterally expressed?: trait frequency and unilateral expression for cranial nonmetric traits in humans. American Journal of Physical Anthropology.

Hallgrimsson, B., Donnabhain, B.O., Walters, G.B., Cooper, D.M., Gudbjartsson, D., Stefansson, K., 2004. Composition of the founding population of Iceland: biological distance and morphological variation in early historic Atlantic Europe. American Journal of Physical Anthropology 124 (3), 257–274.

Hanihara, T., Ishida, H., Dodo, Y., 2003. Characterization of biological diversity through analysis of discrete cranial traits. American Journal of Physical Anthropology 121 (3), 241–251.

Harris, E.F., Sjøvold, T., 2004. Calculation of Smith's mean measure of divergence for intergroup comparisons using nonmetric data. Dental Anthropology 17, 83–93.

Hauser, G., De Stefano, G., 1989. Epigenetic Variants of the Human Skull. Schweizerbart, Stuttgart.

Hefner, J.T., 2003. Assessing Nonmetric Cranial Traits Currently Used in the Forensic Determination of Ancestry. Department of Anthropology, University of Florida, Gainesville, FL.

Hefner, J.T., 2007. The Statistical Determination of Ancestry Using Cranial Nonmetric Traits. Department of Anthropology, University of Florida, Gainesville, FL.

Hefner, J.T., 2009. Cranial nonmetric variation and estimating ancestry. Journal of Forensic Sciences 54 (5), 985–995.

Hefner, J.T., 2015. Cranial morphoscopic traits and the assessment of American Black, American White, and Hispanic ancestry. In: Berg, G.E., Ta'ala, S.C. (Eds.), Biological Affinity in Forensic Identification of Human Skeletal Remains. CRC Press, Boca Raton, FL, pp. 27–42.

Hefner, J.T., Ousley, S.D., 2014. Statistical classification methods for estimating ancestry using morphoscopic traits. Journal of Forensic Sciences 59 (4), 883–890.

Hefner, J.T., Ousley, S.D., Dirkmaat, D.C., 2012. Morphoscopic traits and the assessment of ancestry. In: Dirkmaat, D.C. (Ed.), A Companion to Forensic Anthropology. Wiley-Blackwell, Malden, MA, pp. 287–310.

Hefner, J.T., Pilloud, M.A., Black, C.J., Anderson, B.E., 2015. Morphoscopic trait expression in "Hispanic" populations. Journal of Forensic Sciences 60 (5), 1135–1139.

Hefner, J.T., Spradley, M.K., Anderson, B.E., 2014. Ancestry assessment using random forest modeling. Journal of Forensic Sciences 59 (3), 583–598.

Holliday, R., 1990. DNA methylation and epigenetic inheritance. Philosophical Transactions of the Royal Society B: Biological Sciences 326 (1235), 329–338.

Irish, J., 2010. The mean measure of divergence: its utility in model-free and model-bound analyses relative to the Mahalanobis D^2 distance for nonmetric traits. American Journal of Human Biology.

Irish, J.D., 1997. Characteristic high- and low-frequency dental traits in sub-Saharan African populations. American Journal of Physical Anthropology 102 (4), 455–467.

Irish, J.D., 1998a. Ancestral dental traits in recent sub-Saharan Africans and the origins of modern humans. Journal of Human Evolution 34 (1), 81–98.

Irish, J.D., 1998b. Dental morhpological indications of population discontinuity and Egytptian gene flow in post-Paleolithic Nubia. In: Lukacs, J.R. (Ed.), Human Dental Development, Morphology, and Pathology: A Tribute to Albert A. Dahlberg. Department of Anthropology, University of Oregon, Eugene, OR, pp. 155–172.

Irish, J.D., Turner, C.G., 1990. West African dental affinity of late Pleistocene Nubian peopling of the Eurafrican-South Asian triangle. Homo 41 (1), 42–53.

Jorde, L.B., 1980. The genetic structure of subdivided human populations: a review. In: Mielke, J.H., Crawford, M.H. (Eds.), Current Developments in Anthropological Genetics, Theory and Methods, vol. 1. Plenum Press, New York, pp. 135–208.

Konigsberg, L., 1990. Temporal aspects of biological distance: serial correlation and trend in a prehistoric skeletal lineage. American Journal of Physical Anthropology 82, 45–52.

Konigsberg, L., Blangero, J., 1993. Multivariate quantitative genetic simulations in anthropology with an example from the South Pacific. Human Biology 65, 897–915.

Konigsberg, L., Kohn, L.A., Cheverud, J.M., 1993. Cranial deformation and nonmetric trait variation. American Journal of Physical Anthropology 90, 35–48.

Konigsberg, L.W., Ousley, S.D., 1995. Multivariate quantitative genetics of anthropometric traits from the Boas data. Human Biology 67 (3), 481–498.

Krogman, W.M., İşcan, M.Y., 1986. The Human Skeleton in Forensic Medicine. Charles C. Thomas, Springfiled, Illinois.

Lane, R., 1977. The Allegany Seneca: A Test of the Genetic Reliability of Nonmetric Osteological Traits for Intrapopulation Analysis. Department of Anthropology, Austin, TX. University of Texas.

Lane, R.A., Sublett, A.J., 1972. Osteology of social organization: residence pattern. American Antiquity 37, 186–201.

Mahalanobis, P.C., 1936. On the generalized distance in statistics. In: Proceedings of the National Institute of Science, India, 2, pp. 49–55.

Maier, C.A., Zhang, K., Manhein, M.H., Li, X., 2015. Palate shape and depth: a shape-matching and machine learning method for estimating ancestry from human skeletal remains. Journal of Forensic Science 60 (5), 1129–1134.

Martinez-Abadias, N., Esparza, M., Sjøvold, T., González-José, R., Santos, M., Hernández, M., 2009. Heritability of human cranial dimensions: comparing the evolvability of different cranial traits and biological affinities of North African late Holocene populations. Journal of Anatomy 214 (1), 19–35.

Nikita, E., Mattingly, D., Lahr, M.M., 2012. Sahara: barrier or corridor? Nonmetric cranial traits and biological affinities of North African late Holocenee populations. American Journal of Physical Anthropology 147 (2), 280–292.

Ossenberg, N.S., 1969. Discontinuous Morphological Variation in the Human Cranium. Department of Anthropology, University of Toronto, Toronto.

Ossenberg, N.S., 1970. The influence of artificial cranial deformation on discontinuous morphological traits. American Journal of Physical Anthropology 33 (3), 357–371.
Ossenberg, N.S., 2013. Cranial Nonmetric Trait Database. Nancy S. Ossenberg (Producer). Queen's University Library, Data and Government Information Centre (Distributor), Kingston, Ontario.
Ossenberg, N.S., Dodo, Y., Maeda, T., Kawakubo, Y., 2006. Ethnogenesis and craniofacial change in Japan from the perspective of nonmetric traits. Anthropological Science 114 (2), 99–115.
Oudhof, H.A.J., 1982. Sutural growth. Cells Tissues Organs 112 (1), 58–68.
Ousley, S.D., Hefner, J.T., 2005. The statistical determination of ancestry. In: Proceedings of the 58th Annual Meeting of the American Academy of Forensic Sciences, Seattle, WA.
Perizonius, W.R.K., 1979. Non-metric cranial traits: sex difference and age dependence. Journal of Human Evolution 8 (7), 679–684.
Relethford, J.H., Crawford, M., Blangero, J., 1997. Genetic drift and gene flow in post-famine Ireland. Human Biology 69 (4), 443–465.
Rhine, S., 1990. Non-metric skull racing. In: Gill, G.W., Rhine, S. (Eds.), Skeletal Attribution of Race: Methods for Forensic Anthropology. Maxwell Museum Anthropological Papers No. 4, Albuquerque, N.M., pp. 9–20.
Richtsmeier, J.T., McGrath, J.W., 1986. Quantitative genetics of cranial nonmetric traits in randombred mice: heritability and etiology. American Journal of Physical Anthropology 69 (1), 51–58.
Rightmire, G., 1976. Metric versus discrete traits in African skulls. In: Giles, E., Friedländer, J. (Eds.), The Measures of Man. Peabody Museum Press, Cambridge, Mass, pp. 209–220.
Rightmire, G.P., 1972. Cranial measurements and discrete traits compared in distance studies of African Negro skulls. Human Biology 44, 263–276.
Rogers, A.R., Harpending, H.C., 1986. Migration and genetic drift in human populations. Evolution 1312–1327.
Roseman, C.C., 2004. Detecting interregionally diversifying natural selection on modern human cranial form by using matched molecular and morphometric data. Proceedings of the National Academy of Sciences of the United States of America 101 (35), 12824–12829.
Roseman, C.C., Weaver, T.D., 2004. Multivariate apportionment of global human craniometric diversity. American Journal of Physical Anthropology 125 (3), 257–263.
Rösing, F.W., 1982. Discreta des menschlichen Skeletts—ein kritischer Überblick. Homo 33 (1962), 100–130.
Russell, F., 1900. Studies in cranial variation. The American Naturalist 34 (405), 737–745.
Sanghvi, L., Balakrishnan, V., 1972. Comparison of different measures of genetic distance between human populations. In: Weiner, J.S., Huizinga, J. (Eds.), The Assessment of Population Affinities in Man. Oxford University Press, London, pp. 25–36.
Schillaci, M.A., Irish, J.D., Wood, C.C., 2009. Further analysis of the population history of ancient Egyptians. American Journal of Physical Anthropology 139 (2), 235–243.
Sjøvold, T., 1973. The occurrence of minor non-metrical variants in the skeleton and their quantitative treatment for population comparisons. Homo 24, 204–233.
Sjøvold, T., 1977. Non-metrical divergence between skeletal populations: the theoretical foundation and biological importance of CAB Smith's mean measure of divergences. Ossa 4 (Suppl. 1), 1–133.
Sjøvold, T., 1984. A report on the heritability of some cranial measurements and non-metric traits. In: Van Vark, G.N., Howells, W.W. (Eds.), Multivariate Statistical Methods in Physical Anthropology. D. Reidel Publishing Company, Boston, pp. 223–246.
Sutter, R., Mertz, L., 2004. Nonmetric cranial trait variation and prehistoric biocultural change in the Azapa Valley, Chile. American Journal of Physical Anthropology 123, 130–145.
Sutter, R., Verano, J.W., 2007. Biodistance analysis of the Moche sacrificial victims from Huaca de la Luna Plaza 3C: matrix method test of their origins. American Journal of Physical Anthropology 132 (2), 193–206.
Szilvassy, J., 1986. Eine neue methode zur intraserialen analyse von graberfeldern. Mitteilungen der Berliner Gesellschaft fur Anthropologie, Ethnologie, und Urgeschicte 7, 49–62.

Ta'ala, S.C., 2015. A brief history of the race concept in physical anthropology. In: Berg, G.E., Ta'ala, S.C. (Eds.), Biological Affinity in Forensic Identification of Human Skeletal Remains. CRC Press, Boca Raton, pp. 1–16.

Torres-Rouff, C., Knudson, K.J., Hubbe, M., 2013. Issues of affinity: exploring population structure in the middle and regional developments periods of San Pedro de Atacama, Chile. American Journal of Physical Anthropology 152 (3), 370–382.

Waddington, C.H., 1942. Canalization of development and the inheritance of acquired characters. Nature 150 (3811), 563–565.

Waddington, C.H., 1956. Genetic assimilation of the bithorax phenotype. Evolution 1–13.

Williams-Blangero, S., 1989. Phenotypic consequences of nonrandom migration in the Jirels of Nepal. American Journal of Physical Anthropology 80 (1), 115–125.

Williams-Blangero, S., Blangero, J., 1989. Anthropometric variation and the genetic structure of the Jirels of Nepal. Human Biology 61 (1), 1–12.

Wood-Jones, F., 1931a. The non-metrical morphological characters of the skull as criteria for racial diagnosis: Part I: General discussion of the morphological characters employed in racial diagnosis. Journal of Anatomy 65 (Pt 2), 179–195.

Wood-Jones, F., 1931b. The non-metrical morphological characters of the skull as criteria for racial diagnosis: Part II: The non-metrical morphological characters of the Hawaiian skull. Journal of anatomy 65 (Pt 3), 368–378.

Wright, S., 1951. The genetical structure of populations. Annals of Eugenics 15, 323–354.

CHAPTER

6

Dental Morphology in Biodistance Analysis

M.A. Pilloud[1], H.J.H. Edgar[2], R. George[1], G.R. Scott[1]
University of Nevada, Reno, Reno, NV, United States[1]; University of New Mexico, Albuquerque, NM, United States[2]

CHAPTER OUTLINE HEAD

Dental Morphology 111
  Dental Terminology 111
  Heritability 113
  Dental Development 114
  Threshold Traits 115
  Data Collection and Treatment 116
Population Variation 118
  Sinodont/Sundadont 118
  Afridont 119
  Eurodont 120
Forensic Application 120
Bioarchaeological Application 122
  Intracemetery 123
  Population Level 123
Evolution and Dental Morphology 123
  Hominins 124
  Anatomically Modern Humans 124
Conclusions 125
Endnotes 125
References 126

Dental morphology is the study of the shape and form of teeth. The study of gross morphology has been used extensively in anthropological literature to answer research questions related to archaeology (eg, Hanihara, 2008; Scott and Turner, 1997; Turner, 1990), modern human variation (eg, Edgar, 2002; Hanihara, 2008; Lease, 2003; Scott, 1980), and paleoanthropology (eg, Gómez-Robles et al., 2013; Guatelli-Steinberg and Irish, 2005; Irish and Guatelli-Steinberg, 2003; Martinón-Torres et al., 2007, 2012). With advancements in imaging techniques, studies exploring the tissue dynamics involved with trait expression and development are emerging (eg, Bailey et al., 2011; Skinner et al., 2009). For a brief review of the history of the study of dental morphology, see Chapter 1, this volume.

Biological Distance Analysis. http://dx.doi.org/10.1016/B978-0-12-801966-5.00006-8

Dental morphological traits have been standardized during previous decades, beginning with the work of Dahlberg (1956). Dahlberg created a series of plaques demonstrating variation in the adult dentition to aid in the identification of various morphological traits, with the goal of creating replicable and precise observations (Dahlberg, 1956). Turner et al. (1991) later developed a similar set of plaques for the adult dentition that forms the basis for what is commonly referred to as the Arizona State University Dental Anthropology System (ASUDAS). This system provides a description and scale for the expression of over 30 dental traits. Hanihara (1961) developed similar casts for the deciduous dentition; these descriptions were later supplemented by Sciulli (1998). Tables 6.1 and 6.2 include a list of dental morphological traits of the permanent and deciduous dentition typically considered in anthropological studies and provide sample references for each.

Table 6.1 Morphological Traits of Adult Dentition

Dental Trait	Observed Teeth	References
Winging	Upper central incisors	(Dahlberg, 1963; Enoki and Dahlberg, 1958)
Shoveling	Upper incisors, canines, and lower incisors	(Dahlberg, 1956; Hrdlička, 1920; Scott, 1973)
Labial convexity	Upper incisors	Nichol et al. (1984)
Double shoveling	Upper incisors, canine, first premolar, and lower incisors	Dahlberg (1956)
Interruption groove	Upper incisors	Turner (1967)
Tuberculum dentale	Upper incisors and canine	(Scott, 1973; Turner, 1967)
Canine mesial ridge	Upper canine	Irish and Morris (1996)
Canine distal accessory ridge	Upper and lower canines	Scott (1973)
Premolar mesial and distal accessory cusps	Upper premolars	Turner (1967)
Accessory marginal tubercles	Upper premolars	Scott and Turner (1997)
Tricuspid premolars	Upper premolars	Turner et al. (1991)
Distosagittal ridge (Uto-Aztecan premolar)	Upper third premolar	Morris et al. (1978)
Metacone	Upper molars	Turner et al. (1991)
Hypocone	Upper molars	(Dahlberg, 1951; Larson, 1978; Turner et al., 1991)
Cusp 5 (metaconule)	Upper molars	(Harris, 1977; Harris and Bailit, 1980)
Carabelli's trait	Upper molars	Dahlberg (1956)
Parastyle	Upper molars	Turner et al. (1991)
Enamel extensions	Upper premolars and molars	Turner et al. (1991)
Premolar root number	Upper premolars	Turner (1967)
Upper molar root number	Upper molars	Turner (1967)
Mesial marginal accessory marginal tubercles	Upper molars	Kanazawa et al. (1990)
Radical number	All teeth	Turner (1967)
Peg-shaped incisor	Upper lateral incisor	Turner et al. (1991)
Peg-shaped molar	Upper third molar	Turner et al. (1991)

Table 6.1 Morphological Traits of Adult Dentition—Continued

Dental Trait	Observed Teeth	References
Odontome	Upper and lower premolars	Turner et al. (1991)
Paracone/protoconid accessory ridges	Upper and lower premolars	Scott and Turner (1997)
Congenital absence	Upper lateral and lower central incisors, upper and lower second premolars, and upper and lower third molars	Turner et al. (1991)
Premolar lingual cusp variation	Lower premolars	(Kraus and Furr, 1953; Scott, 1973)
Anterior fovea	Lower first molar	Turner et al. (1991)
Groove pattern	Lower molars	Jorgensen (1955)
Cusp number	Lower molars	Turner (1967)
Deflecting wrinkle	Lower first molar	Turner et al. (1991)
Distal trigonid crest	Lower molars	(Hrdlička, 1924; Turner et al., 1991)
Middle trigonid crest	Lower molars	Wu and Turner (1993)
Protostylid	Lower molars	Dahlberg (1956)
Cusp 5 (hypoconulid)	Lower molars	Turner et al. (1991)
Cusp 6 (entoconulid or tuberculum sextum)	Lower molars	Turner et al. (1991)
Cusp 7 (metaconulid or tuberculum intermedium)	Lower molars	Turner et al. (1991)
Canine root number	Lower canine	Turner (1967)
Tome's root	Lower first premolar	Turner et al. (1991)
Lower molar root number	Lower molars	Turner (1967)

This chapter will not describe dental morphological traits, as such information is present in detail in various other publications (eg, Edgar, 2016; Scott, 2008; Scott et al., 2015; Scott and Turner, 1997; Turner et al., 1991; Van Beek, 1983). Instead, this chapter focuses on how dental morphology can be used as a source of data for biodistance analyses in both forensic anthropology and bioarchaeological studies. This treatment begins with a discussion of key issues in dental morphology that includes dental terminology, heritability, and the way morphological data are collected and treated. Next is a discussion of dental complexes and major trends in population variation. This is followed by a review of how dental morphology is used in forensic and bioarchaeological applications. Finally, research on the evolution of dental morphology is outlined, as is its relevance to biodistance studies.

DENTAL MORPHOLOGY

Dental Terminology

The human dentition is defined by four tooth types (incisor, canine, premolar, molar) and can be divided into four quadrants: upper (maxillary) right and left, and lower (mandibular) right and left. Isomeres are teeth that are opponents in the upper and lower dentitions (maxillary and mandibular), and antimeres are

Table 6.2 Morphological Traits of Deciduous Dentition

Dental Trait	Observed Teeth	References
Shovel shape	Upper and lower incisors and canines	Hanihara (1961, 1963)
Double shovel	Upper incisors and canine	Sciulli (1998)
Winging	Upper central incisors	(Dahlberg, 1963; Enoki and Dahlberg, 1958)
Interruption groove	Upper incisors	Turner (1967)
Tuberculum dentale	Upper incisors and canine and lower canine	Sciulli (1998)
Canine mesial ridge	Upper canine	Irish and Morris (1996)
Canine distal accessory ridge	Upper and lower canines	Scott (1973)
Metacone	Upper molars	Hanihara (1961, 1963)
Hypocone	Upper molars	Hanihara (1961, 1963)
Cusp 5 (metaconule)	Upper second molar	Sciulli (1998)
Carabelli's trait	Upper molars	(Hanihara, 1961, 1963; Sciulli, 1998)
Root sheath	Upper molars	Sciulli (1998)
Cusp number	Lower second molar	Sciulli (1998)
Groove pattern	Lower second molar	Sciulli (1998)
Hypoconulid	Lower second molar	Sciulli (1998)
Deflecting wrinkle (central ridge of the metaconid)	Lower second molar	(Hanihara, 1961, 1963; Sciulli, 1998)
Protostylid	Lower second molar	(Hanihara, 1961, 1963; Sciulli, 1998)
Cusp 6 (tuberculum sextum)	Lower second molar	Sciulli (1998)
Cusp 7 (tuberculum intermedium)	Lower second molar	Sciulli (1998)
Distal trigonid crest	Lower second molar	(Hanihara, 1961, 1963; Sciulli, 1998)
Delta form	Lower first molar	Sciulli (1998)
Double teeth	Lower incisors and canine	Sciulli (1998)
Root groove	All anterior teeth	Sciulli (1998)
Labial deflection	All anterior teeth	Sciulli (1998)

teeth that are correlates in the right and left sides of the dental arcade. For example, left and right mandibular canines are antimeres, whereas the left maxillary and mandibular canines are isomeres. By convention and used within this chapter, teeth are referred to by their positions in the upper or lower dental arcade (U or L) and right or left side (R or L), by tooth type [incisor (I), canine (C), premolar (P), or molar (M)],[1] and by number (first and second incisors, third and fourth[2] premolars, and first through third molars). Therefore, the maxillary left second incisor would be indicated through shorthand as ULI2 (upper left incisor #2).

Anterior teeth (incisors and canines) have an incisal or biting edge. Posterior teeth (premolars and molars) have an occlusal surface with various cusps that make up a broad chewing area. Premolars have

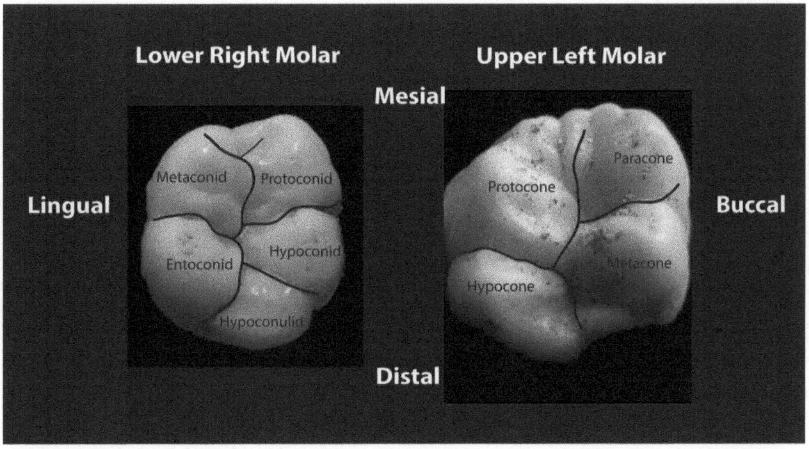

FIGURE 6.1

Major cusps of adult molars.

one buccal cusp and anywhere from zero to three lingual cusps. Molars also vary in cusp number, configuration, and name depending on location (Fig. 6.1). Lower molars have two roots (mesial and distal) and generally four or five cusps. The first molar typically has five cusps, and the second will usually have four plus a reduced or absent distobuccal cusp (hypoconulid), although this can vary greatly between populations. Upper molars have three roots, two buccal and one lingual. The first upper molar usually has four cusps including the hypocone. Moving distally in the tooth row, the hypocone and metacone are often reduced or absent.

The terms used to describe the orientation of teeth are mesial, distal, labial, buccal, and lingual. Mesial refers to the tooth surface toward the midline; distal is the opposite surface. Labial is the surface of the tooth toward the lips on anterior teeth, and buccal is the same surface on posterior teeth (toward the cheek). Lingual refers to the surface of the tooth that is oriented toward the tongue, regardless of tooth type.

Humans have two sets of teeth, deciduous and permanent. Much of the following discussion is focused on the permanent teeth; however, deciduous teeth are addressed when possible.

Heritability

Dental morphological trait expression represents variation in phenotype. To the extent that dental morphological phenotypes reflect genetic variation, dental morphology is useful in biodistance analyses. An early study by Scott (1973) investigated intrafamilial correlations of dental morphology among American White families ($n = 253$). This study found traits to be threshold dichotomies and subject to polygenic modes of inheritance. Later work by Harris (1977) studied the dental morphology of 315 Solomon Island families. This extensive study also found dental traits to be polygenic; however, other factors including epistasis, dominance effects, environment, and possibly sex were also found to have an effect. Berry (1978) found similar results in a study of 91 pairs of monozygous twins and 89 dizygous twins, as well as members from 122 families. Data were collected on 45 morphological variants for each cast. The results of the study indicated that even minor variations in the tooth crown were under strong genetic control. This study also found that the mode of inheritance for dental traits was complex, and there was likely some environmental influence on trait expression. Additionally, anthropological research has found that dental morphological variation corresponds to gene-frequency variation in living and prehistoric populations (Brewer-Carias et al., 1976; Corruccini et al., 2002; Hubbard et al., 2015; Ricaut et al., 2010; Scott, 1992; Shinoda et al., 1998).

Subsequent genetic research and pedigree studies have confirmed these early results and found dental traits to be heritable (eg, Gurri and Balam, 2006; Harris and Bailit, 1980; Nichol, 1990; Sharma, 1992; Zoubov and Nikityuk, 1978); however, there is still much discussion as to the exact rates of heritability for each trait. For Carabelli's trait alone, heritability rates reported have been between 0.909 (Škrinjarić et al., 1985) and 0.069 (Biggerstaff, 1973), with various estimates in between (eg, Aoyagi, 1967; Berry, 1978; Saheki, 1958; Scott and Potter, 1984). The reader is referred to Scott and Turner (1997) and Hughes et al. (2016) for a comprehensive review.

Although studies on the heritability of dental traits have been conducted, the exact mode of their transmission remains elusive, and almost no specific genes signaling dental morphology have been identified. Findings in mice, however, show that dental patterns are established before the dental primordia are perceptible. This may indicate the involvement of homeobox genes in the development of crown morphology, although it is still unclear whether another related system may be responsible (Zhao et al., 2000). More recently, a variant of the ectodysplasin A receptor (EDAR 1540C) was found to account for 18.9% of the total variance observed in the expression of shoveling in two Japanese populations (Kimura et al., 2009). See also Chapter 17, this volume (Edgar and Ousley).

Studies have shown that morphological data of deciduous dentition can discriminate biological relationships in much the same way as traits of the permanent dentition (Kitagawa, 2000; Lease and Sciulli, 2005), and have the potential to identify biologically related individuals (Paul and Stojanowski, 2015). However, it is unclear whether the underlying genetic processes are the same in both sets of dentition (Edgar and Lease, 2007; Hughes et al., 2000), and they are typically analyzed separately.

Dental Development

The role of dental development on crown trait expression was identified early on by Butler (1956). Butler claimed that crown pattern was highly dependent upon the developmental stage in which it formed, and that the timing of cusp formation played a large role in changes to crown patterns, which could be used in studies of phylogeny. Building on this work, Jernvall and Jung (2000) developed the patterning cascade model. This model focuses on spacing and activation differentiation among enamel knots. The genes involved in cusp formation appear to be the same for all individual cusps, so it is unlikely that the cusp's position determines its exact morphology (Jernvall, 2000). Instead, cusp position and size are determined through control of secondary enamel knot spacing (Jernvall and Thesleff, 2000). This spacing is controlled by prior enamel knots, and the exact distance between knots can be regulated by inhibitors or by a decline in activators that diffuse from the enamel knot. Small differences in these inhibitory fields can have cumulative effects on individual teeth in terms of shape, size, and number of cusps (Jernvall, 2000). For example, larger inhibition fields place the formation of subsequent enamel knots further away, likely resulting in fewer cusps. Also, this delay in cusp initiation may lead to a shorter cusp. As this same process is repeated during the formation of each cusp, small differences in spacing lead to increased effects on cusps that develop later (Jernvall and Jung, 2000).

The patterning cascade model was tested by Jernvall (2000) among the Lake Ladoga seal postcanine dentition to determine whether population-level variation could lead to the formation of new cusps and affect dental morphology. This study found that height variation was greatest in smaller cusps, concluding that variation increased in relation to progressing development. Jernvall also tested whether development of the first cusps controlled variation in later-forming smaller cusps. To do this, the angles of the three tallest cusps were measured, and the mean angle was used as a proxy for differences in initial cusp development. Sharp and blunt teeth were identified in this way, such that sharp teeth had large differences in height and blunt teeth did not. The results indicated that among sharp teeth, cusp formation was initiated further apart than it was among blunt teeth. In addition, blunt teeth were more likely to possess extra cusps. The actual number of cusps realized is determined by the termination of crown development and the initiation of root formation. If cusp initiation was below this threshold, no cusp would form. Finally, absolute tooth size did not determine cusp configuration.

While Jernvall (2000) admits that this study is a simplification, since seal teeth are narrow with a triconodont form, the same processes could apply to the more complex molar patterns observed among humans. The emergence of new cusps would not necessitate any new developmental information, but rather small changes in the interactions between knots could change cusp patterns and lead to different morphological expressions (Jernvall and Jung, 2000). Therefore, cusp patterns are highly evolvable so that small developmental changes could lead to large changes in dental morphology (Jernvall, 2000).

The patterning cascade model has been tested on human molars by exploring the spacing of intercusp distances and their relationship to the expression of Carabelli's cusp. These studies found that decreased intercusp distances in the first and second molars were related to the presence of the Carabelli trait (Guatelli-Steinberg et al., 2013; Hunter et al., 2010; Moormann et al., 2013). The authors thereby feel these results are in line with and provide support for the cascade model of dental development. Additional studies on mouse (Harjunmaa et al., 2012) and seal (Salazar-Ciudad and Jernvall, 2010) teeth show promise for documenting evolutionary changes in tooth complexity, which will have further implications for the understanding of human dental development and evolution.

Threshold Traits

In studies of biological distance, dental nonmetric traits are usually expressed as either present or absent. However, most are not simple dichotomous traits, but instead have a range of expression as illustrated in their ranked scales. Wright (1968) distinguished such traits as threshold dichotomies. The expression or nonexpression of these traits is the result of a complex interaction between environment and genes, and depends on how much these factors may push expression to one side or the other at a critical state of development. Grünberg (1952) described a similar condition among skeletal traits of mice, which he termed quasi-continuous. Both Wright and Grünberg recognized that these traits were related to multiple genes and were sensitive to environmental effects.

Occasionally, morphological asymmetry within an individual is found, where antimeres do not express morphological traits in the same way. Studies of morphological asymmetry indicate no evidence for independent genetic trait expression for each side of the dental arcade (Scott and Turner, 1997). Asymmetry may therefore be related to environmental stressors; however, one study found that evidence for asymmetry of Carabelli's trait and the protostylid was likely due to sample size, recording methods, and the extent of development of the trait. Therefore, such asymmetries could not be regarded simply as indicators of environmental stress (Saunders and Mayhall, 1982).

Data Collection and Treatment

Data collection is typically done on the entire dental arcade of maxillary and mandibular teeth. These data can then be quantified in many ways. The tooth count method uses all teeth observed to calculate frequencies, which may be problematic in cases of asymmetry, where a single individual can be treated as two separate phenotypes (Scott and Turner, 1997), and thus genotypes. The tooth count method also artificially enlarges sample size, since trait expression is most often symmetrical. However, in some cases such as with commingled remains, the tooth count method may be most appropriate. The expression count method assigns a coefficient to each grade of expression to calculate a weighted expression frequency (Turner, 1985). For the individual count method, only one expression of a trait is used in analyses. In instances with antimere disagreement, the highest expression is used to characterize an individual, the presumption being that this best characterizes individual genetic potential for trait expression (Scott, 1977). The individual count is the most widely adopted method in dental morphology studies.

Morphological traits can be reported by rank (ordinal data), which can be further dichotomized (present—absent). This dichotomization of traits is based on breakpoints thought to best represent easily recognizable and replicable points on the visible scale of a threshold trait's distribution. Breakpoints may vary between studies, making it critical that they be defined in any study of dental morphology. In addition to breakpoints, each trait has a focal tooth, or rather the tooth recognized within each class as key in population differentiation. Table 6.3 lists commonly used breakpoints and the focal tooth of each trait. However, depending on the research question, these breakpoints can vary. Alternatively, some studies are moving away from the use of breakpoints and instead using the rank scores of the teeth with no dichotomization (Mayhall, 1998; Willermet et al., 2016).

It is important to explore various aspects of dental morphological data before biological distance analyses begin. Such analyses include intertrait correlations, age, and sex. These analyses also serve as a means to check the data for things such as transcription errors or outliers. Correlations are most commonly observed as within-field interactions. When a single trait can be observed on multiple teeth (for example, the hypocone on all upper molars), its appearance on one tooth is often related to its appearance on other teeth in the field (Scott and Turner, 1997). Some of the effects of within-field interactions can be negated by employing focal teeth in analyses, thereby removing redundant data. However, different traits may be correlated within the same field or different fields—eg, hypocone and Carabelli's trait of UM1, Carabelli's trait and protostylid of UM1 and LM1 (Irish, 2008; Khraisat et al., 2011; Scott, 1978, 1979; Tsai et al., 1996). Morphological trait correlations can be found in an entire data set or in subsamples that represent a recognizable group. Exploratory analyses should be conducted to identify trait correlations. If found, at least one correlated trait should be removed from analysis—trait choice would be at the discretion of the researcher and may depend on the research questions of interest.

There are conflicting reports regarding sex differences in dental morphology. For example, several studies on Carabelli's cusp found no significant difference in expression between males and females (Garn et al., 1966; Harris, 2007; Scott, 1980; Turner, 1967), whereas others did find sex-related differences (Goose, 1971; Kaul and Prakash, 1981; Kieser and Preston, 1981; Scott et al., 1983; Tsai et al., 1996). For upper incisor shoveling, some researchers find no sex difference (Gašperšič, 1994; Kieser and Preston, 1981; Turner, 1967) while others do (Harris and Bailit, 1980; Kaul and Prakash, 1981). Such findings likely indicate that sexual dimorphism in dental morphology is population specific. There is, however, one trait that consistently shows sexual dimorphism: the distal accessory ridge (Kaul and Prakash, 1981;

Table 6.3 Dental Morphological Traits Commonly Used in Biological Distance Analysis

Adult Dentition		Deciduous Dentition	
Maxilla	**Mandible**	**Maxilla**	**Mandible**
Winging (UI1):1 Labial convexity (UI1):2-4 Shovel (UI1):3-6 Double shovel (UI1):2-6 Interruption groove (UI2):1 Tuberculum dentale (UI2):1-6 Canine mesial ridge: (UC):1-3 Distal accessory ridge (UC):2-5 Premolar accessory ridges (UP3-4): 1 Hypocone (UM2):2-5 Metaconule (UM1):1-5 Carabelli's trait (UM1):5-7 Parastyle (UM3):1-6 Enamel extension (UM1): 2-3 Root number (UP3):2 Peg-shape (UI2, UM3):1-2 Tri-cusped premolars (UP3, UP4):1 Odontomes (UP3, UP4): 1 Congenital absence (UI2, UM3):1	Lingual cusp number (LP4):2-9 Tome's root (LP3):4-5 Groove pattern (LM2): Y-pattern Deflecting wrinkle (LM1):3 Distal trigonid crest (LM1):1 Anterior fovea (LM1): 2-4 Protostylid (LM1):1-7 Hypoconulid (LM1, LM2):1-5 Cusp 6 (LM1):1-5 Cusp 7 (LM1):1-4 Cusp number (LM1):6 Cusp number (LM2):4+ Congenital absence (LM3, LP3):1	Winging (UI1):1 Shoveling (UI1-UC):2-3 Double shovel (UI1-UC): 1-3 Interruption Groove (UI1-UI2):1 Tuberculum dentale (UI1-UC):1-4 Mesial ridge (UC):1 Distal accessory ridge (UC):1-4 Hypocone (UM1-UM2):4 Cusp 5 (UM2):1 Carabelli's trait (UM2): 2-4 Root groove (UI1-UC):1 Root sheath (UM1-UM2):1 Labial deflection (UI1-UC):1	Shoveling (LI1-LI2): 2-3 Distal accessory Ridge (LC):1-4 Cusp number (LM2):5-8 Groove pattern (LM2): Y Hypoconulid (LM2):1 Deflecting wrinkle (LM2):1 Anterior fovea (LM1): 2-4 Protostylid (LM2):1-2 Hypoconulid (LM2): 1 Cusp 6 (LM2):1-5 Cusp 7 (LM2):1-5 Distal trigonid crest (LM2):1 Delta form (LM1):1 Double teeth (LI1-LC): 1 Root groove (LI1-LC):1 Labial deflection (LI1-LC):1

Parentheses indicate the focal tooth for each trait, and the breakpoints for each trait follow the colon, with the numbers listed indicating the presence of a trait. As described in the text, U indicates upper jaw; L, lower jaw; I, incisor; C, canine; P, premolar; and M, molar.
Based on Turner (1987), Haeussler et al. (1989), Turner et al. (1991), Irish (1993, 1997), Scott and Turner (1997), and Sciulli (1998).

Kieser and Preston, 1981; Scott, 1977). This finding may be tied to the consistent sexual dimorphism in canine mesiodistal diameters (Noss et al., 1983). It is important for the researcher to explore and identify sexual dimorphism in their own study sample prior to biodistance analyses to ensure that biological relationships are being tested and not differences between the sexes.

Finally, age can indirectly affect dental morphological expression. For example, dental wear with advanced age may obscure the presence of a trait. Burnett et al. (2013) found that dental wear can lead to scores of a lower grade or to frequency issues within a sample. Ideally, practitioners should only record data on teeth with visible occlusal morphology and minimal wear. Through such a practice, there should be little correlation between age and morphology. Statistical tests can also be run to explore any such correlation.

Inter- and intraobserver error should also be explored. It is important to know if score differences between individuals (inter-) or single-observer data collection sessions (intra) ultimately result in a different interpretation of the data. Nichol and Turner (1986) outline several ways to report different types of observer error. They assign a critical value that error should not exceed if a set of observations is deemed suitable for analysis. A popular statistical method to assess inter- and intrarater agreement for categorical data is Cohen's kappa (Cohen, 1960). This statistic measures the correlation of agreement between observations or observers after accounting for the proportion of agreement that could happen by chance (Wood, 2007). The value ranges from 0 (no agreement) to 1 (total agreement). To be of value, Landis and Koch (1977) argue that kappa should be at least 0.41.

POPULATION VARIATION

Population-based variation in dental morphology has been thoroughly studied both temporally and spatially. Within this body of literature, a broad outline of "dental complexes" (Hanihara, 1967) has been defined. These complexes are based on a large body of literature documenting trait frequencies across the globe. Scott and Turner (1997) summarize much of this work and illustrate general patterns regarding trait presence and population affiliation (see their table E.1 for an overview). This study of population variation has generally been used to study human evolution, population movement, postmarital residence practices, social structure, and population affinity, and has not been broadly co-opted by practitioners of forensic anthropology.

Various terms have been used over the last several decades to describe these complexes; however, in this treatment, the terms Sinodont/Sundadont, Afridont, and Eurodont are used to describe the morphology of the populations of Asia, Africa, and Europe, respectively. These are very broad patterns of dental morphology and do not account for all global human variation, and in fact do not neatly incorporate all populations. For example, the umbrella term "Asia" incorporates populations from South Asia, East Asia, and Oceania, as well as Native Americans. Such designations are overly simplistic, but they serve as a starting point from which to discuss human dental morphological variation.

The following discussion is focused on permanent teeth. While there is some work on the dental morphology of deciduous teeth (see Hanihara, 1954, 1963; Lease, 2003; Lease and Sciulli, 2005), the patterns are less clear, so they are not incorporated into the descriptions below.

Sinodont/Sundadont

Initially, K. Hanihara (1967, 1968) outlined a dental complex for Asian populations that he termed the "Mongoloid Dental Complex". This complex was characterized by higher frequencies of shovel-shaped upper incisors, cusp 6, protostylid, deflecting wrinkle, cusp 7, and the metaconule. The broad Mongoloid dental complex was refined by Turner (1979, 1987), who divided Asian groups into Sundadont (Southeast Asian/Sunda Shelf) and Sinodont (Northeast Asian and Native American) dental patterns. Turner (1990) defined the differences between these groups based on eight traits. For Sinodonts, he described a higher frequency of shoveling and double shoveling of UI1, single-rooted UP3, enamel extensions (UM1), missing-peg-reduced UM3, deflecting wrinkle (LM1), three rooted LM1, and a low frequency of four-cusped LM2 (Fig. 6.2). Sundadonts showed higher frequencies of the *weaker* grades of

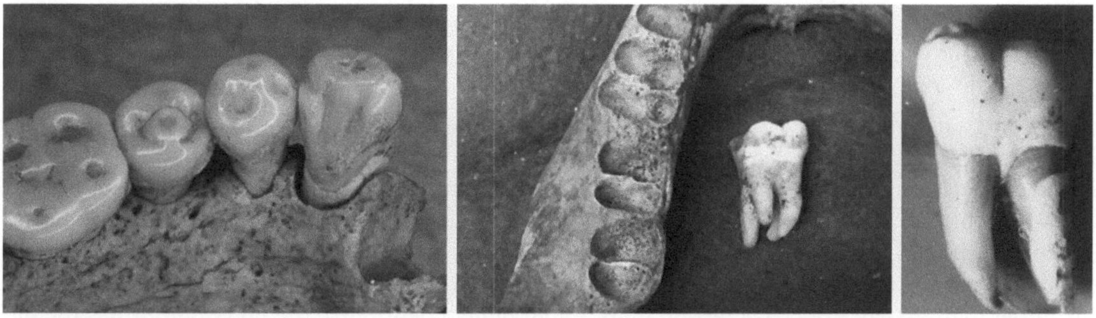

FIGURE 6.2

Morphological traits associated with Sinodont dentition: (left to right) odontome, three-rooted lower first molar, and enamel extensions.

these traits and a higher frequency of four-cusped LM2. The Sundadont pattern was considered to be the conservative pattern exemplifying trait retention, with the Sinodont pattern reflecting intensified and specialized trait expression, sometimes referred to as "mass additive" traits (Irish, 1998).

Afridont

Initially, Irish (1997) outlined a sub-Saharan dental complex that included distinctive frequencies for the Bushman canine (UC), two-rooted UP3, Carabelli's trait (UM1), Y-pattern (LM2), cusp 7 (LM1), Tome's root (LP3), the presence of UM3, and a low incidence of UI1 double shoveling and UM1 enamel extension. This complex was later renamed *Afridont*, although it still focused on sub-Saharan African populations (Fig. 6.3). This latest work defines the Afridont dental complex by these same morphological traits, but also includes two-rooted LM2 and three-rooted UM2 (Irish, 2013).

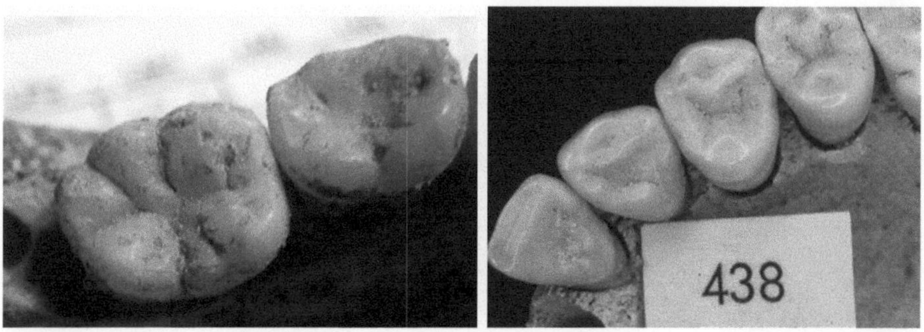

FIGURE 6.3

Morphological traits associated with Afridont dentition: cusp 7 (left) and Bushman's canine (right).

Eurodont

Hanihara (1967) described a "Caucasoid dental complex" that served as a contrast to his Mongoloid dental complex. This complex was characterized by low frequencies of shoveling and winging of the upper incisors, cusps 6 and 7, and the protostylid. Carabelli's cusp was the only high-frequency trait identified. This complex was recently explored by Scott et al. (2013) who proposed the term *Eurodont*. This complex is characterized by a relatively high frequency of two-rooted lower canines, four-cusped lower molars, and Carabelli's cusp on the upper molars (Fig. 6.4). Low-frequency traits include winging, shoveling, and double shoveling of upper incisors; Y-pattern, cusps 6 and 7, protostylid and deflecting wrinkle of lower molars; and enamel extensions of upper molars. In essence, the Eurodont dentition is defined more by the lack rather than presence of characteristic traits. Of all human dentitions, the Eurodont form is the most simplified, showing the fewest morphological bells and whistles, and stands in stark contrast to the Sinodont and Afridont patterns.

FORENSIC APPLICATION

As part of the biological profile (ie, sex, age, stature), forensic anthropologists are asked to provide an estimation of ancestry. While, as biological anthropologists, forensic anthropologists are aware of the typological issues of sorting humans into discrete categories and the issues of biological determinism and scientific racism that may follow, they still perform this task because it is essential in describing an unknown individual so as to limit the possible pool of missing persons for comparison. Generally, forensic anthropologists agree with the American Association of Physical Anthropology statement on race (American Association of Physical Anthropology, 1996), and agree that as a strict biological concept,

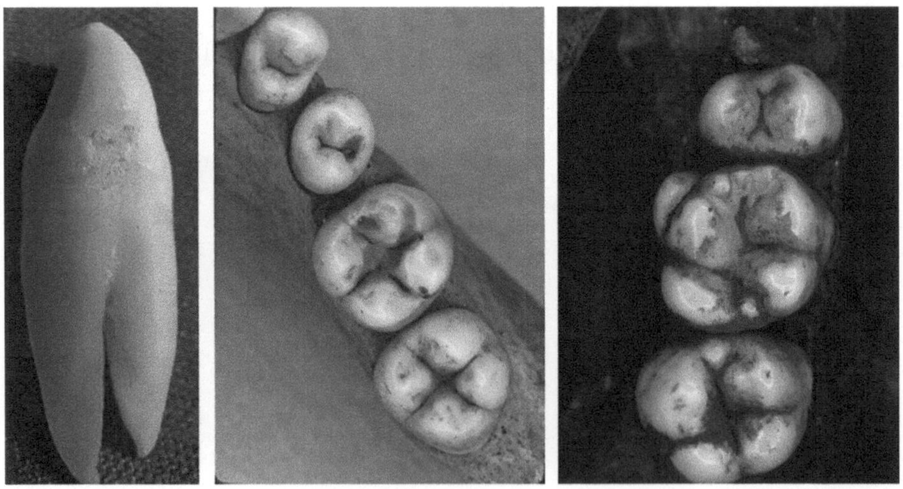

FIGURE 6.4

Morphological traits associated with Eurodont dentition: (left to right) two-rooted lower canine, four-cusped lower molar, and Carabelli's cusp of the upper first molar.

"race" does not exist. However, an individual's self- or community-identified race could be a critical component that leads to identification of a set of unknown remains. Therefore, forensic anthropologists have focused on various skeletal morphological traits that seem to align with geographic population variation (Sauer, 1992). Using methods couched in statistical approaches, they now estimate ancestry in recognition of biological diversity and shared population history.

While there are early reports on population variation in teeth (eg, Campbell, 1925; Klatsky, 1956; Lasker, 1945, 1950; Moorrees, 1957; Nelson, 1938; Shaw, 1931; Tratman, 1938), Lasker and Lee (1957) and Hellman (1928) were among the first to associate morphological traits of the teeth with "race" (or ancestry). In "Mongoloid" dentitions, they identified a higher frequency of marginal ridges on incisors (shoveling), occlusal enamel pearls (odontomes), enamel extensions, cusp 6, and taurodontism. Carabelli's trait and four-cusped lower second molars were characteristic of "Whites." The wrinkling of enamel in maxillary molars (ie, crenulations) is found in "Bushmen and Hottentots" as well as "Mongoloids," and the presence of a fourth molar is more commonly found in "Bushmen and Negroes." Lasker and Lee (1957) make the important point that all the traits they describe as "racial" are simply found at a higher frequency in some populations. It would be unlikely that any one feature would be found exclusively in one group. In Stewart's (1979) seminal publication on forensic anthropology, he mentions shovel-shaped incisors as being only more common in "Mongoloids."

Despite earlier work outlining the various "racial" variants of dental morphology and the creation of the ASUDAS, forensic anthropologists today tend to employ six traits without the use of statistics as part of the biological profile. These traits have a foundation in previous work and were likely popularized among practicing forensic anthropologists based on their appearance in Rhine's (1990) trait lists. Rhine (1990) defined Southwestern Mongoloids as having buccal pits (a low rank of the protostylid in the ASUDAS), enamel extensions, incisor rotation, and shovel-shaped incisors; American Blacks as having crenulated molars; and American Caucasoids as having Carabelli's cusp. This publication solidified the use of these six dental morphological traits within forensic anthropology.

This reliance on "trait lists" to arrive at an estimation of ancestry has received criticism over the past several years. Such an approach is described as having no empirical basis and as being unscientific (Hefner et al., 2012). Furthermore, the reliance on trait lists necessitates a judgment based on experience, particularly when an individual displays multiple phenotypic traits characteristic of several populations. This approach does not provide known error rates as would be needed in a court of law (as per Daubert v. Merrell Dow Pharmaceuticals, 1993). In recent years, there has been a push to develop statistical methods that focus on dental morphology to estimate ancestry, especially as critiques have been levied at the use of only a few traits (Edgar, 2009).

Edgar (2005) developed a method to discriminate between European and African Americans using six morphological traits on eight focal teeth: tuberculum dentale (UC), premolar cusp variation (LP3 and LP4), deflecting wrinkle (LM1), trigonid crest (LM1), cusp 5 (LM2 and LM3), and cusp 7 (LM1). Numerous tables were provided that gave logistic regression and Bayesian probabilities for certain combinations of traits. When using this method, if traits are scored as present, classification is pushed toward African American. These results are based on the nature of the differences between Eurodont and Afridont dentition (as described above). The traits employed in this study are typically found in higher frequencies among individuals of African ancestry and were reported in the study to be of higher frequency in the African American sample.

Edgar (2013) published a subsequent study that included more populations (African American, European American, South Floridian Hispanic, and New Mexican Hispanic) and additional traits. This analysis employed 13 traits recorded on 20 focal teeth: double shovel (UI1, UI2, LI1, LI2), shovel shape (UI2 and UC), distal accessory ridge (UC and LC), tuberculum dentale (UC), hypocone (UM1), metacone (UM1 and UM2), metaconule (UM2), premolar cusp variation (LP3), anterior fovea (LM1), deflecting wrinkle (LM1), protostylid (LM1), cusp 7 (LM1 and LM2), and cusp 5 (LM2). Discriminant function equations are provided in two steps, with step 1 distinguishing Hispanics from African and European Americans and step 2 distinguishing African Americans from European Americans. This work encountered an unexpected difficulty in distinguishing between South Floridian and New Mexican Hispanics based on the dentition alone, and the samples are therefore included together. This method employs breakpoints that are distinct from those presented in Table 6.3. The metacone and hypocone on the upper molars are considered present at a score of 5, and shoveling of the incisors is considered present with a score of 2 on the upper incisors. Upon repeated use of this method, it becomes clear that a score of 5 for the hypocone and metacone for the upper first molar is necessary to classify any individual as Hispanic. Additionally, presence of shoveling leads to a classification of Hispanic.

Irish (2015) created a "simple" method for estimating ancestry based on 10 ASUDAS traits and 5 sample populations: sub-Saharan Africans, Europeans, Chinese—Mongolians, Northern and Southern Native Americans, and Polynesians. Traits were chosen for their ability to discriminate between world samples and their frequencies (ie, overly rare traits were excluded). Populations were chosen based on the likelihood of encountering these groups in the United States. In this method, the analyst records the presence or absence of a trait as identified in the unknown individual, then identifies its frequency in each population. These frequencies are then summed for each population, and whichever population has the highest number is the most likely match to the unknown individual. The advantages to this method are that it is indeed simple and allows for rapid comparison across multiple populations. The disadvantages to this approach are that it has not been validated and does not provide known error rates, which could be problematic in light of the standards placed on admissibility for expert testimony.

Alsolehait (2013) used the mean measure of divergence (MMD) to calculate ancestry among individuals. In this instance, dental morphology was scored for an individual, and the dichotomized score was replaced with either the lowest (for trait absence) or the highest (for trait presence) observed population frequencies. In this way, data on an individual could be treated as if they represented a fictional population. The MMD could then be calculated, with ancestry estimated based on the group to which the individual was found to be most similar. This study suffers from a lack of validation, and the complications of treating an individual as a population should be further considered before this method can be adopted.

While dental morphology is gaining traction within forensic anthropology, there is a need to develop streamlined methods with known error rates that are validated and have a broad comparative sample from which to draw. These initial efforts are certainly a step in the right direction and will form the basis from which further methods will be established. As statistical methods are advanced and comparative data from documented modern collections grow, these methods will certainly expand. It will become increasingly important for forensic anthropology students to be as well versed in dental morphology as they are in skeletal morphology.

BIOARCHAEOLOGICAL APPLICATION

Biodistance can be used to explore several hypotheses within a bioarchaeological framework. These are generally divided into two themes: intracemetery and intercemetery, or population-level analyses. An intracemetery analysis employing dental morphological data can address regional questions such as the relationship between cemetery structure and biological relationships (see Stojanowski and Schillaci, 2006 for an excellent review of intracemetery analyses). Intercemetery approaches can be used to explore broader population relationships and migration.

Intracemetery

Intracemetery analyses that rely on dental morphological variation alone can be problematic due to the binary nature of morphological data. Thus, looking at interindividual differences in morphology is difficult to test statistically. Typically, researchers identify a rare trait and speculate that if two (or more) individuals share this trait, it is likely that they are related (Alt et al., 1997; Christensen, 1998). This analysis can be framed in a probabilistic way to add weight to the analysis. However, this technique of identifying rare traits has been found to be unsuccessful when using a large population with known familial relationships (Kuba, 2006).

If a population can be subdivided into meaningful groups based on archaeological evidence (grave goods, burial location, burial orientation, burial position, etc.) or biological differences (eg, age and sex), then additional analyses become available. A univariate chi-square comparison can be done on a trait-by-trait basis using the Bonferroni correction. However, results from such an analysis may be limited, as these are univariate approaches that do not incorporate multiple variables in understanding population composition. If trait frequencies for each subpopulation are employed, additional analyses can be performed that are more similar to those being used in population-level analyses (Corruccini and Shimada, 2002), although in intracemetery analyses, consideration must be given to small sample sizes.

An alternative to less successful univariate techniques is Gower's coefficient. This statistic compares morphological scores (as 0 or 1) between individuals to arrive at interindividual distances (Gower, 1971) that can be used to explore individual relationships and affinity (eg, Howell and Kintigh, 1996; McClelland, 2003; Paul et al., 2013).

Population Level

Statistical treatments at the population level are easier to apply. Trait frequencies are used for each population. Such an approach has the added benefit of avoiding the problem of missing data. Statistical methods for this type of analysis are described throughout this volume, including MMD (Chapters 5, 20, and 25) and Bray—Curtis (Chapters 21 and 22), among others. These approaches can also be seen in numerous bioarchaeological publications using permanent teeth (Guatelli-Steinberg et al., 2001; Hanihara, 2008; Irish and Konigsberg, 2007; Lukacs and Pal, 2013; Ragsdale and Edgar, 2015; Sutter, 2005; Ullinger et al., 2005) and deciduous teeth (Grine, 1986; Kitagawa et al., 1995; Lukacs and Kuswandari, 2013).

EVOLUTION AND DENTAL MORPHOLOGY

There is clearly an evolutionary and functional basis to tooth morphology. Diet can play a large role in tooth types and enamel thickness (Teaford, 2007). Some animals have very specialized teeth, such as the canine/tusk of the narwhal or the dental comb of most lemurs and lorises. In primate evolution, a decrease in reliance on smell changed the shape of the face (and snout) and in turn affected the dentition. Canines became smaller, and incisors and premolars were reduced in number (Hillson, 2005).

The following is a brief treatment of evolution and dental morphology with a focus on how it can play a role in changing the dental morphology of populations. It is critical to understand the evolutionary process and function of teeth to accurately study dental morphology as a means of exploring human variation (both past and present). If the basis for this variation is not understood, it is possible that data will be used inappropriately. For example, if analyses focus on traits that are overly influenced by environment or culture in their expression, the true genetic variation of the individual is lost, and the focus can become misdirected. The deep evolutionary history of traits needs to be explored to identify those that best distinguish populations. Analyses cannot rely on statistics or observed frequencies alone, but need to consider process in addition to outcome. A review of dental morphology along the human evolutionary line helps demonstrate the traits critical to understanding the range of variation in modern human populations.

Hominins

Dental morphological traits that are of interest in human populations today can be seen in the fossil record beginning with the Australopithecines between 4 and 1 million years ago (Schroer and Wood, 2013), and some traits occur even earlier in primate evolution, such as the Y-5 pattern during the Miocene (Pilbeam et al., 1977). Dental traits can be used in the study of taxonomy and phylogenetic affinity, and there is a vast body of literature exploring these species differences in phylogeny (eg, Bailey et al., 2011; Guatelli-Steinberg and Irish, 2005; Martinón-Torres et al., 2007, 2012; Wood et al., 1983; Wood and Engleman, 1988; Wood and Uytterschaut, 1987). What follows is a brief summary of some of these traits.

Wood and Abbott (1983), in their examination of Australopithecines, found that robust Australopithecines had higher frequencies of cusp 6 on the first lower molar, while gracile Australopithecines had a higher frequency of cusp 7 on the second lower molar. Additionally, the protostylid is more common in the robust Australopithecines, but has a stronger expression in the gracile Australopithecines that exhibit the trait. The new find of *Homo naledi* was found to have a small Carabelli's cusp and protostylid, although neither was as prominent as those found in *Australopithecus* (Berger et al., 2015).

Prominent dental traits in *Homo erectus* include shovel-shaped upper incisors, labial convexity, Y-patterned on LM2, high lingual cusp number on the LP4, deflecting wrinkle, and a well-defined hypoconulid in LM2 and LM3 (Bailey and Hublin, 2013; Zanolli, 2013). Neanderthal dentition has defined midtrigonid crests and anterior fovea on all of the lower molars (Bailey et al., 2011), as well as shovel-shaped upper incisors (Bailey et al., 2009). Additionally, Neanderthals have high frequencies of labial convexity, tuberculum dentale, cusp 5 on UM1, and lingual cusp number on LP4 (Bailey and Hublin, 2013). Like *H. erectus*, the Neanderthal dentition also has a high frequency of Y-patterned LM2, as well as a hypoconulid on both LM2 and LM3 (Bailey, 2006).

Anatomically Modern Humans

It is clear from the fossil record that some dental morphological traits emerged very early in human evolution. These traits have then been shaped by the forces of evolution: drift, flow, and natural selection. It has been thought that among anatomically modern humans, drift has been the prime force acting on dental morphology (Scott and Turner, 1997). Throughout human history as populations became isolated, they became more distinct through random processes. It is presumed that early human populations would have been smaller tens to hundreds of thousands of years ago, and drift could have significant effects. Traits that developed through genetic drift then stay in current ancestral groups because there is no selection against them; however, drift is likely still working on traits, and in conjunction with gene flow, it could change trait frequencies over time.

Conversely, there is another model to suggest that dental traits are subject to the forces of natural selection, and that they are an adaptation to various environmental and cultural factors. Mizoguchi (2013) found a correlation between two traits (incisor shoveling and Carabelli's trait) and environment and diet. Additionally, there is a functional component to teeth that makes them subject to selection in relation to diet, particularly hard foods. To accurately interpret population differences in dental morphology, these evolutionary processes need to be understood. Particularly for anatomically modern human prehistory, because population differences or similarities may be the result of evolutionary forces and may not reflect population affinity. It is also important to consider evolutionary processes within a forensic context, as populations may be experiencing increased gene flow or other microevolutionary processes, thus highlighting the importance of modern reference samples in forensic studies.

CONCLUSIONS

The goal of this chapter was to highlight past research and future directions for using dental morphology in the fields of forensic anthropology and bioarchaeology. This included a discussion of data collection techniques, general trends in population variation, hominin dental morphology, and the evolutionary processes shaping anatomically modern human dental morphology and population variation. While these last two topics may seem outside the scope of interest, they are important areas of study for the accurate interpretation of the results of biodistance studies, because understanding the evolutionary process and function of teeth is critical to studying human variation, evolution, and migration.

One area not discussed herein involves technological advances, such as CT scans and 3-D imaging, that have allowed researchers to explore development and morphology in new and exciting ways. While we acknowledge the importance of this research, this advanced technology is not always readily available and the cost to collect these data can be prohibitive, particularly in large studies of population relationships or in forensic settings. Therefore, we focused on the exploration of gross dental morphology, as we see the ability to take nondestructive data on large numbers of individuals as invaluable to the bioarchaeologist and forensic anthropologist. Furthermore, dental morphological data can be compared across observers and across populations spanning different large expanses of time and space, which also makes these types of studies anthropologically valuable.

Finally, given the potential of dental morphology to discriminate populations coupled with the tendency for teeth to preserve, we see great potential in this field of study. There is certainly room for growth within the realm of forensic anthropology to employ dental morphology as part of the biological profile. We encourage students in physical anthropology to seek training in this area, as it will become increasingly important to include dental morphology within bioarchaeological research and forensic anthropological investigations.

Endnotes

1. For deciduous teeth, letters are in lowercase. Deciduous teeth include no precursors to molars, and therefore only have three tooth classes (incisor, canine, and premolar).
2. Third and fourth are preferred by the authors to indicate their evolutionary placement origin.

References

Alsoleihat, F., 2013. A new quantitative method for predicting forensic racial identity based on dental morphological trait analysis. International Journal of Morphology 31 (2), 418–424.

Alt, K.W., Pichler, S., Vach, W., Klima, B., Vlcek, E., Sedlmeier, J., 1997. Twenty-five thousand-year-old triple burial from Dolni Vestonice: an ice-age family? American Journal of Physical Anthropology 102, 123–131.

American Association of Physical Anthropology, 1996. AAPA statement on biological aspects of race. American Journal of Physical Anthropology 101 (4), 569–570.

Aoyagi, F., 1967. Morpho-genetical studies on similarities in the teeth and dental occlusion of twins. Shikwa Gakuho 67, 606–624.

Bailey, S.E., 2006. Beyond shovel-shaped incisors: neandertal dental morphology in a comparative context. Periodicum Biologorum 108 (3), 253–267.

Bailey, S.E., Hublin, J.-J., 2013. What does it mean to be dentally "modern"? In: Scott, G.R., Irish, J.D. (Eds.), Anthropological Perspectives on Tooth Morphology: Genetics, Evolution, Variation. Cambridge University Press, Cambridge, pp. 222–249.

Bailey, S.E., Skinner, M.M., Hublin, J.-J., 2011. What lies beneath? An evaluation of lower molar trigonid crest patterns based on both dentine and enamel expression. American Journal of Physical Anthropology 145 (4), 505–518.

Bailey, S.E., Weaver, T.D., Hublin, J.-J., 2009. Who made the Aurignacian and other early upper Paleolithic industries? Journal of Human Evolution 57 (1), 11–26.

Berger, L.R., Hawks, J., de Ruiter, D.J., Churchill, S.E., Schmid, P., Delezene, L.K., Kivell, T.L., Garvin, H.M., Williams, S.A., DeSilva, J.M., Skinner, M.M., Musiba, C.M., Cameron, N., Holliday, T.W., Harcourt-Smith, W., Ackermann, R.R., Bastir, M., Bogin, B., Bolter, D., Brophy, J., Cofran, Z.D., Congdon, K.A., Deane, A.S., Dembo, M., Drapeau, M., Elliott, M.C., Feuerriegel, E.M., Garcia-Martinez, D., Green, D.J., Gurtov, A., Irish, J.D., Kruger, A., Laird, M.F., Marchi, D., Meyer, M.R., Nalla, S., Negash, E.W., Orr, C.M., Radovcic, D., Schroeder, L., Scott, J.E., Throckmorton, Z., Tocheri, M.W., VanSickle, C., Walker, C.S., Wei, P., Zipfel, B., 2015. Homo naledi, a new species of the genus Homo from the Dinaledi Chamber, South Africa. eLife 4.

Berry, A.C., 1978. Anthropological and family studies on minor variants of the dental crown. In: Bulter, P.M., Joysey, K.A. (Eds.), Development, Function and Evolution of Teeth. Academic Press, London, pp. 81–96.

Biggerstaff, R.H., 1973. Heritability of the Carabelli cusp in twins. Journal of Dental Research 52 (1), 40–44.

Brewer-Carias, C.A., LeBlanc, S.A., Neel, J.V., 1976. Genetic structure of a tribal population, the Yanomama Indians. XIII. Dental microdifferentiation. American Journal of Physical Anthropology 44 (1), 5–14.

Burnett, S.E., Irish, J.D., Fong, M.R., 2013. Wear's the problem? Examining the effect of dental wear on studies of crown morphology. In: Scott, G.R., Irish, J.D. (Eds.), Anthropological Perspectives on Tooth Morphology: Genetics, Evolution, Variation. Cambridge University Press, Cambridge, pp. 535–554.

Butler, P.M., 1956. The ontogeny of molar pattern. Biological Reviews 31 (1), 30–69.

Campbell, T.D., 1925. The Dentition and Palate of the Australian Aboriginal. Hassell Press, Adelaide.

Christensen, A., 1998. Skeletal evidence for familial interments in the valley of Oaxaca, Mexico. Homo 49, 140–154.

Cohen, J., 1960. A coefficient of agreement for nominal scales. Educational and Psychological Measurement 20 (1), 37–46.

Corruccini, R.S., Shimada, I., 2002. Dental relatedness corresponding to mortuary patterning at Huaca Loro, Peru. American Journal of Physical Anthropology 117, 118–121.

Corruccini, R.S., Shimada, I., Shinoda, K.-I., 2002. Dental and mtDNA relatedness among thousand-year-old remains from Huaca Loro, Peru. Dental Anthropology 16, 9–14.

Dahlberg, A., 1951. The dentition of the American Indian. In: Laughlin, W.S. (Ed.), The Physical Anthropology of the American Indian. The Viking Fund, New York, pp. 138–176.

Dahlberg, A., 1956. Materials for the Establishment of Standards for Classification of Tooth Characteristics, Attributes, and Techniques in Morphological Studies of the Dentition. Zoller Laboratory of Dental Anthropology, University of Chicago, Chicago.

Dahlberg, A., 1963. Analysis of the American Indian dentition. In: Browthwell, D.R. (Ed.), Dental Anthropology. Pergamon Press, London, pp. 149–177.

Daubert v. Merrell Dow Pharmaceuticals, I., 509 U.S. 579, 1993.

Edgar, H.J.H., 2002. Biological Distance and the African American Dentition. Anthropology. The Ohio StateUniversity, Columbus.

Edgar, H.J.H., 2005. Prediction of race using characteristics of dental morphology. Journal of Forensic Sciences 50 (2), 269–273.

Edgar, H.J.H., 2009. Testing the utility of dental morphological traits commonly used in the forensic identification of ancestry. In: Koppe, T., Meyer, G., Alt, K.W. (Eds.), Comparative Dental Morphology. Frontiers of Oral Biology. Karger, Basel, pp. 49–54.

Edgar, H.J.H., 2013. Estimation of ancestry using dental morphological characteristics. Journal of Forensic Sciences 58 (s1), S3–S8.

Edgar, H.J.H., 2016. Dental Morphology: An Illustrated Manual. Left Coast Press, Walnut Creek, CA (in press).

Edgar, H.J.H., Lease, L.R., 2007. Correlations between deciduous and permanent tooth morphology in a European American sample. American Journal of Physical Anthropology 133 (1), 726–734.

Enoki, K., Dahlberg, A., 1958. Rotated maxillary central incisors. Orthodontic Journal of Japan 17, 157–159.

Garn, S., Kerewsky, R.S., Lewis, A.B., 1966. Extent of sex influence on Carabelli's polymorphism. Journal of Dental Research 45, 1823.

Gašperšič, D., 1994. Some principles in the dental crown construction in permanent maxillary centrals of Slovenians. Journal of Oral Rehabilitiation 21 (6), 713–719.

Gómez-Robles, A., Bermúdez de Castro, J.M., Arsuaga, J.-L., Carbonell, E., Polly, P.D., 2013. No known hominin species matches the expected dental morphology of the last common ancestor of Neanderthals and modern humans. Proceedings of the National Academy of Sciences 110 (45), 18196–18201.

Goose, D.H., 1971. The inheritance of tooth size in British families. In: Dahlberg, A.A. (Ed.), Dental Morphology and Evolution. The University of Chicago Press, Chicago, pp. 263–269.

Gower, J.C., 1971. A general coefficient of similarity and some of its properties. Biometrics 27 (4), 857–871.

Grine, F.E., 1986. Anthropolgical aspects of the deciduous teeth of South African blacks. In: Singer, R., Lundy, J.K. (Eds.), Variation, Culture and Evolution in African Populations. Witwatersrand University Press, Johannesburg, pp. 47–83.

Grüneberg, H., 1952. Genetical studies on the skeleton of the mouse. IV. Quasi-continuous variations. Journal of Genetics 51, 95–114.

Guatelli-Steinberg, D., Hunter, J.P., Durner, R.M., Moormann, S., Weston, T.C., Betsinger, T.K., 2013. Teeth, morphogenesis, and levels of variation in the human Carabelli trait. In: Scott, G.R., Irish, J.D. (Eds.), Anthropological Perspectives on Tooth Morphology: Genetics, Evolution, Variation. Cambridge University Press, Cambridge, pp. 69–91.

Guatelli-Steinberg, D., Irish, J.D., 2005. Brief communication: early hominin variability in first molar dental trait frequencies. American Journal of Physical Anthropology 128 (2), 477–484.

Guatelli-Steinberg, D., Irish, J.D., Lukacs, J.R., 2001. Canary islands-north African population affinities: measures of divergence based on dental morphology. Homo 52, 173–188.

Gurri, F.D., Balam, G., 2006. Inheritance of bilateral fusion of the lower central and lateral incisors: a pedigree of a Maya family from Yucatan, Mexico. Dental Anthropology 19 (1), 29–34.

Haeussler, A., Irish, J., Morris, D., Turner, C.G.I., 1989. Morphological and metrical comparison of San and Central Sotho dentitions from southern Africa. American Journal of Physical Anthropology 78, 115–122.

Hanihara, K., 1954. Studies on the deciduous dentition of the Japanese and the Japanese-American hybrids: I. Deciduous incisors. Journal of the Anthropological Society of Nippon 63 (5), 168–185.

Hanihara, K., 1961. Criteria for classification of crown characters of the human deciduous dentition. Journal of the Anthropological Society of Nippon 69, 27–45.

Hanihara, K., 1963. Crown characters of the deciduous dentition of the Japanese–American hybrids. In: Brothwell, D.R. (Ed.), Dental Anthropology. Pergamon, New York, pp. 105–124.

Hanihara, K., 1967. Racial characteristics in the dentition. Journal of Dental Research 46, 923–926.

Hanihara, K., 1968. Mongoloid dental complex in the permanent dentition. In: Proceedings of the VIIIth International Symposium of Anthropological and Ethnological Sciences. Science Council of Japan, Tokyo and Kyoto, pp. 298–300.

Hanihara, T., 2008. Morphological variation of major human populations based on nonmetric dental traits. American Journal of Physical Anthropology 136, 169–182.

Harjunmaa, E., Kallonen, A., Voutilainen, M., Hamalainen, K., Mikkola, M.L., Jernvall, J., 2012. On the difficulty of increasing dental complexity. Nature 483 (7389), 324–327.

Harris, E.F., 1977. Anthropologic and Genetic Aspects of the Dental Morphology of Solomon Islanders, Melanesia. Department of Anthropology: Arizona State University.

Harris, E.F., 2007. Carabelli's trait and tooth size of human maxillary first molars. American Journal of Physical Anthropology 132 (2), 238–246.

Harris, E.F., Bailit, H.L., 1980. The metaconule: a morphological and familiar analysis of a molar cusp in humans. American Journal of Physical Anthropology 53, 349–358.

Hefner, J.T., Ousley, S.D., Dirkmaat, D.C., 2012. Morphoscopic traits and the assessment of ancestry. In: Dirkmaat, D.C. (Ed.), A Companion to Forensic Anthropology. Wiley-Blackwell, Malden, MA, pp. 287–310.

Hellman, M., 1928. Racial characters in human dentition Part I. A racial distribution of the Dryopithecus pattern and its modifications in the lower molar teeth of man. Proceedings of the American Philosophical Society 67 (2), 157–174.

Hillson, S., 2005. Teeth. Cambridge University Press, Cambridge.

Howell, T.L., Kintigh, K.W., 1996. Archaeological identification of kin groups using mortuary and biological data: an example from the American Southwest. American Antiquity 61 (3), 537–554.

Hrdlička, A., 1920. Shovel shaped teeth. American Journal of Physical Anthropology 3, 429–465.

Hrdlička, A., 1924. New data on the teeth of early man and certain fossil European apes. American Journal of Physical Anthropology 7, 109–132.

Hubbard, A.R., Guatelli-Steinberg, D., Irish, J.D., 2015. Do nuclear DNA and dental nonmetric data produce similar reconstructions of regional population history? An example from modern coastal Kenya. American Journal of Physical Anthropology 157 (2), 295–304.

Hughes, T., Dempsey, P., Richards, L., Townsend, G.C., 2000. Genetic analysis of deciduous tooth size in Australian twins. Archives of Oral Biology 45 (11), 997–1004.

Hughes, T., Townsend, G., Bockmann, M., 2016. An overview of dental genetics. In: Irish, J.D., Scott, G.R. (Eds.), A Companion to Dental Anthropology. Wiley & Sons, Inc., Malden, MA, pp. 124–141.

Hunter, J.P., Guatelli-Steinberg, D., Weston, T.C., Durner, R., Betsinger, T.K., 2010. Model of tooth morphogenesis predicts Carabelli cusp expression, size, and symmetry in humans. PLoS One 5 (7), e11844.

Irish, J., Konigsberg, L., 2007. The ancient inhabitants of Jebel Moya redux: measures of population affinity based on dental morphology. International Journal of Osteoarchaeology 17 (2), 138–156.

Irish, J.D., 1993. Biological Affinities of Late Pleistocene Through Modern African Aboriginal Populations: The Dental Evidence. Department of Anthropology. Arizona State University, Tempe, AZ.

Irish, J.D., 1997. Characteristic high- and low-frequency dental traits in sub-Saharan African populations. American Journal of Physical Anthropology 102 (4), 455–467.

Irish, J.D., 1998. Ancestral dental traitis in recent sub-Saharan Africans and the origins of modern humans. Journal of Human Evolution 34, 81–98.

Irish, J.D., 2008. A dental assessment of biological affinity between inhabitants of the Gebel Ramlah and R12 Neolithic sites. In: Man—Millennia—Environment: Studies in Honour of Professor Romuald Schild. Institute of Archaeology and Ethnology, Polish Academy of Sciences, Warsaw, pp. 45–52.

Irish, J.D., 2013. Afridonty: the sub-Saharan African dental complex revisited. In: Scott, G.R., Irish, J.D. (Eds.), Anthropological Perspectives on Tooth Morphology: Genetics, Evolution, Variation. Cambridge University Press, Cambridge, pp. 278–295.

Irish, J.D., 2015. Dental nonmetric variation around the world: using key traits in populations to estimate ancestry in individuals. In: Berg, G.E., Ta'ala, S.C. (Eds.), Biological Affinity in Forensic Identification of Human Skeletal Remains. CRC Press, Boca Raton, FL, pp. 165–190.

Irish, J.D., Guatelli-Steinberg, D., 2003. Ancient teeth and modern human origins: an expanded comparison of African Plio-pleistocene and recent world dental samples. Journal of Human Evolution 45, 113–144.

Irish, J.D., Morris, D.H., 1996. Canine mesial ridge (Bushman canine) dental trait definition. American Journal of Physical Anthropology 99, 357–359.

Jernvall, J., 2000. Linking development with generation of novelty in mammalian teeth. Proceedings of the National Academy of Sciences of the United States of America 97 (6), 2641–2645.

Jernvall, J., Jung, H.-S., 2000. Genotype, phenotype, and developmental biology of molar tooth characters. Yearbook of Physical Anthropology 43, 171–190.

Jernvall, J., Thesleff, I., 2000. Reiterative signaling and patterning during mammalian tooth morphogenesis. Mechanisms of Development 92 (1), 19–29.

Jorgensen, K., 1955. The Dryopithecus pattern in recent Danes and Dutchmen. Journal of Dental Research 34, 195–208.

Kanazawa, E., Sekikawa, M., Ozaki, T., 1990. A quantitative investigation of irregular cuspules in human maxillary permanent molars. American Journal of Physical Anthropology 83, 173–180.

Kaul, V., Prakash, S., 1981. Morphological features of the Jat dentition. American Journal of Physical Anthropology 54, 123–127.

Khraisat, A., Alsoleihat, F., Subramani, K., Taha, S.T., Al-Rabab'ah, M.A., Al-Bitar, Z.B., 2011. Hypocone reduction and Carabelli's traits in contemporary Jordanians and the association between Carabelli's trait and the dimensions of the maxillary first permanent molar. Collegium Antropologicum 35 (1), 73–78.

Kieser, J., Preston, C., 1981. The dentition of the Lengua Indians of Paraguay. American Journal of Physical Anthropology 55, 485–490.

Kimura, R., Yamaguchi, T., Takeda, Y., Kondo, O., Toma, T., Haneji, K., Hanihara, T., Matsukura, H., kawamura, S., Maki, K., Osawa, M., Ishida, H., Oota, H., 2009. A common variation in EDAR is a genetic determinant of shovel-shaped incisors. American Journal of Human Genetics 84 (4), 528–535.

Kitagawa, Y., 2000. Nonmetric morphological characters of deciduous teeth in Japan: diachronic evidence of the past 4000 years. International Journal of Osteoarchaeology 10 (4), 242–253.

Kitagawa, Y., Manabe, Y., Oyamada, J., Rokutanda, A., 1995. Deciduous dental morphology of the prehistoric Jomon people of Japan: comparison of nonmetric characters. American Journal of Physical Anthropology 97, 101–111.

Klatsky, M., 1956. The incidence of six anomalies of the teeth and jaws. Human Biology 28 (4), 420–428.

Kraus, B.S., Furr, M.L., 1953. Lower first premolars. Part 1. A definition and classification of discrete morphological traits. Journal of Dental Research 32, 554–564.

Kuba, C.L., 2006. Nonmetric Traits and the Detection of Family Groups in Archaeological Remains. Department of Anthropology. Arizona State University, Tempe, AZ.

Landis, R.J., Koch, G.G., 1977. The measure of observer agreement for categorial data. Biometrics 33, 159–174.

Larson, M.A., 1978. Dental Morphology of the Gran Quivira Indians. Department of Anthropology. Arizona State University, Tempe.

Lasker, G.W., 1945. Observations on the teeth of Chinese born and reared in China and America. American Journal of Physical Anthropology 3 (2), 129–150.

Lasker, G.W., 1950. Genetic analysis of racial traits of the teeth. In: Cold Spring Harbor Symposia on Quantitative Biology. Cold Spring Harbor Laboratory Press, pp. 191–203.

Lasker, G.W., Lee, M.M., 1957. Racial traits in the human teeth. Journal of Forensic Sciences 2, 401–419.

Lease, L.R., 2003. Ancestral Determination of African American and European American Deciduous Dentition Using Metric and Non-metric Analysis. Department of Anthropology. The Ohio State University, Columbus.
Lease, L.R., Sciulli, P.W., 2005. Brief communication. Discrimination between European-American and African-American children based on deciduous dental metrics and morphology. American Journal of Physical Anthropology 126 (1), 56–60.
Lukacs, J.R., Kuswandari, S., 2013. Crown morphology of Malay deciduous teeth: trait frequencies and biological aflinities. In: Scott, G.R., Irish, J.D. (Eds.), Anthropological Perspectives on Tooth Morphology: Genetics, Evolution, Variation. Cambridge University Press, Cambridge, pp. 453–478.
Lukacs, J.R., Pal, J., 2013. Dental morphology of early Holocene foragers of North India: non-metric trait frequencies and biological affinities. Homo 64 (6), 411–436.
Martinón-Torres, M., De Castro, J.B., Gómez-Robles, A., Arsuaga, J., Carbonell, E., Lordkipanidze, D., Manzi, G., Margvelashvili, A., 2007. Dental evidence on the hominin dispersals during the Pleistocene. Proceedings of the National Academy of Sciences of the United States of America 104 (33), 13279–13282.
Martinón-Torres, M., de Castro, J.M.B., Gómez-Robles, A., Prado-Simón, L., Arsuaga, J.L., 2012. Morphological description and comparison of the dental remains from Atapuerca-Sima de los Huesos site (Spain). Journal of Human Evolution 62 (1), 7–58.
Mayhall, J.T., 1998. Dichotomy in human dental morphology; a plea for complexity. Dental Morphology 43–47.
McClelland, J.A., 2003. Refining the Resolution of Biological Distance Studies Based on the Analysis of Dental Morphology: Detecting Subpopulations at Grasshopper Pueblo. Department of Anthropology. The University of Arizona, Tempe, AZ.
Mizoguchi, K., 2013. Significant among-population associations found between dental characters and environmental factors. In: Scott, G.R., Irish, J.D. (Eds.), Anthropological Perspectives on Tooth Morphology: Genetics, Evolution, Variation. Cambridge University Press, Cambridge, pp. 108–125.
Moormann, S., Guatelli-Steinberg, D., Hunter, J., 2013. Metamerism, morphogenesis, and the expression of carabelli and other dental traits in humans. American Journal of Physical Anthropology 150 (3), 400–408.
Moorrees, C.F.A., 1957. The Aleut Dentition. Harvard University Press, Cambridge, Massachusetts.
Morris, D.H., Hughes, S.G., Dahlberg, A.A., 1978. Uto-Aztecan premolar: the anthropology of a dental trait. In: Bulter, P.M., Joysey, K.A. (Eds.), Development, Function and Evolution of Teeth. Academic Press, London, pp. 69–79.
Nelson, C.T., 1938. The teeth of the Indians of Pecos Pueblo. American Journal of Physical Anthropology 23 (3), 261–293.
Nichol, C.R., 1990. Dental Genetics and Biological Relationships of the Pima Indians of Arizona. Department of Anthropology. Arizona State University, Tempe, AZ.
Nichol, C.R., Turner, C.G., 1986. Intra- and interobserver concordance in classifying dental morphology. American Journal of Physical Anthropology 69 (3), 299–315.
Nichol, C.R., Turner, C.G., Dahlberg, A., 1984. Variation in the convexity of the human maxillary incisor labial surface. American Journal of Physical Anthropology 63, 361–370.
Noss, J.F., Scott, G.R., Potter, R.H., Dahlberg, A.A., 1983. Fluctuating asymmetry in molar dimensions and discrete morphological traits in Pima Indians. American Journal of Physical Anthropology 61 (4), 437–445.
Paul, K.S., Stojanowski, C.M., 2015. Performance analysis of deciduous morphology for detecting biological siblings. American Journal of Physical Anthropology 157 (4), 615–629.
Paul, K.S., Stojanowski, C.M., Butler, M.M., 2013. Biological and spatial structure of an early classic period cemetery at Charco Redondo, Oaxaca. American Journal of Physical Anthropology 152 (2), 217–229.
Pilbeam, D., Meyer, G.E., Badgley, C., Rose, M.D., Pickford, M.H., Behrensmeyer, A., Shah, S.I., 1977. New hominoid primates from the Siwaliks of Pakistan and their bearing on hominoid evolution. Nature 270 (5639), 689–695.
Ragsdale, C.S., Edgar, H.J.H., 2015. Cultural interaction and biological distance in postclassic period Mexico. American Journal of Physical Anthropology 157 (1), 121–133.

Rhine, S., 1990. Non-metric skull racing. In: Gill, G.W., Rhine, S. (Eds.), Skeletal Attribution of Race: Methods for Forensic Anthropology. Maxwell Museum Anthropological Papers No. 4, Albuquerque, NM, pp. 9–20.

Ricaut, F.X., Auriol, V., Von Cramon-Taubadel, N., Sakai, T., Nakaya, H., Yano, W., Kunimatsu, Y., 2010. Comparison between morphological and genetic data to estimate biological relationhsip: the case of the Egyin Gol necropolis (Mongolia). American Journal of Physical Anthropology 143 (3), 355–364.

Saheki, M., 1958. On the heredity of the tooth crown configuration studied in twins. Acta Anatomica Nipponica 33, 456–470.

Salazar-Ciudad, I., Jernvall, J., 2010. A computational model of teeth and the developmental origins of morphological variation. Nature 464 (7288), 583–586.

Sauer, N.J., 1992. Forensic anthropology and the concept of race: if races don't exist, why are forensic anthropologists so good at identifying them? Social Science and Medicine 34, 107–111.

Saunders, S.R., Mayhall, J.T., 1982. Fluctuating asymmetry of dental morphological traits: new interpretations. Human Biology 54 (4), 789–799.

Schroer, K., Wood, B., 2013. Evolution of hominin postcanine macromorphology: a comparative meta-analysis. In: Scott, G.R., Irish, J.D. (Eds.), Anthropological Perspectives on Tooth Morphology: Genetics, Evolution, Variation. Cambridge University Press, Cambridge, pp. 170–200.

Sciulli, P.W., 1998. Evolution of the dentition in prehistoric Ohio valley Native Americans: II. Morphology of the deciduous dentition. American Journal of Physical Anthropology 106, 189–205.

Scott, G.R., 1973. Dental Morphology: A Genetic Study of American White Families and Variation in Living Southwest Indians. Department of Anthropology. Arizona State University, Tempe, AZ.

Scott, G.R., 1977. Classification, sex dimorphism, association, and population variation of the canine distal accessory ridge. Human Biology 49 (3), 453–469.

Scott, G.R., 1978. The relationship between Carabelli's trait and the protostylid. Journal of Dental Research 57 (4), 570.

Scott, G.R., 1979. Annotation association between the hypocone and Carabelli's trait of the maxillary molars. Journal of Dental Research 58 (4), 1403–1404.

Scott, G.R., 1980. Population variation of Carabelli's trait. Human Biology 52, 63–78.

Scott, G.R., 1992. Affinities of prehistoric and modern Kodiak Islanders and the question of Kachemak-Koniag biological continuity. Arctic Anthropology 29 (2), 150–166.

Scott, G.R., 2008. Dental morphology. In: Katzenberg, A., Saunders, S. (Eds.), Biological Anthropology of the Human Skeleton. Wiley-Liss, New York, pp. 265–298.

Scott, G.R., Anta, A., Schomberg, R., De La Rue, C., 2013. Basque dental morphology and the "Eurodont" dental pattern. In: Scott, G.R., Irish, J.D. (Eds.), Anthropological Perspectives on Tooth Morphology: Genetics, Evolution, Variation. Cambridge University Press, Cambridge, pp. 296–318.

Scott, G.R., Maier, C., Heim, K., 2015. Identifying and recording key morphological (nonmetric) crown and root traits. In: Irish, J.D., Scott, G.R. (Eds.), A Companion to Dental Anthropology. John Wiley & Sons, Inc., Hoboken, NJ, pp. 245–264.

Scott, G.R., Potter, R.H., Noss, J.F., Dahlberg, A.A., Dahlberg, T., 1983. The dental morphology of Pima Indians. American Journal of Physical Anthropology 61 (1), 13–31.

Scott, G.R., Potter, R.H.Y., 1984. An analysis of tooth crown morphology in American white twins. Anthropologie 22 (3), 223–231.

Scott, G.R., Turner, C.G., 1997. The Anthropology of Modern Human Teeth. Cambridge University Press, Cambridge.

Sharma, J.C., 1992. Dental morphology and odontometry of twins and the heritability of dental variation. In: Lukacs, J.R. (Ed.), Culture, Ecology and Dental Anthropology. Kamla-Raj Enterprises, Delhi, India, pp. 49–60.

Shaw, J.C.M., 1931. The Teeth, the Bony Palate, and the Mandible in the Bantu Races of South Africa. Bale and Danielsson, London.

Shinoda, K., Matzumura, H., Nishimoto, T., 1998. Genetical and morphological analysis on kinship of the Nakazuma Jomon people using mitochondrial DNA and tooth crown measurements. Zoo-archaeology 11, 1–21.

Skinner, M.M., Wood, B.A., Hublin, J.-J., 2009. Protostylid expression at the enamel-dentine junction and enamel surface of mandibular molars of *Paranthropus robustus* and *Australopithecus africanus*. Journal of Human Evolution 56 (1), 76–85.

Škrinjarić, I., Slaj, M., Lapter, V., Muretic, Z., 1985. Heritability of Carabellis trait in twins. Collegium Antropologicum 9 (2), 177–181.

Stewart, T.D., 1979. Essentials of Forensic Anthropology. Charles C. Thomas, Springfield.

Stojanowski, C.M., Schillaci, M.A., 2006. Phenotypic approaches for understanding patterns of intracemetery biological variation. Yearbook of Physical Anthropology 49, 49–88.

Sutter, R., 2005. The prehistoric peopling of South America as inferred from epigenetic dental traits. Andean Past 7, 183–217.

Teaford, M.F., 2007. What do we know and not know about diet and enamel structure. In: Ungar, P.S. (Ed.), Evolution of the Human Diet: The Known, the Unknown and the Unknowable. Oxford University Press, Oxford, pp. 56–76.

Tratman, E., 1938. Three-rooted lower molars in man and their racial distribution. British Dental Journal 64, 264–274.

Tsai, P.L., Hsu, J.W., Lin, L.M., Liu, K.M., 1996. Logistic analysis of the effects of shovel trait on Carabelli's trait in a Mongoloid population. American Journal of Physical Anthropology 100 (4), 523–530.

Turner, C.G., 1967. The Dentition of Artic Peoples. Department of Anthropology. University of Wisconsin, Madison.

Turner, C.G., 1979. Dental anthropological indications of agriculture among the Jomon people of central Japan. X. Peopling of the Pacific. American Journal of Physical Anthropology 51 (4), 619–635.

Turner, C.G., 1985. Expression count: a method for calculating morphological dental trait frequencies by using adjustable weighting coefficients with standard ranked scales. American Journal of Physical Anthropology 68 (2), 263–267.

Turner, C.G., 1987. Late Pleistocene and Holocene population history of East Asia based on dental variation. American Journal of Physical Anthropology 73, 305–321.

Turner, C.G., 1990. Major features of Sundadonty and Sindodonty, including suggestions about East Asian microevolution, population history, and late Pleistocene relationships with Australian aboriginals. American Journal of Physical Anthropology 82, 295–317.

Turner, C.G., Nichol, C.R., Scott, G.R., 1991. Scoring procedures for key morphological traits of the permanent dentition: the Arizona State University dental anthropology system. In: Kelley, M.A., Larsen, C.S. (Eds.), Advances in Dental Anthropology. Wiley-Liss, New York, pp. 13–31.

Ullinger, J.M., Sheridan, S.G., Hawkey, D.E., Turner, C.G., Cooley, R., 2005. Bioarchaeological analysis of cultural transition in the Southern Levant using dental nonmetric traits. American Journal of Physical Anthropology 128 (2), 466–476.

Van Beek, G.C., 1983. Dental Morphology: An Illustrated Guide. Wright, Bristol.

Willermet, C., Daniels, J., Edgar, H.J.H., 2016. Robust estimator of grade differences: a new statistical solution to an old categorical data problem. American Journal of Human Biology (in press).

Wood, B., Abbott, S., 1983. Analysis of the dental morphology of Plio-pleistocene hominids. I. Mandibular molars: crown area measurements and morphological traits. Journal of Anatomy 136 (Pt 1), 197.

Wood, B., Abbott, S., Graham, S., 1983. Analysis of the dental morphology of Plio-pleistocene hominids. II. Mandibular molars—study of cusp areas, fissure pattern and cross sectional shape of the crown. Journal of Anatomy 137 (Pt 2), 287.

Wood, B., Engleman, C., 1988. Analysis of the dental morphology of Plio-pleistocene hominids. V. Maxillary postcanine tooth morphology. Journal of Anatomy 161, 1.

Wood, B., Uytterschaut, H., 1987. Analysis of the dental morphology of Plio-pleistocene hominids. III. Mandibular premolar crowns. Journal of Anatomy 154, 121.

Wood, J.M., 2007. Understanding Cohen's Kappa: A Tutorial. WebPsychEmpiricist. http://wpe.info/papers_table.html.

Wright, S., 1968. Evolution and the Genetics of Populations, vol. 1. Genetic and Biometric Foundations. University of Chicago Press, Chicago.

Wu, L., Turner, C.G., 1993. Brief communication: variation in the frequency and form of the lower permanent molar trigonid crest. American Journal of Physical Anthropology 91, 245–248.

Zanolli, C., 2013. Additional evidence for morpho-dimensional tooth crown variation in a New Indonesian *H. erectus* sample from the Sangiran Dome (central Java). PLoS One 8 (7), e67233.

Zhao, Z., Weiss, K.M., Stock, D.W., 2000. Development and evolution of dentition patterns and their genetic basis. In: Teaford, M., Smith, M.M., Ferguson, M.W.J. (Eds.), Development, Function and Evolution of Teeth. Cambridge University Press, Cambridge, pp. 152–172.

Zoubov, A.A., Nikityuk, B.A., 1978. Prospects for the application of dental morphology in twin type analysis. Journal of Human Evolution 7, 519–524.

CHAPTER

7

Dental Metrics in Biodistance Analysis

M.A. Pilloud[1], M.W. Kenyhercz[2,3]

University of Nevada, Reno, Reno, NV, United States[1]; University of Tennessee, Knoxville, TN, United States[2]; University of Pretoria, Pretoria, South Africa[3]

CHAPTER OUTLINE HEAD

Dental Development 136
Dental Metrics: The Data 136
  Mesiodistal Diameter 137
  Buccolingual Diameter 137
  Crown Height 137
  Alternative Measurements 139
Heritability 140
Biological Considerations 141
  Sex 141
  Age 142
  Biological Stress 143
Statistical Analysis 143
  Observer Error 143
  Sexual Dimorphism 144
  Methods to Negate Multicollinearity 144
Population Variation and Evolution 146
Forensic Applications 147
Bioarchaeological Applications 148
Conclusions 149
Endnote 149
References 149

The study of dental metrics involves the quantification of tooth dimensions. This study is most commonly achieved through an analysis of the crown length and width (Kieser, 1990). However, alternate measurements have been proposed, such as diagonal or cervical measurements of the crown (Hillson et al., 2005), orthogonal occlusal measurements (Morris, 1986), or measures of the enamel and dentin thickness (Feeney et al., 2010). Analyses can also include studies of how the teeth are apportioned within the jaw (Harris and Rathbun, 1991; Hemphill, 1991). Odontometric analysis extends back to the late 1880s (see, Chapter 1, this volume) and can now be seen throughout anthropology to differentiate anatomically modern human populations in bioarchaeology (Hanihara and Ishida, 2005; Matsumura, 2001;

Biological Distance Analysis. http://dx.doi.org/10.1016/B978-0-12-801966-5.00007-X

Schnutenhaus and Rösing, 1998; Stojanowski et al., 2007), forensics (Harris and Foster, 2015; Lease and Sciulli, 2005; Pilloud et al., 2014), and hominin evolution (Wolpoff, 1971).

This chapter will explore key issues surrounding the use of dental metrics within bioarchaeological and forensic contexts. This treatment will begin with a discussion of dental development and data collection, followed by an evaluation of biological considerations involved in tooth size to include age, sex, stress, and heritability rates. Data collection and various statistical analyses are then explored. Finally, there is a review of population variation and evolution as well as the application of dental metric data in forensics and bioarchaeology.

DENTAL DEVELOPMENT

A full discussion of the embryological development of teeth is beyond the scope of this chapter. However, an exploration of how teeth develop into their various types is germane to this discussion of tooth size. The process of tooth differentiation during development is known as patterning and has been found to be highly consistent. Various homeobox genes have been identified in this process of odontogenesis and the timing and location of tooth formation (Duverger and Morasso, 2008; Ten Cate et al., 2003). Among heterodont humans there are three main classes of tooth: incisiform, caniniform, and molariform (Ten Cate et al., 2003). There are two main theories that focus on how patterning may occur: the field theory and the clone theory.

The field theory states that tooth form is controlled by *morphogens* that induce differentiation. The morphogen concentrates around a key (polar) tooth in the developing jaw and attenuates throughout development. This diffusion means that shape and size may become more variable as teeth are further away from the polar tooth (Butler, 1939). Dahlberg (1945) applied the field theory to study the variation of human dentitions and identify those teeth that were the least variable in morphology, size, and form. These least variable teeth were determined to be the centers of the morphogenetic field (ie, the polar teeth). The polar teeth were identified as the first incisor, canine, third premolar, and first molar among maxillary teeth; and the second incisor, canine, third premolar, and first molar among mandibular teeth.

Alternatively, Osborne (1978) proposed the clone theory. In this model, the dental papilla arises from clones of ectomesenchymal cells. Each tooth class contains its own set of clone cells, and as the tooth class progresses through development, cell divisions accumulate resulting in greater dental variability, similar to the facsimile effect (Kenyhercz, 2014).

The important point to make here is that in either theory of dental development, the polar teeth are recognized as being the most reflective of genetic variation and less so of environmental influence (Alvesalo and Tigerstedt, 1974; Greene, 1967; Kieser, 1990). This distinction is an important one in studies of tooth size and understanding modern human variation.

DENTAL METRICS: THE DATA

Dental metric data may be collected on the entire dental arcade (all 32 teeth); however, antimere[1] size is highly correlated, and data on both teeth should not be included in studies of biodistance to avoid statistical noise due to multicollinearity (Alin, 2010). To avoid redundancy in the data, the convention is to use isomeres on the left side of the dental arcade and to substitute the right if the left antimere is missing.

Dental dimensions of teeth within the same tooth class are also found to be highly correlated (Moorrees and Reed, 1964). Therefore, researchers may only want to include data on the polar teeth; this way, multicollinearity among teeth within the same dental field can be avoided. However, in studies of population variation the more distal teeth (ie, the nonpolar teeth) may be more informative because they tend to show more variation in relation to the environment, which could help to differentiate populations. In such cases the more distal teeth may perform better at classifying groups (Kenyhercz, 2014).

Teeth can be measured in multiple ways; however, the methods described here are concerned with documenting the size of the crown (enamel portion of the tooth) as opposed to measurements of the root or dentin. Crown measurements include the mesiodistal and buccolingual dimensions of the crown.

Mesiodistal Diameter

The mesiodistal diameter can be measured in one of two ways: (1) as the maximum diameter of the tooth crown in the mesiodistal plane or (2) as the distance between the interproximal contact points of the tooth (Mayhall, 1992; Moorrees, 1957; Moorrees and Reed, 1964). Among the anterior teeth, the measurement should be ostensibly the same for either technique employed. However, with the posterior teeth, different measurements will arise based on the method employed. Within the literature, it is most common to see the maximum dimensions as defined by Moorrees and Reed (1964) employed (Hemphill, 2016b). These dimensions are typically preferred, as they are not dependent on accurate observations of contact facets and can be easier to define in cases of malocclusion (Buikstra and Ubelaker, 1994). To take the maximum dimension in the mesiodistal plane, the measurement is taken parallel to the occlusal and buccal surfaces (Fig. 7.1).

During data collection, the researcher should be careful not to collect the mesiodistal measurement on overly worn teeth. The maximum mesiodistal diameter tends to be expressed toward the occlusal surface of the tooth, particularly in anterior teeth. Therefore, interproximal or occlusal wear will effectively "erase" or reduce the maximum mesiodistal dimension. This measurement can also be difficult to take in teeth that are in occlusion, particularly if those teeth are all very close together or show malocclusion. Care must be taken to ensure that the measurements are taken accurately and that they are not overly affected by wear or attrition.

Buccolingual Diameter

The buccolingual measurement is the maximum diameter in the buccolingual, or labiolingual, plane perpendicular to the mesiodistal plane (Mayhall, 1992, 2000; Moorrees and Reed, 1964). Among anterior teeth this measurement is taken parallel to the long axis of the tooth, and not just to the crown itself (Buikstra and Ubelaker, 1994). Care must also be taken when a bulge at the cervical margin of the tooth is present, as is the case in many posterior teeth (Goose, 1963). In order to obtain the maximum diameter, bulges found at buccal or lingual surfaces should be included (Hillson, 1996) (Fig. 7.2).

Crown Height

Crown height is a third common crown measurement. For anterior teeth, the crown height is measured from the most apical point of the cementoenamel junction to the most superior aspect of the occlusal

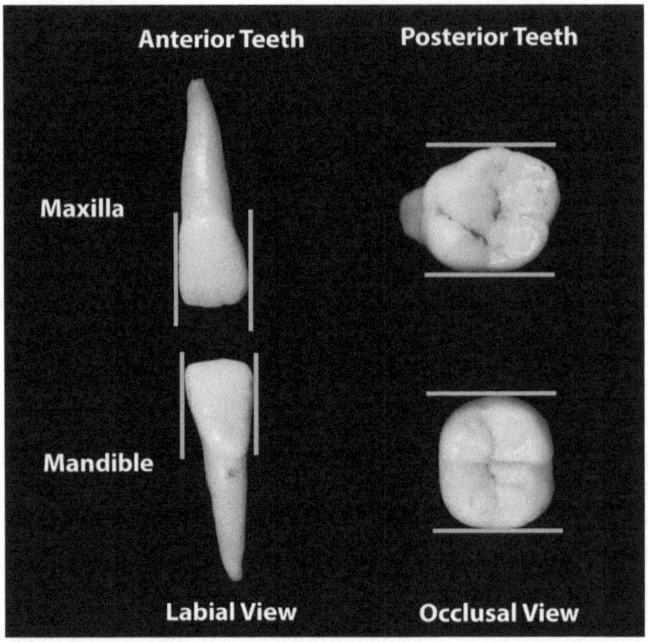

FIGURE 7.1

Maximum mesiodistal dimensions of anterior and posterior teeth.

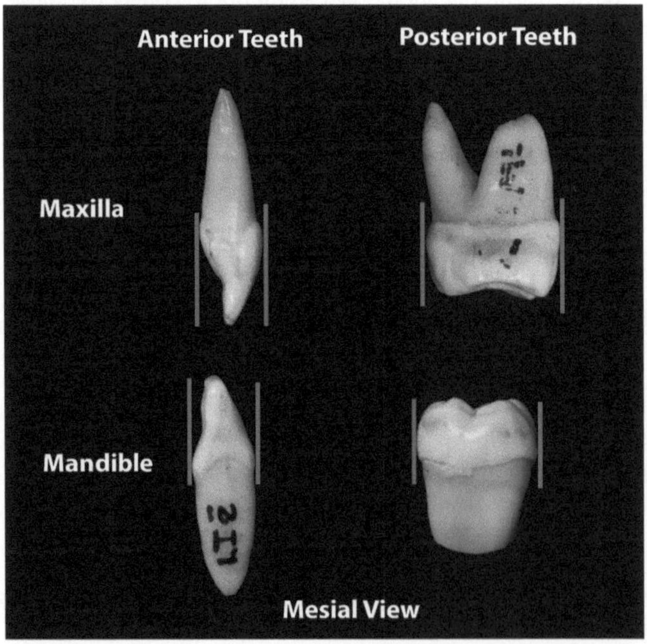

FIGURE 7.2

Maximum buccolingual dimensions of anterior and posterior teeth.

surface (Buikstra and Ubelaker, 1994). For posterior teeth, this measurement is defined as the distance between the apex of the cementoenamel junction on the buccal side of the tooth to the most superior point of the mesiobuccal cusp. This measurement is taken in the plane parallel to the vertical axis of the tooth (Moorrees, 1957). Crown height is not particularly helpful in studies of biodistance as it is directly affected by dental wear and attrition.

Alternative Measurements

Measurements may also be taken at the cervix of the tooth and serve as a means to combat missing data due to dental attrition or wear. These measurements were first introduced by Azouley and Regnault (1893) and were also discussed by Goose (1956, 1963). More recently, these alternative measurements were thoroughly described by Hillson and colleagues (2005). These cervical measurements are taken at the cervicoenamel junction with the caliper points on the enamel. On anterior teeth, the buccolingual measurements are taken at the most apical projection of the enamel, and the mesiodistal measurements are taken at the most occlusal projection of the enamel. For posterior teeth, these cervical measurements are taken at the midpoints of the tooth in each plane (Hillson et al., 2005). Cervical measurements have also been defined for deciduous teeth (Pilloud and Hillson, 2012), reflecting their unique morphology. One drawback to collecting cervical measurements is that they require the use of a specially designed (and costly) caliper, sometimes called the Hillson–Fitzgerald caliper, which is available as the Paleo-Tech dental caliper (www.paleo-tech.com).

Some scholars have explored further ways to measure teeth, criticizing the use of crown dimensions as being overly broad and failing to completely incorporate all the dental variation present. Biggerstaff (1969a,b) made an initial attempt to rectify this issue by establishing additional dental landmarks and incorporating electronic analyses. Building on this work, Morris (1981) introduced a technique to quantify angles within teeth. In Morris's method, a single angle is calculated using the buccal cusp of the third premolar by projecting a line through the midline of the tooth that is intersected by a second line that parallels the mesiobuccal and distobuccal corners of the buccal cusp. This work was later extended to maxillary first molars, wherein cusp tips are connected by lines creating an "occlusal polygon." This polygon's lengths, angles, area, and perimeter can be compared among populations (Morris, 1986). Bailey (2004) and Bailey et al. (2008) refined Morris's occlusal polygons using high-definition photography and computer software to more accurately measure the precise location of molar cusp apices.

Building on occlusal polygons, geometric morphometric techniques have been increasingly used to measure shape with higher fidelity than that of simply maximal measures. Ferrario et al. (1999) used elliptical Fourier analysis (EFA) to examine molar outline shapes among Italian females and males. First molars were photographed in occlusal view and each tooth was outlined before being submitted to EFA. Similarly, Bernal (2007) used occlusal-view photographs to assign coordinate points to maxillary second molar cusp apices and also to generate sliding semilandmarks around the margin of each molar. The raw coordinate data were subjected to a generalized Procrustes analysis to translate, scale, and rotate the data into a common shape space. Kenyhercz et al. (2014) expanded on the work of Bernal (2007) by collecting coordinate data from first and second maxillary and mandibular molars, though their approach directly measured molar cusps via a coordinate digitizer.

Intercusp dimensions of the molar have also been used to investigate variation. Harris and Dinh (2006) examined the efficacy of intercusp distances of the first and second maxillary molars as a means to investigate sexual dimorphism in US Whites. Using high-quality photographs and computer software, the apex of each cusp was marked and then the distances between all cusp pairs calculated. Somewhat similarly, Kenyhercz et al. (2014) collected data from molar cusp apices with a 3-D coordinate digitizer. The digitizer stylus was placed on each molar cusp and that point was collected. Intercusp dimensions were then generated using a simple Euclidean distance function.

HERITABILITY

Heritability is defined as the proportion of phenotypic variance attributable to genotypic variance. As with dental morphology, the genetics of dental metrics are not entirely understood. The various heritability rates in the literature are based on pedigree studies of individuals with known relationships. While these studies have documented relatively high heritabilities of tooth size (as discussed further in this section), more recent work has shifted to focus on the influences of the environment and epigenetics on tooth size (Townsend et al., 2009).

Early pedigree studies in the United Kingdom documented multifactorial genetic inheritance of tooth size with little environmental influence (Bowden and Goose, 1969; Goose, 1971). Some years later, Townsend and Brown (1978) reported heritability rates between 0.5 and 0.81 among Australians. A later study conducted on 261 Australian Aboriginal children found additive genetic effects accounted for 60% of the variation in tooth size. However, environmental factors were also found to strongly contribute to variation (Townsend, 1992). A twin study on incisor crown dimensions found heritability of the mesiodistal diameter to be between 0.81 and 0.91 (Dempsey et al., 1995). A more recent study used mathematical modeling to understand the contributions of genes and environment to the variation in tooth size. This study of nearly 600 monozygotic and dizygotic twins placed the contribution of additive genetic variation at consistently over 80%, with contributions from the environment between 8% and 29% (Dempsey and Townsend, 2001). Hughes et al. (2000) studied deciduous dental metrics among 602 individuals including dizygotic and monozygotic twins as well as siblings. Their results indicated that deciduous dental metrics were under high genetic control, with additive genetic variation accounting for 62%—91% of observed variation, which is similar to findings among adult dentition. In summary, Hughes and colleagues (2016) attribute 59%—62% of crown size to additive genetic variation, with environmental effects ranging from 8% to 29%.

Recent work has also begun to explore the heritability of intercuspal dimensions. Townsend and colleagues (2003) speculated that distances between cusps would show greater variation and lower heritability than would overall crown dimensions due to epigenetic events during odontogenesis. Their study, based on 100 monozygotic and 74 dizygotic twin pairs, found heritability of intercuspal dimensions between 43% and 79%, whereas those of the crown were between 60% and 82%, thereby confirming their hypothesis.

Despite much work on family and twin studies (for review see Hughes et al., 2016; Kieser, 1990), the exact genes involved in controlling tooth size have yet to be identified. However, some work on dental genetics has produced interesting findings. For example, the *EDAR* 370V/A genotype was found to be associated with crown size (Park et al., 2012), as was a version of *PAX9*, a transcription factor involved in dental development (Lee et al., 2012). While more work is needed to identify the genes involved in controlling tooth size, a growing body of literature has established a significant genetic component, which is an important first step in using dental metrics in biological distance studies.

BIOLOGICAL CONSIDERATIONS

Sex

In many animal species including humans, males are larger than females. Body size dimorphism of humans can vary throughout the skeleton, from very little dimorphism to as much as a 20% difference in size (Humphrey, 1998). The amount of sexual dimorphism in human tooth crown dimensions is relatively small (Harris and Couch, 2006), especially when compared with that of many species of nonhuman primates (Garn et al., 1967), with only around a 3%–7% difference between males and females (Harris and Foster, 2015). The level of dimorphism will vary depending on the tooth and the measurement; however, the canine is typically the most sexually dimorphic tooth. The evolutionary reason for sexual dimorphism of tooth size has been extensively argued (eg, Brace and Ryan, 1980; Leutenegger and Shell, 1987) and will not be reviewed here; instead, we give a brief overview of sex-related differences in tooth size relevant to studies of biodistance.

Despite low sexual dimorphism of tooth size, multiple intrapopulation studies have found males to have larger teeth than females (eg, Goose, 1971; Margetts and Brown, 1978; Moorrees, 1959; Zorba et al., 2011). Various studies have tried to take advantage of sex differences in permanent tooth size (both of the crown and the cervix) to establish methods to estimate an individual's sex. These studies report varying success rates, with correct allocation of sex between 78% and 95.5% (Ditch and Rose, 1972; Hassett, 2012; Viciano et al., 2013). Among the deciduous dentition, sexual dimorphism is reportedly low, averaging around 2% (Harris and Lease, 2005). However, discriminant analysis of the deciduous dentition has been shown to provide an accurate estimate of sex with accuracies ranging from 75% to 95% correct in test samples (Black, 1978; DeVito and Saunders, 1990), although another study found deciduous teeth to only correctly identify sex 46%–60% of the time (Cardoso, 2010). Cross-population studies of tooth size have found that levels of sexual dimorphism can be population specific, with some populations showing higher levels of dimorphism than others (Garn et al., 1967; Hanihara, 1978). Such a finding highlights the importance of population-specific standards for the application of methods to estimate sex.

Garn and colleagues (1964) were able to identify differences in dimorphism in relation to dental development among permanent teeth of Ohio children. This study reported metric differences among the sexes to be 3% during development and 5% at the time of eruption. Sexual differences have also been found in the correlation of tooth dimensions. Harris and Bailit (1988) investigated sex-specific multivariate correlation matrices based on dental measurements from 2650 individuals from the Solomon Islands. The results of the principal components analysis (PCA) found significant sexual differences in size intercorrelations, with females showing higher correlations and therefore more integrated dentitions.

Sex differences in tooth size have been identified, but unlike with the skeleton, the effect of sex hormones on sexual dimorphism has been debated. Teeth form prior to puberty and the onset of sex hormones that direct male and female size differences (Harris and Foster, 2015); therefore, teeth should express little to no sexual dimorphism if differences are tied to puberty and hormones. However, some studies have found that females with a twin brother had larger teeth, thereby suggesting that male hormones can affect the female counterpart in utero and influence tooth size (Dempsey et al., 1999; Ribeiro et al., 2013). Moss (1978) proposed that differences in crown dimensions may be the result of prolonged amelogenesis in males. This hypothesis is supported by the fact that male teeth take longer to progress from the formation of the dental papilla to the termination of crown development. Male teeth would deposit enamel at the same rate as females but over a prolonged period, which would result in larger teeth. A study of canine crown formation in extant hominoids found that, among all the hominoids studied except for

Homo, canine crown formation took significantly longer among males than among females based on analysis of histological cross sections of the canines (Schwartz and Dean, 2001).

Alternatively, X and Y chromosomes have been found to have effects on tooth dimensions. The amelogenin gene, a single-copy gene coding for a protein of tooth enamel, is found on the Y chromosome and also in the homologous region of the X chromosome (Hummel and Schultes, 2000). Smaller tooth dimensions have been found among individuals with Turner's syndrome (XO) than among individuals who are XX. Further, males who are XYY exhibit larger teeth than their normal male (XY) counterparts (Kieser, 1990; Mayhall et al., 1998). Alvesalo (1997) argues that there are differential effects of the X and Y chromosomes on tooth growth, which may help to explain sexual dimorphism in dental size and shape. Specifically, the Y chromosome is linked to growth of both the enamel and the dentin, whereas the X chromosome is only involved in enamel growth. Studies of the permanent (Saunders et al., 2007; Schwartz and Dean, 2005) and deciduous (Harris et al., 2001) teeth have found males to have more dentin than females.

Further, a study of Klinefelter males (XXY) found that they had thicker enamel than found in control males or females, and dentin thickness of incisors and canines in between those of control males and females (Alvesalo et al., 1991). A similar study of individuals with androgen insensitivity syndrome (XY females) found that they had larger teeth than found in XX females, and teeth as large as those of XY males (Alvesalo and Varrela, 1980), which again demonstrates the negligible effect of hormones on tooth development and highlights the effect of the sex chromosomes on dental development.

Guatelli-Steinberg et al. (2008) studied published mesiodistal measurements to evaluate sexual dimorphism in tooth dimensions. Their study did not lend support to various models that would indicate an influence of sex hormones on crown size. Instead, they argue that the Y chromosome is responsible for enlarging the boundary between the enamel and dentine to allow greater dentine thickness, likely through cell proliferation (Alvesalo et al., 1991), corroborating the results of Alvesalo (1997).

Age

Age can have a significant impact on tooth size. The most obvious age distinction involves the fact that humans are diphyodont, or have two sets of teeth. The deciduous, or milk, teeth emerge in infancy and all are erupted roughly around 2 years of age. The deciduous teeth are typically shed by 10 years of age. The permanent set of teeth begins to emerge around the age of 5 years, and all permanent teeth with the exception of the third molar are in occlusion by roughly 12 years of age (Schour and Massler, 1940). The third molar is a highly variable tooth with a broad range of eruption ages (eg, Arany et al., 2004; Mincer et al., 1993; Moorrees et al., 1963). In terms of biodistance studies, deciduous and permanent dentition should be considered separately, as it is not entirely clear if the two sets of dentition can be combined due to differences in overall size, tooth type, and genetic control.

Increased age can also alter size through excessive wear. Dental wear is a reduction in tooth crown during life by either dental attrition, or tooth-on-tooth contact; or by abrasion, wear caused by an abrasive object that is not another tooth (Hillson, 1996). As discussed previously, the mesiodistal diameter can decrease significantly with only moderate wear on the occlusal surface of the tooth crown. The buccolingual diameter will be affected by only extreme dental wear (Hillson, 1996). Excessive dental wear can erase any evidence of enamel, making all measurements impossible, which is a common occurrence in archaeological skeletal collections. Dental wear is problematic among both deciduous and adult dentition. In fact, deciduous teeth are likely to wear at a quicker rate than permanent teeth due to having less enamel (Harris and Lease, 2005).

Biological Stress

Selyean, or biological stress, can occur when there is a disruption of homeostasis leading to physiological disruption. Several studies have identified a link between stress and tooth size. Garn et al. (1979, 1980) conducted a study of the deciduous and permanent dentition of 870 participants in the National Collaborative Perinatal Project. Their results indicated that maternal health status was directly correlated to mesiodistal and buccolingual crown dimensions. Larger tooth dimensions were found among children of large birth size and with maternal diabetes or hyperthyroidism. In contrast, they found that smaller tooth dimensions were associated with low birth weight and maternal hypertension. Their results suggest that nearly half of the total variation in tooth size could be accounted for by maternal and fetal factors.

In a study on a Swedish sample, researchers found that preterm children had smaller permanent maxillary and mandibular first molar crowns in both dimensions, whereas incisors were only found to be smaller in the mesiodistal dimension (Paulsson-Björnsson and Bondemark, 2010). Similarly, deciduous teeth were shown to have thinner enamel in preterm children, which resulted in smaller overall tooth dimensions (Seow et al., 2005). However, other studies have found no clear difference between permanent (Harila-Kaera et al., 2001) or deciduous (Harila et al., 2003) tooth dimensions and preterm or full-term children.

Biological stress has also been linked to dental asymmetry within a single individual. Asymmetry of size can occur in three different ways: antisymmetry, in which asymmetry naturally occurs during development, as in handedness among humans; directional asymmetry, where one side will show greater development; and fluctuating asymmetry, in which random deviations from normal symmetry are observed. Dental studies have found that there is no genetic component to fluctuating asymmetry, and that it can develop purely due to developmental noise (Kieser, 1990). What exactly dental fluctuating asymmetry means at a population level is under some debate; however, based on animal studies, increased levels of fluctuating asymmetry appear related to environmental stress (Larsen, 1997). Fluctuating asymmetry in tooth crown dimensions has been used in several studies to identify stress levels of individuals and populations (eg, Barrett et al., 2012; Guatelli-Steinberg et al., 2006; Kieser et al., 1997; Perzigian, 1977).

STATISTICAL ANALYSIS

Dental metric data should be treated in various ways before biological distance analyses can proceed. First, it is important to perform exploratory analyses to ensure that the assumptions of any statistical models being used are not being violated. It is also critical to remove any other biases within the data that may emerge due to observer error, sexual dimorphism, and/or correlation of the data, all of which are discussed in the sections that follow.

Observer Error

Analyses of inter- and intraobserver error are an important and often-overlooked component to metrical studies (Harris and Smith, 2009). Observer error studies typically involve a reanalysis of roughly 10% of the total sample size in the study. Data collection could be separated by a certain length of time, although this has not been shown to have a strong effect on error rates (Kieser et al., 1990). Summary statistics can be generated to report a mean observer error measurement with a standard deviation. The mean measurement error can be further divided by tooth and/or measurement type to more fully understand the source of error. Various other statistical methods can be employed to evaluate measurement error. Harris and Smith (2009) summarize these methods to include correlation coefficients, analysis of variance (ANOVA), the Bland–Altman procedure, or Dahlberg's *d* (also referred to as Solow's error statistic or method error statistic). Other studies have used the student's *t*-test (Stojanowski, 2005; Vodanović et al., 2007), Lin's concordance correlation coefficient (Viciano et al., 2013), or reported the standard error (Kieser, 1990).

Within the study of dental metrics, there are varying opinions on the level of error and how it could affect data sets. Kieser and Groeneveld (1991) conducted an intra- and interobserver error study on the measurement of teeth and found that there was a large error component. They found error to be more marked in the anterior teeth than in the posterior teeth, in the mesiodistal dimensions over the buccolingual, and between observers rather than within a single observer. Pilloud et al. (2014) also found more error between observers and in the mesiodistal dimension; however, this study found low error rates and greater error in the posterior teeth as opposed to the anterior teeth.

Overall, many other studies have reported low mean error rates in crown dimensions. As there are far fewer studies using cervical dental metrics or other alternate measurement types (eg, occlusal polygons), the present discussion of observer error is focused on mesiodistal and buccolingual crown dimensions. Mean intraobserver error rates have been reported between −0.06 and 0.06 mm, with standard deviations between 0.18 and 0.30 (Haddow and Lovell, 2003; Kieser et al., 1986; Kolakowski and Bailit, 1981; Lukacs and Hemphill, 1991; Stojanowski, 2005). Interobserver error rates have been reported between 0.05 and 0.16 mm (Hattab et al., 1997; Kolakowski and Bailit, 1981). These error rates are considerably low, even when appropriately scaled to the overall dimensions of the teeth. Given the relatively low error both between and within observers, dental metrics are valuable data sets for biological distance studies.

Sexual Dimorphism

There are various ways that sexual dimorphism may be handled within a data set. First, males and females could be analyzed completely separately as distinct data sets. However, such a practice is not always preferable in biodistance studies, as it may affect sample sizes or could make it difficult to fully address the proposed research questions. Alternatively, the variables found to be sexually dimorphic (based on univariate analyses with a Bonferroni correction for significance) can be removed from the study. Such a practice may be helpful in pruning data sets, which would be particularly useful with small sample sizes in order to reduce the likelihood of overfitting the data.

Most commonly, sexual dimorphism in data sets is treated through data transformation. In place of the raw data, sex-specific z-scores can be used. Each sex and each sample would be calculated individually to develop z-scores based on the arithmetic mean for each individual. Another common method is to shape transform the data using the log-geometric mean (Darroch and Mosimann, 1985).

Methods to Negate Multicollinearity

Many multivariate analyses, such as discriminant function analysis, assume that variables submitted to the analysis are not highly correlated (Klecka, 1980). Given the strong correlations among teeth within the dental arcade, data must be treated to remove correlations. Such treatment could include the identification and removal of correlated variables before multivariate analyses are conducted. However, there are also several techniques that can transform the raw data into something more useful for investigating variation within and among populations without leading to a reduction in the number of variables used in analyses.

Dental Indices. Populations differ in tooth size in one of two ways: (1) the overall average size of the majority of the variables (ie, a "size difference"); and (2) the relative distribution of size differences within the arcade, or "shape" differences. Wolpoff (1971) put forth the dental robusticity index (RI), which multiplies mesiodistal and buccolingual measures. Wolpoff believed that RI would essentially approximate the total occlusal area. Lukacs (1985) demonstrated the utility of several other dental indices including incisor breadth index, the molarization index, and the step-index. The incisor breadth index examines the relative proportion of incisor breadths by dividing the mesiodistal diameter of the lateral incisor by the mesiodistal diameter of the central incisor. The molarization index divides the buccolingual diameter of the lower second premolar by the buccolingual diameter of the lower first molar, essentially examining the relative "molar-ness" of the second premolar based on relative size. The step-index divides the buccolingual diameter of the second molar by the buccolingual diameter of the first molar, both maxillary and mandibular, to examine the relative size discrepancies. While the use of dental indices improved the utility of odontometric variables, Schmidt et al. (2011) suggested that dental indices, particularly RI, overestimate occlusal area.

PCA and Tooth Size Apportionment (TSA). PCA is a data reduction technique that takes a combination of correlated variables (in this case buccolingual and mesiodistal measures) and transforms them into a smaller subset of uncorrelated variables known as principal components (PCs) (Jolliffe, 2002). In PCA, each of the original variables influences each PC with different weights known as loadings. The relative influence of each variable is judged by the greatest loading, either positive or negative. Typically, the first PC comprises only positive loadings and is then considered to represent the overall size component (Jolliffe, 2002), and subsequent PCs are then thought to represent "shape" data. The number of PCs generated will equal the number of variables in the analysis; however, the first few PCs typically account for the majority of the variability in the sample as judged by eigenvalues. While there is no standard for selecting a particular eigenvalue cutoff for deciding how many PCs to retain, many studies only use PCs with eigenvalues greater than 1 (Kaiser, 1960). However, Jolliffe (2002) noted that PCs with eigenvalues over 0.7 should be retained.

PCA will have the option to rotate the data during the analysis. Rotation has traditionally been used to more easily interpret the PCs because the variance is distributed across the derived components (Kachigan, 1991). Harris (1997) suggests that varimax rotation should be utilized in odontometrics because the loadings for each PC are pushed to either one or zero, which simplifies interpretation. However, Hemphill (1991) argued that no rotation should be employed. Harris (1997) detailed three advantages to using PCA with odontometrics: (1) data are reduced into a compound variable that can be used to show shared variation; (2) developmental and statistical fields controlling tooth size are disclosed when PCA is used; and (3) each PC is statistically independent or uncorrelated. In some instances, PC1 is simply removed from the analysis, however, as noted by Harris (1997), there is still useful "shape" information in PC1.

The relative size of different dental fields, or how size is apportioned throughout the dental arcade, is an important consideration (Irish and Kenyhercz, 2013). TSA analysis examines the relative size of different teeth in the dental arcade within and among populations. TSA analysis has several advantages: (1) it removes the effect of overall size that often obscures odontometric relationships; (2) it is methodologically straightforward; and (3) with only population means necessary for analysis, many more meta-analyses can be conducted from published results.

To conduct TSA, a covariance matrix of mean buccolingual and mesiodistal diameters is submitted to PCA (Irish and Hemphill, 2004). Next, each of the diameters is multiplied by the loading for each tooth dimension. Then the PC scores are regressed on some size measure. To examine the relative effect of size within the dentition, Harris and Rathbun (1989) regressed the PC scores with the sum of mesiodistal measures within the arcade. The resulting regression line then showed the expected PC scores given size. Deviations from this regression line (observed scores minus expected scores, otherwise known as residuals), demonstrate how tooth size has been apportioned. For example, if a group was shown to have positive residuals, or have a relatively greater PC score than estimated through regression, teeth with greater loadings on that PC score are proportionally larger than in other groups with negative residuals (Harris, 1997). However, Harris (1997) later advocated using three size measures to regress the PC scores: the sum of each of the mesiodistal X buccolingual measures, the sum of each of the mesiodistal measures, and the sum of each of the buccolingual measures. Harris (1997) argued that different PCs will be more in line with lengths or widths than simply with area.

POPULATION VARIATION AND EVOLUTION

The potential for tooth size to discriminate populations has been appreciated for some time, beginning with the work of Flower. Using the dental index expressed as:

$$\frac{\text{Dental Length} \times 100}{\text{Basio} - \text{Nasal Length}} \tag{7.1}$$

Flower derived three dental classes: microdonts (dental index <42), mesodonts (dental indices between 42 and 44), and megadonts (dental index >44). Each class was further assigned to a general population; European white groups were identified as microdonts, Asians as mesodonts, and Australian aborigines and American Blacks as megadonts. Comparative odontometrics continued with the work of Selmer-Olsen (1949), who described various populations in relation to one another. In this work, large teeth were considered common of Australians, Melanesians, American Indians, and Eskimos. Lapps and Bushmen were described as having the smallest teeth, and European and White American populations were found to vary greatly in tooth size. Lasker and Lee (1957) summarized much of this early work to succinctly identify "large-toothed and small-toothed races" (p. 403). More recent work by Schnutenhaus and Rösing (1998), using a large data set of dental metrics, discovered that sample populations were largely separated by population, in groups they identified as "Europids, Melanesids, Negrids, and Mongolids" (p. 530). Hanihara and Ishida (2005) described a dental paradigm wherein Australians have the largest teeth, followed by Melanesians, Micronesians, sub-Saharan Africans, and Native Americans. East and Southeast Asians, and Polynesians possess teeth intermediate in size, while Philippine Negritos, Jomon, Ainu, and Western Eurasians have the smallest teeth.

In addition to the absolute size of teeth, there may be differences in the relative sizes of teeth within the dental arcade. For example, Lasker and Lee (1957) summarize research that found Australians have large second molars, as opposed to the first molar being the largest. Other research found that Whites have second lateral incisors that are much smaller than the central ones, whereas "mongoloids" (Asian populations) do not show the same size discrepancy. Pilloud et al. (2014) also found that Asian populations tend to have large anterior teeth.

While there are general population differences in tooth size that can be identified among anatomically modern humans, there has been a general trend of dental reduction during hominin evolution beginning with the Australopithecines (Bermudez de Castro and Nicolas, 1995; Brace et al., 1991). Throughout the Australopith lineage, cheek teeth saw an increase in area relative to overall body size, which was reversed in later *Homo* (McHenry and Coffing, 2000).

Starting 100,000 years ago, tooth size reduction was approximately 1% every 2000 years. Then, beginning 10,000 years ago, this rate of reduction doubled to 1% every 1000 years (Brace et al., 1987). There has been considerable debate as to the exact mechanism of this reduction. Brace (1963, 1964) proposed the probable mutation effect to explain this change in size. Within this model, advances in food preparation technology caused a relaxation of selective forces on masticatory anatomy. This relaxation would result in an accumulation of mutations that ultimately caused tooth size reduction. However, others do not see how probable mutations could logically explain this size reduction and instead offer alternate explanations such as natural selection (Bailit and Friedlaender, 1966; Calcagno and Gibson, 1988). Additionally, Pinhasi and Meiklejohn (2011) argue that there is regional variation in dental reduction trends and the process is likely complex, particularly when considering heritability, dental development, environmental effects, and epigenetics.

FORENSIC APPLICATIONS

While population differences in tooth size have been recognized for some time, the utility of dental metrics for population affinity estimation has not been as thoroughly researched. Much like dental morphology (see, Chapter 6, this volume), dental metrics have not been adopted by forensic anthropologists in standard practice. However, within the forensic anthropological literature, patterned differences in tooth sizes have been reported among ancestral groups. The pattern, similar to the one mentioned earlier, shows that Africans tend to have large teeth (particularly posterior teeth), Asians have intermediate-sized teeth, and Europeans have small posterior teeth with larger anterior teeth (Schmidt, 2008). Several studies have utilized tooth size to differentiate populations and to classify individuals within those populations, all with varying levels of success (eg, Falk and Corruccini, 1982; Harris, 2003; Harris and Rathbun, 1991; Kieser and Groeneveld, 1989; Lavelle, 1973; Lease and Sciulli, 2005; Shields et al., 1989).

Pilloud and colleagues (2014) used a large global data set to explore the allocation power of the maximum dimensions of the dental crown into one of three broad groups: African, Asian, or European. Using a discriminant function analysis, they found that when sex was already known, the cross-validated model was correct in 88% of female cases and 72% of male cases. Their study also provided a series of discriminant function equations that could be used by the forensic anthropologist to estimate ancestry in an individual of known sex. A disadvantage to the Pilloud et al. (2014) method is that the equations provided require a full set of dentition; that is, a complete set of teeth from one-half of the dental arcade (maxilla and mandible), excluding the third molar. Additionally, the sample size for females of African ancestry was quite small, requiring caution in the employment of one of the female discriminant function equations.

Similarly, Harris and Foster (2015) conducted a study on crown dimensions of modern teeth with a smaller sample of American Black and White females from the mid-Southern United States. They provide a series of equations with reported cross-validation rates that can be used to estimate ancestry or sex. These equations have the advantage of only requiring a few measurements; however, they can only distinguish between American Black and White individuals and may only be useful to a small area of the United States.

Kenyhercz (2014) measured the intercusp distances on maxillary and mandibular first and second molars of 480 modern US individuals from three ancestry groups (Black = 119; Hispanic = 198; White = 163). The intercusp distances were submitted to a discriminant function utilizing forward stepwise selection and leave-one-out cross-validation. The discriminant function achieved a total correct classification of 66.3%. Further, two-dimensional coordinates of the same molar cusps were analyzed, which were subjected to a generalized Procrustes analysis, PCA, and discriminant function analysis. Using the geometric morphometric shape variables, the model achieved a total correct classification of 72.3%. These data are freely available by request from the coauthor (Kenyhercz) or on the web (http://michaelkenyhercz.weebly.com).

Discriminant function is a common statistical method within forensic anthropology to classify individuals when using metric data, as these studies have illustrated. However, Lease and Sciulli (2005) used logistic regression to discriminate between African-American and European-American deciduous teeth using dental metrics and morphology with accuracy rates between 90.1% and 92.6%.

Given the ease and repeatability of recording dental metrics, it would be fairly straightforward to incorporate them into a program like Fordisc 3.0 (Jantz and Ousley, 2005), or in the statistical program R. The only requirement would be to have a large reference sample that would be relevant for use in a forensic context. Further, the utility in combining dental metrics with other data sets (eg, craniometrics) has yet to be fully tested as a means of increasing accuracy rates.

BIOARCHAEOLOGICAL APPLICATIONS

Within bioarchaeology, dental metrics have been used extensively in exploring population variation to answer archaeologically relevant research questions. This research can be done at various levels to compare phenotypic similarity between individuals, archaeologically or biologically defined groups within a site, or among populations.

Individuals can be compared with univariate statistics such as ANOVA or with multivariate techniques such as Euclidean distances measures, discriminant function analysis, PCA (eg, Jacobi, 2000; Pilloud, 2009; Thompson et al., 2015), or Q-mode correlation (Adachi et al., 2006). Such methods can be used to identify biological affinity of individuals and explore questions surrounding kinship, cemetery organization, and social structure. Dental metric data have also be used to explore postmarital residence practices, which may involve univariate tests (*F*-test to identify within-group variance, ANOVA) and multivariate analyses (PCA, discriminant function, R-matrix) (eg, Pilloud, 2009, 2013; Schillaci and Stojanowski, 2003).

Dental metrics have also been used to explore biological relationships among populations. Such studies can address the evolutionary forces of gene flow and drift, thereby providing an avenue to address questions surrounding population contact and migration. Such work has been performed in postcontact Spanish Florida (Stojanowski, 2004) and Neolithic Anatolia (Pilloud, 2009), among contemporary South Asian populations (Hemphill, 1991, 2016a), for pre-Hispanic Mesoamerica (Aubry, 2009) and classic period Maya (Scherer, 2007), and to explore the population history of Southeast Asia (Matsumura and Hudson, 2005).

CONCLUSIONS

Dental metrics have been used to answer a variety of anthropological questions, from helping explain a reduction in tooth size through time to examining nebulous population histories and prehistoric social structure. Forensically, dental metrics have been shown to have great success at correctly classifying unknown individuals. Within this discussion of dental metrics, we have tried to highlight the salient points to consider in using these types of data to include factors relating to stress, sex, age, heritability rates, and development. This exploration of tooth size is critical, as fully understanding the data is a first step in implementing appropriate statistical treatment.

Given the relative ease of data collection and the low intra- and interobserver error, dental metrics have great potential for biological distance studies. Continued technical advances in the study of odontometrics, such as advanced imagining techniques and data collection protocols, as well as statistical methods, will only enhance the study of modern human dental variation.

Endnote

1. The reader can refer to, Chapter 6, this volume, for a general overview on dental terminology.

References

Adachi, N., Suzuki, T., Sakaue, K., Takigawa, W., Ohshima, N., Dodo, Y., 2006. Kinship analysis of the Jomon skeletons unearted from a double burial at the Usu-Moshiri site, Hokkaido, Japan. Anthropological Science 114, 29–34.

Alin, A., 2010. Multicollinearity. Wiley Interdisciplinary Reviews: Computational Statistics 2 (3), 370–374.

Alvesalo, L., 1997. Sex chromosomes and human growth: a dental approach. Human Genetics 101, 1–5.

Alvesalo, L., Tammisalo, E., Townsend, G., 1991. Upper central incisor and canine tooth crown size in 47,XXY males. Journal of Dental Research 70 (7), 1057–1060.

Alvesalo, L., Tigerstedt, M.A., 1974. Heritabilities of human tooth dimension. Hereditas 77, 311–318.

Alvesalo, L., Varrela, J., 1980. Permanent tooth sizes in 46,XY females. American Journal of Human Genetics 32 (5), 736–742.

Arany, S., Iino, M., Yoshioka, N., 2004. Radiographic survey of third molar development in relation to chronological age among Japanese juveniles. Journal of Forensic Sciences 49 (3), 534–538.

Aubry, B.S., 2009. Population Structure and Interregional Interaction in Pre-Hispanic Mesoamerica: A Biodistance Study. Department of Anthropology, Columbus. The Ohio State University.

Azouley, O., Regnault, O., 1893. Variation in the form of the teeth. Bulletins et Memoires de la Societe d'Anthropologie de Paris 4, 266.

Bailey, S., Glantz, M., Weaver, T.D., Viola, B., 2008. The affinity of the dental remains from Obi-Rakhmat Grotto, Uzbekistan. Journal of Human Evolution 55 (2), 238–248.

Bailey, S.E., 2004. A morphometric analysis of maxillary molar crowns of Middle-Late Pleistocene hominins. Journal of Human Evolution 47 (3), 183–198.

Bailit, H.L., Friedlaender, J.S., 1966. Tooth size reduction: a hominid trend. American Anthropologist 68 (3), 665–672.

Barrett, C.K., Guatelli-Steinberg, D., Sciulli, P.W., 2012. Revisiting dental fluctuating asymmetry in neandertals and modern humans. American Journal of Physical Anthropology 149 (2), 193–204.

Bermudez de Castro, J.M., Nicolas, M.E., 1995. Posterior dental size reduction in hominids: the Atapuerca evidence. American Journal of Physical Anthropology 96 (4), 335–356.

Bernal, V., 2007. Size and shape analysis of human molars: comparing traditional and geometric morphometric techniques. HOMO—Journal of Comparative Human Biology 58 (4), 279—296.
Biggerstaff, R.H., 1969a. The basal area of posterior tooth crown components: the assessment of within tooth variations of premolars and molars. American Journal of Physical Anthropology 31, 163—170.
Biggerstaff, R.H., 1969b. Electronic models for the analysis of the human post-canine dentition. American Journal of Physical Anthropology 31, 235—242.
Black, T.K., 1978. Sexual dimorphism in the tooth-crown diameters of the deciduous teeth. American Journal of Physical Anthropology 48, 77—82.
Bowden, D., Goose, D., 1969. Inheritance of tooth size in Liverpool families. Journal of Medical Genetics 6 (1), 55.
Brace, C., Smith, S., Hunt, K., 1991. What big teeth you had grandma! Human tooth size past and present. In: Kelley, M., Larsen, C. (Eds.), Advances in Dental Anthropology. Wiley-Liss, New York, pp. 33—58.
Brace, C.L., 1963. Structural reduction in evolution. American Naturalist 39—49.
Brace, C.L., 1964. The probable mutation effect. American Naturalist 453—455.
Brace, C.L., Rosenberg, K.R., Hunt, K.D., 1987. Gradual change in human tooth size in the late Pleistocene and Post-Pleistocene. Evolution 41 (4), 705—720.
Brace, C.L., Ryan, A.S., 1980. Sexual dimorphism and human tooth size differences. Journal of Human Evolution 9 (5), 417—435.
Buikstra, J.E., Ubelaker, D.H. (Eds.), 1994. Standards for Data Collection from Human Skeletal Remains. Arkansas Archeological Survey Research Series No. 44, Fayetteville, Arkansas.
Butler, P., 1939. Studies in the mammalian dentition — and of differentiation of the postcanine dentition. Proceedings of the Zoological Society, London B 107, 130—132.
Calcagno, J.M., Gibson, K.R., 1988. Human dental reduction: natural selection or the probable mutation effect. American Journal of Physical Anthropology 77 (4), 505—517.
Cardoso, H.F.V., 2010. Testing discriminant functions for sex determination from deciduous teeth. Journal of Forensic Sciences 55 (6), 1557—1560.
Dahlberg, A., 1945. The changing dentition of man. Journal of the American Dental Association 32, 676—690.
Darroch, J.N., Mosimann, J.E., 1985. Canonical principal components of shape. Biometrika 72 (2), 241—252.
Dempsey, P.J., Townsend, G.C., 2001. Genetic and environmental contributions to variation in human tooth size. Heredity 86 (6), 685—693.
Dempsey, P.J., Townsend, G.C., Martin, N., Neale, M., 1995. Genetic covariance structure of incisor crown size in twins. Journal of Dental Research 74 (7), 1389—1398.
Dempsey, P.J., Townsend, G.C., Richards, L.C., 1999. Increased tooth crown size in females with twin brothers: evidence for hormonal diffusion between human twins in utero. American Journal of Human Biology 11 (5), 577—586.
DeVito, C., Saunders, S.R., 1990. A discriminant function analysis of deciduous teeth to determine sex. Journal of Forensic Sciences 35 (4), 845—858.
Ditch, L.E., Rose, J.C., 1972. A multivariate dental sexing technique. American Journal of Physical Anthropology 37, 61—64.
Duverger, O., Morasso, M.I., 2008. MIRole of homeobox genes in the patterning, specification, and differentiation of ectodermal appendages in mammals. Journal of Cell Physicology 216, 337—346.
Falk, D., Corruccini, R.S., 1982. Efficacy of cranial versus dental measurements for separating human populations. American Journal of Physical Anthropology 57, 123—127.
Feeney, R.N.M., Zermeno, J.P., Reid, D.J., Nakashima, S., Sano, H., Bahar, A., Hublin, J.-J., Smith, T.M., 2010. Enamel thickness in Asian human canines and premolars. Anthropological Science 118 (3), 191—198.
Ferrario, V.F., Sforza, C., Tartaglia, G.M., Colombo, A., Serrao, G., 1999. Size and shape of the human first permanent molar: a fourier analysis of the occlusal and equatorial outlines. American Journal of Physical Anthropology 108 (3), 281—294.

Garn, S., Osborne, R., Alvesalo, L., Horowitz, L., 1980. Maternal and gestational influences on deciduous and permanent tooth size. Journal of Dental Research 59 (2), 142–143.

Garn, S.M., Lewis, A.B., Kerewsky, R.S., 1964. Sex difference in tooth size. Journal of Dental Research 43, 306.

Garn, S.M., Lewis, A.B., Swindler, D.R., Kerewsky, R.S., 1967. Genetic control of sexual dimorphism in tooth size. Journal of Dental Research 46 (5), 963–973.

Garn, S.M., Osborne, R., McCabe, K., 1979. The effects of prenatal factors on crown dimesions. American Journal of Physical Anthropology 51, 665–678.

Goose, D.H., 1956. Variability in the form of maxillary permanent incisors. Journal of Dental Research 35, 902–908.

Goose, D.H., 1963. Dental measurement: an assessment of its value in anthropological studies. In: Brothwell, D.R. (Ed.), Dental Anthropology. Pergamon, New York, pp. 125–148.

Goose, D.H., 1971. The inheritance of tooth size in British families. In: Dahlberg, A.A. (Ed.), Dental Morphology and Evolution. The University of Chicago Press, Chicago, pp. 263–269.

Greene, D.L., 1967. Genetics, Dentition and Taxonomy, 33. Wyoming Publication, pp. 93–168.

Guatelli-Steinberg, D., Sciulli, P.W., Betsinger, T.K., 2008. Dental crown size and sex hormone concentrations: another look at the development of sexual dimorphism. American Journal of Physical Anthropology 137 (3), 324–333.

Guatelli-Steinberg, D., Sciulli, P.W., Edgar, H.J.H., 2006. Dental fluctuating asymmetry in the Gullah: tests of hypotheses regarding developmental stability in deciduous vs. permanent and male vs. female teeth. American Journal of Physical Anthropology 129 (3), 427–434.

Haddow, S., Lovell, N.C., 2003. Metric analysis of permanent and deciduous teeth from Bronze Age Tell Leilan, Syria. Dental Anthropology 16 (3), 73–80.

Hanihara, K., 1978. Differences in sexual dimorphism in dental morphology among several human populations. In: Bulter, P.M., Joysey, K.A. (Eds.), Development, Function and Evolution of Teeth. Academic Press, London, pp. 127–134.

Hanihara, T., Ishida, H., 2005. Metric dental variation of major human populations. American Journal of Physical Anthropology 128, 287–298.

Harila-Kaera, V., Heikkinen, T., Alvesalo, L., Osborne, R.H., 2001. Permanent tooth crown dimensions in prematurely born children. Early Human Development 62 (2), 131–147.

Harila, V., Heikkinen, T., Alvesalo, L., 2003. Deciduous tooth crown size in prematurely born children. Early Human Development 75 (1–2), 9–20.

Harris, E.F., 1997. A strategy for comparing odontometrics among groups. Dental Anthropology 12 (1), 1–5.

Harris, E.F., 2003. Where's the variation? Variance components in tooth sizes of the permanent dentition. Dental Anthropology 16 (3), 84–94.

Harris, E.F., Bailit, H.L., 1988. A principal components analysis of human odontometrics. American Journal of Physical Anthropology 75, 87–99.

Harris, E.F., Couch, W.M.J., 2006. The relative sexual dimorphism of human incisor crown and root dimensions. Dental Anthropology 19 (3), 87–95.

Harris, E.F., Dinh, D.P., 2006. Intercusp relationships of the permanent maxillary first and second molars in American whites. American Journal of Physical Anthropology 130 (4), 514–528.

Harris, E.F., Foster, C.L., 2015. Size matters: discrimination between American Blacks and Whites, males and females, using tooth crown dimensions. In: Berg, G.E., Ta'ala, S.C. (Eds.), Biological Affinity in Forensic Identification of Human Skeletal Remains. CRC Press, Boca Raton, FL, pp. 209–238.

Harris, E.F., Hicks, J.D., Barcroft, B.D., 2001. Tissue contributions to sex and race: differences in tooth crown size of deciduous molars. American Journal of Physical Anthropology 115 (3), 223–237.

Harris, E.F., Lease, L.R., 2005. Mesiodistal tooth crown dimensions of the primary dentition: a worldwide survey. American Journal of Physical Anthropology 128, 593–607.

Harris, E.F., Rathbun, T.A., 1989. Small tooth sizes in a nineteenth century South Carolina plantation slave series. American Journal of Physical Anthropology 78 (3), 411–420.

Harris, E.F., Rathbun, T.A., 1991. Ethnic differences in the apportionment of tooth sizes. In: Kelley, M.A., Larsen, C.S. (Eds.), Advances in Dental Anthropology. Wiley-Liss, New York, pp. 121–142.

Harris, E.F., Smith, R.N., 2009. Accounting for measurement error: a critical but often overlooked process. Archives of Oral Biology 54, S107–S117.

Hassett, B., 2012. Technical note: estimating sex using cervical canine odontometrics: a test using a known sex sample. American Journal of Physical Anthropology 146, 486–489.

Hattab, F., Al-Momani, A.S., Yassin, O.M., 1997. Odontometric study of deciduous and permanent teeth in Jordanians. Dental News 4, 17–24.

Hemphill, B.E., 1991. Tooth Size Apportionment Among Contemporary Indians: An Analysis of Caste, Language, and Geography. Anthropology: University of Oregon.

Hemphill, B.E., 2016a. Assessing odontometric variation among populations. In: Irish, J.D., Scott, G.R. (Eds.), A Companion to Dental Anthropology. John Wiley & Sons, Inc., Malden, MA, pp. 311–336.

Hemphill, B.E., 2016b. Measurement of tooth size (odontometrics). In: Irish, J.D., Scott, G.R. (Eds.), A Companion to Dental Anthropology. John Wiley & Sons, Inc., Malden, MA, pp. 287–310.

Hillson, S., 1996. Dental Anthropology. Cambridge University Press, Cambridge.

Hillson, S., FitzGerald, C., Flinn, H., 2005. Alternative dental measurements: proposals and relationships with other measurements. American Journal of Physical Anthropology 126, 413–426.

Hughes, T., Dempsey, P., Richards, L., Townsend, G.C., 2000. Genetic analysis of deciduous tooth size in Australian twins. Archives of Oral Biology 45 (11), 997–1004.

Hughes, T., Townsend, G., Bockmann, M., 2016. An overview of dental genetics. In: Irish, J.D., Scott, G.R. (Eds.), A Companion to Dental Anthropology. Wiley & Sons, Inc., Malden, MA, pp. 124–141.

Hummel, S., Schultes, T., 2000. From skeletons to fingerprints – STR typing of ancient DNA. Ancient Biomolecules 3 (2), 103–117.

Humphrey, L.T., 1998. Growth patterns in the modern human skeleton. American Journal of Physical Anthropology 105 (1), 57–72.

Irish, J.D., Hemphill, B.E., 2004. An odontometric investigation of Canary Islander origins. Dental Anthropology 17 (1), 8–17.

Irish, J.D., Kenyhercz, M.W., 2013. Size does matter: variation in tooth size apportionment among major regional North and sub-Saharan African populations. Dental Anthropology 26 (3), 38–44.

Jacobi, K.P., 2000. Last Rites for the Tipu Maya: Genetic Structuring in a Colonial Cemetery. University of Alabama Press, Tuscaloosa.

Jantz, R., Ousley, S., 2005. FORDISC 3: Computerized Forensic Discriminant Functions. The University of Tennessee, Knoxville.

Jolliffe, I., 2002. Principal Component Analysis. Wiley Online Library.

Kachigan, S.K., 1991. Multivariate Statistical Analysis: A Conceptual Introduction. Radius Press, New York, NY.

Kaiser, H.F., 1960. The application of electronic computers to factor analysis. Educational and Psychological Measurement 20 (1), 141–151.

Kenyhercz, M.W., 2014. Molar Size and Shape in the Estimation of Biological Affinity: A Comparison of Relative Cusp Locations Using Geometric Morphometrics and Interlandmark Distances. Department of Anthropology: University of Alaska, Fairbanks.

Kenyhercz, M.W., Klales, A.R., Kenyhercz, W.E., 2014. Molar size and shape in the estimation of biological ancestry: a comparison of relative cusp location using geometric morphometrics and interlandmark distances. American Journal of Physical Anthropology 153 (2), 269–279.

Kieser, J., Groeneveld, H., 1991. The reliability of human odontometric data. The Journal of the Dental Association of South Africa = Die Tydskrif van die Tandheelkundige Vereniging van Suid-Afrika 46 (5), 267–270.

Kieser, J.A., 1990. Human Adult Odontometrics: The Study of Variation in Adult Tooth Size. Cambridge University Press, Cambridge.

Kieser, J.A., Groeneveld, H.T., 1989. Allocation and discrimination based on human odontometric data. American Journal of Physical Anthropology 79 (3), 331–337.

Kieser, J.A., Groeneveld, H.T., Da Silva, P.C., 1997. Dental asymmetry, maternal obesity, and smoking. American Journal of Physical Anthropology 102 (1), 133–139.

Kieser, J.A., Groeneveld, H.T., McKee, J., Cameron, N., 1990. Measurement error in human dental mesuration. Annals of Human Biology 17 (6), 523–528.

Kieser, J.A., Groeneveld, H.T., Preston, C., 1986. Fluctuating dental asymmetry as a measure of odontogenic canalization in man. American Journal of Physical Anthropology 71 (4), 437–444.

Klecka, W.R., 1980. Discriminant Analysis. Sage, Thousand Oaks, CA.

Kolakowski, D., Bailit, H.L., 1981. A differential environmental effect on human anterior tooth size. American Journal of Physical Anthropology 54, 377–381.

Larsen, C.S., 1997. Bioarchaeology: Interpreting Behavior from the Human Skeleton. Cambridge University Press, Cambridge.

Lasker, G.W., Lee, M.M., 1957. Racial traits in the human teeth. Journal of Forensic Sciences 2, 401–419.

Lavelle, C., 1973. Odontometric comparisons between maxillary premolars and molars of different ethnic groups. Human Biology 45 (2), 123–135.

Lease, L.R., Sciulli, P.W., 2005. Brief communication. Discrimination between European-American and African-American children based on deciduous dental metrics and morphology. American Journal of Physical Anthropology 126 (1), 56–60.

Lee, W.-C., Yamaguchi, T., Watanabe, C., Kawaguchi, A., Takeda, M., Kim, Y.-I., Haga, S., Tomoyasu, Y., Ishida, H., Maki, K., Park, S.-B., Kimura, R., 2012. Association of common PAX9 variants with permanent tooth size variation in non-syndromic East Asian populations. Journal of Human Genetics 57 (10), 654–659.

Leutenegger, W., Shell, B., 1987. Variability and sexual dimorphism in canine size of Australopithecus and extant hominoids. Journal of Human Evolution 16 (4), 359–367.

Lukacs, J.R., 1985. Tooth size variation in prehistoric India. American Anthropologist 87 (4), 811–825.

Lukacs, J.R., Hemphill, B.E., 1991. The dental anthropology of prehistoric Baluchistan: a morphometric approach to the peopling of south Asia. In: Kelly, M., Larsen, C.S. (Eds.), Advances in Dental Anthropology. Wiley-Liss, New York, pp. 77–119.

Margetts, B., Brown, T., 1978. Crown diameters of the deciduous teeth in Australian Aboriginals. American Journal of Physical Anthropology 48 (4), 493–502.

Matsumura, H., 2001. Differentials of Yayoi immigration to Japan as derived from dental metrics. HOMO — Journal of Comparative Human Biology 52 (2), 135–156.

Matsumura, H., Hudson, M.J., 2005. Dental perspectives on the population history of Southeast Asia. American Journal of Physical Anthropology 127 (2), 182–209.

Mayhall, J.T., 1992. Techniques for the study of dental morphology. In: Saunders, S.R., Katzenberg, M.A. (Eds.), The Skeletal Biology of Past Peoples: Research Methods. Wiley-Liss, New York, pp. 59–78.

Mayhall, J.T., 2000. Dental morphology: techniques and strategies. In: Katzenberg, M.A., Saunders, S.R. (Eds.), Biological Anthropology of the Human Skeleton. Wiley-Liss, New York, pp. 103–134.

Mayhall, J.T., Alvesalo, L., Townsend, G.C., 1998. Dental morphology of 47,XYY males: molar cusp area, volume, shape, and linear dimensions. In: Lukacs, J.R. (Ed.), Human Dental Development, Morphology and Pathology: A Tribute to Albert A. Dahlberg. University of Oregon, Eugene, pp. 29–39.

McHenry, H.M., Coffing, K., 2000. Australopithecus to Homo: transformations in body and mind. Annual Review of Anthropology 29, 125–146.

Mincer, H.H., Harris, E.F., Berryman, H.E., 1993. The A.B.F.O. study of third molar development and its use as an estimator of chronological age. Journal of Forensic Sciences 38 (2), 379–390.

Moorrees, C., Fanning, E., Hunt, E., 1963. Age variation of formation stages for ten permanent teeth. Journal of Dental Research 42, 1490–1502.

Moorrees, C.F.A., 1957. The Aleut Dentition. Harvard University Press, Cambridge, Massachusetts.

Moorrees, C.F.A., 1959. The Dentition of the Growing Child. Harvard University Press, Cambridge.

Moorrees, C.F.A., Reed, R.B., 1964. Correlations among crown diameters of human teeth. Archives of Oral Biology 9, 685–697.

Morris, D.H., 1981. Maxillary first premolar angular differences between North American Indians and non-North American Indians. American Journal of Physical Anthropology 54 (3), 431–433.

Morris, D.H., 1986. Maxillary molar occlusal polygons in five human samples. American Journal of Physical Anthropology 70 (3), 333–338.

Moss, M.L., 1978. Analysis of developmental processes possibly related to human dental sexual dimorphism. In: Bulter, P.M., Joysey, K.A. (Eds.), Development, Function and Evolution of Teeth. Academic Press, London, pp. 135–144.

Osborne, J., 1978. Morphogenetic gradients: fields versus clones. In: Butler, P., Joysey, K. (Eds.), Development, Function and Evolution of Teeth. Academic Press, London, pp. 171–199.

Park, J.-H., Yamaguchi, T., Watanabe, C., Kawaguchi, A., Haneji, K., Takeda, M., Kim, Y.-I., Tomoyasu, Y., Watanabe, M., Oota, H., Hanihara, T., Ishida, H., Maki, K., Park, S.-B., Kimura, R., 2012. Effects of an Asian-specific nonsynonymous EDAR variant on multiple dental traits. Journal of Human Genetics 57 (8), 508–514.

Paulsson-Björnsson, L., Bondemark, L., 2010. Permanent tooth-crown dimensions in prematurely born children. In: 7th International Orthodontic Congress, Syndey, Australia.

Perzigian, A.J., 1977. Fluctuating dental asymmetry: variation among skeletal populations. American Journal of Physical Anthropology 47 (1), 81–88.

Pilloud, M.A., 2009. Community Structure at Neolithic Çatalhöyük: Biological Distance Analysis of Household, Neighborhood, and Settlement. Department of Anthropology, Columbus, Ohio. The Ohio State University.

Pilloud, M.A., 2013. Postmarital residence in Neolithic Anatolia. American Journal of Physical Anthropology Suppl 150, 221–222.

Pilloud, M.A., Hefner, J.T., Hanihara, T., Hayashi, A., 2014. The use of tooth crown measurements in the assessment of ancestry. Journal of Forensic Sciences 59 (6), 1493–1501.

Pilloud, M.A., Hillson, S., 2012. Brief communication: the use of alternative dental measurements on deciduous teeth. American Journal of Physical Anthropology 149, 299–306.

Pinhasi, R., Meiklejohn, C., 2011. Dental reduction and the transition to agriculture in Europe. In: Pinhasi, R., Stock, J.T. (Eds.), Human Bioarchaeology of the Transition to Agriculture. John Wiley & Sons, Ltd., pp. 451–474

Ribeiro, D.C., Brook, A.H., Hughes, T.E., Sampson, W.J., Townsend, G.C., 2013. Intrauterine hormone effects on tooth dimensions. Journal of Dental Research 92 (5), 425–431.

Saunders, S.R., Chan, A.H., Kahlon, B., Kluge, H.F., FitzGerald, C.M., 2007. Sexual dimorphism of the dental tissues in human permanent mandibular canines and third premolars. American Journal of Physical Anthropology 133, 735–740.

Scherer, A.K., 2007. Population structure of the classic period Maya. American Journal of Physical Anthropology 132 (3), 367–380.

Schillaci, M.A., Stojanowski, C.M., 2003. Postmarital residence and biological variation at Pueblo Bonito. American Journal of Physical Anthropology 120 (1), 1–15.

Schmidt, C.W., 2008. 12 Forensic dental anthropology: issues and guidelines. In: Irish, J.D., Nelson, G.C. (Eds.), Technique and Application in Dental Anthropology. Cambridge University Press, Cambridge, pp. 266–292.

Schmidt, C., Ousley, S., Schmidt, M., 2011. Brief communication: correcting overestimation when determining two-dimensional occlusal area in humanmolars. American Journal of Physical Anthropology 145 (2), 327–332.

Schnutenhaus, S., Rösing, F.W., 1998. World variation of tooth size. In: Alt, K.W., Rösing, F.W., Teschler-Nicola, M. (Eds.), Dental Anthropology: Fundamentals, Limits, and Prospects. Springer, New York, pp. 522–535.

Schour, I., Massler, M., 1940. Studies in tooth development: the growth pattern of human teeth Part II. The Journal of the American Dental Association 27 (12), 1918–1931.

Schwartz, G.T., Dean, C.M., 2001. Ontogeny of canine dimorphsim in extant hominoids. American Journal of Physical Anthropology 115 (3), 269–283.

Schwartz, G.T., Dean, C.M., 2005. Sexual dimorphism in modern human permanent teeth. American Journal of Physical Anthropology 128, 312–317.

Selmer-Olsen, R., 1949. An odontometrical study of the Norwegian Lapps. Skrift Norske Vidensk-Akademi 3, 1–167.

Seow, W.K., Young, W., Tsang, A.K., Daley, T., 2005. A study of primary dental enamel from preterm and full-term children using light and scanning electron microscopy. Pediatric Dentistry 27 (5), 374–379.

Shields, E., Altschuller, B., Choi, E., Michaud, M., 1989. Odontometric variation among American black, European, and Mongoloid populations. Journal of Craniofacial Genetics and Developmental Biology 10 (1), 7–18.

Stojanowski, C., 2004. Population history of native groups in pre- and postcontact Spanish Florida: aggregation, gene flow, and genetic drift on the Southeastern U.S. Atlantic coast. American Journal of Physical Anthropology 123, 316–332.

Stojanowski, C., Larsen, C.S., Tung, T., McEwan, B., 2007. Biological structure and health implications from tooth size at Mission San Luis de Apalachee. American Journal of Physical Anthropology 132 (2), 207–222.

Stojanowski, C.M., 2005. Biocultural Histories in La Florida: A Bioarchaeological Perspective. University of Alabama Press, Tuscaloosa.

Ten Cate, A.R., Sharpe, P.T., Roy, S., Nanci, A., 2003. Development of the tooth and its supporting tissues. In: Nanci, A. (Ed.), Ten Cate's Oral Histology: Development, Structure, and Function. Mosby, St. Louis, Missouri, pp. 79–110.

Thompson, A.R., Hedman, K.M., Slater, P.A., 2015. New dental and isotope evidence of biological distance and place of origin for mass burial groups at Cahokia's mound 72. American Journal of Physical Anthropology 158 (2), 341–357.

Townsend, G., Richards, L., Hughes, T., 2003. Molar intercuspal dimensions: genetic input to phenotypic variation. Journal of Dental Research 82 (5), 350–355.

Townsend, G.C., 1992. Genetic and environmental contributions to morphometric dental variation. In: Lukacs, J.R. (Ed.), Culture, Ecology and Dental Anthropology. Kamla-Raj Enterprises, Delhi, India, pp. 61–72.

Townsend, G.C., Brown, T., 1978. Inheritance of tooth size in Australian Aborigines. American Journal of Physical Anthropology 48, 305–314.

Townsend, G.C., Hughes, T., Luciano, M., Bockmann, M., Brook, A., 2009. Genetic and environmental influences on human dental variation: a critical evaluation of studies involving twins. Archives of Oral Biology 54 (Suppl. 1), S45–S51.

Viciano, J., López-Lázaro, S., Alemán, I., 2013. Sex estimation based on deciduous and permanent dentition in a contemporary Spanish population. American Journal of Physical Anthropology 152 (1), 31–43.

Vodanović, M., Demo, Ž., Njemirovskij, V., Keros, J., Brkić, H., 2007. Odontometrics: a useful method for sex determination in an archaeological skeletal population? Journal of Archaeological Science 34 (6), 905–913.

Wolpoff, M.H., 1971. Metric Trends in Hominid Dental Evolution. Case Western Reserve University, Cleveland.

Zorba, E., Moraitis, K., Manolis, S., 2011. Sexual dimorphsim in permanent teeth of modern Greeks. Forensic Science International 210, 74–81.

CHAPTER

8

Do Biological Distances Reflect Genetic Distances? A Comparison of Craniometric and Genetic Distances at Local and Global Scales

H.F. Smith[1,2], B.I. Hulsey[3], F.L. (Pack) West[3], G.S. Cabana[3]

Midwestern University, Glendale, AZ, United States[1]; Arizona State University, Tempe, AZ, United States[2]; University of Tennessee, Knoxville, TN, United States[3]

CHAPTER OUTLINE HEAD

Background **158**
Methods **161**
- **Samples** 161
  - Local Samples 161
  - Global Population Samples 161
- **Data Collection: Morphological** 161
  - Norris Farms #36 161
  - Global Population Samples 165
- **Data Collection: Genetic** 165
  - Norris Farms #36 165
  - Global Population Samples 167
- **Analytical Methods** 167
  - Linear Cranial Data: Local Norris Farms #36 Individuals Only 167
  - Cranial Landmark Data: All Cranial Samples (Local Norris Farms #36 Individuals and Global Populations) 167
  - Genetic Data 168
  - Genetic vs. Morphological Comparisons 168

Results **169**
- **Local Interindividual Analyses: Norris Farms #36 Individuals** 169
  - Linear Cranial Data: Norris Farms #36 169
  - Local Interindividual Level Analyses: Cranial vs. Genetic Distances 169
  - Cranial vs. Molecular Distances: Global Population-Level Data 169

Discussion **173**
Acknowledgments **176**
References **176**

Biological Distance Analysis. http://dx.doi.org/10.1016/B978-0-12-801966-5.00008-1

Over the past 20 years, numerous studies have established a general congruence between cranial morphological and genetic relatedness among human populations (eg, Relethford, 1994, 2001; Roseman, 2004; Roseman and Weaver, 2004; Harvati and Weaver, 2006; Manica et al., 2007; Smith, 2009; von Cramon-Taubadel, 2009a, 2011a,b; Betti et al., 2009). This relationship is typified by cranial form as captured by standard craniometric dimensions (eg, Relethford, 1994, 2001, 2004; Gonzalez-José et al., 2004; Roseman, 2004; Manica et al., 2007) and by geometric morphometric landmark-based analyses (eg, Harvati and Weaver, 2006; Smith et al., 2007, 2013; Smith, 2009; von Cramon-Taubadel, 2009a,b, 2011a,b). Recently, an increasing number of studies indicate that the degree of correspondence between cranial morphological and genetic data varies, depending not only on cranial region and genetic data type, but also on the quality (ie, degree of informativeness) and quantity (ie, number of measurements or markers) of data collected for both data sources.

Here, we additionally explore the extent to which scale matters. That is, even if robust craniometric and genetic correspondences exist among globally distributed human populations, does this necessarily mean that strong correspondences persist at increasingly localized scales, as some have asserted (ie, von Cramon-Taubadel, 2014)? We explore this question at two geographic scales: (1) global, defined as populations from around the world; and (2) local, defined as individuals from the same spatially and temporally constrained population. We also investigate the idea of scale within genetic and cranial data sets, including: (1) more complete data sets, such as genomic or comprehensive cranial data sets; and (2) partial data sets, including portions of genomes or anatomical regions of skulls (eg, face, neurocranium, mandible).

Furthermore, we investigate the applicability of localized correspondences for the subdiscipline of bioarchaeology, given that bioarchaeological analyses are more often than not limited by the degree of preservation of biological remains. The same is true for ancient DNA analyses, which use these same fragmented and decayed skeletal remains as source material and consequently often rely on mitochondrial DNA (mtDNA) due its higher recovery rate relative to nuclear DNA.

Thus, within the broader discussions on the nature of correspondences between cranial morphology and genetic data in human populations, we focus on two related issues that are tailored to the peculiarities of bioarchaeological and ancient DNA research: suitable data sets and scale. We investigate morphological—genetic correspondences using varied data sets at local (interindividual) and global (interpopulation) scales. Our goal is to advance bioarchaeological inquiry via an enhanced understanding of the ways in which these data sets may co-reveal population relationships at increasingly localized levels, including the intracemetery level.

BACKGROUND

Several studies have assessed whether patterns of modern human cranial variation are consistent with various global-scale evolutionary models (Relethford, 2004; Betti et al., 2010; Smith, 2011; von Cramon-Taubadel, 2014). Neutral evolutionary forces, namely random genetic drift and gene flow, have likely been predominant in shaping cranial morphology beginning with the earliest species of the genus *Homo* (Ackermann and Cheverud, 2004), including Neandertals (Weaver et al., 2007). Evolutionary modeling has shown that much of modern human cranial variation indeed fits with a model of selective neutrality (Betti et al., 2010; Smith, 2011; von Cramon-Taubadel, 2014), although the crania of modern populations deriving from extremely cold regions additionally show signatures of natural selection (Roseman, 2004; Smith, 2009; Betti et al., 2010). These models have demonstrated that local gene exchange explains much of the pattern of between population cranial variation (Relethford, 2004; Betti et al., 2010), especially when cold-adapted populations are excluded from consideration (Betti et al., 2010). Despite using slightly differing climatic adjustments, both Manica et al. (2007) and von Cramon-Taubadel and Lycett (2007) found that between-population variation based on human linear craniometric data is also consistent with a model of African origins followed by iterative founder effects, similar to that which has been described using selectively neutral autosomal genetic data (eg, Prugnolle et al., 2005; Ramachandran et al., 2005; Ray et al., 2005; Liu et al., 2006; Hunley et al., 2016). While these neutral evolutionary patterns appear to hold true at a global scale, individual populations are likely to experience divergent adaptive pressures, and thus patterns of selection may be apparent among smaller subgroups. However, within each subgroup the patterns of adaptive morphology are likely to be relatively constant.

Many of these recent studies comparing among-population cranial morphological and genetic distances have relied upon the same large data set of short tandem repeats (STRs) typed in 52 globally distributed populations from the HGDP-CEPH Human Genome Diversity Cell Line Panel (eg, Rosenberg et al., 2002; Ramachandran et al., 2005). However, other genetic data sets have not yielded comparable results when keeping the craniometric data set constant (eg, Roseman, 2004; Harvati and Weaver, 2006; Smith, 2008). For example, Smith (2008) found that the use of 783 autosomal STRs versus 46 *Alu* insertions produced differing correlations with 3-D cranial shape: the landmark-based morphology of the entire cranium significantly correlated with STR distances, but not with *Alu* insertion distances. In contrast, 3-D basicranial and facial morphology were congruent with *Alu* insertion distances but not those based on STRs. In sum, this dramatic difference in the covariation between cranial shape and various categories of nuclear data suggests that the availability or choice of genetic data type dictates the strength and nature of the correlation between these two types of biological data.

Moreover, most studies investigating morphological and genetic correspondences have done so using globally distributed, matched skeletal and genetic samples. Less than a handful of studies have done the same at smaller geographic scales (eg, Herrera et al., 2014; Hubbard et al., 2015). In Hubbard et al.'s (2015) recent study, they investigated whether variants in dental morphology (9 crown morphology traits) and DNA (42 autosomal STRs) provided similar patterns of intergroup affinity among four contemporary (living) Kenyan populations, two known ethnically as "Swahili" and two known as "Taita." Their results found a positive correlation between distance matrices based on genetic and on dental morphological data. Moreover, biodistance statistics indicated closer affinities between population samples within each ethnic group. Interestingly, very few studies have attempted to quantify the correlation between mtDNA and craniometric distances in humans. This is partly because comparative genetic and morphological studies have only recently been made possible with the availability of large autosomal data sets from globally distributed human populations (eg, Rosenberg et al., 2002; Ramachandran et al., 2005), while comparable mitochondrial data sets have been slower to build (eg, Cann et al., 2002; Cavalli-Sforza, 2005).

To date, only two studies have compared morphological with mtDNA-based distances. The earliest is an intracemetery study by Corruccini et al. (2002). They compared interindividual dental nonmetric traits with 192 DNA bases from the mtDNA D-loop of individuals from the archaeological site of Huaca Loro, Peru. They found a statistically significant but weak correspondence between the two data sources and were able to apply the combined mitochondrial—dental correspondences to identify several separate maternal lineages among the burial clusters at the site.

The more recent study by Herrera et al. (2014) compared cranial and dental traits, mitochondrial data, and Y chromosome data from matched human population samples from the Bering Strait. A divergent pattern was revealed in which craniometric data were most strongly correlated with mtDNA data, while cranial nonmetrics were more highly associated with Y chromosome data. This disparity between the correlations of various types of molecular and cranial data may suggest that different categories of cranial traits may be characterized by different modes of inheritance. Another possibility is that a certain amount of unknown error was introduced to the analysis given the differential degree of information provided by each data source, and/or the use of matched samples at a geographically and culturally constrained scale. Nevertheless, Herrera et al. (2014) suggest that by incorporating various types of biological data into bioarchaeological analyses, a more complete understanding of biological relatedness will be possible.

While the two studies discussed above are among the only research to have focused on directly comparing human population distances calculated using mtDNA with those based on cranial and dental data, several other studies have assessed the concordance between levels of intergroup variation (eg, Relethford, 1994; Relethford and Harpending, 1994). Relethford (2001) found that when human populations were pooled into broad geographic groups, estimates of variation (as measured by F_{ST}) for standard craniometric measurements and mtDNA did not differ markedly. Diversity measures of both craniometrics and mtDNA were higher in sub-Saharan Africa than in the rest of the world, reflecting the deeper evolutionary history of human populations from this region (Relethford and Harpending, 1994).

A few studies have assessed the association between mtDNA macrolineages, or haplogroups, and cranial morphology among individuals (Perez et al., 2007, 2009). In human skeletal remains from Patagonia, Argentina, anterior 2-D facial morphology coincided with mtDNA haplogroup lineage frequencies among archaeological sites, but 2-D landmarks on the neurocranium and lateral face did not (Perez et al., 2007). In a study of early South American specimens from East Central Argentina, Perez et al. (2009) found that mtDNA haplogroup differences were not significantly correlated with 2-D cranial landmarks and semilandmarks. In particular, the older samples in the analysis possessed more elongated crania than the more recent samples, despite belonging to the same haplogroups. These studies suggest that potential concordances between cranial morphology and mtDNA haplogroup data are at best equivocal.

The finding that much of human cranial morphology has been shaped by selectively neutral forces has important implications for its use in biodistance studies when DNA is not obtainable, such as at many archaeological mortuary sites. However, the relationship between cranial morphology and genetic distances, while generally well established for global population-level and even interspecific comparisons, has been less thoroughly investigated at increasingly localized levels. The primary reasons for this oversight are the destructive nature of genetic sampling of skeletal remains, the reluctance of museums to permit such sampling of their valuable morphological collections, and the complications of DNA degradation and contamination in samples even when such permissions are obtained. For these reasons, ancient DNA analyses of bioarchaeological skeletal samples continue to rely on mtDNA due to the inherent difficulties associated with obtaining nuclear DNA relative to mtDNA. Nevertheless, for cranial morphology—including standard craniometric variables and 3-D coordinate-based data—to be reliably employed in studies of individual variation and genetic relatedness, such as in a bioarchaeological context, the relationship between cranial and genetic distances needs to be more thoroughly established.

In addition, the issue of geographic scale, as mentioned above, is crucial in these analyses. While it has been adequately demonstrated that cranial morphology reflects neutral evolution and therefore neutral genetic distances at the global population level (eg, Relethford, 1994, 2001; Roseman, 2004; Harvati and Weaver, 2006; Smith et al., 2007; Smith, 2009; von Cramon-Taubadel, 2009a), this pattern may not hold up at the smaller, more local scales relevant in bioarchaeological contexts. While the adaptive pressures for individuals from a single archaeological site are likely to have been relatively consistent, it is currently unclear how the cranial morphology of these individuals might vary in relation to their genetic distances, and whether the neutral assumptions interpreted from global analyses of cranial morphology can be reasonably extrapolated at the local intracemetery level.

METHODS

Samples

Local Samples

We collected both morphological and genetic (ancient DNA) data from 36 adult individuals from the Norris Farms #36 archaeological mortuary site located in west-central Illinois and dated to ca. AD 1300 (Santure, 1990). The site represents a spatiotemporally constricted cemetery with the remains of 264 skeletons, 119 of which were adults. For various reasons, the Norris Farms #36 sample can be viewed as approximating a single, temporally continuous, biological, and cultural population (Milner et al., 1989; Santure, 1990; Santure et al., 1990). The sample also likely represents a single ethnic/culture group, given that the grave goods associated with the burials were of a single cultural tradition (Oneota) (Santure, 1990). In particular, the individuals are believed to have belonged to a particular regional variant of the Oneota called Bold Counselor (Esarey and Santure, 1990; Conrad, 1991). In addition, Milner et al. (1989) found that the age and sex distribution of skeletons present in this sample correspond to expected human mortality patterns in traditional societies, further supporting the idea of Norris Farms #36 as a population sample. In the present study, only adult individuals were included in order to minimize the effect of ontogenetic changes in cranial morphology.

Global Population Samples

We collated morphological (cranial) and genetic data from 14 globally distributed human population samples (Smith, 2008, 2009, Table 8.1). These populations represent a geographically diverse sample and were chosen based on two criteria: (1) having a close genetic representative that is well typed for neutral genetic loci, and (2) having sufficient number of complete crania available in museum collections [American Museum of Natural History (AMNH), British Natural History Museum (BNHM), and National Museum of Natural History (NMNH)]; see Smith (2009) for further information on these samples.

Data Collection: Morphological

Norris Farms #36

Two types of cranial data were collected on the Norris Farms #36 adult sample: traditional linear cranial dimensions and 3-D landmark-based data; these were collected using a Microscribe G2 digitizer (Immersion Corp.). Adult status was assessed by eruption of the M3s and/or fusion of the spheno—occipital synchondrosis. Linear dimensions were derived from the standard set of craniometric measurements of Howells (1973). Due to incomplete preservation, and to maximize the number of specimens included in this analysis, a subset of Howells's cranial dimensions was used (Table 8.2). The set of 3-D cranial landmarks derived from Smith (2009) also omitted several landmarks to maximize sample size (Table 8.3; Fig. 8.1). These landmarks capture the 3-D morphology of the basicranium, neurocranium, mandible, temporal bone, and upper face. A subset of the landmarks representing all cranial regions was

Table 8.1 ***Human Populations Included in Cranial Global Landmark and Genetic Analyses, Sample Sizes, and Data Locations/Sources***

Cranial			Genetic				
				mtDNA		Autosomal STRs	
Population	*n*	Museum Location(s)	Population	*n*	Data Source	*n*	Data Source
Cameroon	44	AMNH	Biaka, Central African Republic	36	HGDP-CEPH	36	Ramachandran et al. (2005) and Rosenberg et al. (2002)
Khoisan	43	AMNH, BNHM	San, Namibia	7	HGDP-CEPH	7	
Pare	27	AMNH	Bantu (N), Kenya	12	HGDP-CEPH	12	
French	50	NMNH, BNHM	French, France	29	HGDP-CEPH	29	
Russian	36	AMNH, NMNH	Russian, Russia	25	HGDP-CEPH	25	
North Chinese	50	AMNH, NMNH	Han, China	45	HGDP-CEPH	45	
Japanese	40	BNHM, NMNH	Japanese, Japan	31	HGDP-CEPH	31	
Mongolian	44	AMNH	Mongolians, Mongolia	10	HGDP-CEPH	10	
Siberian Natives	51	AMNH, NMNH	Yakut, Siberia	25	HGDP-CEPH	25	
Southern Indians	50	AMNH	Brahui, Pakistan	25	HGDP-CEPH	25	
Australian Aborigine	48	AMNH, NMNH	Australian Aborigine	16	Ingman and Gyllensten (2003)	16	
Papua New Guineans	34	AMNH	Papuan, New Guinea	17	HGDP-CEPH	17	
Solomon Islanders	31	AMNH, NMNH	Bougainville, Solomons	22	HGDP-CEPH	22	
Mexican Indian	44	NMNH	Maya, Mexico	25	HGDP-CEPH	25	

These populations were used for all global analyses in the present study. AMNH, *American Museum of Natural History;* BNHM, *British Natural History Museum;* NMNH, *National Museum of Natural History.*

Table 8.2 Linear Cranial Variables Included in This Study, and the Cranial Subset(s) in Which Each Was Included

Variable	Description	Cranial Portion(s)
AUB	Biauricular breadth	B, N
BBH	Basion bregma height	B, N
BNL	Basion–nasion length	B, N
BPL	Basion–prosthion length	B, N
DKB	Interorbital breadth	F
DKR	Dacryon radius	F
DKS	Dacryon subtense	F
EKB	Biorbital breadth	F
EKR	Ectoconchion radius	N
FMB	Bifrontal breadth	N
FMR	Frontomalare radius	N
FOL	Foramen magnum length	B
FRC	Nasion–bregma chord	F, N
GOL	Glabello–occipital length	N
GLS	Glabella projection	N
IML	Malar length, inferior	F
JUB	Bijugal breadth	F
MDH	Mastoid height	B
NAR	Nasion radius	N
NAS	Nasio–frontal subtense	N
NLB	Nasal breadth	F
NLH	Nasal height	F
NOL	Nasio–occipital length	N
OBB	Orbital breadth	F
OBH	Orbital height	F
OCC	Lambda–opisthion chord	B
PAC	Bregma–lambda chord	N
PRR	Prosthion radius	F
WMH	Cheek height	F
WNB	Simotic chord	F
XCB	Maximum cranial width	N
XFB	Maximum frontal breadth	N
XML	Malar length maximum	F
ZMB	Bimaxillary breadth	F
ZOR	Zygoorbitale radius	F
ZYB	Bizygomatic breadth	F

B, *basicranium*; F, *face*; N, *neurocranium*.
From Howells, W.W., 1973. Cranial variation in man. A study by multivariate analysis of patterns of differences among recent human populations. Papers of the Peabody Museum of Archeology and Ethnology, vol. 67. Peabody Museum, Cambridge, Massachusetts, pp. 259.

Table 8.3 3-D Cranial Landmarks Used in This Study

Landmark	Description
Basicranium	
Basion[a] (ba)	The midline point on the anterior margin of the foramen magnum.
Condyle posterior (cp)	The most posterior points on the occipital condyles.
Mastoidale (ma)	The most inferior point on the mastoid process.
Opisthion (op)	Midline point at the posterior margin of the foramen magnum.
Face—upper	
Dacryon[a] (da)	Point on the medial orbit at which frontal, lacrimal, and maxilla intersect.
Ectoconchion[a] (ec)	Intersection of the most anterior surface of lateral orbital border and a line bisecting the orbit along long axis.
Frontomalare temporale[a] (fmt)	Most laterally positioned point on the fronto-zygomatic suture.
Glabella[a] (gl)	The most anterior midline point on the frontal bone.
Nasion[a] (na)	Point of intersection between the frontonasal suture and midsagittal plane.
Orbitale (left)[a] (or)	The lowest point on the margin of the left orbit.
Mandible	
Condylion laterale (cdl)	The most lateral point on the mandibular condyle.
Coronoid process (co)	The most superior point on the coronoid process of the mandible.
Gnathion (gn)	The most inferior midline point on the mandible.
Gonion (go)	A Point along the rounded posteroinferior corner of the mandible between the ramus and the body.
Infradentale (id)	The midline point at superior tip of septum between the mandibular central incisors.
Mandibular notch (mn)	The most inferior point in the mandibular notch.
Pogonion (pog)	The most anterior point on the mental eminence.
Neurocranium	
Bregma[a] (br)	Ectocranial midline point where the coronal and sagittal sutures intersect.
Frontotemporale[a] (ft)	The point where temporal line reaches its most A-M position on frontal bone.
Glabella[a] (gl)	Most anterior midline point on the frontal bone.
Lambda (la)	Ectocranial midline point where the sagittal and occipital sutures intersect.
Opisthocranion (op)	Most posterior point on the skull not on the external occipital protuberance.
Pterion[a] (pt)	Region in which the sagittal, sphenoidal, temporal sutures overlap.
Vertex (ve)	Highest point on the midsagittal contour.
Temporal bone	
Entoglenoid[a] (ec)	Most inferior point on the entoglenoid process.
Jugular[a] (ju)	Most lateral point of the jugular fossa.
Lateral eminence[a] (lar)	Point on the center of the lateral margin of the articular surface of the articular eminence.
Lateral ovale (lo)	Most lateral point on the margin of the foramen ovale.
Mandibular fossa[a] (mf)	Deepest point within the mandibular fossa.
Mastoidale (ma)	Center of the inferior tip of the mastoid process.

Table 8.3 3-D Cranial Landmarks Used in This Study Continued	
Landmark	**Description**
Medial articular[a] (mar)	Most inferior point on medial margin of articular surface of the articular eminence.
Porion[a] (por)	Most superior point of the external auditory meatus.
Postglenoid[a] (pg)	Most inferior point on the postglenoid process.
Supraglenoid gutter[a] (sg)	Point of inflection where braincase curves laterally into the supraglenoid gutter, in the coronal plane of the mandibular fossa.
Tympanic[a] (ty)	Most inferolateral point on the tympanic element of the temporal.
Zygion (zy)	The most lateral point on the zygomatic arch.

Landmarks are listed more than once if they were included in multiple cranial regions.
[a]Included in "entire cranium" analysis.
From Smith, H.F., 2009. Which cranial regions reflect molecular distance reliable in humans? Evidence from three-dimensional morphology. American Journal of Human Biology 21, 36–47.

combined into an "entire cranium" 3-D landmark set (see Table 8.3). Norris Farms #36 cranial data were collected by two of the authors (HFS and GSC). Interobserver and intraobserver error analyses revealed no significant differences between observers ($p = .846$ to .144) or between either observer's own trials ($p = .169$ to .942); therefore, the data sets were combined.

Global Population Samples

Three-dimensional landmark-based cranial data were collected by HFS on a global sample of 14 modern human populations. Relevant details regarding these populations are in Table 8.1; additional details can be found in Smith (2009).

Data Collection: Genetic

Norris Farms #36

DNA was extracted from 0.25 mg of bone or teeth that had been soaked in 6% sodium hypochlorite for 15 min and then rinsed with water (Quality Biological, Inc.) for 15 min before air-drying. The bone or tooth was ground in a cryogenic mill (SPEX 6770 freezer/mill), before demineralization via a 24 h incubation period at 60°C in a solution of 400 μL of 0.5 EDTA (pH 8.0) and 10 μL of 10 mg/mL proteinase K, with agitation. From there, samples were DNA-extracted using a silica-based protocol (Baker et al., 2001).

We targeted the first hypervariable region (HVI) of the mitochondrial D-loop for polymerase chain reaction (PCR) amplification and sequencing, using 11 overlapping primer sets from Kemp (2006). PCR-amplified samples were visualized by gel electrophoresis on 2% agarose gels containing GelRed (Phenix Research). PCR products were purified using shrimp alkaline phosphatase (Affymetrix/USB) and Exonuclease I (Affymetrix/USB), then run through Sephadex G-10 columns (Sigma-Aldrich), and subsequently sequenced in forward and reverse directions using the BigDye protocol (Applied Biosystems) on an Applied Biosystems 3730 capillary sequencer maintained by the University of Tennessee's Molecular Biology Resource Facility. Sequences were edited using four Peaks (Nucleobytes) and compared against the revised Cambridge Reference Sequence (Andrews et al., 1999) using SeqMan Pro (DNASTAR). All fragments were sequenced in forward and reverse directions from at least two separate extractions and at least two different skeletal elements per individual. Sample preparation, extraction, amplification, visualization, purification, and sequence editing were performed by FLW and BIH. Standard

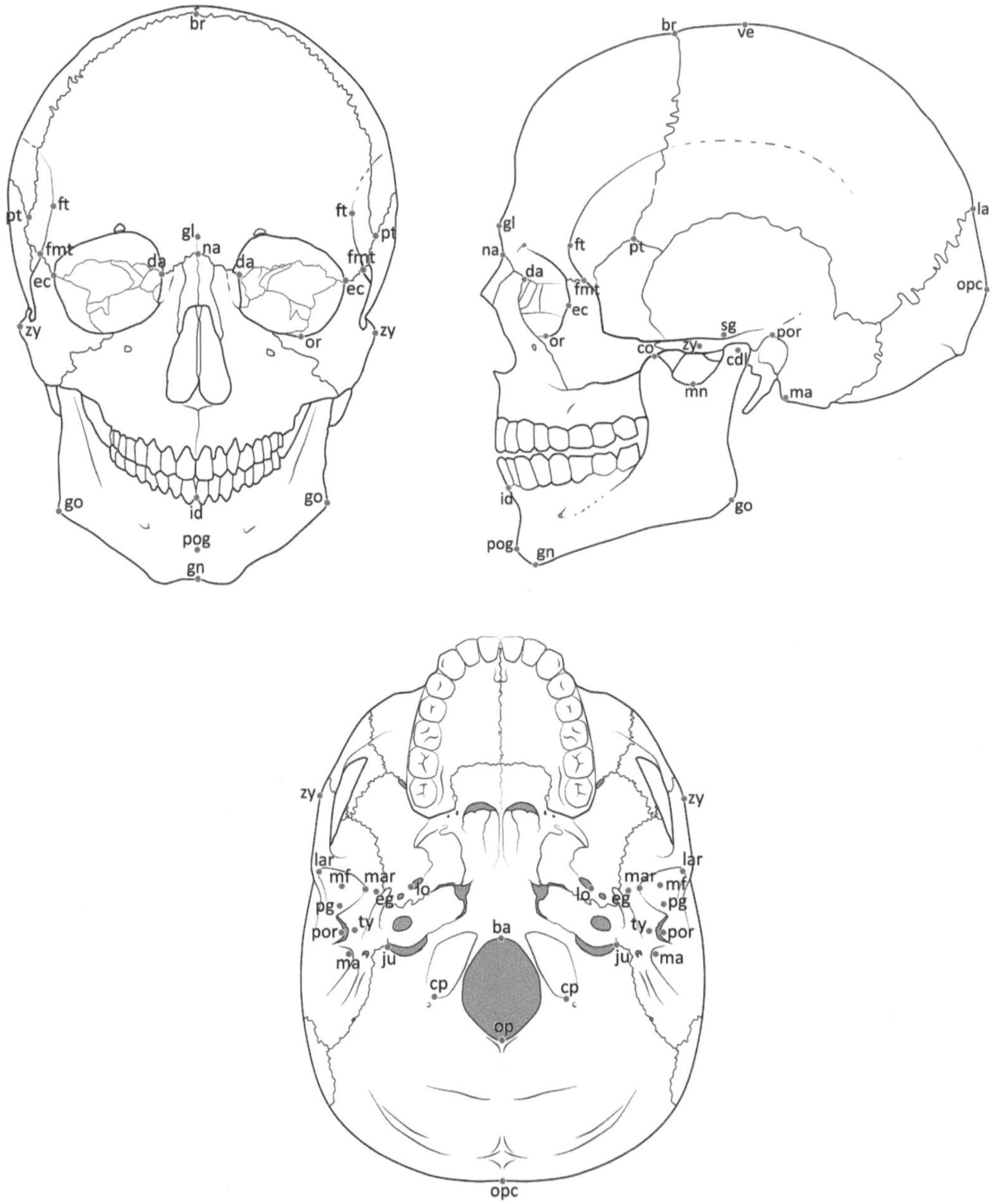

FIGURE 8.1

Cranial landmarks digitized in landmark component of this study. Refer to Table 8.3 for abbreviations and complete descriptions.

best practices were followed for preventing and detecting exogenous DNA contamination in these ancient samples (Cooper and Poinar, 2001). We were able to obtain HVI sequences for a large number of Norris Farms #36 individuals. While we also obtained other types of genetic data for some specimens, we chose to focus our individual-level analysis on HVI in order to maximize the number of individual specimens that we could include in the paired genetic–morphological comparison.

Global Population Samples

Genetic data from either the same population or a closely related population were compiled from the literature and online databases (see Table 8.1). These data consisted of 783 STRs and complete mtgenomes. The complete mtgenomes were analyzed in their entirety, as well as in partitions [HVI, HVII, HVIII, and the coding region (CR)]. These genetic regions were analyzed with the aim of replicating the fragmentary nature of bioarchaeological samples, in which entire genomes are rarely preserved. The inclusion of both complete mtgenomes and regions of the mtgenome permitted a direct comparison of these complete versus incomplete genetic data sets.

Analytical Methods

Linear Cranial Data: Local Norris Farms #36 Individuals Only

Linear craniometric data for the Norris Farms #36 sample were subjected to several different analytical steps. First, to determine whether individuals belonging to particular genetic haplogroup lineages differed significantly in their cranial dimensions, a multivariate analysis of variance (MANOVA) was conducted among the individuals in the four mtDNA major haplogroups (A, B, C, D) present in the Norris Farms #36 sample. Tukey post hoc pairwise comparisons were subsequently conducted to assess whether significant differences existed in cranial dimensions between any pairs of haplogroups. Next, a discriminant function analysis (DFA) was conducted among haplogroups to determine whether linear cranial dimensions could be used to reliably sort Norris Farms #36 individuals into the correct haplogroups. Classification rates for the DFA were cross-validated. Linear dimensions from the basicranium, neurocranium, and facial skeleton were considered separately as well as combined into an "entire cranium" analysis in which all cranial regions were considered together. The MANOVA and DFA analyses were conducted using PASW Statistics 18 (SPSS Inc.). Finally, Euclidean distances among the Norris Farms #36 individuals based on linear dimensions of the basicranium, neurocranium, face, and entire cranium were calculated using PopTools v.3.2.5 (Hood, 2010) and entered into four separate individual linear cranial distance matrices.

Cranial Landmark Data: All Cranial Samples (Local Norris Farms #36 Individuals and Global Populations)

The landmark data were first registered in Morphologika v2.5 (O'Higgins and Jones, 1998) using a generalized Procrustes analysis (GPA) (Gower, 1975), in which specimens are statistically scaled to the same size, rotated to the same orientation, and translated on top of each other, such that the only remaining differences among them are attributed to shape, removing size from the analysis. This analysis was run separately for each landmark set: basicranium, mandible, neurocranium, temporal bone, upper face, and the entire cranium. The global population-level data were analyzed twice: once using the entire landmark data set from Smith (2009), and again using only the landmarks for which the Norris Farms #36 sample was complete.

Following the GPA, a principal components analysis was conducted, and Procrustes distances calculated in Morphologika v2.5. Procrustes distances among individual specimens were recorded for the Norris Farms #36 data, while population distances were calculated for the global sample. Procrustes distances were subsequently entered into individual 3-D cranial distance matrices and population-level 3-D cranial distance matrices.

Genetic Data

Sequence alignment of mtgenome data followed the recommendations of Wilson et al. (2002a,b) and Bandelt and Parson (2008). In addition, all analyses excluded any inserts between nucleotide positions (np) 315 and 316, 520 and 525, 573 and 574, and 161193 and 16194, to either temper any potential confounding effects of sequence heteroplasmy (c.f., Irwin et al., 2009), or to avoid giving excess analytical weight to certain regions of the mitochondrial genome (eg, Pfeiffer et al., 1999). To partition mtgenomes, HVI was defined as encompassing np 16024 to 16365, HVII as np 73 to 340, and HVIII as np 438 to 574 (Butler, 2009).

For the mtDNA-based analyses, interindividual and interpopulation genetic distances were estimated as Φst genetic distances using the Tamura–Nei evolutionary model (Tamura and Nei, 1993) with the gamma distribution parameter alpha (α) set to 0.26 (Meyer et al., 1999). All genetic distance analyses were performed using Arlequin, version 3.5.1.3 (Excoffier and Lischer, 2010).

Genetic vs. Morphological Comparisons

The genetic vs. morphological comparisons were conducted using a multitiered approach:

(1) Local individual-level analyses (Norris Farms #36 individuals only):
- **(A)** mtDNA HVI vs. entire cranium (all regions of the cranium combined).
- **(B)** mtDNA HVI vs. cranial regions (ie, basicranium, face, mandible, neurocranium, temporal bone).

(2) Global population-level analyses (see Table 8.1):
- **(A)** Genetic regions [mtDNA (HVI, HVII–III, and CR) and autosomal STRs] each separately compared with the morphology of the entire cranium (all regions of the cranium combined).
- **(B)** Genetic regions [mtDNA (HVI, HVII–III, and CR) and autosomal STRs] each separately compared with the cranial regions/subsets (ie, basicranium, face, mandible, neurocranium, temporal bone), including a subset of only those landmarks preserved in the Norris Farms #36 sample.
- **(C)** Complete mtgenome vs. entire cranium (all regions of the cranium combined).
- **(D)** Complete mtgenome vs. cranial regions/subsets (ie, basicranium, face, mandible, neurocranium, temporal bone), including a subset of only those landmarks preserved in the Norris Farms #36 sample.

In each comparison, the relevant morphological matrices were statistically compared with the corresponding molecular distance matrices using a Mantel test (Mantel, 1967) in PopTools v.3.2.5 (Hood, 2010). The Norris Farms #36 individual-level cranial matrices were compared with the HVI distance matrix of the same individuals. The global population cranial matrices were compared with the population-level molecular matrices based on published data for: complete mtgenome, mtDNA (HVI, HVII–HVIII, and CR) and autosomal STRs. A sequential Bonferroni correction (Holm, 1979) was applied to each set of analyses to correct for multiple comparisons.

RESULTS

Local Interindividual Analyses: Norris Farms #36 Individuals

Linear Cranial Data: Norris Farms #36

The MANOVA of linear cranial data revealed no significant differences in any of the included linear craniometric measurements among the four mtDNA haplogroups present in the Norris Farms #36 sample. Tukey post hoc pairwise comparisons revealed only a single variable that differed significantly between one pair of haplogroups. In particular, only maximum cranial width differed between haplogroups A and B ($p = .035$).

The cross-validated DFAs revealed relatively poor classification rates of individuals into haplogroups (16.7–44.0%; Table 8.4). The DFA of the entire cranial data set provided the highest level of discrimination (44.0%; see Table 8.4; Fig. 8.2). The classification rates varied slightly among the cranial regions (basicranium: 22.7%, face: 16.7%, neurocranium: 22.7%), but were all extremely low (see Table 8.4).

Local Interindividual Level Analyses: Cranial vs. Genetic Distances

(1A) Local Norris Farms #36 mtDNA HVI vs. Entire Cranium (All Cranial Regions)

The local individual-level comparisons of mtDNA HVI distances with traditional craniometric dimensions and 3-D landmark-based morphology in Norris Farms #36 specimens yielded few significant results (Table 8.5). The Howells measurements capturing the morphology of the entire skull (all regions considered together) were not significantly correlated with the HVI matrix (see Table 8.5). Similarly, the Norris Farms #36 landmark-based data from the entire cranium were not correlated with the HVI matrix (see Table 8.5).

(1B) Local Norris Farms #36 mtDNA HVI vs. Cranial Regions

The Norris Farms #36 individual cranial region distance matrices (ie, basicranium, face, mandible, neurocranium, temporal bone) were found to have varying degrees of correlation with the HVI individual matrix in the Mantel tests (see Table 8.5). The correlation between the matrix based on the Howells variables of the cranial neurocranium and the HVI matrix was significant but low ($r = 0.227$, $p = .021$); however, it was not significant following the sequential Bonferroni correction (see Table 8.5). The measurements of the face and basicranium were not significantly correlated with the HVI matrix (see Table 8.5). For the landmark-based data, none of the cranial regions were significantly correlated with the HVI matrix (see Table 8.5).

Cranial vs. Molecular Distances: Global Population-Level Data

The Mantel tests between the 3-D cranial distances and the various genetic distance matrices for the global population sample revealed a more complicated relationship between these two types of biological data (Table 8.6).

(2A) Genetic Regions [mtDNA (HVI, HVII–III, and CR) and Autosomal STRs] Each Separately Compared with the Entire Cranium (All Cranial Regions Together)

The Mantel tests comparing the morphology of the entire cranium with each of the various genetic distances revealed several significant correlations at the population level with r values ranging from 0.436 (STRs) to 0.637 (HVI) (see Table 8.6). Each of the genetic subsets was found to have a significant

Table 8.4 ***Results from Discriminant Function Analysis (DFA) of Linear Cranial Dimensions Among the mtDNA Haplogroups Present at Norris Farms (A–D)***

Cranial Region	Overall Correct (%)	A Prior Probability (%)	A Correctly Classified (%)	B Prior Probability (%)	B Correctly Classified (%)	C Prior Probability (%)	C Correctly Classified (%)	D Prior Probability (%)	D Correctly Classified (%)
Entire cranium	44.0	20.0	40.0	20.0	60.0	44.0	54.5	16.0	0.0
Basicranium	22.7	22.7	40.0	22.7	0.0	40.9	33.3	13.6	0.0
Facial skeleton	16.7	20.8	60.0	20.8	0.0	41.2	0.0	16.7	25.0
Neurocranium	22.7	18.2	75.0	22.7	0.0	45.5	20.0	13.6	0.0

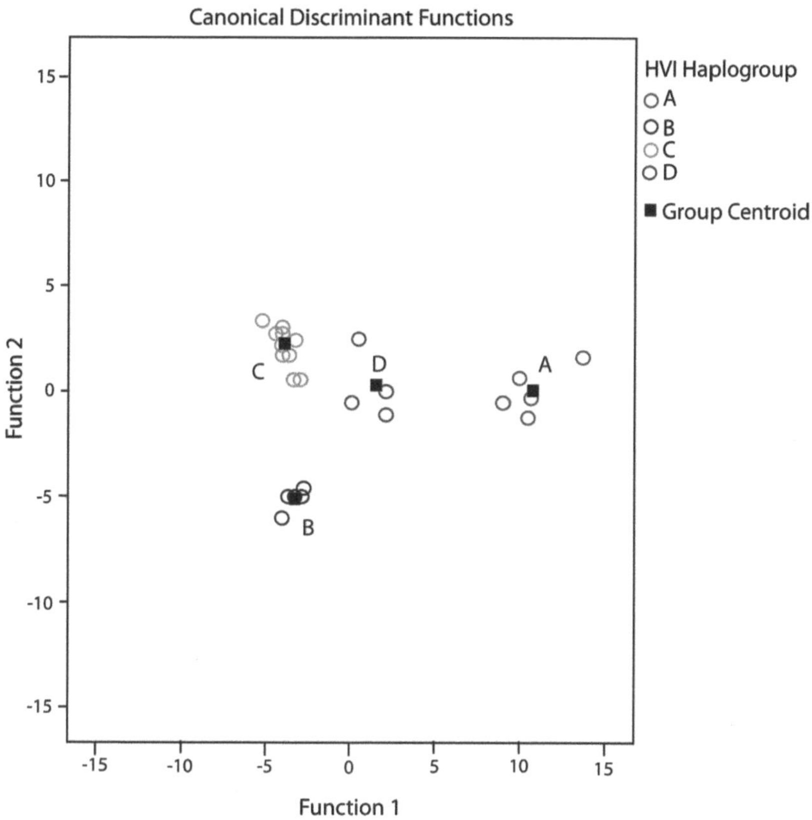

FIGURE 8.2

Plot of Discriminant Functions 1 and 2 from discriminant function analysis of the entire set of linear cranial dimensions among the four Norris Farms #36 mtDNA haplogroups A–D. Haplogroup A separated most notably from the other haplogroups along Function 1, which primarily reflected EKR and FRC. Haplogroup B separated out from the others along Function 2, which strongly reflected FRC, DKR, FMR, ZOR, XCB, ZMR, WNB, ZMB, and WMH. Refer to Table 8.2 for abbreviations and complete descriptions.

Table 8.5 Results of Mantel Tests Indicating Correlations Between Morphological and mtDNA Distances in the Norris Farms #36 Sample

	Howells Traditional Linear Measurements vs. HVI			Cranial Landmarks vs. HVI		
	r	*p*	Bonferroni Critical *α*	*r*	*p*	Bonferroni Critical *α*
Entire cranium	0.011	.436	0.0500	0.160	.085	0.0100
Basicranium	0.106	.085	0.0167	0.183	.054	0.0083
Face	0.039	.291	0.0250	0.095	.241	0.0250
Temporal bone	N/A			0.090	.216	0.0167
Neurocranium	**0.165**	**.021**	0.0125	0.168	.093	0.0125
Mandible	N/A			0.060	.265	0.0500

Howells linear measurements are indicated in the first two columns, while 3-D landmark-based morphology is indicated in the last two columns. The single significant correlation is indicated in bold, but this correlation was not significant following a Sequential Bonferroni correction. Bonferroni critical alpha levels (those that would be required for significance to be achieved) are also indicated for each comparison.

Table 8.6 ***Results of Mantel Tests Indicating Correlations Between Morphological and Molecular Distances in the Global Population Sample Using the Complete Set of Landmarks***

	Autosomal STRs		mtDNA HVI		mtDNA HVII-III		mtDNA HVI, II, III		mtDNA Coding Region (CR)		mtgenome	
	r	*p*	*r*	*p*	*r*	*p*	*r*	*p*	*r*	*p*	*r*	*p*
Entire cranium	**0.436**	**.012**	**0.637**	**<.001***	**0.524**	**.013**	**0.600**	**.013**	**0.571**	**.013**	**0.585**	**<.001***
Basicranium	**0.421**	**.027**	0.159	.261	0.084	.356	0.123	.294	0.206	.209	0.182	.230
Face—upper	**0.369**	**.009**	0.257	.069	0.127	.191	0.203	.108	0.145	.185	0.161	.147
Temporal	**0.378**	**.014**	0.318	.055	0.334	.070	0.331	.054	0.314	.083	0.320	.075
Neurocranium	0.169	.230	0.323	.059	0.236	.128	0.289	.079	0.240	.108	0.249	.123
Mandible	0.237	.127	**0.399**	**.034**	0.294	.053	**0.358**	**.035**	**0.334**	**.023**	**0.342**	**.020**

Significant correlations are indicated in bold. Correlations that remained significant after a Sequential Bonferroni correction are indicated with an asterisk.
From Smith, H.F., 2009. Which cranial regions reflect molecular distance reliable in humans? Evidence from three-dimensional morphology. American Journal of Human Biology 21, 36–47.

correlation with morphology of the entire cranium (see Table 8.6); however, only the correlation with HVI distances remained significant after a sequential Bonferroni correction.

(2B) Genetic Regions [mtDNA (HVI, HVII–III, and CR) and Autosomal STRs] vs. Cranial Regions and Reduced Landmark Set

In the population-level genetic subset comparisons, the STR distances were found to be correlated with the most cranial regions: basicranium, upper face, and temporal (see Table 8.6). The population-level mtDNA HVI, HVI–III, HVII–III, and CR distance matrices were all significantly correlated with the mandible, although none of these correlations were significant following the sequential Bonferroni correction (Table 8.6). However, as noted above, the entire cranium data set was significantly correlated with the HVI and entire mtgenome data sets (see Table 8.6).

In the analyses in which only the landmarks utilized for the Norris Farms #36 sample were included, the correlations between cranial and genetic distances dropped substantially (Table 8.7). For this reduced landmark set, the population-level mtDNA HVI, HVII–III, HVI-III, and complete mtgenome distance matrices were each significantly correlated with the entire cranium distance matrix (see Table 8.7). The mtDNA CR distances were also significantly associated with the upper face matrix (see Table 8.7). The worldwide STR matrix was significantly correlated with only the mandibular data set ($r = 0.531, p = .014$; see Table 8.7). None of the reduced-landmark correlations remained significant after a sequential Bonferroni correction.

DISCUSSION

The goals of this study were to (1) quantify and (2) preliminarily evaluate the observed correspondence between genetic (mtDNA) and morphological (cranial) data at the local scale, such as in intracemetery analyses, and draw comparisons with analogous population-level correlations. Specifically, we sought to assess how the use of limited biological data sets, both morphological and genetic, such as those often used by necessity in bioarchaeological analyses, might affect the reliability of interpretations about past populations.

At the local intracemetery level, the cranial morphology of Norris Farms #36 site individuals did not reflect interindividual mtDNA distances with high reliability (see Table 8.5). Only the linear dimensions of the neurocranium were correlated with mtDNA distances, and even that correlation was low and not significant after a correction for multiple comparisons. Additionally, cranial dimensions could not be used to reliably sort individuals into mitochondrial haplogroups, suggesting that deep maternal ancestry as captured by HVI is not correlated with cranial shape among the individuals in this sample (see Table 8.4).

We simultaneously conducted a comparable global, population-level analysis. This is because the relationships among large population data sets of selectively neutral autosomal markers (STRs) and craniometric data have been both previously ascertained and contextualized within evolutionary frameworks (eg, Relethford, 1994, 2001; Roseman, 2004; Ramachandran et al., 2005; Harvati and Weaver, 2006; Manica et al., 2007; Hunley et al., 2009; Smith, 2009; Betti et al., 2009; von Cramon-Taubadel, 2009a, 2011a,b). We conducted this set of comparisons using two data sets: (1) a comprehensive set of landmarks used in previous studies to capture cranial morphology of well-preserved museum specimens; (2) a slightly reduced landmark set representative of those present in the Norris

***Table 8.7** Results of Mantel Tests Indicating Correlations Between Morphological and Molecular Distances in the Global Population Sample for the Reduced Landmark Set, Including Only Landmarks that Were Represented in the Norris Farms #36 Sample*

	Autosomal STRs		mtDNA HVI		mtDNA HVII–III		mtDNA HVI, II, III		mtDNA Coding Region (CR)		mtgenome	
	r	p	r	p	r	p	r	p	r	p	r	p
Entire cranium	0.282	.073	**0.430**	**.014**	**0.351**	**.017**	**0.403**	**.019**	**0.407**	**.021**	**0.414**	**.016**
Basicranium	0.249	.134	0.089	.311	0.065	.353	0.076	.352	0.207	.174	0.172	.214
Face—upper	0.286	.089	0.299	.080	0.252	.124	0.284	.086	**0.368**	**.046**	0.352	.065
Temporal	0.067	.397	0.256	.110	0.319	.087	0.288	.091	0.338	.084	0.328	.098
Neurocranium	−0.062	.376	0.323	.059	0.236	.128	0.289	.079	0.240	.108	0.249	.123
Mandible	**0.531**	**.014**	0.333	.058	0.262	.129	0.307	.094	0.318	.084	0.320	.079

Significant correlations are indicated in bold. None of the correlations remained significant after a sequential Bonferroni correction.

Farms #36 sample. This procedure allowed us to assess the effect of relying on the cranial metrics of somewhat fragmentary bioarchaeological specimens compared with the complete crania that have typically formed the basis for many previous studies on the relationship between cranial and genetic data.

In conducting these population-level analyses, we expected to mirror previous findings and also find significant correlations between autosomal STRs and craniometric distances at the global population level. Against these expected results, we hoped to compare the relative correlation between complete and partitioned mtgenomes (see Tables 8.6 and 8.7). We revealed some differences between the complete and reduced landmark data set that may shed some light onto the use of craniometrics in fragmentary samples. Most notably, the complete "entire cranium" landmark set (including data from all portions of the cranium) was significant after the Bonferroni correction (see Table 8.6), while the reduced landmark set (including only those landmarks preserved in the Norris Farms #36 sample) was not (see Table 8.7).

The dramatic reduction in correspondence between cranial morphology as captured by the reduced landmark set and the various genetic distances compared with the complete set (Table 8.6 vs. Table 8.7) suggests that analyses using fragmentary cranial morphology should be approached with caution. Results obtained and patterns identified using well-preserved museum specimens may not be as broadly applicable to bioarchaeological contexts as one might hope.

For the individual-level analyses, a potentially complicating factor is the expected limited nature of genetic information of these archaeological mortuary specimens. Recent studies have demonstrated that Native American craniometric and genetic samples exhibit the lowest global values of craniometric and genetic (autosomal STR) within-population heterozygosities (Ramachandran et al., 2005; Hunley et al., 2009), suggesting that the power of our statistical findings should be much reduced relative to comparable analyses conducted on samples from outside the Americas. Also, since only mtDNA was sequenced in these ancient skeletons, many individuals exhibited identical mitochondrial haplotypes and therefore presented a genetic distance of 0. Since no two crania can ever have morphological distances of 0, this led to an inconsistency between the two data set types. In the Norris Farms #36 sample, the mean interindividual Procrustes distance for the cranial data was 0.361, compared with a Φst estimate of 0.014 for the HVI data. While these two types of data rely on different distance measures and consequently should not be expected to yield identical distance values, the discrepancy between the two distance measures ranges widely, from 0 to 1. Clearly, the estimate of interindividual genetic distances using HVI should be considered an underestimate of the overall level of genetic diversity at this mortuary site. Cranial distance measures at this site do not experience the same constraints and are hypothesized to reflect neutral evolution within a population. Therefore, the levels of local variability based on cranial data in this case are more likely to accurately reflect the overall levels of genetic diversity than the HVI data. This discrepancy did not occur in the population-level analyses in which no two populations were identical for any genetic data set, and more complete and varied subsets of genetic data, including autosomal data and complete mtgenomes, could be included.

Clearly, much more work is needed to assess the nature of the correspondence between morphological and (ancient) DNA data for bioarchaeological purposes. To address these issues at both local and global scales, (1) we are currently typing autosomal SNPs in the Norris Farms #36 sample to better evaluate the evolutionary significance of the mtDNA results, and (2) Cabana and Hunley (in prep) are investigating the global pattern of mtgenomes, autosomal STRs, and Y chromosome STRs in an evolutionary framework work.

Acknowledgments

This research was supported by NSF SES-0730808 and by funds from the University of Tennessee, Knoxville (both to GSC), and Midwestern University funds (to HFS). Special thanks go to the Illinois State Museum for permission to study the Norris Farms #36 osteological collection and to George & Claire Milner for their hospitality during our visits to the collection. Fig. 8.1 was created by Brent Adrian.

References

Ackermann, R.R., Cheverud, J.M., 2004. Detecting genetic drift versus selection in human evolution. Proceedings of the National Academy of Sciences of the United States of America 101, 17946–17951.

Andrews, R.M., Kubacka, I., Chinnery, P.F., Lightowlers, R.N., Turnbull, D.M., Howell, N., 1999. Reanalysis and revision of the Cambridge reference sequence for human mitochondrial DNA. Nature Genetics 23, 147.

Baker, L.E., McCormick, W.F., Matteson, K.J., 2001. A silica-based mitochondrial DNA extraction method applied to forensic hair shafts and teeth. Journal of Forensic Sciences 46, 126–130.

Bandelt, H.-J., Parson, W., 2008. Consistent treatment of length variants in the human mtDNA control region: a reappraisal. International Journal of Legal Medicine 122, 11–21.

Betti, L., Balloux, F., Amos, W., Hanihara, T., Manica, A., 2009. Distance from Africa, not climate, explains phenotypic diversity in humans. Proceedings. Biological Sciences 276, 809–814.

Betti, L., Balloux, F., Hanihara, T., Manica, A., 2010. The relative role of drift and selection in shaping the human skull. American Journal of Physical Anthropology 141, 76–82.

Butler, J.M., 2009. Fundamentals of Forensic DNA Typing. Academic Press, Burlington, Massachusetts.

Cann, H.M., de Toma, C., Cazes, L., Legrand, M.-F., Morel, V., Piouffre, L., Bodmer, J., et al., 2002. A human genome diversity cell line panel. Science 296, 261–262.

Cavalli-Sforza, L.L., 2005. The Human Genome Diversity Project: past, present and future. Nature Reviews Genetics 6, 333–340.

Conrad, L.A., 1991. The Middle Mississippian cultures of the central Illinois valley. In: Emerson, T.E., Lewis, R.B. (Eds.), Cahokia and the Hinterlands. University of Illinois Press, Urbana, pp. 119–156.

Cooper, A., Poinar, H.N., 2001. Ancient DNA: do it right or not at all. Science 289, 1139.

Corruccini, R.S., Shimada, I., Shinoda, K., 2002. Dental and mtDNA relatedness among thousand-year-old remains from Huaca Loro, Peru. Dental Anthropology 16, 9–14.

Esarey, D., Santure, S.K., 1990. The Morton site Oneota component and the bold counselor phase. Reports of Investigations No. 45. In: Santure, S.K., Harn, A.D., Esarey, D. (Eds.), Archaeological Investigations at the Morton Village and Norris Farms 36 Cemetery. Illinois State Museum, Springfield, pp. 162–166.

Excoffier, L., Lischer, H.E.L., 2010. Arlequin suite ver 3.5: a new series of programs to perform population genetics analyses under Linux and Windows. Molecular Ecology Resources 10, 564–567.

González-José, R., Van der Molen, S., González-Pérez, E., Hernandez, M., 2004. Patterns of phenotypic covariation and correlation in modern humans as viewed from morphological integration. American Journal of Physical Anthropology 123, 69–77.

Gower, J.C., 1975. Generalized procrustes analysis. Psychometrika 40, 33–51.

Harvati, K., Weaver, T.D., 2006. Human cranial anatomy and the differential preservation of population history and climate signatures. The Anatomical Record 288, 1225–1233.

Herrera, B., Hanihara, T., Godde, K., 2014. Comparability of multiple data types from the bering strait region: cranial and dental metrics and nonmetrics, mtDNA, and Y-chromosome DNA. American Journal of Physical Anthropology 154, 334–348.

Holm, S., 1979. A simple sequential rejective multiple test procedure. Scandinavian Journal of Statistics 6, 65–70.

Hood, G.M., 2010. PopTools Version 3.2.5. http://www.poptools.org.

Howells, W.W., 1973. Cranial variation in man. A study by multivariate analysis of patterns of differences among recent human populations. In: Papers of the Peabody Museum of Archeology and Ethnology, vol. 67. Peabody Museum, Cambridge, Massachusetts, p. 259.

Hubbard, A.R., Guatelli-Steinberg, D., Irish, J.D., 2015. Do nuclear DNA and dental nonmetric data produce similar reconstructions of regional population history? An example from modern coastal Kenya. American Journal of Physical Anthropology 157, 295–304.

Hunley, K.L., Healy, M.E., Long, J.C., 2009. The global pattern of gene identity variation reveals a history of long-range migrations, bottlenecks, and local mate exchange: implications for biological race. American Journal of Physical Anthropology 139, 35–46.

Hunley, K.L., Cabana, G.S., Long, J., 2016. The apportionment of human diversity revisited. American Journal of Physical Anthropology (in press).

Ingman, M.M., Gyllensten, U.U., 2003. Mitochondrial genome variation and evolutionary history of Australian and New Guinean aborigines. Genome Research 13, 1600–1606.

Irwin, J.A., Saunier, J.L., Niederstätter, H., Strouss, K.M., Sturk, K.A., Diegoli, T.M., Brandstätter, A., Parson, W., Parsons, T.J., 2009. Investigation of heteroplasmy in the human mitochondrial DNA control region: a synthesis of observations from more than 5000 global population samples. Journal of Molecular Evolution 68, 516–527.

Kemp, B.M., 2006. Mesoamerica and Southwest Prehistory, and the Entrance of Humans into the Americas: Mitochondrial DNA Evidence (Unpublished Ph.D. dissertation). University of California, Davis.

Liu, H., Prugnolle, F., Manica, A., Balloux, F., 2006. A geographically explicit genetic model of worldwide human-settlement history. American Journal of Human Genetics 79, 230–237.

Manica, A., Amos, W., Balloux, F., Hanihara, T., 2007. The effect of ancient population bottlenecks on human phenotypic variation. Nature 448, 346–349.

Mantel, N., 1967. The detection of disease clustering and a generalized regression approach. Cancer Research 27, 209–220.

Meyer, S., Weiss, G., von Haeseler, A., 1999. Pattern of nucleotide substitution and rate heterogeneity in the hypervariable regions I and II of human mtDNA. Genetics 152, 1103–1110.

Milner, G.R., Humpf, D.H., Harpending, H.C., 1989. Pattern matching of age-at-death distributions in paleodemographic analysis. American Journal of Physical Anthropology 80, 49–58.

O'Higgins, P., Jones, N., 1998. Facial growth in *Cercocebus torquatus*: an application of three dimensional geometric morphometric techniques to the study of morphological variation. Journal of Anatomy 193, 251–272.

Perez, S.I., Bernal, V., Gonzalez, P.N., 2007. Morphological differentiation of aboriginal human populations from Tierra del Fuego Patagonia: implications for South American peopling. American Journal of Physical Anthropology 133, 1067–1079.

Perez, S.I., Bernal, V., Gonzalez, P.N., Sardi, M., Politis, G.G., 2009. Discrepancy between cranial and DNA data of early Americans: implications for American peopling. PLoS One 4, e5746.

Pfeiffer, H., Brinkmann, B., Hühne, J., Rolf, B., Morris, A.A., Steighner, R., Holland, M.M., Forster, P., 1999. Expanding the forensic German mitochondrial DNA control region database: genetic diversity as a function of sample size and microgeography. International Journal of Legal Medicine 112, 291–298.

Prugnolle, F., Manica, A., Balloux, F., 2005. Geography predicts neutral genetic diversity of human populations. Current Biology 15, R159–R160.

Ramachandran, S., Deshpande, O., Roseman, C.C., Rosenberg, N.A., Feldman, M.W., Cavalli-Sforza, L.L., 2005. Support from the relationship of genetic and geographic distance in human populations for a serial founder effect originating in Africa. Proceedings of the National Academy of Sciences of the United States of America 102, 15942–15947.

Ray, N., Currat, M., Berthier, P., Excoffier, L., 2005. Recovering the geographic origin of early modern humans by realistic and spatially explicit simulations. Genome Research 15, 1161–1167.

Relethford, J.H., 1994. Craniometric variation among modern human populations. American Journal of Physical Anthropology 95, 53–62.
Relethford, J.H., 2001. Global analysis of regional differences in craniometric diversity and population substructure. Human Biology 73, 629–636.
Relethford, J.H., 2004. Boas and beyond: migration and craniometric variation. American Journal of Human Biology 16, 379–386.
Relethford, J.H., Harpending, H.C., 1994. Craniometric variation, genetic theory, and modern human origins. American Journal of Physical Anthropology 95, 249–270.
Roseman, C.C., 2004. Detecting interregionally diversifying natural selection on modern human cranial form by using matched molecular and morphometric data. Proceedings of the National Academy of Sciences of the United States of America 101, 12825–12829.
Roseman, C.C., Weaver, T.D., 2004. Multivariate apportionment of global human craniometric diversity. American Journal of Physical Anthropology 125, 257–263.
Rosenberg, N.A., Pritchard, J.K., Weber, J.L., Cann, H.M., Kidd, K.K., Zhivotovsky, L.A., Feldman, M.W., 2002. Genetic structure of human populations. Science 298, 2381–2385.
Santure, S.K., 1990. Norris Farms 36: a bold counselor phase Oneota cemetery. Reports of Investigations 45. In: Archaeological Investigations at the Morton Village and Norris Farms 36 Cemetery. Illinois State Museum, Springfield, Illinois, pp. 66–74.
Santure, S.K., Harb, A.D., Esarey, D., 1990. Archaeological Investigations at the Morton Village and Norris Farms 36 Cemetery. Reports of Investigations No. 45. Illinois State Museum, Springfield.
Smith, H.F., 2008. An Evaluation of the Association between Three-dimensional Cranial Morphology and Molecular Distances in Humans (Ph.D. dissertation). Arizona State University, Tempe, AZ.
Smith, H.F., 2009. Which cranial regions reflect molecular distance reliable in humans? Evidence from three-dimensional morphology. American Journal of Human Biology 21, 36–47.
Smith, H.F., 2011. The role of genetic drift in shaping modern human cranial variation: a test using microevolutionary modeling. International Journal of Evolutionary Biology 2011. http://dx.doi.org/10.4061/2011/145262.
Smith, H.F., Ritzman, T., Otárola-Castillo, E., Terhune, C.E., 2013. A 3-D geometric morphometric study of intraspecific variation in the ontogeny of the temporal bone in modern *Homo sapiens*. Journal of Human Evolution 65, 479–489.
Smith, H.F., Terhune, C.E., Lockwood, C.A., 2007. Genetic, geographic, and environmental correlates of human temporal bone variation. American Journal of Physical Anthropology 134, 312–322.
Tamura, K., Nei, M., 1993. Estimation of the number of nucleotide substitutions in the control region of mitochondrial DNA in humans and chimpanzees. Molecular Biology and Evolution 10, 512–526.
von Cramon-Taubadel, N., 2009a. Congruence of individual cranial bone morphology and neutral molecular affinity patterns in modern humans. American Journal of Physical Anthropology 140, 205–215.
von Cramon-Taubadel, N., 2009b. Revisiting the homoiology hypothesis: the impact of phenotypic plasticity on the reconstruction of human population history from craniometric data. Journal of Human Evolution 57, 179–190.
von Cramon-Taubadel, N., 2011a. The relative efficacy of functional and developmental cranial modules for reconstructing global human population history. American Journal of Physical Anthropology 146, 83–93.
von Cramon-Taubadel, N., 2011b. Global human mandibular variation reflects differences in agricultural and hunter-gatherer subsistence strategies. Proceedings of the National Academy of Sciences of the United States of America 108, 19546–19551.
von Cramon-Taubadel, N., 2014. Evolutionary insights into global patterns of human cranial diversity: population history, climatic and dietary effects. Journal of Anthropological Sciences 92, 43–77.
von Cramon-Taubadel, N., Lycett, S., 2007. Brief Communication: human cranial variation fits iterative founder effect model with African origin. American Journal of Physical Anthropology 136, 108–113.

Weaver, T.D., Roseman, C.C., Stringer, C.B., 2007. Were neandertal and modern human cranial differences produced by natural selection or genetic drift? Journal of Human Evolution 53, 135–145.

Wilson, M.R., Allard, M.W., Monson, K., Miller, K.W.P., Budowle, B., 2002a. Recommendations for consistent treatment of length variants in the human mitochondrial DNA control region. Forensic Science International 129, 35–42.

Wilson, M.R., Allard, M.W., Monson, K., Miller, K.W.P., Budowle, B., 2002b. Further discussion of the consistent treatment of length variants in the human mitochondrial DNA control region. Forensic Science Communications 4 (4).

CHAPTER

9

Missing Data Imputation Methods and Their Performance With Biodistance Analyses

M.W. Kenyhercz[1,2], N.V. Passalacqua[3]

University of Tennessee, Knoxville, TN, United States[1]; University of Pretoria, Pretoria, South Africa[2]; Western Carolina University, Cullowhee, NC, United States[3]

CHAPTER OUTLINE HEAD

Materials **182**
Methods **183**
Imputation Methods 183
Hot Deck 183
Iterative Robust Model-Based Imputations 183
k-Nearest Neighbor 184
Variable Mean 185
Results **186**
Missing Data at 25% 186
Imputation 186
Biodistance 187
Missing Data at 50% 189
Imputation 189
Biodistance 191
Discussion **192**
Conclusions **193**
Acknowledgments **194**
References **194**

Biological anthropologists often work with incomplete skeletal specimens due to taphonomic and other destructive processes. Unfortunately, many multivariate analyses require complete data sets and are thus not applicable to many bioarchaeological (incomplete) data sets. This is not a new problem; Howells (1973) suggested three potential approaches to handle missing data in craniometrics: (1) use the mean of the series for a particular variable; (2) use an estimate from regression formulae; or (3) make a "careful guess" (p. 34) based on overall skull size and shape (this was Howells's preferred method). However, each of Howells's suggestions is problematic. First, replacement of missing data with a mean is not suitable given the ease with which outliers skew mean values. Second, the regression formulae, specifically the widely used BMDP statistical software (Dixon, 1990), are not appropriate when more than a few variables are

Biological Distance Analysis. http://dx.doi.org/10.1016/B978-0-12-801966-5.00009-3

missing (Pietrusewsky, 2000). Third, a "careful guess" is inherently subjective with no mathematical basis. Since the time of Howells's suggestions, considerable advances in computing technology and statistics have allowed for more sophisticated algorithms that better assess and quantify missing data. The goal of this study was to test several different data imputation techniques on the same data set in order to examine which method had the least difference from the actual data set and thus is best suited for bioanthropological analyses.

MATERIALS

The sample consisted of 352 individuals representing four population groups from Howells's publicly available craniometric data set (Howells, 1973—see Appendix of this volume). The four groups were selected to represent different geographic populations and include the Ainu ($n = 86$), Arikara ($n = 69$), Dogon ($n = 99$), and Zalavar ($n = 98$) (Howells, 1973). Twenty variables were selected to represent the entire cranium (Table 9.1).

Table 9.1 Craniometric Variables Included in the Study and Their Abbreviations

Craniometric Variable	Abbreviation
Biasterionic breadth	ASB
Biauricular breadth	AUB
Basion–bregma height	BBH
Basion–nasion length	BNL
Basion–prosthion length	BPL
Interorbital breadth	DKB
Glabello–occipital length	GOL
External palate breadth	MAB
Nasal breadth	NLB
Nasal height	NLH
Nasio–occipital length	NOL
Nasion–prosthion height	NPH
Orbit breadth	OBB
Orbit height	OBH
Minimum cranial breadth	WCB
Simotic chord (minimum nasal breadth)	WNB
Maximum cranial breadth	XCB
Maximum frontal breadth	XFB
Bimaxillary breadth	ZMB
Bizygomatic breadth	ZYB

METHODS

Each individual included in this study contained complete craniometric data. Rinker (2012) wrote an R function to randomly delete data, which was modified for the current study and is available from the authors upon request. Simply put, the function uses a predefined proportion that is set by the user, and then it iteratively replaces values with NA. Due to the function, some contiguous blocks of data may be replaced at the beginning and end of a data frame. Using the complete four-group data set, two subsets of the data were created using the modified Rinker function. These subsets were randomly created with 25% and 50% missing data (Figs. 9.1 and 9.2). The missing data sets were subjected to various imputation methods, and the original data matrix was subtracted from the imputed data set in order to evaluate the efficacy of each imputation method.

The imputation methods tested include hot deck, iterative robust model-based imputation (IRMI), *k*-nearest neighbor (kNN), and individual variable means. All analyses were conducted in R (R Core Team, 2013), and each imputation method, excluding variable means computed in base R, was conducted with the VIMGUI package (Schopfhauser et al., 2014). Data imputation was conducted on the entire sample (geographic populations pooled) as well as individually for each Howells population group.

Additionally, Mahalanobis distances (D^2) were calculated for each population group of the original data set and each imputed data set in order to explore the impact of different imputation methods on biodistance. Each D^2 matrix was subjected to hierarchical cluster analysis to visualize the impact that each imputation method had on the calculation of biological distance. Lastly, the complete and imputed data sets were subjected to a linear discriminant function analysis (LDFA) with leave-one-out cross-validation, as this offers a more realistic view of model performance.

Imputation Methods

Little and Rubin (2002) explained that the goal of data imputation is to generate plausible replacement values, and not to explicitly generate the most accurate prediction of missing data. We argue that when working with incomplete craniometric data sets, the most accurate imputation is favorable over simply a plausible value, particularly in forensic applications (Passalacqua et al., 2013).

Hot Deck

Hot deck imputation replaces missing values for *n* variables with observations from a similar, complete individual known as a donor, based on each variable present (Andridge and Little, 2010). A suitable donor is randomly selected in the data set, again with the criteria that present values between individuals are similar. In this way, hot deck imputation does not rely on model building and is thus less sensitive to the inherent misspecification that is an issue in parametric models such as regression (Andridge and Little, 2010). However, given the hot deck procedure, multivariate relationships among data are not considered, which may be problematic considering the goals of analyses involving craniometrics.

Iterative Robust Model-Based Imputations

IRMIs use the one missing data value as a response variable, and the remaining variables are designated as the regressors (Templ et al., 2011). In this way, the multivariate model of the entire data set is used to

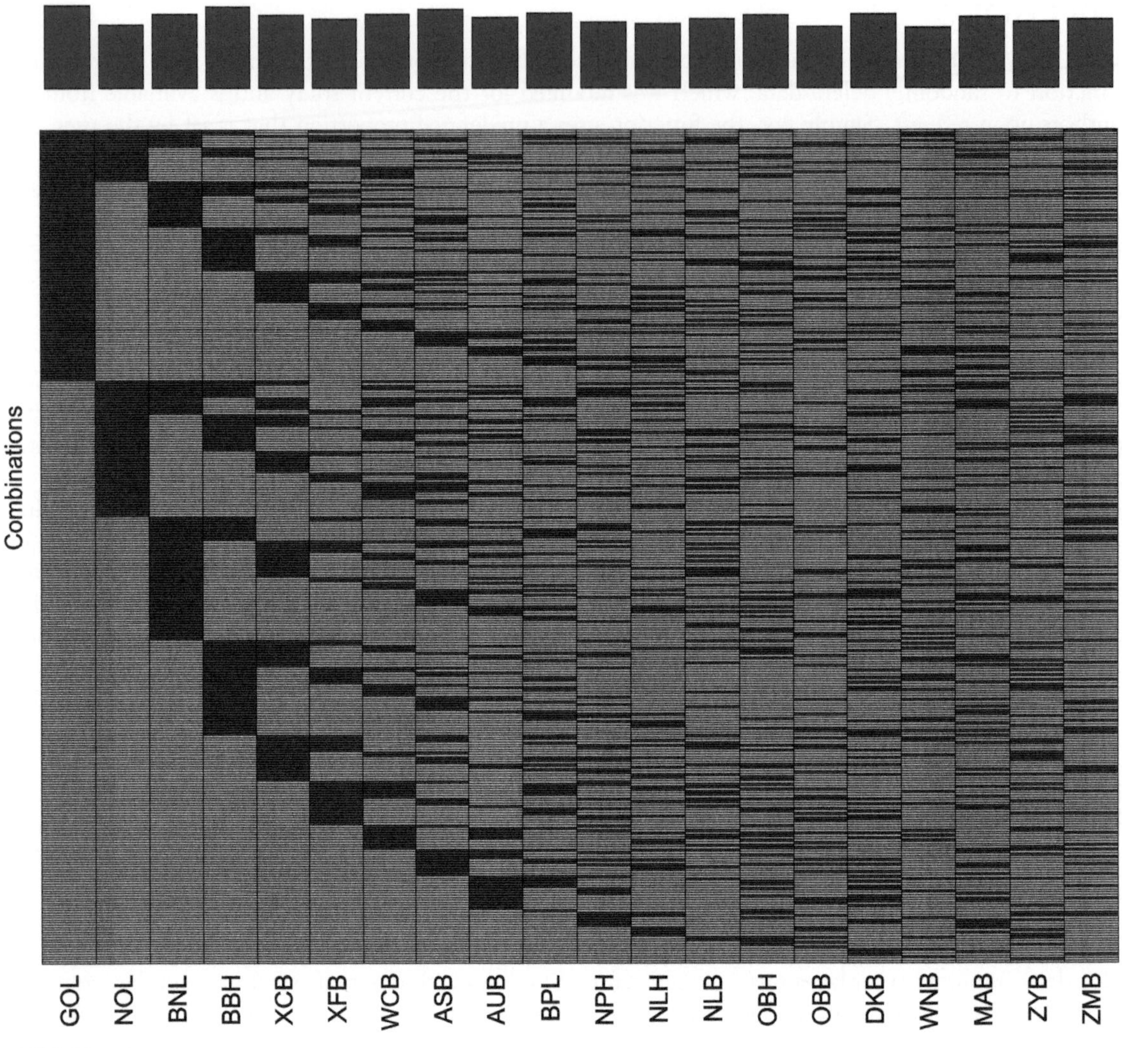

FIGURE 9.1

Visualization of 25% missing data by variable for entire data set. The bars at the top of the figure represent proportions of data missing from individual variables.

impute the missing response variable. Furthermore, IRMI does not require that one variable be completely present in order to predict response variables. However, because IRMI models the data from a multivariate normal distribution, imputed values can become so large or small that they are not biologically meaningful.

k-Nearest Neighbor

The kNN imputation method uses the kNN algorithm to search the entire data set for the *k* number of most similar cases, or neighbors, that show the same patterns as the row with missing data. An average of missing

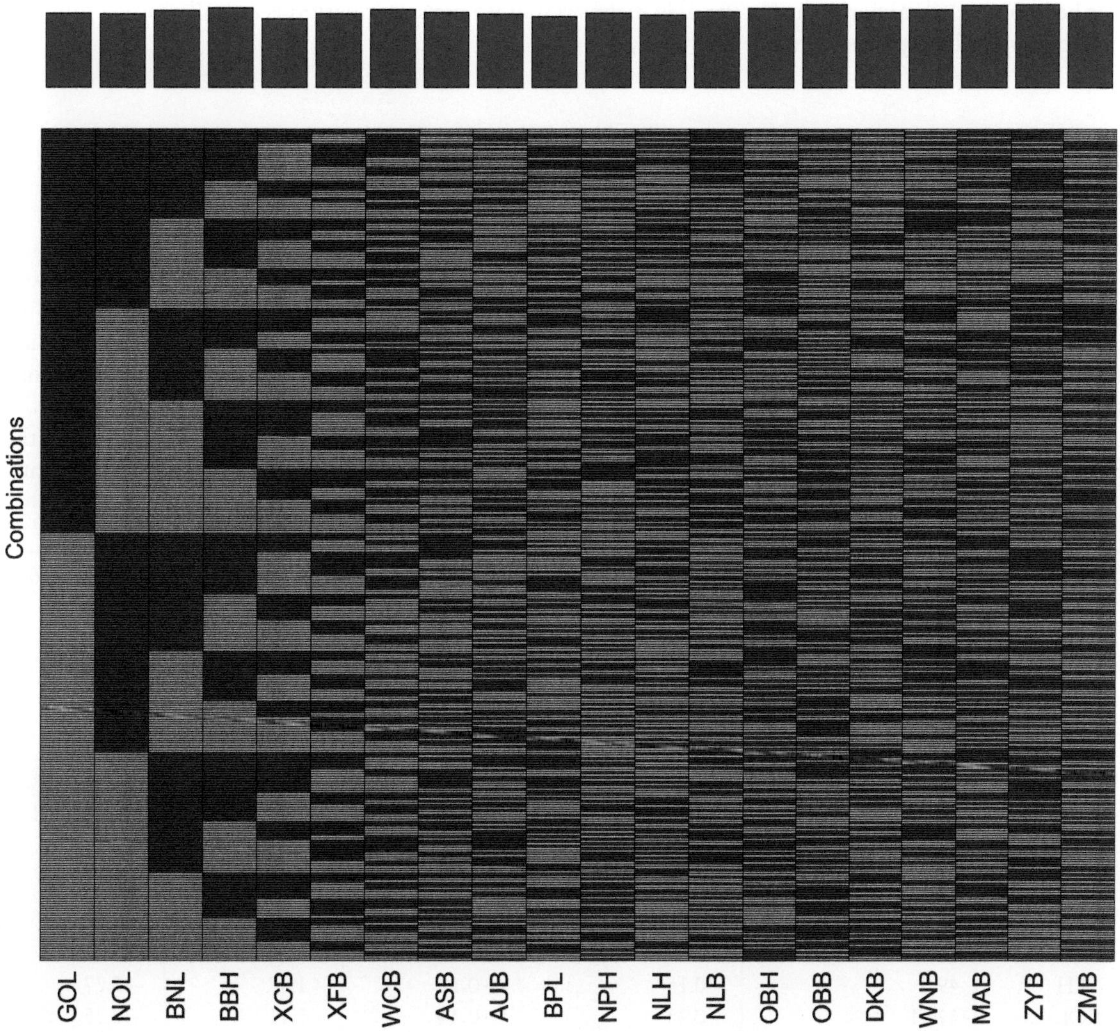

FIGURE 9.2

Visualization of 50% missing data by variable for entire data set. The bars at the top of the figure represent proportions of data missing from individual variables.

data variables was derived from the kNNs and used for each missing value (Batista and Monard, 2002). In the current study, $k = 5$, where the five closest individuals were used to impute missing data; this has previously been shown to be adequate (Hastie et al., 1999). One disadvantage of kNN is that an appropriate number of values from present data is necessary for each variable, which in the current study is five.

Variable Mean

The column mean for each variable was inserted in place of any missing data. Means were derived from the entire data set and not by group, because in a true unknown context, group demographic information may not be known. A detriment of using variable means is that no new information is actually gained from the replacement. The replaced data are essentially noise.

RESULTS

Missing Data at 25%

Imputation

The differences between the actual data set and the 25%-imputed data sets with geographic populations pooled are shown in Table 9.2. These results indicate that kNN most frequently had the smallest absolute difference from the original data set, while IRMI consistently had the greatest. For each imputation technique, there was a bias toward estimates that were greater than the original values. Further, kNN had the smallest average absolute difference from the original data set, and IRMI had the greatest (Table 9.3).

When the populations were kept separate and data were imputed, kNN and IRMI resulted in the lowest average absolute differences (see Table 9.3). In the Ainu subset, column means most consistently

***Table 9.2** Mean Values for Craniometric Variables and Differences Between Imputation Methods Using 25% Missing Data Set and Original Data Set*

Variable	Howells (Mean)	Column Mean	Hot Deck	IRMI	kNN
ASB	107.1	0.12	0.35	−1.81	**−0.03**
AUB	120.5	−0.39	−0.26	−1.24	**−0.01**
BBH	132.2	0.15	0.22	−1.44	**−0.02**
BNL	99.8	**0.07**	0.23	−1.22	−0.18
BPL	97.8	−0.22	−0.22	−1.61	**−0.20**
DKB	21.5	0.24	0.07	−1.06	**0.06**
GOL	179	0.67	0.74	−2.08	**−0.45**
MAB	63.6	0.03	0.17	−0.90	**−0.02**
NLB	26.7	−0.05	**0.01**	−0.17	−0.02
NLH	49.7	−0.15	**−0.10**	−1.47	−0.27
NOL	177.1	−0.23	**−0.14**	−2.11	−0.25
NPH	66	−0.05	0.13	−1.88	**−0.04**
OBB	39.7	−0.05	**−0.01**	−0.42	−0.09
OBH	33.6	−0.09	−0.03	−0.32	**<0.01**
WCB	71.5	−0.22	−0.23	−1.03	**−0.12**
WNB	9	0.10	0.17	0.24	**0.06**
XCB	138.3	**0.17**	0.22	−0.40	−0.34
XFB	115.3	−0.31	−0.26	−0.97	**−0.15**
ZMB	95.4	−0.31	**−0.26**	−1.85	−0.33
ZYB	130.9	−0.09	**0.05**	−0.81	**0.05**

IRMI, *Iterative robust model;* kNN, *k-nearest neighbor.*
The smallest differences for each variable are in bold. All measurements in mm.

Table 9.3 Average Method Absolute Differences with 25% Missing Data				
	Column Mean	Hot Deck	IRMI	kNN
All groups	0.19	0.19	1.15	**0.14**
Ainu	0.37	0.44	0.21	**0.20**
Arikara	0.04	0.10	0.03	**0.001**
Dogon	**0.12**	0.29	**0.12**	0.19
Zalavar	0.33	0.23	**0.19**	0.22

IRMI, *Iterative robust model;* kNN, *k-nearest neighbor.*
Smallest difference is in bold.

had the lowest absolute differences. However, kNN still had the lowest average absolute difference. Furthermore, the majority of the lowest differences from column means centered on variables from the facial skeleton—particularly the midface (NPH, NLB, NLH, OBH, WNB, ZYB). Similarly, the Arikara subset also showed that column means had the greatest number of smallest absolute differences, though it was followed closely by kNN. Just as in the Ainu, while column means had the greatest number of smallest differences, kNN still had the smallest average absolute difference. Furthermore, the Arikara had the smallest differences between actual and imputed values, compared with each other individual population. Column means showed the smallest differences in variables centered on the nasal aperture (NPH, NLB, NLH), while kNN's smallest differences were centered around the palate and midface (MAB, ZYB, ZMB). In the Dogon, both column means and IRMI had the most instances of the lowest absolute difference from actual values and also shared the lowest average absolute difference (Table 9.3). Following previous trends, column means most accurately recreated facial skeleton variables, while IRMI most accurately estimated cranial vault variables. Lastly, in the Zalavar, IRMI had the lowest average absolute difference. Overall, kNN imputation had the most instances of lowest absolute difference from the actual data set.

Biodistance

The D^2 matrix for the entire data set (no missing variables), generated using each of the 20 variables, is shown in Table 9.4. Each D^2 value between populations is significant at $p < .001$. The Dogon and Arikara have the greatest distance among the groups, with Zalavar and Ainu having the smallest. The D^2 matrices calculated using the imputations imposed on the 25% missing data set are visualized in Fig. 9.3. Each

Table 9.4 Mahalanobis D^2 Matrix of Complete Howells Data Set				
Group	Ainu	Arikara	Dogon	Zalavar
Ainu	–	12.47	11.53	7.34
Arikara	<0.001	–	22.40	12.41
Dogon	<0.001	<0.001	–	19.69
Zalavar	<0.001	<0.001	<0.001	–

Distances are above the diagonal and p *values are below the diagonal.*

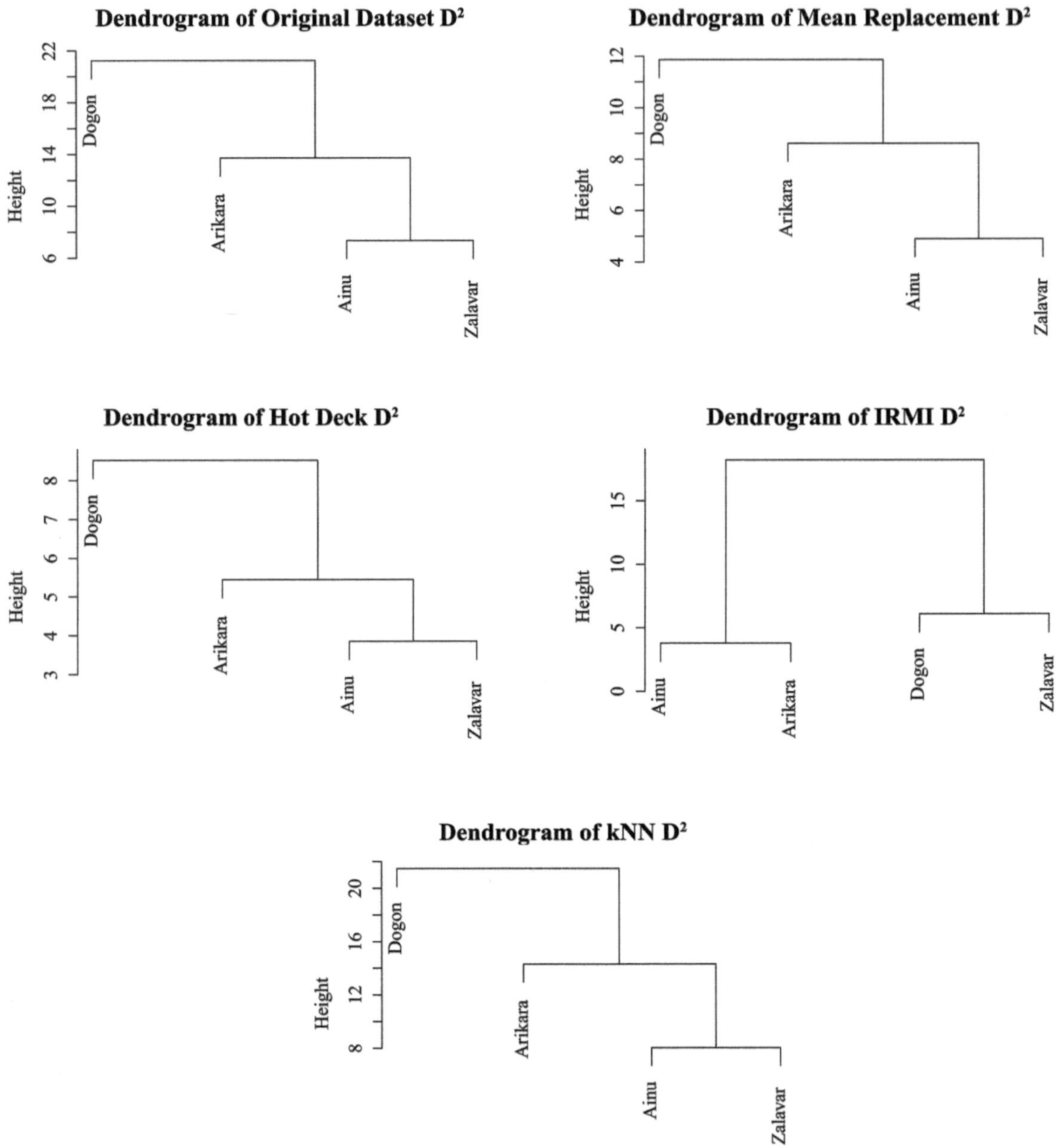

FIGURE 9.3

Comparison of D^2 matrices as visualized through hierarchical cluster analysis for the various imputation methods with 25% missing data.

imputation technique produces similar relationships among the groups with the exception of IRMI, which changes the overall cluster pattern. Virtually all imputation methods decrease the D^2 between populations, essentially making them more similar. The only imputation method resulting in increases in D^2 values is kNN. Still, each D^2 value generated from the various imputation techniques is significantly different at $p < .001$. The mean D^2 for each group and imputation technique was subtracted from the complete data set, and the absolute differences can be seen in Table 9.5. Hot deck imputation has the highest mean difference from actual values, and kNN has the lowest (Table 9.5).

Actual and imputed data sets were subjected to LDFA, the results of which are shown in Table 9.6. The complete data set has a total correct classification of 87.5%, cross-validated. The single highest total correct classification is from the kNN data set at 88.1%, which corroborates the increase in D^2 due to this imputation technique. The poorest classification is from hot deck at 68.2%.

Missing Data at 50%

Imputation

Differences between the actual data set and 50%-imputed data sets are shown in Table 9.7. With half the data missing, hot deck imputation most frequently had the smallest differences from the complete data set, followed by mean replacement. Just as in the 25% imputation, there was a bias to overestimate values for all variables in all groups. Hot deck imputation had the lowest average absolute difference for the entire sample, though mean replacement generally had the lowest average absolute difference for all but one of the individual populations (Table 9.8).

***Table 9.5** Mean Absolute Difference in D^2 Values Between Complete Data Set and Each 25% Imputation Technique*

Column Mean	Hot Deck	IRMI	kNN
5.75	8.32	4.69	0.61

IRMI, *Iterative robust model;* kNN, *k-nearest neighbor.*

***Table 9.6** Total Correct Classification Percentages (%) Using Linear Discriminant Function Analysis for Howells and 25%-imputed Data Sets*

Data Set	Ainu	Arikara	Dogon	Zalavar	Total Correct
Howells	80.2	89.9	93.9	85.7	87.5
Hot deck	54.7	69.6	76.8	70.4	68.2
IRMI	50.0	81.2	85.9	81.6	75.0
kNN	84.9	87.0	90.9	88.8	88.1
Mean	68.6	81.2	82.8	75.5	77.0

***Table 9.7** Mean Values for Craniometric Variables and Differences Between Imputation Methods Using the 50% Missing Data Set and the Complete Data Set*

Variable	Howells (Mean)	Column Mean	Hot Deck	IRMI	kNN
ASB	107.1	0.05	−0.56	−1.82	**−0.02**
AUB	120.5	0.33	**0.21**	−2.19	−0.57
BBH	132.2	**0.19**	0.26	−2.22	−0.49
BNL	99.8	**0.08**	0.57	−1.23	−0.73
BPL	97.8	**0.01**	0.03	−2.39	−0.43
DKB	21.5	−0.3	**−0.03**	−1.07	−0.15
GOL	179	−0.85	**−0.24**	−3.64	−1.96
MAB	63.6	−1.84	**−0.12**	−1.24	**−0.12**
NLB	26.7	−0.22	**−0.13**	−0.83	−0.26
NLH	49.7	−0.14	**0.08**	−1.39	−0.22
NOL	177.1	**−0.16**	−0.39	−2.43	−1.29
NPH	66	**0.09**	0.32	−2.37	−0.39
OBB	39.7	−0.17	**−0.02**	−0.83	−0.19
OBH	33.6	−0.23	**0.09**	−0.5	−0.17
WCB	71.5	−0.25	−0.24	−2.11	**−0.15**
WNB	9	**0.13**	0.23	−0.43	0.28
XCB	138.3	0.19	**0.14**	−1.55	−0.45
XFB	115.3	**−0.46**	−0.47	−2.41	−0.81
ZMB	95.4	−0.44	**−0.18**	−1.61	−0.41
ZYB	130.9	0.84	**0.49**	−2.01	−0.59

IRMI, *Iterative robust model;* kNN, *k-nearest neighbor.*
The smallest differences for each variable are in bold. All values in mm.

When imputation was performed on individual populations, column mean generally exhibited the least differences from the actual data set. The only population in which mean replacement did not have the smallest differences was the Zalavar, where hot deck outperformed mean replacement. Generally, pooled sample-imputed data sets showed that vault variables have the least differences from actual values, while midface variables (XFB, ZMB, ZYB) have greater differences. However, when populations were kept separate, differences between actual and imputed values dropped off, particularly in the midface.

***Table 9.8** Average Method Absolute Differences with 50% Missing Data*

	Column Mean	Hot Deck	IRMI	kNN
All groups	0.35	**0.24**	1.71	0.48
Ainu	**0.23**	0.55	0.41	0.44
Arikara	**0.39**	0.52	0.48	0.56
Dogon	**0.39**	0.49	0.43	0.48
Zalavar	0.32	0.36	**0.29**	0.34

IRMI, *Iterative robust model;* kNN, *k-nearest neighbor.*
The smallest differences for each variable are in bold. All values in mm.

Biodistance

The D^2 matrix for each imputed data set is visualized in Fig. 9.4. Each D^2 value between populations is significant at $p < .05$ except in the IRMI imputation data set, where the p value for the Arikara–Zalavar D^2 equals 0.273, and for Dogon–Zalavar equals 0.866. Each imputation method decreases the D^2 between groups, though the overall relationship among groups is the same (see Fig. 9.4). The mean difference

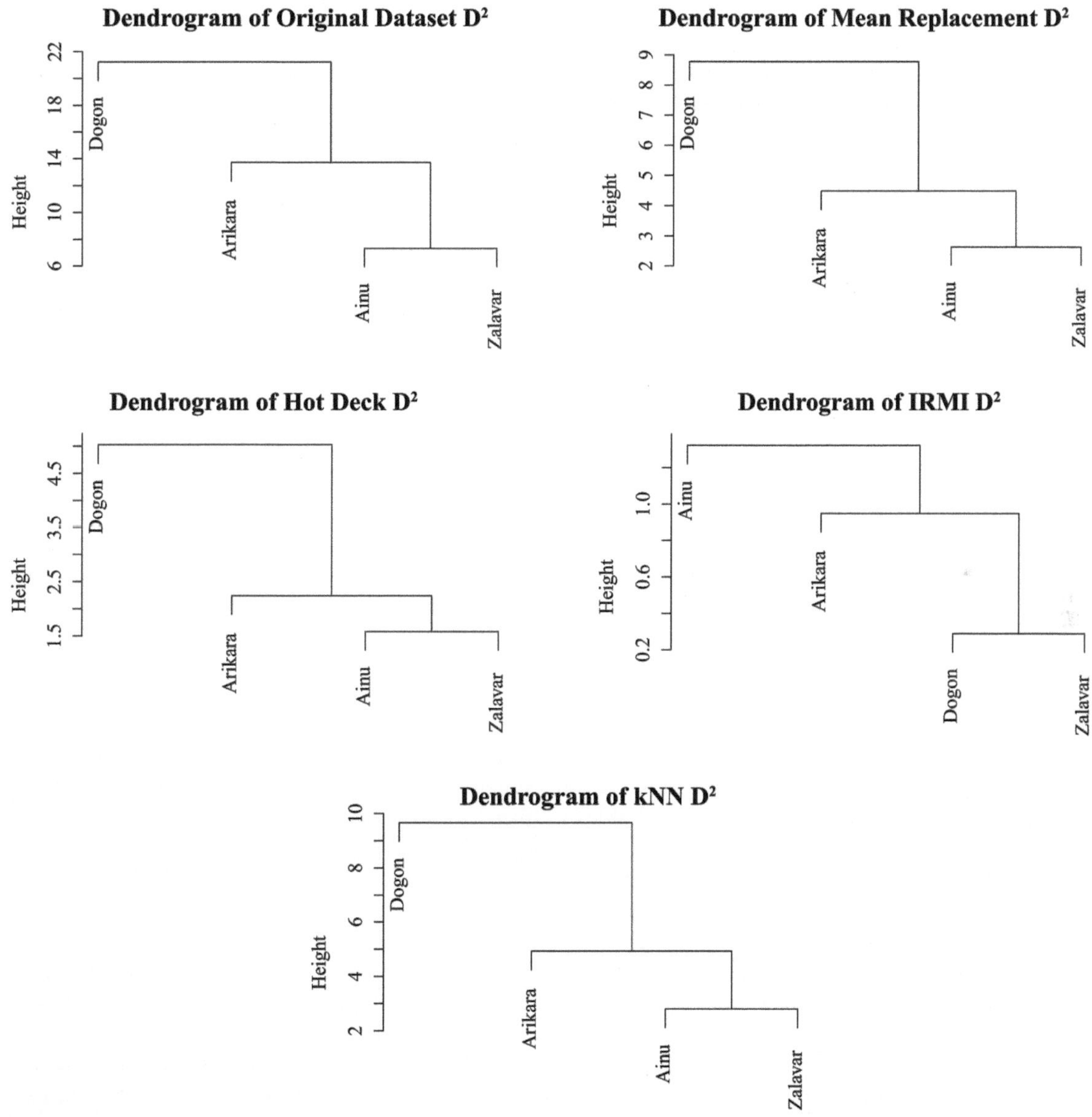

FIGURE 9.4

Comparison of D^2 matrices as visualized through hierarchical cluster analysis for the various imputation methods with 50% missing data.

***Table 9.9** Mean Absolute Difference in D^2 Values Between Complete Data Set and Each 50% Imputation Technique*

Column Mean	Hot Deck	IRMI	kNN
8.77	11.23	13.41	8.25

IRMI, *Iterative robust model;* kNN, *k-nearest neighbor.*

***Table 9.10** Total Correct Classification Using Linear Discriminant Function Analysis for Howells and 50%-imputed Data Sets*

Data Set	Ainu	Arikara	Dogon	Zalavar	Total Correct
Howells	80.2	89.9	93.9	85.7	87.5
Hot deck	44.2	47.8	67.7	53.1	54.0
IRMI	7.0	37.7	63.6	43.9	39.2
kNN	58.1	63.8	81.8	64.3	67.6
Mean	59.3	65.2	84.8	55.1	66.5

between complete and 50%-imputed data sets is available in Table 9.9. The smallest difference between actual and imputed data is from kNN, followed by mean replacement, and the largest difference occurs using IRMI.

Each data set was subjected to LDFA, and the results are shown in Table 9.10. Of the imputation methods, kNN has the highest total correct classification at 67.6% cross-validated, a decrease from the 87.5% of the complete data set. The lowest total correct classification is observed with IRMI-imputed data at 39.2%. Of note, IRMI imputation is the only instance of a group being misclassified more often than correctly classified: the Ainu achieve only a 7.0% total correct classification.

DISCUSSION

Missing data are an inherent problem in biological anthropology due to the fragile nature of osseous material. When poorly preserved remains are encountered, most often these specimens are either completely excluded from study, or the variables in question are dropped from the analysis. However, when approaching incomplete data sets for analytical work, the goal of the project should not be changed because of missing values in the data set. Unfortunately, missing-data analysis receives little attention, particularly within biological anthropology, and listwise deletion remains the most common method used to handle cases with missing values. By their statistical nature, imputation methods reduce the overall variance present in sample variables, decreasing overall heterogeneity. Because of this, when comparing groups that may vary only slightly between variable measurements, imputation may obscure the already narrow margin of group variable differences. Here we have examined the affect of missing data on biodistance analyses using four different data imputation methods. Our results demonstrate that when a researcher has a partial cranium from an unknown population, kNN is a viable option for the reliable imputation of missing data.

In both the 25% and 50% imputations, kNN exhibited the smallest absolute difference between actual and imputed D^2 values (Tables 9.5 and 9.9). The utility of kNN in data imputation is logical given the algorithm; that is, the five cases most similar to the one with missing data are used to generate a mean to replace the missing value. Assuming that the phenotypic expression of craniometrics is related to genetics (Relethford, 2004, 2010), the relatively geographically isolated Howells populations should exhibit craniometric similarities. In situations where the population of an unknown specimen is used, kNN is more appropriate than using mean replacements because the mean will take the entire sample into account, not just specimens most similar to the unknown, effectively creating noise in the data. Even though kNN is more robust than mean replacement, mean values outperform the other imputation methods in population-specific contexts.

While kNN had the smallest absolute difference from actual D^2 matrices in both the 25% and 50% imputation sets, the utility of mean replacement is more pronounced in the 50% missing data. However, hot deck imputation did show the smallest amount of differences between actual and imputed values with 50% missing data. Nevertheless, in hot deck, a suitable donor (specimen) with full data is taken at random. If there are only a few individuals with complete data sets and one happens to be an outlier, hot deck could replace missing data with data that are significantly different from those of most individuals in the sample.

The IRMI imputation method consistently performed the worst for craniometric data. The poor performance of IRMI is likely due to the manner in which missing data are modeled—that is, the missing value is treated as the response variable, and the remaining variables are regressors. Specifically, in the complete sample, the remaining regressor variables will be from several populations, often replacing the missing value with one that is expected given the entire population. Additionally, IRMI often models missing data at values too large or too small to be biologically feasible (creating outliers), which diminishes its performance on both complete and population-specific models.

In the 25% missing data model, kNN-imputed data achieved a higher total correct classification than was the case with the actual data set. However, kNN should be used with caution because the algorithm introduces artificial bias by replacing missing data with those from the most closely related individuals, thus reducing the variability in the model and introducing ascertainment bias. Still, in both the 25% and 50% models, kNN had the highest classification of any of the other imputation methods and the least differences from actual data. The IRMI imputation method struggled when 50% of the data were missing, especially in population-specific models where it achieved the lowest total correct classification (Ainu = 7.0%).

CONCLUSIONS

While several imputation methods exist for treating missing data, not all imputation methods are suitable for the craniometric data often encountered in biological anthropology. We have argued that omitting data via listwise deletion is not necessary given advancements in data-imputation techniques. Based on the methods compared here, it is suggested that kNN imputation be used in place of other data-imputation methods whenever possible. The kNN algorithm is conceptually and computationally simple, thus giving it greater power over the other multiple imputation methods, and is more robust than using simple mean replacement. Furthermore, when it is unclear which population a cranium may have belonged to mean replacement offers little more than statistical noise. The kNN-imputation method had the least effect on biodistance analyses and classification accuracy.

Acknowledgments

Thanks to Drs. Marin Pilloud and Joseph Hefner for inviting us to participate in this edited volume, and to the anonymous reviewer for their helpful suggestions.

References

Andridge, R.R., Little, R.J., 2010. A review of hot deck imputation for survey non-response. International Statistical Review 78 (1), 40–64.

Batista, G.E.A.P.A., Monard, M.C., 2002. A study of k-nearest neighbour as an imputation method. In: Abraham, A., del Solar, J.R., Köppen, M. (Eds.), HIS, vol. 87 of frontiers in artificial intelligence and applications. IOS Press, Santiago, Chile, pp. 251–260.

Dixon, W.J., 1990. BMPD Statistical Software Manual. University of California Press, Berkeley, CA.

Hastie, T., Tibshirani, R., Sherlock, G., Eisen, M., Brown, P., Botstein, D., 1999. Imputing Missing Data for Gene Expression Arrays. Stanford University Statistics Department Technical Report.

Howells, W.W., 1973. Cranial variation in man. A study by multivariate analysis of patterns of difference. Among recent human populations. In: Papers of the Peabody Museum of Archaeology and Ethnology, vol. 67, pp. 1–259.

Little, R.J.A., Rubin, D.B., 2002. Statistical Analysis with Missing Data. Wiley-Interscience, Hoboken.

Passalacqua, N.V., Zhang, Z., Pierce, S.J., 2013. Sex determination of human skeletal populations using latent profile analysis. American Journal of Physical Anthropology 151 (4), 538–543.

Pietrusewsky, M., 2000. Metric analysis of skeletal remains: methods and applications. In: Katzenberg, M.A., Saunders, S.R. (Eds.), Biological Anthropology of the Human Skeleton. Wiley-Liss, New York, pp. 375–415.

R Core Team, 2013. R: A Language and Environment for Statistical Computing. R Foundation for Statistical Computing, Vienna, Austria, ISBN 3-900051-07-0. URL: http://www.R-project.org.

Relethford, J.H., 2004. Boas and beyond: migration and craniometric variation. American Journal of Human Biology 16 (4), 379–386.

Relethford, J.H., 2010. Population-specific deviations of global human craniometric variation from a neutral model. American Journal of Physical Anthropology 142 (1), 105–111.

Rinker, T., 2012. Function to Generate a Randon Data Set. Available from: http://www.r-bloggers.com/function-to-generate-a-random-data-set/.

Schopfhauser, D., Templ, M., Alfons, A., Kowarik, A., Prantner, B., 2014. VIMGUI: Visualization and Imputation of Missing Values. R package version 0.9.0. http://cran.r-project.org/web/packages/VIMGUI/index.html.

Templ, M., Kowarik, A., Filzmoser, P., 2011. Iterative stepwise regression imputation using standard and robust methods. Computational Statistics & Data Analysis 55 (10), 2793–2806.

SECTION

2

Biodistance in a Forensic Setting

CHAPTER

10

Forensic Classification and Biodistance in the 21st Century: The Rise of Learning Machines

S.D. Ousley
Mercyhurst University, Erie, PA, United States

CHAPTER OUTLINE HEAD

Introduction 197
Estimating Classification Accuracy 198
Overfitting 199
Finding the Best Measurements 200
Other Traditional Classification Methods 201
Resampling 202
Machine Learning 204
Materials and Methods 206
Results and Discussion 206
Summary 210
Acknowledgments 211
References 211

INTRODUCTION

Linear discriminant function analysis (LDFA), the first multivariate statistical classification method, was invented by R.A. Fisher in 1936. LDFA is predominantly used in bioarchaeology and biological anthropology to assess biodistance (relationships) among groups (called descriptive discriminant analysis or DDA) and in forensic anthropology to classify unidentified individuals (called predictive discriminant analysis or PDA). Both of these approaches to group relationships are provided in LDFA, because individual classifications are based on a cohesive and limited model of intragroup variation and distances based on them. LDFA is a member of the family of classification methods known as supervised learning, because group membership of individuals is used during the process of maximizing group differences. Overviews of LDFA are available in Affifi and Clark (1997), Hand (1997), Huberty (1994), Huberty and Olejnik (2006), Klecka (1980), and Tabachnik and Fidel (2007). LDFA specific to forensic anthropology is outlined in Ousley and Jantz (2012).

The LDFA model utilizes group-specific means and a pooled within-group variance—covariance matrix (VCM), representing the relationships among measurements within groups, to calculate

Biological Distance Analysis. http://dx.doi.org/10.1016/B978-0-12-801966-5.00010-X

multivariate distances among groups. In this paper, which is centered on craniometrics, "measurements" will be used often when measurements are meant, and "variables" will be used when any kind of variables can be referred to, which may be measurements, binary, ordinal, or nominal observations, or transformations of measurements; in most cases the two terms are interchangeable. The measurement means for each group and the pooled VCM are calculated directly from the data, and the pooled VCM is the average VCM from each group weighted by sample size. Using matrix multiplication, vectors of differences in group means are multiplied by the inverse of the VCM to combine and scale all differences into one number, the Mahalanobis distance. If all Mahalanobis distances are significantly greater than zero, then the distances reflect all variation in the measurements in the most objective way. Canonical variates analysis can be used to compare groups using two- or three-dimensional plots that show the most important axes that separate groups, and dendrograms can be constructed from the distances that illustrate complex group relationships (Albrecht, 1980; Affifi and Clark, 1997). These graphical methods are especially illuminating in biodistance studies.

There are important assumptions of LDFA—in other words, requirements—in order for the Mahalanobis distances to best represent intergroup relationships. LDFA requires multivariate normality of each group's data, which is usually limited to continuous measurements. As it turns out, interpreting multivariate normality tests is not straightforward, because they depend on sample sizes, the number of measurements analyzed, and other factors. Multivariate normality is simply assumed when each measurement is normally distributed; a more basic requirement is that the discriminant scores themselves are normally distributed within groups. Of course, the normal distribution is also a model, and in fact is based on an infinite sample size, and small deviations from multivariate normality do not affect LDFA accuracy very much (Huberty, 1994). Outliers often affect LDFA models more than normality per se, and there are methods to detect and quantify outliers using the LDFA model and typicality probabilities (Ousley and Jantz, 2012). Additionally, osteometric data appear to be normally distributed as long as sample sizes are large enough and outliers are removed, which is true for nearly any other metric data from animals or plants. Another requirement of LDFA is that variation in each group is more or less the same, and has been described as being "in the same ballpark" (Huberty and Olejnik, 2006, p. 83). As with normality, testing for the homogeneity of VCMs is not especially straightforward. For example, Box's M test for homogeneity is notoriously oversensitive to slight heterogeneity and to small departures from normality (Huberty and Olejnik, 2006; Tabachnik and Fidel, 2007). Importantly, small deviations from homogeneity do not seem to affect the estimated relationships or classification accuracy. Classification accuracy is central to evaluating any classification function, because with a potentially large number of measurements available, many unique combinations of measurements could be analyzed, and some combinations will be more accurate than others. As it turns out, estimating classification accuracy is not as straightforward as it may seem.

ESTIMATING CLASSIFICATION ACCURACY

Intuitively, we will always want to use the most accurate classification function available, whether LDFA or any other method, and accuracy will vary depending on how many and which specific variables are used in an analysis. Classification accuracy is an important part of assessing a method's validity, which is especially important after the Supreme Court's 1993 *Daubert* decision, because validity, especially the error rate of a method, needs to be quantified when possible. Classification accuracy must be estimated, and ideally the accuracy would apply to the next case we analyze or to an independent sample of additional individuals. Large samples will produce better estimates of the characteristics of the population that the group samples represent. Ideally, one would have two independent and large samples of groups, calculate a classification function using one of them, and apply it to the other to estimate accuracy, because larger samples also provide better estimates of classification accuracy. Similarly, having a large total sample would allow one part to be designated the reference or training sample (also known as the calibration sample), with, say, 75% of each group, which would be used to calculate the function. The function would then be applied to the other 25% of the total sample, known as the validation sample, to estimate classification accuracy. But sample sizes are rarely large enough to partition them (especially in anthropology); ideally, the training sample should be as large as possible to get the best group estimates for classifications, but the validation sample should also be as large as possible to get the best estimates of classification accuracy.

The simplest method of estimating classification accuracy is the accuracy when a function is applied to the reference sample, known as the resubstitution method. Resubstitution produces positively biased estimates of accuracy, because each classified individual was part of the training sample. The most popular method of avoiding bias is to use a resampling method known as leave-one-out cross-validation (LOOCV), also known as jackknifing. With LOOCV, each individual is sequentially removed from the total sample, the classification function is calculated using all remaining individuals, and then the function is applied to the removed individual. The accuracy rate is derived from tabulations of the individual classifications. LOOCV is an example of resampling, because a reference sample of size $N - 1$ is analyzed N times, each time with a slightly different composition. LOOCV removes the positive bias but shows high estimation variance, meaning that the actual accuracy may be quite different from the estimated accuracy (Efron, 1979). Another method of estimating accuracy is known as K-fold cross-validation (KFCV), and likewise involves resampling. With $k = 10$, or 10-fold cross-validation, the sample is divided into tenths; nine-tenths of the total sample is used as the training sample, and the remaining tenth is used as the validation sample. The $k = 10$ accuracy estimates in this example are averaged and the variance calculated, so a confidence interval on the accuracy can also be obtained. KFCV shows low bias and a lower variance in estimating classification accuracy.

OVERFITTING

There is a further concern with all classification methods related to sample size. Analyzing more measurements allows more differences among groups to be detected. Very large samples allow the simultaneous analysis of numerous available measurements, because larger samples simply contain more information. In forensic anthropology, typically there are a large number of measurements that can be taken from remains: Howells (1973) defined 81 measurements and calculated angles that can be collected, and using a three-dimensional digitizer can enable the calculation of thousands of ILDs (interlandmark distances) and angles. However, classifications are often made using rather small samples: the Howells worldwide craniometric database, for example, has 35 groups, most of which have sample sizes of about 50 males and 50 females (Howells, 1996). LDFA involves calculating parameters (means, variances, and covariances) from the sample, and the number of calculated parameters is $[m^*(m + 1)]/2 + m$, where m is the number of measurements analyzed. To classify using 5 measurements requires 20 calculated parameters; using 10 measurements requires 65; using 20 measurements requires 230. Naturally, we want to use as many measurements as we can to utilize the most information and maximize classification accuracy, but trying to extract a lot of information from a small sample is known as overfitting, and is like trying to get water from a dry sponge. The consequence of overfitting is called the "curse of dimensionality" and is clearly seen as a decline in classification accuracy after a certain point as more and more measurements are added to a classification function. As with most statistical models, simpler is better, and more measurements do not necessarily better delineate groups or improve classification accuracy because of redundancy in interrelated measurements, especially in craniometrics, due to morphological integration (Klingenberg, 2009). In fact, adding more measurements that do not improve classifications or increase distances could make more of the distances nonsignificant, muddling group relationships. Also, with more measurements, more individuals in the reference groups appear to be outliers, because the high dimensionality reduces their typicality probabilities. The most extreme example of overfitting would be to have more measurements than there are individuals, thus producing a singular VCM that cannot be inverted and making the calculation of Mahalanobis distances impossible under normal conditions. There are ways of dealing with singular VCMs, but the consequences are rather unpredictable. SAS, for example, automatically uses a variant of a generalized inverse or pseudo-inverse of the VCM, the quasi-inverse, which adjusts calculated VCM values slightly to remove singularities when a singular matrix is detected (SAS Institute, 2002). One recommended limit to the number of measurements that should be used is $\min(n_g)/3$, the minimum group sample size divided by 3 (Huberty, 1994), so to classify using n_g of 50, 70, and 100, one should use a maximum of 17 measurements. Though the limit is not absolute, and other suggested limits have been proposed, limiting the number of measurements improves classification accuracy and consistency (Tabachnik and Fidel, 2007).

We can appreciate the effects of overfitting through appropriate validation methods. For instance, using 231 ILDs in LDFA on a sample of 50 males and 50 females black and white digitized crania classifies 100% correctly using resubstitution. However, the estimated overall accuracy using LOOCV is only 40%; the function was overfit, optimized for the test sample only, and failed when even one individual was removed, which does not bode well for accuracy of the next individuals to be classified. Classifying the same sample using 23 measurements results in an overall classification accuracy rate of 84%. If accuracies are much higher when the number of measurements is reduced, it is a good indicator of model overfitting. Another way to check for overfitting is by examining the amount of independent information in a VCM through its determinant; in the example using 231 ILDs, it is less than 10^{-217}, but with 23 measurements it is more than 3×10^{19}. Clearly, overfitting and redundant measurements are to be avoided. How can we avoid them?

FINDING THE BEST MEASUREMENTS

Because the number of measurements that can be used in forensic anthropology will often be limited by sample sizes, statistical methods for finding the most valuable measurements are important. These are termed subset selection or feature selection methods, the most popular of which has been stepwise selection. With LDFA, forward stepwise selection is used most often, first classifying by using each single measurement, and retaining the one that classifies the most accurately or shows the greatest group differences using multivariate measures such as Wilks's lambda. Then the best single measurement is analyzed pairwise with every other measurement so that the best two measurements are retained. The procedure keeps testing additional measurements until no further classification improvements can be made. Stepwise procedures are relatively fast, because to find the best 10 measurements of 18, for example, only

18 + 17 + 16 + 15 + 14 + 13 + 12 + 11 + 10 + 9 = 135 functions need to be run. Importantly, there is no guarantee that the stepwise procedure will find the best possible combination, because not all combinations are tested. To do that requires testing of all possible subset selections, and finding the best 10 of 18 measurements requires running 18!/10! = 43,758 functions. Each time a function is run, individuals with all tested measurements are used, but sampling variation is a concern, because one combination of measurements may show a small advantage with fewer individuals and be retained for further analysis. One other method of avoiding overfitting is to convert the original measurements into principal component scores, which more efficiently represent variation in the original measurements and can be analyzed using LDFA or other methods. Using far fewer principal component scores than measurements usually captures the vast majority of the original variation and avoids overfitting due to measurement redundancy and the smaller number of variables analyzed. It is important to remember is that principal components represent the variation among individuals, while classification functions utilize the variation among groups, so the most valuable principal component scores to use in a classification function (separating groups) will not always come from the lowest-numbered principal components (which separate individuals). The most useful principal component scores for classification can be chosen using stepwise selection methods.

Clearly, LDFA has a number of requirements and analytical concerns that often cannot be met. Why use LDFA? Because when measurements are analyzed using LDFA, it generally performs very well. LDFA provides intuitive classifications and relationships among groups and provides the most accurate way to graphically and numerically compare groups. LDFA uses the simplest multivariate model for group variation, and as a result it provides more stable and consistent parameter estimates, even with different group sample sizes and when groups are 100% separated, unlike some other methods (James et al., 2013). In fact, if the requirements are met, then no other method can calculate intergroup relationships more accurately than those given by Mahalanobis distances, canonical variates plots, and dendrograms, which are essential in biodistance studies. Also, when the requirements are more or less met, virtually no other method provides more accurate classifications, and accuracy is the key to the forensic value of LDFA. LDFA also provides intuitive posterior probabilities, the probabilities of group membership for each group in an analysis. Other classification methods with fewer requirements may be necessary at times, but lack the rich results of LDFA.

OTHER TRADITIONAL CLASSIFICATION METHODS

When the requirements for LDFA are not met, there are other traditional methods that one can use with various theoretical advantages and disadvantages. When the variation in groups is not the same, **quadratic discriminant function analysis** (QDFA) is one possible solution. QDFA calculates a separate VCM for each group, and classifications are made using the variation unique to each group. With QDFA there are no objective distances among groups, and relationships among groups cannot be easily represented graphically because the levels of variation are so different. Further insights into the levels of variation within groups can be gained by performing R matrix analysis (Relethford and Blangero, 1990). However, QDFA using craniometrics nearly always shows far worse classification accuracy than that of LDFA because of the additional parameters required (group-specific VCMs) and the curse of dimensionality. While some authors have found that LDFA performs well compared with other numerous methods (Maroco et al., 2013), others recommend the use of QDFA instead of LDFA as a general rule based on results from simulations (Finch and Schneider, 2006, 2007). However, the simulations have not been appropriate for forensic anthropology—for instance, using categorical survey data, a maximum of five predictors, very large disparities in VCMs, and large sample sizes.

Another traditional classification method is **logistic regression** (LR), which calculates probabilities of group membership directly rather than by calculating distances. Data used for classification using LR need not be normally distributed, are less affected by outliers, ordinal and binary data can be used along with continuous data, and the variation within groups need not be similar, so it has many theoretical advantages over LDFA. As with QDFA, some authors assert that LR should be used instead of LDFA: "[discriminant analysis] is considered an anachronistic procedure and does not currently represent a best practice. Instead, researchers should use logistic regression..." (Osborne, 2015, p. 16—17). However, LR has its own set of disadvantages. Multicollinearity (high correlations among measurements) can be problematic, and function estimates are less stable than they are in LDFA: ideally, the smallest n_g using LR should be at least 10 times the number of analyzed measurements in two-group classification (Agresti, 2007; Peduzzi, 1996). LR classification rates can be apparently high in two-group classifications, but they are calculated indirectly and differently depending on the software package. When craniometric data from more than two groups are analyzed, LR classification accuracies are often far lower than those of LDFA.

Two other methods of classification are termed nonparametric because they do not use group means to classify individuals; rather, to classify an individual, they find similar individuals and examine their group memberships. As a result, the methods do not require multivariate normality or the same level of variation in each group. **K-nearest neighbor** analysis (kNN) classifies an individual by finding the closest k individuals (morphological "neighbors") in a reference data set. Distances are based on Euclidean distance or the pooled within-group VCM, so within-group variation can play a role but distance to the mean for a group is not used to classify. K can be any integer ≥ 1, and depending on the data and groups involved, using different values for k results in different classification accuracies, so the optimal value for k can be discovered. **Kernel probability density** classification (KPD) is similar, but the "neighbors" are chosen differently. KPD classifies an individual using the probabilities of group membership based on the most similar individuals within a chosen distance (known as the radius), which is calculated using either the pooled VCM or group-specific VCMs. Once again, an individual's distances to group means are not calculated; rather, kernel probability densities for each group are calculated using the summed kernel probabilities of individuals within the chosen distance. The individual is simply classified into the group that shows the highest probability as in LDFA, but the probability for each group is calculated quite differently. Kernel probability densities are small-scale densities, often similar to miniature normal distribution curves, centered on each individual, though differently shaped kernels can be used. The choice of VCM and radius influences the number of similar individuals included, and the type of kernel influences the calculated probabilities at any one point (SAS Institute, 2002). Like kNN classification, depending on the data and groups involved, the choices involved in KPD classification can be optimized for classification accuracy.

RESAMPLING

LDFA and the methods outlined so far have certain requirements and choices to be made that affect group relationships and classification accuracy, and this is not always acknowledged. Additionally, transformations of original data can be performed in any number of ways, which may improve classification accuracies. As with all statistical analyses, sample size is the most important factor: larger samples are better than smaller samples, and we should make the most of any samples we work with. Limited sample sizes also restrict the number of variables that can be used in every classification method with confidence. Sampling variation is a concern when either training or validation samples are limited, as at least one of them often is. Large training samples are better for DDA and parameter estimates, and large validation samples are better for PDA. Huge sample sizes would solve the problem, but sample sizes are often limited in bioarchaeology and forensic anthropology, making statistical significance less likely for distances, and classification accuracies less certain in forensic anthropology. We are thus faced with a Goldilocks dilemma: we need to use as many variables as we can to more objectively compare groups and increase classifications, so we want large reference sample sizes; but using more variables reduces accuracy at a certain point, and we need large validation samples to better estimate classification accuracy. Samples are typically limited, so we need samples that are just right. Thanks to the rise of computer hardware and software, resampling is a solution to our sampling needs.

Resampling includes a family of techniques that involve fewer theoretical assumptions and form the core of machine learning (Efron and Tibshirani, 1993; Good, 2006, 2008; Manly, 2007; Roff, 2006). Data-centric randomization and resampling methods have been around for a long time, including permutation (sampling without replacement) methods (since 1923), jackknifing (LOOCV) and Monte Carlo (simulation) methods (both since 1949), and bootstrapping (since 1979). These methods were first used to derive and test theoretical distributions while avoiding excess computation (by hand) required for assumptions that often could not be met. For instance, Fisher's exact test (a permutation test) for contingency tables showed that chi-square test results were unreliable for small samples (Berry et al., 2014). Monte Carlo simulation has been used extensively to objectively test hypotheses based on large-scale empirical distributions. "Bootstrapping" usually refers to the nonparametric bootstrap and is particularly useful in estimating parameters empirically through sampling with replacement n times from the original n individuals hundreds or thousands of times, mimicking sampling variation through the many generated data sets. Bootstrap methods are also used to estimate confidence and prediction intervals (locally weighted scatter-plot smoother regression) for outlier tests (studentized residuals in regression), and especially, statistical classification and biodistance methods, including significance tests for intergroup distances (resampled multivariate distances), testing model assumptions (VCM homogeneity tests), model building (bootstrapped support for dendrogram branches), and estimating classification accuracies (LOOCV, KFCV). Once parameters are estimated, another type of bootstrapping, the parametric bootstrap, is used to generate simulated data sets with specified parameters (Cole et al., 2002; Efron and Tibshirani, 1993; Good, 2008).

One essential method for estimating the classification accuracy of classification methods uses bootstrapping and is called bootstrapped cross-validation (BSCV), one version of which is known as the 0.632 + estimator (Efron and Tibshirani, 1997). With BSCV, n_g individuals from each group are bootstrapped to form the reference groups. On average the bootstrapped sample has 63.2% of the original individuals, meaning 36.8% of the original individuals are not part of the bootstrapped sample and are used for the validation sample. The number of bootstrapped sample repeats can be hundreds or thousands, with the training and validation samples changing somewhat every time. BSCV shows very low bias and very low variance in estimated accuracy. A bootstrapped sample is usually the same size as the original sample that was sampled with replacement, so each bootstrapped sample perturbs the data or changes the sample composition somewhat in terms of means, variances, and distributions of the original measurements. Because sampling variation is always a concern, bootstrapping in some ways provides "insurance" against sampling variation in the training and validation samples, because many, sometimes thousands, of bootstrapped samples are analyzed. For classification purposes, the total sample can be bootstrapped, which will change the number in each group each time, or each group can be bootstrapped, preserving the original sample sizes in each. Many classification methods do not perform as well when the data are imbalanced; that is, when there are large differences in group sample sizes. When data are unbalanced, as is often the case in anthropology, the original data from groups can be bootstrapped into samples smaller than the original sample sizes, known as subsampling, or bootstrapped into larger sample sizes than the original, known as oversampling, in order to make the group sample sizes similar.

Resampling provides a solution to another major concern in multivariate analysis, that of missing data. Multivariate methods require all variables to be present in an analysis, but taphonomic factors often prevent complete preservation of all measurements in human remains. If only 1 measurement is missing in a reference individual, then none of the data from that individual can be used in classifications. Multiple Imputation methods generate multiple estimates for missing values in individuals, and those data are integrated into multiple data sets for analysis, which further perturbs the reference data (Carpenter and Kenward, 2013; Graham, 2012; see Kenyhercz and Passalacqua, Chapter 9, this volume).

Resampling methods have grown in popularity with the increase in computing power through faster hardware and hardware availability: as of 2011, there are more desktops, laptops, tablets, and smartphones than there are people in the United States (Pew Research Center, 2015); before long there will be more of such devices than people in the world (Cisco Inc., 2015; TechCrunch, 2015). Computers will only get faster with greater use of parallel programming, which executes tasks simultaneously, and faster multiple-core processors. Software improvements, especially in algorithms and programming languages, have made statistical analyses easier and faster as well.

MACHINE LEARNING

Machine learning (ML) methods are computer-intensive and use resampling and iterative methods extensively to classify individuals. ML methods have few assumptions, can perform better subset selection, and avoid problems of traditional classification methods such as overfitting and distributional requirements of variables. ML methods, which originated in computer science, involve more logic and basic math than statistics, because ML methods do not calculate group characteristics or distances; instead, they begin with random group separators and then tune them repeatedly ("learn") until the best criteria for classifying groups are found. ML analyses must be run many times in order to tune them, and while individual ML functions can be unstable, averaging them makes them more applicable. Because of their nonstatistical nature, ML methods can utilize any kind of data in combination, including nominal data, and often produce very high classification accuracies. Estimating classification accuracies for ML methods generally involves bootstrapping, though any number of validation methods can be used. The newest ML methods consistently produce classification accuracies near 100%, but the results are largely limited to classification per se, have involved classification into one of two groups, and are less valuable for biodistance studies.

ML methods include neural networks (NNets), recursive partitioning (RecPart), random forests, and support vector machines (SVMs). Details of these methods can be found in Bishop (2006), Hastie et al. (2009), and James et al. (2013), and their application in forensic anthropology is outlined in Hefner and Ousley (2014). Each method has somewhat different ways of combining, weighing, classifying, and reusing observations through the use of different algorithms to optimize classification rules. For example, RecPart emphasizes relatively few binary decisions about the measurement boundaries, sectioning points, or cutoffs that best separate groups; SVMs iteratively and repeatedly apply greater and greater emphasis on individuals near classification boundaries; NNets apply algorithms derived from neuroscience to weigh different variables in order to create accurate classification boundaries; the **random forests** method iteratively uses numerous combinations of relatively few measurements with initially random boundaries to determine the best measurements and boundaries for classification. Ensemble methods use the results of multiple ML analyses to create a consensus classification based on the idea that assessing results from several classifiers is better than assessing results from only one classification (Bannerman-Thompson et al., 2013; Okun et al., 2011; Rokach, 2010). The best known ensemble methods are boosting and bagging, which repeatedly use ML results to calculate an optimal classifier through averaging or voting. **Bagging** optimizes ML functions and bootstrapped data sets in a consensus classification function using the non-bootstrapped, or out-of-bag (OOB), individuals to calculate accuracy. **Boosting** uses ML classification results to repeatedly and sequentially reclassify, each time applying greater weight to misclassified observations, then calculates a consensus classifier based on all functions used.

A recurrent theme in all classification methods is that more data are better, and the available data need to be maximized. Ideally, one would have very large training, tuning, and validation samples, which is rare in anthropology. The usual proportional mixture for ML methods is 70%/15%/15% (training/tuning/validation) or 90%/10% (training/validation) for KFCV. A large validation sample is more representative, avoids sampling bias, and makes it easier to detect noisy variables that often hurt classification; a large validation sample provides a measure of how realistic the classification model is, helps us avoid overfitting, and tells us how accurate the function will be for future cases. As a result of the relatively small validation sample used by ML methods, estimates of accuracy suffer from a coarse resolution, because smaller samples have larger variances for estimated accuracies. For example, with a reference sample of 100 individuals, often considered a sufficient sample size, using a 15% validation sample means that each incorrect classification decreases the estimated accuracy by 7% (1/15). Given the requirements for large training and validation samples, a larger total sample is clearly needed, but skeletal samples are limited and data collection costs money and time. How can we make greater use of the samples we have? Through simulation.

ML methods utilize a back-end approach to resampling, limiting the bootstrapped samples to the original sample size. But introducing simulated data at the front end may have several advantages (Ousley, 2015). Most statistical methods work with parameters estimated from the available samples, finite samples will show sampling variability, and there is also biological variability represented in every sample. Smaller samples will show relatively greater sample variability in terms of the calculated standard deviations, but will represent less of the biological variation in a group, because all things being equal, smaller samples are less representative. Smaller samples also limit the number of measurements we can use in an analysis. Bootstrapping adds variability into samples that mimics normal biological variation and can be thought of as insurance that our samples better represent the variation in groups, which is a useful feature for future classifications. With every bootstrapped sample, we can use the parametric bootstrap to simulate much larger reference samples and apply various statistical classification methods to them, as Ousley (2015) did. Simulated data sets are not true external validation samples, but are quasi-independent from the original data because there are no duplicated individuals. Importantly, the original data can also be used as a semi-independent validation sample for functions derived from the simulated samples. In Ousley's analysis, he discovered that large simulated data sets can be used to improve classification accuracy in the original sample and break the curse of dimensionality.

MATERIALS AND METHODS

To examine the performance of numerous classification methods using craniometric data, the complete set of 81 Howells (1973) craniometrics, including angles, were calculated through digitizing 19th-century black females ($n = 75$), black males ($n = 74$), white females ($n = 75$), and white males ($n = 98$). No apparent outliers were removed. The complete sample was bootstrapped 10 times, changing the sample sizes and composition for each group each time. The group means and pooled VCM were calculated from each bootstrapped sample, which were then used as the basis for simulated samples of 500 each from the four groups. Stepwise selection methods (using classification accuracy and Wilks's lambda) and numerous classification and validation methods were used on the original and simulated data sets. Validation methods included LOOCV, 10-fold cross-validation (10FCV), 0.632+, and validation methods specific to certain classification methods. kNN methods classified using Euclidean distance, because it classified better than using Mahalanobis distance, and using various numbers of nearest neighbors ($k = 3,9,15$), and the highest accuracies are reported. The ML methods (RecPart and random forest) used training, tuning, and validation proportions of 70/15/15. Numerous other adjustments are possible for the ML methods; the default settings were used in most cases, but the neural network method required adjustments; adjustments to the decision tree and random forest methods could well improve their rather poor results. All classification methods used equal prior probabilities in classifying. Fordisc 3.1 (Jantz and Ousley, 2005), *R* version 3.0.1 (R Development Core Team, 2014), and SAS version 9.1 (SAS Institute, 2002) were used in analyses. Numerous *R* packages were used: mvtnorm was used to simulate data sets from group means and the pooled VCM; for the classification methods, Rattle was used to call several ML packages such as randomForest and neuralnet; the caret package was also used to create training and validation sets; class was used for kNN classification, ipred and rpart were used for bagging, and e1071 was used for SVM classification.

RESULTS AND DISCUSSION

Table 10.1 shows the results of the classification methods used on the original data. The number of measurements (81) exceeded all but one of the group sample sizes. The curse of dimensionality can be immediately appreciated by the fact that the LDFA classification accuracy using all 81 measurements was 82% but using 40 stepwise-selected measurements resulted in 90% accuracy, the highest accuracy of all the classification methods used on the original data. QDFA showed stronger curse of dimensionality effects, with the poorest classification using LOOCV (40%). To be more certain of the poor classification, which is a common finding when using QDFA on multiple groups, 10-fold cross-validation was used for both LDFA and QDFA, with both estimates near their LOOCV estimates (81% and 36%, respectively). The very poor performance of QDFA likely reflects its need for more calculated parameters, such as group-specific VCMs, and in this case three of the determinants of the four groups were negative because the number of measurements exceeded the number of group members. Of the remaining traditional classification methods, KPD was the most accurate (82%), followed by LR (70%) and kNN (69%). ML methods performed about as well as the traditional methods, with the highest accuracies seen in neural net (83%), SVM (80%), and random forest (75%).

Every method showed an increase in estimated accuracy using the simulated data sets, as shown in Table 10.2. KPD was the most accurate method overall with 98.5% accuracy, and LDFA, using several

Table 10.1 *Classification Accuracies Using the Original Data*

Method	Validation Data	Accuracy (%)
LDFA	LOOCV	82
LDFA	10FCV	81
LDFA (SW15)	LOOCV	84
LDFA (SW40)	LOOCV	90
QDFA	LOOCV	40
QDFA	10FCV	36
kNN	10FCV	69
KPD	LOOCV	82
LR	10FCV	70
SVM	10FCV	80.3
RecPart	0.15(N)	65
Bagging	OOB	71
Random forest	0.15(N)	75
NNet	0.10(N)	83

For abbreviations see the text.

Table 10.2 *Classification Accuracies Using the Simulated Data*

Method	Validation	Mean Acc (%)	SD (Acc)
LDFA	LOOCV	98.0	0.7
LDFA	10FCV	98.0	0.7
LDFA	0.632+	98.0	0.6
LDFA (SW15)	LOOCV	91.0	–
LDFA (SW40)	LOOCV	94.7	–
QDFA	LOOCV	93.0	1.6
kNN	LOOCV	80.9	2.3
KPD	LOOCV	98.5	0.7
LR	10FCV	94.7	1.8
Bagging	OOB	82.3	1.7
SVM	10FCV	93.9	1.1
SVM	0.632+	95.4	0.9
RecPart	0.15(N)	68.2	4.3
Random forest	0.15(N)	83.2	2.9
NNet	10FCV	95.8	1.6

Acc, *accuracy;* SD, *standard deviation.*
For other abbreviations see the text.

measures of validation, was nearly as accurate at 98.0%. Both methods showed the lowest standard deviations of accuracies, less than 0.7%, and therefore had the most consistent accuracies. Also, there were far fewer outliers indicated by low typicality probabilities ($p < 0.01$) in the simulated data sets than in the original data sets. Stepwise LDFA showed small improvements, but the greatest improvement in accuracy was seen in QDFA, which classified 93% correctly with a standard deviation of 1.6%. All four simulated groups had log determinants of their VCM greater than 70, representing far more information than contained in the original data. LR also showed a large improvement, with 94.7% accuracy. The neural net (95.8%) and SVM (95.4% using 0.632+) methods showed the highest ML accuracies. Bagging using RecPart improved somewhat on RecPart alone, but the random forest classification did best of the three remaining ML methods at 83.2%; accuracy in all three could likely be improved through tuning.

Stepwise selection was performed on the original data set, and the first simulated data set and the maximum accuracy in each for a given number of measurements using LOOCV are shown in Fig. 10.1. At every step, the simulated data show higher accuracy. Using more measurements increases accuracy in both the original and simulated data up to a point, each showing a dip in accuracy when using 27 measurements. In the original data, classification accuracy peaked at 90% using 27 measurements, then fell with more and more measurements, showing the effects of the curse of dimensionality. Using the simulated data, the dips in accuracy were at most 0.1% in any one step, and accuracy always recovered until stabilizing at 98% when using at least 73 measurements. In contrast, Wilks's lambda values in both the original and the simulated data decrease monotonically with more measurements, with a slight advantage to the simulated data. The Wilks's lambda value for 81 measurements using the simulated data (0.015) is

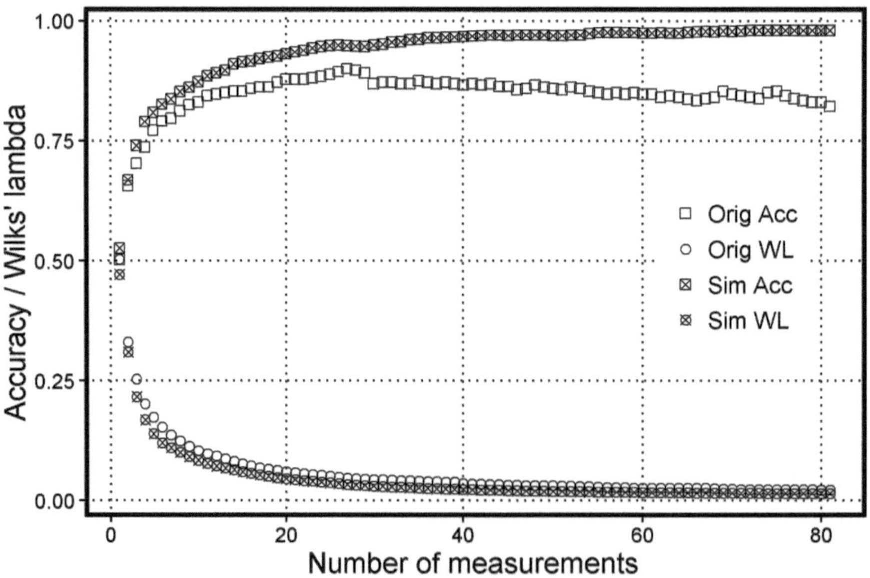

FIGURE 10.1

Accuracy and Wilks's lambda in original and simulated data using stepwise selection. *Acc*, accuracy; *Orig*, original data; *Sim*, simulated data; *WL*, Wilks's lambda.

slightly lower than that of the original data (0.0225), indicating somewhat better group separation in the simulated data. In the original data, it is notable that Wilks's lambda keeps decreasing after classification accuracy peaks at 27 measurements, suggesting that estimated accuracy is affected more by the curse of dimensionality.

When applying classification functions derived from the simulated data sets to the original data (Table 10.3), the results are striking: All the classification accuracies but one are higher than those using the functions derived from the original data. The simulated data samples, remember, are quasi-independent of the original data and represent variation expected from additional individuals from the same underlying populations. The simulated samples are very similar to the original sample, but the groups have larger sample sizes, so the simulated samples seem to break the curse of dimensionality through better estimated functions of traditional methods. The LDFA function using all simulated measurements improved classification of the original data to 89.5%, but applying the stepwise LDFA functions from 40 simulated measurements to the original data was less accurate, at 86.2%. These results indicate that stepwise methods apparently work best when samples are limited: LDFA using stepwise methods worked better than using all measurements only when based on the original data. However, the apparent higher accuracy of stepwise methods when data are limited may be due somewhat to sampling variation, and the accuracy figures may be higher than what one can expect when applied to a new case. QDFA showed a huge improvement in classification accuracy, increasing from 40% to 87%, clearly reflecting better function estimates thanks to having more data, which is also seen in the much higher determinants for all group VCMs. LR, like QDFA, showed a large improvement in accuracy, from 70% to 85.6%. Both QDFA and LR clearly require larger samples to classify more accurately. The higher classification accuracies in kNN and KPD methods, which do not use within-group variation directly, are likely due to better smoothing of probabilities when more individuals are present, especially when many measurements are being analyzed. The ML methods also showed higher classification accuracies than when based on the original data, except for the random forest method, though ML methods are supposed to perform well even

***Table 10.3** Classification Accuracies Applied to the Original Data Using Functions From the Simulated Data*

Method	Mean Acc (%)	SD (Acc)
LDFA	89.5	0.8
LDFA (SW15)	81.4	1.5
LDFA (SW40)	86.2	2.6
QDFA	87.1	2.1
kNN	78.8	1.7
KPD	89.2	0.7
LR	85.6	1.9
SVM	86.9	1.2
NNet	88.8	1.5
Random forest	65.3	1.4

Acc, *accuracy;* SD, *standard deviation.*
For other abbreviations see the text.

when analyzing small sample sizes and many variables. The NNet classification rate was the third highest at 88.8%. All classification accuracies in Table 10.3 are lower than those in Table 10.2 when accuracies are based on other members of the same simulated sample.

SUMMARY

There are many ways to analyze data from groups depending on the goals of the analysis. As long as the assumptions of LDFA are more or less met, which is very often the case with craniometric data, LDFA provides important information for assessing group relationships. Other groups may show differences in within-group craniometric variation. If the goal is to classify remains using craniometrics, LDFA showed the highest accuracies in this study and has additional advantages over other methods. Accuracy is how we should judge classification functions, especially the estimated accuracy when applied to new cases. It is self-evident that we should use the most accurate method for the data we have at hand. When analyzing other kinds of data with different sample compositions, other classification methods will no doubt perform better than LDFA, depending on the kinds of data analyzed, groups compared, and sample composition, as found by Hefner and Ousley (2014) in their analysis of cranial morphoscopic data, in which NNet and SVM classified better than other ML and traditional methods, by Hefner et al. (2014) in their analysis of mixed craniometric and morphoscopic data, in which random forest modeling performed slightly better (90%) than LDFA (86%), and by Edgar and Ousley (2013) in their analysis of dental morphology data (in which LR performed best among traditional methods).

Though ML methods are supposed to perform better when sample sizes are small and dimensionality is high, QDFA, LR, and ML methods showed higher classification accuracies when the sample size was increased. Improved classification rates when using the larger simulated data sets were not a surprise, but better classification by functions based on the simulated data sets applied to the original than by those derived from the original data tells us that all of these methods are sensitive to sample size and can be improved through larger simulated data sets. For LDFA, the much higher determinants of the group VCMs are partly the result of generating them using the pooled VCM of the original data. However, as long as not too many measurements are used, the VCMs of these groups are rarely significantly different using the Kullback (1959) test for homogeneity. Adding more and more measurements to limited samples causes failure of the homogeneity test, which would necessitate using QDFA or some other method rather than LDFA. But as we saw, VCMs are often poorly conditioned when QDFA is used with relatively small samples. QDFA accuracy was doubled when functions derived from simulated data were applied to the original data, even though the groups in the simulated data had a common VCM. Therefore, the poor performance of QDFA on the original data cannot be due to a flawed theoretical model of QDFA, but to practical concerns such as sample size. Software has made statistical analyses much better but should not be used blindly. Because SAS uses the quasi-inverse automatically when a singular matrix is detected, classification accuracies with the original data and 81 measurements using QDFA in SAS were abysmally low ($\sim$25%). Using simulated data sets in this study outperformed the pseudo-inverse by a large margin, at least with these data. Also, as mentioned, many of the ML methods can be tuned in ways that could increase their accuracies. Further tests need to be run with various other simulations.

Thanks to resampling, especially bootstrapping, we can better estimate expected classification accuracies. Thanks to simulations, we can estimate missing data, improve classifications, and understand aspects of statistical classification methods like never before. Thanks to computers, we can resample and simulate faster and faster, allowing us to choose from numerous classification methods and making even more computationally intense ensemble methods more practical. But simulations run on computers must reflect the data we work with. It is mistaken to apply conclusions to forensic anthropology and biodistance analyses from simulations that use data with very different characteristics.

This paper has illustrated not only the value of resampling and simulation in appreciating certain aspects of classification, but also revealed that simulated samples can improve classification accuracies. Skeletal data from human groups will always be limited and unbalanced, and we still need to collect as many data as we can before analyzing, but resampling can help us maximize our data.

Acknowledgments

The author benefitted from several discussions with Richard Jantz and Lyle Konigsberg.

References

Afifi, A.A., Clark, V., 1997. Computer-Aided Multivariate Analysis, third ed. Chapman and Hall, London.

Agresti, A., 2007. An Introduction to Categorical Data Analysis, second ed. Wiley, New York.

Albrecht, G.H., 1980. Multivariate analysis and the study of form, with special reference to canonical variate analysis. American Zoologist 20, 679–693.

Bannerman, H., Rao, M.B., Kasala, S., 2013. Bagging, boosting, and random forests using R. In: Govindaraju, V., Rao, C.R. (Eds.), Handbook of Statistics 31. Machine Learning: Theory and Applications. Elsevier, New York, pp. 101–149.

Berry, K.J., Johnston, J.E., Mielke Jr., P.W., 2014. A Chronicle of Permutation Statistical Methods. Springer, New York.

Bishop, C.M., 2006. Pattern Recognition and Machine Learning. Springer, New York.

Carpenter, J.R., Kenward, M.G., 2013. Multiple Imputation and its Application. Wiley, New York.

Cisco, Inc., 2015. Cisco Visual Networking Index: Global Mobile Data Traffic Forecast Update, 2014–2019. http://www.cisco.com/c/en/us/solutions/collateral/service-provider/visual-networking-index-vni/white_paper_c11-520862.pdf.

Cole, T.M., Lele, S., Richtmeier, J.T., 2002. A parametric bootstrap approach to the detection of phylogenetic signals in landmark data. In: MacLeod, N., Foley, P.L. (Eds.), Morphology, Shape and Phylogeny. Taylor and Francis, New York, pp. 194–219.

Edgar, H.J.H., Ousley, S.D., 2013. New approaches to the use of dental morphology in forensic contexts. In: Scott, J.R., Irish, J. (Eds.), Anthropological Perspectives on Tooth Morphology: Genetics, Evolution, Variation. Cambridge University Press, London, pp. 510–534.

Efron, B., Tibshirani, R., 1993. An Introduction to the Bootstrap. Chapman and Hall, London.

Efron, B., Tibshirani, R., 1997. Improvements on cross-validation: the .632+ bootstrap method. Journal of the American Statistical Association 92, 548–560.

Efron, B., 1979. Bootstrap methods: another look at the jackknife. The Annals of Statistics 7, 1–26.

Finch, W.H., Schneider, M.K., 2006. Misclassification rates for four methods of group classification impact of predictor distribution, covariance inequality, effect size, sample size, and group size ratio. Educational and Psychological Measurement 66, 240–257.

Finch, W.H., Schneider, M.K., 2007. Classification accuracy of neural networks vs. discriminant analysis, logistic regression, and classification and regression trees: three- and five-group cases. Methodology 3, 47–57.

Fisher, R.A., 1936. The use of multiple measurements in taxonomic problems. Annals of Eugenics 7 (2), 179–188.

Good, P.I., 2006. Resampling Methods, third ed. Birkhaeuser, Boston.

Good, P.I., 2008. Permutation, Parametric and Bootstrap Tests of Hypotheses, third ed. Springer, New York.
Graham, J.W., 2012. Missing Data. Springer, New York.
Hand, D.J., 1997. Construction and Assessment of Classification Rules. Wiley, New York.
Hastie, T., Tibshirani, R.J., Friedman, J., 2009. The Elements of Statistical Learning, second ed. Springer, New York.
Hefner, J.T., Ousley, S.D., 2014. Statistical classification methods for estimating ancestry using morphoscopic traits. Journal of Forensic Sciences 59, 883–890.
Hefner, J.T., Spradley, M.K., Anderson, B., 2014. Ancestry assessment using random forest modeling. Journal of Forensic Sciences 59, 583–589.
Howells, W.W., 1973. Cranial variation in man. In: Papers of the Peabody Museum of Archeology and Ethnology, vol. 67. Peabody Museum, Cambridge, Mass.
Howells, W.W., 1996. Howells' craniometric data on the Internet. American Journal of Physical Anthropology 101, 441–442.
Huberty, C.J., Olejnik, S., 2006. Applied MANOVA and Discriminant Analysis. Wiley, New York.
Huberty, C.J., 1994. Applied Discriminant Analysis. Wiley, New York.
James, G., Witten, D., Hastie, T., Tibshirani, R., 2013. An Introduction to Statistical Learning with Applications in R. Wiley, New York.
Jantz, R.L., Ousley, S.D., 2005. FORDISC 3: Computerized Forensic Discriminant Functions. Version 3.1. The University of Tennessee, Knoxville.
Klecka, W.R., 1980. Discriminant Analysis. Sage, Beverly Hills, CA.
Klingenberg, C.P., 2009. Morphological integration and developmental modularity. Annual Review of Ecology, Evolution, and Systematics 39, 115–132.
Kullback, S., 1959. Information Theory and Statistics. Wiley and Sons, New York.
Manly, B.F.J., 2007. Randomization, Bootstrap and Monte Carlo Methods in Biology, third ed. Chapman and Hall, Boca Raton.
Maroco, J., Silva, D., Guerreiro, M., de Mendonca, A., Santata, I., 2013. Prediction of dementia patients: a comparative approach using parametric versus nonparametric classifiers. In: da Silva, J.L., Caeiro, F., Natario, I., Brauman, C.A. (Eds.), Advances in Regression, Survival Analysis, Extreme Values, Markov Processes and Other Statistical Applications. Springer, New York, pp. 269–280.
Okun, O., Valentini, G., Re, M., 2011. Ensembles in Machine Learning Applications. Springer, New York.
Osborne, J.W., 2015. Best Practices in Logistic Regression. Sage Publications, Thousand Oaks, CA.
Ousley, S.D., Jantz, R.L., 2012. Fordisc 3 and statistical methods for estimating sex and ancestry. In: Dirkmaat, D.C. (Ed.), A Companion to Forensic Anthropology. Wiley-Blackwell, London, pp. 311–329.
Ousley, S.D., 2015. Forensic classification and biodistance in the 21st century: why the machines will win. American Journal of Physical Anthropology 156 (s60), 244.
Peduzzi, P., 1996. A simulation study of the number of events per variable in logistic regression analysis. Journal of Clinical Epidemiology 49, 1373–1379.
Pew Research Center, 2015. Device Ownership over Time. http://www.pewinternet.org/data-trend/mobile/device-ownership/.
R Development Core Team, 2015. R: A Language and Environment for Statistical Computing. R Foundation for Statistical Computing, Vienna, Austria.
Relethford, J.H., Blangero, J., 1990. Detection of differential gene flow from patterns of quantitative variation. Human Biology 63, 629–641.
Roff, D.A., 2006. Introduction to Computer-Intensive Methods of Data Analysis in Biology. Cambridge University Press, Cambridge.
Rokach, L., 2010. Pattern Classification Using Ensemble Methods. World Scientific Publishing, Singapore.
SAS Institute, 2002. SAS/STAT Version 9.0. SAS Institute Inc., Cary, NC.
Tabachnick, B.G., Fidell, L.S., 2007. Using Multivariate Statistics, fifth ed. Pearson, New York.
TechCrunch, 2015. 6.1B Smartphone Users Globally by 2020, Overtaking Basic Fixed Phone Subscriptions. http://techcrunch.com/2015/06/02/6-1b-smartphone-users-globally-by-2020-overtaking-basic-fixed-phone-subscriptions/.

CHAPTER

11

Forensic Ancestry Assessment Using Cranial Nonmetric Traits Traditionally Applied to Biological Distance Studies

C.M. Pink
Metropolitan State University of Denver, Denver, CO, United States

CHAPTER OUTLINE HEAD

Introduction ... 213
Materials and Methods ... 215
  Variable Selection ... 215
  Statistical Models ... 215
  Machine Learning ... 215
  Decision Tree ... 218
  Random Forest ... 218
  Support Vector Machines ... 219
Results ... 219
Discussion ... 221
  SVM Models ... 223
  The Nature of Phenotypic Variation in Cranial Nonmetric Traits ... 223
  Biological Distance and Cranial Nonmetric Trait Data ... 225
Conclusions ... 226
Acknowledgments ... 226
References ... 226

INTRODUCTION

Cranial nonmetric trait data often form the basis of bioarchaeological studies that make inferences about prehistoric social organization. Over the past five decades studies have repeatedly demonstrated the usefulness of these data for such inquiries (Berry and Berry, 1967; Birkby, 1973; Blom et al., 1998; Buikstra, 1976; Buikstra et al., 1990; Jantz, 1973; Hallgrímsson et al., 2004; Irish, 2010; Konigsberg, 1987, 1990; Konigsberg et al., 1993; Lane and Sublett, 1972; Ossenberg, 1969, 1976; Spence, 1974). The importance of this class of data is so well recognized that nonmetric traits are included in the standard data collection manual utilized by many biological anthropologists (Buikstra and Ubelaker, 1994). Despite their utility for

Biological Distance Analysis. http://dx.doi.org/10.1016/B978-0-12-801966-5.00011-1

analyses of biological distance, cranial nonmetric traits have not been extensively researched for potential application to forensic ancestry estimation.

Although not common in the literature, there have been attempts to distinguish largely unrelated populations using cranial nonmetric traits. Many studies made simple comparisons of trait frequencies between populations (Dodo, 1987; Hanihara and Ishida, 2001a,b,c,d; Kellock and Parsons, 1970; Milne et al., 1983). Most notably, Hauser and De Stefano (1989) presented an extensive summary of known trait frequencies in worldwide populations as a part of their comprehensive volume, *Epigenetic Variants of the Human Skull*. More sophisticated statistical treatments of population differences on the continental scale have tended to be the by-product of biological distance analyses.

Most analyses of populations without recent common ancestry resulted in uninterpretable patterns (eg, see Thoma, 1981; Wijsman and Neves, 1986). However, others have had success in discriminating between ancestral groups on the continental scale. In her early work, Ossenberg (1976) was able to distinguish groups with African ancestry from Amerinds. Berry and Berry (1967) also suggested cranial nonmetric trait frequencies could be used to differentiate human ancestral groups. Notably, Corruccini (1974) found that 72.5% of the between-group variance (African vs European ancestry) in nonmetric trait frequencies was due to ancestry, followed by sex (18.2%). This sampling of studies tangentially related to ancestry estimation based on cranial nonmetric traits suggests there is potential in pursuing this methodology for ancestry classification. However, it is also clear that caution should be taken in the application of statistical classification models to cranial nonmetric data and the interpretation of any results.

In terms of forensic ancestry estimation, anthropologists have focused on another group of nonmetric traits collectively referred to as morphoscopic traits (see Pink et al., , Chapter 5, this volume). Certainly all biological anthropologists are familiar with the trait lists published by Gill and Rhine (1990). Forensic anthropological methodology has recently been undergoing reevaluation to meet current standards as defined by the Daubert ruling (Grivas and Komar, 2008). Another part of the motivation for methodological advancement is in improved accessibility to powerful statistical software such as R, which is analogous to the rapid advancements seen in the 1960s with the first relatively easy access to computers. Following this trend, morphoscopic traits have been treated with much more statistical rigor, and classification methods have been applied to the data rather than relying on a more post hoc approach based on the experience of the practitioner (Hefner, 2009; Hefner and Ousley, 2014).

This study applies machine learning statistical classification methods to cranial nonmetric data that are typically used in biological distance analyses. Machine learning is exceptionally good at accurately classifying unknown data using a model developed on a known dataset where the underlying structure is complex. These methods have been very successful with text categorization, face detection, and biomedical applications (Hearst et al., 1998). This study addresses the hypothesis that machine learning classification methods will expose patterned differences in cranial nonmetric trait frequencies between two ancestral groups and generate a model that successfully classifies unknown individuals based on a set of these traits.

Although this study focuses on classification of ancestry for unknown cases, it is important to note that the approach is not intended to imply there are discrete ancestral groups among humans. The term "classification" is used here in the statistical, not taxonomic, sense. Human phenotypic variation is best conceived of as clinal in nature, and by definition no clear divisions exist between populations (Bolnick, 2008; Endler, 1977). However, many traits are found in relatively higher frequencies among various populations and thus are potentially informative of an individual's ancestry. This facet of the biological profile is absolutely useful in the identification of unknown human remains (see Sauer, 1992).

The methods described in the remainder of this chapter are intended as a tool to be used by trained forensic anthropologists to aid in ancestry estimation.

MATERIALS AND METHODS

Data were collected from a subset of the Robert J. Terry Anatomical Collection curated at the Smithsonian National Museum of Natural History. This collection was selected for its well-documented specimens, relatively balanced demographic profile, and because the collection has previously been studied with respect to cranial nonmetric traits (Corruccini, 1974; Hunt and Albanese, 2005). A summary of the study sample by sex, age, and ancestry is presented in Table 11.1.

Variable Selection

Thirty-five cranial nonmetric traits were scored on 200 Terry specimens. Three traits were removed from analysis due to zero variation within the sample (bregmatic bone, Inca bone, and auditory exotoses). The remaining 32 traits were tested for potential effects of age and sex on trait expression using a series of logistic regression analyses following Konigsberg (1987). Age was broken down into three categories following Buikstra and Ubelaker (1994, p. 36; see Table 11.1). The significance level for removal of traits from the analysis was adjusted from $\alpha \leq 0.05$ using the Šidák correction for multiple comparisons. Two additional traits were removed from analysis due to a significant effect of sex on the expression of the trait (Table 11.2). The remaining 30 nonmetric traits were used in the classification analyses. All calculations were made using R Statistical Computing software (R Core Team, 2014).

Statistical Models

Since the statistical methods can accommodate multilevel categorical data, two datasets were used to test the hypothesis that an uncompressed raw-score dataset would result in better classification performance than a binary dataset. The first dataset consisted of binary trait scores where the raw score was recoded and then collapsed to a score of 1 (present), 0 (absent), or NA (unobservable) [see Pink (2013) for scoring format]. The compressed dataset is consistent with those most commonly used in biological distance analyses. The second dataset used the raw scores originally assigned for each trait. For each dataset a side was randomly selected for bilaterally expressed traits. In the case of a bilateral trait where one side was not observable, the other side was used.

Machine Learning

The concept of machine learning was developed in the mid-1970s by Vapnik and Chervonekis (Statnikov et al., 2011, p. 16). In supervised machine learning the algorithm is given labeled training data with which to build a predictive model using data-driven decisions (Bishop, 2006). Supervised learning, the approach used in this analysis, is different from unsupervised learning where no example is given and the goal of the algorithm is to find patterns in the data. Machine learning is particularly good at generalization, or accurately classifying unknown data using a model developed on a known dataset, without overfitting the model. As with all statistical methods, it is important to consider the appropriateness of the methods for addressing the hypothesis based on the available data (Kotsiantis et al., 2007). This study utilized three

Table 11.1 *Sample Summary*

	Males					Females				
	Age (Years)					Age (Years)				
	19–34	35–49	50+	Adult (Unknown Age)	Subtotals	19–34	35–49	50+	Adult (Unknown Age)	Subtotals
African ancestry	17	17	13	0	47	11	12	29	1	53
European ancestry	1	6	42	1	50	1	2	47	0	50
Totals	18	23	55	1	97	12	14	76	1	103

Table 11.2 Results of Analysis of Sex and Age Influence on the Expression of Traits

Traits		*n*	Sex[a]	Age[a]	Sex × Age[a]
T1	Metopic suture	198	0.194	0.503	0.376
T2	Supraorbital notch	198	0.010	0.120	0.716
T3	Supraorbital foramen	198	0.792	0.384	0.488
T4	**Infraorbital suture**	198	**$4.98\ e^{6}$**	0.660	0.178
T5	Multiple infraorbital foramina	198	0.055	0.727	0.934
T6	Multiple zygomatico-facial foramina	198	0.008	0.769	0.666
T7	Parietal foramen	198	0.007	0.605	0.867
T8	Epiteric bone	168	0.536	0.578	0.305
T9	Coronal ossicle	178	0.987	0.256	0.958
T11	Sagittal ossicle	153	0.424	0.778	0.453
T12	Apical bone	177	0.831	0.997	0.850
T13	Lambdoid ossicle	170	0.574	0.453	0.525
T14	Asterionic bone	183	0.995	0.423	1.000
T15	Ossicle in the occipito-mastoid suture	166	0.285	0.058	0.510
T16	Parietal notch bone	191	0.220	0.616	0.994
T18	Os japonicum	197	0.997	0.308	1.000
T20	Condylar canal	195	0.103	0.854	0.235
T21	Divided hypoglossal canal	197	0.183	0.670	0.931
T22	Superior sagittal sulcus flex right	192	0.695	0.903	0.624
T23	Foramen ovale incomplete	198	0.458	0.368	0.209
T24	Foramen spinosum incomplete	198	0.018	0.493	0.358
T25	Pterygospinous bridge	198	0.804	0.211	0.926
T26	Pterygoalar bridge	198	0.042	0.889	0.050
T27	Tympanic dehiscence	185	0.184	0.143	0.552
T29	**Mastoid foramen**	198	**$3.71\ e^{8}$**	0.308	0.403
T30	Double condylar facet	196	0.458	0.545	0.044
T31	Bridging of jugular foramen	197	0.461	0.816	0.234
T32	Pharyngeal tubercle	197	0.971	0.689	0.209
T33	Palatine torus	196	0.011	0.097	0.322
T34	Mental foramen	196	0.695	0.157	0.485
T35	Mandibular torus	165	0.794	0.961	0.125
T37	Mylohyoid bridge	196	0.898	0.617	0.253

The traits in bold were removed from further analysis.
[a]$\alpha \leq 0.0003$.

supervised machine learning methods to develop classification models based on cranial nonmetric trait data: decision trees, random forest, and support vector machines (SVMs).

Three machine learning classification models were constructed on a training subset of each dataset. The training dataset consisted of 140 (70%) randomly selected cases. A validation subset of 60 (30%) individuals was held out to test the models built from the training datasets. Decision trees cannot handle missing data and any cases in the validation set with missing data were omitted. In this case, the validation set was less than 60 individuals. The three models were compared across both datasets on the basis of sensitivity, specificity, and correct classification rate (accuracy).

Decision Tree

The classification decision tree creates a set of binary splits contingent on the predictor variables (traits) to create a tree that can be used to classify new observations into one of two groups (Tan et al., 2006). Decision trees have potential in forensic ancestry estimation in that the model can be graphically represented in a flowchart that is simple to follow, thus reducing user error (Tan et al., 2006). Furthermore, the algorithm used to construct a decision tree works well with categorical data and does not recognize implicit order in the data (Tan et al., 2006). Some cranial nonmetric traits are scored on an ordinal scale to include most of the hypo- and hyperostotic traits (trait expression due to excessive or diminished bone formation, respectively), but the majority of the traits used in this study were not scored on an ordinal scale. Thus, splitting decisions that do not consider order in the scoring system are an advantage.

In this analysis, the tree was built by choosing a predictor variable that best split the data into the two ancestral groups so that the homogeneity (purity) of the outcome groups was maximized. Based on Hunt's algorithm the process was then repeated for the subgroups until no further splits improved the homogeneity of the subgroups. Multiple trees were constructed and the tree with the lowest 10-fold cross-validated prediction error was chosen as the final pruned tree. Observations with missing values for a trait were omitted from the analysis resulting in training and validation datasets variably smaller than the respective 140 and 60 individuals used in the random forest and SVM models. The decision trees were built and pruned using the *rpart* package (Therneau et al., 2013).

Random Forest

The random forest method builds on decision trees. A large number of decision trees is created by sampling individuals and variables in the training dataset. A key difference from the decision tree is that each node is split by the best of a random subset of variables, rather than the best of all the variables (Liaw and Wiener, 2002). Each individual is classified by each tree and the most common outcome is used as the final classification. This approach performs well compared to other classification methods including discriminant analysis, which is used extensively in forensic ancestry estimation (Liaw and Wiener, 2002). Another advantage of random forest classification is that it is robust to overfitting (Breiman, 2001; Liaw and Wiener, 2002). In this analysis, 500 decision trees were produced by sampling the training dataset with replacement (bootstrapping). Missing values were replaced by the modal value for the trait during the model-building phase. Once a model was built the validation datasets were then classified using the random forest. For model validation, individuals with missing data were omitted if they could not be classified by all the decision trees in the random forest. The random forest models were built using the *randomForest* package (Liaw and Wiener, 2002).

A useful result obtained from random forest modeling was relative variable importance. In this analysis the Mean Decrease Gini based on the Gini impurity index was used. Each split at a node (nonmetric trait variable) should increase the homogeneity (purity) of the two descendant nodes resulting in a reduction of the Gini impurity criterion. The average decrease in the Gini for each variable over all the trees gives an accurate picture of the relative importance of the variables in the model. However, one should keep in mind that true variable importance can be obscured by complex variable interactions (Breiman, 2001; Liaw and Wiener, 2002).

Support Vector Machines

SVMs are a relatively new class of data analysis tools in the machine learning family. They have gained popularity, especially in the biomedical research field, for their ability to handle datasets with a large number of predictor values compared to a relatively smaller sample size, to learn very complex models, and for their robusticity to overfitting (Statnikov et al., 2011, p. ix). A drawback to SVMs is that they are difficult to interpret (Kotsiantis et al., 2007). SVMs are primarily used, as they were in this analysis, to generate classification models. However, they are also used for variable selection, outlier (novelty) detection, prediction of a continuous value (regression), and clustering (Statnikov et al., 2011).

In a classification analysis, the SVM looks for the optimal hyperplane to separate two groups in a multidimensional space. In this case, the hyperplane maximized the margin between the closest points of the two ancestral groups (Statnikov et al., 2011). The optimal hyperplane has N-1 dimensions. Since the datasets have 30 traits (predictor variables) the optimal hyperplane had 29 dimensions. Because the data were fundamentally nonlinear, a kernel function was used to transform the data to be more linearly separable. The SVM was tuned by adjusting gamma (the kernel parameter controlling the shape of the hyperplane) and cost (the penalty for errors in classification). The SVMs were produced and tuned using the *e1071* package (Meyer et al., 2014).

RESULTS

The classification performance for decision trees, random forests, and SVMs are summarized for both datasets in Table 11.3. When all measures of performance are considered, the random forest based on the raw-score dataset produced the best model (73% correct allocation) (see Table 11.3).

Table 11.3 Results of the Three Classification Methods Based on the Binary-Score (Binary) and Raw-Score (Raw) Datasets

	Sensitivity		Specificity		Correct Classification Rate	
	Binary	Raw	Binary	Raw	Binary	Raw
Decision tree	0.56	0.62	0.57	0.65	0.57	0.63
Random forest	0.73	0.71	0.67	0.75	0.69	0.73
Support Vector Machine	0.67	0.67	0.73	0.38	0.69	0.47

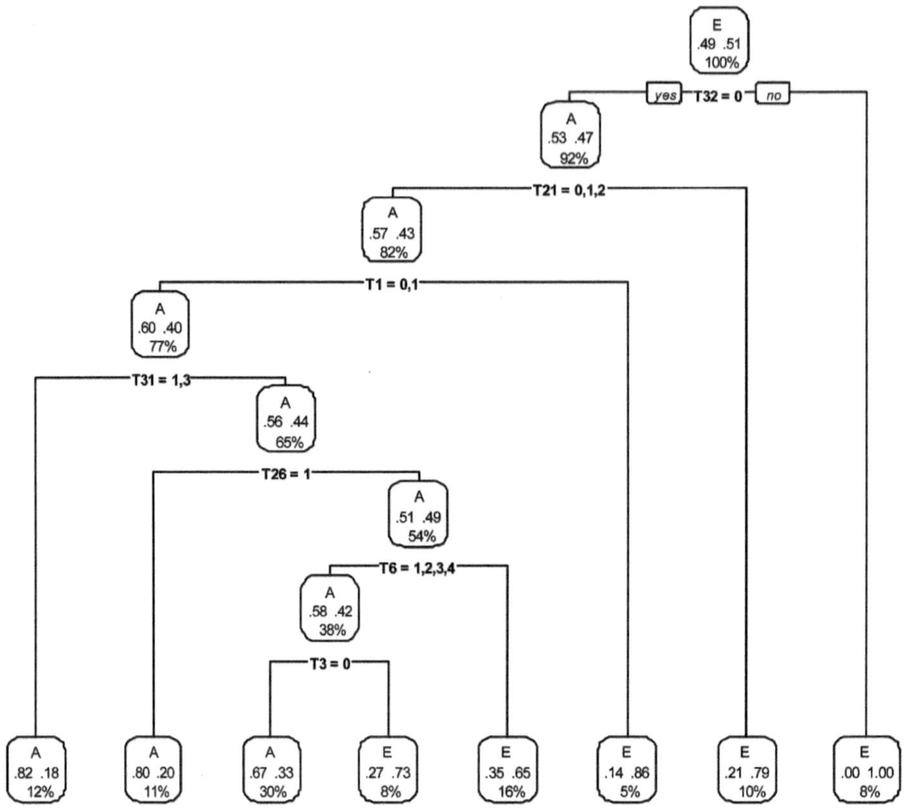

FIGURE 11.1

Decision tree based on raw-score dataset. Starting at the top of the tree, move left if the condition is true and right otherwise. The observation is classified at the terminal node. Each node has the probability of each class in the node [African (A) or European (E) ancestry] and the percentage of the sample.

The most accurate decision tree, based on the raw-score dataset, is illustrated in Fig. 11.1. Each node shows the decision criterion for the partition, the probability of each class (ancestral group), and the percentage of the sample remaining in the subset. The decision tree also illustrates the traits that were important in the classification model as the nodes for each split (see Fig. 11.1). The important traits for the model based on raw scores includes the pharyngeal tubercle (T32), divided hypoglossal canal (T21), metopic suture (T1), bridging of the jugular foramen (T31), pterygoalar bridge (T26), multiple zygomatico-facial foramina (T6), and supraorbital foramen (T3). Not surprisingly, these important traits were all shared with the random forest models.

Figs. 11.2 and 11.3 illustrate the relative importance of the 30 traits included in the random forest models. The most important traits according to the Mean Decrease Gini are summarized in Table 11.4. The condylar canal (T20) and palatine torus (T33) are included in Table 11.4 as important variables identified in the random forest models in addition to six that were also identified in the decision tree

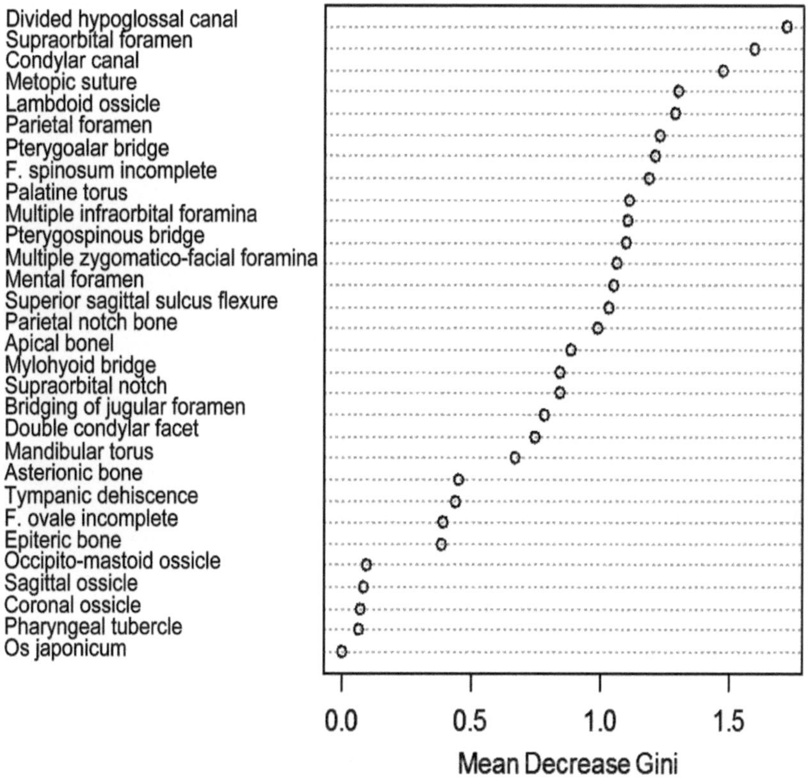

FIGURE 11.2

Variable importance in the random forest based on the binary dataset.

(see Fig. 11.1). The majority of these traits (55.5%) were observations of cranial foramina. The implications of important variables in the decision tree and random forest models are discussed in the next section.

Given the sophistication of the SVM method, the expectation was that these models would have relatively better performance compared to the decision tree and random forest models. However, this was not the observed result. The SVM classification model performed similarly to the random forest based on the binary dataset, but failed completely on the raw-score dataset (see Table 11.3). Further consideration of the applicability of this methodology to cranial nonmetric trait data is questionable given these results.

DISCUSSION

The three classification methods all performed poorly on both binary and raw-score datasets. Less accurate methods are still valuable in forensic contexts, especially when remains are fragmentary and the technique is the only one available (Christensen and Crowder, 2009). Decision trees and random forest models were

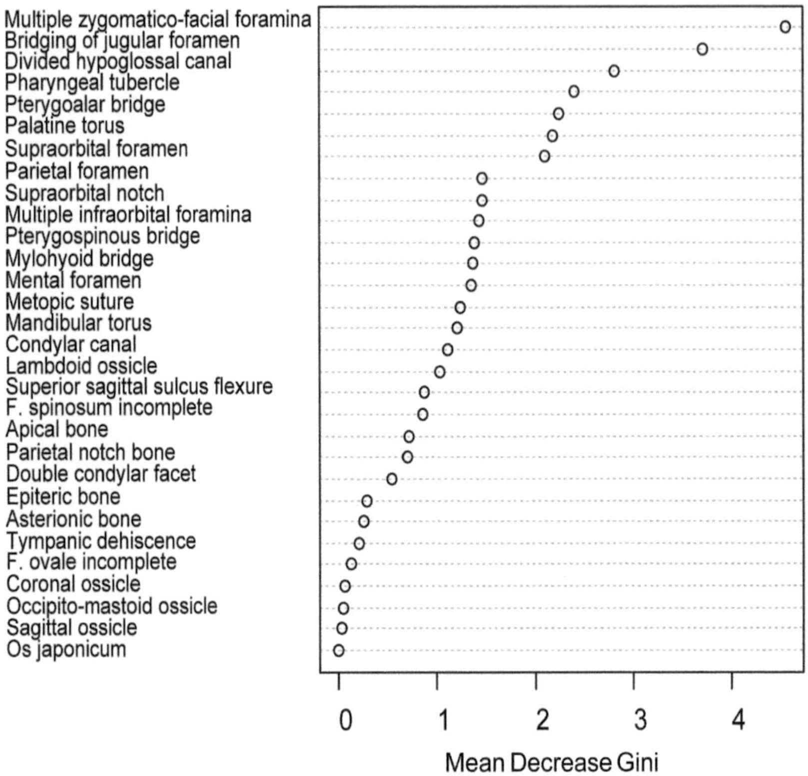

FIGURE 11.3

Variable importance in the random forest based on the raw dataset.

Table 11.4 Important Variables in the Random Forests

Traits	
T3	Supraorbital foramen
T6	Multiple zygomatico-facial foramina
T20	Condylar canal
T21	Divided hypoglossal canal
T26	Pterygoalar bridge
T31	Bridging of the jugular foramen
T32	Pharyngeal tubercle
T33	Palatine torus

more successful when built on the raw-score dataset. These results support the hypothesis that using raw scores, which retain more data about phenotypic variation, would strengthen the ability to classify unknown individuals. Random forest models, as an extension of the decision tree, tend to be more accurate when compared to other classification methods in general (Kabacoff, 2015). However, the best random forest model misclassified 27% of the validation sample (see Table 11.4).

While this analysis failed to achieve highly accurate ancestry classification using cranial nonmetric trait data, further research is warranted with the random forest method. A benefit of this method is the ability to examine variable importance, although caution should be exercised in that traits with more levels in their scoring may appear more influential in the Mean Decrease Gini calculation. Four of the influential traits listed in Table 11.4 (zygo-matico facial foramen, divided hypoglossal canal, bridging of the jugular foramen, and palatine torus) are scored with more levels than the majority of the remaining 26 traits used in the analysis. These results should guide future consideration of trait selection and scoring approaches. Recent studies have explored combined datasets with cranial morphoscopic and metric variables (Hefner and Ousley, 2014). There is merit in testing mixed-variable models with the addition of cranial nonmetric traits that are influential and demonstrate independence from confounding factors such as age and sex.

SVM Models

The SVM models performed similarly to the decision tree and random forest models based on the traditional binary dataset. However, performance was much worse with the raw-score dataset resulting in a correct classification rate lower than random chance (see Table 11.3). These results reject the hypothesis that models using the raw-score data would have superior performance. The failure of SVM models was also somewhat unexpected given the sophistication of the method, and success others have had with similar classes of data. Hefner and Ousley (2014) found this method to work well for ancestry classification using cranial morphoscopic trait data. In this study, it is argued that the particularly poor performance of the SVM method with raw-score data can be reduced to incompatibility between the statistical treatment of the data and the nature of cranial nonmetric trait expression.

Predictor variables with a large variance have greater influence as the SVM model is built. Therefore, the svm() function in the *e1071* package scales variables. The scaling is more appropriately applied to ordinal data, and likely had an effect on the model's performance. Although some cranial nonmetric traits are scored on an ordinal scale, this is not uniformly the case. Not surprisingly, the SVM model performed better with the binary data where scaling was applied to an already compressed dataset (see Table 11.3). A classification model built using variables that are ordinal in nature and others that are not, but have been scaled as though they are, would have the observed result of a model that fails to classify between groups.

The Nature of Phenotypic Variation in Cranial Nonmetric Traits

The overall failure of cranial nonmetric trait data to demonstrate ancestry on the continental scale between even two populations points toward a more fundamental dilemma. Classification methods that perform with relatively large error rates are not necessarily useless in a forensic context. However, according to the Daubert ruling the theoretical underpinning of a method or technique must be sound for results to be admissible as evidence in court (Christensen and Crowder, 2009). This principle is also at the root of good science. If the nature of cranial nonmetric trait expression between populations is not theoretically compatible with statistical classification methods, then the techniques explored in this chapter would not meet the Daubert standard for forensic evidence. Early on, Jantz (1970) cautioned the need for a more robust understanding of cranial nonmetric trait expression before any studies should rely exclusively on this class of data. Similarly, Finnegan (1972) suggested that limits exist in the utility of cranial nonmetric traits for accurately demonstrating biological affinities when the populations being compared are not closely related. Corruccini (1974) also expressed reservations about relying on these data to distinguish between European and African American groups in his study based on specimens from the same collection considered here. He advised that cranial nonmetric trait data may be better used as a validation dataset for biological affinity studies based on craniometric data (Corruccini, 1974).

Since the 1970s many have tested assumptions that cranial nonmetric traits are highly heritable and reflect genetic, more so than environmental, variation; are uncorrelated; and are independent of sex and age. All of these assumptions have been found to vary by trait and between populations (Corruccini, 1974; Cosseddu et al., 1979; Green et al., 1979; Hallgrímsson et al., 2005; Hauser and De Stefano, 1989; Korey, 1980; McGrath et al., 1984; Ossenberg, 1970; Perizonius, 1979; Trinkaus, 1978). Trait intercorrelation and correlation with age and sex can be controlled for relatively easily. The degree to which phenotypic variation reflects actual genetic variation, however, is an issue that is still being addressed in the literature (Carson, 2006; Cheverud, 1982; Cheverud et al., 1979; Cheverud and Buikstra, 1981b; Martínez-Abadías et al., 2009; Ricaut et al., 2010).

The expression of polygenic traits is affected by an array of variables for which we have a relatively low-resolution understanding of the direction and magnitude of influence. Many studies acknowledge that both genetic and nongenetic factors influence phenotypic variation in both metric and nonmetric cranial traits; however, these factors are usually not explicitly addressed and phenotypic expression is often assumed to reflect genes more than the environment (Šešelj et al., 2015; Sherwood et al., 2008). Several studies have addressed the heritability of cranial nonmetric traits in humans and other nonhuman primates to understand the relative importance of genes and environment in the variation of traits within and between populations. If phenotypic variance (σ_P^2) is the sum of the underlying genetic (σ_G^2) and environmental (σ_E^2) variances, then heritability (h^2) (in the narrow sense) is the proportion of phenotypic variation (σ_P^2) explained by the additive genetic effects (σ_A^2).

$$h^2 = \frac{\sigma_A^2}{\sigma_P^2} \tag{11.1}$$

Intuitively, cranial nonmetric traits that tend to have high h^2 values would be preferable for building ancestry classification models. However, it is important to point out some misconceptions about heritability before continuing. Visscher et al. (2008) neatly summarize the major common misinterpretations of heritability that are pertinent to this discussion. In particular, low heritability has been presented as though it indicates there is little additive genetic variance (Visscher et al., 2008, p. 257). A low heritability means only that the proportion of observed phenotypic variation explained by genetic variation is small. The implication for this study is that genetic variance was not well represented in the phenotypic variation of the groups under consideration.

The second misconception is that when heritabilities are high, differences in mean expression between two groups necessarily indicate genetic differences (Visscher et al., 2008, p. 257). At the root of this misunderstanding is the fact that heritabilities are calculated for a particular population and do not speak to the environments of other populations. It is argued here that cranial nonmetric traits demonstrating high heritabilities in various populations, or in nonhuman models, should not be relied on more heavily in this, or any analysis. Inclusion of a maximum number of traits may help to diminish confounding environmental variables that are not easily controlled for.

The well-known work of Cheverud and Buikstra (1981a, 1982) (see also Cheverud, 1981) examined heritability of cranial metric and nonmetric traits in a population of rhesus macaques (*Macaca mulatta*) laying a foundation for further studies. Although most traits had moderate heritability, they found that hypo- and hyperostotic traits had higher heritability relative to foraminal traits (Cheverud and Buikstra, 1981a, p. 46). They hypothesized that lower heritability for foraminal traits was due to the etiology of the traits during growth and development, but cautioned that the pattern may not be generalizable to humans (Cheverud and Buikstra, 1982). An alternative to the trait etiology hypothesis is that traits with higher fitness should have lower heritabilities following Fisher's (1930, p. 37) theorem of natural selection stating, "The rate of increase in fitness of any organism at any time is equal to its genetic variance in fitness at that time" (see also Fisher, 1958; Falconer, 1960, 1989). This pattern has indeed been demonstrated across multiple ecto- and endothermic species (Mousseau and Roff, 1987). In a study of biological affinity, such as this one, the primary goal is to clarify population history as reflected by gene flow and genetic drift. Therefore, the optimal approach is to use neutral traits, or those not undergoing selection [Roseman, 2004 (in reference to craniometric variables)].

In general, heritability studies of cranial nonmetric traits in humans have shown them to have low to moderate heritabilities (Carson, 2006; Sjøvold, 1984). Cranial nonmetric traits may have large genetic variances; however, they are not well reflected in the phenotypic variation. Therefore, phenotypic variation is affected enough by environmental factors that in a comparison of two or more unrelated groups any patterned genetic variance is not easily interpretable. This explains why two largely unrelated groups living in early 1900s St. Louis, Missouri would be difficult to distinguish on the basis of cranial nonmetric trait frequencies. A similar physical and nutritional environment could potentially homogenize phenotypic variation in trait expression and obscure genetic variation due to different ancestral backgrounds. Also worth noting is potential admixture in the African ancestry sample. African American populations have been demonstrated to have appreciable admixture with European American populations without a reciprocal effect in the populations of European ancestry (Parra et al., 1998; Shriver et al., 1997; Workman et al., 1963). The genetic admixture serves to further diminish expectations for any structured between-group variation. Ultimately, with significant overlap in phenotypic variation between distantly related populations most statistical approaches will not result in an effective classification model based on cranial nonmetric traits alone.

Biological Distance and Cranial Nonmetric Trait Data

Constraints clearly exist for the use of cranial nonmetric traits to compare unrelated groups. However, decades of biological distance studies have demonstrated their usefulness for exploring biological affinity on the regional scale where recent common ancestry is a reasonable assumption (Buikstra et al., 1990; Konigsberg, 2006). In regional studies, environmental influence should be relatively constant. Therefore, even if genetic variance is minimally expressed in trait phenotype, the observed between-group variation should be reflective of genetic variation (ideally) due to gene flow and genetic drift. In the case of common ancestry the assumption of similar effects of genes and environment on the expression of a threshold trait is a more valid assumption than with unrelated groups. Biological distance studies also take different statistical approaches to the data than classification models. For instance, Euclidean methods such as the Mahalanobis D^2 consider distances between group centroids with overlap in phenotypic variation. Therefore, within- and between-group variation is measurable and interpretable in a quantitative genetic theoretical framework. These differences regarding basic assumptions in the research question and statistical approaches are important implications for the continued use of cranial nonmetric trait data in bioarchaeology.

CONCLUSIONS

The failure of the classification methods to reliably sort individuals on the basis of cranial nonmetric data indicates that the nature of the data itself is not well suited to ancestry estimation. There is sufficient overlap in trait frequencies that unrelated groups are difficult to separate. Of primary concern in this analysis is the role of environmental variables on the expression of a threshold trait. The effects of environment on the phenotypic expression of cranial nonmetric traits are essentially a black box. Without knowledge the effect in direction and/or magnitude that environmental variables have on trait expression, it is difficult to say to what degree phenotypic variation reflects genetic differences.

This study should not dissuade future considerations of biological distance based on cranial nonmetric traits. The literature clearly demonstrates analyses in regional populations yield results that are interpretable in archaeological and historical frameworks. Furthermore, the data have real advantages, especially for archaeological assemblages. One cautionary tale from this research is in the use of an out group. It is likely that including a group with little known biological relationship to those under study is of dubious utility, and will probably amount to no more than an analytical distraction.

Cranial nonmetric traits will continue to form the basis for inquires of biological affinity. However, the results of this study indicate that models built on these data do not meet the Daubert standard for forensic ancestry estimation. The reliability of studies based on cranial nonmetric traits would be greatly aided by a better understanding of the specific genes and genetic interactions that play a role in trait expression relative to developmental and environmental influences. Unfortunately, unless cranial nonmetric trait expressions are found to correlate with cancer it is unlikely major funding for such research will be forthcoming anytime soon.

Acknowledgments

I would like to thank the editors of this volume for the invitation to contribute to an excellent volume. I am appreciative of the anonymous peer reviewers for their helpful comments on earlier drafts of this chapter. Thanks are also in order to Dr. David Hunt of the National Museum of Natural History for facilitating data collection. This research was partially funded by the Defense POW/MIA Accounting Agency.

References

Berry, C.A., Berry, R.J., 1967. Epigenetic variation of the human cranium. Journal of Anatomy 101, 361–379.

Birkby, W.H., 1973. Discontinuous Morphological Traits of the Skull as Population Markers in the Prehistoric Southwest (Ph.D. dissertation). The University of Arizona, Tucson. University Microfilms, Ann Arbor.

Bishop, C.M., 2006. Pattern Recognition and Machine Learning. Springer.

Blom, D.E., Hallgrimsson, B., Keng, L., Lozada, C.M.C., Buikstra, J.E., 1998. Tiwanaku 'colonization': bioarchaeological implications for migration in the Moquegua Valley, Peru. World Archaeology 30 (2), 238–261.
Bolnick, D.A., 2008. Individual ancestry inference and the reification of race as a biological phenomenon. In: Revisiting Race a Genomic Age, pp. 70–85.
Breiman, L., 2001. Random forests. Machine Learning 45 (1), 5–32.
Buikstra, J.E., 1976. Hopewell in the lower Illinois valley. In: Northwestern University Archeological Program Scientific Papers, No. 2.
Buikstra, J.E., Frankenberg, S.R., Konigsberg, L.W., 1990. Skeletal biological distance studies in American physical anthropology: recent trends. American Journal of Physical Anthropology 82 (1), 1–7.
Buikstra, J.E., Ubelaker, D.H., 1994. Standards for Data Collection from Human Skeletal Remains. Arkansas Archeological Survey Research Series No. 44, Fayetteville, AR.
Carson, E.A., 2006. Maximum-likelihood variance coordinates analysis of heritabilities of cranial nonmetric traits. Human Biology 78, 383–402.
Cheverud, J.M., 1981. Variation in highly and lowly heritable morphological traits among social groups of rhesus macaques (*Macaca mulatta*) on Cayo Santiago. Evolution 35 (1), 75–83.
Cheverud, J.M., 1982. Phenotypic, genetic, and environmental morphological integration in the cranium. Evolution 36 (3), 499–516.
Cheverud, J.M., Buikstra, J.E., 1981a. Quantitative genetics of nonmetric traits in the rhesus macaques on Cayo Santiago. I. Single trait heritabilities. American Journal of Physical Anthropology 54 (1), 43–49.
Cheverud, J.M., Buikstra, J.E., 1981b. Quantitative genetics of nonmetric traits in the rhesus macaques on Cayo Santiago. II. Phenotypic genetic and environmental correlations between traits. American Journal of Physical Anthropology 54 (1), 51–58.
Cheverud, J.M., Buikstra, J.E., 1982. Quantitative genetics of skeletal nonmetric traits in the rhesus macaques of Cayo Santiago. III. Relative heritability of skeletal nonmetric and metric traits. American Journal of Physical Anthropology 59, 151–155.
Cheverud, J.M., Buikstra, J.E., Twichell, E., 1979. Relationships between non-metric skeletal traits and cranial size and shape. American Journal of Physical Anthropology 50 (2), 191–198.
Christensen, A.M., Crowder, C.M., 2009. Evidentiary standards for forensic anthropology. Journal of Forensic Sciences 54 (6), 1211–1216.
Corruccini, R.S., 1974. An examination of the meaning of cranial discrete traits for human skeletal biological studies. American Journal of Physical Anthropology 40 (3), 425–446.
Cosseddu, G.G., Floris, G., Vona, G., 1979. Sex and side differences in the minor nonmetrical cranial variants. Journal of Human Evolution 8 (7), 685–692.
Dodo, Y., 1987. Supraorbital foramen and hypoglossal canal bridging: the two most suggestive nonmetric traits in discriminating major racial groupings in man. Journal of the Anthropological Society of Nippon 95, 19–35.
Endler, J.A., 1977. Geographic Variation, Speciation, and Clines (No. 10). Princeton University Press, Princeton.
Falconer, D.S., 1960. Introduction to Quantitative Genetics. Oliver and Boyd, Edinburgh.
Falconer, D.S., 1989. Introduction to Quantitative Genetics, third ed. Longman Scientific & Technical, Edinburgh.
Finnegan, M.J., 1972. Population Definition on the Northwest Coast by Analysis of Discrete Character Variation (Ph.D. dissertation). University of Colorado.
Fisher, R.A., 1930. The Genetical Theory of Natural Selection: A Complete Variorum Edition. Oxford University Press, Oxford.
Fisher, R.A., 1958. The Genetic Theory of Natural Selection. Oxford University Press, Oxford.
Gill, G.W., Rhine, S., 1990. Skeletal attribution of race: methods for forensic anthropology. In: Anthropological Papers of the Maxwell Museum of Anthropology, No. 4.
Green, R.F., Suchey, J.M., Gokhale, D.V., 1979. The statistical treatment of correlated bilateral traits in the analysis of cranial material. American Journal of Physical Anthropology 50 (4), 629–634.

Grivas, C.R., Komar, D.A., 2008. Kumho, Daubert, and the nature of scientific inquiry: implications for forensic anthropology. Journal of Forensic Sciences 53 (4), 771–776.

Hallgrímsson, B., Ó Donnabháin, B., Walters, G.B., Cooper, D.M., Guðbjartsson, D., Stefánsson, K., 2004. Composition of the founding population of Iceland: biological distance and morphological variation in early historic Atlantic Europe. American Journal of Physical Anthropology 124 (3), 257–274.

Hallgrímsson, B., Donnabhain, B.O., Blom, D.E., Lozada, M.C., Willmore, K.T., 2005. Why are rare traits unilaterally expressed? Trait frequency and unilateral expression for cranial nonmetric traits in humans. American Journal of Physical Anthropology 128 (1), 14–25.

Hanihara, T., Ishida, H., 2001a. Frequency variations of discrete cranial traits in major human populations. I. Supernumerary ossicle variations. Journal of Anatomy 198 (6), 689–706.

Hanihara, T., Ishida, H., 2001b. Frequency variations of discrete cranial traits in major human populations. II. Hypostotic variations. Journal of Anatomy 198 (6), 707–725.

Hanihara, T., Ishida, H., 2001c. Frequency variations of discrete cranial traits in major human populations. III. Hyperostotic variations. Journal of Anatomy 199 (3), 251–272.

Hanihara, T., Ishida, H., 2001d. Frequency variations of discrete cranial traits in major human populations. IV. Vessel and nerve related variations. Journal of Anatomy 199 (3), 273–287.

Hauser, G., De Stefano, G.F., 1989. Epigenetic Variants of the Human Skull. E. Schweizerbartsche Verlagsbuchhandlung.

Hearst, M.A., Dumais, S.T., Osman, E., Platt, J., Scholkopf, B., 1998. Support vector machines. Intelligent Systems and Their Applications, IEEE 13 (4), 18–28.

Hefner, J.T., 2009. Cranial nonmetric variation and estimating ancestry. Journal of Forensic Sciences 54 (5), 985–995.

Hefner, J.T., Ousley, S.D., 2014. Statistical classification methods for estimating ancestry using morphoscopic traits. Journal of Forensic Sciences 59 (4), 883–890.

Hunt, D.R., Albanese, J., 2005. History and demographic composition of the Robert J. Terry anatomical collection. American Journal of Physical Anthropology 127 (4), 406–417.

Irish, J.D., 2010. The mean measure of divergence: its utility in model-free and model-bound analyses relative to the Mahalanobis D^2 distance for nonmetric traits. American Journal of Human Biology 22, 378–395.

Jantz, R.L., 1970. Change and Variation in Skeletal Populations of Arikara Indians (Ph.D. dissertation). University of Kansas, Lawrence.

Jantz, R.L., 1973. Microevolutionary change in Arikara Crania: a multivariate analysis. American Journal of Physical Anthropology 38 (1), 15–26.

Kabacoff, R., 2015. R in Action, second ed. Manning Publications Co., Greenwich.

Kellock, W.L., Parsons, P.A., 1970. A comparison of the incidence of minor nonmetrical cranial variants in Australian aborigines with those of Melanesia and Polynesia. American Journal of Physical Anthropology 33 (2), 235–239.

Konigsberg, L.W., 1987. Population Genetic Models for Interpreting Prehistoric Intra-cemetery Biological Variation (Unpublished Ph.D. dissertation). Department of Anthropology, Northwestern University.

Konigsberg, L.W., 1990. Analysis of prehistoric biological variation under a model of isolation by geographic and temporal distance. Human Biology 62, 49–70.

Konigsberg, L.W., 2006. A post-Neumann history of biological and genetic distance studies in bioarchaeology. In: Bioarchaeology: The Contextual Analysis of Human Remains. Academic Press, New York, pp. 263–279.

Konigsberg, L.W., Kohn, L.A.P., Cheverud, J.M., 1993. Cranial deformation and nonmetric trait variation. American Journal of Physical Anthropology 90 (1), 35–48.

Korey, K.A., 1980. The incidence of bilateral nonmetric skeletal traits: a reanalysis of sampling procedures. American Journal of Physical Anthropology 53 (1), 19–23.

Kotsiantis, S.B., Zaharakis, I., Pintelas, P., 2007. Supervised Machine Learning: A Review of Classification Techniques. IOS Press, Amsterdam.

Lane, R.A., Sublett, A.J., 1972. Osteology of social organization: residence pattern. American Antiquity 37 (2), 186–201.

Liaw, A., Wiener, M., 2002. Classification and regression by randomForest. R News 2 (3), 18–22.

Martínez-Abadías, N., Esparza, M., Sjøvold, T., González-José, R., Santos, M., Hernández, M., 2009. Heritability of human cranial dimensions: comparing the evolvability of different cranial regions. Journal of Anatomy 214 (1), 19–35.

McGrath, J.W., Cheverud, J.M., Buikstra, J.E., 1984. Genetic correlations between sides and heritability of asymmetry for nonmetric traits in rhesus macaques on Cayo Santiago. American Journal of Physical Anthropology 64 (4), 401–411.

Meyer, D., Dimitriadou, E., Hornik, K., Weingessel, A., Leisch, F., 2014. e1071: Misc Functions of the Department of Statistics. TU Wien. R package version 1.6-4. http://CRAN.R-project.org/package=e1071.

Milne, N., Schmitt, L.H., Freedman, L., 1983. Discrete trait variation in Western Australian Aboriginal skulls. Journal of Human Evolution 12 (2), 157–168.

Mousseau, T.A., Roff, D.A., 1987. Natural selection and the heritability of fitness components. Heredity 59 (Pt 2), 181–197.

Ossenberg, N., 1969. Discontinuous Morphological Variation in the Human Cranium (Ph.D. dissertation). University of Toronto.

Ossenberg, N., 1970. The influence of artificial cranial deformation on discontinuous morphological traits. American Journal of Physical Anthropology 33 (3), 357–371.

Ossenberg, N., 1976. Within and between race distances in population studies based on discrete traits of the human skull. American Journal of Physical Anthropology 45 (3), 701–715.

Parra, E.J., Marcini, A., Akey, J., Martinson, J., Batzer, M.A., Cooper, R., Shriver, M.D., 1998. Estimating African American admixture proportions by use of population-specific alleles. The American Journal of Human Genetics 63 (6), 1839–1851.

Perizonius, W.R.K., 1979. Nonmetric cranial traits: sex difference and age dependence. Journal of Human Evolution 8 (7), 679–684.

Pink, C.M., 2013. Striking Out and Digging in: A Bioarchaeological Perspective on Regional Impacts of Wari Imperialism in the Peruvian Central Andes (Ph.D. dissertation). University of Tennessee.

R Core Team, 2014. R: A Language and Environment for Statistical Computing. R Foundation for Statistical Computing, Vienna, Austria. http://www.R-project.org/.

Ricaut, F.X., Auriol, V., von Cramon-Taubadel, N., Keyser, C., Murail, P., Ludes, B., Crubézy, E., 2010. Comparison between morphological and genetic data to estimate biological relationship: the case of the Egyin Gol necropolis (Mongolia). American Journal of Physical Anthropology 143 (3), 355–364.

Roseman, C.C., 2004. Detecting interregionally diversifying natural selection on modern human cranial form by using matched molecular and morphometric data. Proceedings of the National Academy of Sciences of the United States of America 101 (35), 12824–12829.

Sauer, N.J., 1992. Forensic anthropology and the concept of race: if races don't exist, why are forensic anthropologists so good at identifying them? Social Science & Medicine 34 (2), 107–111.

Šešelj, M., Duren, D.L., Sherwood, R.J., 2015. Heritability of the Human Craniofacial Complex. The Anatomical Record 298 (9), 1535–1547.

Sherwood, R.J., Duren, D.L., Demerath, E.W., Czerwinski, S.A., Siervogel, R.M., Towne, B., 2008. Quantitative genetics of modern human cranial variation. Journal of Human Evolution 54, 909–914.

Shriver, M.D., Smith, M.W., Jin, L., Marcini, A., Akey, J.M., Deka, R., Ferrell, R.E., 1997. Ethnic-affiliation estimation by use of population-specific DNA markers. American Journal of Human Genetics 60 (4), 957.

Sjøvold, T., 1984. A report on the heritability of some cranial measurements and nonmetric traits. In: Multivariate Statistical Methods in Physical Anthropology. Springer Netherlands, Amsterdam, pp. 223–246.

Spence, M.W., 1974. Residential practices and the distribution of skeletal traits in Teotihuacan, Mexico. Man 9, 262–273.

Statnikov, A., Aliferis, C.F., Hardin, D.P., 2011. A Gentle Introduction to Support Vector Machines in Biomedicine: Theory and Methods, vol. 1. World Scientific.

Tan, P.N., Steinbach, M., Kumar, V., 2006. Classification: basic concepts, decision trees, and model evaluation. Introduction to Data Mining 1, 145–205.

Therneau, T., Atkinson, E.J., Ripley, B., 2013. rpart: Recursive Partitioning, R package, version 4.1-1. R Foundation for Statistical Computing, Vienna, Austria.

Thoma, A., 1981. The pattern of quasi-continuous variation in *Homo sapiens*. Journal of Human Evolution 10 (4), 303–310.

Trinkaus, E., 1978. Bilateral asymmetry of human skeletal non-metric traits. American Journal of Physical Anthropology 49 (3), 315–318.

Visscher, P.M., Hill, W.G., Wray, N.R., 2008. Heritability in the genomics era—concepts and misconceptions. Nature Reviews Genetics 9 (4), 255–266.

Wijsman, E.M., Neves, W.A., 1986. The use of nonmetric variation in estimating human population admixture: a test case with Brazilian blacks, whites, and mulattos. American Journal of Physical Anthropology 70 (3), 395–405.

Workman, P.L., Blumberg, B.S., Cooper, A.J., 1963. Selection, gene migration and polymorphic stability in a US white and negro population. American Journal of Human Genetics 15 (4), 429.

CHAPTER

12

Biological Distance, Migrants, and Reference Group Selection in Forensic Anthropology

K. Spradley
Texas State University, San Marcos, TX, United States

CHAPTER OUTLINE HEAD

Background 233
Materials and Methods 234
  Population Groups 234
    Migrant Groups 234
    Forensic Reference Groups 235
    Craniometric Data 235
  Analyses 236
    Arizona and Texas Migrants 236
    Arizona and Texas Migrants and Forensic Reference Groups 236
  Results 236
    Arizona and Texas Migrants 236
    Arizona and Texas Migrants and Forensic Reference Groups 238
    Combining Groups for Discriminant Function Analysis 238
Discussion 241
References 243

Biological distance, or biodistance, has been a useful way to aid in the reconstruction of population structure within prehistoric populations and to gain further knowledge about processes that affect the biological relationships of historic or recent population groups. In prehistoric populations, biodistance can provide information otherwise unavailable (Jantz, 1977; Jantz and Owsley, 2001; Powell and Neves, 1999; Stojanowski and Schillaci, 2006). Biodistance in historical investigations can help corroborate historical documentation (Edgar, 2009; Ousley et al., 2005). Biodistance studies involving recent groups can inform forensic anthropological practice by gaining a better understanding of reference samples used in classification statistics and to understand the relationship of an unknown individual to known reference groups (Jantz and Moore-Jansen, 1988; Ousley et al., 2009; Ross et al., 2004; Spradley, 2014).

Classification statistics, including discriminant function analysis (DFA) or machine learning techniques such as random forest modeling can provide an estimate of geographic origin for an unknown individual. However, the major assumption that goes along with any classification statistic is that the

Biological Distance Analysis. http://dx.doi.org/10.1016/B978-0-12-801966-5.00012-3

unknown individual belongs to one of the reference groups. Therefore, having appropriate reference groups and understanding where those reference groups are from, how they biologically relate to one another, and how the unknown relates to the reference groups is the key to a good classification. No matter the method, an important consideration is the appropriateness of reference groups. This is a pressing issue as a classification (estimate) of geographic origin (where in the world the person is from) is produced for use within the medico-legal community and will be compared against missing persons records, making accuracies in such classifications important. As such, the reference groups need to represent the population groups they are applied to, necessitating a need to fully understand the reference groups themselves and their biological similarities to one another. If groups are similar, pooling may be the appropriate option given the nature of the desired outcome. For example, is a broad classification (African, European, Native American) enough to assist with identification, or is something more specific needed that denotes the actual geographic origin and self-described group membership (American Black, American White, Central American)? If a broad classification is desired, pooling groups may be appropriate if they are from the same or similar geographic areas and temporal period. If a more specific classification is desired, pooling may not be the best solution.

Along the US/Mexico border there is a continual flow of migration and, unfortunately, an increasing number of deaths. In recent years, the majority of migrants who die crossing the US/Mexico border are found in Arizona and Texas. Previous research supports the supposition that the majority of migrants that cross the Arizona/Mexico border are from Mexico (Anderson, 2008; Pima County Office of the Medical Examiner, 2013), predominantly central and south Mexico. Within Texas, the majority of migrants are termed by the US Border Patrol (USBP) as "other than Mexican," or OTMs. Apprehension statistics indicate the majority of migrants who cross the Texas/Mexico border are from Honduras, El Salvador, and Guatemala followed by Mexico (U.S. Customs and Border Patrol, 2012). The majority of anthropological analyses on the undocumented migrants have been focused within a forensic context, generating case reports and attempting to facilitate identifications and repatriations. Systematic data collection during forensic anthropological analysis has provided valuable information for better understanding of the biological variation within and among these migrant populations (Birkby et al., 2008; Hughes et al., 2013; Hurst, 2012; Spradley, 2013, 2014, 2015; Spradley et al., 2015; Tise et al., 2013).

In order to discuss migrant populations, an understanding of migration is important. Until recently, few definitions of migration were provided in the biological anthropology literature (Cabana and Clark, 2011). Clark defines migration as "a long-term residential relocation by one or more social groups across community boundaries in response to spatially uneven changes in social and economic conditions" (2011, p. 84). Within bioarchaeology, the investigator is typically trying to reconstruct the act and rate of migration, using model-bound methods. Model-bound methods have more assumptions, incorporate measures of similarity, and are meant to provide estimates of specific parameters such as admixture and kinship, while model-free methods evaluate the degree and pattern among groups (Relethford and Lees, 1982, p. 176). However, both are used to quantitatively assess populations that have already experienced the act and long-term effects of migration. The present study differs from most studies of migration in that it uses model-free methods to assess the structure and scale of migration (Cabana and Clark, 2011). Structure and scale are defined by Cabana and Clark as addressing questions relating to who is migrating, what border is traversed, and how the migrant groups are organized.

The purpose of this chapter is to use biodistance techniques to better understand the biological variation of these migrants and to further explore biological relationships of migrants who die in Arizona versus those who die in Texas. As forensic anthropologists are called to estimate geographic origin of unidentified individuals, biological distance is also used to understand the biological relationships of these migrants to other reference groups commonly used in forensic anthropological practice.

BACKGROUND

Migration (as defined by Clark, 2011) is a natural process in the course of human history and is a continual process along the US/Mexico border. The United States has a long history with migration at the US/Mexico border, both authorized and unauthorized. During the late 1930s, the Bracero program was initiated within the US to recruit workers from Mexico and provide them with temporary visas, mostly for work in agriculture within border states (Brick et al., 2011). Central Americans also took advantage of the program. The Bracero program ended in 1964 and subsequent changes in US policy fueled a demand for immigrant labor beginning in the 1970s. The demise of the Bracero program meant that the majority of Mexicans and Central Americans supplying the continued labor demand were unauthorized. Mexico currently makes up the largest group of naturalized and unauthorized immigrants in the United States followed by Central American countries, particularly El Salvador, Guatemala, and Honduras (Brick et al., 2011; Ramirez and de la Cruz, 2002).

Currently, the demand for immigrant labor has not diminished and it is estimated that without immigrant labor the US would be short 7.3 million workers in the workforce over the next decade (Myers et al., 2013, p. 5). There are a number of reasons why Mexicans and Central Americans continue to migrate to the United States, including escaping economic circumstances and violence. In response to unauthorized migration, in 1994 the USBP adopted the policy "Prevention through Deterrence" as their operational strategy of choice for securing the US/Mexico border. This strategy deterred migrant crossings in populated areas that were relatively safe and instead forced migrants to cross in more remote and dangerous areas such as the Sonoran Desert (Haddal, 2010). As a result, a funnel effect was created that led to an increase in migrant apprehensions and deaths (Martinez et al., 2013). Although USBP strategies have historically aimed to stop migrants before entering the United States, migration continues and the problem remains: deaths continue, creating a humanitarian crisis at the US/Mexico border. Until recently the majority of migrant deaths occurred in Arizona despite the fact that the Texas/Mexico border covers 1254 miles of the 1900 miles of the entire border. However, in 2012 Texas surpassed Arizona in deaths. The majority of these deaths occur in the Rio Grande Valley and more specifically in Brooks County, Texas (U.S. Customs and Border Patrol, 2012).

The Pima County Office of the Medical Examiner (PCOME) located in Tucson, Arizona receives the majority of migrant remains, due to their proximity to the border. The PCOME also keeps official statistics on border deaths. In 2000, as a result of "Prevention through Deterrence," migrant death rates began to rise. Between 1990 and 1999, 129 deaths occurred along the Arizona/Mexico border in contrast to 802 deaths that occurred over the next 5 years (Martinez et al., 2013). The identification rate of the migrants at the PCOME is approximately 60%. Based on information collected by the PCOME, the majority of migrants analyzed in the W.H. Birkby Forensic Anthropology Laboratory since 2001 were from Mexico (1285/85%), followed by Guatemala (120/8%), and El Salvador (40/3%) (Pima County Office of the Medical Examiner, 2013).

In Texas, unlike Arizona, not all migrant deaths are sent to a medical examiner's office. Brooks County, Texas (942 mi^2) receives the highest reported number of undocumented migrant deaths each year (80 in 2011, 129 in 2012, and 87 in 2013). These deaths fall under the jurisdiction of a justice of the peace (JP), since there is no medical examiner within the county. Due to the lack of a centralized location for medico-legal investigation of migrant remains, there exists a lack of centralized record keeping on information pertaining to the identification rate of migrants and their countries of origin. Therefore, the USBP apprehension rates are used as a proxy for country of origin. As stated previously, the majority of apprehensions are from Central America, specifically Honduras, El Salvador, and Guatemala.

Because the geographic origins of apprehensions should correlate with the geographic origins of decedents, these two migrant samples offer a unique insight into biodistance studies. Both source populations are from Latin America, a broad geographic location; however, Arizona receives high numbers of Mexicans while Texas receives high numbers of Central Americans. Cranial morphology has been shown to be a proxy for genetic data, in that quantitative continuous traits can provide information about genetic similarities (Carson, 2006; Devor, 1987; Herrera et al., 2014; Relethford, 2004; Relethford and Blangero, 1990; Strauss and Hubbe, 2010). Because Arizona and Texas migrants represent Mexico and Central American groups, respectively, craniofacial morphology from these migrant groups can be used to explore among and within group biological variation and their morphometric similarities to other forensic reference groups.

The objective of this research is to ascertain, through biological distance measures, how the migrant groups are organized in terms of population structure. Can the migrants who cross into Arizona be distinguished from the migrants who cross into Texas? As these groups represent active forensic anthropology cases it is important to establish if these two groups can be distinguished from other relevant reference groups for purposes of improving ancestry estimation.

MATERIALS AND METHODS

Population Groups

Migrant Groups

Two migrant groups representing deaths along the Arizona and Texas borders are from (1) the PCOME located in Tucson, Arizona and (2) from exhumations carried out in Brooks County, Texas housed at the Forensic Anthropology Center at Texas State (FACTS). Due to the high volume of migrant deaths along the border and because these deaths are taken to the PCOME for anthropological or pathological examination, systematic craniometric data collection was possible (see Spradley, 2013). In the late 2000s, Texas saw in increase in migrant deaths, most notable in the USBP Rio Grande Valley Sector. Due to this dramatic increase in deaths and lack of resources, the local JP and Brooks County Sheriff's Office were overwhelmed with deaths and began to bury the deceased individuals, most without proper analyses or collection of DNA samples, leaving little chance for identification and repatriation.

During the summers of 2012 and 2013, Drs. Lori Baker (Baylor University) and Krista Latham (University of Indianapolis) and their students performed voluntary exhumations of burials within Brooks County for the purposes of skeletal analysis and DNA sampling in hopes of facilitating positive identifications. From these exhumations and the cases sent from a South Texas Medical Examiner, a total of 80 migrant individuals were sent to Texas State University for processing and analyses. The majority of these individuals had significant amounts of flesh that required extensive processing prior to analysis. To date, 40 individuals have been processed and analyzed.

Table 12.1 Sample Sizes[a]	
Group	**N**
Migrants	
Arizona female	39
Arizona male	182
Texas female	19
Texas male	20
Forensic reference groups	
Guatemalan male	87
American Black female	86
American Black male	151
American White female	306
American White male	543

[a]*These sample sizes reflect the starting sample sizes; each analysis will have a different sample size based on missing data due to trauma, taphonomic factors, or age-related changes.*

The undocumented migrants from the PCOME (Arizona) and from FACTS (Texas) are used in all subsequent analyses (Table 12.1). The PCOME data come from two sources, the Forensic Anthropology Data Bank (FDB), and a long-term data collection project between Texas State University and the PCOME (Spradley, 2013). Because various aspects of biological variation between males and females are of interest, only individuals with known sex from DNA or from pelvic morphology were used in the present analyses. Many individuals from the PCOME are crania only and sexing reliability from cranial morphology alone has been shown to be difficult for this particular population group. Both samples contain identified and unidentified individuals.

Forensic Reference Groups

Additional forensic reference groups include American Black and White males and females and Guatemalan males (see Table 12.1). The American Black and White groups are from the FDB (Jantz and Moore-Jansen, 1988); the Guatemalan sample was collected by the author at the Forensic Anthropology Foundation of Guatemala on behalf of the FDB. The FDB is a repository of data collected by forensic anthropologists, curated by Dr. Richard Jantz at the University of Tennessee. While the cases in the FDB are predominantly from the United States, it does contain a southeastern bias as the majority of the data were collected through the efforts of Dr. Jantz. The Guatemalan sample contains only males and represents Mayans who were victims of Guatemala's Civil War. These particular forensic reference groups were chosen based on the fact that they contain birth-years post-1930 and minimally contain the standard craniometric data found in Moore-Jansen et al. (1994).

Craniometric Data

The craniometric data selected for use in the subsequent analyses were collected according to standards found in Moore Jansen et al. (1994) or Howells (1973). The migrant and Guatemalan data were all collected with the Microscribe digitizer and the program 3Skull (SD Ousley, 2004). For the FDB,

Table 12.2 Interlandmark Distances

Glabella-occipital length (GOL)	Bimaxillary subtense (SSS)
Basion-nasion length (BNL)	Dacryon subtense (DKS)
Basion-bregma height (BBH)	Inferior malar length (IML)
Biasteronic breadth (ASB)	Minimum malar height (WMH)
Minimum frontal breadth (WFB)	Frontal chord (FRC)
Basion-prosthion length (BPL)	Frontal subtense (FRS)
Nasion-prosthion height (NPH)	Parietal chord (PAC)
Nasal height (NLH)	Parietal subtense (PAS)
Nasal breadth (NLB)	Occipital chord (OCC)
Maximum alveolar breadth (MAB)	Occipital subtense (OCS)
Orbital breadth (OBB)	Bregma radius (BRR)
Interorbital breadth (DKB)	Basion radius (BAR)

some data were collected with calipers while in other instances data were collected using the Microscribe. The craniometric data selected for the following analyses are presented in Table 12.2 and were selected for representing the overall craniofacial morphology and to maximize sample sizes.

Analyses

Arizona and Texas Migrants

In order to assess similarity among the Arizona and Texas males and females, Mahalanobis squared Euclidean distance (D^2) was obtained as a measure of biological similarity between the two groups. A canonical discriminant analysis (CANDISC) was used to reduce the dimensionality of the data and assess the overall morphological similarities and dissimilarities between the two migrant groups. The variables chosen for the CANDISC include 24 interlandmark distances representing the overall craniofacial complex and maximize sample sizes (see Table 12.2). A discriminant function analysis (DFA) with cross-validated classification rates was used to determine how well the two groups classify. Prior to running the DFA, a stepwise variable selection procedure was employed, by sex, to reduce the number of variables as to not overfit the data.

Arizona and Texas Migrants and Forensic Reference Groups

The same procedures described for Arizona and Texas migrants were employed for the comparison of the migrant groups to other forensically relevant reference groups, American Black and White males and females and Guatemalan males. Because the Arizona and Texas migrants and Guatemalans are all from Latin America, it is expected, based on an isolation by distance model, that they will be more similar to one another than to the American Black and White groups. Therefore, the Mahalanobis D^2 was evaluated for all groups. If the distances between the groups are small and insignificant, then the analyses are repeated by combining the groups with small D^2 values.

Results

Arizona and Texas Migrants

The D^2 values (Table 12.3) derived from the DFA suggest that the Arizona and Texas females are the most similar to each other followed by the Arizona males. The Arizona males and females are more similar to

Table 12.3 Mahalanobis D^2 for Arizona and Texas Groups[a]

Group	Arizona Female	Texas Female	Arizona Male
Arizona female	–		
Texas female	4.94	–	
Arizona male	11.45	13.74	–
Texas male	10.28	8.00	5.20

[a]*Variables:* GOL, BNL, BBH, ASB, WFB, BPL, NPH, NLH, NLB, MAB, OBB, DKB, SSS, DKS, IML, WMH, FRC, FRS, PAC, PAS, OCC, OCS, BRR, *and* BAR.

each other than the Texas males and females; this could be due to differences in sample size. However, the Texas group has a more equal distribution of males to females than the Arizona group. The canonical plot (Fig. 12.1) represents 93% of the total variation. The males and females are separated on the first axis while the two population groups on the second axis. Based on the first axis, the males exhibit larger values for all variables in the between canonical structure with the exception of the frontal subtense (FRS). The second axis is separating the Texas males and females from the Arizona males and females based on larger values for parietal subtense (PAS), FRS, interorbital breadth (DKB), and minimum frontal breadth (WFB).

The DFA (Table 12.4) results produce good classification, higher than random chance, with 78% of the Arizona migrant females correctly classified and 76% of the Texas migrant females. The variables used

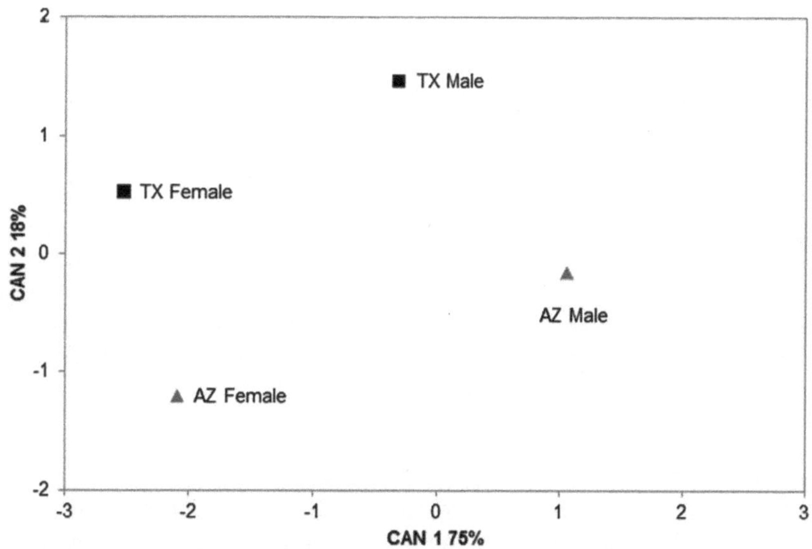

FIGURE 12.1 Plot of canonical means for Arizona and Texas males and females.

Variables: GOL, BNL, BBH, ASB, WFB, BPL, NPH, NLH, NLB, MAB, OBB, DKB, SSS, DKS, IML, WMH, FRC, FRS, PAC, PAS, OCC, OCS, BRR, and BAR.

Table 12.4 DFA Results for Arizona and Texas Groups[a, b]

Group	N	Cross-Validated Classification Rate (%)
Arizona female	18	76.47
Texas female	17	77.78
Arizona male	77	80.52
Texas male	15	73.33

[a]*Stepwise selected variables for females: BAR, DKS, MAB, IML, OCS, OCC, and PAS.*
[b]*Stepwise selected variables for males: IML, BAR, NLB, DKS, WFB, MAB, OBB, and DKB.*

for discrimination include basion radius (BAR), dacryon subtense (DKS), maximum alveolar breadth (MAB), inferior malar length (IML), occipital subtense (OCS), occipital chord (OCC), and PAS. The Arizona migrant males have an 81% classification rate and the Texas migrant males a 73% classification rate. The variables used to discriminate male migrants include IML, BAR, nasal breadth (NLB), DKS, WFB, MAB, orbital breadth (OBB), and DKB.

Arizona and Texas Migrants and Forensic Reference Groups

The D^2 values indicate that the smallest distances are found among the Texas, Arizona, and Guatemalan groups (Table 12.5). In the canonical plot (Fig. 12.2), the first axis separates American White females and males from all other groups, with American Black males intermediate. The American White group is the most differentiated based on larger values for DKS, frontal chord (FRC), FRS, biasterionic breadth (ASB), basion-bregma height (BBH), WFB, glabella-occipital length (GOL), bregma radius (BRR), parietal chord (PAC), basion-nasion length (BNL), OCC, BAR, bimaxillary subtense (SSS), and OCS. The second axis separates American Black and White, Arizona, and Guatemalan males from all other groups. The second axis separates males and females with the exception of the Texas males.

The American Black males are most differentiated from all other groups on the second axis based on larger values for basion-prosthion length (BPL), IML, DKB, nasion-prosthion height (NPH), MAB, NLB, and nasal height (NLH). Fig. 12.2 The American Black and White males and American White females are differentiated from all other groups on the plot with the American Black females clustering with the Arizona and Texas migrants and Guatemalan males.

The DFA results classify 50% of the Arizona migrant females correctly, as well as 53% of the Texas migrant females, 80% of the American Black females, and 89% of the American White females. (Table 12.6) of the males, 52% of the Arizona migrant males classified correctly, as well as 74% of the Guatemalan males, 80% of the American Black males, 40% of the Texas migrant males, and 79% of the American White males.

Combining Groups for Discriminant Function Analysis

Due to the small D^2 values among the Arizona, Texas, and Guatemalan migrants, these groups were combined into a general Hispanic group. The term Hispanic is a generic category that erases cultural identity and nationality. These groups are combined and labeled Hispanic due to the small D^2 values

Table 12.5 Mahalanobis D^2 *for Arizona, Texas, and Other Forensic Reference Groups*[a]

Group	Arizona Female	American Black Female	Texas Female	American White Female	Arizona Male	American Black Male	Guatemalan Male	Texas Male
Arizona female	–							
American Black female	6.37	–						
Texas female	4.01	8.00	–					
American White female	9.98	8.52	11.09	–				
Arizona male	7.69	6.78	9.62	11.01	–			
American Black male	19.34	8.47	21.04	20.25	7.35	–		
Guatemalan male	7.01	8.78	7.06	13.70	3.46	12.62	–	
Texas male	7.67	7.91	6.23	6.18	3.75	12.86	4.46	–
American White male	17.49	11.52	20.69	6.98	6.52	9.32	13.76	7.70

[a]*Variables: GOL, BNL, BBH, ASB, WFB, BPL, NPH, NLH, NLB, MAB, OBB, DKB, SSS, DKS, IML, WMH, FRC, FRS, PAC, PAS, OCC, OCS, BRR, and BAR.*

Table 12.6 DFA Cross-Validation Classification Rates for Arizona, Texas, and Other Forensic Reference Groups

Group	Female N	Female Classification Rate (%)[a]	Male N	Male Classification Rate (%)[b]
Arizona	18	50	75	52
Texas	17	53	15	40
Guatemalan	–	–	66	74
American Black	20	80	44	80
American White	71	89	177	79

[a]*Female stepwise selected variables:* NLB, GOL, IML, BPL, BNL, BPL, BRR, FRS, MAB, BBH, ASB, *and* PAS.
[b]*Male stepwise selected variables:* GOL, DKS, MAB, IML, BNL, BPL, FRS, DKB, WFB, NLB, OCS, PAC,PAS, OBB, BAR.

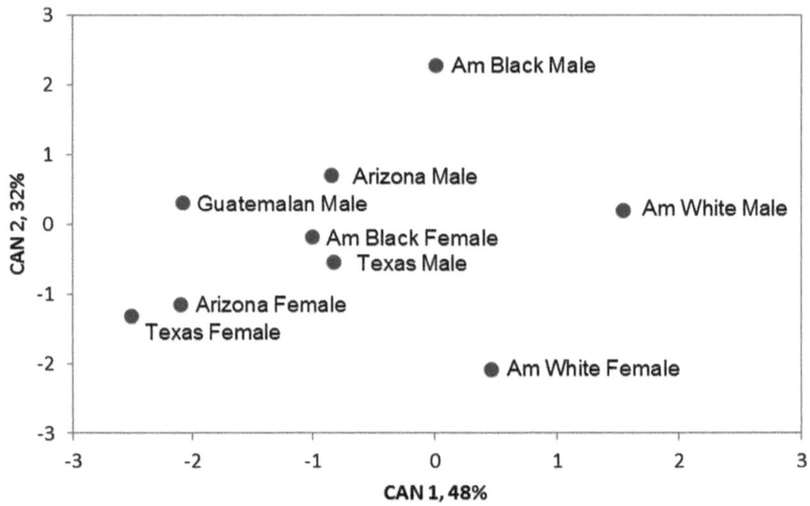

FIGURE 12.2 Plot of canonical means for Arizona and Texas and other forensic reference groups.

Variables: GOL, BNL, BBH, ASB, WFB, BPL, NPH, NLH, NLB, MAB, OBB, DKB, SSS, DKS, IML, WMH, FRC, FRS, PAC, PAS, OCC, OCS, BRR, and BAR.

indicating similarity to one another. The plot of the canonical means (Fig. 12.2), showing 80% of the total variation, indicates that the Hispanic groups cluster together on the first axis along with the American Black females.

The first axis also separates American White females and males from all other groups, with American Black males intermediate. The American White group is the most differentiated based on larger values for DKS, FRC, FRS, ASB, BBH, WFB, GOL, BRR, PAC, BNL, OCC, BAR, SSS, and OCS. The second axis

Table 12.7 DFA and Cross-Validated Classification Rates for Combined Hispanic Groups and Other Forensic Reference Groups[a, b, c]

Group	Female N	Female Classification Rate (%)[b]	Male N	Male Classification Rate (%)[c]
Hispanic	36	79	194	84
American Black	19	19	48	85
American White	71	71	189	83

[a]*Including Guatemalan males (n = 66) separately with TX and AZ combined results in AMB 81%, Guatemalan 68%, Hispanic 51%, and White 82%.*
[b]*Stepwise selected variables for females: GOL, BNL, BPL, BBH, NLB, MAB, DKB, IML, FRS, ASB and BRR.*
[c]*Stepwise selected variables for males: GOL, BNL, BPL, DKB, NLB, MAB, OBB, IML, WMH, WFB, ASB, FRC, FRS, PAS, and OCS.*

separates American Black and White, Arizona, and Guatemalan males from all other groups. The second axis separates males and females with the exception of the Texas males. The American Black males are most differentiated from all other groups on the second axis based on larger values for BPL, IML, DKB, NPH, MAB, NLB, and NLH.

The classification results for females and males improved when combining the population specific groups into a broad Hispanic category. For the Hispanic females 79% classified correctly, as well as 78% for the American Black, and 92% for the American White. The Hispanic males achieved an 84% classification rate, American Black males achieved 85%, and American White males achieved 83% (Table 12.7).

DISCUSSION

Addressing issues of structure and scale as defined by Cabana and Clark (2011), partitioning the migrant groups by the location where they were found, Arizona and Texas, suggests both demographic and morphological differences are evident between the groups. Texas receives an equal male-to-female distribution while Arizona receives an unequal sex distribution, with more males than females. The D^2 values and DFA indicate that the Texas and Arizona migrants are morphologically dissimilar enough for classification accuracy, suggesting that it is possible to distinguish the two groups from one another, as previously suggested using craniometric data and genetic data.

Spradley (2014), using smaller sample sizes and geometric morphometric methods, found that Texas migrants were dissimilar from Arizona migrants based on several facial features and more projecting anterior vault landmarks including metopion (FRS point), bregma, and PAS in the Texas migrants. The present analyses found the crania of the Texas migrants larger than Arizona migrants based on overall values for anterior vault measurements, including FRS and PAS and DKB, allowing these two groups to achieve good classification rates. Further, Salazar-Flores et al. (2015) using short tandem repeats and Nei genetic distances found that although Central American and Mexican Mestizos are genetically more similar to each other than South Americans and Caribbeans, the two groups are still genetically differentiated from one another.

When the migrants are compared to the forensic reference samples, the migrants cluster together and classification rates drop for the migrants and Guatemalans. This clustering and drop in classification rates are primarily related to size with the American White males and females and American Black males exhibiting larger values for all variables. When the migrant groups are pooled with the Guatemalan group to form a broad Hispanic group, classification rates increase. These results suggest that the Latin American groups are more similar to one another than to the other groups. Further, these groups are considered complex population groups having Spanish, Native American, and some African admixture and often show an intermediate position between parental groups, making them more challenging to classify.

Though pooling the Latin American groups does not address the structure or scale of migration, it does inform forensic anthropological practice. Using nonmetric traits, Hefner et al. (2015) previously found that when a broad classification is needed, it is statistically sound to pool the groups considered Hispanic. While pooling specific groups from Latin America may be useful to achieve a broad classification of Hispanic in general anthropological practice within the United States, when working with individual cases with enough circumstantial evidence that fits the profile of a migrant, a more specific classification may be of greater use.

Thus, once the classification of Hispanic is identified, it may be useful to attempt a separate DFA using more population-specific groups. At present, positively identified Mexican and Guatemalan reference groups exist. However, for Central American groups (ie, Honduran, El Salvadoran) enough data do not exist. Rather, these data are contextually inferred in that the Texas migrants are from Central America and can be differentiated from Arizona migrants predominantly from Mexico.

The issue of the mass disaster along the US/Mexico border and the humanitarian crisis it has created suggests that anthropologists need to know that an individual fits the overall migrant profile; in this case the designation of Hispanic in addition to other contextual information (see Birkby et al., 2008 for a discussion of the cultural profile of migrants) may be helpful. However, saying someone is Hispanic on the border is not necessarily helpful if the goal is to figure out where they are from within Latin America. Collecting data on these migrants can further research and development in forensic anthropological practice while also informing modern human variation and issues of population structure through morphological analysis.

Arizona and Texas are not the primary destinations for all migrants. While the states that traditionally receive Latin American immigration vary based on country of origin, California and Texas are the states with the largest immigrant communities from all four countries. However, as of 2010 Mexicans and Central Americans began to settle in Georgia, Nevada, North Carolina, New York, Colorado, New Jersey, Washington, and Florida (Telford, 2014). Therefore, these immigrants, authorized or unauthorized, are no longer heavily clustered within certain regions of the United States. While it was once forensic anthropologists in the Southwest who were faced with the majority of immigrants or naturalized citizens from Latin America, today practitioners from all over the country are likely to see an increase of Latin Americans in their casework. The data collected by forensic anthropologists used in the present research highlight the role forensic anthropologists play in the data collection that is used to further understanding of modern human variation, migration, and practice.

The results presented here suggest that within the United States, the use of a broad Hispanic reference sample will increase classification accuracy. However, if the goal is to estimate where in the world the individual is from, comparing the unknown forensic case to more specific geographically defined groups will be more informative.

References

Anderson, B.E., 2008. Identifying the dead: methods utilized by the Pima County (Arizona) Office of the medical examiner for undocumented border crossers: 2001–2006. Journal of Forensic Sciences 53, 8–15.

Birkby, W.H., Fenton, T.W., Anderson, B.E., 2008. Identifying Southwest Hispanics using nonmetric traits and the cultural profile. Journal of Forensic Sciences 53, 29–33.

Brick, K., Challinor, A., Rosenblum, M.R., 2011. Mexican and Central American Immigrants in the United States. Migration Policy Institute, p. 24.

Cabana, G.S., Clark, J.J. (Eds.), 2011. Rethinking Anthropological Perspectives on Migration. University of Florida, Gainsville.

Carson, E.A., 2006. Maximum likelihood estimation of human craniometric heritabilities. American Journal of Physical Anthropology 131, 169–180.

Clark, J.J., 2011. Disappearance and diaspora: contrasting two migrations in the Southern U.S. Southwest. In: Cabana, G.S., Clark, J.J. (Eds.), Rethinking Anthropological Perspectives on Migration. University of Florida, Gainsville, pp. 84–110.

Devor, E.J., 1987. Transmission of human craniofacial dimensions. Journal of Craniofacial Genetics and Developmental Biology 7, 95–106.

Edgar, H.J.H., 2009. Biohistorical approaches to "race" in the United States: biological distances among African Americans, European Americans, and their ancestors. American Journal of Physical Anthropology 139, 58–67.

Haddal, C.C., 2010. Border Security: The Role of the U.S. Border Patrol. Congressional Research Service, p. 36.

Hefner, J.T., Pilloud, M.A., Black, C.J., Anderson, B.E., 2015. Morphoscopic trait expression in "Hispanic" populations. Journal of Forensic Sciences 60, 1135–1139.

Herrera, B., Hanihara, T., Godde, K., 2014. Comparability of multiple data types from the bering strait region: cranial and dental metrics and nonmetrics, mtDNA, and Y-chromosome DNA. American Journal of Physical Anthropology 154, 334–348.

Howells, W.W., 1973. Cranial Variation in Man: A Study by Multivariate Analysis of Patterns of Difference Among Recent Human Populations. Harvard University Press.

Hughes, C.E., Tise, M.L., Trammell, L.H., Anderson, B.E., 2013. Cranial morphological variation among contemporary Mexicans: regional trends, ancestral affinities, and genetic comparisons. American Journal of Physical Anthropology 151, 506–517.

Hurst, C.V., 2012. Morphoscopic trait expressions used to identify Southwest Hispanics. Journal of Forensic Sciences 57, 859–865.

Jantz, R.L., Moore-Jansen, P.H., 1988. A Data Base for Forensic Anthropology: Structure Content and Analysis. Department of Anthropology, The University of Tennessee, Knoxville.

Jantz, R.L., Owsley, D.W., 2001. Variation among early North American crania. American Journal of Physical Anthropology 114, 146–155.

Jantz, R.L., 1977. Craniometric relationships of plains populations: historical and evolutionary implications. Plains Anthropology 114, 146–155.

Martinez, D.E., Reineke, R.C., Rubio-Goldsmith, R., Anderson, B.E., Hess, G.L., Parks, B.O., 2013. In: Institute, B.M. (Ed.), A Continued Crisis at the Border: Undocumented Border Crosser Deaths Recorded by the Pima County Office of the Medical Examiner, 1990–2012. The University of Arizona, p. 23.

Moore-Jansen, P.H., Ousley, S.D., Jantz, R.L., 1994. Data Collection Procedures for Forensic Skeletal Material. Department of Anthropology, The University of Tennessee, Knoxville.

Myers, D., Levy, S., Pitkin, J., 2013. The Contributions of Immigrants and Their Children to the American Workforce and Jobs of the Future. Center for American Progress.

Ousley, S.D., Billeck, W.T., Hollinger, R.E., 2005. Federal repatriation legislation and the role of physical anthropology in repatriation. American Journal of Physical Anthropology 128, 2–32.

Ousley, S., Jantz, R., Freid, D., 2009. Understanding race and human variation: why forensic anthropologists are good at identifying race. American Journal of Physical Anthropology 139, 68–76.

Ousley, S., 2004. 3Skull 2.0.77. http://math.mercyhurst.edu/~sousley/Software/.

Pima County Office of the Medical Examiner, 2013. Pima County Office of the Medical Examiner Annual Report 2013. Pima County Office of the Medical Examiner, Tucson, Arizona, p. 34.

Powell, J.F., Neves, W.A., 1999. Craniofacial morphology of the first Americans: pattern and process in the peopling of the new world. Yearbook of Physical Anthropology 49 (42), 158–188, 2006.

Ramirez, E., de la Cruz, G., 2002. In: Reports, C.P. (Ed.), The Hispanic Population in the United States: March 2002. U.S. Census Bureau, Washington DC.

Relethford, J.H., Blangero, J., 1990. Detection of differential gene flow from patterns of quantitative variation. Human Biology 62, 5–25.

Relethford, J.H., Lees, F.C., 1982. The use of quantitative traits in the study of human population structure. American Journal of Physical Anthropology 25, 113–132.

Relethford, J., 2004. Boas and beyond: migration and craniometric variation. American Journal of Human Biology 16, 379–386.

Ross, A.H., S, D., Ubelaker, D.H., Falsetti, A.B., 2004. Population affinities of 19th century Cuban crania: implications for identification criteria in South Floridian Cuban Americans. Journal of Forensic Sciences 49, 1–6.

Salazar-Flores, J., Zuñiga-Chiquette, F., Rubi-Castellanos, R., Álvarez-Miranda, J.L., Zetina-Hérnandez, A., Martínez-Sevilla, V.M., et al., 2015. Admixture and genetic relationships of Mexican Mestizos regarding Latin American and Caribbean populations based on 13 CODIS-STRs. HOMO 66, 44–59.

Spradley, M.K., Anderson, B.E., Tise, M.L., 2015. Postcranial sex estimation criteria for Mexican Hispanics. Journal of Forensic Sciences 60, S27–S31.

Spradley, M.K., 2013. Project Identification: Developing Accurate Identification Criteria for Hispanics. US Department of Justice. Washington, D.C.

Spradley, M.K., 2014. Toward estimating geographic origin of migrant remains along the United States-Mexico border. Annals of Anthropological Practice 38, 101–110.

Spradley, M.K., 2015. Ancestry estimation from the postcranial skeleton. In: Berg, G.E., Ta'ala, S.C. (Eds.), Biological Affinity in Forensic Identification of Human Skeletal Remains: Beyond Black and White. CRC Press, Boca Raton, FL.

Stojanowski, C.M., Schillaci, M.A., 2006. Phenotypic approaches for understanding patterns of intracemetery biological variation. Yearbook of Physical Anthropology 49 (49), 49–88.

Strauss, A., Hubbe, M., 2010. Craniometric similarities within and between human populations in comparison with nuetral genetic data. Human Biology 82.

Telford, M., 2014. Central American Immigrants in the U.S.: Fact Sheet. Center for Immigration Studies.

Tise, M.L., Spradley, M.K., Anderson, B.E., 2013. Postcranial sex estimation of individuals considered Hispanic. Journal of Forensic Sciences 58, S9–S14.

U.S. Customs and Border Patrol, 2012. United States Border Patrol Sector Profile – Fiscal Year 2012. U.S. Border Patrol.

CHAPTER

13

The Craniometric Implications of a Complex Population History in South Africa

K.E. Stull[1,4], M.W. Kenyhercz[2,4], M.L. Tise[3], E.N. L'Abbé[4], P. Tuamsuk[5]
University of Nevada, Reno, Reno, NV, United States[1]; University of Tennessee, Knoxville, TN, United States[2]; History Flight, Inc., Marathon, FL, United States[3]; University of Pretoria, Pretoria, South Africa[4]; Khon Kaen University, Khon Kaen, Thailand[5]

CHAPTER OUTLINE HEAD

Introduction 245
Population History of South Africa 246
Genetic Composition of Modern South African Populations 248
Materials 248
Methods 251
Results 252
  All Groups Pooled Sexes 252
  Females 253
  Males 253
Discussion and Conclusions 255
Acknowledgments 260
References 260

INTRODUCTION

Population diversity is considered greatest within all of Africa but specifically in southern Africa (Tishkoff and Kidd, 2004; Tishkoff and Williams, 2002). The Bantu expansion (intracontinental migration) and later colonization that introduced Europeans and slaves from numerous African and Asian countries (intercontinental migration) to the indigenous groups (Khoe-San) formed a collective population with high levels of admixture (Petersen et al., 2013). Multifaceted colonization history, extensive mineral wealth (eg, diamonds, gold, and coal), the general geographic location of Cape Town as a base for major trade routes (De Wit et al., 2010; Mountain, 2003; Tishkoff et al., 2009), along with the apartheid era has provided South Africa with an extensive diversity of people, culture, and self-identities when compared to other African countries.

The patterns of global craniometric variation are well recognized and often provide a reasonable reconstruction of population structure and population history (Relethford, 2009). The neutral model of

Biological Distance Analysis. http://dx.doi.org/10.1016/B978-0-12-801966-5.00013-5

population structure assumes the majority of human variation can be attributed to genetic drift and mutation as opposed to natural selection. Population level craniometric variation largely follows the neutral model theory and mirrors patterns observed with DNA polymorphism and genetic markers (Relethford, 2002). The range of human variation within a population is also modified by social practices and as such, culture affects biology. Groups within the same geographic region or nation may show differing trait frequencies due to assortative mating (Ousley et al., 2009). The disparity in phenotypic frequencies does not imply that biological differences exist, only that sociocultural barriers do, or did, exist and have affected the distribution of genes and the resulting morphological features. Because culture and society are founded on historical circumstances, population history may provide explanations for the distribution of human variation within the current population. South Africa, in particular, offers an example of institutionalized segregation through apartheid, in which systemic racism acted as a barrier for gene flow among social groups. Yet, the complexities of South Africa's population history began long before colonization and the apartheid regime.

POPULATION HISTORY OF SOUTH AFRICA

Archaeological, linguistic, and genetic data indicate significant migration events in Africa during the mid-to-late Holocene that shaped the pattern of human variation within southern Africa and created the foundation for modern, black South African (SA) groups (De Filippo et al., 2012; Tishkoff and Williams, 2002; Tishkoff et al., 2009; Vansina, 1995). One of the most significant migrations involved Bantu-speaking groups, commonly referred to as the Bantu expansion, which originated in Nigeria and Cameroon and traveled down into southern Africa approximately 3000—5000 years ago (De Filippo et al., 2012; González-Santos et al., 2015; Li et al., 2014). Because agriculture and new economies were spread rather than just language, the Bantu expansion is considered a demic diffusion (Berniell-Lee et al., 2009; Li et al., 2014; Petersen et al., 2013; Ribot, 2004; Tishkoff and Williams, 2002). Some debate exists around the nature of dispersal (ie, people, culture, and/or languages) and the trajectory and geographic routes of the dispersal (Robertson and Bradley, 2000; Russell and Steele, 2009). The population movement is recognized as having led to the spread of Bantu languages (representing the largest linguistic family in Africa), greater genetic diversity, and agricultural technologies across southern Africa (De Filippo et al., 2011, 2012). Small genetic distances as demonstrated by mitochondrial DNA, Y-chromosome, and autosomal markers are present among Bantu populations even when the geographic distance is large, which reflects the demic diffusion model with some regional variations between western and eastern regions (ie, selective pressures) (De Filippo et al., 2012; González-Santos et al., 2015; Tishkoff et al., 2009).

In contrast to the observed linguistic and genetic homogeneity within Bantu-speaking sub-Saharan Africans, the phenotypic data, shown through craniometrics, revealed differences among the populations instead of a founder effect phenomenon (Ribot, 2004; Franklin et al., 2010). Recent studies captured a larger amount of variation and dissimilarity between Bantu-speaking groups, which might be attributed to the use of shape variables rather than only size variables as seen in De Villiers (1968), Rightmire (1970) and Franklin et al. (2010). Franklin et al. (2010) suggested that the diversity within the Bantu-speaking groups resulted in part from differential admixture with adjacent groups in relation to various historical processes and geographical proximity. For example, southern African Bantu speakers and east African populations, rather than the San, greatly influenced both Venda and Shangaan groups

(L'Abbé et al., 2006). In contrast, other groups, such as the Xhosa, Southern Sotho, and Zulu, exhibited greater morphological contributions from the Khoe-San, particularly in relation to the facial skeleton and shape of the cranial vault (Franklin et al., 2010).

Presently, modern black SAs are generally subdivided based on factors associated with ethnicity, namely kinship, religion, and language (Treiman, 2007). Nine of the 11 official SA languages belong to the Niger-Kordofanian linguistic family with the two largest sublanguages being isiZulu and isiXhosa (Patterson et al., 2010; Treiman, 2007). The click sounds present in isiXhosa language and approximately 40% of Khoe-San shared mtDNA indicates interactions, and thus gene flow, between Bantu-speakers and historic groups (Barbieri et al., 2013; Petersen et al., 2013).

Prior to the Bantu expansion, the Khoikhoi had arrived in southern Africa around 2000 BP and settled among the indigenous hunter-gatherer San groups in the region (Smith et al., 1991; Whitelaw and Moon, 1996). The two indigenous populations are commonly merged into the Khoe-San, reflecting both the Khoikhoi and the San. The combination of these morphologically and culturally distinct groups are primarily based on their similar click-languages (Khoisan linguistic family) (Petersen et al., 2013; Schlebusch, 2010). While the San, a hunter-gatherer society, is recognized as the earliest group to populate southern Africa, the Khoikhoi, a pastoralist society, is also considered indigenous to southern Africa. Mitochondrial DNA, Y-chromosome, and autosomal chromosome diversity studies demonstrated the most divergent contemporary lineages in southern Africa Khoe-San populations (Jakobsson et al., 2008; Li et al., 2008; Schlebusch et al., 2012; Tishkoff et al., 2009). Recent genetic studies revealed precolonial population histories of the Khoikhoi and San to be complex with various phases of admixture with groups from eastern regions within Africa and west Eurasia (Petersen et al., 2013; Pickrell et al., 2014; Schlebusch, 2010). Though no significant shape or size differences have been noted between the crania of Khoikhoi and San (Franklin et al., 2010; Stynder, 2009), craniometric studies substantiated the genetic claims of the Khoe-San being the most divergent population groups, such that significant size and shape differences exist between sub-Saharan Africans and the Khoikhoi (Franklin et al., 2010).

In 1652, the Dutch East India Company, along with immigrants and sailors therein, colonized the southern tip of Africa, known then as *Cabo das Tormentas* (Cape of Storms) and today as Cape Town. The majority of settlers subsisted as semimigratory cattle herders around Cape Town with some farms as far as Worcester (Patterson et al., 2010; Treiman, 2007). Most European settlers were Dutch, though some French Huguenots and Germans were also present among them. After the Napoleonic Wars in 1820, larger groups of English settlers arrived in South Africa. Separate settlement periods, and two Anglo-Boer wars later, instituted the primary cultural division between Afrikaners and English-speakers within white SAs.

The initial European settlers to arrive at the Cape were predominantly men, and almost all recorded mixed marriages were between a male settler and either a Free Black or indigenous female (Van der Ross, 2005). The indigenous Khoikhoi or San were not enslaved, but often acted as indentured laborers on farms (Mountain, 2003; Shell, 1994). Cape slaves encompassed individuals from many different geographic locations that provided both genetic and ethnic contributions to the modern populations. Specifically, political exiles were brought in from Indonesia and Malaysia and slaves came from the Indian subcontinent (25.9%), the east coast of Africa (26.4%), Madagascar (25.1%), and Indonesia (22.7%) (Mountain, 2003; Patterson et al., 2010; Shell, 1994; Treiman, 2007). A law that was abolished in 1823 stated that slaves were prohibited to marry unless a man bought the slave their freedom or they bore an unwed child. In contrast, marriage was freely possible with an indigenous female (Patterson et al., 2010). Between 1652 and 1672, an estimated 75% of children born in the colony had slave mothers and

European fathers (Marquard, 1952). When extended to 1796, 1350 settler—Free Black marriages were recorded whereas only 137 Free Black marriages were recorded. Because the social divide was based mostly on religion and not skin color, a significant proportion of mixed-ancestry children were raised as Christian and accepted as equal members of the European community (Inwood and Masakure, 2009). Particularly after 1700, the children of the mixed marriages were assimilated into the growing "colored group" (De Wit et al., 2010; Mountain, 2003). The peer-reported term "colored" is legally recognized and has been socially used in the country since 1808 (Van der Ross, 2005).

GENETIC COMPOSITION OF MODERN SOUTH AFRICAN POPULATIONS

A sex-biased gene flow in the SA colored population has been documented in the genetic literature and supports historical accounts of marriage prior to and after slavery within the Cape colony (De Wit et al., 2010; Patterson et al., 2010; Quintana-Murci et al., 2010). Specifically, the X-chromosome exhibits a greatly reduced European contribution and a greatly increased Khoe-San contribution. In contrast, the Y-chromosome exhibits a reduced Khoe-San contribution and pronounced contributions from Europeans and Bantu-speakers (Patterson et al., 2010; Quintana-Murci et al., 2010). The four major populations that comprise colored SA genetic variation are non-Khoe-San African, Khoe-San, European, and Southeast Asian (De Wit et al., 2010; Pritchard et al., 2000; Quintana-Murci et al., 2010; Tishkoff et al., 2009). Because sex-biased asymmetry has been shown in the genetic composition of SA coloreds, and craniometrics can act as a proxy for genetic variation, different patterns of craniometric variation should exist between SA colored males and females.

Craniometric patterns among three SA groups highlight the vast heterogeneity in SA coloreds in comparison to homogeneity in SA blacks and whites (L'Abbé et al., 2013; Stull et al., 2014). SA coloreds were shown to be more similar in size to white SAs through craniometric analysis, but were more similar in shape to black SAs, via geometric morphometric analysis (Stull et al., 2014). Additionally, SA colored males and females show different misclassification patterns, further indicating a potential sex-bias asymmetry. The purpose of this chapter is to evaluate the craniometric patterns of possible parental groups and modern SAs to explore the idea of a sex-bias among SA colored males and females. Given the population history and associated genetic structure, SA colored females should be more similar to the indigenous SA groups and the SA colored males should be more similar to the historic European groups.

MATERIALS

The total sample was composed of 897 crania (Table 13.1). Modern SA groups included black, colored, and white crania and parental groups included Bahutu, Basuku, San, Thai, and historic white (English) crania. All groups, except Thai, are considered possible parental groups to modern SA coloreds based on previous STRUCTURE analysis (De Wit et al., 2010; Pritchard et al., 2000; Tishkoff et al., 2009).

Criteria for selected parental populations were based on availability of data and the historical relationships between the parental group and the modern population. The parental groups included Bantu-speaking central and east Africans, the historic San, and historic white (English). Although modern, the Thai sample was also treated as a parental population and used as a proxy for the Indonesian genetic

Table 13.1 Population and Sample Size for the Parental and Modern Groups

Pop-Sex and Abbreviation	n	Time Period	Social Race in South Africa
South African (SA) black males (SABM)	110	Modern	Black
SA black females (SABF)	48		
Bahutu females (BHF)	47	Historic	
Bahutu males (BHM)	37		
Basuku females (BSF)	86		
Basuku males (BSM)	57		
SA colored males (SACM)	160	Modern	Colored
SA colored females (SACF)	88		
San female (SF)	21	Historic	
San male (SM)	27		
Thai females (TF)	17	Modern	
Thai males (TM)	36		
SA white female (SAWF)	46	Modern	White
SA white male (SAWM)	60		
Historic white female (HWF)	21	Historic	
Historic white male (HWM)	36		

component of the SA coloreds, primarily because it has the greatest geographic proximity. The sex of the three historic parental groups was evaluated on the basis of the pelvis and/or cranium.

Parental groups associated with the Bantu-speaking expansion include the Bahutu (BH, $n = 84$) and the Basuku (BS, $n = 143$), which are both housed in the Royal Institute of Natural Sciences in Brussels. The Basuku population is a central African group from the Feshi territory in the South-west Democratic Republic of the Congo that dates to within the last two centuries. The Bahutu is an east African population from Rwanda (Bugoye and Ruhengeri) and dates to within the last century (Fig. 13.1) (Ribot, 2003). The two historic black samples represent the largest and best-documented cranial data of central and east Africans (Ribot, 2003; 2004). Multivariate statistical analyses previously conducted on the Basuku and Bahutu demonstrated that the two populations share relatively similar lengths and breadths of vaults, but the populations differ for features such as the protrusion and height of face, size of orbits, and nasal width (Ribot, 2003).

The San population (S, $n = 48$) was from the Orange River Valley (Northern Cape Province) that dated from the 1600s through the 1800s (Morris, 1992). While the skeletons were not all well documented during the excavations in the 1920s and 1930s, historical documentation, oral accounts, and skeletal morphology confidently support a San origin (Morris, 1992). All skeletons were removed near Koffientein and the Riet River and, in life, the groups were suggested to have been of a mixed economy of hunting and gathering and herding.

The Thai sample (T, $n = 53$) was used as a proxy for the Indonesian genetic component and is housed at the Medical School at Khon Kaen University in Khon Kaen, Thailand. The collection at Khon Kaen University contains over 700 contemporary skeletons with known demographic information and is primarily composed of individuals from northeastern Thailand. The Thai data for the present sample contain 17 females and 36 males.

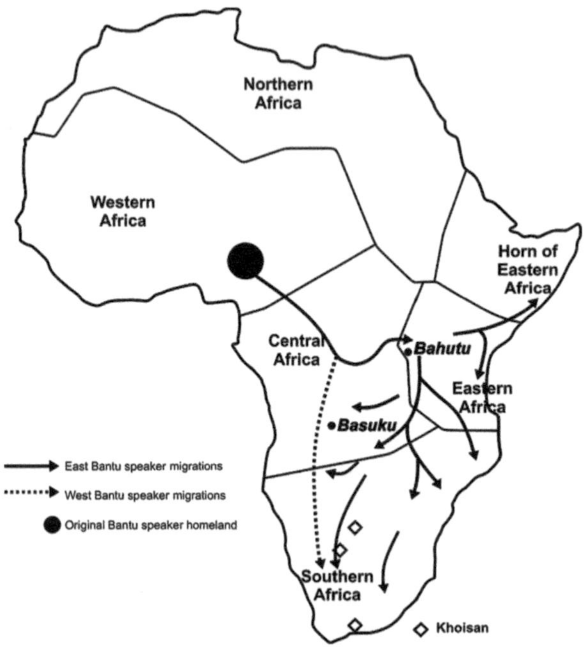

FIGURE 13.1

Geographic patterns of the Bantu expansion and location of three parental groups.

The historic white (Hist. White) sample was composed of 57 individuals (females = 21, males = 36) from Spitalfields with dates of birth ranging from 1646 to 1852. The sample was used as a proxy for the white settlers of the Cape. There may be some issues with the appropriateness of the sample considering the Dutch were the primary settlers and the English did not arrive until years later. While Dutch craniometric variation may not be captured, the Spitalfields collection does contain French Huguenots, which were present during initial colonization, though fewer in number than Dutch (Thompson, 2001).

Craniometric data from the three largest modern SA population groups were collected from the Pretoria Bone Collection at the University of Pretoria, Raymond A. Dart Collection of Human Skeletons at the University of Witswatersrand, and Kirsten Skeletal Collection at Stellenbosch University and totaled 519 individuals (SA black = 158, SA colored = 248, SA white = 106). Data were collected from SA coloreds from the Kirsten Collection, all white SAs from the Pretoria Bone Collection, and SA blacks from both the Pretoria Bone Collection and Raymond A. Dart Collection. The random sampling resulted in slightly more males ($n = 333$, 64%) than females ($n = 186$, 36%). All groups are of known age, sex, and self-identified ancestry.

In sum, the total study sample contains 897 individual crania. There is a slight male bias ($n = 523$; 58%) to females ($n = 374$; 42%). Exclusion criteria included persons younger than 18 years of age, macroscopic pathology, traumatic injuries, and extensive antemortem tooth loss that would have obliterated prosthion.

METHODS

Craniometrics from the historic samples were collected with spreading and sliding calipers and recorded to the nearest half millimeter following the Howells standards (Howells, 1973) (Table 13.2). Craniometrics from the modern SA and Thai crania were all collected with a coordinate digitizer. Because of the poor preservation and small sample sizes of the historic San, missing values were addressed in the dataset. The *k* nearest neighbor approach for missing number imputation was used to estimate missing data (Kenyhercz and Passalacqua, 2015; Chapter 9, this volume). A robust sequential nearest neighbor imputation was utilized that sequentially estimated the missing values by minimizing the determinant of the covariance of the augmented data matrix while decreasing the influence of outliers through robust estimates of location and scatter (Todorov, 2012).

Aggregating the possible parental groups (historic white, Thai, San, Basuku, and Bahutu) and modern (black, white, and colored) datasets resulted in a limited number of predictor variables due to the paucity of complete crania in the historical record. Of the 13 variables available, 9 were stepwise selected and included GOL, maximum cranial breadth (XCB), BBH, BPL, NPH, NLH, NLB, orbital height (OBH), and DKB. Stepwise selection was necessary to ensure the smallest sample size was three times larger than the number of measurements to avoid overfitting the models (Huberty, 1994). Because a larger set of variables could not be analyzed to determine the variables that maximized separation of groups, the variables available to analyze might not be ideal for group separation. The variables captured the overall dimensions of the cranium even if the variables did not include the entire craniometric suite.

The means of all measurements were used to measure the degree of dissimilarity among groups and transform the data into a distance matrix. Due to the use of mean-centered variables and to satisfy requirements of the Ward's method for hierarchical clustering, squared Euclidean distance (D^2) was used (Jobson, 1992; Murtagh and Legendre, 2011). The distance matrix was then subjected to hierarchical

***Table 13.2** Cranial Measurements Collected on All Skeletal Samples and Used in the Analyses, Prior to Stepwise Selection*

Measurement	Abbreviation
Maximum cranial length	GOL
Maximum cranial breadth	XCB
Bizygomatic breadth	ZYB
Basion-bregma height	BBH
Cranial base length	BNL
Basion-prosthion length	BPL
Upper facial height	NPH
Nasal height	NLH
Nasal breadth	NLB
Orbital height	OBH
Interorbital breadth	DKB
Frontal chord	FRC
Parietal chord	PAC

cluster analysis (HCA) and classical multidimensional scaling (MDS). Both HCA and MDS are exploratory data analysis techniques, though the two analyses have different objectives.

The objective of HCA is to partition the data based on similarities and then partition groups based on the dissimilarity measure derived from the measurements. Hierarchical cluster analysis proceeds sequentially, such that at each agglomeration only one group is added to the previous group. The process begins with the same number of clusters as groups and ends with one cluster that contains all groups (Jobson, 1992). A clustering is computed at each step in the HCA process to determine the two groups to be joined (Jobson, 1992). The authors chose to use Ward's minimum variance as it aims to find compact, spherical clusters, is less sensitive to extremes and/or outliers, and has a greater tendency to form equal-sized and/or smaller clusters (Jobson, 1992; R Core Team, 2013; Ward, 1963). Dendrograms are used to illustrate the HCA.

The most basic concept of MDS is the relation of objects to one another given by the proximity matrix using a low dimensional graphical representation. The proximity matrix, which summarizes the degree of similarity among pairs, is used to generate a sum of squares and cross products matrix. The proximity matrix is then used to generate the underlying dimensions (Jobson, 1992). The major objective is to minimize the number of dimensions and preserve the relationships from the dissimilarity matrix. More specifically, MDS configures n points in Euclidean space based on the distances between n points (Mardia et al., 1979). The distances between points equates to the dissimilarity among the objects and thus conveys the relationships among the objects (Cox and Cox, 2000; Jaworska and Chupetlovska-Anastasova, 2009; Mardia et al., 1979). The MDS illustrates the similarity between the groups and thus the estimates of biological divergence. Therefore, the genetic variation is assumed to be more similar in groups that are closer to one another. Both 2D and 3D MDS plots were used to visualize the relationships among groups. Although the added dimension increases the difficulty for interpretation, it provides an additional value to compare the groups.

A normal mixtures clustering analysis (NMCA) was performed in JMP 7.0.1 (SAS Institute, 2007) to examine the inter- and intrapopulation variation per individual of the three modern SA groups to the parental groups. The NMCA provides clustering probabilities for each individual into three preassigned centers that include three of the parental groups. The San, Basuku/Bahutu, and historic white were the chosen groups as these were the most valid and appropriate of the parental populations. Furthermore, the Bahutu and Basuku populations were combined to represent a non-Khoe-San African population. The probabilities are visualized with ternary plots for both male and female individuals to illustrate the distribution of each individual among the three parental groups. The three parental groups are located at each vortex of the triangle representing the three preassigned centers for the normal mixtures analysis (Wang et al., 2008). The coordinates on each axis indicate the proportions derived from the NMCA for each individual (represented by each marker), summing to 100%. The process enables each modern SA to partially belong to each of the three parental groups and visualizes the distribution of the modern SA groups in relation to three of the parental groups.

RESULTS

All Groups Pooled Sexes

The D^2 matrix is available in Table 13.3. The dendrogram associated with the HCA of the pooled sexes displays the similarity between the SA colored and San and the SA blacks and Bahutu, while SA whites

Table 13.3 The Euclidean D^2 *Values When Males and Females Are Pooled*

	South African (SA) Black	Bahutu	Basuku	SA Colored	Hist. White	San	Thai	SA White
SA black	0.000							
Bahutu	8.286	0.000						
Basuku	16.913	14.843	0.000					
SA colored	7.918	8.238	11.834	0.000				
Hist. white	46.903	44.170	34.788	39.942	0.000			
San	12.682	10.263	9.671	6.020	35.994	0.000		
Thai	16.760	15.506	17.805	15.858	45.240	17.636	0.000	
SA white	12.009	13.509	19.160	9.319	43.058	13.789	16.073	0.000

share a parent node with the latter. Further, the Thai form an out-group from the rest of the African groups and the historic white group form an out-group from all other groups (Fig. 13.2A). In the 2D MDS (Fig. 13.2B), the SA coloreds are intermediate between the San and Bahutu, and are most dissimilar to the Thai. As expected, the same trends persist in the 3D MDS visualizations (Fig. 13.2C). The most apparent result in the 3D MDS when the sexes are pooled is the disparity in the *z*-axis between the SA white and all other populations.

Females

The D^2 matrix for females is shown in Table 13.4. The dendrogram associated with the HCA for females show the SA colored females being most similar to the San, the SA blacks to the Bahutu, and the Thai and historic whites remain as out-groups (Fig. 13.3A). The 2D MDS shows the SA colored females are most similar to San females and more similar to the other modern SA groups and the Bahutu. SA colored females are most dissimilar to historic whites, Basuku, and Thai (Fig. 13.3B). The 3D MDS (Fig. 13.3C) reflects the same pattern, though, interestingly, SA colored females are intermediate in the *z*-axis between the San and SA white females. The ternary plot from the NMCA (Fig. 13.4) illustrates that the majority of SA colored females exhibit contributions from African and San parental populations, seen by the clustering on the left of the triangle. Surprisingly, a substantial number of SA white females show higher admixture rates and fewer SA colored females demonstrate high percentages from the San parental group.

Males

The D^2 for males is available in Table 13.5. The dendrogram associated with the HCA of the males shows the same general pattern as that of the females—SA blacks are most similar to the Bahutu and SA colored males are more similar to the San (Fig. 13.5A). As with the previous analyses, the Thai and historic white males form out-groups. It should be acknowledged that the shorter vertical lines indicate smaller distances between the groups. As expected from the distance matrix, in the 2D and 3D MDS visualizations SA colored males display a greater intermediacy between each of the modern SA males and historic African males (Fig. 13.5B and C). The NMCA using the male raw measurements (Fig. 13.6) results in SA colored

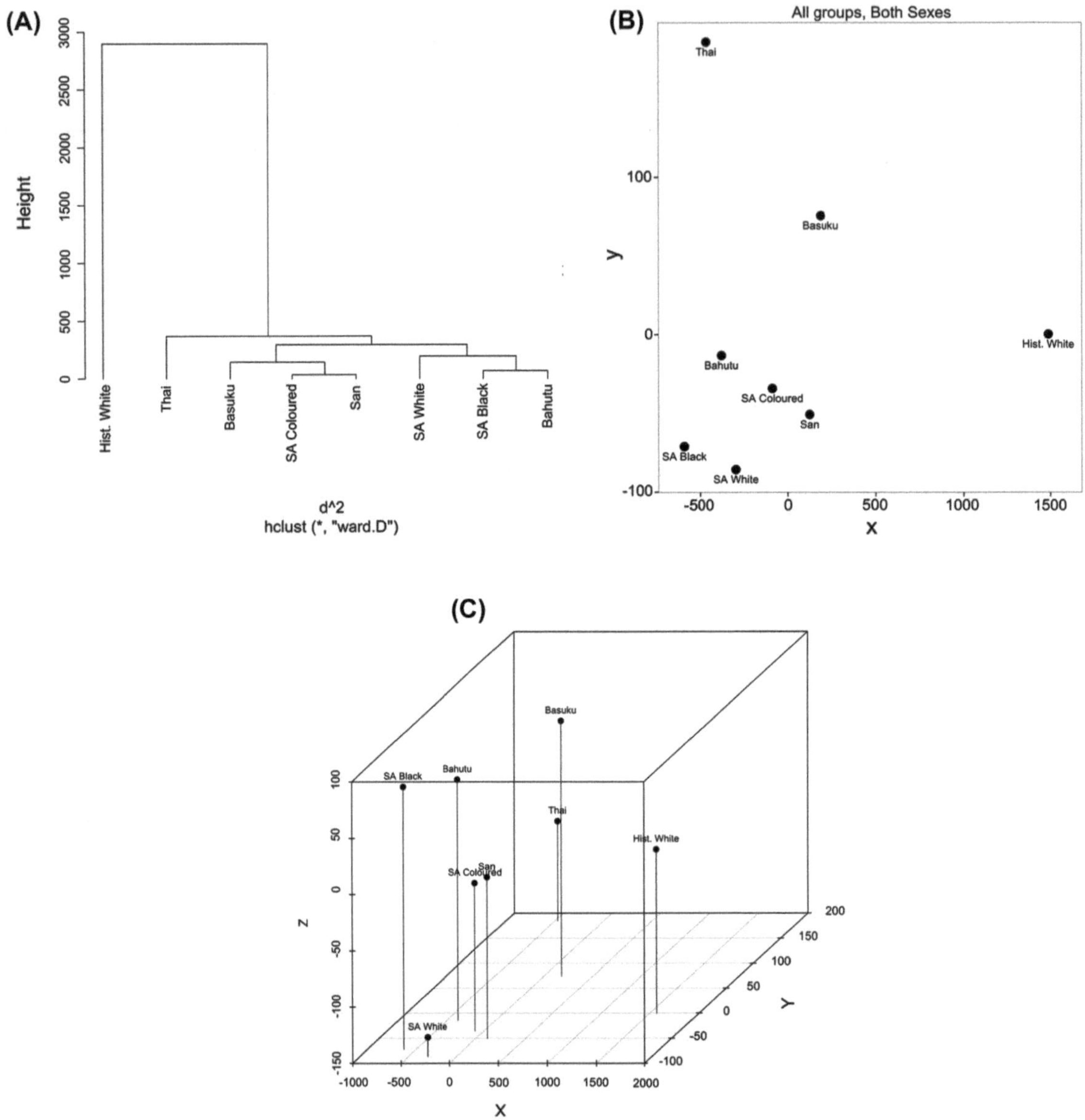

FIGURE 13.2

Visualizations associated with the relationships among all contemporary and possible paternal groups, with the sexes pooled: (A) dendrogram; (B) two-dimensional multidimensional scaling (MDS); and (C) three-dimensional MDS.

Table 13.4 The Euclidean D^2 *Values for Only Females in All Populations*

	South African (SA) Black	Bahutu	Basuku	SA Colored	Hist. White	San	Thai	SA White
SA black	0.000							
Bahutu	4.710	0.000						
Basuku	11.716	14.881	0.000					
SA colored	5.791	9.367	9.525	0.000				
Hist. white	34.872	37.274	26.357	30.954	0.000			
San	7.716	9.927	10.381	4.977	30.030	0.000		
Thai	15.903	16.720	16.325	16.655	39.284	17.444	0.000	
SA white	11.357	13.053	16.193	8.905	34.113	11.413	18.163	0.000

males expressing higher percentages of historic white and African admixture, as demonstrated by the clustering on the right side of the ternary plot. Overall, SA colored males display more intrapopulation variation compared to the SA colored females.

DISCUSSION AND CONCLUSIONS

The phenotypic expression of craniometrics, as explored by HCA, MDS, and NMCA, reflects the genetic and population history data. With the sexes pooled, the modern SA groups form a cluster with Bahutu and San, while the Thai, Basuku, and historic whites are the most dissimilar. When separated by sex, the trends change. The results are expected due to the numerous studies exploring the sex-biased genotype of the SA colored population (Quintana-Murci et al., 2010). Within SA coloreds, the genetic pattern substantiates colonial history. Specifically, the X-chromosome exhibits a greatly reduced European contribution and a greatly increased Khoe-San contribution, whereas the Y-chromosome exhibits a reduced Khoe-San contribution and pronounced contributions from Europeans and Bantu-speakers (Patterson et al., 2010; Quintana-Murci et al., 2010).

SA colored females are most similar to the San, though they also demonstrate similarities to SA black, Bahutu, and SA white, though it is substantially less. Specifically, the visualizations from the MDS and NMCA illustrate the SA colored females' stronger affiliations to the San and historic black groups. The observed trends are similar to the genetic data; approximately 60% of colored SAs' mtDNA are specific to Khoe-San groups and are autochthonous to South Africa. African lineages (Bantu-speakers) contribute 20% of the mtDNA and the remaining contributions are from India and Southeast Asia (16.3%) and Europe (4.6%) (Quintana-Murci et al., 2010). The relatively low level of European contribution to the modern SA female genetic pool is reflected in the D^2 value.

The males show a different pattern of variation; as a group they demonstrate nearly equal degrees of similarity between the San, SA blacks, Bahutus, Basukus, and SA whites. The ternary plot highlights the stronger affiliation to the African and historic white parental populations rather than the San. In strong contrast with mtDNA, a negligible portion of Y-chromosome genetics can be firmly attributed to the Khoe-San (5.3%). The negligible European component in mtDNA (<5%) is also in contrast to the

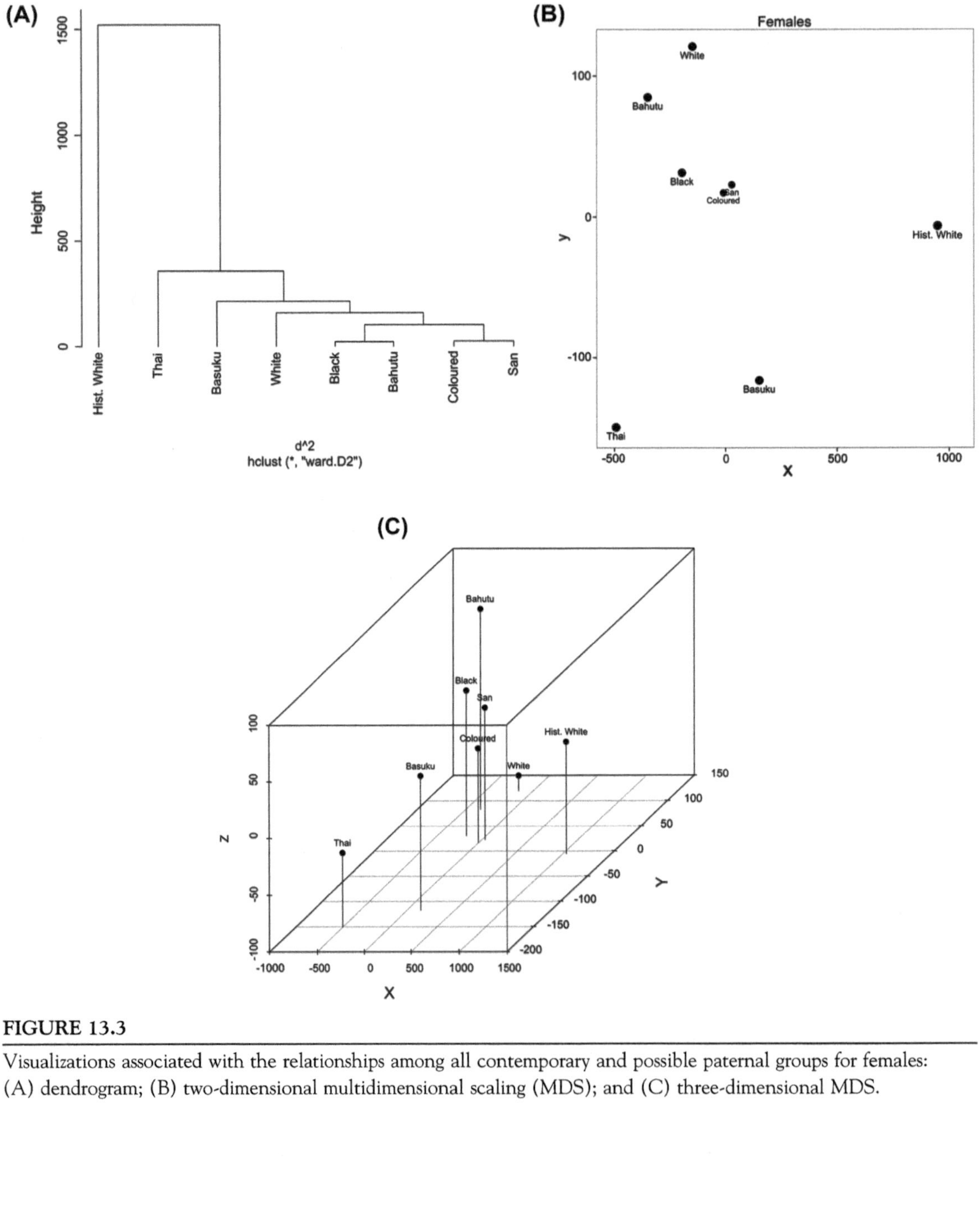

FIGURE 13.3

Visualizations associated with the relationships among all contemporary and possible paternal groups for females: (A) dendrogram; (B) two-dimensional multidimensional scaling (MDS); and (C) three-dimensional MDS.

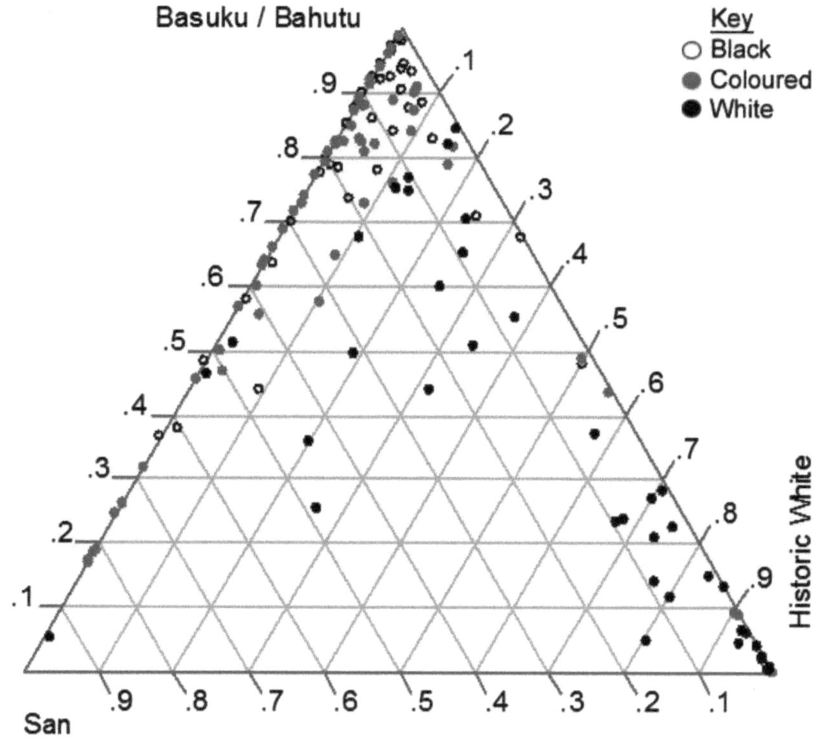

FIGURE 13.4

NMCA ternary plot of parental proportion distribution of all female individuals within the modern South African groups.

Table 13.5 The Euclidean D^2 Values for Only Males in All Populations

	South African (SA) Black	Bahutu	Basuku	SA Colored	Hist. White	San	Thai	SA White
SA black	0							
Bahutu	9.985	0						
Basuku	12.908	13.868	0					
SA colored	8.449	10.168	8.76	0				
Hist. white	52.925	51.42	43.736	45.437	0			
San	13.469	13.277	8.063	6.273	41.305	0		
Thai	17.422	15.64	14.552	15.542	49.077	17.563	0	
SA white	12.247	14.496	18.229	11.144	50.839	16.332	16.066	0

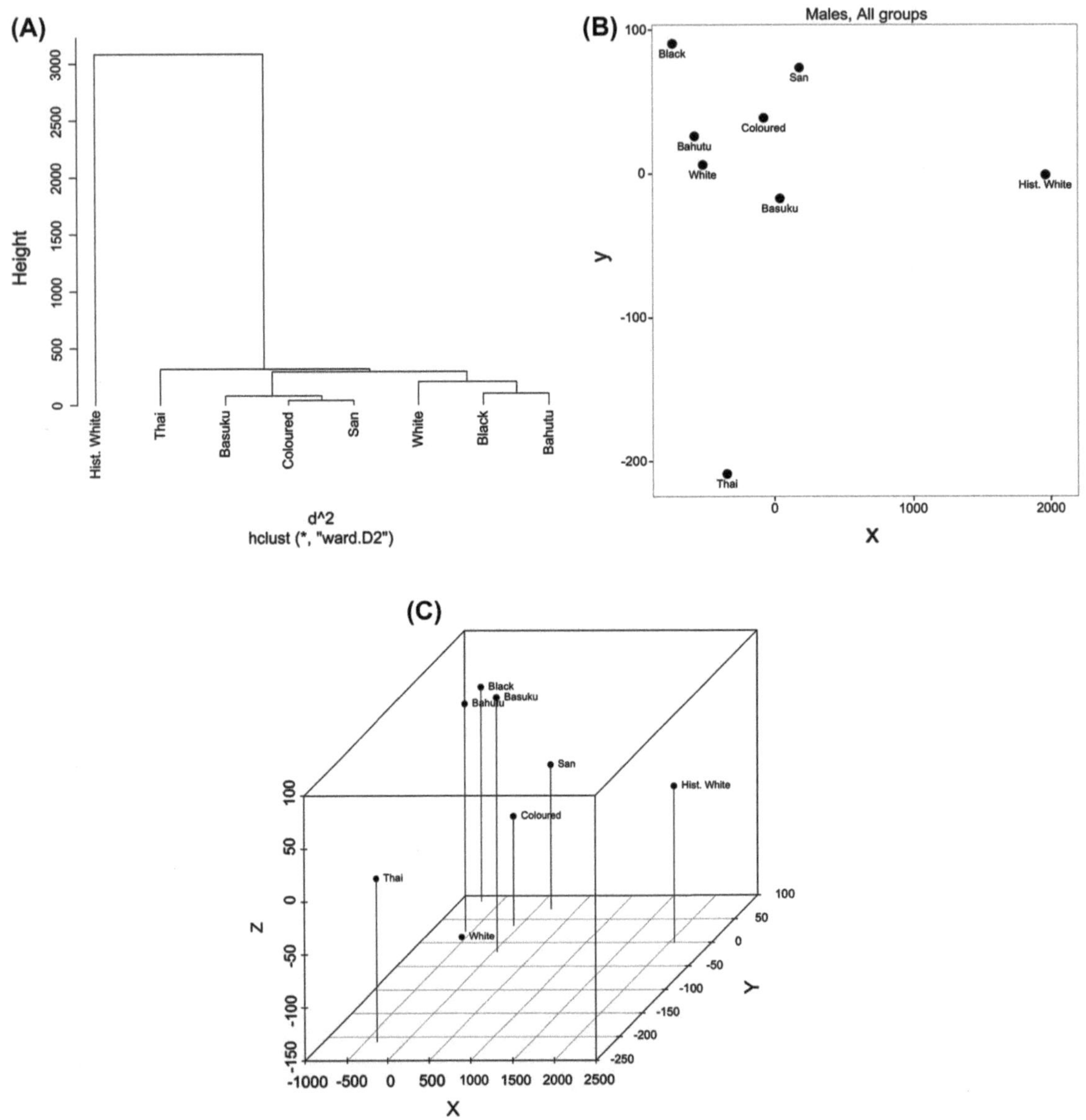

FIGURE 13.5

Visualizations associated with the relationships among all contemporary and possible paternal groups for males: (A) dendrogram; (B) two-dimensional multidimensional scaling (MDS); and (C) three-dimensional MDS.

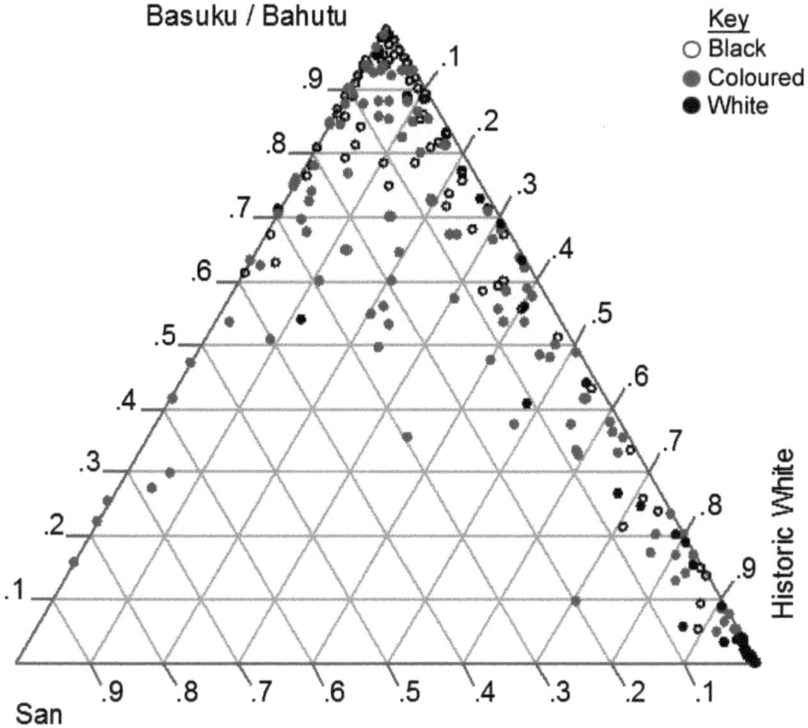

FIGURE 13.6

NMCA ternary plot of parental proportion distribution of all male individuals within the modern South African groups.

paternal contribution of European genetics found in colored males with contributions greater than 32.5%. However, the highest contribution in the genotype is the African lineage, which was greater than 40% (Quintana-Murci et al., 2010).

Some relationships that exist may not be expressed in the current study because of limitations associated with available skeletal samples and available landmarks. The Southeast Asian affinity was not observed in the current study and may be because of one of two reasons: (1) the modern Thai sample is not an appropriate analog for a possible parental group considering most sources cite Indonesia, India, and/or Malaysia as the geographic locations for the Southeast Asian genetic contributions, and/or (2) a bias exists in the available skeletal material, specifically in temporality. We would expect the SA colored males to be more similar to the historic white males than SA black groups in the HCA and MDS analyses. This result may also be due do to sampling limitations, considering the population may not be the most appropriate parental sample. For example, the primary male settlers were Dutch, not English. Further, in the ternary plots the SA colored females clustered between San and African parental groups, which is expected. Based on the genetic data, we would anticipate a greater number of SA colored females to demonstrate higher proportions of San. Though the Khoikhoi and San are commonly pooled as a group, previous researchers have recognized that the Khoikhoi are often stronger and taller than the San and contribute more than the San to the modern gene pool of colored SAs (Patterson et al., 2010). However, due to accessible crania, only a San sample was available. Still, the San consistently showed the greatest similarity to the colored groups, both male and female, though the females showed stronger affinity than the males.

While the clustering trends reflect the complex, multifaceted colonization and overall population history of South Africa, the importance of understanding the predictor variables and how that will affect probability of group membership should be noted. Misclassification trends differed when SA coloreds were explored with raw measurements and geometric morphometrics (Stull et al., 2014). Thus, the clustering trends may be dependent on the type of predictor variable used. Furthermore, it is important to consider the differential phenotypic expressions from each allosome. Given the phenotypic expressions noted in the current study, population history has shaped modern SA craniometric variation, specifically between SA colored females and males. The observed variation, particularly the differential sex biases among groups, must be considered when estimating ancestry in a forensic setting within South Africa. Finally, craniometrics can elucidate population history and corroborate genetic trends.

Acknowledgments

The authors are grateful to Isabelle Ribot, who provided the craniometric data for some of the possible parental groups, specifically the data from Basuku, Bahutu, and Spitalfields.

References

Barbieri, C., Butthof, A., Bostoen, K., Pakendorf, B., 2013. Genetic perspectives on the origin of clicks in Bantu languages from southwestern Zambia. European Journal of Human Genetics 21, 430–436. http://dx.doi.org/10.1038/ejhg.2012.192.

Berniell-Lee, G., Calafell, F., Bosch, E., Heyer, E., Sica, L., Mouguiama-Daouda, P., van der Veen, L., Hombert, J.-M., Quintana-Murci, L., Comas, D., 2009. Genetic and demographic implications of the Bantu expansion: insights from human paternal lineages. Molecular Biology and Evolution 26, 1581–1589. http://dx.doi.org/10.1093/molbev/msp069.

Cox, T.F., Cox, M.A.A., 2000. Multidimensional Scaling, second ed. CRC Press, Boca Raton, FL.

De Filippo, C., Barbieri, C., Whitten, M., Mpoloka, S.W., Gunnarsdóttir, E.D., Bostoen, K., Nyambe, T., Beyer, K., Schreiber, H., de Knijff, P., Luiselli, D., Stoneking, M., Pakendorf, B., 2011. Y-chromosomal variation in sub-Saharan Africa: insights into the history of Niger-Congo groups. Molecular Biology and Evolution 28, 1255–1269.

De Filippo, C., Bostoen, K., Stoneking, M., Pakendorf, B., 2012. Bringing together linguistic and genetic evidence to test the Bantu expansion. Proceedings of the Royal Society B: Biological Sciences 279, 3256–3263. http://dx.doi.org/10.1098/rspb.2012.0318.

De Villiers, H., 1968. The Skull of the South African Negro. Witwatersrand University Press, Johannesburg.

De Wit, E., Delport, W., Rugamika, C.E., Meintjes, A., Möller, M., van Helden, P.D., Seoighe, C., Hoal, E.G., 2010. Genome-wide analysis of the structure of the South African coloured population in the Western Cape. Human Genetics 128, 145–153.

Franklin, D., Cardini, A., Oxnard, C.E., 2010. A geometric morphometric approach to the quantification of population variation in sub-Saharan African crania. American Journal of Human Biology 22, 23–35.

González-Santos, M., Montinaro, F., Oosthuizen, O., Oosthuizen, E., Busby, G.B.J., Anagnostou, P., Destro-Bisol, G., Pascali, V., Capelli, C., 2015. Genome-Wide SNP analysis of Southern African populations provides new insights into the dispersal of Bantu-speaking groups. Genome Biology and Evolution 7, 2560–2568. http://dx.doi.org/10.1093/gbe/evv164.

Howells, W.W., 1973. Cranial Variation in Man: A Study by Multivariate Analysis of Patterns of Difference Among Recent Human Populations. Papers of the Peabody Museum of Archaeology and Ethnolgy. Harvard University Press, Cambridge, Mass.

Huberty, C., 1994. Applied Discriminant Analysis. Wiley and Sons, New York.

Inwood, K., Masakure, O., 2009. The Historical Roots of Poverty and Inequality in South Africa: The Coloured Population. Economic History Association, Tucson, AZ.

Jakobsson, M., Scholz, S.W., Scheet, P., Gibbs, J.R., VanLiere, J.M., Fung, H.-C., Szpiech, Z.A., Degnan, J.H., Wang, K., Guerreiro, R., Bras, J.M., Schymick, J.C., Hernandez, D.G., Traynor, B.J., Simon-Sanchez, J., Matarin, M., Britton, A., van de Leemput, J., Rafferty, I., Bucan, M., 2008. Genotype, haplotype and copy-number variation in worldwide human populations. Nature 451, 998–1003. http://dx.doi.org/10.1038/nature06742.

Jaworska, N., Chupetlovska-Anastasova, A., 2009. A review of multidimensional scaling (MDS) and its utility in various psychological domains. Tutorials in Quantitative Methods for Psychology 5, 1–10.

Jobson, J.D., 1992. Applied Multivariate Data Analysis: Volume II: Categorical and Multivariate Methods. Springer, New York, Heidelberg.

Kenyhercz, M.W., Passalacqua, N.P., In press. Missing data imputation methods and their performance with biodistance analyses. Forensic and Bioarchaeological Perspectives on Biological Distance, Elsevier.

L'Abbé, E., Kenyhercz, M., Stull, K., 2013. Craniometric variation among 20th century black, white and coloured South Africans. Anatomical Society of Southern African Annual Meeting: Kruger National Park.

L'Abbé, E.N., Ribot, I., Steyn, M., 2006. A craniometric study of the 20th century Venda. The South African Archaeological Bulletin 61, 19–25.

Li, J.Z., Absher, D.M., Tang, H., Southwick, A.M., Casto, A.M., Ramachandran, S., Cann, H.M., Barsh, G.S., Feldman, M., Cavalli-Sforza, L.L., Myers, R.M., 2008. Worldwide human relationships inferred from genome-wide patterns of variation. Science 319, 1100–1104. http://dx.doi.org/10.1126/science.1153717.

Li, S., Schlebusch, C., Jakobsson, M., 2014. Genetic variation reveals large-scale population expansion and migration during the expansion of Bantu-speaking peoples. Proceedings of the Royal Society of London B: Biological Sciences 281, 20141448. http://dx.doi.org/10.1098/rspb.2014.1448.

Mardia, K.V., Kent, J.T., Bibby, J.M., 1979. Multivariate Analysis. Academic Press, London, New York.

Marquard, L., 1952. The Peoples and Policies of South Africa. Oxford University Press, London, New York.

Morris, A.G., 1992. The skeletons of contact: a study of protohistoric burials from the lower Orange River Valley, South Africa. Witwatersrand University Press, Johannesburg, p. 228.

Mountain, A., 2003. The First People of the Cape, first ed. David Philip Publishers, Cape Town, South Africa.

Murtagh, F., Legendre, P., 2011. Ward's Hierarchical Clustering Method: Clustering Criterion and Agglomerative Algorithm arXiv:1111.6285 [cs, stat].

Ousley, S., Jantz, R., Freid, D., 2009. Understanding race and human variation: why forensic anthropologists are good at identifying race. American Journal of Physical Anthropology 139, 68–76.

Patterson, N., Petersen, D.C., van der Ross, R.E., Sudoyo, H., Glashoff, R.H., Marzuki, S., Reich, D., Hayes, V.M., 2010. Genetic structure of a unique admixed population: implications for medical research. Human Molecular Genetics 19, 411–419. http://dx.doi.org/10.1093/hmg/ddp505.

Petersen, D.C., Libiger, O., Tindall, E.A., Hardie, R.-A., Hannick, L.I., Glashoff, R.H., Mukerji, M., Fernandez, P., Haacke, W., Schork, N.J., Hayes, V.M., Indian Genome Variation Consortium, 2013. Complex patterns of genomic admixture within southern Africa. PLoS Genetics 9, e1003309. http://dx.doi.org/10.1371/journal.pgen.1003309.

Pickrell, J.K., Patterson, N., Loh, P.-R., Lipson, M., Berger, B., Stoneking, M., Pakendorf, B., Reich, D., 2014. Ancient west Eurasian ancestry in southern and Eastern Africa. Proceedings of the National Academy of Sciences of the United States of America 111, 2632–2637. http://dx.doi.org/10.1073/pnas.1313787111.

Pritchard, J.K., Stephens, M., Donnelly, P., 2000. Inference of population structure using multilocus genotype data. Genetics 155, 945–959.

Quintana-Murci, L., Harmant, C., Quach, H., Balanovsky, O., Zaporozhchenko, V., Bormans, C., van Helden, P.D., Hoal, E.G., Behar, D.M., 2010. Strong maternal Khoisan contribution to the South African coloured population: a case of gender-biased admixture. American Journal of Human Genetics 86, 611–620. http://dx.doi.org/10.1016/j.ajhg.2010.02.014.

R Core Team, 2013. R: A Language and Environment for Statistical Computing. R Foundation for Statistical Computing, Vienna, Austria.

Relethford, J., 2002. Apportionment of global human genetic diversity based on craniometrics and skin color. American Journal of Physical Anthropology 118, 393–398.

Relethford, J.H., 2009. Race and global patterns of phenotypic variation. American Journal of Physical Anthropology 139, 16–22.

Ribot, I., 2003. Craniometrical analysis of Central and East Africans in relation to history: a case study based on unique collections of known ethnic affiliation. Anthropologica et Praehistorica 114, 25–50.

Ribot, I., 2004. Differentiation of modern sub-Saharan African populations: craniometric interpretations in relation to geography and history. Bulletins et Mémoires de la Société d'Anthropologie de Paris 16, 143–165.

Rightmire, G.P., 1970. Bushman, Hottentot and South African Negro crania studies by distance and discrimination. American Journal of Physical Anthropology 33, 169–195.

Robertson, J., Bradley, R., 2000. A new paradigm: the African Early Iron age without Bantu migrations. History in Africa 27, 287–323.

Russell, T., Steele, J., 2009. A geo-referenced radiocarbon database for Early Iron Age sites in sub-Saharan Africa: initial analysis. Southern African Humanities 21, 327–344.

SAS Institute, 2007. JMP Software (Cary, NC).

Schlebusch, C., 2010. Issues raised by use of ethnic-group names in genome study. Nature 464, 487. http://dx.doi.org/10.1038/464487a.

Schlebusch, C.M., Skoglund, P., Sjödin, P., Gattepaille, L.M., Hernandez, D., Jay, F., Li, S., Jongh, M.D., Singleton, A., Blum, M.G.B., Soodyall, H., Jakobsson, M., 2012. Genomic variation in seven Khoe-San groups reveals adaptation and complex African history. Science 338, 374–379. http://dx.doi.org/10.1126/science.1227721.

Shell, R., 1994. Children of Bondage. Witwatersrand University Press, Johannesburg, South Africa.

Smith, A.B., Sadr, K., Gribble, J., Yates, R., 1991. Excavations in the South-Western Cape, South Africa, and the archaeological identity of prehistoric hunter-gatherers within the last 2000 years. The South African Archaeological Bulletin 46, 71–91.

Stull, K.E., Kenyhercz, M.W., L'Abbé, E.N., 2014. Ancestry estimation in South Africa using craniometrics and geometric morphometrics. Forensic Science International 245, 206.e1–206.e7. http://dx.doi.org/10.1016/j.forsciint.2014.10.021.

Stynder, D.D., 2009. Craniometric evidence for South African later Stone Age herders and hunter–gatherers being a single biological population. Journal of Archaeological Science 36, 798–806. http://dx.doi.org/10.1016/j.jas.2008.11.001.

Thompson, L., 2001. A History of South Africa, third ed. Yale University Press, New Haven, CT.

Tishkoff, S., Kidd, K., 2004. Implications of biogeography of human populations for "race" and medicine. Nature Genetics Supplement 36, S21–S27.

Tishkoff, S.A., Reed, F.A., Friedlaender, F.R., Ehret, C., Ranciaro, A., Froment, A., Hirbo, J.B., Awomoyi, A.A., Bodo, J.-M., Doumbo, O., Ibrahim, M., Juma, A.T., Kotze, M.J., Lema, G., Moore, J.H., Mortensen, H., Nyambo, T.B., Omar, S.A., Powell, K., Pretorius, G.S., Smith, M.W., Thera, M.A., Wambebe, C., Weber, J.L., Williams, S.M., 2009. The genetic structure and history of Africans and African Americans. Science 324, 1035–1044. http://dx.doi.org/10.1126/science.1172257.

Tishkoff, S.A., Williams, S.M., 2002. Genetic analysis of African populations: human evolution and complex disease. Nature Reviews Genetics 3, 611–621. http://dx.doi.org/10.1038/nrg865.

Todorov, V., 2012. rrcovNA: Scalable Robust Estimators with High Breakdown Point for Incomplete Data.

Treiman, D.J., 2007. The legacy of apartheid: racial inequalities in the new South Africa. In: Heath, A.F., Cheung, S.Y. (Eds.), Unequal Chances: Ethnic Minorities in Western Labour Markets. Published for the British Academy by Oxford University Press, Oxford, pp. 401–447.

Van der Ross, R.E., 2005. Up From Slavery Slaves at the Cape: Their Origins, Treatment and Contribution. Ampersand Press in association With the University of the Western Cape, Kenilworth [South Africa].

Vansina, J., 1995. New linguistic evidence and "the Bantu expansion". The Journal of African History 36, 173–195.

Wang, S., Ray, N., Rojas, W., Parra, M.V., Bedoya, G., Gallo, C., Poletti, G., Mazzotti, G., Hill, K., Hurtado, A.M., Camrena, B., Nicolini, H., Klitz, W., Barrantes, R., Molina, J.A., Freimer, N.B., Bortolini, M.C., Salzano, F.M., Petzl-Erler, M.L., Tsuneto, L.T., Dipierri, J.E., Alfaro, E.L., Bailliet, G., Bianchi, N.O., Llop, E., Rothhammer, F., Excoffier, L., Ruiz-Linares, A., 2008. Geographic patterns of genome admixture in Latin American Mestizos. PLoS Genetics 4, e1000037. http://dx.doi.org/10.1371/journal.pgen.1000037.

Ward, J.H., 1963. Hierarchical grouping to optimize an objective function. Journal of the American Statistical Association 58, 236–244. http://dx.doi.org/10.1080/01621459.1963.10500845.

Whitelaw, G., Moon, M.A., 1996. The ceramics and distribution of pioneer agriculturists in KwaZulu-Natal. Southerrin African Humanities 8, 53–79.

CHAPTER

Complexity of Assessing Migrant Death Place of Origin

14

A.H. Ross[1], C.A. Juarez[1], P. Urbanová[2]
North Carolina State University, Raleigh, NC, United States[1]; Masaryk University Brno, Brno, Czech Republic[2]

CHAPTER OUTLINE HEAD

The Unidentified Decedents in the United States 266
Demographic Profiles of the Foreign-Born Latinos 266
Deceased Undocumented Latinos in the United States 267
Medical Examiner and Coroner's Offices' Casework Issues 268
Arizona Unidentified Decedents Versus North Carolina Unidentified Decedents 268
Sample 269
Methods 269
Geometric Morphometrics 269
Results 271
The Two-Pronged Approach to Provenance: Geometric Morphometrics and Isotopes 274
A Case Example Using the Two-Pronged Approach 275
Isotope Methods 277
Results 277
Conclusion 279
References 279

Deaths of undocumented Latinos are concentrated in large numbers at the US/Mexico border. Since 1993, as many as 5000 border deaths have been recorded (Anderson, 2010, 2013; Martinez et al., 2013). However, the deaths of undocumented Latinos extend well beyond the US/Mexico border. Undocumented populations travel and reside throughout the country, and as a result states such as Florida, North Carolina, Georgia, and Illinois are among the top states with the highest undocumented populations (Passel and Cohn, 2011a,b). The purpose of this study is to (1) explore the possible origins of undocumented border crossers (UBCs) who died in transit investigated by PCOME (Pima County Office of the Medical Examiner, Arizona) and compare these data to unidentified decedents (UIDs) from North Carolina and Georgia whose distance from the border makes their migration status uncertain; (2) explore whether the UBCs from Arizona differ morphologically from the NC UIDs; and (3) present a two-pronged approach to region of origin using Geometric Morphometrics and isotope analysis to narrow provenance for UIDs.

Biological Distance Analysis. http://dx.doi.org/10.1016/B978-0-12-801966-5.00014-7

THE UNIDENTIFIED DECEDENTS IN THE UNITED STATES

According to the FBI's National Crime Information Center (NCIC) missing person and unidentified person files, as of December 31, 2014 there were 84,924 active missing person records and 8311 unidentified persons records. Of the 8311 records, 876 were entered in 2014 of which 650, or 74.2%, are deceased unidentified records; 23, or 3%, are unidentified catastrophe victims; and 200, or 22.8%, are living unidentified persons (Federal Bureau of Investigation National Crime Information Center, 2014). Many of those in the missing persons records are thought to be deceased, but remains have not yet been located or identified. Experts estimate there are approximately 40,000 to 50,000 unidentified dead in the United States, most believed to be victims of homicides (Federal Bureau of Investigation National Crime Information Center, 2014; Ritter, 2007). This means that only 2.4% of the unidentified dead are accounted for by the NCIC database. According to the National Missing and Unidentified Persons System (NamUs), the problem of UIDs is compounded annually. Nationwide, over 4000 UIDs are found every year and about one-fourth of these remain unidentified after 1 year. UID cases turn into cold cases when the investigative leads for the case have been exhausted (Heurich, 2008; Davis et al., 2011). The longer the period between death and identification, the more difficult case resolution becomes (Davis et al., 2011). This situation has become so overwhelming for law enforcement in local jurisdictions that many UID websites and databases are cropping up at medical examiner offices around the country (eg, Florida Unidentified Decedent Database, Unidentified Decedent Reporting System, Fulton County Medical Examiner, Doe Network, etc.). This crisis ultimately led to the establishment of the national database system NamUs, a project sponsored by the National Institute of Justice (NIJ) (US Department of Justice, 2010).

Human remains are thought to go unidentified for many reasons including understaffed and underfunded law enforcement agencies, lack of interagency communication, and the foreign-born or undocumented status of individuals (Welford et al., 1999). According to Kimmerle et al. (2010), the missing who end up as our unidentified are predominantly male, adult, foreign-born, minorities, and at-risk individuals such as the mentally ill, elderly, and infants. The foreign-born and undocumented status of many of the unidentified presents a unique challenge in the process of identification as conventional forensic identification tools such as missing person reports and family DNA reference databases focus on US citizens with next of kin. Thus, although the ability to solve a cold case is multifactorial, region of origin data is a critical component in successfully beginning the identification process (Kimmerle et al., 2010).

DEMOGRAPHIC PROFILES OF THE FOREIGN-BORN LATINOS

According to the 2010 US Census, Latinos make up the largest percentage of foreign-born persons in the United States. Within that context, Mexicans make up approximately 29% of the total Hispanic foreign-born population in the United States, Cubans 3.0%, Dominican Republic 2.0%, Guatemalans 2.0%, and El Salvadorans 3.0% (US Census Bureau, 2011). Including the US-born Latinos, one in six people in the United States are of Latin-American origin (US Census Bureau, 2011). Latinos are more geographically concentrated in specific regions of the United States and are more likely to live in central cities of metropolitan areas than non-Hispanic Whites with approximately 54.6% of Latinos of Mexican origin residing in the West and 34.3% residing in the South (Ennis et al., 2011; Brown and Lopez, 2013). In the Northeast, 58% are Puerto Ricans and 31.5% are Central and South Americans. Seventy-five percent of Cubans are concentrated in the South, making up 66% of the total population of Miami and 90% of the total population of the city of Hialeah (US Census Bureau, 2004).

Mestizos, or individuals of mixed European and Amerindian ancestry, had become the largest group in Mexico by the end of the 19th century even though they were discriminated against during the three centuries of Spanish colonization. Today, 60% of Mexicans are *mestizos*, 30% are indigenous, and 9% are European (CIA World Factbook, 2013). The primary sources of migration into the United States from Mexico originate in North Central Mexico including Jalisco, Michoacán, Guanajuato, Zacatecas, Durango, San Luis Potosi, and Aguas-Calientes. Chihuahua, North East Federal District including Mexico City and Oaxaca, have become new important sources of emigration (Passel and Cohn, 2011b).

Currently, North Carolina has the ninth largest Latino population in the nation (Pew Research Center, 2012; Motel and Patten, 2012). This follows almost two decades of rapid growth among Latinos in North Carolina. Between 1990 and 2000, the state's Hispanic population grew by 302,237 individuals, a growth rate of nearly 400% (Pew Research Center, 2012; Motel and Patten, 2012). The 2010 US Census recorded 421,157 Hispanics in North Carolina, a 111% increase from the 2000 census. The geographic origin of Hispanics in North Carolina is approximately 61% Mexican, 7.1% other Hispanic or Latino, 9% Puerto Rican, 13% Central American, 5.7% South American, 2.2% Cuban, and 2% from the Dominican Republic.

DECEASED UNDOCUMENTED LATINOS IN THE UNITED STATES

Since the start of the United States border enforcement strategy (Operation Hold the Line) in El Paso in 1994, border movement patterns and points of entry at the US/Mexico border have significantly changed from unauthorized entries using mostly residential areas along the border to more inhospitable areas of the American Southwest (Androff and Tavassoli, 2012; Cornelius, 2001, 2005; Eschbach et al., 2011, 1999). This US border enforcement strategy has led to an increase in border crosser deaths. According to the US Customs and Border Protection, as US/Mexico border enforcement strategies continue to militarize, the number of migrants apprehended has decreased, but the number of deaths has remained stable, increasing the ratio of deaths to apprehensions to approximately 11% in 2011 (Moreno, 2012). Unauthorized entry into the United States does not begin at the Southwest border. Mexico acts as the starting route of entry from around Latin America as the 750 mile shared border between Mexico and Guatemala and Belize has few checkpoints along the crossing (Walser et al., 2011). A better understanding of the region of origin of undocumented migrants could assist in the identification efforts that have become a major human rights issue in the United States.

As the numbers of Latinos (documented and undocumented) rise in the general population, increases will likely be observed at medical examiner facilities. The Pew Hispanic Center estimates that there are 10.3 million unauthorized immigrants as of 2004 (Passel, 2005). They also estimate that the majority of these unauthorized persons are from Latin America—57% (5.9 million) from Mexico and 24% (2.5 million) from other Latin American countries (primarily from Central America). States that are new destinations for Latino communities such as North Carolina and Georgia are seeing dramatic increases in their population of undocumented Latinos. Estimates from Georgia State Fiscal Policy briefs estimate that as many as half the current Latino population in Georgia (200,000–250,000) is undocumented (Rioja et al., 2006). Because of this overwhelming increase in the Latino population, and because it is likely that many decedents in coroners'/medical examiners' offices may be undocumented, it is imperative to devise a plan that will increase the likelihood of identification.

MEDICAL EXAMINER AND CORONER'S OFFICES' CASEWORK ISSUES

Many medical examiners' offices have UIDs dating back to the 1960s or earlier. These remains, primarily skeletonized, are boxed and stored at these facilities. However, many remains have been destroyed via cremation or buried in potter's fields due to insufficient storage space and thus, will probably remain unidentified. In addition, many of the initial biological profiles (or complete skeletal analyses) derived for cold cases were not performed by vetted forensic anthropologists. Thus, the biological information that is available is inaccurate, which adds yet another dimension to an already complex problem. Fortunately, however, more medical examiner offices now routinely consult with or have a forensic anthropologist on staff to perform full skeletal analyses and provide accurate biological profiles, which will ultimately aid the identification process. In the past year, several law enforcement agencies, working with the North Carolina Office of the Chief Medical Examiner, have requested new analyses in order to help resolve some of the cold cases around the state. During this process we have discovered that incorrect age-at-death estimates and ancestry assessments have been made in all the cases, which would have hindered identification. This situation underscores the necessity to reexamine our cold cases with new methods. Currently, in North Carolina we have 130 known cases dating back to the 1970s that remain unidentified.

Beyond the incorrect profiles assigned to cold cases, there are two major obstacles in the identification of unknown or UIDs: (1) the increase in foreign-born immigrants in the United States, and (2) the increased mobility of US citizens over the last few decades (Kimmerle et al., 2010). Forensic approaches to human identification traditionally rely on biological data such as DNA, fingerprints, and radiographic comparisons, all of which require comparative records. In the case of UIDs the lack of comparative records can be crippling to identification efforts. Difficulties resulting from reliance on DNA and familial matching have been learned from tragedies like Hurricane Katrina and the World Trade Center (Brenner and Weir, 2003; Brunkard et al., 2008; Donkervoort et al., 2008).

Forensic anthropological assessments of unknown or unidentified individuals can be particularly helpful with issues of provenance. The first indication of foreign-born or undocumented status may come from ancestry assessments with the use of NIJ sponsored programs such as 3D-ID. In the case of deceased individuals that are not local or possibly foreign-born, there are several obstacles in the identification process including (1) no indication of a region within the probable country of origin to locate records or family; (2) possible lack of a national and/or international database for missing persons in actual countries of origin (eg, Mexico and Central and South America); (3) with a few exceptions (most notably PCOME), limited communication between forensic investigators and the appropriate agencies (eg, consulates, NGOs collecting information on the undocumented missing, etc.) that have information regarding the missing (Anderson, 2008). Although provenance data is not a silver bullet for identification, it is a helpful start in the aforementioned instances with persons that are high risk to remain unidentified.

ARIZONA UNIDENTIFIED DECEDENTS VERSUS NORTH CAROLINA UNIDENTIFIED DECEDENTS

In the following sections we compare UIDs from Pima County, Arizona to UIDs in North Carolina using Geometric Morphometrics, with the goal of investigating regional differences in Latino UID populations.

Table 14.1 Sample Composition	
Sample	***n***
UBD PCOME, AZ	129
PCOME identified	28
NC/GA UID	22
Panama	24
Guatemala	77
Cuba	19
Mexico Merida Peabody	44
Mexico Morton Collection	6
Peru	7

SAMPLE

The sample includes 356 (Table 14.1) modern individuals (UBC $n = 129$; PCOME known $n = 28$; NC/GA UID $n = 22$; Panama $n = 24$; Perú $n = 7$; Guatemala $n = 77$; Cuba $n = 19$, Mexico Merida $n = 44$; Mexico Morton Collection $n = 6$). The sample for PCOME and Guatemala were provided by Kate Spradley as part of the collaboration between the University of Tennessee and the development of the software 3D-ID (Slice and Ross, 2009). In addition, coordinate data collected by Ross can be downloaded from http://www.3d-id.org/forensic-3d-coordinates.

METHODS

Geometric Morphometrics

Fourteen Type 1 and Type 2 standard craniofacial homologous coordinate landmarks were used in the analysis and are listed in Table 14.2 and depicted in Fig. 14.1 (Ross and Williams, 2008).

Table 14.2 Type 1 and 2 Craniofacial Anatomical Landmarks Used	
Landmarks	
1. Left asterion	8. Right ectoconchion
2. Right asterion	9. Left frontomalare anterior
3. Basion	10. Right frontomalare anterior
4. Bregma	11. Glabella
5. Left dacryon	12. Lambda
6. Right dacryon	13. Nasion
7. Left ectoconchion	14. Opisthion

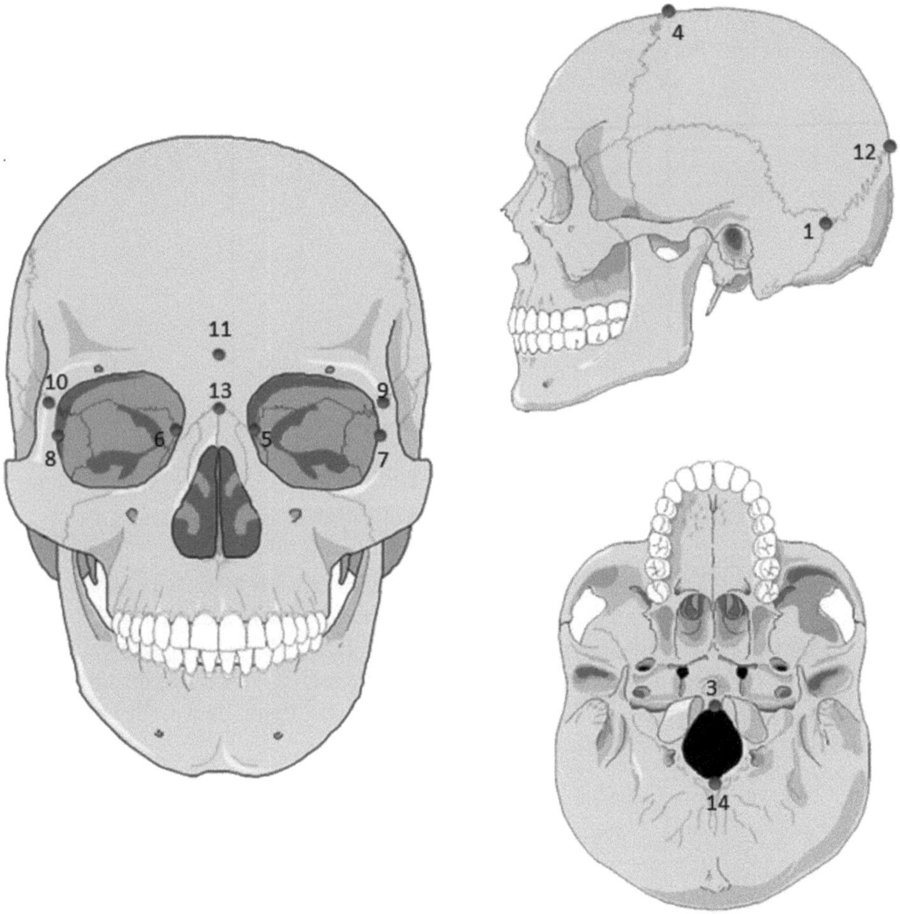

FIGURE 14.1

Landmark locations.

The shareware program MorphoJ (http://www.flywings.org.uk/MorphoJ_page.htm) developed by Klingenberg (2011) was used to translate, rotate, and scale all coordinates into a common coordinate system using a Generalized Procrustes Analysis (GPA). Group comparisons were explored with a Canonical Variates Analysis of the newly derived Procrustes coordinates. A Mahalanobis distance was used to examine the similarity between the groups. MorphoJ uses distance values that can be interpreted as distance measures scaled by the within-group standard deviations. In addition, individual analyses for the 22 North Carolina/Georgia (NC/GA) UIDs were performed and were inputted into 3D-ID (www.3d-id.org), which uses geometric morphometrics to assign an unknown to one of several groups including geographic regions such as MesoAmerica, South America, and CircumCaribbean. The entire reference sample ($n = 2166$) is first subjected to a GPA. 3D-ID assigns an unknown to the group with the smallest squared Euclidean distance (D^2), which uses the Moore—Penrose inverse rather than

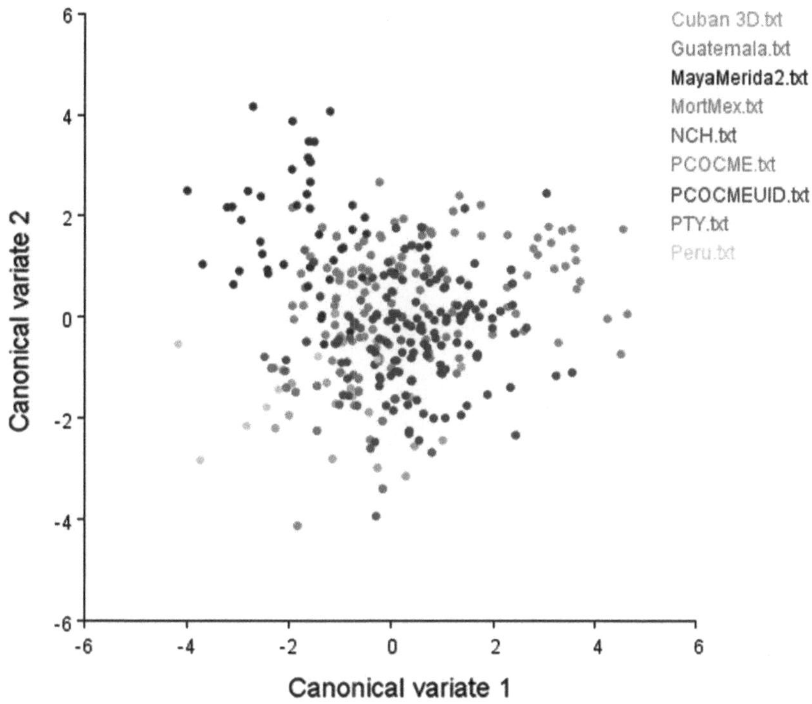

FIGURE 14.2

Canonical variates 1 and 2 showing 61% of the total variation.

the standard matrix inverse to avoid problems with reference and sample size limitations (Ross et al., 2004, 2015, 2014; Slice and Ross, 2009).

RESULTS

The MorphoJ results show that approximately 83% of the total variation is accounted for on the first four canonical variates using the newly derived Procrustes coordinates. Fig. 14.2 illustrates the separation between the first and second canonical variates accounting for 61% of the total variation, which shows a clear separation of the Arizona identified and the other groups. Furthermore, the Arizona UBCs cluster with the Guatemalan sample and the NC/GA UIDs who also separate out. A Mahalanobis distance was used to examine the similarity between the groups and show that all groups are significantly different from one another based on 1000 permutations (Table 14.3). Interestingly, the Arizona UBCs are closest to the Guatemalan sample. The NC/GA sample is closest to Panama, then to Arizona UBC, followed by Guatemala. Difference vectors depict the direction and magnitude of change of deforming one mean configuration onto another. Fig. 14.3 illustrates the difference between the Guatemalan and Mexican mean configurations onto the NC/GA mean configuration and show that bregma is more anteriorly placed in the Guatemalan sample and is more anteroinferiorly placed in the Mexican sample from Merida.

Table 14.3 Mahalanobis Distance Matrix

	Cuba	Guatemala	Merida	Morton	NC/GA	PCOME ID	PCOME UBC	Panama
Guatemala	3.459							
Merida	3.982	2.695						
Morton	4.492	3.702	4.882					
NC/GA	3.138	2.592	3.480	3.612				
PCOME ID	4.896	3.733	4.891	5.703	4.157			
PCOME UBC	2.836	1.755	3.317	3.836	2.352	3.219		
Panama	2.774	3.045	3.684	4.144	2.282	4.825	2.928	
Peru	4.549	4.510	4.663	4.646	3.918	6.573	4.565	4.143

Note: All distances significant at the 0.01–0.0001 level based on 1000 permutations.

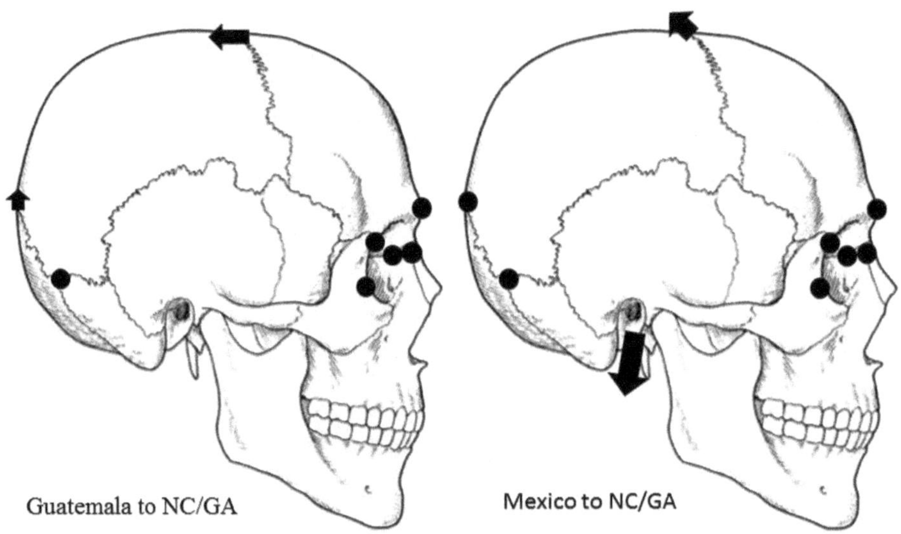

FIGURE 14.3

Vector plot magnified by the power of two illustrating the difference between the Guatemalan and the Mexican consensus forms into NC/GA consensus configuration.

In addition, basion is more superiorly placed in the Mexican sample. The vector plots show less variation between the Guatemalan and the Mexican mean configurations and PCOME UBC consensus configuration (Fig. 14.4). Fig. 14.5 illustrates that there are significant differences in vault shape and glabella between the Guatemalan and Mexican consensus configurations and the Peruvian mean form.

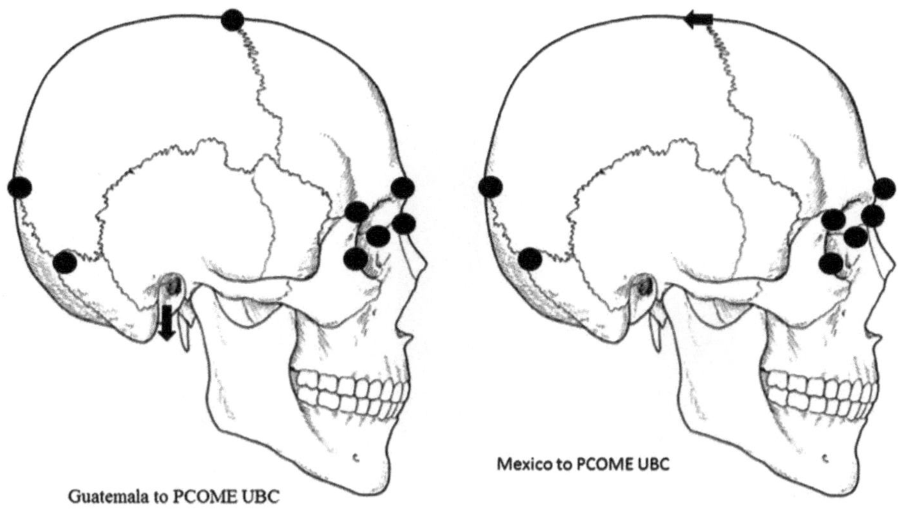

FIGURE 14.4

Vector plot magnified by the power of two showing the deformation of Guatemalan mean configuration into PCOME UBC.

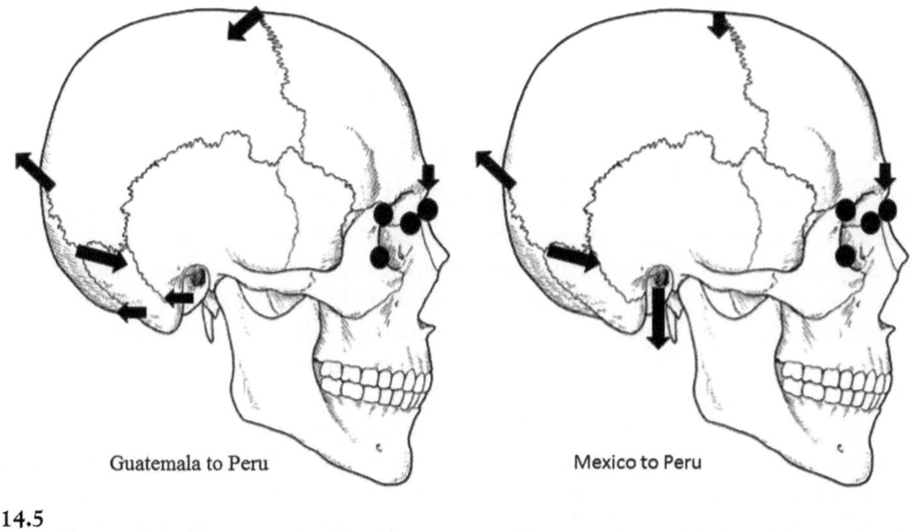

FIGURE 14.5

Vector plot magnified by the power of two illustrating the difference between the Guatemalan and the Mexican consensus forms into Peruvian consensus form.

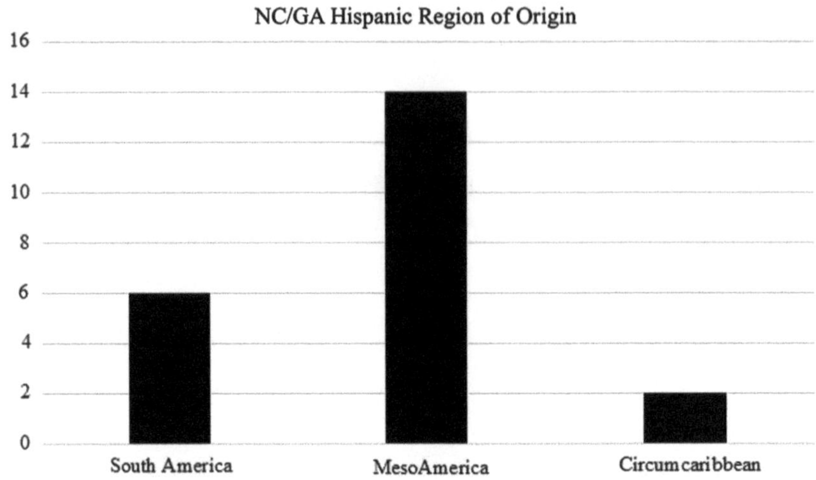

FIGURE 14.6

Classification of NC/GA cases using 3D-ID.

3D-ID classified the majority of the individuals as MesoAmerican. However, our reference sample is composed primarily of Guatemalan and Mexican individuals and the generally low typicalities suggest other possible geographic sources not accounted for in the reference database such as Honduras and El Salvador. Six individuals classified as South American and two as CircumCaribbean (Fig. 14.6).

The results of these analyses show that the 2010 Census may not adequately reflect the country of origin of undocumented and unidentified migrants in the United States. The following case example provides a window into the undocumented cases in North Carolina and the utility of a multifactorial analysis to initiate identifications.

THE TWO-PRONGED APPROACH TO PROVENANCE: GEOMETRIC MORPHOMETRICS AND ISOTOPES

In UID cases, forensic anthropological assessments of ancestry and isotope analysis of tissues may provide valuable indications on provenance. While neither technology can generate a unique identification profile, together they confer a level of regional specificity that neither method can produce in isolation. This estimate of region of origin can initiate the identification process by linking unidentified bodies with a location(s) where the investigation can begin the arduous process of contacting foreign agencies. For a discussion on Geometric Morphometrics please refer to the previous section (and Chapter 4, by Urbanová and Ross, this volume); in the following we briefly detail how the isotopes of carbon, oxygen, and strontium are related to provenance.

Isotopes found in the hard tissues of the body are incorporated through consumption of foodstuffs. Consumption of foodstuffs from a person's local environment transfers local isotope values into the body tissues. Although isotope values are not unique, analysis of multiple isotopes can assist in identifying provenance (Pollard, 2011; Slater et al., 2014). Isotope analysis employed in forensic cases in North Carolina focus on strontium, carbon, and oxygen isotopes.

Variation in strontium isotope ^{87}Sr is produced by radioactive decay of rubidium ^{87}Rb. This decay has produced distinct abundances of strontium for different regions of the earth (Capo et al., 1998; Vitousek et al., 1999; Beard and Johnson, 2000). When an individual consumes locally, and the region has enough distinct abundances, they may be used to differentiate localities (Bentley et al., 2004; Pollard, 2011; Price et al., 2008; Slater et al., 2014). Oxygen and hydrogen isotopes in body tissues are obtained primarily from drinking water ($\sim$70%) (Longinelli, 1984; Daux et al., 2008). Depending on the population, the intake source of imbibed water may be related to local aquifers, which are related to the oxygen and hydrogen concentrations in meteoric precipitation (Bowen et al., 2007; Thompson et al., 2010). Meteoric waters are geographically and climatically dependent and these dependencies produce predictable patterns in water isotopes that can be recorded in human tissues (Bowen et al., 2007; Buzon and Bowen, 2010; Ehleringer et al., 2008; Thompson et al., 2010). Carbon isotopes become part of human tissues through dietary intake. Carbon isotope values in terrestrial food webs vary depending on the photosynthetic pathways used by plants (C3, C4, CAM), and traditionally have been utilized as a dietary indicator (Al-Shorman, 2004; O'Leary, 1988; Schwarcz and Schoeninger, 1991; Sponheimer et al., 2009).

Each of these isotopes represents a unique vantage point from which to determine provenance. However, even with multiple isotopes, a lack of uniqueness in isotope values may result in several disparate regions of origin attributable to a single individual. For this reason, the two approaches, Geometric Morphometric and isotope analysis, are critical partners in narrowing down probable regions of origin. In the following section, we discuss a case example demonstrating this two-pronged approach.

A CASE EXAMPLE USING THE TWO-PRONGED APPROACH

In July of 2003 skeletonized human remains were found by a farmworker in a semiwooded agricultural area near a well-traveled highway in rural North Carolina. The region is known for agriculturally intensive crops like tobacco, strawberries, melons, and tree fruits, and is home to a large mixed community of Latino immigrants, African Americans, and European Americans. At the time they were located, the remains were completely skeletonized with limited associated personal effects (eg, boots, leather belt). No identification was found with the remains. The medical examiner's office received the skeletal material, and the initial analysis determined that the remains were consistent with a single, white, adult male, of possible Hispanic origin with one gunshot wound to the cranium. The case was ruled a homicide. Although several potential leads were investigated none were a DNA match to the victim. The case was entered into NamUs, and within a year the case went cold. In November of 2012 the remains were transported to the North Carolina State University (NCSU) Forensic Analysis Laboratory for provenance evaluation, biological profile, and trauma assessment. Currently, this individual is unidentified; however, it remains an ongoing investigation by multiple law enforcement agencies. The following section presents the findings of that analysis to highlight how the two-pronged approach to provenance is conducted at the NCSU Forensic Analysis Laboratory.

Although the cranium was relatively small, assessment of the gross morphological characteristics demonstrated a series of features consistent with male (eg, prominent superciliary arches, square mandible, sloping forehead, and overall rugosity), which was quantitatively substantiated using FORDISC 3.0 (Jantz and Ousley, 2005) and 3D-ID (Fig. 14.7). Gross craniofacial morphology demonstrated a suite of characteristics found in high frequencies in Asian and European individuals; this mix suggested an individual of possible Hispanic ancestry such as narrow interorbital distance and complex cranial sutures (Birkby

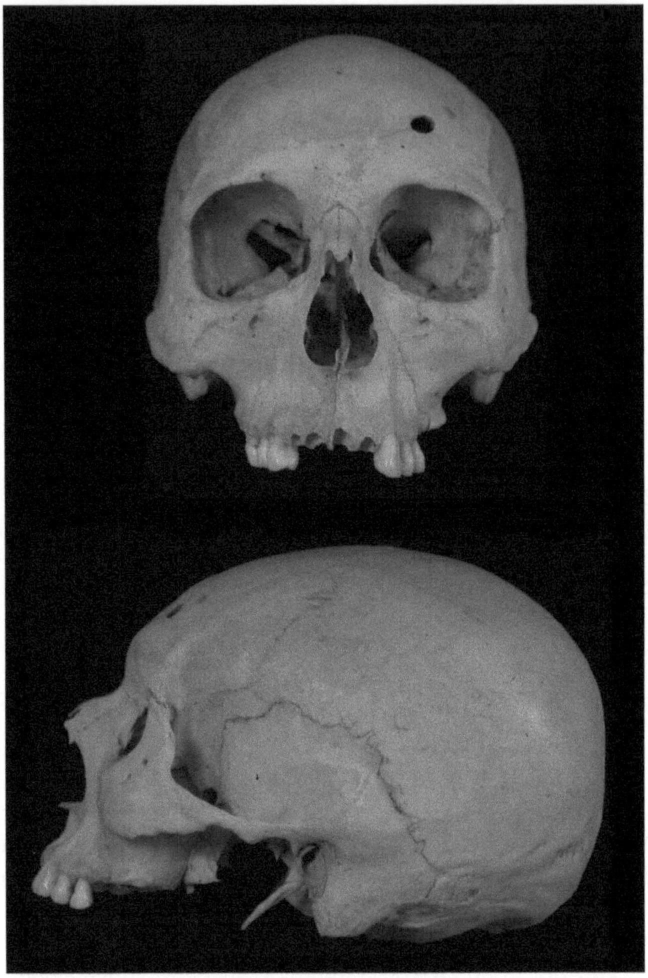

FIGURE 14.7

Frontal and lateral view of unidentified.

et al., 2008; Rhine, 1990). Metric and geometric morphometric ancestry assessment was conducted using both FORDISC 3.0 and 3D-ID with similar, but critically distinct results. Using FORDISC 3.0 the individual classified as a Hispanic male with posterior (0.476) and typicality (0.655) probabilities. The software 3D-ID classified this individual as South American male with posterior (0.704) and typicality (0.831) probabilities. Based on the ancestral estimation of Hispanic/South American the dental aging method for single rooted teeth by Ubelaker and Parra (2008) for Peruvians was used. The periodontal regression was 2.37 mm, tooth height was 14 mm, and root transparency was 5.99 consistent with a mean age of 47.8 years and a range of 41.9—53.7 years. Trauma assessment revealed the presence of three penetrating gunshot wounds and two exit defects. One lead slug consistent with a 0.22 caliber bullet was lodged in the right greater wing of the sphenoid.

In order to clarify region of origin, enamel samples of tooth #30, a portion of the cortical bone from the right femoral shaft, and a portion of the sternal end of right rib #12 were sampled for carbon, oxygen, and strontium isotopes. The specific goals of this analysis were the following: (1) to investigate the possibility that this individual was born in North Carolina, (2) to examine the length of time this individual resided in North Carolina, and (3) to provide alternative possibilities for provenance if the individual was nonnative.

ISOTOPE METHODS

Although the samples were recent, diagenetic alteration was still a concern. Samples were prepared using mechanical cleaning and weak acid protocols to limit the potential impacts of diagenetic alteration (Koch et al., 1997). Sample digestion for strontium analysis was conducted according to the protocol from Slater et al. (2014). All strontium samples were analyzed at the University of Illinois on the Nu Plasma MC-ICP-MS. Strontium samples reported in this study are reported using the value of the $^{87}Sr/^{86}Sr$ ratio and reported in parts per 1000, or per mil (‰). Ratios were corrected for mass bias fractionation using an internal normalization to $^{86}Sr/^{87}Sr = 0.1194$. All $^{86}Sr/^{87}Sr$ isotope ratios were normalized using the within run values of the NBS 987 standard (accepted $^{86}Sr/^{87}Sr = 0.710255$) every six samples (average for the runs reported here 0.71025 ± 0.0000876). For carbonate preparation the protocol described in Clementz et al. (2009) was used. All carbonate analysis was conducted for the tooth and bone samples at the Duke DEVIL Lab using a Thermo Finnegan Gas Bench II and completed in one run. Replicates of NBS-19 resulted in a reproducibility of 0.1‰ and 0.2‰ for $\delta^{18}O$ and $\delta^{13}C$. Oxygen and carbon isotopes are reported using the delta notation:

$$\delta^h X = ((R_{sample}/R_{standard}) - 1) * 1000 \qquad (14.1)$$

where X is the element, h is the high mass number, R is the high-mass to low-mass isotope ratio, and $R_{standard}$ is V-PDB (a marine carbonate) for carbon and V-SMOW (standard mean ocean water) for oxygen.

RESULTS

Values for $^{86}Sr/^{87}Sr$ were generated for the femur and tooth enamel. The $^{86}Sr/^{87}Sr$ for the femur was 0.70802, and the value for $^{86}Sr/^{87}Sr$ from the tooth enamel was 0.70813. Both samples had a standard error of $\pm$ 0.00001. Femur $\delta^{13}C$ value was -9.5 ± 0.265‰; rib $\delta^{13}C$ value was -11.1 ± 0.363‰; and the enamel $\delta^{13}C$ value was -5.8 ± 0.184‰. The value of $\delta^{18}O$ for the femur was 22.7 ± 0.341‰. The value of $\delta^{18}O$ for the rib sample was 22.5 ± 0.107‰. The value of $\delta^{18}O$ for the enamel sample was 22.4 ± 0.269‰. Measurements of strontium isotope values in human bone and teeth are a reflection of the biologically available strontium in foods and water in the region, and in this case were compared directly to available values for drinking water for the region (Bataille and Bowen, 2012; Bowen et al., 2007; Chesson et al., 2012; Sillen and Kavenaugh, 1982). Although carbon isotope data was generated, analysis of these dietary isotopes is not the focus here; the following discussion will focus on the strontium and oxygen results.

Several researchers have utilized the relationship between oxygen isotopes in body tissues and drinking water to assess possible region of origin by using the conversion developed by Levinson et al. (1987) or the more recent example by Daux et al. (2008) that estimates the drinking water source by analyzing body phosphates. Similar conversions have successfully been utilized in a forensic context (Meier-Augenstein and Fraser, 2008). To estimate drinking water values from tooth and bone values, the equations from Iacumin et al. (1996) and Daux et al. (2008) were used, respectively:

$$\delta^{18}\text{O carbonate}_{(\text{VSMOW})} = (8.5 + (\delta^{18}\text{O phosphate}))/0.98, \quad (14.2)$$

$$\delta^{18}\text{O drinking water}_{(\text{VSMOW})} = \left(1.54 \times \left(\delta^{18}\text{O phosphate}_{(\text{VSMOW})}\right)\right) - 33.72 \quad (14.3)$$

The oxygen results generated show that the average $\delta^{18}O$ bone and tooth values are mechanistically indistinguishable and as such will be treated as an average value of 22.5 ± 1.429‰. The $\delta^{18}O$ value of potential drinking water sources from body tissues was estimated to be −11.11‰. This estimation is inconsistent with $\delta^{18}O$ values for drinking water and precipitation for North Carolina, where $\delta^{18}O$ for tap water ranges from 0‰ to −3.9‰ and precipitation ranges from −4‰ to −7.9‰ (Bowen, 2008; Bowen and Revenaugh, 2003; Bowen et al., 2007). The estimated drinking water values generated from bone and tooth enamel are moderately low and from a precipitation standpoint they are consistent with an inland, semiarid and/or high elevation environment.

Although studies analyzing archaeological material have reported meaningful differences in strontium values in the fourth significant figure, modern populations offer a unique challenge. Although the strontium results generated in this analysis do show a slight difference in the fourth significant figure, the average bone and tooth values are relatively unchanged. According to Chesson et al. (2012), the biologically available strontium for North Carolina generated from drinking water ranged from 0.720 to 0.707, which overlaps the values of strontium identified in the case materials. However, when strontium and oxygen results are combined, the results clearly indicate a nonnative birthplace and the consistency of isotope values among tissue types suggests that this individual spent less than 6 years in North Carolina, failing to acclimate to the local isotope values.

The final step to this analysis was to generate possible regions of provenance based on the 3D-ID reference data and the isotope values for strontium and estimated drinking water. Very few public sources currently exist for drinking water values for Central and South America. Using data from http://waterisotopes.org on precipitation values, as well as Mexican water samples collected by Juarez (2014), we identified five regions from Mexico and Central and South America with drinking water values or precipitation values for $\delta^{18}O$ that overlapped with the estimated drinking water value derived from the victim's tissues (Andrushko et al., 2011; Conlee et al., 2009; Knudson et al., 2014, 2009, 2005). These regions include drinking water values for Central Mexico (State of Morelos), and precipitation values for the West Coast of Colombia, Ecuador, Peru, and Chile. In addition, drinking water values were located for Southern Peru, which helped to refine $\delta^{18}O$ values for this region. Strontium isotopes used for comparison were gleaned from the literature (Andrushko et al., 2011; Conlee et al., 2009; Juarez, 2008; Knudson and Torres-Rouff, 2009; Knudson et al., 2014, 2009, 2005; Slovak et al., 2009). When strontium isotopes were combined with the oxygen values the Mexican regions were eliminated and the best overlap was found with the region of southern Peru (Cuzco) to Northern Chile which demonstrated a $^{86}Sr/^{87}Sr$ range of 0.70728 to 0.70906 and $\delta^{18}O$ range for drinking water of −11.1‰ to −12.6‰. This isotope assessment supports the 3D-ID assignment of South American Male and adds a second line of evidence to the provenance data. This case example demonstrates how the two-pronged approach works to refine and inform the provenance data of each method.

CONCLUSION

This chapter and case example demonstrate two important themes that need to be considered when working with UIDs of Latino origin. First, it is critical to understand the limitations of our commonly utilized tools and the necessity to incorporate other analytical options into the common repertoire. In this example, 3D-ID helped to narrow the ancestry assessment in a manner that informed other lines of evidence. Other studies have generated similar cautionary tales. For example, Hughes et al. (2012) showed that modern Guatemalan Maya exhibit combinations of morphoscopic traits that forensic practitioners have traditionally used to assess the antiquity of remains such as dental wear, shovel-shaped incisors, and enamel extensions, which could lead to misidentifications of Latin American decedents. They also found that out of nine standard traditional craniometric variables, face breadth, nasal height, and parietal chord measures were the most classificatory in separating California Native Americans from modern Guatemalans. Humphries et al. (2013) found that there is continuity of prehistoric indigenous populations to modern Mexican samples and found that the biological European influence is higher in the eastern coastal Mexican samples.

Second, in as much as possible, multiple lines of evidence that speak to provenance need to become commonplace in case analysis. Latino populations are not homogeneous and methodological approaches to identification founded in this idea will not produce successful identifications. Both the regional comparison and the case presented here were specifically chosen to illustrate the reality of the difficulties encountered when dealing with foreign-born UIDs of suspected Latino origin. In order for forensic anthropology to truly assist with identifications, we must understand our regional population differences and work collaboratively to create multimodal approaches.

References

Al-Shorman, A., 2004. Stable carbon isotope analysis of human tooth enamel from the Bronze Age cemetery of Ya'amoun in Northern Jordan. Journal of Archaeological Science 31, 1693–1698. http://dx.doi.org/10.1016/j.jas.2004.05.002.

Anderson, B.E., 2008. Identifying the dead: methods utilized by the Pima County (Arizona) office of the medical examiner for undocumented border crossers: 2001–2006. Journal of Forensic Sciences 53, 8–15.

Anderson, S., 2010. Death at the Border. Arlington, VA. Available from: https://www.carnegie.org/media/filer_public/aa/c4/aac4d522-ae48-47e4-a346-ca336b41ef3d/ccny_report_2010_death.pdf.

Anderson, S., 2013. How Many More Deaths? The Moral Case for a Temporary Worker Program. Policy Br (Internet). Available from: http://www.nfap.com/researchactivities/studies/.

Androff, D.K., Tavassoli, K.Y., 2012. Deaths in the desert: the human rights crisis on the US-Mexico border. Social Work (United States) 57, 165–173. http://dx.doi.org/10.1093/sw/sws034.

Andrushko, V.A., Buzon, M.R., Gibaja, A.M., McEwan, G.F., Simonetti, A., Creaser, R.A., 2011. Investigating a child sacrifice event from the Inca heartland. Journal of Archaeological Science 38, 323–333. http://dx.doi.org/10.1016/j.jas.2010.09.009.

Bataille, C.P., Bowen, G.J., 2012. Mapping $^{87}Sr/^{86}Sr$ variations in bedrock and water for large scale provenance studies. Chemical Geology 304–305, 39–52. http://dx.doi.org/10.1016/j.chemgeo.2012.01.028.

Beard, B.L., Johnson, C.M., 2000. Strontium isotope composition of skeletal material can determine the birthplace and geographic mobility of humans and animals. Journal of Forensic Sciences 45, 1049–1061.

Bentley, R.A., Price, T.D., Stephan, E., 2004. Determining the "local" $^{87}Sr/^{86}Sr$ range for archaeological skeletons: a case study from Neolithic Europe. Journal of Archaeological Science 31, 365–375. http://dx.doi.org/10.1016/j.jas.2003.09.003.

Birkby, W.H., Fenton, T.W., Anderson, B.E., 2008. Identifying Southwest Hispanics using nonmetric traits and the cultural profile. Journal of Forensic Sciences 53, 29–33.

Bowen, G.J., Revenaugh, J., 2003. Interpolating the isotopic composition of modern meteoric precipitation. Water Resources Research 39. http://dx.doi.org/10.1029/2003WR002086.

Bowen, G.J., Ehleringer, J.R., Chesson, L.A., Stange, E., Cerling, T.E., 2007. Stable isotope ratios of tap water in the contiguous United States. Water Resources Research 43, 1–12. http://dx.doi.org/10.1029/2006WR005186.

Bowen, G., 2008. The Online Isotopes in Precipitation Calculator. http://www.waterisotopes.org.

Brenner, C.H., Weir, B.S., 2003. Issues and strategies in the DNA identification of World Trade Center victims. Theoretical Population Biology 63, 173–178. http://dx.doi.org/10.1016/S0040-5809(03)00008-X.

Brown, A., Lopez, M.H., 2013. Mapping the Latino Population, by State, County and City. Pew Hispanic Center.

Brunkard, J., Namulanda, G., Ratard, R., 2008. Hurricane Katrina deaths, Louisiana, 2005. Disaster Medicine and Public Health Preparedness 2, 215–223. http://dx.doi.org/10.1097/DMP.0b013e31818aaf55.

Buzon, M.R., Bowen, G.J., 2010. Oxygen and carbon isotope analysis of human tooth enamel from the new kingdom site of tombos in Nubia. Archaeometry 52, 855–868. http://dx.doi.org/10.1111/j.1475-4754.2009.00503.x.

Capo, R.C., Stewart, B.W., Chadwick, O.A., 1998. Strontium isotopes as tracers of ecosystem processes: theory and methods. Geoderma 82, 197–225.

Central Intelligence Agency, 2013. The World Factbook 2013–14 (WWW Document). https://www.cia.gov/library/publications/the-world-factbook/index.html.

Chesson, L.A., Tipple, B.J., Mackey, G.N., Hynek, S.A., Fernandez, D.P., Ehleringer, J.R., 2012. Strontium isotopes in tap water from the coterminous USA. Ecosphere 3, 1–17. http://dx.doi.org/10.1890/ES12-00122.1.

Clementz, M.T., Fox-Dobbs, K., Wheatley, P.V., Koch, P.L., Doak, D.F., 2009. Revisiting old bones: coupled carbon isotope analysis of bioapatite and collagen as an ecological and palaeoecological tool. Geological Journal 44, 605–620. http://dx.doi.org/10.1002/gj.1173.

Conlee, C.A., Buzon, M.R., Gutierrez, A.N., Simonetti, A., Creaser, R.A., 2009. Identifying foreigners versus locals in a burial population from Nasca, Peru: an investigation using strontium isotope analysis. Journal of Archaeological Science 36, 2755–2764. http://dx.doi.org/10.1016/j.jas.2009.08.016.

Cornelius, W.A., 2001. Death at the border: efficacy and unintended consequences of US immigration control policy. Population and Development Review 27, 661–685. http://dx.doi.org/10.1111/j.1728-4457.2001.00661.x.

Cornelius, W.A., 2005. Controlling "unwanted" immigration: sessons from the United States, 1993–2004. Journal of Ethnic and Migration Studies 31, 775–794. http://dx.doi.org/10.1080/13691830500110017.

Daux, V., Lécuyer, C., Héran, M.A., Amiot, R., Simon, L., Fourel, F., Martineau, F., Lynnerup, N., Reychler, H., Escarguel, G., 2008. Oxygen isotope fractionation between human phosphate and water revisited. Journal of Human Evolution 55, 1138–1147.

Davis, R., Jensen, C., Kitchens, K., Corporation, R., 2011. Cold Case Investigations: An Analysis of Current Practices and Factors Associated With Successful Outcomes, Executive Summary. Available from: https://www.ncjrs.gov/App/AbstractDB/AbstractDBDetails.aspx?id=260008.

Donkervoort, S., Dolan, S.M., Beckwith, M., Northrup, T.P., Sozer, A., 2008. Enhancing accurate data collection in mass fatality kinship identifications: lessons learned from Hurricane Katrina. Forensic Science International: Genetics 2, 354–362. http://dx.doi.org/10.1016/j.fsigen.2008.05.008.

Ehleringer, J.R., Bowen, G.J., Chesson, L.A., West, A.G., Podlesak, D.W., Cerling, T.E., 2008. Hydrogen and oxygen isotope ratios in human hair are related to geography. Proceedings of the National Academy of Sciences of the United States of America 105, 2788–2793. http://dx.doi.org/10.1073/pnas.0712228105.

Ennis, S.R., Rios-Vargas, M., Albert, N.G., 2011. The Hispanic Population: 2010, p. 201, Washington, DC. http://dx.doi.org/10.1016/j.mhpa.2012.10.005.

Eschbach, K., Hagan, J., Rodriguez, N., Hernandez-leon, R., Bailey, S., 1999. Death at the border. International. Migration Review 33, 430–454. http://dx.doi.org/10.2307/2547703.

Eschbach, K., Hagan, J., Rodriguez, N., Hernandez-leon, R., 2011. Death at the Border. The Center for Migration Studies of New York, Inc.. http://www.jstor.org/stable/2547703

Federal Bureau of Investigation National Crime Information Center, 2014. NCIC Missing Person and Unidentified Person Statistics for 2014. National Crime Information Center.

Heurich, C., 2008. Cold cases: resources for agencies, resolution for families. National Institute of Justice Journal 20–23.

Hughes, C., Juarez, C., Zephro, L., Fowler, G., Chacon, S., 2012. Past or present? Differentiating California prehistoric Native American remains from forensic cases: an empirical approach. International Journal of Osteoarchaeology 22, 110–118.

Humphries, A., Maxwell, A., Ross, A.H., Ubelaker, D.H., 2013. A geometric morphometric study of regional craniofacial variation in Mexico. International Journal of Osteoarchaeology 25, 795–804.

Iacumin, P., Bocherens, H., Mariotti, A., Longinelli, A., 1996. Oxygen isotope analyses of co-existing carbonate and phosphate in biogenic apatite: a way to monitor diagenetic alteration of bone phosphate? Earth Planetary Science Letters 142, 1–6.

Jantz, R.L., Ousley, S.D., 2005. FORDISC 3.0 Personal Computer Forensic Discriminant Functions. University of Tennessee Knoxville.

Juarez, C.A., 2008. Strontium and geolocation, the pathway to identification for deceased undocumented Mexican border-crossers: a preliminary report. Journal of Forensic Sciences 53, 46–49.

Juarez, C., 2014. Creating the Mexican Isoscape: using water isotopes for region of origin identification in Mexico. In: Proceedings of the American Academy of Forensic Sciences. IPV, vol. XVV. Seattle, Washington.

Kimmerle, E.H., Falsetti, A., Ross, A.H., 2010. Immigrants, undocumented workers, runaways, transients and the homeless: towards contextual identification among unidentified decedents. Forensic Science Policy and Management: An International Journal 1, 178–186.

Klingenberg, C.P., 2011. MorphoJ: an integrated software package for geometric morphometrics. Molecular Ecology Resources 11, 353–357.

Knudson, K.J., Torres-Rouff, C., 2009. Investigating cultural heterogeneity in San Pedro de Atacama, northern Chile, through biogeochemistry and bioarchaeology. American Journal of Physical Anthropology 138, 473–485. http://dx.doi.org/10.1002/ajpa.20965.

Knudson, K.J., Tung, T.A., Nystrom, K.C., Price, T.D., Fullagar, P.D., 2005. The origin of the Juch'uypampa Cave mummies: strontium isotope analysis of archaeological human remains from Bolivia. Journal of Archaeological Science. http://dx.doi.org/10.1016/j.jas.2005.01.007.

Knudson, K.J., Williams, S.R., Osborn, R., Forgey, K., Williams, P.R., 2009. The geographic origins of Nasca trophy heads using strontium, oxygen, and carbon isotope data. Journal of Anthropological Archaeology 28, 244–257. http://dx.doi.org/10.1016/j.jaa.2008.10.006.

Knudson, K.J., Goldstein, P.S., Dahlstedt, A., Somerville, A., Schoeninger, M.J., 2014. Paleomobility in the Tiwanaku diaspora: biogeochemical analyses at Rio Muerto, Moquegua, Peru. American Journal of Physical Anthropology 155 (3), 405–421. http://dx.doi.org/10.1002/ajpa.22584.

Koch, P.L., Tuross, N., Fogel, M.L., 1997. The effects of sample treatment and diagenesis on the isotopic integrity of carbonate in biogenic hydroxyapatite. Journal of Archaeological Science 24, 417–429. http://dx.doi.org/10.1006/jasc.1996.0126.

Levinson, A.A., Luz, B., Kolodny, Y., 1987. Variations in oxygen isotopic compositions of human teeth and urinary stones. Applied Geochemistry 2, 367–371.

Longinelli, A., 1984. Oxygen isotopes in mammal bone phosphate: a new tool for paleohydrological and paleoclimatological research? Geochimica et Cosmochima Acta 48, 385–390.

Martinez, D.A., Reineke, R.C., Rubio-Goldsmith, R., Anderson, B.E., Hess, G.L., Parks, B.O., 2013. A Continued Humanitarian Crisis at the Border: Undocumented Border Crosser Deaths Recorded by the Pima County Office of the Medical Examiner. Tuscon.

Meier-Augenstein, W., Fraser, I., 2008. Forensic isotope analysis leads to identification of a mutilated murder victim. Science and Justice 48, 153–159. http://dx.doi.org/10.1016/j.scijus.2007.10.010.

Moreno, C., 2012. Border Crossing Deaths More Common as Illegal Immigration Declines. Huffington Post.

Motel, S., Patten, E., 2012. The 10 Largest Hispanic Origin Groups: Characteristics, Rankings, Top Counties. Pew Research, Washington, DC.

O'Leary, M., 1988. Carbon isotopes in photosynthesis. Bioscience 38, 328–336. http://dx.doi.org/10.2307/1310735.

Passel, J.S., Cohn, D., 2011a. How Many Hispanics? Comparing New Census Counts With the Latest Census Estimates. Pew Research Center.

Passel, J.S., Cohn, D., 2011b. Unauthorized Immigrant Population: National and State Trends 2010, Population, English ed. Washington, DC.

Passel, J.S., 2005. Estimates of the Size and Characteristics of the Undocumented Population. Pew Research Center.

Pew Research Center, 2012. Pew Research Center Hispanic Trends Demographic Profile of Hispanics in North Carolina, 2011. Available from: http://www.pewhispanic.org/states/state/nc/.

Pollard, A.M., 2011. Isotopes and impact : a cautionary tale. Antiquity 85, 631–638.

Price, T.D., Burton, J.H., Fullagar, P.D., Wright, L.E., Buikstra, J.E., Tiesler, V., 2008. Strontium isotopes and the study of human mobility in ancient Mesoamerica. Latin American Antiquity 19, 1–14.

Rhine, S., 1990. Non-metric skull racing. In: Gill, G., Rhine, S. (Eds.), Skeletal Attribution of Race. Maxwell Museum of Anthropology, Albuquerque, pp. 9–18.

Rioja, F., Valev, N., Wilske, A., 2006. The Demographics of Georgia IV: Hispanic Immigration Economic Policy Issues. Atlanta.

Ritter, N., 2007. Missing persons and unidentified remains: the Nation's silent mass disaster. National Institute of Justice Journal 2–7.

Ross, A.H., Williams, S., 2008. Testing repeatability and error of coordinate cranial landmark data acquired from skulls. Journal of Forensic Sciences 53, 782–785.

Ross, A.H., Slice, D.E., Ubelaker, D.H., Falsetti, A., 2004. Population affinities of 19th Century Cuban crania: implications for identification criteria of Cuban Americans in South Florida. Journal of Forensic Sciences 49, 11–16.

Ross, A.H., Hale, A., Slice, D.E., 2014. 3D-ID – geometric morphometric software for ancestry and sex determination. In: Delabarde, T. (Ed.), C'est L'histoire D'un Squelette: Manuel Practique D'anthropologie Médico-légal. ESKA, Paris, France.

Ross, A.H., Slice, D.E., Ubelaker, D.H., 2015. Population affinities of Hispanic crania. Implications for forensic identification. In: Berg, G., Ta'ala, S. (Eds.), Biological Affinity in Forensic Identification of Human Skeletal Remains: Beyond Black and White. CRC Press, Boca Raton, FL, pp. 155–164.

Schwarcz, H.P., Schoeninger, M.J., 1991. Stable isotope analyses in human nutritional ecology. American Journal of Physical Anthropology 34, 283–321. http://dx.doi.org/10.1002/ajpa.1330340613.

Sillen, A., Kavanagh, M., 1982. Strontium and paleodietary research: a review. American Journal of Physical Anthropology 25, 67–90.

Slater, P.A., Hedman, K.M., Emerson, T.E., 2014. Immigrants at the Mississippian polity of Cahokia: strontium isotope evidence for population movement. Journal of Archaeological Science 44, 117–127. http://dx.doi.org/10.1016/j.jas.2014.01.022.

Slice, D.E., Ross, A.H., 2009. 3D-ID.org (WWW Document). http://www.3d-id.org/home.

Slovak, N.M., Paytan, A., Wiegand, B.A., 2009. Reconstructing Middle Horizon mobility patterns on the coast of Peru through strontium isotope analysis. Journal of Archaeological Science 36, 157–165. http://dx.doi.org/10.1016/j.jas.2008.08.004.

Sponheimer, M., Codron, D., Passey, B.H., De Ruiter, D.J., Cerling, T.E., Lee-Thorp, J.A., 2009. Using carbon isotopes to track dietary change in modern, historical, and ancient primates. American Journal of Physical Anthropology 140, 661–670. http://dx.doi.org/10.1002/ajpa.21111.

Thompson, A.H., Chesson, L.A., Podlesak, D.W., Bowen, G.J., Cerling, T.E., Ehleringer, J.R., 2010. Stable isotope analysis of modern human hair collected from Asia (China, India, Mongolia, and Pakistan). American Journal of Physical Anthropology 141, 440–451. http://dx.doi.org/10.1002/ajpa.21162.

US Department of Justice, 2010. NaMus the Unidentified Persons Database. Available from: http://namus.gov/about.htm.

US Census Bureau, 2004. 2000 Census of Population and Housing, Population and Housing Unit Counts PHC-3-1, United States Summary. Washington, DC.

US Census Bureau, 2011. 2010 Census Demographic Profile Summary File. Washington, DC. Available from: https://www.census.gov/prod/cen2010/doc/dpsf.pdf.

Ubelaker, D.H., Parra, R.C., 2008. Application of three dental methods of adult age estimation from intact single rooted teeth to a Peruvian sample. Journal of Forensic Science 53, 608–611.

Vitousek, P.M., Kennedy, M.J., Derry, L.A., Chadwick, O.A., 1999. Weathering versus atmospheric sources of strontium in ecosystems on young volcanic soils. Oecologia 121, 255–259.

Walser, R., McNeill, J.B., Zuckerman, J., 2011. The Human Tragedy of Illegal Immigration: Greater Efforts Needed to Combat Smuggling and Violence. Herit Found, pp. 1–18.

Welford, C., Cronin, J., Brandl, S., Bynum, T., Eversen, T., Galeria, S., 1999. An Analysis of Variables Affecting the Clearance of Homicides: A Multistate Study. Washington, DC.

CHAPTER

15

Estimating Ancestry of Fragmentary Remains Via Multiple Classifier Systems: A Study of the Mississippi State Asylum Skeletal Assemblage

N.P. Herrmann[1], A. Plemons[2], E.F. Harris[3]

Texas State University, San Marcos, TX, United States[1]; Mississippi State University, Mississippi State, MS, United States[2]; The University of Tennessee Health Science Center, Memphis, TN, United States[3]

CHAPTER OUTLINE HEAD

Introduction 285
Mississippi State Asylum History 286
Materials and Methods 287
Reference Datasets 287
Dental Metrics 287
Dental Morphology 287
Cranial Macromorphoscopic Traits 288
Data Collection and Analysis 288
Results 289
Discussion 297
Conclusions 297
References 298

INTRODUCTION

The estimation of ancestry in historic skeletal samples and forensic cases from the United States is complicated by diverse population histories of communities. Reference datasets are often temporally varied and geographically limited. Researchers have recognized these limitations and have focused on expanding reference databases to improve assessments for modern forensic casework and historical bioarchaeology.

Recent research on ancestry estimation has examined dental metrics (Harris and Foster, 2015; Pilloud et al., 2014), dental morphological traits (Edgar, 2005, 2013), and cranial macromorphoscopic traits (Hefner, 2009, 2015; Hefner and Ousley, 2014; Hefner et al., 2015). The methods proposed in these referenced studies include, but are not limited to, discriminant function analysis (DFA), optimized

Biological Distance Analysis. http://dx.doi.org/10.1016/B978-0-12-801966-5.00015-9

summed scored attributes (OSSA), logistic regression, random forest modeling, and Bayesian classifiers (Hefner and Ousley, 2014; Hefner et al., 2014). The accuracy of the methods presented ranged from roughly 70% to approximately 95% for the various reference samples examined.

These refined approaches and datasets form the basis for the examination of a series of burials from the Mississippi State Asylum (MSA) Cemetery located in Jackson, Mississippi. The MSA skeletal sample is extremely fragmentary due to the burial context, and craniometric and cranial morphological observations are limited. Based on these conditions, the assessment of ancestry posed a particular challenge for the MSA sample. However, as these are largely unmarked graves, the assessment of ancestry for these individuals is critical to the interpretation of this collection, and may ultimately aid in the identification of these unmarked graves.

MISSISSIPPI STATE ASYLUM HISTORY

The origins of the MSA can be traced to mid-19th century America when the need for asylums and other similar institutions became apparent as populations expanded and financial burdens posed by society's unwanted and supposedly incurable individuals shifted from family or community responsibility to state governments. In 1848, the Mississippi State Legislature passed an act to establish a lunatic asylum for the state of Mississippi. The legislation provided an appropriation of $10,000 and land near the city of Jackson for the construction of the institution (Milner, n.d.). After several years and additional appropriations, the institution was completed and opened on January 8, 1855. The asylum design followed a Kirkbride floor plan, which was significantly modified in the late 19th and early 20th centuries to accommodate additional patients. The asylum was one of several mental institutions established in Mississippi in the 19th century, but it received patients from across the state. In 1870, the MSA began receiving black patients, and segregated wards appeared on the 1895 Sanborn Insurance Map for Jackson, Mississippi (Sanborn Fire Insurance Map, 1895). In total, over 30,000 patients were admitted to the hospital and over 9000 patients died in the institution. As a result of overcrowding, dilapidated conditions, and health concerns, the Mississippi legislature appropriated new funds in 1926 to construct a new facility, Whitfield, which opened in 1935. Patients were transferred to the new facility, but burial continued at the MSA cemetery until 1936, when a cemetery was established at Whitfield.

The exact number of burials at the MSA cemetery is unknown, but archaeological geophysical prospection and subsurface testing has demonstrated over 1200 graves across the cemetery area (Cureton et al., 2014). It is likely that over 6000 burials are present in the cemetery given the historical records. The MSA cemetery sample ($n = 67$) was derived from archaeological investigations of a road right-of-way and subsurface testing for a proposed garage for the University of Mississippi Medical Center. In total, 66 intact hexagonal coffin burials were identified, documented, and excavated within the road right-of-way, and one additional sample was collected during subsurface testing for the proposed parking garage. Analysis of the burials continues, but the data described here represent the analysis of the cranial and dental remains. Overall, bone preservation ranges from poor to good, but the collapse and compression of the pine coffins typically resulted in severe fragmentation of the skeletal remains. The fragmentation limited our skeletal metric and morphological observations, but dental remains are represented and are well preserved.

MATERIALS AND METHODS

Due to the high degree of fragmentation and poor preservation of the MSA skeletal assemblage, this study focused on methods of ancestry estimation using dentition, specifically dental metrics and morphological traits, and cranial macromorphoscopic traits when the cranium could be moderately reconstructed. Individuals with no dentition were excluded, reducing the sample size to 57 individuals. Sex was determined using cranial and pelvic morphology prior to assessments of ancestry in order to decrease the influence of sexual dimorphism.

Examining the asylum historical records, including death and admission records, we noted that the institutionalized population was divided into two socially defined races (white and black); therefore, a binary classification was developed using European American/White and African American/Black reference datasets. As result of this dichotomous classification, techniques like OSSA in a modified form were favored over other approaches for both cranial and dental morphological traits. In addition, Harris and Foster (2015) published an extensive dental metric reference dataset from Memphis, Tennessee that could be utilized within FORDISC 3.0 (Jantz and Ousley, 2005) for customized discriminant functions based on the measures that were available from each burial.

Reference Datasets

As previously discussed, the MSA operated in Jackson, Mississippi between 1855 and 1935. However, the dendrochronology results largely date the excavated portion of the cemetery later than 1900. In order to account for secular change, all reference datasets utilized in this study date between the late 19th and early 20th centuries. The reference datasets used for each method of ancestry estimation are described in the following.

Dental Metrics

The MSA dental metrics were referenced to a collection of dental casts taken during routine orthodontic work at the University of Tennessee, Memphis, College of Dentistry. The collection consists of maximum tooth crown dimensions of fully developed adolescent dentition who do not exhibit wear or dental modifications. A total of 126 American Black and 198 American White individuals are represented (Harris and Foster, 2015). Missing measurements for individuals were imputed with the norm package within R (RCoreTeam, 2013). Only individuals with three or fewer imputed missing measures were included in the final dataset. While the Memphis sample is the primary reference dataset, we also explore the population dichotomy presented by Pilloud et al. (2014) for the worldwide dataset developed by Hanihara (Hanihara and Ishida, 2005; Pilloud et al., 2014). Pilloud et al. (2014) grouped regional populations from the worldwide dataset into three broad geographical populations (ie, European, African, and Asian) in order to create a classification system based on evolutionary concepts to determine ancestry. The authors graciously provided access to the original dataset and we were able to import this into FORDISC 3.0 and perform a similar assessment as the Memphis sample. Classifications for the worldwide sample will be compared to the Memphis data.

Dental Morphology

The frequencies and sectioning points of 20 dental morphological traits used for this study were derived from Edgar (2013). In this study, data were derived from four locations, including (1) Case Western Reserve

University; (2) University of Tennessee, Memphis, College of Dentistry; (3) Nova Southeastern University; and (4) Economides Orthodontic Collection. The latter two collections are Hispanic collections and were not included in this project. Case Western Reserve University houses a collection of dental casts from 44 American Whites born in Cayuga County, Ohio from 1920 to 1945. The University of Tennessee, Memphis collection was described in the dental metrics section, earlier. However, the sample was reduced to 90 American Black and 101 American White individuals of the complete collection.

Cranial Macromorphoscopic Traits

Cranial macromorphoscopic trait frequencies of seven traits were used in this study as defined by Hefner (2009). These traits include anterior nasal spine, inferior nasal aperture, interorbital breadth, nasal aperture breadth, nasal bone contour, nasal overgrowth, and postbregmatic depression. The reference dataset in this study is based on Hefner (2015), which consists of 180 American Black and 100 American White individuals from the Terry Collection and 38 American Blacks and 46 American Whites from the William M. Bass Donated Skeletal Collection. In his study, Hefner also established cranial morphological trait frequencies for Hispanic individuals from the Pima County Medical Examiner's Office, but these individuals were excluded from this study. The Terry Collection represents American Blacks and Whites from the 19th and 20th centuries while the William M. Bass Donated Skeletal Collection represents a modern population.

Data Collection and Analysis

The methods for measuring maximum mesiodistal and buccolingual dimensions follow that described in Moorrees (1957) and Hillson (1996). All third molars were excluded from the analysis of the MSA assemblage due to the lack of representativeness from extraction in the University of Tennessee, Memphis collection. Dental metrics for each MSA individual were entered into FORDISC 3.0 and referenced to the dataset of American Blacks and Whites from the University of Tennessee, Memphis, College of Dentistry using the custom import feature that generates posterior and typicality probabilities. The left dental arcades were selected for analysis with measurements for right arcade being utilized only in instances of missing data within the left arcades. This allowed for specific groups, specifically Black male, Black female, White male, and White female, to be run within FORDISC 3.0 using the Stepwise Wilks analysis to calculate posterior and typicality probabilities. For example, if the individual is known to be female, we simply select only the Black female and White female groups in which to reference the target individual. This same methodology was applied to the worldwide metric dataset in order to compare the consistency of classifications between populations across the world and the regional population used in the Memphis dataset.

A total of 20 dental morphological traits were assessed using the Arizona State University Dental Anthropology System and associated reference plaques (Turner et al., 1991). The 20 traits selected for this study as well as their breakpoints were based on the study by Edgar (2013). A score was entered into Microsoft Excel for each observable trait and referenced against the trait frequencies provided by Edgar (2013). Within Microsoft Excel, a formula was created to calculate a posterior probability using Bayes' Theorem. Bayesian formula calculates the posterior probability of each ancestral group tested based on given trait frequencies for each group (Edgar, 2005).

Finally, cranial macromorphoscopics were assessed using the previously mentioned seven traits established by Hefner (2009). All observed macromorphoscopic traits were incorporated into a Bayesian classifier to calculate posterior probabilities within Microsoft Excel, as described for the dental morphological trait analysis. Hefner (2009) recommends using OSSA summed scores. However, a Bayesian classifier was utilized because OSSA summed scores require the complete set of traits to be present, which is not feasible with MSA assemblage due to the high degree of fragmentation and poor preservation.

Given that the reference datasets are derived from three published samples, which do not contain the same samples or individuals, a single classification using multiple indicator types (dental metric, dental morphology, craniometric, or cranial morphoscopic) as recommended by Hefner et al. (2014) or Lease and Sciulli (2005) could not be performed. Lease and Sciulli (2005) used logistic regression of metric and morphological traits in deciduous dentition to assess ancestry of early 20th century and modern US children. Hefner et al. (2014) use random forest modeling to assess classification rate of American Black, American White, and Hispanic individuals. For our analysis, three separate posterior probabilities were derived by various techniques (DFA or a naïve Bayesian classifier) based on the reference samples either provided by the authors of those studies (Pilloud et al., 2014; Harris and Foster, 2015) or based on published trait frequencies (Hefner, 2009; Edgar, 2013). Therefore, available posterior probabilities from the three methods of ancestry estimation (dental metrics, dental morphological traits, and cranial morphoscopic traits) were averaged by ancestral group. We are essentially producing a simple Bayes average where the various contributors are equally weighted (Subhasini et al., 2013). Ultimately, each individual is assigned to an ancestral group, either American White or American Black or indeterminate, based on the averaged posterior probability for the three utilized binary classifications. Two sectioning points were arbitrarily defined to assign ancestry. The American Black posterior probabilities are used to calculate the average. An average between 0 and 0.399 classifies the individual as American White, 0.400—0.599 as indeterminate, and 0.60—1.00 as American Black.

All posterior values were tabulated by burial and imported into R for visualization and analysis (RCoreTeam, 2013). Average posterior probabilities were calculated and the range of posterior probability values determined. Due to the limited number of cranial macromorphoscopic trait assessments, plots were limited to dental metric and morphology posterior comparisons. As an exploratory visual aid, histograms of average posterior probabilities and the range of posterior probabilities were generated. Finally, average posterior probabilities were linked to the burial distribution map. The average posterior probability value was assessed for spatial autocorrelation using a Moran's I statistic to determine if the pattern of average values is dispersed, random, or clustered. If the pattern is clustered then it may suggest that the cemetery was segregated by socially defined race.

RESULTS

Of the 57 burials with dental remains, all individuals could be assessed for metric and morphological observations. However, only eight individuals could be assessed for cranial macromorphoscopic traits. Table 15.1 provides a breakdown of the posterior probabilities and the average posterior probabilities for the sample. Average posterior probabilities ranged from 0.172 to 1 with a mean of 0.685.

Fig. 15.1 provides a histogram of the averaged posterior probabilities. Using the arbitrary classification ranges previously defined, a total of 40 individuals were classified as American Black, 11 as American White, and 6 as indeterminate ancestry. If more conservative sectioning points were used, the number of indeterminate estimates would have increased. For example, if the sectioning point of American White is shifted to 0.333 rather than 0.399 and the American Black point is shifted to 0.666 rather than 0.600, the

Table 15.1 Classification of the MSA Burials

			Memphis Metrics		Dental Morphology	Cranial Morphology	Average	Pilloud et al. (2014)	
Burial	Sex	Ancestry	Posterior Prob	AA_Typ	Posterior Prob	Posterior Prob	Posterior Prob	Posterior Prob	AA_Typ
1	F	AA	0.551	0.943	0.952	0.522	0.675	0.784	0.722
2	F	EA	0.200	0.229	0.427		0.314	0.098	0.376
3	M	AA	0.994	0.662	0.980	0.777	0.917	0.973	0.063
4	F	AA	0.995	0.457	0.973	0.934	0.967	0.751	0.028
5	F	AA	0.830	0.555	0.846	0.934	0.870	0.841	0.525
6	M	AA	0.993	0.916	0.776	0.975	0.915	0.904	0.307
7	M	AA	0.735	0.778	0.851	–	0.793	0.208	0.737
8	M	EA	0.307	0.006	0.347	–	0.327	0.474	0.649
9	F	AA	0.997	0.410	0.981	–	0.989	0.996	0.213
10	F	AA	0.827	0.870	0.621	–	0.724	0.769	0.314
11	F	AA	0.813	0.924	0.741	–	0.777	0.131	0.093
12	M	AA	0.755	0.582	0.577	–	0.666	0.854	0.453
13	M	AA	0.808	0.610	0.849	–	0.829	0.935	0.080
14	M	AA	0.918	0.430	0.999	–	0.959	0.939	0.414
15	U	EA	0.039	0.897	0.402	–	0.220	0.264	0.501
16	M	IND	0.619	0.632	0.408	–	0.513	0.658	0.483
17	M	EA	0.109	0.230	0.288	–	0.198	0.926	0.927
18	U	AA	0.385	0.153	0.987	–	0.686	0.393	0.330
19	F	IND	0.813	0.731	0.356	–	0.584	0.888	0.337
21	U	AA	0.991	0.783	0.440	–	0.715	0.953	0.554
22	U	EA	0.154	0.032	0.189	–	0.172	0.239	0.026
24	F	AA	0.972	0.384	0.605	–	0.789	0.985	0.044
25	F	AA	0.916	0.729	0.974	–	0.945	0.959	0.702
28	M	EA	0.330	0.158	0.214	–	0.272	0.915	0.859
30	F	AA	0.785	0.202	0.792	–	0.789	0.270	0.241
32	M	IND	0.267	0.412	0.760	–	0.513	0.302	0.568

33	M	AA	0.786	0.336	0.948	–	0.867	0.344	0.696
34	M	AA	0.819	0.112	0.950	–	0.885	0.825	0.287
35	F	AA	0.725	0.743	0.682	–	0.704	0.831	0.725
36	M	AA	0.827	0.850	0.716	–	0.772	0.434	0.213
37	F	AA	0.538	0.598	0.963	–	0.750	0.079	0.136
38	M	AA	0.894	0.931	1.000	–	0.947	0.692	0.555
39	M	AA	0.834	0.859	0.879	0.770	0.828	0.909	0.988
40	F	AA	0.053	0.477	0.933	0.934	0.640	0.483	0.277
41	M	AA	0.986	0.784	1.000	–	0.993	0.950	0.063
43	M	EA	0.296	0.092	0.302	–	0.399	0.516	0.330
45	U	AA	0.644	0.558	0.998	–	0.821	0.971	0.096
46	M	AA	1.000	0.482	0.999	–	1.000	0.968	0.153
47	U	AA	0.766	0.806	0.817	–	0.791	0.994	0.499
48	F	AA	0.582	0.897	0.772	–	0.677	0.987	0.358
49	M	AA	0.490	0.707	0.636	0.772	0.633	0.163	0.205
50	F	AA	0.999	0.843	0.626	–	0.812	0.999	0.156
51	F	EA	0.167	0.034	0.230	–	0.199	0.171	0.065
52	F	AA	0.952	0.715	0.964	–	0.958	0.935	0.363
53	F	EA	0.297	0.649	0.452	–	0.375	0.210	0.739
54	U	AA	0.813	0.664	0.988	–	0.901	0.350	0.035
55	F	EA	0.255	0.747	0.452	–	0.354	0.966	0.129
56	F	EA	0.060	0.068	0.285	–	0.173	0.072	0.015
57	M	AA	0.998	0.126	0.891	–	0.944	0.821	0.603
58	U	AA	0.958	0.899	0.535	–	0.747	0.849	0.823
59	M	AA	0.957	0.218	0.574	–	0.766	0.048	0.044
60	U	AA	0.816	0.059	0.717	–	0.766	0.271	0.061
61	F	IND	0.420	0.083	0.589	–	0.505	0.910	0.447
62	U	IND	0.636	0.499	0.327	–	0.481	0.756	0.793
63	F	AA	0.989	0.825	0.992	–	0.990	0.979	0.355
64	M	AA	0.598	0.912	0.881	–	0.740	0.785	0.839
65	M	IND	0.311	0.655	0.838	–	0.575	0.624	0.152

Individuals without dentition are not represented.

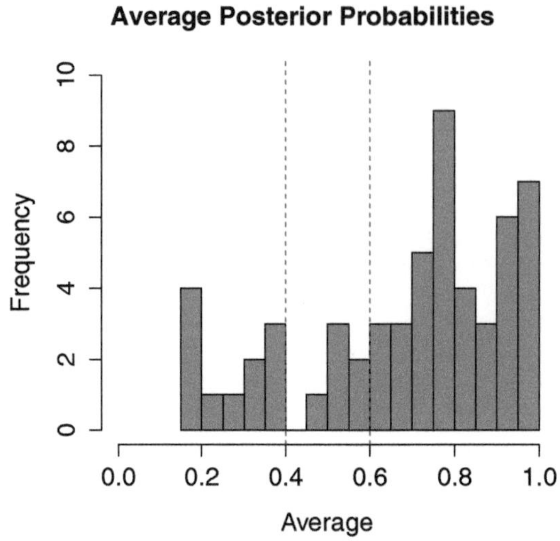

FIGURE 15.1

Histogram of average posterior probabilities for the MSA sample with sectioning lines at 0.4 and 0.6. Individuals below 0.4 ($n = 11$) were considered American White and individuals above 0.6 ($n = 40$) were considered American Black. The remaining individuals were considered indeterminate ($n = 6$).

ancestry classifications would be 37 American Black, 11 American White, and 9 indeterminate individuals. Conversely, a less conservative approach would decrease the number of indeterminate estimates. Had we set a 50% threshold, then the ancestry ratio would have been 45 American Black to 12 American White assessments with no indeterminate individuals.

The classification rates varied between methods. The dental metric analysis using the Memphis dataset classified 36 individuals as American Black, 15 as American White, and 6 as indeterminate. Dental morphological analysis classified 38 individuals as American Black, equivalent to the dental metric analysis, and 8 as American White. The number of individuals with indeterminate ancestry increased from the dental metric assessment to 11 individuals. The final method of ancestry determination, cranial macromorphoscopic traits, estimated seven American Black and no American White individuals and one indeterminate estimate. All methods found the highest classification to be American Black with various rates of White and indeterminate ancestry. Dental morphology established the highest rate of individuals who could not be classified.

The range of posterior probability values for any one individual spanned from 0.001 to 0.881 with an average range of 0.213, which suggests general agreement between multiple assessments. Fig. 15.2 is a histogram of the posterior probability ranges by burial and clearly shows a positive skew (1.23) with a majority of the values between 0 and 0.25. Two cases have extreme ranges, which are greater than 0.6. Burial 40 is the individual with the highest range with the dental metric assessment (0.053) divergent from the dental morphology (0.933) and cranial morphology (0.934) posteriors. Burial 18 is the other extreme range with only dental morphology (0.987) and dental metric (0.385) assessments available. A closer examination of the dental metric and dental morphology posterior probabilities provides some insight into the problematic cases. Fig. 15.3 presents the two posteriors plotted with a central axis representing a one-

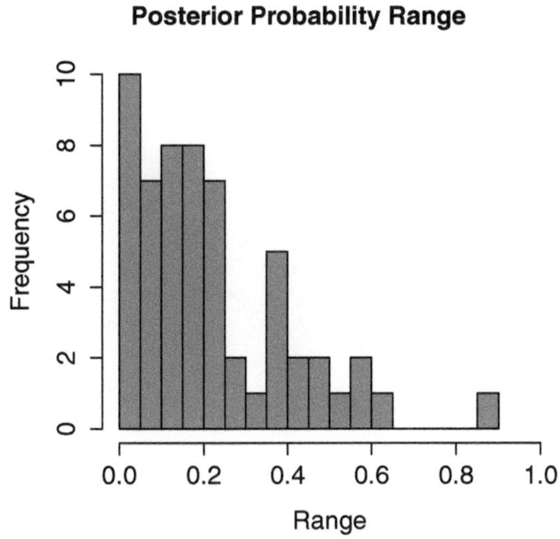

FIGURE 15.2

Histogram of the posterior probability range by individual.

to-one relationship for the probability values. Two symmetrical triangles represent the areas where the posterior probability pairs are problematic. Burials 40 and 18 are clearly visible in the plot but additional burials fall in these areas including burials 1, 19, 21, 32, 37, 58, and 65. The burials primarily classify as American Black ($n = 6$), and the remaining three burials are indeterminate. Only two of these individuals (Burials 1 and 40) have cranial macromorphoscopic traits to contribute to the average posterior probability. The individuals with disparate probabilities and who fall within the two triangles on the margins of the plot on average have a similar number of available measurements as the other burials (Student's $t = 0.489$, $df = 55$, $p = .627$). Thus, the different posteriors are not a result of lower number of data points available for their assessment. Overall, most posteriors ($n = 48$) correlate well and support the individual ancestry assessments.

As a final comparison, we examine the method presented by Pilloud et al. (2014) using Hanihara's worldwide database. For their analysis, the authors provided two-step discriminant function equations divided by sex. In the first set, the European sample is compared to a combined African and Asian sample. Using this same dichotomy, we imported the provided dataset into FORDISC 3.0 and performed a similar classification of each burial as we had done with Harris' Memphis dataset. The worldwide database reference determined 36 individuals to be African, 17 European, and 4 with indeterminate ancestry. Fig. 15.4 presents a histogram of the absolute difference between the two posterior probability estimates. There are four samples with extreme values (>0.6 difference); once again these do not distinguish themselves from the other burials based on the available metrics. Overall, the metric posterior probabilities from these two analyses have a low but significant correlation ($r = 0.469$, $p < .0003$). A scatterplot of the two classification probabilities (Fig. 15.5) shows the extreme values but for the most part posteriors appear to align. In fact when the four extreme values are removed, the correlation coefficient increases substantially to 0.644 ($p < .0001$). It is worth noting that the worldwide database includes a large number individuals from Asian populations while the Memphis dataset is only American Black and American White populations.

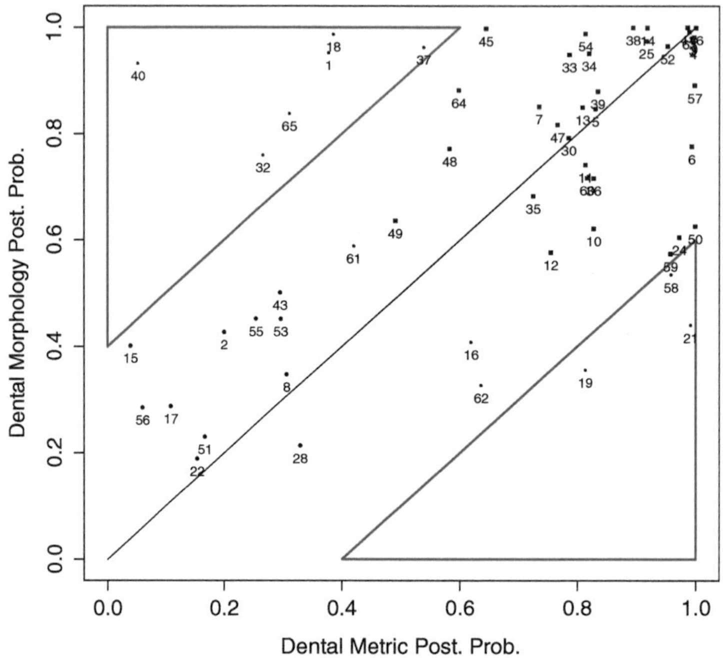

FIGURE 15.3

Posterior probability comparison by burial. The opposite triangles represent areas where the posterior probability differs by 0.4 or greater, and the line represents 1:1 agreement of the two posterior probability measures.

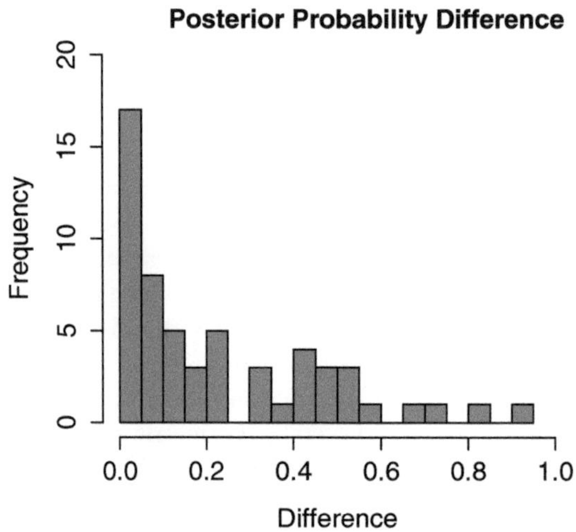

FIGURE 15.4

Posterior probability difference between the Memphis dataset assessment and the Hanihara dataset assessment.

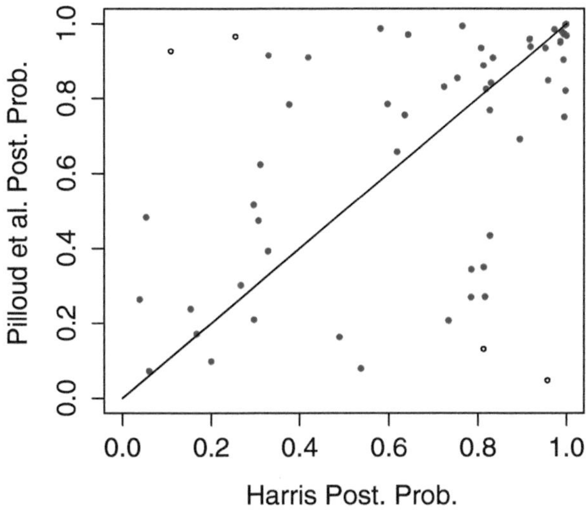

FIGURE 15.5

A comparison of the Memphis dataset classifications to the Hanihara worldwide dichotomy classification. The unfilled markers represent the four extreme values from the histogram. The *line* represents the one-to-one correspondence and not the linear fit of the data.

Additionally, based on the MSA historical records, the likelihood of encountering an individual of Asian descent is near zero. Therefore, further analysis was conducted to remove the Asian population from the worldwide database to determine whether discrepancy between reference datasets is driving the low correlation of the posterior probabilities. The modified dataset was imported into FORDISC 3.0 and the burials were classified in the same manner as the previous analyses. Overall, the classification rates changed little from those established with the Asian populations included. The results estimated 37 African and 19 European individuals and 1 of indeterminate ancestry. However, it must be noted that while the classifications between the dataset with and without the Asian populations are significantly correlated ($r = 0.800$, $p < .0001$) with an average posterior difference of only 0.146 (s.d. = 0.164), six individuals contained inconsistent ancestry estimations. When compared to the Memphis dataset, the correlation is similar to the previous assessment with a low but significant correlation ($r = 0.514$, $p < .0001$). A scatterplot of the comparison of posterior probabilities is provided in Fig. 15.6.

Bridging the average posterior probability values back to the MSA cemetery layout allows an examination of the cemetery structure. Based on recent dendrochronological analysis of the coffin wood (Harley, Personal Communication), it is known that the excavated section of the cemetery postdates 1910. During this time we know from the Sanborn Insurance maps that the institution maintained segregated wards by sex and socially defined race. Based on this knowledge, we wanted to examine the pattern of interments at the cemetery. A map of the posterior probability values by burial is presented in Fig. 15.7. The pattern appears random with individuals classified as American White and American Black occurring across the excavation. In order to test this visual assessment an inspection of spatial autocorrelation was performed on the average posterior probability values in order to obtain the Moran's Index statistic within Spatial Analyst extension of ESRI ArcGIS 10.2 (ESRI, 2014). The resulting Moran's

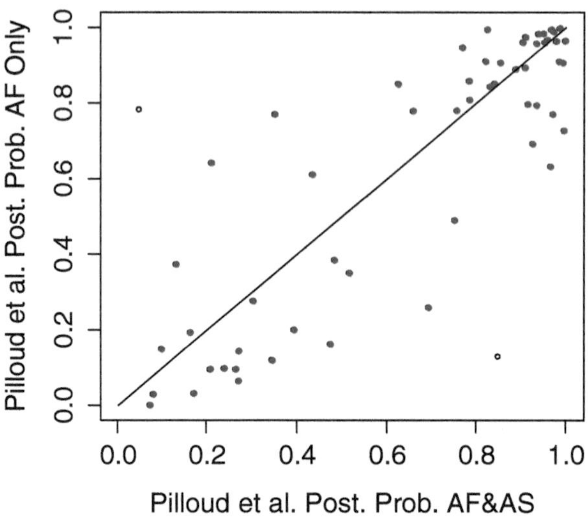

FIGURE 15.6

Posterior probability comparison of the complete Hanihara worldwide dichotomy (Europeans vs. All Other Samples) classification with the European/African population dichotomy. The line represents the one-to-one correspondence and not the linear fit of the data.

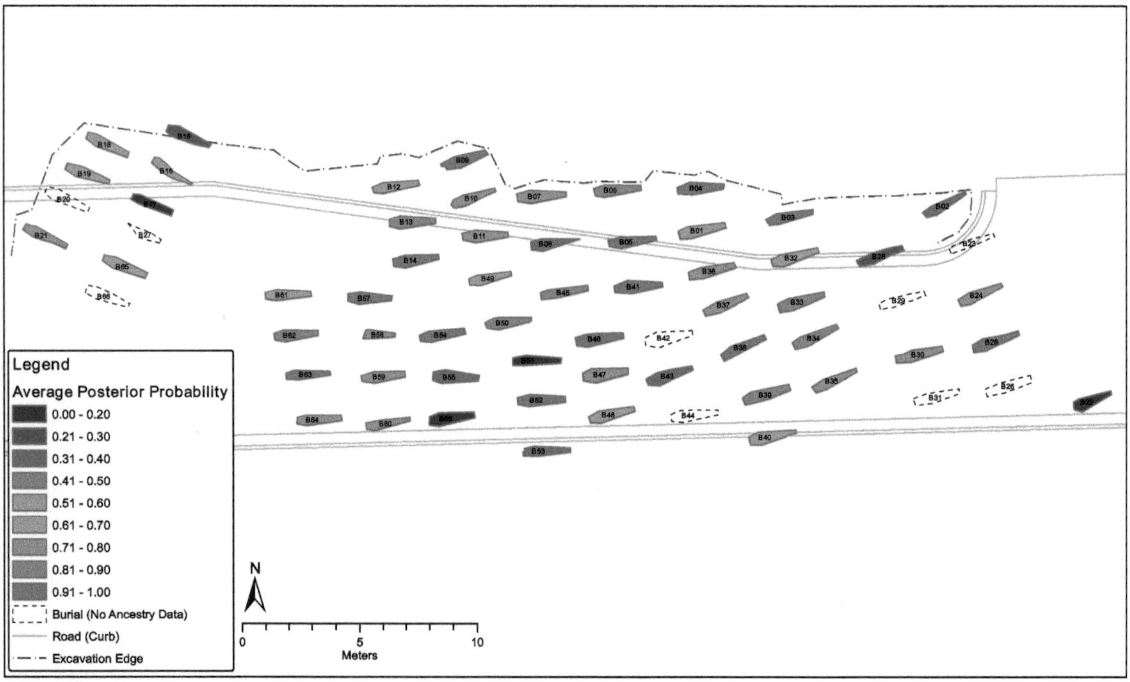

FIGURE 15.7

Average posterior probably assigned to coffins within the excavated burial area of the MSA.

Index was 0.087 ($p = .125$), indicating a random distribution of posterior probability scores across the excavated cemetery area. Although the excavation block was small, it appears that individuals were buried at death without regard to ancestry. So individuals were treated differently in death as compared to life in the asylum. This pattern is consistent with the Greenwood Cemetery located in downtown Jackson, Mississippi, which remained integrated throughout its long history (Gordon, 1984).

DISCUSSION

The MSA burial sample represents an important skeletal collection for the history of the State of Mississippi. Although the graves are unidentified, they provide a critical record of an institutionalized population, which originated from communities across Mississippi. Ancestry assessments employing an averaged posterior probability provide a means to include available classifications from numerous reference samples. The posterior values per individual are relatively consistent, but a few burials present disparate values. In addition, the Memphis dataset appears to provide good classifications relative to the other indicators (cranial macromorphoscopic and dental morphology), but the Hanihara worldwide sample produces similar posterior values as the Memphis dataset. For the individuals identified through this analysis with divergent posterior probabilities based on dental metrics, it is anticipated that the postcranial metrics will be examined to see if they can provide additional evidence to clarify our classifications; however, such assessments will be limited given the typically poor preservation of the MSA postcranial remains.

The classifications reported here provide a basis for further analysis of the MSA sample, including paleopathological and demographic comparisons. Interestingly, a majority of the burials classify as American Black. While this is not unexpected, the partially transcribed discharge by death records and biennial reports for the asylum indicate greater African American mortality. Indeterminate ancestry assessments may relate to a greater level of admixture across the American South. DNA analysis has shown that modern African American populations in the southern United States display as high as 22% European genetic ancestry (Parra et al., 1998; value for New Orleans, Louisiana). Currently, the MSA admission and discharge by death records are being transcribed and once these are complete we will have a better understanding of the structure of the patient population. Preliminary results from 1907 to 1923 suggest that American Black patients did have higher mortality rates during the first 5 years of institutionalization as compared to their White counterparts, but it is unclear if this corresponded with a higher number of deaths. The higher percentage of Black individuals in the burial sample may also point to socioeconomic factors contributing to their burial at the asylum. It may be that families were not notified of their relative's death or they did not have the financial resources to retrieve their deceased family member. Finally, there could be a spatial sampling bias, and the excavation block may happen to be an area where American Blacks were preferentially buried.

CONCLUSIONS

The full osteological analysis of the MSA burial sample is underway, but the appropriate assessment of ancestry is a critical first step in understanding the context of this skeletal collection. The use of multiple techniques to classify the burials has produced several posterior probability values. Averaging these values per burial has provided a way to equally weight the available indicators and examine the pattern of posteriors across the sample. Ideally, multiple indicators would be integrated into a single classification system like those presented by Hefner et al. (2014) and Lease and Sciulli (2005). We are currently pursuing the individual dental morphology data for the Memphis sample and will reassess the sample based on a combined dental reference dataset, which will include both metric and morphological observations. Based on our analysis the MSA burial sample is primarily of African ancestry with 40 individuals (70.2%) classifying as American Black. Eleven individuals (19.3%) are of European ancestry and classify as American White. The remaining six individuals (10.5%) could not be specifically classified as American White or Black. One additional finding of this research supports the conclusion that the cemetery was not segregated, suggesting that burials were placed on an as-needed basis without regard to ancestry.

References

Cureton, T., Harris, S., Herrmann, N.P., Warner, M., Johnshon, J.K., 2014. Archaeological Survey of Site 22Hi859: A Historic Cemetery on the University of Mississippi Medical Center Campus. Jackson, Mississippi (Report prepared for University of Mississippi Medical Center, Construction Office No. CAR 2014-01). University of Mississippi and Mississippi State University, Oxford, MS.

Edgar, H.J., 2005. Prediction of race using characteristics of dental morphology. Journal of Forensic Sciences 50 (2), 269–273.

Edgar, H.J., 2013. Estimation of ancestry using dental morphological characteristics. Journal of Forensic Sciences 58 (s1), S3–S8.

ESRI, 2014. ArcGIS 10.2.2 for Desktop. Environmental Systems Research Institute, Redlands, California.

Gordon, P.A., 1984. Greenwood Cemetery, City Cemetery, Old Cemetery, Jackson, Mississippi. Jackson Mississippi Department of Archives and History 31. This is a National Register of Historic Places Inventory Nomination for the Greenwood Cemetery, Jackson, Mississippi by Ana Gordon dated April 1984 and Certified by the State Historic Preservation Officer on November 8, 1984. Submitted to United States Department of the Interior, National Park Service.

Hanihara, T., Ishida, H., 2005. Metric dental variation of major human populations. American Journal of Physical Anthropology 128, 287–298.

Harris, E.F., Foster, C.L., 2015. Size matters: discrimination between American Blacks and Whites, males and females, using tooth crown dimensions. In: Berg, G.E., Ta'ala, S.C. (Eds.), Biological Affinity in Forensic Identification of Human Skeletal Remains. CRC Press, Boca Raton, FL, pp. 209–238.

Hefner, J.T., Ousley, S.D., 2014. Statistical classification methods for estimating ancestry using morphoscopic traits. Journal of Forensic Sciences 59 (4), 883–890.

Hefner, J.T., Spradley, M.K., Anderson, B.E., 2014. Ancestry assessment using random forest modeling. Journal of Forensic Sciences 59 (3), 583–598.

Hefner, J.T., Pilloud, M.A., Black, C.J., Anderson, B.E., 2015. Morphoscopic trait expression in "Hispanic" populations. Journal of Forensic Sciences 60 (5), 1135–1139.

Hefner, J.T., 2009. Cranial nonmetric variation and estimating ancestry. Journal of Forensic Sciences 54 (5), 985–995.

Hefner, J.T., 2015. Cranial morphoscopic traits and the assessment of American black, American white, and Hispanic ancestry. In: Berg, G.E., Ta'ala, S.C. (Eds.), Biological Affinity in Forensic Identification of Human Skeletal Remains. CRC Press, Boca Raton, FL, pp. 27–42.

Hillson, S., 1996. Dental Anthropology. Cambridge University Press, Cambridge.

Jantz, R., Ousley, S., 2005. FORDISC 3: Computerized Forensic Discriminant Functions. The University of Tennessee, Knoxville.

Lease, L.R., Sciulli, P.W., 2005. Brief communication: discrimination between European-American and African-American children based on deciduous dental metrics and morphology. American Journal of Physical Anthropology 126 (1), 56–60.

Milner, J., n.d. Whitfield Marks 100th Anniversary. Clarion-Ledger, Jackson.

Moorrees, C.F.A., 1957. The Aleut Dentition. Harvard University Press, Cambridge, Massachusetts.

Parra, E.J., Marcini, A., Akey, J., et al., 1998. Estimating African American Admixture Proportions by Use of Population-Specific Alleles. The American Journal of Human Genetics 63 (6), 1839–1851.

Pilloud, M.A., Hefner, J.T., Hanihara, T., Hayashi, A., 2014. The use of tooth crown measurements in the assessment of ancestry. Journal of Forensic Sciences 59 (6), 1493–1501.

RCoreTeam, 2013. R: A Language and Environment for Statistical Computing. R Foundation for Statistical Computing, Vienna, Austria.

Sanborn Fire Insurance Map, 1895. Sheet 12. Mississippi, Jackson.

Subhasini, P., Ane, B.K., Roller, D., Krishnaveni, M., 2013. Intelligent classifiers fusion for enhancing recognition of genes and protein pattern of hereditary diseases. In: Information Resources Management Association (Ed.), Bioinformatics: Concepts, Methodologies, Tools, and Applications. IGI Global, Hershey, PA, USA, pp. 1570–1598.

Turner, C.G., Nichol, C.R., Scott, G.R., 1991. Scoring procedures for key morphological traits of the permanent dentition: the Arizona State University dental anthropology system. In: Kelley, M.A., Larsen, C.S. (Eds.), Advances in Dental Anthropology. Wiley-Liss, New York, pp. 13–31.

CHAPTER

Biological Distance Analysis, Cranial Morphoscopic Traits, and Ancestry Assessment in Forensic Anthropology

16

J.T. Hefner
Michigan State University, East Lansing, MI, United States

CHAPTER OUTLINE HEAD

Introduction 301
Materials and Methods 302
  Sample Descriptions 303
  Canonical Analysis of the Principal Coordinates 304
Results 306
Discussion 313
Acknowledgments 314
References 314

INTRODUCTION

Forensic anthropology and morphoscopic trait analysis are rarely considered in biodistance literature, in part because forensic anthropology is a field primarily concerned with an individual rather than with populations, but also because forensic anthropologists rarely incorporate biodistance measures in the analysis of morphoscopic trait data. Likewise, differences between the traits used in biodistance studies (traditional cranial nonmetric data) and forensic analyses (morphoscopic traits) have resulted in hesitancy on the part of forensic anthropologists to apply biodistance measures to morphoscopic trait data.

Traditional cranial nonmetric, or discrete, trait data (covered in detail in this volume by Pink et al., Chapter 5, and Pink, Chapter 11) differ significantly from the morphoscopic (macromorphoscopic) traits used by forensic anthropologists to assess ancestry. Following Buikstra and Ubelaker (1996), cranial nonmetric traits are "dichotomous, discontinuous, epigenetic traits; nonpathological variations of skeletal tissues that can be better classified as present or absent (or as a point on a morphological gradient; e.g., small to large) rather than quantified by a measurement." These traits fall into one of five major categories, including (1) extrasutural bone (eg, Inca bone); (2) proliferative ossifications (eg, pterygo-alar bridging); (3) ossification failure (eg, septal aperture); (4) suture variation (eg, metopic suture); and (5) foramina variation (eg, zygomaticofacial foramen number) (Buikstra and Ubelaker, 1996).

Noting a contrast between these traits and the traits used by forensic anthropologists, Ousley and Hefner (2005) applied the term macromorphoscopic traits to those morphologies used in forensic

Biological Distance Analysis. http://dx.doi.org/10.1016/B978-0-12-801966-5.00016-0

anthropological research that are distinct from the discrete traits just described. Macromorphoscopic traits are quasicontinuous variables of the cranium reflected as soft-tissue differences in the living. Hefner (2009) simplified Ousley and Hefner's term to morphoscopic traits, while maintaining the original characterization of the variables. Morphoscopic traits are subdivided into five classes: (1) assessing bone shape (eg, nasal bone structure); (2) bony feature morphology (eg, inferior nasal aperture morphology); (3) suture shape (eg, zygomaticomaxillary suture); (4) presence/absence data (eg, postbregmatic depression); and (5) feature prominence/protrusion (eg, anterior nasal spine) (Hefner, 2009).

Of course, morphoscopic traits have been used broadly in typological trait lists (eg, Rhine, 1990) for the assessment of ancestry in forensic settings. Morphoscopic traits, generally offered as character states to undergraduate and graduate students to support the assessment of ancestry, are rarely, if ever, quantified in any meaningful way beyond the expertise of the individual forensic anthropologist. To significantly reduce the inherent subjectivity in scoring these traits for ancestry, a system was developed by Hefner (2007, 2009). Although Hefner (2009) advocated and modernized this standardization, Hooton (1936) was the first to recognize this inherent subjectivity in a morphoscopic approach and he recommended sweeping changes in the collection and analysis of that data. Unfortunately, his recommendations were overlooked for nearly 50 years. Finnegan and McGuire (1979) tackled morphoscopic trait analysis (they also included several cranial nonmetric traits) using relatively modern statistical methods, including discriminant function analysis and the Rubison Procedure. Even their work was not adopted by the forensic anthropology community, most likely because the statistics were too challenging for many practitioners at that time.

The purpose of this chapter is to demonstrate the applicability of morphoscopic trait data in biodistance studies and to fill a gap in the analysis of that data in a forensic setting. While Hefner and Ousley (2014) and Hefner et al. (2014) demonstrated the applicability of various statistical methods for morphoscopic trait analysis, this chapter builds on that earlier work and establishes morphoscopic traits in a broader, population-based analysis. While the focus is predominately establishing the ancestry of an unknown individual in a forensic setting, as with any biodistance analysis, the relationships between the populations used as reference samples must be understood prior to the classification of an individual. Therefore, between-group variability in morphoscopic trait expression is first explored using canonical analysis of principal coordinates (CAP), an approach first advocated by Anderson (2002) and Anderson and Willis (2003). CAP provides constrained and unconstrained ordinations that maximize between-group (a priori) differences and tests for no differences in multivariate location among groups using a trace statistic of canonical discriminant analysis and the associated *p*-value with permutations (Anderson and Willis, 2003).

Following that analysis, the applicability of morphoscopic trait data for the assessment of ancestry using a classification function is demonstrated. Morphoscopic trait data are incorporated into several discriminant function analyses and the models are assessed using cross-validation procedures.

MATERIALS AND METHODS

Morphoscopic trait data for 728 individuals were obtained from the Macromorphoscopic Databank (NIJ, 2015-DN-BX-K012). Seven morphoscopic traits were utilized in subsequent analyses. These include the anterior nasal spine, inferior nasal aperture width, interorbital breadth, nasal aperture width, nasal bone structure, nasal overgrowth, and postbregmatic depression (Table 16.1). These traits were previously

Table 16.1 Morphoscopic Traits (With Accompanying Abbreviations) Used in the Current Study	
Morphoscopic Trait	
Anterior nasal spine (ANS)	Nasal bone contour (NBC)
Inferior nasal aperture (INA)	Nasal overgrowth (NO)
Interorbital breadth (IOB)	Postbregmatic depression (PBD)
Nasal aperture width (NAW)	Zygomaticomaxillary suture (ZS)

defined and illustrated by Hefner (2009). All data were collected using the Macromorphoscopic module in Osteoware (Smithsonian Institution, 2010), a computer program for the collection of osteological data freely available (http://osteoware.si.edu/). No missing data are present and no individuals with pathology or trauma are included in this analysis. Table 16.2 provides a breakdown of each sample by ancestry and sex.

Sample Descriptions

Samples representative of the ancestry groups most frequently encountered in forensic anthropology cases in the United States are used in all subsequent analyses. The American Black and American White samples comprise 20th century individuals from the William M. Bass Donated Skeletal Collection housed at the University of Tennessee, Department of Anthropology, Knoxville, TN. The Asian sample comprises modern individuals from Japan, Thailand, and North America. These data are supplemented with additional samples from the National Museum of Natural History, to include a Japanese sample from the Tokyo prefecture donated by Tokyo Imperial University to the Smithsonian Institution and Chinese crania obtained by Hrdlička from a cannery cemetery in Karluk, Alaska. All Hispanic data ($n = 39$) were obtained from the Pima County Office of the Medical Examiner, in Tucson, Arizona, which houses and identifies unidentified border crossers using a "pre-established profile…that indicates the decedent was engaged in the undocumented crossing of [the U.S.] southern border" (Anderson, 2008, p. 12). As such, these individuals pooled into one broad category: Hispanic. Justification for this pooling is provided in Birkby et al. (2008), who demonstrate the efficacy of the model used in that office.

Table 16.2 Sample Distribution, by Ancestry and Sex

Group	Female	Male	Unknown	Total
American Black	132	149	0	281
American White	110	110	0	220
Asian	31	41	0	72
Hispanic	37	101	17	155
Total	**310**	**401**	**17**	**728**

Canonical Analysis of the Principal Coordinates

Legendre and Legendre (1998) first proposed a canonical discriminant analysis performed on the transformed values of the principal coordinates. In short, a CAP applies a principal coordinate analysis using any one of several distance measures (Anderson and Willis, 2003), which is essentially a transformation of categorical variables into continuous, normally distributed variables. In that way, the CAP method is highly effective for dealing with morphoscopic data and enables classification and visualization of the groups in a manner approximating craniometric analyses. The following mathematical description of the CAP method is a summarization of Anderson and Willis's (2003) treatment of the same.

Consider an $N \times p$ matrix (**Y**) comprising morphoscopic trait data for a population, where $N =$ number of individuals and $p =$ the number of morphoscopic traits. Consider also an $N \times q$ matrix (**X**) representing the populations. CAP performs a nonparametric canonical analysis for the effect of **X**, if any, on **Y** using a distance measure. Since **X** contains predictor (explanatory) variables, the result is a generalized discriminant analysis.

The first step in a CAP analysis is to calculate a distance matrix. So, let $\mathbf{D} = (d_{ij})$ be an $(N \times N)$ distance matrix calculated from trait values from **Y**, using distance measure, **J**. Then we allow $\mathbf{A} = (a_{ij}) = \left(-1/2d_{ij}^2\right)$. Now we calculate Gower's (1966) centered matrix (**G**) by centering the elements of **A**:

$$\mathbf{G} = \left(\mathbf{I} - \left(\frac{1}{N}\right)1 \cdot 1'\right)\mathbf{A}\left(\mathbf{I} - \left(\frac{1}{N}\right)1 \cdot 1'\right) \tag{16.1}$$

where 1 is a column of 1's the length of N and **I** is an identity matrix in the form $(N \times N)$. Decomposing matrix **G** into component eigenvalues and corresponding orthonormal eigenvectors, we get **Q**. A subset of these eigenvectors ($\boldsymbol{m}$) is then selected to form a matrix ($\mathbf{Q}_m$) for the canonical analysis. To avoid overfitting the model, $\boldsymbol{m}$ is kept small relative to N. To avoid this issue and issues of subjectivity in the selection of $\boldsymbol{m}$, the derived diagnostic information for appropriate dimensionality recommended by Anderson (2002) was used for the successive canonical analyses. Next, we calculate the influence, or hat, matrix which is idempotent; thus by definition, $\mathbf{H}^2 = \mathbf{HH} = \mathbf{H}$. So, for our purposes the hat matrix is

$$\mathbf{H} = \mathbf{X}\left[\mathbf{X}'\mathbf{X}\right]^{-1}\mathbf{X}' \qquad (16.2$$

[which Anderson (2002) attributes to Johnson and Wichern (1992)]. We can now calculate the canonical test statistic as the trace:

$$tr\left(\mathbf{Q}_m'\mathbf{H}\mathbf{Q}_m\right) \tag{16.3}$$

Two issues should be addressed: (1) choosing the number of appropriate axes $\boldsymbol{m}$, and (2) selecting the most appropriate distance/dissimilarity measure for the analysis. Anderson and Willis (2003) consider the selection of the number of principal coordinate (PCO) axes retained to be one of the most fundamental issues in a CAP analysis. If the number of axes is too small, then pertinent information contained in the data may be lost; if the number is too large, overfitting the data to the model may occur. To remedy this, they suggest increasing the value of $\boldsymbol{m}$ until the residual error or the misclassification rate (for generalized discriminant functions) is minimized. In addition, Anderson and Willis (2003) suggest that the selected $\boldsymbol{m}$ axes should explain at least 60% of the variation in the dataset, but should never reach 100%, as would be the case for an overfit to the model.

The second issue is only briefly discussed by Anderson and Willis (2003), who suggest using a methodological approach similar to that used for the selection of PCOs. They analyze their datasets using multiple distance measures and then plot the proportion of correct allocations against the number of axes (1-misclassification). The measure that provides the highest proportion correct using the lowest value m provides the best fitting model. At any rate, the authors believe that multiple dissimilarity measures should be used to explore various aspects of the dataset. An example may clarify this issue: the Chi-square metric highlights compositional rather than abundance information in the dataset, whereas Bray—Curtis dissimilarities highlight relative abundance information. In a sense, both types of information may be important, particularly when dealing with morphoscopic traits across populations. Which variables comprise Europeans or what is the proportional distribution of an inferior nasal morphology score of 2? When establishing a model to answer questions like these, each dissimilarity measure may provide information not captured by another. Underlying assumptions about the data should always be considered when selecting a distance/dissimilarity measure, but one is not automatically selected over another because of possible violations.

The Euclidean distance measure is usually used with continuous variables and is defined as the shortest distance between two points. The calculation of the Euclidean distance is similar to the Pythagorean distance (a straight line connecting A to B). The Manhattan Block distance is suitable for use with discreet data (although it is not restricted to just that type of data) and is calculated as whole units (eg, three units may equal three individuals, etc.). The Canberra distance is usually reserved for nonnegative variables only. This distance measure sums the ratios between corresponding values and accounts for not only the distance between the two points but also their relationship to an origin (0,0). The Chi-square metric computes distances based on compositional data obtained from contingency table profiles (the computed percentages for the response variables and each category) and is extremely useful for visualizing patterns, relative dispersions, and total variance within a dataset (Hefner and Ousley, 2006). The Chi-square distance measure is likely the most appropriate measure for use with categorical, nonmetric cranial traits. Most importantly, the distance measure selected for analysis should be robust and capable of emphasizing patterns in the dataset. There are many ways to calculate the distance between two points in multidimensional space and, of the multiple distance measures to choose from, one or several measures may provide classification rates that meet the criterion necessary for a particular research paradigm.

Second, the CAP method accounts for variable correlations, unlike other statistics (eg, naïve Bayesian) that assume all response variables are independent. This is particularly important in light of earlier research by Hefner (2003), who demonstrated intertrait correlations between morphoscopic variables. By accounting for the correlative structure in the response matrix, significant patterns in the data set may be elucidated, particularly with regard to a priori labels. The complex relationship of morphoscopic traits, environment, genetics, and head form should and can be explored more thoroughly if the interrelationships of the data are properly understood.

The final advantage of the CAP method is that unknown individuals can be assigned to a group through a generalized discriminant analysis (Anderson and Willis, 2003). This is particularly useful to forensic anthropologists who seek to identify the ancestry of an unknown skeleton using morphoscopic traits. Although traditional discriminant function analysis can produce admirable results using categorical variables (Hefner and Ousley, 2014), the underlying assumptions of multivariate normality and equal variance-covariance may not be met. Krzanowski (2002) reviews the use of categorical data in multivariate discriminant analysis and acknowledges that underlying assumptions will be violated, but he also points out that the method may be appropriate for descriptive purposes and as an exploratory method. However, the CAP method circumvents this issue by transforming data values from categorical variables to principal coordinate scores; in a sense, the data are changed from categorical responses to continuous variables (Anderson and Willis, 2003).

RESULTS

Frequency distribution data (by population) are presented in Table 16.3. All traits varied significantly between groups ($p < 0.05$) but no statistically significant differences were noted between males and females. Therefore, all subsequent analyses incorporate pooled male/female data. No data transformations were necessary and the data does not need to be standardized. An initially multivariate analysis of the data utilized the Chi-square distance measure between all pairs of observations, followed by an unconstrained ordination using the principal coordinates on the similarity matrix. The first two axes explained slightly over 60% of the variability in the matrix. A scatterplot of these data (Fig. 16.1) demonstrates few significant differences between groups (a high degree of overlap), a pattern also observed in several other unconstrained analyses. However, categorized histograms (Fig. 16.2 is one example) and nonparametric tests for significant differences in trait expression between groups (KWANOVA $-$ $\mathbf{H}\,[3, n = 728] = 41.28$ to 152.36, $p < 0.001$, with 1999 permutations) indicate significant differences exist in trait manifestation. The next step is a series of constrained ordination procedures. Using the same data, and again using the Chi-square distance measure, a canonical analysis (constrained) produced three canonical axes with squared canonical correlations of $\boldsymbol{\delta}_1^2 = 0.43267$, $\boldsymbol{\delta}_2^2 = 0.10150$, and $\boldsymbol{\delta}_3^2 = 0.03925$. All post hoc tests were significant ($p = 0.005$; 999 permutations). A scatterplot of these axes demonstrates how effectively the constrained ordination procedure clusters members in multivariate space, while still reducing overall dimensionality from $p = 8$ to $\boldsymbol{m} = 3$ dimensions in the CAP analysis (Fig. 16.3). The final step is the implementation of multiple similarity/dissimilarity and distance measures. Table 16.4 presents the results of 12 such analyses.

To explore between-group variability in morphoscopic trait expression, the parameters derived from the canonical analysis were used for the three- and four-group analyses using $\boldsymbol{m} = 6$, no transformations of the dataset, and the Chi-square dissimilarity measure. The results of the four-group analysis of American Black ($n = 277$), American White ($n = 202$), Asian ($n = 68$), and Hispanic ($n = 186$) samples are summarized in Tables 16.5 and 16.6. Randomization and permutation tests of the trace statistic ($tr = 0.609$) and the first squared canonical correlation $\left(\delta_1^2 = 0.478\right)$ were both significant at the $\alpha = 0.001$ level using 999 permutations of the test (random seed = 1234). Generally, there is good separation between groups. The classification component of the CAP model correctly allocated 56.2% of the sample (408/733), a low value but still higher than random chance (25%). American Blacks (60.6) and American Whites (58.9) had the highest classification rates, followed by the Asian (51.4) and Hispanic (46.2) samples. Fig. 16.4 is a plot of the first two roots, explaining slightly over 80% of the variation. The first axis separates the American Black and Hispanic samples from the American White and Asian samples; the second axis separates the American Black and Asian samples from the American White and Hispanic samples. The Hispanic sample is markedly close to the American White sample in multivariate space. Given the composition of the Hispanic sample (predominately from Northern Mexico), this is not surprising. Researchers demonstrated a higher European genetic component among those populations (Hughes et al., 2011). The principal coordinate axes plot (constrained) demonstrates

Table 16.3 Frequency Distribution of Morphoscopic Traits by Population

	Character State					
	1		2		3	
Anterior Nasal Spine	*n*	%	*n*	%	*n*	%
American Black	167	59.4	80	28.5	34	12.1
American White	61	27.7	86	39.1	73	33.2
Asian	59	81.9	8	11.1	5	6.9
SW Hispanic	21	13.5	88	56.8	46	29.7

	1		2		3		4	
Inferior Nasal Aperture	*n*	%	*n*	%	*n*	%	*n*	%
American Black	136	48.4	59	21.0	61	21.7	25	8.9
American White	7	3.2	31	14.1	78	35.5	104	47.3
Asian	12	19.0	46	73.0	3	4.8	2	3.2
SW Hispanic	8	5.2	22	14.2	82	52.9	43	27.7

	1		2		3	
Interorbital Breadth	*n*	%	*n*	%	*n*	%
American Black	30	10.7	101	35.9	150	53.4
American White	71	32.3	134	60.9	15	6.8
Asian	30	41.7	37	51.2	5	6.9
SW Hispanic	54	34.8	87	56.1	14	9.0

	1		2		3	
Nasal Aperture Width	*n*	%	*n*	%	*n*	%
American Black	10	3.6	115	40.9	156	55.5
American White	100	45.5	95	43.2	25	11.4
Asian	1	1.4	63	87.5	8	11.1
SW Hispanic	33	21.3	107	69.0	15	9.7

	0		1		2		3		4	
Nasal Bone Contour	*n*	%	*n*	%	*n*	%	*n*	%	*n*	%
American Black	122	43.4	61	21.7	25	8.9	48	17.1	25	8.9
American White	8	3.6	38	17.3	24	10.9	81	36.9	69	31.4
Asian	17	23.6	17	23.6	28	38.9	9	12.5	1	1.4
SW Hispanic	7	4.5	48	31.0	4	2.6	72	46.5	24	15.5

Continued

Table 16.3 Frequency Distribution of Morphoscopic Traits by Population Continued				
	0		1	
Nasal Overgrowth	*n*	%	*n*	%
American Black	198	70.5	83	29.5
American White	126	57.3	94	42.7
Asian	53	73.6	19	26.4
SW Bispanic	46	29.7	109	70.3
	0		1	
Postbregmatic Depression	*n*	%	*n*	%
American Black	160	56.9	121	43.1
American White	171	77.7	49	22.3
Asian	65	90.3	7	9.7
SW Hispanic	120	77.4	35	22.6

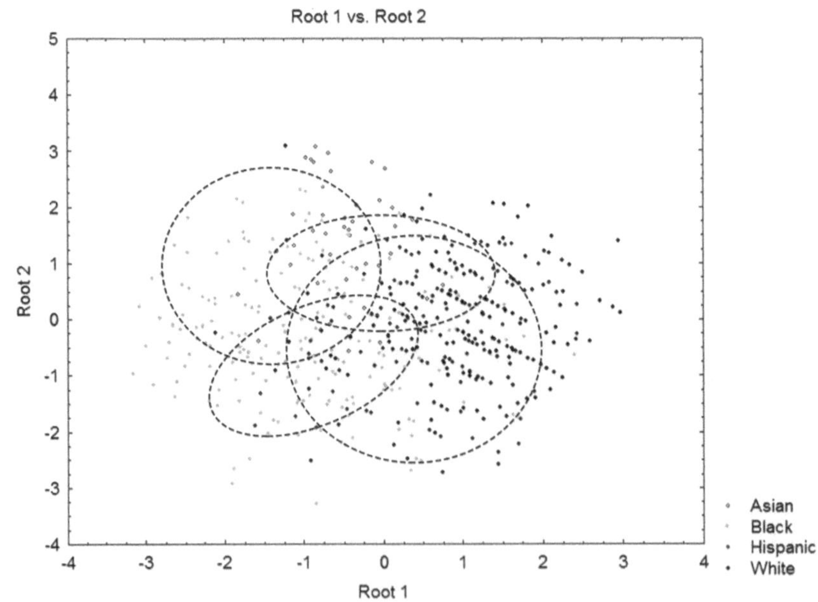

FIGURE 16.1

Unconstrained ordination scatterplot of the morphoscopic data for four groups.

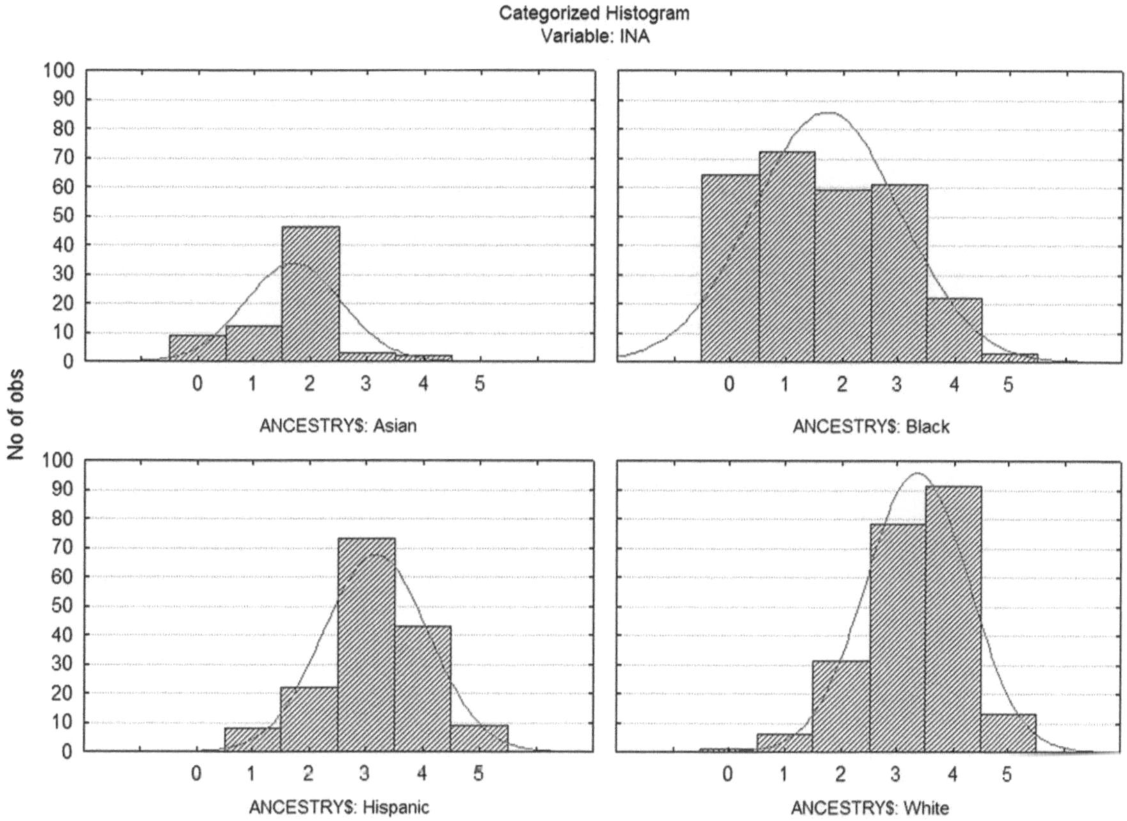

FIGURE 16.2

Categorized histogram of inferior nasal aperture morphologies between Asian, American Black and White, and Hispanic samples.

moderate separation between samples although clear similarities are noted between the Hispanic and American White samples (Fig. 16.4). In fact, classification rates (leave-one-out ×-validation) of the Hispanic sample indicate nearly 37% of that sample is misclassified as American White and nearly 27% of the American White sample is misclassified as Hispanic.

Correlations between the original seven variables and the canonical axes indicate the midface (NAW and IOB) is of greatest importance for separating American Blacks and Asians (PCO1) from the other two populations, and that postbregmatic depression and nasal overgrowth are important for separating American Blacks from Hispanics (PCO2).

The results of a three-group analysis comparing American Black, American White, and Asian samples were similar to the four-group, although, overall classification accuracies were higher. The results of that analysis are not presented. A third analysis was used to tease out differences between the American Black ($n = 277$), American White ($n = 202$), and Hispanic ($n = 186$) samples. Those data are summarized in Tables 16.7 and 16.8. Randomization and permutation tests of the trace statistic ($tr = 0.530$) and the first squared canonical correlation $\left(\delta_1^2 = 0.486\right)$ were both significant at the $\alpha = 0.002$ level using 499

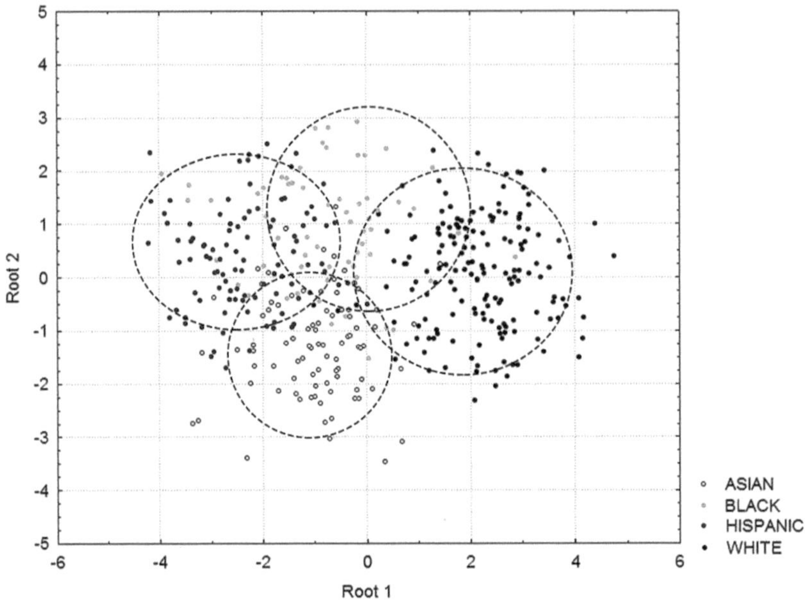

FIGURE 16.3

Constrained ordination scatterplot of the morphoscopic data for four groups derived from the CAP analysis.

Table 16.4 Four-Group CAP Analysis of Morphoscopic Data Using Several Different Distance and Dissimilarity Measures

Measure	*m*	Proportion of SSt	δ_1^2	δ_2^2	Correct (%)
Bray–Curtis	3	0.99327	0.45102	0.23891	55.907
Canberra	3	0.97514	0.38925	0.04135	51.374
Chi-square	6	1.00000	0.43267	0.10152	55.357
Chi-square dist	6	1.00000	0.43267	0.10152	55.357
Euclidean	6	0.96287	0.47647	0.14741	58.104
CY dissimilarity	2	0.83267	0.35305	0.03701	48.764
Gower	3	0.90181	0.44824	0.15285	57.418
Hellinger	7	0.99088	0.46166	0.12992	60.440
Jaccard	2	0.75872	0.23719	0.02993	46.566
Kulczynski	3	0.90426	0.44744	0.04836	54.396
Manhattan (city-block)	4	0.99483	0.46264	0.15611	57.418
Orloci's chord	6	0.98514	0.46333	0.09914	56.593

Note: "Proportion of SSt" is the proportion of the total sum of squared interindividual dissimilarities divided by the total variance explained by the first **m** *PCO axes. The last column indicates the overall correct classification rate obtained using a leave-one-out procedure. No data transformations and no data standardizations were necessary.*

Table 16.5 *Four-Group CAP Analysis of Morphoscopic Trait Data Using Chi-Square Distance Measure*

m	Prop. G	Prop. SSt	δ_1^2	δ_2^2	δ_3^2	Correct (%)
1	0.42119	3.70325	0.38279	0.00000	0.00000	46.658%
2	0.62911	3.69472	0.38293	0.02835	0.00000	46.794%
3	0.80116	3.69894	0.38916	0.04050	0.02554	50.068%
4	0.91541	3.79388	0.47712	0.04150	0.02962	54.843%
5	0.96218	3.77604	0.47719	0.07843	0.03077	54.434%
6	1.00000	3.77097	0.47791	0.08392	0.04778	55.662%

Table 16.6 *Leave-One-Out Allocation of Observations to Groups (for the Choice of* m = 6*)*

Group	Asian	Black	Hispanic	White	Total	Correct (%)
Asian	35	23	9	1	68	51.4
Black	49	168	29	31	277	60.6
Hispanic	23	9	86	68	186	46.2
White	17	12	54	119	202	58.9

Error = 44.34 (*permutations* = 999); tr = 0.609609; $p < 0.001$; $\delta_1^2 = 0.477911$; $p < 0.001$.

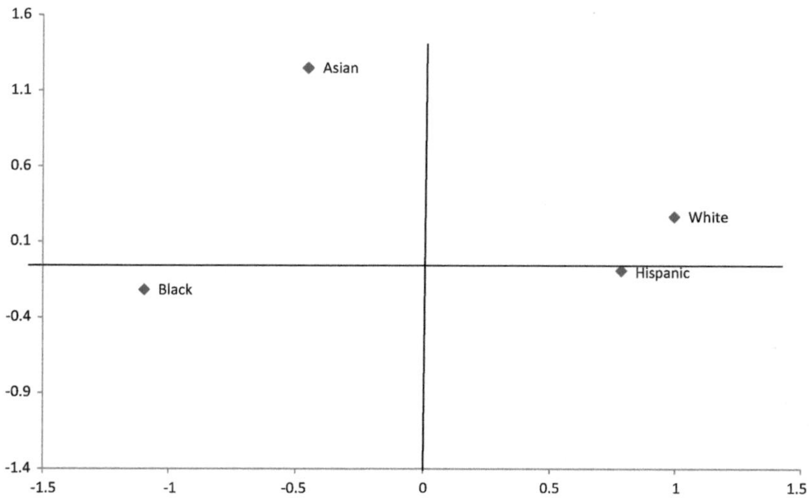

FIGURE 16.4

Canonical plot of centroid data derived from the CAP analysis of four groups.

Table 16.7 Three-Group CAP Analysis of Morphoscopic Trait Data Using Chi-Square Distance Measure

m	Prop. G	Prop. SSt	δ_1^2	δ_2^2	δ_3^2	Correct (%)
1	0.40544	3.09158	0.39970	0.00000	0.00000	47.39
2	0.60364	3.11681	0.40199	0.03131	0.00000	49.72
3	0.76384	3.13859	0.40250	0.03336	0.00374	49.45
4	0.88992	3.14144	0.42368	0.03377	0.02314	50.00
5	0.96602	3.14049	0.43217	0.06133	0.03113	53.02
6	1.00000	3.11091	0.43267	0.10150	0.03925	55.35

Table 16.8 Leave-One-Out Allocation of Observations to Groups (for the Choice of m = 6)

Group	Black	Hispanic	White	Total	Correct (%)
Black	203	45	29	277	73.28
Hispanic	17	101	68	186	54.30
White	22	54	126	202	62.38

Error = 35.34 (permutations = 999); tr = 0.530245; p = 0.002; $\delta_1^2 = 0.486016$; *p = 0.002.*

permutations of the test (random seed = 658). The classification component of the CAP model correctly allocated 65.6% of the sample (430/665). Again, the Hispanic sample is predominately misclassifying with the American White sample. However, in the three-group analysis we see better separation in space. In Fig. 16.5, the first axis separates American Whites and Hispanics from the American Black sample, with loadings on NAW (0.8626), IOB (0.8305), and INA (−0.7558), highlighting the wider nasal aperture

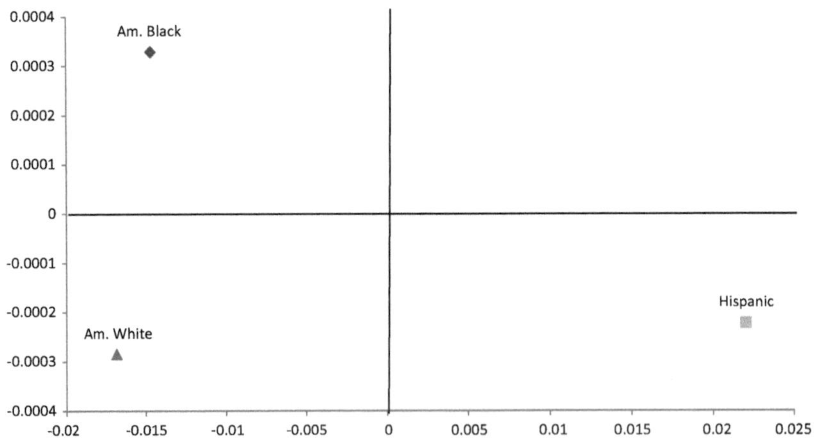

FIGURE 16.5

Canonical plot of centroid data derived from the CAP analysis of three groups.

width and interorbital breadth of American Blacks and the higher (ordinal) scores of inferior nasal aperture morphology among the American White and Hispanic samples. The second axis separates the Hispanic sample from the American Black and White samples, loading nasal overgrowth (0.8957), a trait observed in higher frequencies within the Hispanic sample and previously associated with that group (Birkby et al., 2008).

DISCUSSION

Morphoscopic trait data have been used in forensic anthropology, but predominately only in a trait-list driven approach to ancestry estimation that gives little regard to the actual distribution of these traits among groups and only moderate efforts to understand wider patterns of human variation in trait manifestation. Few, if any, studies have used these traits in biodistance analyses. However, as demonstrated earlier, that need not be the case. The CAP method is a novel approach to biodistance data analysis. The flexibility of the model to handle continuous and categorical data is ideal for all types of anthropological data and the ability to use any dissimilarity (distance) matrix allows data exploration in multivariate space since each of these measures highlights different aspects of the dataset.

The application of statistical classification methods and biodistance analysis using cranial morphoscopic data has been explored here. These results demonstrate that cranial morphoscopic traits can be used to assess ancestry successfully and can provide estimated error rates, but more importantly, these same data can be used to assess population relatedness through an exploration of biodistance measures. Finally, while Hefner's (2009) revised definitions and illustrations reduce subjectivity in trait scoring, methods like CAP go one step further to reduce subjectivity in how these traits are used to assess ancestry. Properly weighing the importance of a morphoscopic trait in a final assessment is only achieved using a statistical model. While some may argue that the new distributions presented in Hefner (2009) can be used for a majority-vote trait-list approach, statistical models utilizing these traits do not seem to support that sentiment.

As illustrated by the CAP analysis, some traits are more important for correct classifications and the joint distributions of these traits provide better classification information than any single trait. Morphoscopic data require different statistical approaches compared to their metric counterparts. Fortunately, substantial progress in numerical ecology and other fields exploring similar data types has led to a wealth of analytical methods like the CAP analysis, which forensic anthropologists can employ in analyses. The next step for the utilization of the CAP method in forensic anthropology is exploration of data transformation methods.

The results of the CAP are also promising when using morphoscopic data in biodistance analysis. Several distance measures produced acceptable results, but the Chi-square distance measure performed best overall. Chi-square distance measures have been used extensively in anthropological data analysis. In the CAP analysis, the Chi-square distance measure likely works better than others because it emphasizes compositional differences rather than accumulation differences, for example, the Bray—Curtis measure, which is commonly used for genetic data, the CY distance measure (a log transformed Bray—Curtis), or the Gower and Canberra measures, which standardize each variable by the range.

The benefits of a statistical approach to classification using morphoscopic traits are obvious. Subjectivity in trait scoring is minimized, effectively decreasing the importance and emphasis traditionally placed on observer experience for arriving at a correct classification. Any statistical method will optimize classification accuracies in ancestry assessment because they more appropriately weigh variable importance in the final model. In so doing they also provide support for the true nature of human biological variation rather than lending credence to the old typological model.

Acknowledgments

The author wishes to express gratitude and thanks to Stephen D. Ousley, Richard L. Jantz, and M. Kate Spradley for critically questioning morphoscopic trait analysis. Kandus Linde provided useful insight and comments on early manifestations of this manuscript. Lee Meadows Jantz, David Hunt, Bruce Anderson, and Atsuko Hayashi provided access to collections and/or portions of the data used in this analysis. Finally, I would like to thank the anonymous reviewer of this manuscript for very useful comments and criticisms. All mistakes and oversights are my own. This study was funded in part by the National Institute of Justice, Office of Justice Programs, United States Department of Justice (2015-DN-BX-K012). The opinions, findings, and conclusions expressed in this publication are those of the author and do not necessarily reflect the views of the Department of Justice.

References

Anderson, M.J., Willis, T.J., 2003. Canonical analysis of principal coordinates: a useful method of constrained ordination for ecology. Ecology 84, 511–525.

Anderson, M.J., 2002. CAP: A Computer Program (Auckland, New Zealand).

Anderson, B., 2008. Identifying the dead: methods utilized by the Pima County (Arizona) Office of the Medical Examiner for undocumented border crossers: 2001–2006. Journal of Forensic Sciences 53 (1), 8–15.

Birkby, W.H., Fenton, T.W., Anderson, B.E., 2008. Identifying Southwest Hispanics using nonmetric traits and the cultural profile. Journal of Forensic Sciences 53 (1), 29–33.

Buikstra, J., Ubelaker, D., 1996. Standards for data collection from human skeletal remains. In: Proceedings of a Seminar at the Field Museum of Natural History. In: Arkansas Archeological Survey Research Series, vol. 44. Arkansas.

Finnegan, M., McGuire, S.A., 1979. Classification systems for discrete variables used in forensic anthropology. American Journal of Physical Anthropology 51, 547–553.

Gower, J.C., 1966. Some distance properties of latent root and vector methods used in multivariate analysis. Biometrika 53, 325–338.

Hefner, J.T., Ousley, S.D., 2006. Morphoscopic traits and the statistical determination of ancestry II. In: Proceedings of the 58th Annual Meeting of the American Academy of Forensic Science, Seattle, WA.

Hefner, J.T., Ousley, S.D., 2014. Statistical classification methods for estimating ancestry using morphoscopic traits. Journal of Forensic Sciences 59 (4), 883–890.

Hefner, J.T., Spradley, M.K., Anderson, B.E., 2014. Ancestry assessment using random forest modeling. Journal of Forensic Sciences 59 (3), 583–598.

Hefner, J.T., 2003. Assessing Nonmetric Cranial Traits Currently Used in the Forensic Determination of Ancestry (Master's thesis). The University of Florida, Gainesville, FL.

Hefner, J.T., 2007. The statistical determination of ancestry using cranial nonmetric traits (unpublished Ph.D. dissertation). Department of Anthropology, University of Florida, Gainesville.

Hefner, J.T., 2009. Cranial nonmetric variation and estimating ancestry. Journal of Forensic Sciences 54 (5), 985–995.

Hooton, E.A., 1936. Lecture Notes of EA Hooton (Unpublished manuscripts of the Peabody Museum archives of E.A. Hooton. Cambridge, MA).

Hughes, C.E., Juarez, C.A., Hughes, T.L., Galloway, A., Fowler, G., Chacon, S., 2011. A simulation for exploring the effects of the "trait list" method's subjectivity on consistency and accuracy of ancestry estimations. Journal of Forensic Sciences 56 (5), 1094–1106.

Johnson, R.A., Wichern, D.W., 1992. Applied multivariate statistical analysis, third ed. Prentice-Hall, Englewood Cliffs, New Jersey.

Krzanowski, W.J., 2002. Principles of Multivariate Analysis: A User's Perspective. Oxford University Press, London.

Legendre, P., Legendre, L., 1998. Numerical Ecology In: Developments in Environmental Modelling, second English ed., vol. 20. Elsevier.

Ousley, S.D., Hefner, J.T., 2005. The statistical determination of ancestry. In: Proceedings of the 56th Annual meeting of the American Academy of Forensic Sciences. Seattle, WA.

Rhine, S., 1990. Nonmetric skull racing. In: Gill, Rhine (Eds.), Skeletal Attribution of Race: Methods for Forensic Anthropology. Maxwell Museum of Anthropology, Albuquerque, New Mexico, pp. 7–20.

Smithsonian Institution, 2010. Osteoware. Computer software. In: Dudar, J.C. (Ed.). Smithsonian Institution, Washington, DC.

CHAPTER 17

Dominance in Dental Morphological Traits: Implications for Biological Distance Studies

H.J.H. Edgar[1], S.D. Ousley[2]
University of New Mexico, Albuquerque, NM, United States[1]; Mercyhurst University, Erie, PA, United States[2]

CHAPTER OUTLINE HEAD

Background 318
Developmental Influences on Dental Morphology 319
Genes Influencing Dental Morphology 319
Quantitative Analyses of Genetic Effects 320
Statistical Issues 321
Materials 322
Methods 323
Results 324
Discussion 326
Conclusions 329
Acknowledgments 329
References 329

Dental anthropologists have consistently asserted that dental morphological variables are highly heritable traits, with threshold expression, resulting from equal and additive genetic effects that are evolutionarily conservative and selectively neutral (Larsen and Kelley, 1991; Hillson, 1996; Scott and Turner, 1997). Heritability, while not generalizable, has been repeatedly investigated for several tooth crown characteristics collected from families (Harris, 1977; Scott and Potter, 1984; Nichol, 1989). Dental morphology and skeletal nonmetric trait observations have also been collected from groups with estimated interrelationships using genetic markers to test their utility for estimating genetic distances (Hubbard et al., 2015; Sofaer et al., 1972; Turner, 1969; Wijsman and Neves, 1986). The remaining components of this assertion rely mostly on observations and experience, rather than formal tests in humans. Animal experiments involving crossing different strains show differential effects on dental morphology. One tantalizing study involves hybrid pigs, whose second molars present a shape intermediate between their wild and domestic progenitors. However, third molars in the hybrids are shaped more like their wild parent's proportionally narrower teeth than those of the domesticated parent. The size of both the second and third molars is more similar to the domesticated parent's smaller teeth (Elvin et al., 2015).

Heritability, the degree of genetic influence on trait variability, must be qualified. Broad-sense heritability includes all genetic influences on variation, including additive, dominance, epistasis, and genetic—environmental interaction effects; in sibling and twin studies, broad-sense heritability includes

Biological Distance Analysis. http://dx.doi.org/10.1016/B978-0-12-801966-5.00017-2

the effects of a shared environment. Narrow-sense heritability includes only the additive effects of variation, and therefore represents the more predictable outcomes when two parents reproduce, or two populations exchange genes (Falconer, 1989). When estimating heritability using siblings and especially twins, sharing a common environment (environmental covariance) and dominance effects make siblings and twin pairs more similar and inflates broad-sense heritability estimates; discerning between dominance and shared environmental effects, both of which are nonadditive effects, is difficult. There have been a few tests of the additive genetic assumption, which require data not only from twins, but from parents as well (reviewed in Scott and Turner, 1997).

Dental morphology is believed to change slowly (or at least, slowly enough for dental anthropologists working with hominines) because many of the traits seen in contemporary humans have homologues in other primates (Skinner and Gunz, 2010; Hardin and Legge, 2013; Irish et al., 2014). Dental traits are also thought to be selectively neutral because they are so small (but see Mizoguchi, 1985 for an opposing view of shovel-shaped incisors), because many do not affect overall tooth size, and because throughout most of human history they mainly have worn away with normal tooth use. Dental morphological variables are thought to be threshold traits that develop due to equal, additive genes, because those models seem to fit the variation we see when we look at lots of dentitions (Berry, 1968; Sofaer, 1970; Scott and Turner, 1997).

Because they represent an admixed population, dentitions of Hispanic Americans can provide a test of the assumptions described previously. Hispanic New Mexicans are known to primarily descend from Europeans and Native Americans (the latter descend from late Pleistocene/early Holocene Asian populations), with only a very small African component to their ancestry (Bonilla et al., 2004a,b; Klimentidis et al., 2009). In contrast, South Florida Hispanic Americans are thought to be primarily of Cuban and Caribbean descent, with more African and European ancestry than Native American (Hanis et al., 1991). Given these two distinct population histories, dental morphological data, which reflects population history and admixture, could be used to discern the group membership of an unknown individual. However, previous research has shown that dental morphology in Hispanics from New Mexico and South Florida are not discernibly different (Edgar, 2013). Why might this be? If our assumption about the overwhelmingly additive genetic nature of the variation in dental trait expression is incorrect, dominance may provide an explanation for this phenomenon. If, instead of equal and additive genetic effects, dental traits show dominance, the shared ancestry in New Mexico and Florida Hispanics would be overestimated at the sample and individual level. This would be especially true if the expressions with dominant inheritance were associated with Native American/Asian-derived ancestry. Here, using samples of estimated genetic ancestry admixture proportions, we test the assumption of the equal, additive contribution of genes in dental morphology. We ask, is there evidence of dominance in dental morphological trait expression?

BACKGROUND

To appreciate why dental morphologists have made assumptions about inheritance, it is useful to see what is known about the development and genetics of trait expression. Until relatively recently, very little was understood about the factors that shape tooth form. Researchers have been pursuing two distinct routes to understand the causes of dental morphological variability. First, evolutionary developmental biological (evo-devo) approaches have been employed to understand the processes by which dental variants form.

Second, specific allelic variation has been examined for covariation with dental trait frequencies. Although applying evo-devo and genetic approaches have facilitated great progress in our understanding of the factors that influence dental characteristics, it is important not to lose sight of the environmental variables that may also be influential (Mizoguchi, 2013).

Developmental Influences on Dental Morphology

Townsend et al. (2012) provide an excellent and concise discussion of dental development. They argue that an understanding of genetic, epigenetic, and environmental factors that shape tooth morphology is imperative for studies of population relationships as well as forensic analyses. They further argue that many dental phenotypes such as size and shape are interrelated. Brook (2009) has proposed a relationship between the overall size of teeth in a dentition with the likelihood of supernumerary or congenitally absent teeth. This relationship may be complicated by the possibility of negative size interactions between two adjacent teeth, due to arch constraints on joint tooth size (Sofaer et al., 1971; Yamada et al., 2010).

Cusp number seems determined by an interaction between tooth size and cusp size, which are in turn determined by an interaction of the basic tissues of tooth morphogenesis, dental epithelium, and ectomesenchyme (Cai et al., 2007). Because cusps develop iteratively from enamel knots using the same combination of genes and developmental processes (the patterning cascade model; Jernvall and Jung, 2000), there is no single gene responsible for the presence or absence of most dental traits. However, the likelihood of new cusps to form is increased by the modular nature of enamel knot formation (Jernvall and Jung, 2000). In fact, the hypocone has evolved in over 20 mammal species independently (Hunter and Jernvall, 1995). Instead of cusp formation being controlled by allelic gene variants, new cusps may develop due to interaction between the inhibitory cusp-forming space that surrounds preexisting cusps and overall tooth size (Jernvall, 2000). Such appears to be the mechanism that explains Carabelli's trait presence and size in humans (Hunter et al., 2010; Hunter and Jernvall, 1995; Moormann et al., 2013), and may explain variation in mandibular molar cusp six expression in chimpanzees (Skinner and Gunz, 2010).

As mentioned previously, genetic and environmental forces (such as hormones, disease, and dietary stress) all affect the final outcome of tooth morphology (Townsend et al., 2012; Sperber, 2004; Thesleff, 2006; Brook and Brook O'Donnell, 2011). Interestingly, the two traits that have been the primary subjects of these two different research approaches, shovel-shape incisors and Carabelli's trait, may themselves be related (Tsai et al., 1996). Genetic and developmental relationships among less studied variants are just beginning to be considered (ie, Brook, 2009; Tan et al., 2014). While our knowledge of the genetics and development of teeth is rapidly improving, in general these studies are in their infancy. We cannot yet apply this knowledge to actually understand the complex inheritance of any particular dental trait, much less apply that knowledge to bioarchaeological or forensic questions.

Genes Influencing Dental Morphology

There are over 300 genes known to be involved in odontongenesis (Thesleff, 2006). Most of these influence the timing of specific events in dental development, which shapes cusp number, size, and final tooth form. Only a few genes have been implicated in the presence or absence of specific dental variants. Some of these genes have been investigated to determine whether they influence trait expression in an additive or other fashion. For example, promoter polymorphism C of PAX9, a gene that has been shown to be related to autosomal dominant forms of systemwide agenesis, has also been shown to be associated with the much more common third molar agenesis (Bianchi et al., 2007).

The ectodysplasin A receptor gene (EDAR) has famously been shown to be associated with dental morphological variants, especially shoveling and double shoveling on incisors in Koreans, Japanese (Kimura et al., 2009), and Uyghurs (Tan et al., 2014). EDARV370A is a missense variant that appears to have arisen in East Asia about 30,000 ya. This variant is present in up to 95% of Han Chinese and nearly absent from Europeans (Sabeti et al., 2007). Variation in the number of EDARV730A copies explains 18.9% of variation in the eight grades of shoveling expression in Japanese dentitions, about one-fourth of the heritable component (Kimura et al., 2009).

EDARV370A is also significantly associated with incisor shoveling, double shoveling, and maxillary canine mesial ridge in Uyghurs from the Xinjiang autonomous region, accounting for 18% of the variation of these traits. Tan et al. (2014) looked at 28 mostly standard dental characteristics in 242 Uyghur students. Uyghurs are a Eurasian population with admixture of approximately 48% East Asian and 52% European contributions (Xu and Jin, 2008). They found that mandibular first molar cusp six occurred at a rate similar to that seen in Europeans. Several traits were seen at rates similar to East Asians, including maxillary first incisor double shoveling, mandibular second molar Y-groove, and mandibular first molar deflecting wrinkle. Still other traits were seen at rates that exceeded those seen in either parental population, including first molar Carabelli's trait and maxillary canine mesial ridge.

The authors then compared dental trait observations, the majority of which were scored using at least five grades of expression, with genetic data for EDARV370A using a general linear model, testing additive, dominant, and recessive models of inheritance (Tan et al., 2014). While an additive effects model was the best fitting, all three models returned similar results, showing that EDARV370A was significantly associated with a composite phenotype (indicating pleiotropy) consisting of shoveling on the first and second maxillary incisor, first and second maxillary incisor double shovel, and maxillary canine mesial ridge. An additive effects model was also the best fitting to explain variation in hypocone expression in Australian twins (Higgins et al., 2009).

Unlike the inheritance pattern associated with EDARV370A, several previous reports have indicated that dominance explains the pattern of inheritance for specific traits, such as aspects of tooth size, peg, and absent maxillary lateral incisors (Alvesalo and Portin, 1969) but not others, such as Carabelli's trait (Townsend and Martin, 1992). Through pedigree studies, Alvesalo and Portin (1969) determined that congenitally absent, peg, and reduced maxillary lateral incisors were all part of the same trait. They contend the characteristic is determined through a single autosomal dominant allele with 72% penetrance. A nonadditive genetic model also best explained variation in mesiodistal canine breadth in permanent canine size in Australian twins (Dempsey and Townsend, 2001).

Quantitative Analyses of Genetic Effects

Genetic studies using grades of expression indicate additive effects and an underlying normal distribution for most traits (Scott, 2008; Scott and Turner, 1997). Different results may be found, however, when the trait expressions are converted into dichotomized values before analysis. Using complex segregation analysis, Nichol (1989) found that many of the dichotomized traits analyzed in the current research showed dominance effects in their inheritance, and that the cutoff points chosen for dichotomization greatly affect estimates of transmissibility. Scott and Potter (1984) analyzed dental traits scored using at least five grades for each in monozygotic (MZ; identical) and dizygotic (DZ; fraternal) twins, and estimated heritabilities for several traits between 0.19 and 0.40, cautiously remarking that dental traits show large environmental effects. However, they also calculated concordances of 13 dichotomous traits between twins, and found that nearly all MZ concordances were much higher than a sample of random pairs, and except for the canine tubercle, first molar metaconule, and second molar hypocone, the DZ twins had concordances very close to those for MZ twins, implying strong dominance and/or shared environmental effects in dichotomized traits.

Falconer (1989) provides a formula to estimate narrow-sense heritability, $2(r_{MZ} - r_{DZ})$, where r is the correlation coefficient, in this case equivalent to the concordance. Using this equation, estimated narrow-sense heritabilities from their figures range between 0.0 and 0.46 for the 13 traits. Falconer (1989) also provides a way to estimate the effects of a shared environment or dominance on traits by subtracting the estimated narrow-sense heritability from the MZ correlation, r_{MZ}. Because the effects of a shared environment cannot be separated from the effects of dominance, the figure represents the effects of both, and using Scott and Porter's traits, it ranged between 0.46 and 0.87 with a median of 0.68, much higher than the narrow-sense heritability for every trait except the canine tubercle. So dental traits dichotomized this way represent a good deal of nonadditive variation. Similarly, Higgins et al. (2009) found additive effects when scoring six grades of expression of the hypocone in first and second maxillary molars, but the relatively high concordance in DZ twins (67%) compared to MZ twins (80%) suggested substantial nonadditive variation present when traits are dichotomized. Likewise, Kolakowski et al. (1980) found evidence for dominance and shared environmental effects using a trichotomy of Carabelli's trait, in contrast to Townsend and Martin (1992). Clearly, reducing the degrees of expression in dental traits changes the nature of the data.

To add to the distorting effects of dichotomizing, there is no consensus on where to divide traits into presence and absence, different authors dichotomize differently, and there are no objective standards, only "fuzzy" ones (Scott, 2008, p. 284). Breakpoints can be adjusted according to the needs of the particular study (Scott, 2008; Scott and Turner, 1997). As Harris (2008) and Scott (2008) point out, different cutoff points for the dichotomies will bias results in different ways. For instance, Scott (2008) remarked that relatively low frequency traits such as cusp seven seem to be recessive while high-frequency traits such as Carabelli's trait seem to be dominant. In any event, the genetics of dichotomized dental traits are quite variable and are more complicated than has been assumed. Clearly, interpretation of the mode of inheritance can be made problematic by data format and source. This has downstream consequences for our ability to rely on the results of biological distance analyses.

Statistical Issues

Despite the evidence that the graded expression scores show additive effects in contrast to dichotomized data, which apparently inflate the effect of nonadditive genetic variation, for computational simplicity dental anthropologists have overwhelmingly analyzed dichotomized traits. C.A.B. Smith's Mean Measure of Divergence (MMD) has been traditionally used, despite numerous and considerable problems (Harris, 2008). The MMD was used initially because the statistical methods involved with mixes of nominal and ordinal observations were intractable. Because the MMD works only with binary traits, original scores showing grades of expression must be dichotomized, which discards information. While some authors described the use of standardized breakpoints for dichotomization (ie, Pilloud and Larsen, 2011), in fact no such standard breakpoints have been presented in the literature. Instead, breakpoints have either been used because they were used by previous authors (ie, Hubbard et al., 2015; Huffman, 2014; Irish, 2005) or because they made sense based on average expressions in the samples used in authors' particular studies (ie, Ragsdale and Edgar, 2015; Sołtysiak and Bialon, 2013). Many of the breakpoints in the first case come from Turner (1987) and other subsequent papers citing that work. Additional problems with the use of MMD include its sensitively to intertrait correlations (sometimes ignored by researchers), that negative distances are possible, and that an interpretable test for significance of distances is lacking. Harris and Sjøvold (2004) have solved some additional problems with published errors in the equation and confusion regarding statistical transformations (Irish, 2010). Whatever the source of the dichotomies, the end effect is to make groups with dominant traits appear more similar. Because those traits are more often found in Asian and Native American groups, their ancestry will be overestimated.

MATERIALS

Data derive from three sources: dental casts of contemporary Hispanic Americans, teeth in skeletal samples from populations ancestral to Hispanic Americans, and published admixture estimates based on genetic data (Table 17.2). One author (H.E.) collected all the dental morphological data. The dental models of the contemporary samples are curated at several universities, and derive from orthodontic clinics and practices. These included observations of 48 dental morphological variants in Hispanics from Los Angeles, California (University of Southern California); Ft. Lauderdale, Florida (Nova Southeastern University); Albuquerque, New Mexico (University of New Mexico); and New York, New York (New York University) ($n = 454$; Table 17.1). Individual dental models were identified as representing a Hispanic American by the treating orthodontist. This identification can be thought of as community identification, wherein a subject's ethnicity is Hispanic relative to the standards of their local community. These data were compared to expected values computed from frequencies of ancestry-informative markers in ancestral populations: Native Americans (including Native Mexicans), Western Europeans, and West Africans ($n = 1025$; Table 17.1) and the genetic admixture estimates. The ancestral group samples consist of human skeletal remains curated at several institutions in England, France, Mexico, Senegal, Spain, and the United States. In order to best represent those populations that contributed to contemporary Hispanic Americans, these samples dated prior to 1492 whenever possible. Due to provenience uncertainty and sample availability, there are likely to be some individuals, especially in the West African sample, that lived after this date.

Table 17.1 Dental Morphological Samples

Sample	n
West African	233
Western Europe/Early European American	176
Native American and Mexican	616
California Hispanic	82
Florida Hispanic	201
New Mexico Hispanic	91
New York Hispanic	80

METHODS

Observed frequencies (O) of dental traits in the contemporary Hispanic samples were compared to expected frequencies. The expected frequencies (*E*) were calculated through multiplying the frequencies of dental traits observed in ancestral samples by published proportional estimates of genetic ancestry in Hispanic Americans from the geographic areas from which the dental trait samples were taken (Table 17.2). For example, dental trait frequencies from Latino Americans in Los Angeles were compared with genetic data from a Los Angeles Latino sample (Shtir et al., 2009). The frequencies for the maxillary first incisor labial curvature trait in Native Americans, Europeans, and West Africans of 0.092, 0.223, and 0.278, respectively, were multiplied by estimated ancestry proportions in the Los Angeles Latino sample of 0.44, 0.48, and 0.08, respectively, to get the expected frequency of 0.170 ($0.092 \times 0.44 + 0.223 \times 0.48 + 0.278 \times 0.08$) in the sample. Likewise, New Mexican Hispanic Americans were compared with a genetic sample of New Mexican Hispanics (Klimentidis et al., 2009). The New York dental morphology sample was compared with a genetic sample taken from New York Puerto Ricans (Bonilla et al., 2004a,b). However, the Florida Latino dental sample was compared with samples of both Cubans and Puerto Ricans (Hanis et al., 1991), as a genetic sample specific to Florida Latinos has not yet been published. Our use of the terms Latino and Hispanic follow the most common terms used by members of the population in each geographic location. Observed minus expected frequencies divided by the expected frequencies, $(O - E)/E$, the deviation, is the basis for the Chi-squared test and provides a straightforward, standardized estimate of the magnitude and direction of a divergence in trait frequency. Large deviations from expected trait frequencies indicate nonadditive effects, which include dominance. A positive mean deviation is evidence of trait expression dominance because the observed trait frequency is higher than expected based on the genetic proportions. Overdominance or underdominance occurs when the admixed group's trait frequency is higher or lower than both ancestral groups' frequencies, respectively.

Table 17.2 Published Estimates of Ancestral Genetic Contributions in Admixed Samples

			Ancestry Proportion				
Location	Origin	Study Description	NatAm	Eur	Afr	Asian	NatAm/ Asian
Bonilla et al. (2004a,b)							
New York NY	Caribbean	Puerto Ricans	0.176	0.533	0.291		
Hanis et al. (1991)							
Cuba	Caribbean	Cubans	0.18	0.622	0.198		
Puerto Rico	Caribbean	Puerto Ricans	0.181	0.45	0.369		
Klimentidis et al. (2009)							
New Mexico	Mexico/SW	Hispanics	0.327	0.616	0.057		
Shtir et al. (2009)							
Los Angeles CA	Mexico/SW	Latinos	0.452	0.401	0.049	0.098	0.55

It is important to note that the expected frequencies of traits (the trait frequencies in the related samples multiplied by the estimated ancestral genetic proportions in each group) presented in Tables 17.4 and 17.5 are artificially high because calculation assumes that there is no threshold for dental traits. In other words, the traits have complete penetrance and behave like Mendelian traits. Actual frequencies lower than the expected frequencies should be the norm.

To create a rough estimate of what effects specific dental traits have on overall tooth morphology, we developed a simple two-part scoring scheme to relatively rank whether a trait adds mass or complexity to a tooth. Scores for each characterization could run from −2 to +3. A positive score indicates that a trait being observed adds complexity or mass to the tooth crown. A negative score means that the presence of a trait makes a tooth smaller or simpler. For example, mandibular molar trigonid crest is scored at 2 for complexity, but since it does not add significantly to tooth size, it is scored at zero for mass. Scores for congenitally absent teeth and peg shape were multiplied by −1 so that a higher score reflects greater complexity and mass when the teeth are present or normally shaped. These scores are presented independently and summed in Table 17.5. A comparison of summed complexity/mass with (O − E)/E provides an indication of the relationship between these two factors.

RESULTS

Table 17.3 lists the 14 dental characteristics with observed frequencies that do not deviate greatly from the expected frequencies (<0.25 deviation). These observations constitute 29.2% of all observations made. Maxillary observations dominate the list, including all observations of incisor labial curvature, tuberculum dentale, hypocone, and maxillary molar cusp 5.

On the other end of the spectrum, Table 17.4 describes the seven traits (14.6% of all traits studied) with mean (O − E)/E values that diverge from expected by at least 0.75. The table shows the observed

Table 17.3 Traits With Mean Dominance Effects <0.25

Tooth	Trait
UI1	Labial curve
UI1	Tuberculum dentale
UI2	Tuberculum dentale
UC	Tuberculum dentale
UM1	Hypocone
UM2	Hypocone
UM1	Cusp 5
UM2	Cusp 5
UM1	Carabelli's trait
UM3	Absence
LP4	Lingual complexity
LM1	Deflecting wrinkle
LM1	Cusp 5
LM2	Groove pattern

Table 17.4 Traits in Groups With Mean Deviations From Expected Frequencies by At Least 0.75, Their Associated Ancestral Groups, and Mean Effects

Genetic Comparison Group	Dental Sample		UI1 Double Shovel	UI2 Peg	UC Distal Ridge	UM2 Metacone	LI1 Shovel Shape	LM1 Anterior Fovea	LM1 Groove
	Native Am/ Mexican	Freq	0.912	0.044	0.654	0.09	0.961	0.51	0.316
	Europe	Freq	0.039	0.008	0.101	0.19	0.089	0.246	1
	W Africa	Freq	0.057	0.057	0.474	0.332	0.189	0.58	0.87
Cubans	FL Latino	Obs	0.587	0.051	0.595	0.591	0.627	0.672	0.139
		Exp	0.2	0.024	0.274	0.2	0.266	0.36	0.851
		(O – E)/E	**1.939**	**1.085**	**1.167**	**1.953**	**1.359**	**0.87**	**–0.837**
Puerto Ricans	FL Latino	Obs	0.587	0.051	0.595	0.591	0.627	0.672	0.139
		Exp	0.204	0.033	0.339	0.224	0.284	0.417	0.828
		(O – E)/E	**1.882**	**0.543**	**0.755**	**1.636**	**1.21**	**0.613**	**–0.833**
LA Latino	LA Latino	Obs	0.425	0.013	0.72	0.394	0.436	0.884	0.054
		Exp	0.424	0.028	0.374	0.158	0.481	0.389	0.689
		(O – E)/E	0.001	**–0.543**	**0.925**	**1.504**	–0.093	**1.274**	**–0.922**
NM Hispanics	NM Hispanic	Obs	0.73	0.044	0.718	0.324	0.83	0.704	0.079
		Exp	0.325	0.023	0.303	0.166	0.38	0.351	0.769
		(O – E)/E	**1.245**	**0.953**	**1.369**	**0.959**	**1.184**	**1.003**	**–0.897**
NY Puerto Ricans	NY Latino	Obs	0.388	0.079	0.724	0.176	0.628	0.63	0.151
		Exp	0.198	0.029	0.307	0.214	0.272	0.39	0.842
		(O – E)/E	**0.959**	**1.752**	**1.358**	–0.178	**1.313**	**0.618**	**–0.821**
Mean (O – E)/E			**1.205**	**0.758**	**1.115**	**1.175**	**0.995**	**0.876**	**–0.862**

(O – E)/E *deviations more than 0.75 are in bold; positive values are in italics.*

frequencies of dental traits in ancestral and admixed samples, the expected frequencies given the proportion of genetic contribution from each ancestral group, and the $(O - E)/E$ deviation for each sample and for each trait's mean. Four maxillary and three mandibular observations are included. High deviations are generally in the same direction for all samples. Second molar Carabelli's trait is higher than expected for all groups, as is the expression of first molar anterior fovea. The exception to this pattern is maxillary lateral incisor peg shape, in which the deviation is high in all comparisons except Los Angeles Latinos. Overall, six of the seven traits with high deviations diverge positively in their actual values. Additionally, first molar anterior fovea shows overdominance in all groups, second molar metacone and maxillary canine distal ridge show overdominance in three of the five groups. Given that the expected frequencies are inflated, it is remarkable that the observed frequencies show a clear positive trend for the traits that deviate from expectations.

Table 17.5 summarizes the results in traits for which observed frequencies diverge from expected by at least 0.25. Each trait's scores for its relative contribution to complexity and mass are presented, together with the sum of these scores. Based on these sums, the traits are described as making the tooth crown either more simple or complex. Nine of the top 10 traits add complexity, while only 6 of the bottom 10 traits add complexity. Finally, each dental trait's mean deviation was compared with the observed trait frequencies in the ancestral groups. Each trait is described as being on average more similar to Native Americans, West Africans, or Western Europeans than expected, according to the direction and magnitude of its deviation. Six of the top 10 traits are associated with Native Americans, as are 4 of the bottom 10 traits. Only six total traits have deviations that make these Hispanic American samples more similar than expected to Europeans.

Fig. 17.1 provides a smoothed density plot of deviations and the summed characterization of relative complexity and mass that is associated with each trait. Interestingly, the trait with nearly the greatest positive mean deviation from expected, maxillary central incisor double shovel, scores highest for adding relative complexity and mass. The greatest concentration of dominance values for complex traits is in the upper right quadrant of the plot, indicating that there is a positive relationship between relative dominance and relative added complexity and mass.

DISCUSSION

Many dental trait frequencies in Hispanic Americans deviate significantly from what is expected from genetic estimates of admixture and trait frequencies in ancestral populations. Of the 48 traits we included in this analysis, 34 (70.8%) show mean deviations greater than 0.25. Out of those 34 traits, 21 (61.8%) show positive average deviations. Only 9 of these 34 traits (26.7%) decrease the mass or complexity of tooth crowns. When the 25 traits are observed, they describe factors that make tooth surfaces more complex or add mass to a tooth overall. It appears that traits that add complexity or mass to a tooth show dominance.

Clearly, the observation that dental morphological traits may not result from straightforward additive genetic variation points out a related issue in the statistical analyses of these traits. Dichotomization of data, a requirement of most contemporary methods of analysis, exacerbates biodistance distortions related to dominance. The recognition of the need to use ordinal dental morphological data is not new (Mayhall, 1999), but methods to address the issue have been slow in development. Biodistance using dental morphology traits should be conducted using ordinal scores in a multivariate framework, similar to that

Table 17.5 Traits Deviating From Expected Frequencies by At Least 0.25, Their Associated Ancestral Groups, and Tooth Effects

Tooth	Trait	Mean (O − E)/E	Makes the Expression More Like...	Makes the Tooth More...	Relative Complexity/Mass		
					Complexity	Mass	Sum
LM2	**Cusp 7**	***1.217***	**Afr**	**Complex**	2	0	2
UI1	**Double shovel**	***1.205***	**NatAm**	**Complex**	3	2	5
UM2	**Metacone**	***1.175***	**Afr**	**Complex**	1	3	4
UC	**Distal ridge**	***1.115***	**NatAm**	**Complex**	2	1	3
LI1	**Shovel shape**	**0.995**	**NatAm**	**Complex**	1	1	2
LM1	**Anterior fovea**	**0.876**	**NatAm Afr**	**Complex**	2	0	2
LM1	**Groove pattern**	**0.862**	**NatAm**	**Complex**	1	0	1
UI2	**Peg**	**−0.758**	**NatAm Afr**	**Simple**	1	1	2
LM3	Absence	*0.736*	Afr	Complex	2	2	4
UM2	Carabelli's trait	*0.727*	Eur Afr	Complex	2	3	5
LI2	Shovel shape	*0.704*	NatAm	Complex	1	1	2
UM2	Parastyle	−0.672	Afr	Simple	2	2	4
LM1	Cusp 7	*0.65*	Afr	Complex	2	0	2
UM1	Parastyle	*0.645*	NatAm	Complex	2	2	4
UI2	Double shovel	*0.587*	NatAm	Complex	3	1	4
UI2	Interruption groove	−0.554	Afr	Complex	3	0	3
UP4	Accessory cusps	*0.539*	NatAm	Complex	2	0	2
LM2	Protostylid	−0.539	Eur	Simple	2	3	5
LP3	Lingual complexity	−0.515	NatAm	Simple	3	0	3
LM2	Trigonid crest	−0.513	NatAm	Simple	2	0	2
UI1	Shovel shape	*0.474*	NatAm	Complex	2	2	4
LC	Distal ridge	*0.461*	NatAm Afr	Complex	1	1	2
LM1	Metacone	*0.382*	Eur	Complex	1	3	4
LM1	Trigonid crest	−0.375	Eur	Simple	2	0	2
UI2	Absence	−0.345	Eur	Simple	2	2	4
LM1	Protostylid	−0.302	Afr	Simple	2	3	5
UI2	Shovel shape	*0.3*	NatAm	Complex	2	2	4
UC	Shovel shape	*0.298*	NatAm	Complex	1	1	2
LM2	Cusp 6	−0.291	Eur	Simple	2	0	2
UC	Mesial ridge	*0.288*	Afr	Complex	2	1	3
UP3	Accessory cusps	*0.277*	NatAm	Complex	2	0	2

Traits are ordered by the mean absolute deviations (O − E)/E, with the seven traits described in Table 17.4 at the top, in bold. Traits with positive mean (O − E)/E values are in italics.

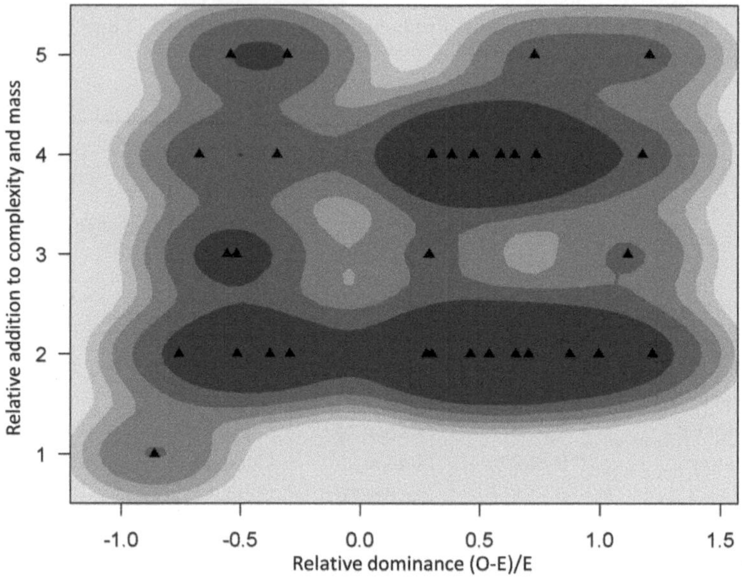

FIGURE 17.1

Contour map of dental trait $(O - E)/E$ deviation, by relative contribution to tooth complexity and mass. *Triangles* show values for individual traits that deviate by more than 0.25.

explored by Nikita (2015), who, using simulation, showed that calculating Mahalanobis distances from ordinal dental traits reflected actual relationships far better than using the MMD. Much more research is expected using this promising approach. Some dental morphology traits scored on ordinal scales apparently show true genetic dominance using pedigrees, and the dominance must be better estimated for multiple traits, but it could theoretically be compensated for in future distance calculations.

Of course, quasicontinuous traits such as dental morphological variants are subject not just to genetic effects but to important developmental effects such as diet and disease as well. How these factors interact to produce a final tooth is, at the moment, poorly understood. However, advancements in our knowledge are rapidly developing. In the meantime, bioarchaeological and forensic investigations that rely on dental morphological analyses should be cautious when studying groups with continentally diverse ancestries, which may have changed over time (Ousley and Edgar, 2012).

One-half of the traits with more than 0.25 average deviations from expected are seen more commonly in Native American dentitions. For this reason, the component of Native American/Asian-derived ancestry in Hispanic Americans is likely to be overestimated. This may explain why it is not statistically possible to determine whether an unknown individual is New Mexican Hispanic American or Florida Hispanic American; the genetic differences between the two groups are masked by the Native American contribution, because the traits we use to measure that contribution show dominance.

A study comparing biodistances calculated from genetic and dental morphological variation among East African samples indicated that the two systems gave similar results, though the patterns discerned from the dental data were more coarse-grained (Hubbard et al., 2015). Of the nine traits in that study, eight are included here; two show deviations <0.25, and two deviate >0.75. Given the close, non-Asian ancestry among their African groups, it is unclear of the relationship between that study and this one. Possibly, dominance was not an issue for Hubbard et al. (2015) because the samples in that study are all East African, with no significant Asian component suspected. There may be little to no dominance effect because no group is likely to show much higher levels of heterozygosity in these traits, unlike the Hispanic samples that were used in the present study.

CONCLUSIONS

It remains to be seen how our increasing knowledge of the inheritance of dental morphological characteristics will be incorporated in biological distance and forensic analyses. In the meantime, we present a few caveats that should be considered when conducting biodistance or forensic analyses using dental morphological traits in samples or individuals thought to have widely disparate continental ancestries:

- Traits that appeared dominant are more often associated with added complexity and mass, regardless of the geographic origin of the associated group.
- Biodistance studies of groups that include Native American/Asian-derived and non-Asian-derived ancestry will overestimate the contribution of Asian-derived ancestry.
- Biodistance studies of groups of primarily Asian-derived ancestry will provide results that make groups appear to be more similar than they actually are.
- Biodistance analyses that use dental morphological data or other data requiring dichotomization are severely hampered. Even without true dominance, dichotomization of traits alone may make groups that are somewhat similar appear to be more similar, and groups that are different may appear to be more different.
- Forensic assessments will overestimate Asian-derived ancestry in individuals with Asian or Native American admixture; non-Asian-derived ancestry will be masked.

Acknowledgments

Our thanks go to Anthony Koehl for gathering published estimates of genetic admixture. Thank you to the University of Tennessee Forensic Anthropology Center and the University of New Mexico Research Allocations Committee for funding data collection. We are also grateful to Drs. Hefner and Pilloud for organizing the symposium in which this paper originated.

References

Alvesalo, L., Portin, P., 1969. The inheritance pattern of missing, peg-shaped, and strongly mesio-distally reduced upper lateral incisors. Acta Odontologia Scandinavia 27 (6), 563–575.

Berry, R.J., 1968. The biology of non-metrical variation in mice and men. In: Brothwell, D.R. (Ed.), Skeletal Biology of Earlier Human Populations. Pergamon Press, New York, pp. 103–133.

Bianchi, F.J., Franco de Oliviera, T., Borges Pereira Saito, C., Rocha Peres, R.C., Peres Line, S.R., 2007. Association between polymorphism in the promoter region (G/C-915) of PAX9 gene and third molar agenesis. Journal of Applied Oral Science 15 (5), 382–386.

Bonilla, C., Shriver, M.D., Parra, E.J., Jones, A., Fernández, J.R., 2004a. Ancestral proportions and their association with skin pigmentation and bone mineral density in Puerto Rican women from New York City. Human Genetics 115, 57–68.

Bonilla, C., Parra, E.J., Pfaff, C.L., Dios, S., Marshall, J.A., Hamman, R.F., Ferrell, R.E., Hoggart, C.L., McKeigue, P.M., Shriver, M.D., 2004b. Admixture in the Hispanics of the San Luis Valley, Colorado and its implications for complex trait gene mapping. Annals of Human Genetics 68, 139–153.

Brook, A.H., Brook O'Donnell, M., 2011. Modeling the complexity of the dentition. In: Townsend, G., Kanazawa, E., Takayama, H. (Eds.), New Directions in Dental Anthropology: Paradigms, Methodologies and Outcomes. University of Adelaide Press, Adelaide.

Brook, A.H., 2009. Multilevel complex interactions between genetic, epigenetic and environmental factors in the aetiology of anomalies of dental development. Archives of Oral Biology 54S, S3–S17.

Cai, J., Cho, S.-W., Kim, J.-Y., Lee, M.-J., Cha, Y.-G., Jung, H.-S., 2007. Patterning the size and number of tooth and its cusps. Developmental Biology 304, 499–507.

Dempsey, P.J., Townsend, G.C., 2001. Genetic and environmental contributions to variation in human tooth size. Heredity 86, 685–693.

Edgar, H.J.H., 2013. Estimation of ancestry using dental morphological characteristics. Journal of Forensic Science 58 (s1), s3–s8. PMCID: PMC3548042.

Elvin, A., Dobney, K., Schafberg, R., Owen, J., Strand Vidarsdottir, U., Larson, G., Cucchi, T., 2015. Phenotype and animal domestication: a study of dental variation between domestic, wild, captive, hybrid and insular *Sus scrofa*. BMC Evolutionary Biology 15, 6.

Falconer, D.S., 1989. Introduction to Quantitative Genetics, third ed. Wiley, New York.

Hanis, C.L., Hewett-Emmett, D., Bertin, T.K., Schull, W.J., 1991. Origins of US Hispanics: implications for diabetes. Diabetes Care 14, 618–627.

Hardin, A.M., Legge, S.S., 2013. Geographic variation in nonmetric dental traits of the deciduous molars of Pan and Gorilla. International Journal of Primatology 34 (5), 1000–1019.

Harris, E.F., Sjøvold, T., 2004. Calculation of Smith's mean measure of divergence for intergroup comparisons using nonmetric data. Dental Anthropology 17, 83–93.

Harris, E.F., 1977. Anthropologic and Genetic Aspects of the Dental Morphology of Solomon Islanders, Melanesia (Ph.D. dissertation). Arizona State University.

Harris, E.F., 2008. Statistical applications in dental anthropology. In: Irish, J.D., Nelson, G.C. (Eds.), Technique and Application in Dental Anthropology. Cambridge University Press, Cambridge, pp. 35–67.

Higgins, D., Hughes, T.E., James, H., Townsend, G.C., 2009. Strong genetic influence on hypocone expression of permanent maxillary molars in South Australian twins. Dental Anthropology 22 (1), 1–7.

Hillson, S., 1996. Dental Anthropology. Cambridge University Press, Cambridge.

Hubbard, A.R., Guatelli-Steinberg, D., Irish, J.D., 2015. Do nuclear DNA and dental non-metric data produce similar reconstructions of regional population history? An example from modern coastal Kenya. American Journal of Physical Anthropology 157, 295–304.

Huffman, M.M., 2014. Biological Variation in South American Populations Using Dental Non-Metric Traits: Assessment of Isolation by Time and Distance (Ph.D. dissertation). The Ohio State University.

Hunter, J.P., Jernvall, J., 1995. The hypocone as a key innovation in mammalian evolution. Proceedings of the National Academy of Sciences 92, 10718–10722.

Hunter, J.P., Guatelli-Steinberg, D., Weston, T.C., Durner, R., Bestsinger, T.K., 2010. Model of tooth morphogenesis predicts Carabelli feature expression, size, and symmetry in humans. PLoS One 5 (7), e11844.

Irish, J.D., Guatelli-Steinberg, D., Legge, S.S., de Ruiter, D.J., Berger, L.R., 2014. News and views: response to "non-metric dental traits and hominin phylogeny" by Carter et al., with additional information on the Arizona State University Dental Anthropology System and phylogenetic "place" of Australopithecus sediba. Journal of Human Evolution 69, 129–134.

Irish, J.D., 2005. Population continuity vs. discontinuity revisited: dental affinities among late Paleolithic through Christian-era Nubians. American Journal of Physical Anthropology 128, 520–535.

Irish, J.D., 2010. The mean measure of divergence: its utility in model-free and model-bound analyses relative the Mahalanobis D^2 distance for nonmetric traits. American Journal of Human Biology 22, 378–398.

Jernvall, J., Jung, H.-S., 2000. Genotype, phenotype, and developmental biology of molar tooth characters. Yearbook of Physical Anthropology 43, 171–190.

Jernvall, J., 2000. Linking development with generation of novelty in mammalian teeth. Proceedings of the National Academy of Sciences 97, 2641–2645.

Kimura, R., Yamaguchi, T., Takeda, M., Kondo, O., Toma, T., Haneji, K., et al., 2009. A common variation in EDAR is a genetic determinant of shovel-shaped incisors. American Journal of Human Genetics 85, 528–535.

Klimentidis, Y.C., Miller, G.F., Shriver, M.D., 2009. Genetic admixture, self-reported ethnicity, self-estimation, and skin pigmentation among Hispanics and Native Americans. American Journal of Physical Anthropology 138, 375–383.

Kolakowski, D., Harris, E.F., Bailit, H.L., 1980. Complex segregation analysis of Carabelli's triat in a Melanesian population. American Journal of Physical Anthropology 53 (2), 301–308.

Larsen, C.S., Kelley, M.A., 1991. Introduction. In: Kelley, M.A., Larsen, C.S. (Eds.), Advances in Dental Anthropology. Wiley-Liss, New York, pp. 1–7.

Mayhall, J.T., 1999. Dichotomy in human dental morphology: a plea for complexity. In: Mayhall, J.T., Heikkenen, T. (Eds.), Dental Morphology 98. Oulu University Press, Oulu, Finland, pp. 43–47.

Mizoguchi, Y., 1985. Shoveling: A Statistical Analysis of its Morphology. University of Tokyo Press, Tokyo.

Mizoguchi, Y., 2013. Significant among-population associations found between dental characters and environmental characters. In: Scott, G.R., Irish, J.D. (Eds.), Anthropological Perspectives on Tooth Morphology: Genetics, Evolution, Variation. Cambridge University, Cambridge, pp. 108–125.

Moormann, S., Guatelli-Steinberg, D., Hunter, J., 2013. Metamerism, morphogenesis, and the expression of Carabelli and other dental traits in humans. American Journal of Physical Anthropology 150, 400–408.

Nichol, C.R., 1989. Complex segregation analysis of dental morphological variants. American Journal of Physical Anthropology 78, 37–59.

Nikita, E., 2015. A critical review of the mean measure of divergence and Mahalanobis distances using artificial data and new approaches to the estimation of biodistances employing nonmetric traits. American Journal of Physical Anthropology 157, 284–294.

Ousley, S., Edgar, H.J.H., 2012. Secular changes in discrete dental traits on three continents. American Journal of Physical Anthropology (Suppl. 44), 230. Manuscript in progress.

Pilloud, M.A., Larsen, C.S., 2011. "Official" and "practical" kin: inferring social and community structure from dental phenotype at Neolithic Catalhoyuk, Turkey. American Journal of Physical Anthropology 145, 519–530.

Ragsdale, C.S., Edgar, H.J.H., 2015. Cultural interaction and biological distance in postclassic period Mexico. American Journal of Physical Anthropology 157, 121–133.

Sabeti, P.C., Varilly, P., Fry, B., Lohmueller, J., Hostetter, E., Cotsapas, C., Xie, X., Byrne, E.H., McCarroll, S.A., Gaudet, R., et al., 2007. Genome-wide detection and characterization of positive selection in human populations. Nature 449, 913–918.

Scott, G.R., Potter, R.H.Y., 1984. An analysis of tooth crown morphology in American white twins. Anthropologie 22, 223–231.

Scott, G.R., Turner II, C.G., 1997. The Anthropology of Modern Human Teeth: Dental Morphology and Its Variation in Recent Human Populations. Cambridge University Press, Cambridge.

Scott, G.R., 2008. Dental morphology. In: Katzenberg, M.A., Saunders, S.R. (Eds.), Biological Anthropology of the Human Skeleton, second ed. John Wiley and Sons, New York, pp. 265–298.

Shtir, C.J., Marjoram, P., Azen, S., Conti, D.V., LeMarchand, L., Haiman, C.A., Varma, R., 2009. Variation in genetic admixture and population structure among Latinos: the Los Angeles Latino eye study (LALES). BMC Genetics 10, 1–13.

Skinner, M.M., Gunz, P., 2010. The presence of accessory cusps in chimpanzee lower molars is consistent with a patterning cascade model of development. Journal of Anatomy 217, 245–253.

Sofaer, J.A., Chung, C.S., Niswander, J.D., Runck, D.W., 1971. Developmental interaction, size and agenesis among permanent maxillary incisors. Human Biology 43, 36–45.

Sofaer, J.A., Niswander, J.D., MacLean, C.J., Workman, P.L., 1972. Population studies on Southwestern Indian tribes. V. Tooth morphology as an indicator of biological distance. American Journal of Physical Anthropology 37, 357–366.

Sofaer, J.A., 1970. Dental morphological variation and the Hardy-Weinberg law. Journal of Dental Research 49, 1505–1508.

Sołtysiak, A., Bialon, M., 2013. Population history of the middle Euphrates valley: dental non-metric traits at Tell Ashara, Tell Masaikh and Jebel Mashtale, Syria. HOMO 64, 341–356.

Sperber, G.H., 2004. The genetics of odontogenesis: implications in dental anthropology and palaeo-odontology. Dental Anthropology 17, 1–7.

Tan, J.Z., Peng, Q.Q., Li, J.X., Guan, Y.Q., Zhang, L.P., Jiao, Y., Yang, Y.J., Wang, S.J., Jin, L., 2014. Characteristics of dental morphology in the Xinjiang Uyghur and correlation with the EDARV370A variant. Science China Life Sciences 57, 510–518. http://dx.doi.org/10.1007/s11427-014-4654-x.

Thesleff, I., 2006. The genetic basis of tooth development and dentaldefects. American Journal of Medical Genetics 140A, 2530–2535.

Townsend, G.C., Martin, N.G., 1992. Fitting genetic models to Carabelli trait data in South Australian twins. Journal of Dental Research 71 (2), 403–409.

Townsend, G.C., Bockmann, M., Hughes, T., Brook, A., 2012. Genetic, environmental and epigenetic influences on variation in human tooth number, size and shape. Odontology 100, 1–9.

Tsai, P.L., Hsu, J.W., Liu, K.M., 1996. Logistic analysis of the effects of shovel trait on Carabelli's trait in a Mongoloid population. American Journal of Physical Anthropology 100, 523–530.

Turner II, C.G., 1969. Microevolutionary interpretations from the dentition. American Journal of Physical Anthropology 30 (3), 421–426.

Turner II, C.G., 1987. Late Pleistocene and Holocene population history of East Asia based on dental variation. American Journal of Physical Anthropology 73, 305–321.

Wijsman, E.M., Neves, W.A., 1986. The use of nonmetric variation in estimating human population admixture: a test case with Brazilian blacks, whites, and mulattos. American Journal of Physical Anthropology 70, 395–405.

Xu, S., Jin, L., 2008. A genome-wide analysis of admixture in Uyghurs and a high-density admixture map for disease-gene discovery. American Journal of Human Genetics 83 (3), 322–336.

Yamada, H., Kondo, S., Hanamura, H., Townsend, G.C., 2010. Tooth size in individuals with congenitally missing teeth: a study of Japanese males. Journal of Anthropological Science 118, 87–93.

SECTION

3

Biodistance and Population Studies

CHAPTER

Postmarital Residence Analysis

18

L.W. Konigsberg, S.R. Frankenberg
University of Illinois at Urbana-Champaign, Urbana, IL, United States

CHAPTER OUTLINE HEAD

Introduction 335
The Assessment of Quantitative Trait Phenotypic Variability in Males and in Females 337
Analysis of Postmarital Residence in Prehistoric West Central Illinois 338
Analyzing Male and Female Within-Site Haplotypic Diversity 338
Analyzing Male and Female Within-Site Phenotypic Diversity for Dichotomous Traits 339
Discussion 344
References 345

INTRODUCTION

Postmarital residence patterns are of interest to anthropologists because of the relationships of certain adult residential patterns and forms of mate exchange to the sexual division of labor, household structures, subsistence strategies, and alliance and bond formation (see Walker, 2015 for a review). Archaeologists, in particular, are interested in prehistoric postmarital residence patterns as a proxy indicator of subsistence strategies and village composition (eg, Burns et al., 2012; Cook and Aubry, 2014; Miró-Herrans et al., 2014). However, the analysis of prehistoric postmarital residence is a difficult undertaking because of assumptions contained in certain terms, issues in modeling the effects of differential migration over generations, and difficulties in specifying other variables that may be correlated with residence patterns. This chapter examines prehistoric postmarital residence analyses based on phenotypic and genotypic (haplotypic) information from human skeletal remains. The analysis involves various comparisons between males and females within a single archaeological site.

The use of the term "postmarital residence" in prehistory is problematic in that the real distinction is between an individual's place of birth and his/her adult place of residence. These two places may not be the same for any number of reasons, in addition to the form and state of some type of marriage institution. Additionally, there is an assumption here that the adult place of residence is fairly stable. In the end, all that we can do is assess whether or not residence patterns differed depending on the sex of individuals. Such differences in residence pattern may fit the classic anthropological distinctions between virilocal and uxorilocal residence (Adam, 1947). Here virilocal refers to residence of the husband and wife at the husband's place of birth or childhood, while uxorilocal refers to residence of the husband and wife at the

Biological Distance Analysis. http://dx.doi.org/10.1016/B978-0-12-801966-5.00018-4

wife's place of birth or childhood. Adam (1947) pointed out that these terms were preferable to patrilocal (for virilocal) and matrilocal (for uxorilocal) as the terms patrilocal and matrilocal require that the couple have produced at least one child, and would seem to imply that the residence pattern patrilocal would mean that the child lives with the father and that both have a separate residence from the mother. Similarly, the use of the terms husband and wife implies a certain form of marriage institution. Be this as it may, virilocal and uxorilocal are the more useful terms to contrast residence patterns based on higher female migration rates versus higher male migration rates.

Aside from terminology, two broad issues must be dealt with in discussing the analysis of postmarital residence patterns. First is the problem of modeling the effects of differential migration by sex on population structure. The issue of generational effects raised by Kennedy (1981) in her MA thesis was largely addressed by Konigsberg (1988, 1990b, 2006) within a population genetics framework. Konigsberg's modeling was in contrast to a number of earlier studies from bioarchaeology that had argued by analogy to the evolution of ceramic styles. Rogers and Harpending (1986) gave a more formal basis to models of genetic drift and migration by distinguishing between stochastic events due to sampling of alleles (reproductively) between generations versus stochastic events due to sampling of alleles within generations via migration. Marital residence pattern is therefore sometimes given as the explanation for differing male and female variances, particularly at the between-group level. Rothhammer et al. (1973) have suggested that the greater among-village dermatoglyphic variability for male Yanomama Indians as compared to females is due to the patrilocal (ie, virilocal) residence pattern. But we cannot necessarily make simplistic assumptions about the relationships between male and female migration rates and differences in male and female genetic variation at the within-site or between-site level. Effective population size also has an effect on within-site variation through its relationship to genetic drift, and consequently genetic variation. Williams-Blangero and Blangero (1990, pp. 140–141) note the complications of assuming that it is migration rate alone that drives within-group variation:

> In populations in which there are differences in variances among subdivisions, both the pattern and magnitude of migration are important determinants of within residence variability and the relative relationship between female and male variance. If migrants come from villages with lower variance, variance can actually be decreased in the receiving village after migration.

A second problem is that of specifying other variables that may be correlated with residence patterns. This is generally a necessary first step in an analysis of archaeological material, as we must be able to posit some possible proxy or proxies for residence pattern. Murdock (1949) in particular argued that there was a relationship between virilocal versus uxorilocal residence and the subsistence mode, with virilocality being related to a hunting and gathering subsistence economy, whereas uxorilocality is related to an agricultural subsistence pattern. Naroll refers to this rather simple assumption of a relationship between sexual division of labor and residence pattern as being part of the "main sequence" theory. In his words, "Where the role of the man is predominant, newly married couples tend to live with or near the parents of the groom. Where that of the woman is predominant, they tend instead to live with or near the parents of the bride" (Naroll, 1970, p. 1239). That the male role may be predominant among hunting economies and the female role among agricultural economies is an older idea from the anthropological literature. For example, Driver (1956, p. 4) wrote in regard to American Indians that "hunting and fishing were nearly everywhere chiefly the work of men" while "In the eastern half of the United States women consistently did most of the farming." Further, he found positive correlations between societies classified as having a matridominant division of labor and matrilocal residence as well as between those societies with a patridominant division of labor and patrilocal residence. Indeed, it was not until Ember and Ember (1971) expanded the analysis to a worldwide level that alternative relationships were suggested. The Embers in particular stressed a relationship between internal warfare and virilocal residence. But they (Ember and Ember, 1971, p. 575) also noted that when they restricted their analysis to North America their results were "strikingly similar to that obtained by Driver and Massey."

Korotayev (2003) has suggested a more nuanced version of Murdock's and Driver's association between division of labor and residence pattern. Specifically, he (Korotayev, 2003, p. 364) has stated that in his worldwide analysis, "A very low female contribution to subsistence predicts strongly a nonmatrilocal residence and less strongly patrilocal residence." Additionally, work by Walker (2015) and Flinn and Low (1986) amply demonstrate both the high degree of variability in adult residence pattern, even when certain patterns are preferred or prescribed, and the myriad factors other than division of labor and subsistence strategies that come into play in these decisions.

Although archaeological evidence is generally less informative than the ethnographic record, Bentley et al. (2005, p. 878) write in regard to prehistoric Thailand that "the isotopic evidence from Ban Chiang skeletons is consistent with a transition to matrilocality that, if true, suggests a potential link between marital residence pattern and the prehistoric spread of agriculture." Hart (2001) argues that there was coevolution of maize agriculture and matrilocality among the Iroquois. For West Central Illinois, it remains clear, as it did in the late 1970s (Van der Merwe and Vogel, 1978), that maize agriculture did not become an important component in the subsistence economy until the Mississippian Period. Indeed, Claassen (2013, p. 536) has written more generally for the eastern woodlands that "It was not until the Mississippian Period that maize took on the role of food for native easterners." The question remains as to whether this shift in subsistence strategy was accompanied by a shift in postmarital residence pattern.

The Assessment of Quantitative Trait Phenotypic Variability in Males and in Females

In the most simplistic of models, we expect greater phenotypic variability at the within-group level for the sex with a higher migration rate and greater phenotypic variability at the between-group level for the sex with the lower migration rate. There is broad consensus over the appropriate method for comparing quantitative trait phenotypic variability within males and within females. The basis for comparing quantitative trait variation uses ratios of determinants of variance-covariance matrices. Konigsberg (1988) described a rather crude form of this type of analysis, but it was Petersen (2000) who gave the correct approach based on Zhivotovsky's *F*-ratio. This method had been presaged by Key and Jantz (1990a,b). Petersen also implemented a parametric bootstrap and a nonparametric bootstrap test that could be used in place of Zhivotovsky's test when sample sizes are smaller. Jaffari (2012, p. 299) has referred to Zhivotovsky's ratio of two generalized variances as "better than other existing methods" and has extended the method to include calculation of confidence intervals for the ratio. Unfortunately, Petersen's methods have been applied all too rarely (Morita et al., 2012; Scherer and Wright, 2015). As Zhivotovsky's *F*-test and the parametric and nonparametric bootstraps are available as R scripts at http://konig.la.utk.edu/Rstuff.htm it is hoped that these methods will see greater use in the future for analyzing quantitative trait phenotypic variability.

Analysis of Postmarital Residence in Prehistoric West Central Illinois

In her doctoral dissertation, Bolnick (2005, p. 129) described the following procedure for comparing male and female DNA variation within the Pete Klunk site:

> ...the mean number of pairwise differences (p) for each sex was calculated, and the ratio of these means (p_m/p_f) was used to characterize the relative levels of male and female genetic variation (following Konigsberg, 1988). The statistical significance of this ratio was assessed through nonparametric bootstrapping, in which the observed ratio was compared to a distribution of ratios obtained through 1000 random permutations of the original data matrix with replacement.

The procedure Bolnick described, which was reiterated in Bolnick and Smith (2007), did follow Konigsberg (1988) in many respects. The formation of a ratio and the permutation of cases (so that sexes got reassigned across the DNA data) was the method used in Konigsberg (1988), though he was working with dichotomous phenotypic traits. Bolnick's analysis was partly based on DNA sequence data, and as such it made use of the mismatch distributions within the sexes. In this sense, her analysis differed from Konigsberg's, and it suggests an alternative mode of analysis that could be applied to dichotomous traits as well. In the following section we describe the basic methods, beginning with a reanalysis of Bolnick's DNA data and then showing how to extend the method to analyze dichotomous traits.

Analyzing Male and Female Within-Site Haplotypic Diversity

Bolnick suggested, among other methods, finding the average pairwise difference in nucleotide sequences within males and within females. In her example, she formed the triangular matrix (excluding the diagonal) for pairwise comparisons among 10 Middle Woodland males and among 12 Middle Woodland females from the Pete Klunk mound group. This analysis was done using mtDNA nucleotides 16,016–16,367, though one nucleotide (16,183) was deleted because it is correlated with another site in the sequence. Bolnick consequently found the number of base differences across 351 nucleotide sites for $N_m(N_m-1)/2$ pairwise comparisons in males and $N_f(N_f-1)/2$ pairwise comparisons in females. She then averaged across the 45 male pairwise comparisons and across the 66 female pairwise comparisons and found that the average number of pairwise base differences was 7.133 for males and 5.800 for females. We reanalyzed her summarized sequence data (Bolnick and Smith, 2007, Table 2) using the package "ape" in "R" and found a value of 6.667 for males and 5.606 for females, slightly different from Bolnick's results. As she had done her analysis in Arlequin 2.0, we also calculated mean pairwise differences in Arlequin 3.5.1.2 and again found values of 6.667 and 5.606. It therefore seems that there are some minor errors in Bolnick and Smith's Table 2.

Instead of forming a ratio of the mean pairwise male and female differences and permuting cases, we use an approach more common among DNA sequence data, which is bootstrap sampling across the nucleotides. Felsenstein (1985) and Hasegawa and Kishino (1989) have described this bootstrap procedure where the strategy is to sample with replacement across nucleotide sites. With Bolnick's data, this amounts to sampling with replacement from the 351 nucleotide sites, and calculating the mean pairwise differences within males and within females for each bootstrap sample. Fig. 18.1 shows the results from 10,000 bootstrap samples for males and females where the histograms represent the 10,000 draws and the dotted vertical lines are for the observed values. The 2.5, 50.0, and 97.5 percentile values for male average pairwise differences from the bootstrap samples were 3.889, 6.578, and 9.844 and for females they were 2.954, 5.515, and 8.621. Fig. 18.2 shows how an empirical cumulative density plot can be used to

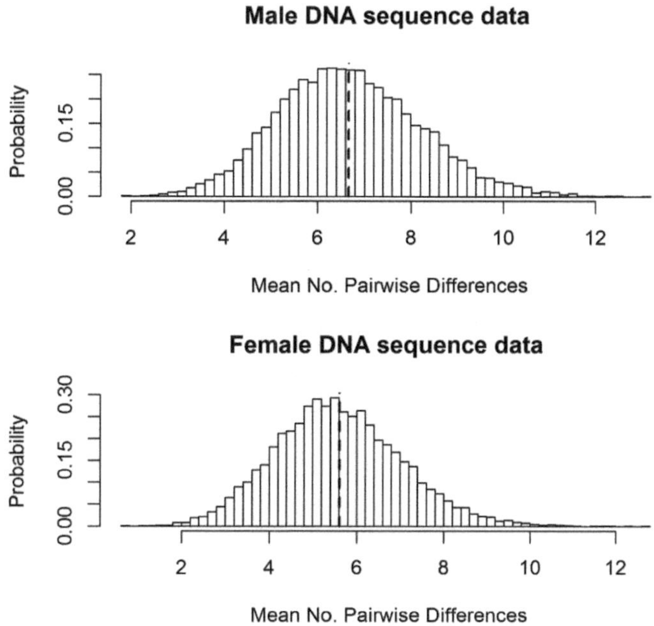

FIGURE 18.1

Histograms of 10,000 bootstrap samples (across nucleotides) for mean number of mtDNA pairwise differences within males and within females for Bolnick and Smith's (2007) Middle Woodland samples from the Pete Klunk Mound Group. The *dashed vertical lines* are the observed male and female values.

summarize this type of information without having to bin the bootstrap samples. Given the extensive overlap between male and female bootstrap distributions in Fig. 18.1, it is clear that either the sample size is too small to detect a difference in male versus female variability or that such a difference in variability did not exist.

Any calculated statistics from the bootstrap sampling can be used to establish confidence intervals, so for example we could form a bootstrap confidence interval on the ratio of average male and female pairwise differences. This is shown in Fig. 18.3 where the 0.025 and 0.975 percentile values are 0.899 and 1.669, which includes the null hypothesis value of 1.0. An advantage of this particular approach is that we can extend it so as to consider male and female variability on a within-archaeological site basis. Konigsberg's (1988) treatment did not deal effectively with this problem of combining information across sites. In the following section we show the extension to analysis of dichotomous traits.

Analyzing Male and Female Within-Site Phenotypic Diversity for Dichotomous Traits

It is a simple matter to treat the coding of dichotomous traits using the codes that are typically used for DNA data. Specifically, we coded the presence of a trait as a C (cytosine) for complete and the absence of a trait as an A (adenine) for absent. Unobservable traits were scored as a ?, which is the code usually used

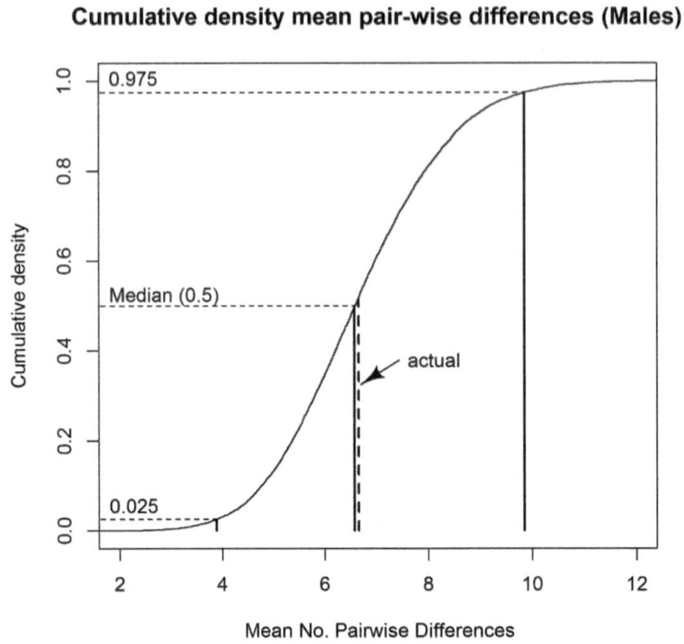

FIGURE 18.2

Empirical cumulative density representation of the 10,000 bootstrap samples for males in Fig. 18.1. The 2.5th, 50th, and 97.5th percentile values are marked, as is the actual observed value.

when bases cannot be read in a particular DNA sequence. We do this particular recoding for the sole reason that it makes available a wide host of nuclear sequence analysis methods, and because the coding of C for complete, A for absent, and ? for unobservable is intuitive. Twenty-three dichotomous cranial traits were analyzed in Konigsberg (1987) and are available for males and females from 11 pre-Mississippian sites and 3 Mississippian sites (Table 18.1). Sixteen of the 23 traits were scored bilaterally, but were collapsed to single traits by random side selection when both sides were available and by using the available side when only one side was available. Numbers of available individuals listed in Table 18.1 differ from Konigsberg (1987, Table 6), Konigsberg (1988, Table 4), and Konigsberg (1990a, Table 1). More individuals were listed as available in Konigsberg (1987) because he included individuals on whom the osteologically assessed sex was indeterminate. Fewer individuals were listed as available in Konigsberg (1988, 1990a,b) as those studies used only a portion of the 23 traits used here, which led to the elimination of individuals who had no observations for the retained traits.

For the sites in Table 18.1, the cultural periods have been listed as Middle Woodland, Late Woodland, Emergent Mississippian, and Mississippian following Konigsberg (1987). The designation of Emergent Mississippian has since fallen out of favor (Fortier and McElrath, 2002) and has been largely replaced with the designation Terminal Late Woodland or Late Late Woodland (Studenmund, 2000). For the purposes of this chapter we will refer to sites simply as Pre-Mississippian (which we take to include the old Emergent Mississippian, now Terminal Late Woodland or Late Late Woodland) versus Mississippian. We do this to distinguish between sites that predate the adoption of intensive maize agriculture and those sites that

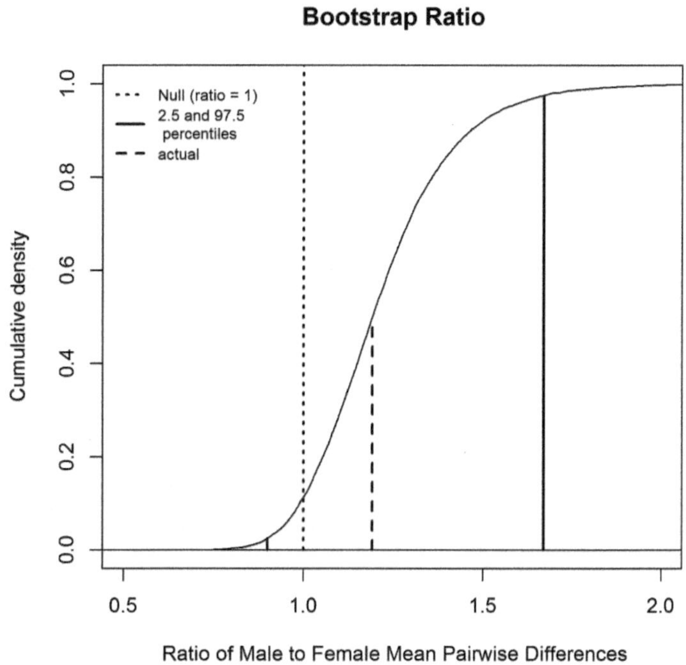

FIGURE 18.3

Empirical cumulative density plot of the 10,000 bootstrap samples where the plotted statistic is the ratio of male-to-female mean pairwise differences.

Table 18.1 Sites, Temporal Components, and Numbers of Males and Females Used in the Cranial Nonmetric Analyses

Site	Time Period	Males	Females
Elizabeth	MW	21	26
Gibson	MW	35	43
Pete Klunk	MW	75	92
Ray	MW	25	25
Koster	LW/EM	44	39
Helton	EM	47	28
Ledders	EM	34	23
Elizabeth	LW	17	20
Pete Klunk	LW/EM	10	17
Schild	EM	36	45
Yokem	EM	15	20
Hacker So. Md. 2	MI	27	19
Schild	MI	61	69
Yokem	MI	18	30

EM, *Terminal Late Woodland (formerly Emergent Mississippian)*; LW, *Late Woodland;* MI, *Mississippean;* MW, *Middle Woodland.*

postdate the adoption. This distinction may be related to a shift in division of labor by sex, and as a consequence it may also be related to a shift in postmarital residence pattern. The distinction that intensive maize agriculture only appears with full-blown Mississippian has generally been borne out for both the Central Illinois (VanDerwarker et al., 2013) and Lower Illinois River valleys and American Bottoms (Hedman et al., 2002). What is problematic is the position of Hacker South Mound 2. Both Konigsberg (1987) and Conner (1990) treated the mound as dating to the Mississippian Period based on the four radiocarbon dates reported in Conner's (1984) doctoral dissertation. But Farnsworth and Koldehoff (2007, p. 41) have called the dates into question and write instead that "Taken together, the artifact associations in Hacker Mound #2 tend to suggest a Terminal Late Woodland age for Hacker South Mound #2...." Given the uncertainty surrounding Hacker South Mound 2's assignments, we initially analyze the data treating Hacker South Mound 2 as Mississippian and then as Pre-Mississippian.

For a comparison to Bolnick and Smith's (2007) results, we begin with a reanalysis of the dichotomous cranial traits from the Middle Woodland component of the Pete Klunk mounds. Fig. 18.4 shows the results from the bootstrap analysis (with 10,000 bootstrap samples) using just the Pete Klunk Middle Woodland individuals. As with Bolnick and Smith's (2007) results from mtDNA, the pairwise differences from dichotomous traits do not provide support for an argument that male and female variances differ for the archaeological site. Interestingly, the directionality differs, as Bolnick and Smith's (2007) analysis of

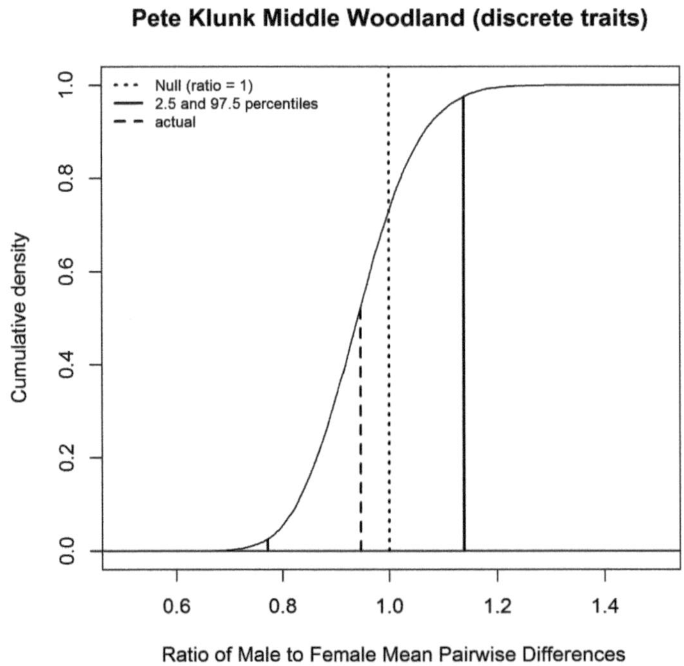

FIGURE 18.4

Empirical cumulative density plot of 10,000 bootstrap samples for the Pete Klunk Middle Woodland Site where the plotted statistic is the ratio of male-to-female mean pairwise differences for cranial discrete traits. Note that the observed ratio value (0.946) is near the 1.0 ratio, indicating equivalent variation in the sexes.

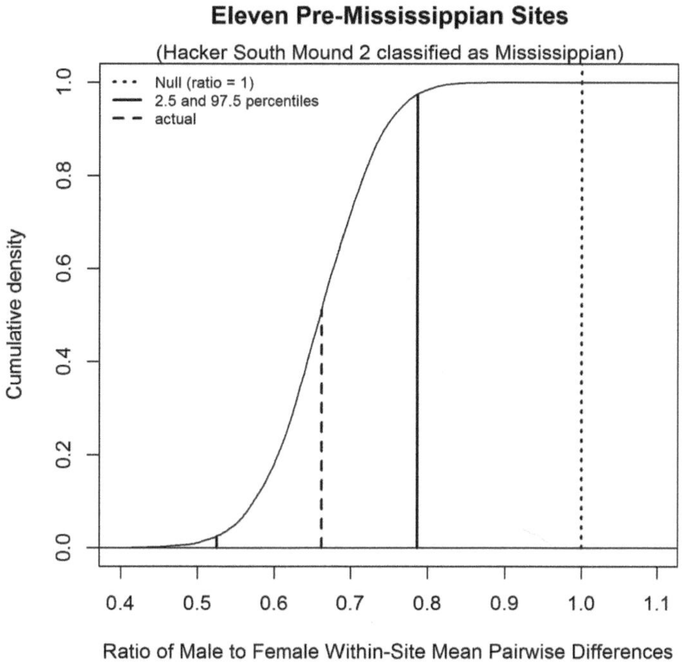

FIGURE 18.5

Empirical cumulative density plot of 10,000 bootstrap samples for 11 pre-Mississippian sites where the plotted statistic is the ratio of male-to-female mean pairwise differences for cranial discrete traits.

pairwise differences suggests that males are the more variable, while the phenotypic analysis suggests the opposite. Bolnick and Smith (2007, p. 638) noted this in comparison to earlier results from Buikstra (1980) and Konigsberg (1988): "males exhibit significantly greater mtDNA diversity than females. This finding is surprising since females exhibit greater morphological variation than males at the Klunk site" (Buikstra, 1980; Konigsberg, 1988).

An advantage of the current approach is that we can find the average within archaeological site pairwise differences for males and for females, and then pool within the sexes. In this way, the pairwise comparisons within the sexes are only done within individual archaeological sites. This is in keeping with Konigsberg's (1988, p. 477) previous comment on the inherent problem with between-site comparisons, where he wrote that "only within-group variances will be considered, since it is virtually impossible to delineate mating networks in prehistoric samples (which would be required in most between-group analyses)." Fig. 18.5 shows the bootstrap analysis for 11 pre-Mississippian sites (treating Hacker South Mound 2 as Mississippian). It shows that the observed ratio of male-to-female average mismatches, equal to 0.6624, is well below the null hypothesis of a ratio equal to 1.0. This is an indication that for the pre-Mississippian sites in general, males are phenotypically more homogenous for cranial discrete traits than are females, at the within-site level. The 95% bootstrap confidence interval is 0.5251–0.7868, which does not include the null hypothesis ratio of 1.0. If Hacker South Mound 2 is treated as being from the Terminal Late Woodland, then the analysis for 12 pre-Mississippian sites is little changed. The observed ratio is 0.6449 and the 95% bootstrap confidence interval is from 0.5112 to 0.7661.

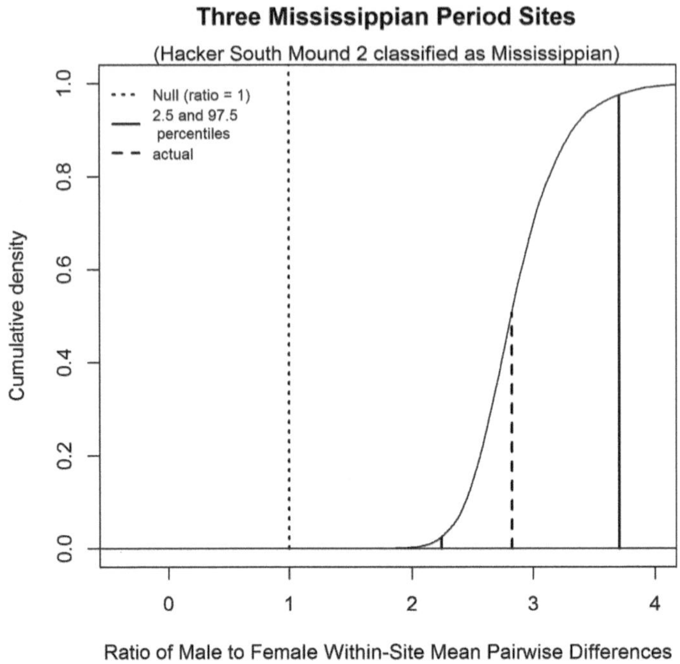

FIGURE 18.6

Empirical cumulative density plot of 10,000 bootstrap samples for three Mississippian sites where the plotted statistic is the ratio of male-to-female mean pairwise differences for cranial discrete traits.

Fig. 18.6 shows the bootstrap analysis for three Mississippian sites (treating Hacker South Mound 2 as Mississippian). The observed ratio of male-to-female average mismatches within sites is 2.8222, which with a 95% bootstrap confidence interval of from 2.2440 to 3 is well above the null hypothesis ratio of 1. Removing Hacker South Mound 2 from the sample does lower the observed ratio to 1.2283, but the 96% bootstrap confidence interval from 1.0544 to 1.4022 does not include a ratio of 1.0. The data consequently support a finding that females are phenotypically more homogenous than males for cranial discrete traits at the within-site level during the Mississippian.

DISCUSSION

The results from the reanalysis of Konigsberg's (1988) study do provide support for an argument that there was a shift from virilocality to uxorilocality in prehistoric West Central Illinois. This shift appears to have coincided with the adoption of intensive maize agriculture during the Mississippian Period. The results from the current study are stronger than those from the earlier study because the randomization procedure in the newer study was across traits rather than across individuals. This allowed for data to be pooled so that the contrasts were between males and females *within* multiple archaeological sites. The use of within-site (archaeological) comparisons is important because between-site comparisons carry the risk of drawing comparisons across different migration networks and across samples that may not be synchronic. From this standpoint, while the use of aDNA is a very welcome addition to the tools we can use to assess postmarital residence patterns, it does have limitations. The primary limitation is the cost in both time and money of obtaining aDNA data. It is this limitation that presumably led to the very small sample size of only 10 Middle Woodland males and 12 Middle Woodland females in the Bolnick and Smith (2007) study. In a more recent study, Dong et al. (2015) had a smaller sample size than Bolnick and Smith (16 total individuals vs Bolnick and Smith's 22). Dong et al. (2015) did not statistically analyze their data partitioned by sex, and instead referred to a heuristic table (their Table 4) that gave glosses of similar versus diverse for mtDNA.

While the information contained in nonmetric traits is much less than that contained in DNA sequence data, nonmetric traits can be rapidly collected and analyzed. When we consider the additional lines of evidence that can be called into play, such as isotopic evidence for residence pattern (Bentley et al., 2005), it becomes clear that genetic data are, at best, still only a supplement to the other resources available for analysis. Given that we may ultimately be interested in differences in migration rates between the sexes, the collection of aDNA data from a limited sample of individuals may be insufficient to characterize these differences. We do not view this comment as limiting future research on aDNA, but rather as emphasizing the fact that it is time to begin integrating different lines of evidence into examinations of prehistoric residence patterns.

References

Adam, L., 1947. Virilocal and uxorilocal. American Anthropologist 49 (4), 678.

Bentley, R.A., Pietrusewsky, M., Douglas, M.T., Atkinson, T.C., 2005. Matrilocality during the prehistoric transition to agriculture in Thailand? Antiquity 79 (306), 865–881.

Bolnick, D.A., Smith, D.G., 2007. Migration and social structure among the Hopewell: evidence from ancient DNA. American Antiquity 72, 627–644.

Bolnick, D.A., 2005. The Genetic Prehistory of Eastern North America: Evidence from Ancient and Modern DNA, Anthropology, University of California, Davis.

Buikstra, J.E., 1980. Epigenetic distance: a study of biological variability in the Lower Illinois River region. In: Browman, D. (Ed.), Early Native Americans. Mouton, Paris, pp. 271–299.

Burns, G.R., Talcott, S., Demps, K., Edmonds, J.L., Lambert, J.M., Tremayne, A., Eerkens, J.W., Bartelink, E.J., 2012. Isotopic evidence for changing residence patterns through the middle to late holocene in central California. Proceedings of the Society for California Archaeology 26, 164–171.

Claassen, C., 2013. Gender in the prehistory of the Eastern United States. In: Bolger, D. (Ed.), A Companion to Gender Prehistory. John Wiley & Sons, Hoboken, NJ, pp. 526–543.

Conner, M.D., 1984. Population Structure and Biological Variation in the Late Woodland of West-Central Illinois. Anthropology, University of Chicago.

Conner, M.D., 1990. Population structure and skeletal variation in the Late Woodland of west-central Illinois. American Journal of Physical Anthropology 82 (1), 31–43.

Cook, R.A., Aubry, B.S., 2014. Aggregation, interregional interaction, and postmarital residence patterning: a study of biological variation in the late prehistoric middle Ohio Valley. American Journal of Physical Anthropology 154 (2), 270–278.

Dong, Y., Li, C., Luan, F., Li, Z., Li, H., Cui, Y., Zhou, H., Malhi, R.S., 2015. Low mitochondrial DNA diversity in an ancient population from China: insight into social organization at the Fujia site. Human Biology 87 (1), 71–84.

Driver, H.E., 1956. An Integration of Functional, Evolutionary, and Historical Theory by Means of Correlations, vol. 12. Indiana University Publications in Anthropology and Linguistics, pp. 1–35.

Ember, M., Ember, C.R., 1971. The conditions favoring matrilocal versus patrilocal residence. American Anthropologist 73 (3), 571–594.

Farnsworth, K.B., Koldehoff, B., 2007. Kingfisher-effigy bone hairpins: clues to Late Woodland iconography and social complexity in west-central Illinois. Illinois Archaeology 15 & 16, 30–57.

Felsenstein, J., 1985. Confidence limits on phylogenies: an approach using the bootstrap. Evolution 39 (4), 783–791.

Flinn, M.V., Low, B.S., 1986. Resource distribution, social competition, and mating patterns in human societies. In: Rubenstein, D.I., Wrangham, R.W. (Eds.), Ecological Aspects of Social Evolution: Birds and Mammals. Princeton University Press, Pinceton, NJ, pp. 217–243.

Fortier, A.C., McElrath, D.L., 2002. Deconstructing the emergent Mississippian concept: the case for the terminal Late Woodland in the American bottom. Midcontinental Journal of Archaeology 171–215.

Hart, J.P., 2001. Maize, matrilocality, migration, and northern Iroquoian evolution. Journal of Archaeological Method and Theory 8 (2), 151–182.

Hasegawa, M., Kishino, H., 1989. Confidence limits of the maximum-likelihood estimate of the hominoid tree from mitochondrial-DNA sequences. Evolution 43 (3), 672–677.

Hedman, K., Hargrave, E.A., Ambrose, S.H., 2002. Late Mississippian diet in the American bottom: stable isotope analyses of bone collagen and apatite. Midcontinental Journal of Archaeology 237–271.

Jafari, A.A., 2012. Inferences on the ratio of two generalized variances: independent and correlated cases. Statistical Methods & Applications 21 (3), 297–314.

Kennedy, B., 1981. Marriage Patterns in an Archaic Population: A Study of Skeletal Remains from Port au Choix, Newfoundland. National Museums of Canada, Ottawa, Canada.

Key, P., Jantz, R., 1990a. Statistical measures of intrasample variability. Human Evolution 5 (5), 457–469.

Key, P.J., Jantz, R.L., 1990b. Statistical assessment of population variability: a methodological approach. American Journal of Physical Anthropology 82 (1), 53–59.

Konigsberg, L.W., 1987. Population Genetic Models for Interpreting Prehistoric Intra-cemetery Biological Variation. Anthropology, Northwestern University, Evanston, IL.

Konigsberg, L.W., 1988. Migration models of prehistoric postmarital residence. American Journal of Physical Anthropology 77, 471–482.

Konigsberg, L.W., 1990a. Analysis of prehistoric biological variation under a model of isolation by geographic and temporal distance. Human Biology 62, 49–70.

Konigsberg, L.W., 1990b. Temporal aspects of biological distance: serial correlation and trend in a prehistoric skeletal lineage. American Journal of Physical Anthropology 82, 45–52.

Konigsberg, L.W., 2006. A post-Neumann history of biological and genetic distance studies in bioarchaeology. In: Buikstra, J.E., Beck, L.A. (Eds.), Bioarchaeology: The Contextual Analysis of Human Remains. Academic Press, Amsterdam, pp. 263–280.

Korotayev, A., 2003. Division of labor by gender and postmarital residence in cross-cultural perspective: a reconsideration. Cross-Cultural Research 37 (4), 335–372.

Miró-Herrans, A.T., Al-Meeri, A., Mulligan, C.J., 2014. Human migration patterns in Yemen and implications for reconstructing prehistoric population movements. PLoS One 9 (4), 1–9.

Morita, W., Kusaka, S., Yano, W., Nakatsukasa, M., 2012. Dental metric variability associated with human migration from skeletal remains of two Jomon sites (Yoshigo and Inariyama) in the Atsumi Peninsula area. Anthropological Science 120 (2), 167–177.

Murdock, G.P., 1949. Social Structure. Macmillan, New York, NY.

Naroll, R., 1970. What have we learned from cross-cultural surveys? American Anthropologist 72 (6), 1227–1288.

Petersen, H.C., 2000. On statistical methods for comparison of intrasample morphometric variability: Zalavár revisited. American Journal of Physical Anthropology 113 (1), 79–84.

Rogers, A.R., Harpending, H.C., 1986. Migration and genetic drift in human populations. Evolution 40, 1312–1327.

Rothhammer, F., Neel, J., Da Rocha, F., Sundling, G., 1973. The genetic structure of a tribal population, the Yanomama Indians. 8. Dermatoglyphic differences among villages. American Journal of Human Genetics 25 (2), 152–166.

Scherer, A.K., Wright, L.E., 2015. Dental morphometric and strontium isotope evidence for population history at Tikal, Guatemala. In: Cucina, A. (Ed.), Archaeology and Bioarchaeology of Population Movement Among the Prehispanic Maya. Springer, New York, NY, pp. 109–118.

Studenmund, S., 2000. Late Woodland occupations in the Lower Illinois Valley: research questions and data sets. In: Emerson, T.E., McElrath, D.L., Fortier, A.C. (Eds.), Late Woodland Societies: Tradition and Transformation Across the Midcontinent. University of Nebraska Press, Lincoln, NE, pp. 301–343.

Van der Merwe, N.J., Vogel, J.C., 1978. 13C content of human collagen as a measure of prehistoric diet in woodland North America. Nature 276, 815–816.

VanDerwarker, A.M., Wilson, G.D., Bardolph, D.N., 2013. Maize adoption and intensification in the central Illinois River valley: an analysis of archaeobotanical data from the Late Woodland to early Mississippian periods (AD 600–1200). Southeastern Archaeology 32 (2), 147–168.

Walker, R.S., 2015. Human residence patterns. In: Scott, R., Kosslyn, S. (Eds.), Emerging Trends in the Social and Behavioral Sciences. John Wiley & Sons, New York, NY, pp. 1–8.

Williams-Blangero, S., Blangero, J., 1990. Effects of population structure on within-group variation in the Jirels of Nepal. Human Biology 62, 131–146.

CHAPTER

19

Population Structure During the Collapse of the Moche (AD 200–850): A Comparison of Results Derived From Deciduous and Permanent Tooth Trait Data From San José de Moro, Jequetepeque Valley, Perú

R.C. Sutter, T. Chhatiawala
Indiana University-Purdue University Fort Wayne, Fort Wayne, IN, United States

CHAPTER OUTLINE HEAD

Introduction 349
Background 351
Materials and Methods 352
  Biodistance and Population Structure Analyses 353
Results 356
  Biodistances and Population Structure 356
Discussion and Conclusions 358
References 359

INTRODUCTION

Despite recommendations to the contrary (Lasker, 1950), numerous investigators have explored deciduous tooth crown and root morphological variation (Aguirre et al., 2006; Aragón et al., 2008; Bailey et al., 2014; Benazzi et al., 2010; Brabant, 1967; Brook and Winter, 1970; Grine, 1986; Hanihara, 1956, 1961, 1963, 1965, 1970; Jørgensen, 1956; Kitagawa, 2000; Kitagawa et al., 1995, 1996; Lease and Sciulli, 2005; Lucacks and Kuswandari, 2013; Lucacks and Walimbe, 1984; Nelson and Griffin, 1996; Paul and Stojanowski, 2015; Saunders and Mayhall, 1982; Sciulli, 1977, 1979, 1990, 1998; Suzuki and Sakai, 1973; Tocheri, 2002). Although most of the cited studies are largely descriptive in nature, some have explored biodistances derived using deciduous dentitions (Aragón et al., 2008; Kitagawa, 2000; Lucacks and Walimbe, 1984; Paul and Stojanowski, 2015; Sciulli, 1998). Recently, Edgar and Lease (2007) and

Biological Distance Analysis. http://dx.doi.org/10.1016/B978-0-12-801966-5.00019-6

Pilloud and Larsen (2011) provided empirical support for other studies (Saunders and Mayhall, 1982; Smith and Garn, 1987) that document a close correspondence between levels of expression and biodistance results derived from deciduous and adult nonmetric tooth crown and root traits. To date, however, no studies have specifically examined the correspondence between population structure estimates (ie, *R*-matrix, biodistances, and F_{st}) derived using deciduous and adult dentitions. Here, we examine population structure estimates derived from deciduous dentitions for three temporal samples from the Moche (AD 200–850) site, San José de Moro (Fig. 19.1), and compare those estimates to those previously reported for the region by Sutter and Castillo (2015). We also compare the results derived from the

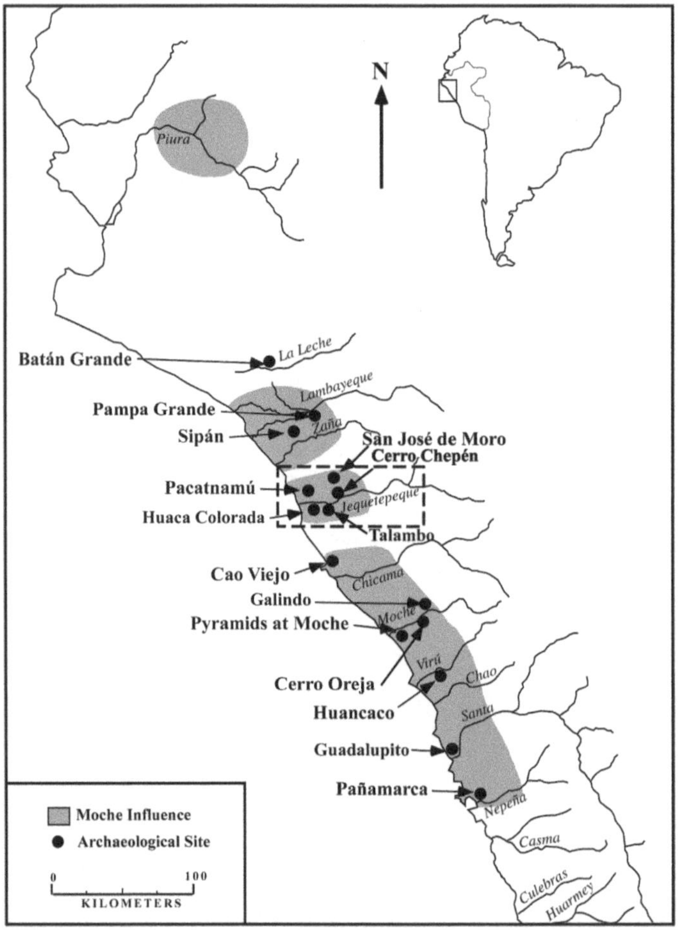

FIGURE 19.1

Moche regions of influence.

After Castillo, L.J., Quilter, J., 2010. Many Moche models: an overview of past and current theories and research on Moche political organization. In: Quilter, J., Castillo, L.J. (Eds.), New Perspectives on Moche Political Organization, Dumbarton Oaks, Washington, DC, p. 3.

deciduous dentitions to population structure estimates derived for adult dentitions from the same site. Our goal is to determine if deciduous tooth traits produce similar estimates of genetic variability and biodistance results as those derived using adult dentitions from the same as reported by Sutter and Castillo (2015): similar results may suggest that deciduous tooth traits are useful for the estimation of population structure and genetic relatedness (ie, *R*-matrix biodistances and F_{st} values).

BACKGROUND

The Moche were a number of complex societies that likely represented nascent states or shifting confederations of competing complex polities (Castillo, 2001; Castillo and Quilter, 2010; Castillo and Uceda, 2008) within the coastal valleys of the north coast of Perú. The nature of these polities and their degree of sociopolitical integration remains the source of continued investigations. General consensus suggests that there were two independent spheres of influence: one in the north (Piura to Jequetepeque valleys), and one in the south (ie, Chicama to Huarmey valleys). Although sociopolitical developments in the southern Moche valleys likely resulted from the expansion of a multivalley state with its seat of power in the Moche Valley, the Jequetepeque Valley was characterized by the sociopolitical fragmentation of competing Moche polities, each with their own independent irrigation canals and fortified settlements (Castillo, 2010; Castillo and Uceda, 2008).

For the Jequetepeque Valley (Fig. 19.2), although the cultural sequence is similar to those reported for the southern Moche, some important differences exist. Namely, Castillo (2003) has developed a three-phase Moche ceramic chronology for the Jequetepeque Valley that only broadly corresponds to the traditional five-phase ceramic chronology developed for the southern Moche (Fig. 19.3). Unlike elsewhere in the region, the Moche persisted at San José de Moro for another 150 years, where a proposed lineage of ruling elite priestesses carried on Moche feasting and sacrificial traditions (Castillo, 2001, 2006). Through his excavations at San José de Moro, Castillo has uncovered nearly 1300 burials dating to the Middle Moche (~AD 550–700), Late Moche (~AD 700–850), and the Transitional (~AD 850–950) periods. While clusters of boot tombs associated with Middle Moche ceramics typify burials of the Middle Moche period, the subsequent Late Moche period is characterized by tombs that often contain a new style of Moche fineline wares and imported styles from the central coastal Nievería, adjacent highland Cajamarca, and southern highland Wari traditions. The Transitional period is associated with the collapse of the Moche polity at San José de Moro and the subsequent emergence of the north coast Lambayeque influence. During the Transitional period, Castillo (2000) hypothesizes that an absence of centralized power at San José de Moro permitted a diversification of cultural expression. The early Transitional period is marked by eclecticism, with local ceramics blending with foreign styles from the central coast, adjacent highlands, and distant Ayacucho region. Both in terms of quantity and quality, the exotic wares included as funerary offerings at San José de Moro are unparalleled in the north coast region (Castillo and Uceda, 2008).

Sutter and Castillo (2015) reported population structure analyses based upon genetically influenced nonmetric tooth cusp and root traits for adults interred at San José de Moro as compared to other samples from the region. Their results indicate that during the Middle Moche period, Moche skeletal populations from both the Jequetepeque and Moche valleys exhibited relatively low levels of genetic variability and that all populations were part of a relatively homogenous breeding population. However, beginning with the Late Moche period, individuals interred at San José de Moro exhibited greater genetic variability and

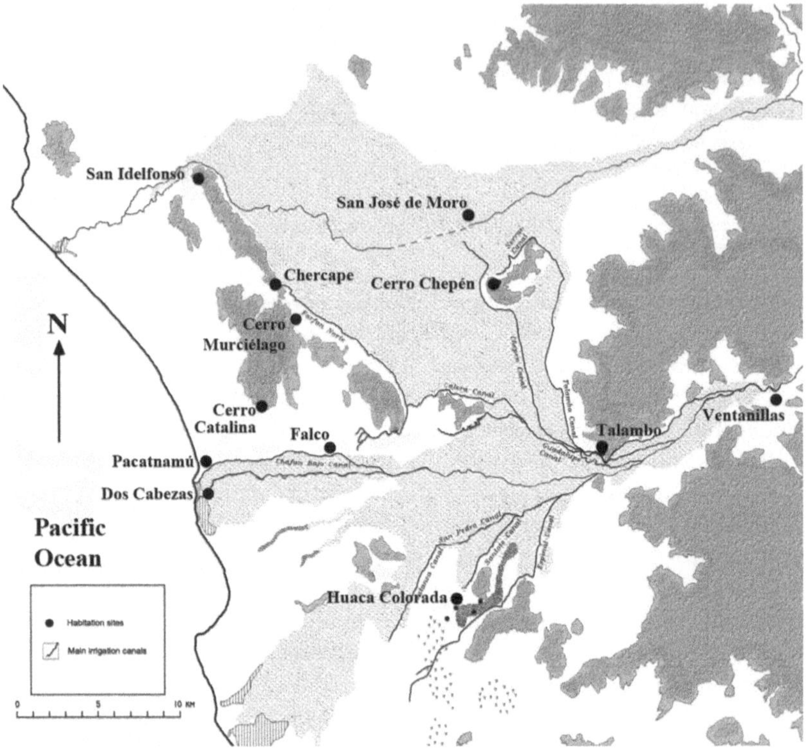

FIGURE 19.2

Archaeological sites of the Jequetepeque Valley.

Modified from *Rosas, M., 2010. Cerro Chepén and the Late Moche collapse in the Jequetepeque Valley, North Coast of Perú (Ph.D. dissertation). Department of Anthropology, University of New Mexico, Albuquerque*, Fig. 5.2, 927–930.

received more extralocal gene flow than both previous and other contemporaneous Moche populations. These trends increased during the subsequent Transitional period.

MATERIALS AND METHODS

Human nonmetric dental trait data are used to derive estimates of genetic distance and variation among subadult skeletal samples from the Middle Moche ($n = 9$), Late Moche ($n = 23$), and Transitional ($n = 23$) periods at San José de Moro. Data for 21 deciduous nonmetric tooth traits (Table 19.1) were scored using standardized descriptions (Hanihara, 1961; Kitagawa, 2000; Sciulli, 1998). Nonmetric tooth trait variation for permanent teeth from subadults that had mixed dentition is not utilized by this study, therefore—given that all individuals were roughly six skeletal years of age or younger—tooth wear is not considered to be a factor in tooth trait variation. The deciduous tooth crown and root traits scored by this study were selected based upon their ease of scoring and inferred intra- and interobserver replicability: although no formal intra- nor interobserver error study was conducted, other studies have reported

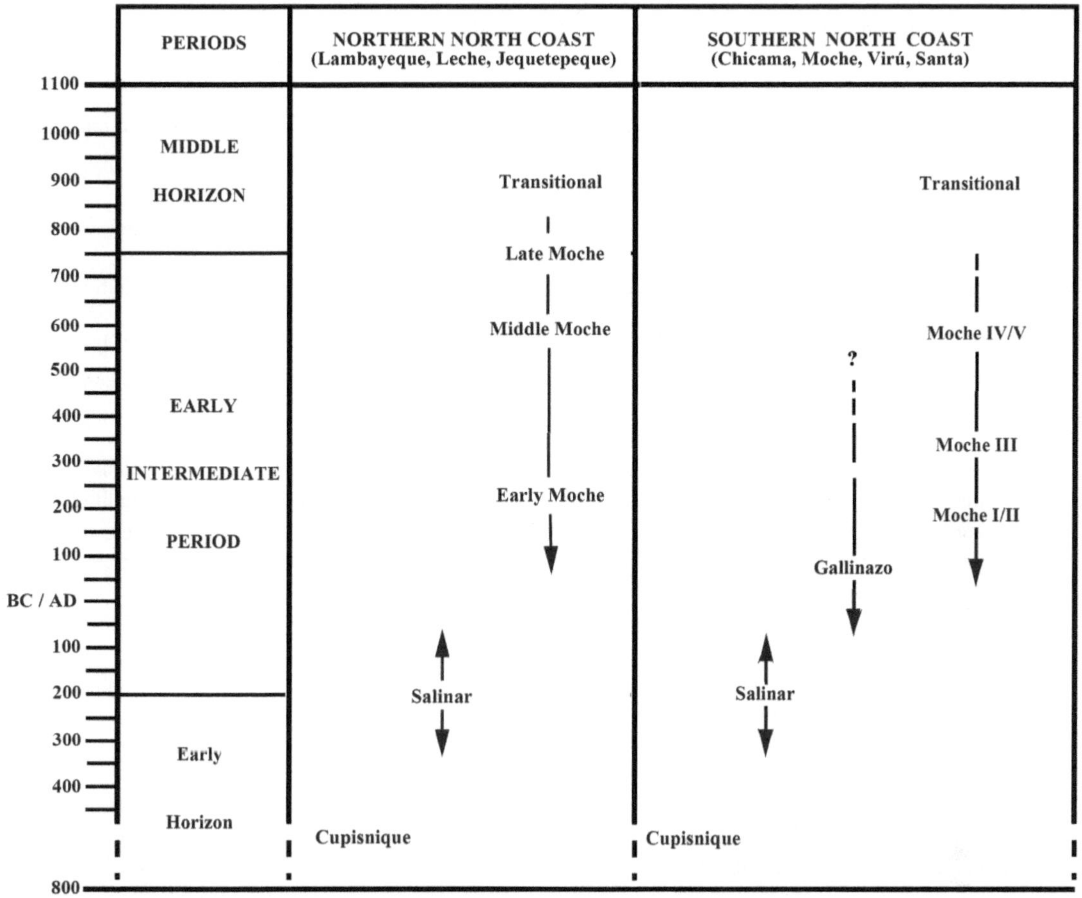

FIGURE 19.3

Southern versus Northern Moche ceramic chronologies.

After Castillo, L.J., Quilter, J., 2010. Many Moche models: an overview of past and current theories and research on Moche political organization. In: Quilter, J., Castillo, L.J. (Eds.), New Perspectives on Moche Political Organization, Dumbarton Oaks, Washington, DC, p. 3.

relatively low rates of error, especially when the traits observed are either present/absent or when they have fewer grades of variation to be scored (Nichol and Turner, 1986).

Biodistance and Population Structure Analyses

For the biodistance analyses, teeth were scored according to the individual count method described by Turner and Scott (1977). In cases where an individual exhibited asymmetry in the expression of a given trait the greatest level of expression is used. Given the small sample sizes for the three skeletal populations considered here, those traits where fewer than 10 observations were possible for more than one of the three samples were eliminated from further analyses.

Table 19.1 Deciduous Tooth Traits Examined by This Study

Maxillary Traits	Deciduous Teeth Examined for Trait Presence	Range	Presence	Reference
Winging	Maxillary central incisors	[a]0–1	[a]1	Sciulli (1998)
Shoveling	Maxillary incisors and canines	0–3	2–3	Kitagawa (2000)
Double shoveling	Maxillary incisors and canine	0–3	1–3	Scuilli (1998)
Interruption groove	Maxillary incisors	[b]0–1	[b]1	Scuilli (1998)
Cusp number	Maxillary deciduous molars	2–4	4	Kitagawa (2000)
Metaconule	Maxillary dm2	0–1	1	Kitagawa (2000)
Cusp 5	Maxillary dm2	0–1	1	Scuilli (1998)
Carabelli's trait	Maxillary dm2	0–4	2–4	Sciulli (1998)
Enamel extensions	Maxillary dm2	0–3	2–3	Kitagawa (2000)
Mandibular Traits	**Deciduous Teeth Examined for Trait Presence**	**Range**	**Presence**	**Presence**
Double teeth (twinning/fusion)	Mandibular incisors and canines	0–1	1	Sciulli (1998)
Shoveling	Mandibular incisors	0–3	2–3	Kitagawa (2000)
Delta-shaped crown	Mandibular dm1	0–1	1	Kitagawa (2000)
Deflecting wrinkle	Mandibular dm2	0–3	1–3	Kitagawa (2000)
Protostylid	Mandibular dm2	0–2	1–2	Sciulli (1998)
Hypoconulid (cusp 5)	Mandibular dm2	0–3	1–3	Sciulli (1998)
Entoconulid (cusp 6)	Mandibular dm2	0–3	1–3	Kitagawa (2000)
Metaconulid (cusp 7)	Mandibular dm2	0–3	1–3	Kitagawa (2000)
Enamel extension	Mandibular dm2	0–3	2–3	Kitagawa (2000)
Distolingual root	Mandibular dm2	0–1	1	Kitagawa (2000)
Distal trigonid crest	Mandibular dm2	0–1	1	Kitagawa (2000)

[a]*Rather than scoring winging as 1 = unilateral and 2 = bilateral, left and right UI1 were scored independently. For subsequent biodistance analyses, any presence was considered present for this study.*
[b]*For simplicity, the scoring of this trait was modified to a simple present/absent (1/0). Additional qualitative information regarding location of the interruption groove was recorded on the data sheets. For subsequent biodistance analyses, any presence was considered present for this study.*

This study estimates levels of genetic diversity (F_{st}) and its standard error (Relethford, 1996, 2003; Relethford and Blangero, 1990; Relethford et al., 1997; Williams-Blangero, 1989a,b; Williams-Blangero and Blangero, 1989) as well as estimates of genetic distances between the samples being studied using the *R*- (relational) matrix method (Relethford, 2003; Relethford and Blangero, 1990; Relethford et al., 1997) using a code written by Lyle Konigsberg for the statistical program R 2.15.2. The *R*-matrix provides an estimate of sample variability and the degree of similarity to other samples being compared (Relethford and Blangero, 1990). The *R*-matrix is a matrix of average kinship coefficients between populations (off the diagonal or r_{ij}) and within populations (on the diagonal or r_{ii}). Therefore, samples with positive r_{ij} values are genetically more similar, while those with negative values are less similar than average (Irish, 2010).

R-matrix analysis is also used to derive both phenetic distances (Mahalanobis' distance), which reveal the patterns of genetic relatedness primarily due to gene flow and ancestral-descent relationships among the samples, and estimates of the effects of genetic drift and gene flow, or F_{st}. The Mahalanobis' generalized distance (d^2) for binary epigenetic traits (Konigsberg, 1990) is calculated as a biodistance measure between two skeletal samples *i* and *j*, which represent the minimum genetic distance between two groups being compared (Williams-Blangero, 1989a). This distance is determined using the following equation:

$$d_{ij}^2 = (z_{ik} - z_{jk})' T^{-1} (z_{ik} - z_{jk}), \tag{19.1}$$

where, as Konigsberg (1990, p. 60) explains, "z_{ik} represents the threshold value corresponding to a trait frequency of p_{ik} for trait *k* in site *i*, z_{jk} is the threshold value for trait *k* in site *j*, and *T* is a pooled tetrachoric correlation matrix between the *k* traits."

Using *R*-matrix analysis, we generated both phenetic distances, which reveal the patterns of genetic relatedness primarily due to gene flow and ancestral-descent relationships among the samples, and estimates of the effects of regional genetic drift and gene flow, or F_{st}. Theoretically, populations that frequently shared mates will be characterized by smaller phenetic distances between them than those populations that rarely shared mates. Subsequently, those populations that frequently shared mates should have small F_{st} values (populations exhibiting no differences between them will have an $F_{st} = 0$) while comparisons between those populations that rarely shared mates will have large F_{st} values.

Once differences in effective population size are accounted for, any changes in heterozygosity will reflect effects of migration and population history (Relethford, 1996). Proportional estimates of effective population sizes are necessary for bias-correction of the *R*-matrix, and are either estimated from historic records (Relethford, 2003; Relethford et al., 1997; Stojanowski, 2003, 2005, 2009) or archaeologically derived estimates of population densities or site habitation areas (Nystrom, 2006). Unbiased estimates of both the *R*-matrix and F_{st} were then calculated using formulae from Relethford et al. (1997). Effective population sizes used by this study are based upon relative differences from estimates of settlement pattern studies and irrigable land estimates for the Moche era within the Jequetepeque Valley (Castillo, 2010; Wilson, 1999) and are the same estimates as those used by Sutter and Castillo (2015), which assumed equal population size estimates for the three temporal samples from San José de Moro. Although not presented here, other varying population size estimates for the three temporal samples from San José de Moro were also modeled, but none were found to have any meaningful effect on either the resulting deciduous F_{st} nor its standard error (ie, varying population size estimates for each of the three temporal samples resulted in differences that were <0.001 for both the F_{st} and its standard error).

R-matrix analyses for this preliminary study were conducted using a conservative heritability estimate of 1, which produces the minimum F_{st} (Relethford and Blangero, 1990). Significance tests for differences in F_{st} were derived from standard error calculations (Relethford et al., 1997). While future analyses might explore F_{st} using different estimates of heritability, previous studies have demonstrated that patterns of *R*-matrix analyses are largely unaffected by different heritability estimates and bias corrections (Nystrom, 2006; Stojanowski, 2005). Further, for purposes of comparability, a heritability estimate of 1 was also used in a study by Sutter and Castillo (2015) that examined phenetically derived regional levels of genetic diversity (F_{st}) and biodistances for north coast Moche adult skeletal populations that also included the adult samples from San José de Moro.

RESULTS

Biodistances and Population Structure

Twenty-five of the original 36 tooth trait combinations for 27 traits were eliminated for biodistance analyses due to insufficient sample sizes (>10 observations for more than two of the three samples). Nine tooth trait combinations were retained for subsequent biodistance and population structure analyses. These include groove pattern (Ldm2 Groove), presence of the protostylid (Ldm2 Proto) and hypoconulid (Ldm2 Hypo) for the deciduous lower second molars, shoveling and double shoveling for the deciduous upper central incisor (Udi1 Shovel and Udi1 DShov), shoveling and double shoveling for the deciduous upper canine (Udc Shovel and Udc DShov), and cusp number for each of the deciduous upper molars (Udm1 Cusp No and Udm2 Cusp No). Trait frequencies for the three temporal subadult skeletal populations from San José de Moro reported here are presented in Table 19.2. Inspection of the matrix of tetrachoric correlations among the nine remaining traits indicated that all intertrait correlations were low (<0.27).

The results of the unadjusted (biased) Mahalanobis' d^2 values and F_{st} analyses for subadult samples from San José de Moro are presented in Table 19.3, and the unadjusted values for three adult temporal samples from the site are presented in Table 19.4. Adjusted (unbiased) intersite distances and F_{st} values for subadult and adult dentitions are presented in Tables 19.5 and 19.6, respectively. The biased (uncorrected) phenotypic F_{st} for the subadult skeletal samples from San José de Moro is 0.037 (S.E. = 0.015), while the uncorrected F_{st} derived from adult dentitions from San José de Moro is 0.049 (S.E. = 0.0.11): the unadjusted F_{st} estimates for both the deciduous and permanent dentitions are significantly different from 0 at the 0.05 level. The Mantel matrix test was run for the two uncorrected subadult and adult distance matrices dentitions using 999 iterations and produced an $r = 0.997$ ($p = .001$). The unbiased F_{st} for the subadult skeletal samples from San José de Moro is 0.037 (S.E. = 0.038), while the unbiased for F_{st}

Table 19.2 Dental Crown and Root Trait Frequencies for the Three Temporal Subadult Skeletal Populations From San José de Moro for the Nine Traits Retained for This Study

Nonmetric Tooth Trait	Middle Moche Period (%)	Late Moche Period (%)	Transitional Period (%)
Ldm2 groove	71 (5/7)	75 (15/20)	89 (18/16)
Ldm2 proto	86 (6/7)	94 (17/18)	81 (13/16)
Ldm2 hypo	86 (6/7)	95 (19/20)	100 (20/20)
Udi1 shovel	100 (7/7)	100 (12/12)	100 (19/19)
Udi1 double shovel	71 (5/7)	54 (7/13)	28 (5/18)
Udc shovel	100 (8/8)	100 (19/19)	100 (15/15)
Udm1 cusp no.	100 (8/8)	100 (19/19)	100 (15/15)
Udm2 cusp no.	100 (7/7)	95 (19/20)	100 (20/20)
Udc double shovel	75 (6/8)	100 (8/8)	100 (15/15)

Table 19.3 The Unadjusted Mahalanobis' Squared Distances (Below the Diagonal) and the R-Matrix (Diagonal and Above) for Three Subadult Skeletal Samples Analyzed by This Study From San José de Moro, Peru [The r_{ii} Values Are the Diagonal Values in Bold, While the r_{ij} Values Are Above the Diagonal. The Unadjusted F_{st} = 0.037 (S.E. = 0.015)]

	Middle Moche	Late Moche	Transitional
Middle Moche	**0.053**	−0.017	−0.037
Late Moche	1.959	**0.018**	−0.002
Transitional	3.077	1.113	**0.038**

Table 19.4 The Unadjusted Mahalanobis' Squared Distances (Below the Diagonal) and the R-Matrix (Diagonal and Above) for Three Adult Skeletal Samples From San José de Moro, Peru [The r_{ii} Values Are the Diagonal Values in Bold, While the r_{ij} Values Are Above the Diagonal. The Unadjusted F_{st} = 0.049 (S.E. = 0.0.11)]

	Middle Moche	Late Moche	Transitional
Middle Moche	**0.083**	−0.018	−0.066
Late Moche	1.856	**0.008**	0.009
Transitional	3.946	0.665	**0.056**

Table 19.5 The Unbiased Mahalanobis' Squared Distances (Below the Diagonal) and the R-Matrix (Diagonal and Above) for Three Subadult Skeletal Samples Analyzed by This Study From San José de Moro, Peru [The r_{ii} Values Are the Diagonal Values in Bold, While the r_{ij} Values Are Above the Diagonal. The Unbiased F_{st} = 0.037 (S.E. = 0.038)]

	Middle Moche	Late Moche	Transitional
Middle Moche	**0.018**	0.002	0.008
Late Moche	0.105	**0.061**	0.003
Transitional	0.165	0.060	**0.013**

Table 19.6 The Unbiased Mahalanobis' Squared Distances (Below the Diagonal) and the R-Matrix (Diagonal and Above) for Three Adult Skeletal Samples From San José de Moro, Peru [The r_{ii} Values Are the Diagonal Values in Bold, While the r_{ij} Values Are Above the Diagonal. The Unbiased F_{st} = 0.049 (S.E. = 0.012)]

	Middle Moche	Late Moche	Transitional
Middle Moche	**0.028**	0.002	0.001
Late Moche	0.126	**0.003**	0.001
Transitional	0.270	0.045	**0.019**

derived using permanent dentitions from the same site is 0.049 (S.E. = 0.012). The Mantel test for the two unbiased subadult and adult distance matrices using 999 iterations also produced an $r = 0.997$ ($p = .001$). In this case, however, only the F_{st} estimate from adult dentitions is significantly different from 0. On the other hand, strictly on statistical grounds, there is little evidence that either gene flow or genetic drift impacted the population structure for the three subadult temporal samples, and that, through time, the parent populations were a relatively coherent breeding population. In other words, most of the variation exists within the subadult samples and not between them.

Although there is a strong concordance in the patterns and magnitudes of the R-matrix, F_{st}, and biodistances for the subadult and adult dental samples from San José de Moro, the lack of a statistically significant F_{st} for the subadult samples is likely due to the relative paucity of remains relative to adults for each of the three temporal samples. Overall, however, the magnitude of the F_{st} reported here for the three temporal subadult samples from San José de Moro is similar to that compared to F_{st} values reported for other prehistoric skeletal populations (see Nystrom, 2006; Stojanowski, 2005) as well as those for the three adult temporal samples from the site reported by Sutter and Castillo (2015). Trends for both the unbiased R-matrix and biodistance results (Tables 19.5 and 19.6) indicate that genetic differentiation increased in the Jequetepeque Valley during both the Late Moche period and even more so during the Transitional period. Inspection of the average kinship coefficients between populations (off diagonal or r_{ij} values) indicates that, through time, the temporal samples become increasingly less similar to one another, as we might expect among sequential temporal samples. However, Sutter and Castillo (2015) report that the adult Transitional sample is least similar, which suggests increasing gene flow into the region during the period covering the Late Moche and Transitional periods. Although not significant, the results derived from deciduous dentitions lend support to this interpretation and exhibit similar trends. This corresponds well with the archaeological evidence for increased extralocal influence during the Transitional period.

DISCUSSION AND CONCLUSIONS

Results of this study indicate that population structure analyses based upon deciduous nonmetric tooth traits exhibit a high correspondence with those derived using adult dentitions as indicated by high and significant correlations between the deciduous and permanent tooth trait data sets ($r = 0.997$; $p = .001$). Given the similar patterns we report here to the population structure estimates derived using permanent tooth traits for both the region (Sutter and Castillo, 2015) and adults from the same site, we argue that the population structure results reported here for deciduous dentitions are robust.

Further, the population structure results reported here derived using deciduous traits also provide support for the archaeological evidence and results from Sutter and Castillo (2015) that point to external gene flow into the Jequetepeque Valley following the Middle Moche period. As the Moche's influence began to wane throughout the region during the Late Moche period, evidence for external contacts in the form of exotic ceramics from the Central coast (ie, Nievería) and highlands (ie, Cajamarca, Chachapoyas, Wari) become evident from grave lots at San José de Moro. Both the biodistance and R-matrix results (Table 19.5) indicate that the Late Moche sample from San José de Moro received extralocal gene flow. The levels of external gene flow and genetic differentiation continued to increase during the subsequent Transitional Period at San José de Moro. Importantly, Castillo and Uceda (2008) emphasize that the appearance of exotic wares is unique to San José de Moro and that such wares are largely absent from other Late Moche and Transitional period sites from the north coast of Perú. Therefore, the corresponding levels of external gene flow and culture contact evident during the Late and Transitional periods at San José de Moro may not reflect changes at other contemporaneous north coast sites.

However, given the relatively small subadult sample sizes, the conclusions drawn by this study should be considered tentative. Indeed, while the unadjusted F_{st} results for deciduous teeth significantly differed from zero, the unbiased F_{st} results did not, likely due to the relatively small sample sizes and limited phenetic variation exhibited for the nine deciduous tooth traits we examined: we found that well over half of the subadults that we examined for deciduous tooth traits either lacked their anterior teeth or that their deciduous molars were still developing at the time of death and, therefore, their traits were unobservable. While the results reported here are promising, we suspect that small sample sizes and limited tooth trait variation will also be an issue for other investigators who attempt to use deciduous dentitions for population structure analyses. On the other hand, it may simply be the case that relatively little variation exists in the dentitions of prehistoric north coast Andeans. We encourage other investigators to explore the viability of using deciduous teeth as an additional means of assessing population structure of skeletal populations by comparing estimates from both deciduous and permanent dentition samples from the same site(s).

References

Aguirre, L., Castillo, D., Solarte, D., Moreno, F., 2006. Frequency and variability of five non-metric dental crown traits in the primary and permanent dentitions of a racially mixed population from Cali, Colombia. Dental Anthropology 19 (2), 39–48.

Aragón, N., Bastidas, C., Bedón, L.K., Duque, P., Sánchez, M., Rivera, S., Triana, F., Bedoya, N., Moreno, F., 2008. Rasgos Morfológicos Dentales Coronales en Dentición Temporal y Permanente: Distancia Biológica Entre Tres Grupos Indígenas del Amazonas Colombiano. Revista Odontológica Mexicana 12 (1), 13–28.

Bailey, S.E., Benazzi, S., Astorino, C., Paul, K.S., Hublin, J.-J., 2014. Taxonomic difference in decidous upper second molar crown outlines of Homo sapiens, Homo neanderthalensis, and Homo erectus. Journal of Human Evolution 72, 1–9.

Benazzi, S., Buti, L., Franzo, I., Kullmer, O., Winzen, O., Gruppioni, G., 2010. Report of three fused primary human teeth in an Archaeological material. International Journal of Osteoarchaeology 20, 481–485.

Brabant, H., 1967. Comparison of the characteristics and anomalies of the deciduous and the permanent dentition. Journal of Dental Research 46 (Suppl. 5), 897–902.

Brook, A.H., Winter, S.B., 1970. Double teeth: a retrospective study of "germinated" and "fused" teeth in children. British Dental Journal 129, 123–130.

Castillo, L.J., Quilter, J., 2010. Many Moche models: an overview of past and current theories and research on Moche political organization. In: Quilter, J., Castillo, L.J. (Eds.), New Perspectives on Moche Political Organization. Dumbarton Oaks, Washington, DC, pp. 1–16.

Castillo, L.J., Uceda, S., 2008. The Mochicas. In: Silverman, H., Isbell, W. (Eds.), Handbook of South American Archaeology. Springer, New York, pp. 707–730.

Castillo, L.J., 2000. La Presencia de Wari en San Jose de Moro. Boletín de arqueología PUCP 4, 143–179.

Castillo, L.J., 2001. The Last of the Mochicas: a view from the Jequetepeque Valley. In: Pillsbury, J. (Ed.), Moche Art and Archaeology in Ancient Peru. Yale University Press, New Haven, pp. 307–332.

Castillo, L.J., 2003. Los últimos Mochicas en Jequetepeque. In: Uceda Castillo, S., Mujica, E. (Eds.), Moche: hacia el final del milenio. Universidad Nacional de Trujillo y Pontificia Universidad Catolica del Peru, Lima, pp. 65–123.

Castillo, L.J., 2006. Five Sacred Priestesses from San Jose de Moro: Elite Women Funerary Ritual on Peru's Northern Coast. Revista Electronica de Arqueologia Pontificia Universidad Catolica del Peru 1 (3), 1–10.

Castillo, L.J., 2010. Moche politics in the Jequetepeque Valley: a case for political opportunism. In: Quilter, J., Castillo, L.J. (Eds.), New Perspectives on Moche Political Organization. Pontificia Universidad Católica del Perú, Dumbarton Oaks, and Museo Arqueológico Rafael Larco Herrera, Washington, DC, pp. 83–109.

Edgar, H.J.H., Lease, L.R., 2007. Correlations between deciduous and permanent tooth morphology in a European American sample. American Journal of Physical Anthropology 133, 726–734.

Grine, F.E., 1986. Anthropological aspects of the deciduous teeth of African Blacks. In: Singer, I., Lundy, J.K. (Eds.), Variation, Culture, and Evolution in African Populations. Witwatersrand University Press, Johanessburg, pp. 47–83.

Hanihara, K., 1956. Studies on the deciduous dentition of the Japanese and Japanese-American Hybrids. III. Deciduous lower molars. Anthropological Science 64, 95–116.

Hanihara, K., 1961. Criteria for classification of crown characters of the human deciduous dentitions. Journal of the Anthropological Society of Nippon 72, 1–8.

Hanihara, K., 1963. Crown characters of deciduous dentition of Japanese-American hybrids. In: Brothwell, D.R. (Ed.), Dental Anthropology. Pergamon Press, New York, pp. 105–124.

Hanihara, K., 1965. Tuberculum accessorium mediale internum in the human deciduous lower second molars. Anthropological Science 73, 9–19.

Hanihara, K., 1970. Mongoloid dental complex in the deciduous dentition, with special reference to the dentition of the Ainu. Anthropological Science 78, 3–17.

Irish, J., 2010. The mean measure of divergence (MMD): its utility in model-free and model-bound analyses relative to the Mahalanobis D^2 for nonmetric traits. American Journal of Human Biology 22 (3), 378–395.

Jørgensen, K.D., 1956. The deciduous dentition, a descriptive and comparative anatomical study. Acta Odontologica Scandinavica 14, 1–202.

Kitagawa, Y., Manabe, Y., Oyamada, J., Rokulanda, A., 1995. Deciduous dental morphology of the prehistoric Jomon people of Japan: comparion of nonmetric characters. American Journal of Physical Anthropology 97, 101–111.

Kitagawa, Y., Manabe, Y., Oyamada, J., Rokulanda, A., 1996. Morphological and anthropological aspects of human triangular deciduous lower first molar teeth. Archives of Oral Biology 41, 387–391.

Kitagawa, Y., 2000. Nonmetric morphological characters of deciduous teeth in Japan: diachronic evidence of the past 4000 years. International Journal of Osteoarchaeology 10, 242–253.

Konigsberg, L.W., 1990. Analysis of prehistoric biological variation under a model of isolation by geographic and temporal distance. Human Biology 62, 49–70.

Lasker, G.W., 1950. Genetic analysis of racial traits of the teeth. Cold Spring Harbor Symposia on Quantitative Biology 15, 191–203.

Lease, L.R., Sciulli, P.W., 2005. Brief communication: discrimination between European-American and African-American children based on deciduous dental metrics and morphology. American Journal of Physical Anthropology 126, 56–60.

Lucacks, J.R., Kuswandari, S., 2013. Crown morphology of Malay deciduous teeth. In: Scott, G.R., Irish, J.D. (Eds.), Anthropological Perspectives on Tooth Morphology: Genetics, Evolution, Variation. Cambridge University Press, New York, pp. 453–478.

Lucacks, J.R., Walimbe, S.R., 1984. Deciduous dental morphology and the biological affinities of a Late Chalcolithic skeletal series from Western India. American Journal of Physical Anthropology 6 (10), 23–30.

Nelson, A.M., Griffin, M.C., 1996. Adult and deciduous dental morphology in Four U.S. Amerindian population samples: a comparative study. American Journal of Physical Anthropology 22 (Suppl.), 175.

Nichol, C.R., Turner, C.G., 1986. Intra- and interobserver concordance in classifying dental morphology. American Journal of Physical Anthropology 69 (3), 299–325.

Nystrom, K.C., 2006. Late Chachapoya population structure prior to Inka Conquest. American Journal of Physical Anthropology 131 (3), 334–342.

Paul, K.S., Stojanowski, C.M., 2015. Performance analysis of deciduous morphology for detecting biological siblings. American Journal of Physical Anthropology 157 (4), 615–629.

Pilloud, M.A., Larsen, C.S., 2011. "Official" and "Practical" kin: inferring social community structure from dental phenotype at Neolithic Çatalhöyük, Turkey. American Journal of Physical Anthropology 145, 519–530.
Relethford, J.H., Blangero, J., 1990. Detection of differential gene flow from patterns of quantitative variation. Human Biology 68, 29–44.
Relethford, J.H., Crawford, M., Blangero, J., 1997. Genetic drift and gene flow in Post-Famine Ireland. Human Biology 69 (4), 443–465.
Relethford, J.H., 1996. Genetic drift can obscure population history: problem and solution. Human Biology 68, 29–44.
Relethford, J.H., 2003. Anthropometric data and population history. In: Herring, D.A., Swedlund, A.C. (Eds.), Human Bioloigists in the Archives: Demography, Health, Nutrition, and Genetics in Historical Populations. Cambridge University Press, Cambridge, pp. 32–52.
Saunders, S.R., Mayhall, J.T., 1982. Developmental patterns of human dental morphological traits. Archives of Oral Biology 27, 45–49.
Sciulli, P.W., 1977. A descriptive and comparative study of the deciduous dentition of prehistoric Ohio Valley Amerindians. American Journal of Physical Anthropology 47, 71–80.
Sciulli, P.W., 1979. Size and morphology of the permanent dentition in prehistoric Ohio Valley Amerindians. American Journal of Physical Anthropology 50, 615–628.
Sciulli, P.W., 1990. Deciduous dentition of a late archaic population of Ohio. Human Biology 62, 221–245.
Sciulli, P.W., 1998. Evolution of the dentition in prehistoric Ohio Valley Native Americans: II. Morphology of the deciduous dentition. American Journal of Physical Anthropology 106, 189–205.
Smith, B.H., Garn, S.M., 1987. Polymorphisms in eruption sequence of permanent teeth in American children. American Journal of Physical Anthropology 742, 89–303.
Stojanowski, C.M., 2003. Matrix decomposition model for investigating prehistoric intracemetery biological variation. American Journal of Physical Anthropology 122, 216–231.
Stojanowski, C.M., 2005. Apalachee mortuary practices: biological structure of the San Pedro de Patale Mission Cemetery. Southeastern Archaeology 24, 165–179.
Stojanowski, C.M., 2009. Bridging histories: the bioarchaeology of identity in Postcontact Florida. In: Knudson, K.J., Stojanowski, C.M. (Eds.), Bioarchaeology and Identity in the Americas. University of Florida Press, Gainesville, pp. 59–81.
Sutter, R.C., Castillo, L.J., 2015. Population structure during the Demise of the Moche (AD 550–850). Current Anthropology 56 (5), 762–771.
Suzuki, M., Sakai, T., 1973. Occlusal surface pattern of the lower molars and the second deciduous molar among the Living Polynesians. American Journal of Physical Anthropology 39, 305–316.
Tocheri, M.W., 2002. The effects of sexual dimorphism, asymmetry and inter-trait association on the distribution of thirteen deciduous non-metric traits in a sample of Pima Amerindians. Dental Anthropology 15 (2–3), 1–8.
Turner II, C.G., Scott, G.R., 1977. Dentition of Easter Island. In: Dahlberg, A.A., Graber, T.M. (Eds.), Orofacial Growth and Development. Mouton Publishers, Chicago, pp. 229–250.
Williams-Blangero, S., Blangero, J., 1989. Anthropometric variation and the genetic structure of the Jirels of Nepal. Human Biology 61, 1–12.
Williams-Blangero, S., 1989a. Clan-structured migration and phenotypic differentiation in the Jirels of Nepal. Human Biology 61, 143–157.
Williams-Blangero, S., 1989b. Phenotypic consequences of non-random migration in the Jirels of Nepal. American Journal of Physical Anthropology 80, 115–125.
Wilson, D.J., 1999. Indigenous South Americans of the Past and Present. Westview Press, Boulder.

CHAPTER

20

Alternate Methods to Assess Phenetic Affinities and Genetic Structure Among Seven South African "Bantu" Groups Based on Dental Nonmetric Data

J.D. Irish
Liverpool John Moores University, Liverpool, United Kingdom

CHAPTER OUTLINE HEAD

Materials ... **364**
- A Brief History ... 365
- Samples and Context ... 365

Methods ... **366**
- Dental Trait Recording ... 366
- Model-Free Quantitative Analyses ... 367
- Model-Bound Quantitative Analyses ... 368
- Population Hypotheses/Expectations ... 370

Results ... **370**
- Model-Free Quantitative Analyses ... 374
- Model-Bound Quantitative Analyses ... 375

Discussion ... **379**
Summary and Conclusions ... **385**
Acknowledgments ... **386**
References ... **386**

The purpose of this chapter is to detail and expand upon the quantitative methods used in Irish (2016) to assess the credibility of ethnic group affiliations assigned to individuals in seven "Bantu" samples from the Raymond A. Dart Collection of Human Skeletons: Ndebele, Sotho, Swazi, Tswana, Venda, Xosa, and Zulu. In this case ethnic group is deemed synonymous with population in consideration of the approach. Model-free and model-bound analyses, based on and derived from comparisons of dental nonmetric traits using the mean measure of divergence (MMD), yielded indicative phenetic and, by extension, genetic intersample affinities (see Irish, 2010) that could be compared with documented population relationships. Where credibility was reasonably established, the findings serve to supplement published data on biological relatedness among these South African peoples (Irish, 2016).

Biological Distance Analysis. http://dx.doi.org/10.1016/B978-0-12-801966-5.00020-2

Here, the "nuts and bolts" of the MMD (Sjøvold, 1977) are presented in comparing these samples; as well, the same are provided for the other most common biodistance methods used by biological anthropologists, the Mahalanobis D^2 for nonmetric traits (Konigsberg, 1990). Again, only the MMD was used above (Irish, 2016); the rationale for doing so is covered in Irish (2010). Now the D^2 is given equal time. Phenetic distance matrices from both methods, their fit with intersample geographic distances (ie, relative to the isolation-by-distance model), the derived genetic relationship or R-matrices, and Sewall Wright's fixation index, or F_{st} are presented with the results compared and contrasted.

By way of some background the motivation for this research is to help address concerns, real and perceived, that many skeletons in the Dart Collection (University of the Witwatersrand, Johannesburg) may not be what they seem. It is acknowledged that the collection is thoroughly documented, substantial (ie, >2600 skeletons), and particularly valuable for its many African remains ($n = 1390$) (Dayal et al., 2009). The latter fact encouraged the author to record dental data in "Bantu" skeletons with the goal of creating representative samples in this key region for a National Science Foundation-funded project on the "Bantu" expansion (BCS-0840674). However, most remains are from cadavers of 20th century individuals who died near Johannesburg rather than their native homelands; as such, ethnic (or tribal) identification was often based on appearance, name, or other subjective factors (Tal and Tau, 1983; Dayal et al., 2009). Other curation-related issues affecting ethnic identification also existed (Dayal et al., 2009). Thus, with the aforementioned focus on methodology, individuals in the seven samples are considered further (after Irish, 2016) regarding their originally assigned affiliations—though with additional phenetic affinity and genetic structure results based on the nonmetric D^2. Evidence of credible ethnic/population identity, at least as demonstrated for (most) individuals in these samples is, of course, critical for use of the Collection by researchers in addressing anthropological problems on regional and broader scales.

MATERIALS

The Arizona State University Dental Anthropology System (next) was used to record traits in 408 Africans from the Collection (Dayal et al., 2009). For the few Ndebele and Venda individuals (see sample sizes in Table 20.1), all of the applicable crania were observed and scored. For the Sotho, Swazi, Tswana, Xosa, and Zulu ethnic groups with more identified individuals, every second specimen was recorded until a minimum, representative number for each trait was attained (counts provided in Table 20.2).

Table 20.1 Basic Background Information on the Seven "Bantu" Samples in the Study

Sample	Ethnic Group	Date Established	Ancestral/Language Group	n
NDB	Ndebele	19th century	Nguni	38
SOT	(Southern) Sotho	19th century	Sotho	66
SWZ	Swazi	18th century	Nguni	58
TSW	Tswana (Western Sotho)	17th–18th centuries	Sotho	63
VEN	Venda	16th–17th centuries	Venda	51
XOS	Xosa (a.k.a., Xhosa)	15th–17th centuries	Nguni	65
ZUL	Zulu	18th century	Nguni	67

A Brief History

All populations under study are descendants of migrants from eastern Africa, who in turn were part of the ancient, continent-wide "Bantu" expansion (July, 1992; Ruhlen, 1994; Newman, 1995; Vogel, 1997). "Bantu" refers to their language group but has long been used to identify the peoples and cultures as well; though incorrect, this practice is maintained here for consistency with previous studies. The first of two main routes from eastern to South Africa was near the coast (Maylam, 1986), and was taken by speakers of the Nguni "Bantu" language. Their arrival in country occurred by 1100 AD (Huffman, 2007). The second East African route, inland along the western side of Lake Malawi (Monnig, 1967; Sutton, 1981; Nurse et al., 1985), was followed by Sotho speakers. They reached what is today's Limpopo Province in the 13th–14th centuries (Monnig, 1967; Huffman, 1989; Hall, 2010; Warren et al., 2014).

Samples and Context

Information concerning populations on which the seven samples are based is detailed in Irish (2016) and summarized in Table 20.1. All are of relatively recent derivation from many, often significant historical events prompting group fission and fusion (Van Warmelo, 1962; Seligman, 1967; Davidson, 1974; July, 1992; Byrnes, 1996). The result to varying degrees is a combination of peoples, as the original two immigrant populations interbred with previous (western) "Bantu" migrants, indigenous Khoesan-speaking peoples, and each other (Tobias, 1974; Denbow, 1981; Parkington, 1981; Nurse et al., 1985; Loubser, 1989; Newman, 1995). Yet, ancestral Nguni and Sotho biocultural divisions remain to some extent (see Table 20.1).

The Ndebele, Swazi, Xosa, and Zulu all speak an Nguni language (Van Warmelo, 1962; Byrnes, 1996), so are descendants of the coastal-route migrants. The Ndebele, most of whom live near KwaNdebele (Fig. 20.1) alongside many Sotho, first settled by Zululand (Fig. 20.1), and may be Zulu offshoots (Van Warmelo, 1962; Seligman, 1967; Byrnes, 1996). Swazi have lived in the Swaziland region (Fig. 20.1) for hundreds of years, during which time they dominated nearby Nguni and Sotho-speakers (Van Warmelo, 1962; Byrnes, 1996). The Xosa language is similar to that of the Zulu (Byrnes, 1996); however, since moving to their far southern location (Fig. 20.1) they have, of all four Nguni groups, interbred most extensively with Khoesan peoples (ie, Khoekhoe) (Van Warmelo, 1962; Byrnes, 1996). And, the Zulu, though present in the 18th century, were not a true ethnic group until the 19th century, during the most important of historic population-changing events—the Mfecane (see Davidson, 1974; Maylam, 1986; Byrnes, 1996).

The (Southern) Sotho, who differ from their Northern Sotho relatives near KwaNdebele, and Tswana are both Sotho-speaking populations; they would have derived from eastern African immigrants who followed the inland route to South Africa. The (Southern) Sotho began moving southward in the 15th century (Byrnes, 1996; Hall, 2010) to their eventual Lesotho homeland; on the way they interbred with Khoesan peoples (ie, San), and eventually some Nguni displaced by the Mfecane (Van Warmelo, 1962; Byrnes, 1996). Rather than south, the Tswana (or Western Sotho) moved westward several hundred years ago toward their current home (Fig. 20.1), but also interbred extensively with San (Van Warmelo, 1962).

Lastly, the Venda of the Soutpansberg area (Fig. 20.1) had a separate origin from these groups; they are likely comprised of later arriving Zimbabwean Shona and Singo peoples who interbred with local Northern Sotho over the course of two centuries (Loubser, 1989).

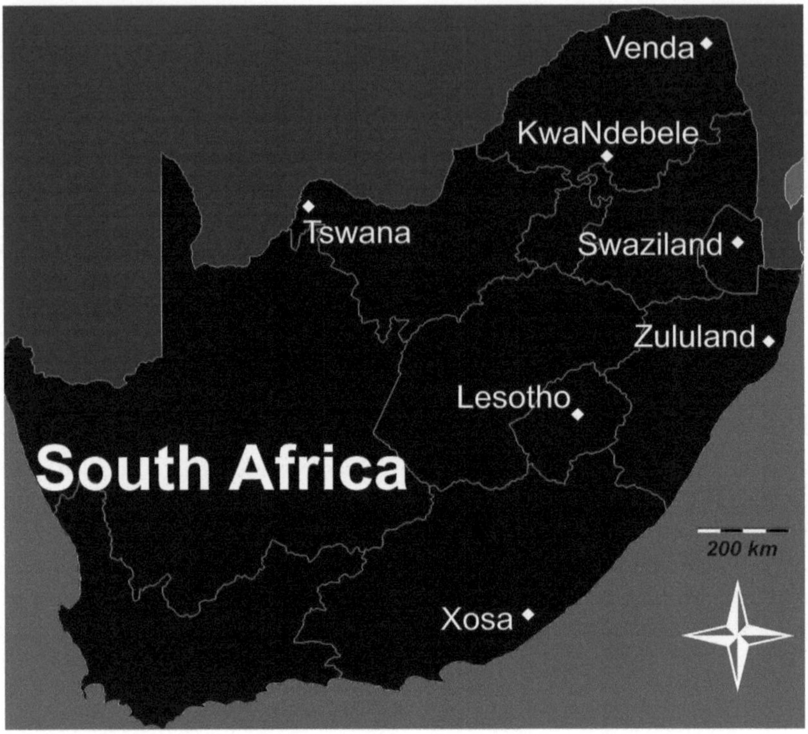

FIGURE 20.1

Locations of historic homelands of the seven South African "Bantu" populations used in the present study.

Modified from Irish, J.D., 2016. Who were they really? Model-free and model-bound dental nonmetric analyses to affirm "known" population affiliations of seven South African "Bantu" samples. American Journal of Physical Anthropology 159, 655–670.

METHODS

Dental Trait Recording

Thirty-six nonmetric traits were recorded in each dentition for use in the analyses (see list in Table 20.2); all were previously used by the author (Irish, 1993, 1997, 2005, 2006, 2013) and make up the Arizona State University Dental Anthropology System (ASUDAS) (Turner et al., 1991; Scott and Turner, 1997). Traits are recorded using 23 rank-scale reference plaques that help to standardize scoring by illustrating the minimum, maximum, and intermediate expressions (Turner et al., 1991). As described in the preceding references, the reasons for using these traits are numerous; among others, they (1) can, with caution, be observed despite some attrition or, with osseous and root traits, are unaffected by it; (2) were shown to have minimal inter- and intraobserver recording error; (3) are readily identifiable; (4) represent all the dental morphogenetic fields; (5) have a high genetic component in expression(s) (Scott, 1973; Larsen, 1997; Scott and Turner, 1997; Rightmire, 1999; Martinon-Torres et al., 2007; Hughes and Townsend, 2011); (6) are evolutionarily conservative, which makes them excellent markers for biodistance analyses (Larsen, 1997); and (7) exhibit little or no sexual dimorphism (Scott, 1973, 1980; Smith and Shegev,

1988; Bermudez de Castro, 1989; Hanihara, 1992; Irish, 1993), to permit pooling of the sexes to maximize sample sizes.

Model-Free Quantitative Analyses

Before comparing samples, all rank-scale ASUDAS trait data were divided into present/absent categories following standard procedure (eg, Turner et al., 1991; Scott and Turner, 1997; Irish, 1993, 1997). This step is necessary to calculate intersample distances with the MMD and nonmetric D^2 statistics (see Irish, 2010). By definition, these statistics yield measures of among-sample phenetic distance, where small distance values equate with similitude and larger values indicate dissimilarity.

The MMD formula used here contains the Freeman and Tukey angular transformation to correct for low ($\leq$0.05) or high ($\geq$0.95) trait frequencies and small sample sizes ($n \geq 10$) (Sjøvold, 1973, 1977; Green and Suchey, 1976).

$$\mathrm{MMD} = \frac{\sum_{i=1}^{r} (\theta_{1i} - \theta_{2i})^2 - (1/(n_{1i} + 1/2) + 1/(n_{2i} + 1/2))}{r} \tag{20.1}$$

where r = number of uncorrelated traits; θ = angular transformation, where the observed proportion, p, is an unbiased estimator of the population proportion, P, that here $\theta = ½ \sin^{-1} (1 - (2k)/(n + 1)) + ½ \sin^{-1} (1 - 2 (k + 1)/(n + 1))$; k = count of positive observations for trait i; n = number of individuals examined for trait i.

To determine if sample pairs differ significantly from one another, the MMD value is compared with its standard deviation [ie, $\sqrt{\mathrm{Var(MMD)}}$]. If the MMD $>2 \times s$, then the null hypothesis of $P_1 = P_2$ (where P = sample population) is rejected at the 0.025 level (Sjøvold, 1977).

$$\mathrm{Var(MMD)} = \frac{2\sum_{i=1}^{r} (1/(n_{1i} + 1/2) + 1/(n_{2i} + 1/2))^2}{r^2} \tag{20.2}$$

The nonmetric D^2 extends the original Mahalanobis generalized distance by including a tetrachoric correlation matrix for dichotomized data. Correlations are calculated within samples and then pooled by using sample size for each trait pair to yield a weighted average correlation (Konigsberg, 1990).

$$D_{ij}^2 = (Z_{ik} - Z_{jk})' T^{-1} (Z_{ik} - Z_{jk}) \tag{20.3}$$

where z_{ik} = threshold value (ie, presence) for a trait frequency of p_{ik} for trait k in sample i; z_{jk} = threshold value for a trait frequency of p_{jk} for trait k in sample j; $'$ = transpose; T^{-1} = inverse of pooled tetrachoric correlation matrix between the k traits.

Thus, the distance measure addresses variation in sample sizes, but unlike the MMD does not incorporate a correction factor specifically for small samples, so it is not an unbiased estimator of population divergence (Irish, 2010; Nikita, 2015). Further, the nonmetric D^2 used here does not have a significance test [ie, several can be used, but all provide less than satisfactory results (Nikita, 2015)]. However, it does adjust for intertrait correlation so as to avoid undue weight on groups of traits that cooccur. Additional details are available elsewhere (Konigsberg, 1990; Konigsberg et al., 1993; Irish, 2010).

In brief, both the MMD and D^2 have pros and cons (as earlier, and expanded upon later; details in Irish, 2010), including handling of problematic data; thus, it is important to edit traits before conducting analyses. The author routinely edits data in three steps (eg, Irish, 2005, 2006). First, traits with numerous missing data are deleted. The MMD's Freeman and Tukey transformation was not designed to correct for sample sizes smaller than 10 (Green and Suchey, 1976; Greene et al., 1979). This step is of critical importance when selecting traits for the D^2, because the inclusion of many traits having considerable missing data can adversely affect calculation of the tetrachoric correlation matrix (Schillaci et al., 2009). Second, fixed and largely invariant traits are dropped. They have no contributory information to identify among-sample differences (Harris and Sjøvold, 2004, p. 91), and can generate negative MMD values; the latter is a statistical artifact of the bias correction that has no biological meaning (Harris and Sjøvold, 2004, p. 91). If negative MMD distances still occur after removal of such traits, they are set to 0.0 (ie, no divergence), following standard procedure (Harris and Sjøvold, 2004). Traits with little discriminatory value can further be identified quantitatively (eg, principal components analysis in the present study). Lastly, Kendall's tau-*b* is used on the rank-scale trait data to identify highly correlated ($\tau_b \geq 0.5$) trait pairs, though only when using the MMD. It is held that as many traits as possible should be used with this statistic but, unlike the D^2, they must not be correlated or differential weighting of the underlying dimensions may produce inaccurate results (Sjøvold, 1977).

Finally, beyond simply presenting the among-sample MMD or D^2 distance matrices, the latter were submitted to multidimensional scaling (MDS) to illustrate the intersample phenetic affinities (SPSS 21.0 Procedure Alscal). Interval-level metric MDS was used because the large number of traits causes the distance values to emulate continuous data. As such, the sum of the squared differences between Euclidean values derived from the MMD or D^2 distance matrix (ie, d_{ij}) and those in the resulting $(\hat{d}_{ij})$ matrix are minimized, or optimally scaled (Hintze, 2007). From the latter, plots between 1 and n dimensions can be made, where a group of points in space suggests a close intersample relationship, and vice versa (Kruskal and Wish, 1978; Cox and Cox, 1994; Borg and Groenen, 1997).

Model-Bound Quantitative Analyses

As noted, nonmetric data can be used to approximate a genetic relationship matrix (R-matrix) and Sewall Wright's fixation index (F_{st}), using a method (Konigsberg, 2006) fashioned after that for phenotypic quantitative data (Williams-Blangero and Blangero, 1989; Relethford and Blangero, 1990). Nonmetric data may actually have an advantage over metric, in that they are more likely selectively neutral, such that they may best compare with genetic markers in measuring among-sample variation (Leigh et al., 2003). Briefly, off-diagonal r_{ij} values of the R-matrix are scaled variances and covariances about the mean of all samples, or regional centroid; values on the diagonal — r_{ii}, are standardized estimates of each sample = s genetic distance to the centroid (Relethford and Blangero, 1990; Relethford, 1994). Thus, r_{ij} values provide a measure of intersample genetic distance (Relethford and Crawford, 1995; Leigh et al., 2003), where the positive numbers indicate greater genetic similarity than average, and negative numbers less (Relethford and Harpending, 1994; Relethford et al., 1997). The r_{ii} values can be used to evaluate internal variation; samples near the centroid exhibit greater heterogeneity (ie, heterozygosity), whereas those farther away should be more homogeneous as a result of genetic drift and lower migration (Relethford and Crawford, 1995; Konigsberg, 2006). The mean of the r_{ii} values yields F_{st}, which provides an overall measure of population differentiation in the form of among-sample variation (Relethford and Harpending, 1994).

To obtain this output from the D^2 values, Konigsberg's (2006) approach was followed, where the distance matrix was used to calculate a C- or codivergence-matrix and, from that, an R-matrix and F_{st}, as follows:

$$C = -0.5(I - 1w')D^2(I - 1w')' \quad (20.4)$$

where $I = g \times g$ identity matrix, g = number of groups; $1 = g \times 1$ column vector of 1s; $D^2 = a \cdot g \times g$ matrix of squared distances based on t traits; $w = g \times 1$ column vector of relative population sizes (if known); $'$ = transpose.

$$F_{st} = \frac{w' \text{diag}\{\mathbf{C}\}}{2t + w' \text{diag}\{\mathbf{C}\}} \tag{20.5}$$

where diag{·} = an operator that places the diagonal of a matrix into a column vector weighting with w, relative population size, corrects for the otherwise equivalent influence of small groups; the latter tend to be farther away from the regional centroid as a result of drift (Relethford and Crawford, 1995; Leigh et al., 2003). Of course, w is generally not known for premodern populations, and is also unknown in this study of recent peoples; again, the South African census categories do not differentiate among various groups of Africans (Christopher, 2011; Stats SA, 2014).

There are estimates (eg, Byrnes, 1996), but they differ by source and otherwise do not appear reliable for the 20th century Dart Collection groups. Thus, following Relethford (1994), $w = 1/g$ in the analyses. Including the heritability of traits also affects r_{ii}, r_{ij}, and F_{st}, in that they decrease as h^2 increases (Relethford and Blangero, 1990; Relethford, 1994; Relethford et al., 1997). If unknown, it is standard to use $h^2 = 1$, to yield minimum F_{st}. If known, estimated F_{st} may be calculated using Relethford's (1994) formula:

$$\text{Est } F_{st} = \frac{\text{Min } F_{st}}{\text{Min } F_{st} + h^2(1 - \text{Min } F_{st})} \tag{20.6}$$

Minimum and estimated F_{st} are calculated in the present study, with the latter using a midrange estimate of $h^2 = 0.65$; the latter is higher than 0.55 used for craniometric variables (Relethford, 1994) but lower than that found for highly heritable dental traits such as Carabelli's cusp (ie, 0.80; Hughes and Townsend, 2011).

This same output from differently scaled non-Euclidean MMD distances is obtained with the approach of Irish (2010), where the optimally scaled Euclidean intersample distance matrix from MDS (or recreated from coordinates/eigenvectors) replaces D^2 in Eq. (20.4). Given the high correlation between D^2 and MMD distances (Irish, 2010), and because MDS optimal values are rescaled and provide as close of a match as possible to those in the original distance matrix, the R-matrix is proportionate to that obtained directly from the D^2. Because results are related to the MDS solution, dimensionality may need to be increased to yield a stress value of less than 0.10 (Kruskal and Wish, 1978), which is considered an excellent fit (Borgatti, 1997). Another approach was suggested by Nikita (2015), where the distances from the optimally scaled MDS matrix are replaced with the total measures of divergence (TMD); the formula for two populations based on r traits (de Souza and Houghton, 1977, p. 164) is:

$$\text{TMD} = \sum_{i=1}^{r} (\theta_{1i} - \theta_{2i})^2 - (1/(n_{1i} + 1/2) + 1/(n_{2i} + 1/2)) \tag{20.7}$$

However, this approach is not used here because the negative-turned-0.0 values (see earlier) that result from the bias correction, whether MMD (Eq. (20.1)) or TMD, adversely affect estimation of the R-matrix. For example, using the TMD matrix (not shown but available from author), two of the r_{ii} diagonal values are negative, which is theoretically impossible; thus, as expected, the F_{st} values are smaller than those based on the preceding methods (including D^2) by nearly a factor of 10.

A final quantitative approach to substantiate ethnic group identities is the isolation-by-distance model (eg, Wright, 1943). Genetic, and here phenetic, similarity among populations should decrease exponentially as geographic distance increases as a result of decreasing gene flow (Relethford, 2004). Among-sample distances in km were determined from the approximate center of each group's homeland (eg, De Villiers, 1968; Lane et al., 2002) with the Geographic Distance Matrix Generator (v. 1.2.3) (Ersts, 2014). Because of these general approximations, the linear unidimensional stepping-stone variant of the model was used (Konigsberg, 1990). To calculate correlations between the geographic, MMD, and D^2 distance matrices a Mantel test (Smouse et al., 1986) was employed.

Population Hypotheses/Expectations

Based on what is known about the regional history, several outcomes concerning sample affinities would be expected if the samples are representative of their populations. However, as briefly noted and detailed elsewhere (Irish, 2016), gene flow and population movements during historic times likely complicate matters beyond that documented. Therefore, instead of treating these expected outcomes as hypotheses to be tested, they serve as bases from which to interpret the quantitative results.

The first hypothesis/expectation is that samples will evidence some measure of similarity based on common ancestry; so Nguni samples of Ndebele, Swazi, Xosa, and Zulu should show a closer affinity to one another, compared to related Sotho and Tswana, and separately originating Venda. Second, samples from populations in geographic proximity, regardless of ancestry and modern ethnic identity, will exhibit closer affinities than to those farther away in relation to the isolation-by-distance model. And third, specific pairwise affinities should be evident based on ancestry and geographic proximity, but in particular due to events that have transpired since the 13th and 14th centuries AD (again, see Irish, 2016), as summarized in the following scenarios for each of the seven samples.

With regard to Nguni samples, Ndebele should be least like Xosa, more akin to Swazi, and most like Zulu from whom they diverged; similarities to Sotho and neighboring Venda may be possible. Swazi will be most comparable to Zulu and least like Xosa; regarding non-Nguni, some affinity with Sotho may be indicated via historic contact. Zulu will be more similar to Ndebele and Swazi than Xosa, and more divergent from other geographically distant samples. Xosa will appear somewhat distinct from Ndebele, Swazi, and Zulu, though may be pushed toward Sotho and Tswana from parallel contact with Khoesan.

Concerning the Sotho samples, Tswana will be akin to Sotho, while the Khoesan influence may, as earlier, push them toward the Nguni Xosa. Sotho will be close to Tswana and, based on their location near the region's geographic center (Fig. 20.1), should be the most similar sample to all others.

Finally, Venda will be divergent given separate origins; however, the sample may show some similarity to nearby Ndebele and, through contact with Northern Sotho peoples, the Sotho and Tswana samples.

RESULTS

The trait percentages and ASUDAS presence and absence dichotomies from Irish (2016) are tabulated (Table 20.2). There is general uniformity across samples, although some variation is evident, including traits differing by >30%: NDB and VEN for Bushman Canine, Tswana (TSW) and Zulu (ZUL) for UC distal accessory ridge, VEN and ZUL for LM1 cusp 7. Of all samples, ZUL, NDB, and VEN exhibit the most contrary occurrences.

Table 20.2 Dental Trait Percentages (%) and Number of Individuals Scored (n) for the Seven South African "Bantu" Samples[a]

	Trait[b]	Sample[c]	NDB	SOT	SWZ	TSW	VEN	XOS	ZUL
1)	Winging UI1	%	0.00	1.92	2.94	4.17	10.53	3.45	0.00
	(+ = ASU 1)	n	27	52	34	48	38	58	57
2)	Labial curvature UI1	%	71.43	60.61	61.11	68.57	60.71	61.54	77.78
	(+ = ASU 2–4)	n	14	33	18	35	28	39	36
3)	Palatine torus	%	0.00	0.00	0.00	0.00	2.13	0.00	0.00
	(+ = ASU 2–3)	n	35	63	53	60	47	60	61
4)	Shoveling UI1	%	0.00	12.12	11.11	20.69	5.00	8.11	2.70
	(+ = ASU 2–6)	n	17	33	18	29	20	37	37
5)	Double shoveling UI1	%	6.67	2.70	0.00	0.00	0.00	0.00	0.00
	(+ = ASU 2–6)	n	15	37	19	34	25	43	36
6)	Interruption groove UI2	%	9.09	4.65	4.00	0.00	3.70	2.63	15.79
	(+ = ASU +)	n	22	43	25	38	27	38	38
7)	Tuberc. dentale UI2	%	30.43	36.59	34.48	37.50	34.62	44.44	29.73
	(+ = ASU 2–6)	n	23	41	29	32	26	36	37
8)	Bushman canine UC	%	8.00	24.44	35.00	37.78	45.16	31.58	23.40
	(+ = ASU 1–3)	n	25	45	40	45	31	38	47
9)	Distal acc. ridge UC	%	38.10	39.02	44.12	60.61	37.04	31.43	26.32
	(+ = ASU 2–5)	n	21	41	34	33	27	35	38
10)	Hypocone UM2	%	77.42	93.65	74.47	77.55	90.48	93.44	91.07
	(+ = ASU 3–5)	n	31	63	47	49	42	61	56
11)	Cusp 5 UM1	%	22.22	22.03	17.39	17.02	14.63	21.15	18.37
	(+ = ASU 2–5)	n	27	59	46	47	41	52	49
12)	Carabelli's trait UM1	%	31.03	49.15	51.06	47.06	34.15	52.63	58.00
	(+ = ASU 2–7)	n	29	59	47	51	41	57	50
13)	Parastyle UM3	%	0.00	0.00	0.00	2.33	2.94	1.92	2.38
	(+ = ASU 1–5)	n	25	52	41	43	34	52	42
14)	Enamel extension UM1	%	3.45	4.76	2.08	3.92	5.00	1.85	1.72
	(+ = ASU 1–3)	n	29	63	48	51	40	54	58
15)	Root number UP1	%	64.29	74.36	64.52	57.14	76.19	60.61	68.97
	(+ = ASU 2+)	n	14	39	31	35	21	33	29

Continued

Table 20.2 *Dental Trait Percentages (%) and Number of Individuals Scored (n) for the Seven South African "Bantu" Samples*[a]*—Continued*

	Trait[b]	Sample[c]	NDB	SOT	SWZ	TSW	VEN	XOS	ZUL
16)	Root number UM2	%	92.86	83.33	77.27	65.00	83.33	60.87	84.62
	(+ = ASU 3+)	n	14	24	22	20	12	23	26
17)	Peg-reduced UI2	%	0.00	3.28	2.13	1.85	7.69	3.17	3.17
	(+ = ASU *P* or *R*)	n	30	61	47	54	39	63	63
18)	Odontome P1–P2	%	0.00	1.56	0.00	1.64	0.00	0.00	0.00
	(+ = ASU +)	n	36	64	57	61	44	64	63
19)	Congenital abs. UM3	%	5.56	4.55	3.77	7.14	13.04	6.35	6.78
	(+ = ASU −)	n	36	66	53	56	46	63	59
20)	Midline diastema UI1	%	20.69	8.47	11.11	2.13	5.88	4.92	10.17
	(+0.5 mm)	n	29	59	36	47	34	61	59
21)	Lingual cusp LP2	%	65.52	66.67	68.75	68.63	54.29	75.00	54.72
	(+ = ASU 2–9)	n	29	57	48	51	35	48	53
22)	Anterior fovea LM1	%	68.97	68.75	70.27	74.42	66.67	73.33	54.00
	(+ = ASU 2–4)	n	29	48	37	43	33	45	50
23)	Mandibular torus	%	0.00	1.54	1.79	0.00	2.13	0.00	0.00
	(+ = ASU 2–3)	n	34	65	56	61	47	63	63
24)	Groove pattern LM2	%	75.86	64.81	65.85	75.56	80.56	64.29	72.00
	(+ = ASU Y)	n	29	54	41	45	36	56	50
25)	Rocker jaw	%	2.94	1.52	0.00	5.17	2.13	1.59	3.23
	(+ = ASU 1–2)	n	34	66	57	58	47	63	62
26)	Cusp number LM1	%	6.45	13.79	2.27	6.25	12.50	0.00	1.85
	(+ = ASU 6+)	n	31	58	44	48	40	56	54
27)	Cusp number LM2	%	88.46	83.64	77.50	76.60	71.43	87.50	90.00
	(+ = ASU 5+)	n	26	55	40	47	35	56	50
28)	Deflecting wrinkle LM1	%	10.34	30.00	42.50	26.67	26.47	31.25	31.37
	(+ = ASU 2–3)	n	29	50	40	45	34	48	51
29)	C1–C2 crest LM1	%	6.90	1.89	0.00	2.22	5.56	2.08	1.96
	(+ = ASU +)	n	29	53	40	45	36	48	51

30)	Protostylid LM1	%	0.00	0.00	2.27	0.00	2.50	3.64	7.14
	(+ = ASU 1–6)	n	31	59	44	49	40	55	56
31)	Cusp 7 LM1	%	31.25	37.93	33.33	37.50	18.42	42.84	49.09
	(+ = ASU 2–4)	n	32	58	45	48	38	55	55
32)	Tomes' root LP1	%	15.79	10.53	25.00	5.71	14.29	8.57	7.41
	(+ = ASU 3–5)	n	19	38	36	35	21	35	27
33)	Root number LC	%	0.00	0.00	0.00	0.00	0.00	0.00	0.00
	(+ = ASU 2+)	n	21	32	31	29	23	40	33
34)	Root number LM1	%	0.00	0.00	0.00	0.00	5.56	0.00	0.00
	(+ = ASU 3+)	n	17	26	25	22	18	25	28
35)	Root number LM2	%	100.00	92.86	100.00	89.29	94.12	100.00	72.73
	(+ = ASU 2+)	n	16	28	21	28	17	26	22
36)	Torsomolar angle LM3	%	0.00	8.00	6.82	8.11	5.71	11.54	8.33
	(+ = ASU +)	n	23	50	44	37	35	52	48

[a]*Modified from Irish (2016).*
[b]*ASU rank-scale trait breakpoints from Irish (1993, 1997, 2005, 2006) and Scott and Turner (1997).*
[c]NDB = *Ndebele;* SOT = *Sotho;* SWZ = *Swazi;* TSW = *Tswana;* VEN = *Venda;* XOS = *Xhosa;* ZUL = *Zulu (see text for sample details).*

Table 20.3 MMD (Bottom Diagonal) and D^2 (Top Diagonal) Distance Matrices for the Seven South African "Bantu" Samples Based on 36 Dental Traits

	NDB	SOT	SWZ	TSW	VEN	XOS	ZUL
NDB	0	2.629	2.845	3.279	3.463	2.979	3.209
SOT	0.000	0	1.931	2.143	2.191	2.237	2.806
SWZ	0.003	0.000	0	2.267	2.617	1.846	3.127
TSW	0.035	0.000	0.000	0	2.569	2.196	3.439
VEN	0.011	0.000	0.000	0.000	0	2.904	3.489
XOS	0.027	0.000	0.000	0.000	0.014	0	3.043
ZUL	0.019	0.004	0.023	0.036	0.024	0.018	0

NDB = *Ndebele;* SOT = *Sotho;* SWZ = *Swazi;* TSW = *Tswana;* VEN = *Venda;* XOS = *Xhosa;* ZUL = *Zulu (see text for sample details).*
Underlined MMD distances indicate significant difference at the 0.025 level.

Model-Free Quantitative Analyses

Prior to trait editing, MMD and D^2 comparisons were conducted with all 36 traits to give an initial indication of intersample affinities. The two matrices are combined in Table 20.3. General uniformity is reflected by small values, particularly the bottom diagonal where only two sample pairs differ significantly; all 0.00s were negative MMD values reset to specify no divergence (as earlier), which resulted from traits with no, or minimal, discriminatory value influencing the bias correction. The MDS solution for the MMD matrix (Fig. 20.2) yields a Kruskal's stress formula 1 value of 0.062 and r^2 of 0.972 (Irish, 2016). The stress and r^2 for the MDS of D^2 distances (Fig. 20.3) are 0.056 and 0.961. Sample locations vary between figures, but some of the aforementioned trait variation is visualized, such as the divergence of NDB, VEN, and ZUL.

Next, the full complement of 36 traits was edited (Irish, 2016). All are of sufficient sample size (>10), so none were deleted. However, some traits that are largely invariant were removed: palatine torus (0.00–2.13% across samples), UI1 double shoveling (0.00–6.67%), UM3 parastyle (0.00–2.94%), mandibular torus (0.00–2.13%), LM1 C1–C2 crest (0.00–6.90%), LM1 protostylid (0.00–7.17%), LC root number (0.00%), and LM1 root number (0.00–5.56%). The remaining 28 trait percentages were submitted to PCA to identify additional minimally discriminatory traits or, conversely, those that drive variation. Six components that account for 100% of the variance were attained. However, the component matrix (not shown) reveals a marked drop-off of strong (ie, >|0.5|) loadings in components 4–6, so just the first three (70.77% of variance) are listed in Table 20.4; the group component scores are plotted in Fig. 20.4, which as can be seen looks similar to Fig. 20.2. On Comp 1, seven strongly positive loadings, particularly UI2 interruption groove (0.894) and LM2 cusp number (0.846), push the samples with high occurrences of these traits (ie, NDB and ZUL) toward the positive end of the *x*-axis (Fig. 20.4). Strong negative loadings for seven additional traits, notably UI1 winging (−0.816) and Bushman Canine (−0.864), push others [VEN and Tswana (TSW)] toward the negative side. Important traits, relative to the component variance, were likewise identified in Comp 2 (*y*-axis), such as LM2 groove pattern (0.794) and LM1 cusp 7 (−0.734), and Comp 3 (*z*-axis) [LM2 root number (−0.746)]. As such, five more traits were dropped: UM2 hypocone, P1-P2 odontome, rocker jaw, LM1 deflecting wrinkle, and LP1 Tomes' root. Finally, two remaining trait-pairs were found to be strongly correlated (>0.5)—UI1 shoveling/UI2

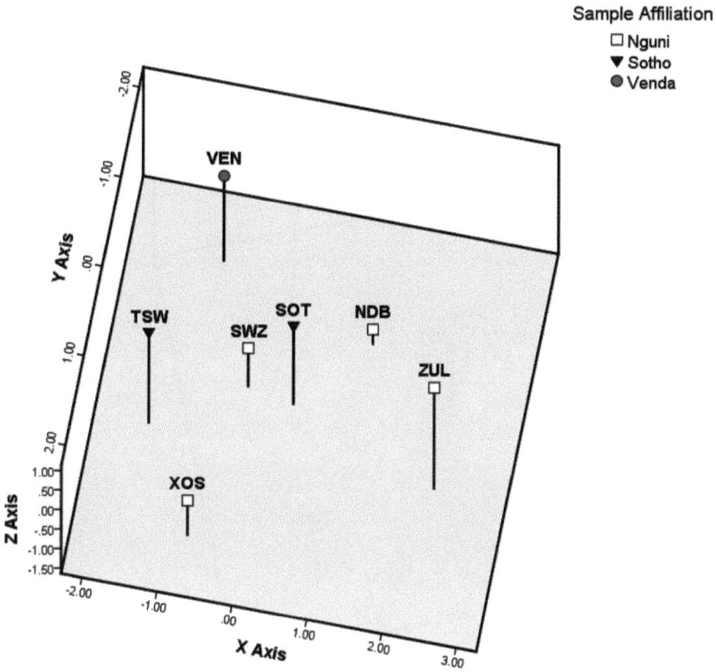

FIGURE 20.2

Three-dimensional MDS of 36-trait MMD distances among the seven "Bantu" samples. The three-letter sample abbreviations are defined in Table 20.1 and the text.

Modified from Irish, J.D., 2016. Who were they really? Model-free and model-bound dental nonmetric analyses to affirm "known" population affiliations of seven South African "Bantu" samples. American Journal of Physical Anthropology 159, 655–670.

interruption groove ($\tau_b = 0.558$) and UI2 interruption groove/UI2 tuberculum dentale ($\tau_b = 0.751$), so shoveling and tuberculum dentale were deleted. Thus, 21 traits, denoted by asterisks in Table 20.4, were used for a second round of MMD and D^2 analyses.

After trait editing MMD values increased, with six indicating a significant difference, while D^2 decreased (Table 20.5); thus, the results appear more concordant. Indeed, the intermatrix correlation is 0.920 ($p = .000$) using the Mantel test. Comparable intermethod results are also apparent in the MDS plots (Figs. 20.5–20.6). The 21-trait D^2 sample locations are more like those of the 21-trait MMD, which, in turn, appear essentially unchanged from the 36-trait version (Fig. 20.2). In both cases the MDS solutions provide excellent representations (ie, fit); for the MMD Kruskal's stress is 0.056 and r^2 is 0.965, and for the D^2 the equivalent values are 0.046 and 0.982. Further, the sample positions are to some degree suggestive of the population locations in Fig. 20.1 (Irish, 2016).

Model-Bound Quantitative Analyses

Two sets of R-matrices from the MDS optimally scaled matrix of MMD distances and D^2 distances, based on 21 traits, are presented (Tables 20.6 and 20.7). Minimum and estimated F_{st} are listed in each table and,

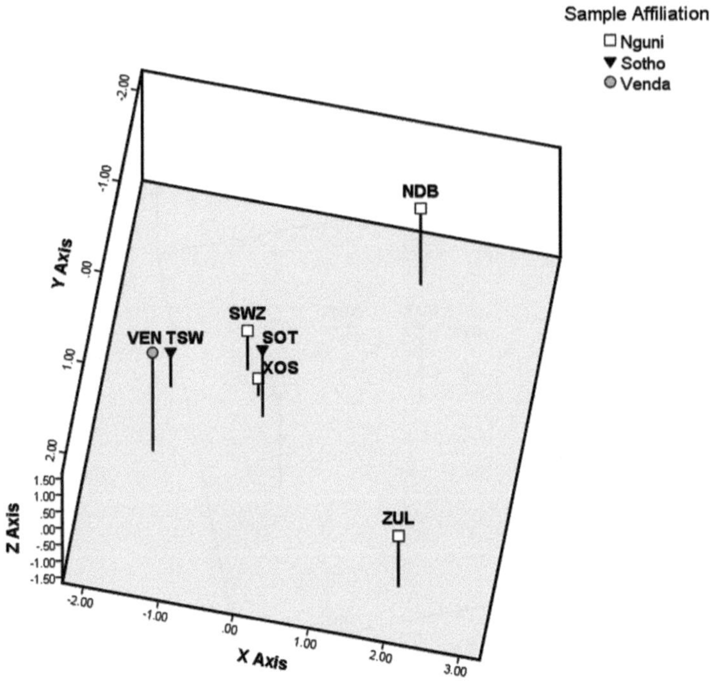

FIGURE 20.3

Three-dimensional MDS of 36-trait D^2 distances among the seven "Bantu" samples. The three-letter sample abbreviations are defined in Table 20.1 and the text.

as mentioned, the magnitudes do increase when $h^2 = 0.65$. By comparing tables it can be seen that the corresponding values are concordant; for example, in both bottom diagonals ZUL ($R_{ii} = 0.061$ vs. 0.047) is farthest from the centroid, with the SOT (0.020, 0.022) and SWZ (0.023, 0.021) samples closest. The correlation between R_{ii} values from MMD and D^2 is 0.964 ($p = .000$), which accounts for the similar F_{st} values; when R_{ij} measures of genetic distance are included, the correlation of R-matrices between tables is 0.979 ($p = .000$). A strongly negative relationship also occurs between the R_{ij} and respective MMD ($r = -.713$; $p = .000$) and D^2 ($r = -.832$; $p = .000$) values [negative because higher positive R_{ij} values signify greater (genetic) similarity]; the R_{ij}-D^2 correlation is slightly greater because the actual distance matrix was used in calculations (earlier).

As would be expected, the estimated genetic differentiation parallels that of the model-free phenetic affinities (Irish, 2016); the lower diagonal values in Tables 20.6 and 20.7 are approximated in Figs. 20.7 and 20.8 for comparison to phenetic sample variation (Figs. 20.5 and 20.6). They are approximations because the negative and positive R_{ij} values were first submitted to the proximities function in SPSS 21.0 to acquire Euclidean distances; the latter were then submitted to MDS. As such, visualization of the R-matrix is two steps removed from that of the MMD and D^2 distance matrices. So, among-sample variation (Figs. 20.7 and 20.8) results from R_{ij} measures and the R_{ii} distances are represented by lines to each figure's centroid. Minimum and estimated F_{st} imply that of the total genetic variation, 3.8% (MMD Est$F_{st} = 0.038$) or less (D^2 Min$F_{st} = 0.0211$) is the result of differences among groups.

Table 20.4 Component Loadings, Eigenvalues, and Variance Explained for 28 Traits in Seven South African "Bantu" Samples[a]

Trait	Comp 1	Comp 2	Comp 3
Winging UI1[c]	**−0.816**[b]	0.481	0.181
Labial curvature UI1[c]	**0.741**	0.068	0.194
Shoveling UI1	**−0.681**	−0.492	−0.067
Interruption groove UI2[c]	**0.894**	0.241	0.363
Tuberc. dentale UI2	**−0.613**	**−0.605**	0.047
Bushman canine UC[c]	**−0.864**	0.060	0.395
Distal acc. ridge UC[c]	**−0.573**	−0.144	−0.487
Hypocone UM2	−0.016	0.041	**0.597**
Cusp 5 UM1[c]	**0.535**	−0.416	−0.369
Carabelli's trait UM1[c]	0.115	**−0.720**	**0.611**
Enamel extension UM1[c]	−0.493	**0.601**	−0.232
Root number UP1[c]	0.007	**0.685**	0.344
Root number UM2[c]	**0.576**	**0.715**	−0.177
Peg-reduced UI2[c]	**−0.530**	**0.515**	**0.602**
Odontome P1−P2	−0.390	−0.246	−0.112
Congenital abs. UM3[c]	−0.425	**0.701**	0.371
Midline diastema UI1[c]	**0.763**	0.287	**−0.531**
Lingual cusp LP2[c]	−0.212	**−0.807**	−0.499
Anterior fovea LM1[c]	**−0.637**	−0.359	**−0.647**
Groove pattern LM2[c]	−0.093	**0.794**	−0.048
Rocker jaw	0.031	0.087	0.056
Cusp number LM1[c]	−0.356	**0.628**	−0.131
Cusp number LM2[c]	**0.846**	−0.389	0.065
Deflecting wrinkle LM1	−0.329	−0.442	0.464
Cusp 7 LM1[c]	**0.500**	**−0.734**	0.391
Tomes' root LP1	0.007	0.200	−0.471
Root number LM2[c]	−0.362	−0.094	**−0.746**
Torsomolar angle LM3[c]	−0.377	**−0.636**	**0.661**
Eigenvalue	7.931	7.009	4.875
Variance (%)	28.327	25.033	17.410
Total variance	28.327	53.360	70.770

[a]*Modified from Irish (2016).*
[b]*Values in boldface indicate strong loadings (ie, >|.5|) as detailed in text.*
[c]*21 traits used for the final distance analyses after trait editing.*

Finally, the matrix of geographic distances in km (Table 20.8) was compared with those of the MMD and D^2 distances as described. The Mantel correlations are weak to none [ie, 0.195 ($p = .100$) and −0.005 ($p = .246$), respectively], despite suggestions of resemblance in geographic and phenetic patterning (summarized in Fig. 20.9A–C); the most divergent samples in all MDS plots are, clockwise from top,

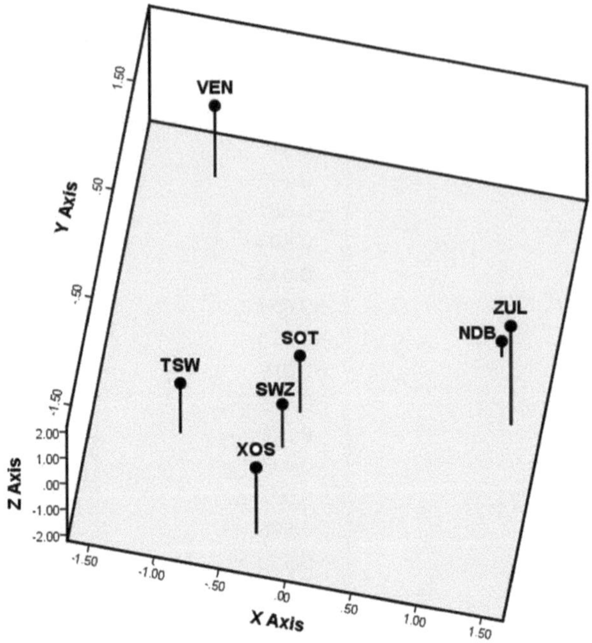

FIGURE 20.4

Three-dimensional scatterplot of the first three components among the seven "Bantu" samples for 28 dental traits accounts for 70.77% of the total variance (28.33% on *x*-axis, 25.03% on *y*-axis, and 17.77% on *z*-axis). Methodological details and the sample abbreviations are defined in Table 20.1 and the text.

Modified from Irish, J.D., 2016. Who were they really? Model-free and model-bound dental nonmetric analyses to affirm "known" population affiliations of seven South African "Bantu" samples. American Journal of Physical Anthropology 159, 655–670.

Table 20.5 MMD (Bottom Diagonal) and D^2 (Top Diagonal) Distance Matrices for the Seven South African "Bantu" Samples Based on 21 Dental Traits After Editing

	NDB	SOT	SWZ	TSW	VEN	XOS	ZUL
NDB	0	1.742	1.885	2.611	2.622	2.508	2.355
SOT	0.000	0	1.343	1.596	1.810	1.888	2.213
SWZ	0.000	0.000	0	1.544	1.951	1.221	2.465
TSW	<u>0.052</u>	0.001	0.000	0	1.732	1.886	2.801
VEN	0.031	0.000	0.000	0.005	0	2.395	3.117
XOS	0.038	0.008	0.000	0.006	<u>0.044</u>	0	2.597
ZUL	0.033	0.013	<u>0.037</u>	<u>0.060</u>	<u>0.062</u>	<u>0.054</u>	0

NDB = *Ndebele*; SOT = *Sotho*; SWZ = *Swazi*; TSW = *Tswana*; VEN = *Venda*; XOS = *Xhosa*; ZUL = *Zulu (see text for sample details)*.
Underlined MMD distances indicate significant difference at the 0.025 level.

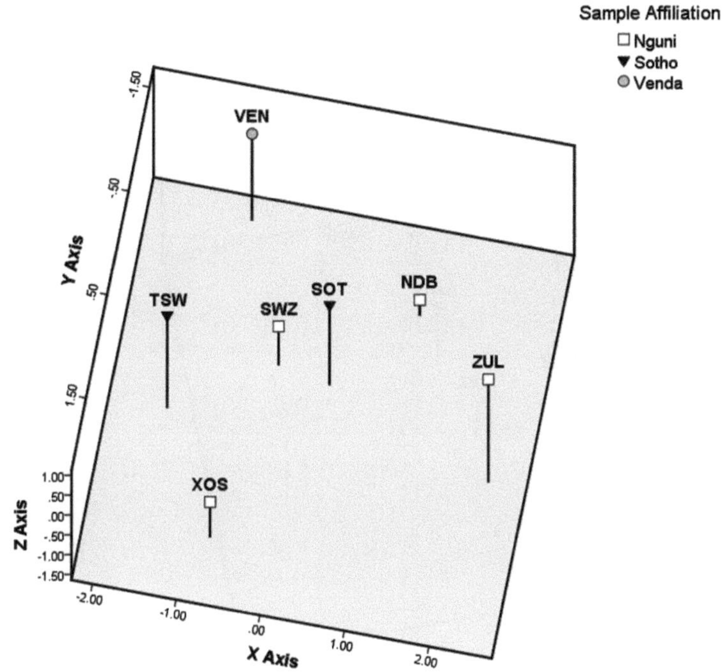

FIGURE 20.5

Three-dimensional MDS of 21-trait MMD distances among the seven "Bantu" samples. The three-letter sample abbreviations are defined in Table 20.1 and the text.

Modified from Irish, J.D., 2016. Who were they really? Model-free and model-bound dental nonmetric analyses to affirm "known" population affiliations of seven South African "Bantu" samples. American Journal of Physical Anthropology 159, 655–670.

VEN, ZUL, XOS, and TSW, while SOT is in more of a central location. The most obvious exceptions in sample location based on geographic versus phenetic distances, are SWZ and NDB (Fig. 20.9B–C). If SWZ is removed the r-values become 0.242 ($p = .097$) and 0.055 ($p = .212$). With SWZ and NDB both dropped, the values increase to 0.308 ($p = .097$) for the MMD—a moderately positive correlation, and 0.136 ($p = .177$) for the D^2 distances, a weak positive relationship (Cohen, 1988).

DISCUSSION

Revisiting the introduction, the comparisons of quantitative results from the MMD and D^2 are supportive of several conclusions in Irish (2010). First, the 36-trait MMD intersample affinities are similar to those from the 21-trait comparison; therefore the statistic is capable of yielding reliable results even when minimally variant, highly correlated, and other problematic traits are included (also see Nikita, 2015). Following trait editing, the D^2 distances are highly correlated with those from the MMD. Second, although requiring an extra step (ie, using MDS-produced distances), an R-matrix can be estimated from the MMD; it is highly correlated with the R-matrix from D^2 distances, though relatively less concordant with the original (MMD) matrix from which it is secondarily derived. Third, the among-sample geographic distances are more closely

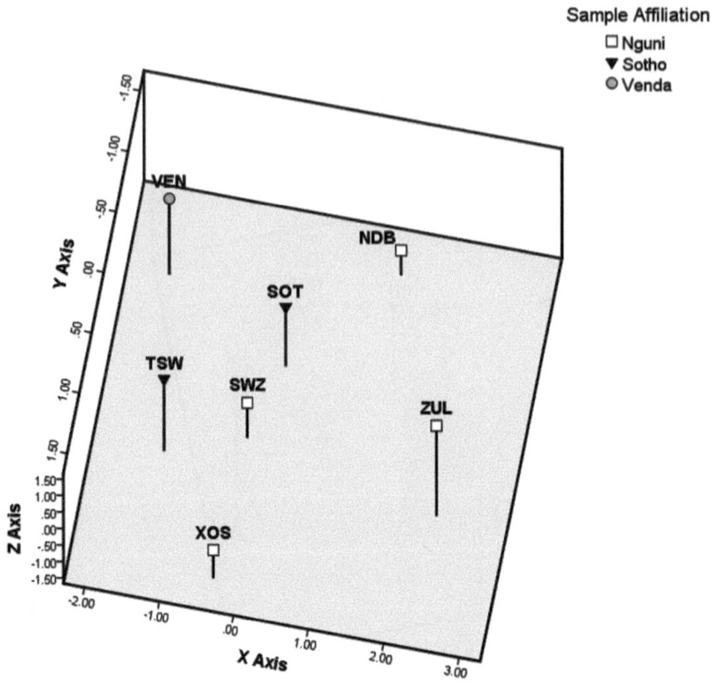

FIGURE 20.6

Three-dimensional MDS of 21-trait D^2 distances among the seven "Bantu" samples. The three-letter sample abbreviations are defined in Table 20.1 and the text.

Table 20.6 **R-Matrices From MDS Optimally Scaled Matrix of MMD Distances Using Overall Trait Heritability of $h^2 = 0.65$ for Calculation of Estimated F_{st} [Bottom Diagonal (in boldface)] and $h^2 = 1.0$ for Minimum F_{st} [Top Diagonal (in boldface)] for the Seven South African "Bantu" Samples Based on 21 Dental Traits**

	NDB	SOT	SWZ	TSW	VEN	XOS	ZUL	
	0.028	0.000	0.001	−0.015	−0.006	−0.008	0.000	NDB
		0.013	−0.007	−0.002	−0.001	−0.004	0.000	SOT
NDB	**0.043**		**0.015**	−0.001	0.000	0.000	−0.008	SWZ
SOT	0.000	**0.020**		**0.025**	0.003	0.003	−0.012	TSW
SWZ	0.001	−0.010	**0.023**		**0.027**	−0.011	−0.012	VEN
TSW	−0.023	−0.003	−0.002	**0.038**		**0.028**	−0.008	XOS
VEN	−0.009	−0.001	0.000	0.004	**0.041**		**0.040**	ZUL
XOS	−0.012	−0.006	0.001	0.005	−0.017	**0.042**		
ZUL	0.000	0.001	−0.012	−0.019	−0.018	−0.013	**0.061**	
	NDB	SOT	SWZ	TSW	VEN	XOS	ZUL	

Minimum $F_{st} = 0.0252$.
Estimated $F_{st} = 0.0382$.

Table 20.7 ***R-Matrices From D^2 Distance Matrix Using Overall Trait Heritability of $h^2 = 0.65$ for Calculation of Estimated F_{st} [Bottom Diagonal (in boldface)] and $h^2 = 1.0$ for Minimum F_{st} [Top Diagonal (in boldface)] for the Seven South African "Bantu" Samples Based on 21 Dental Traits***

	NDB	SOT	SWZ	TSW	VEN	XOS	ZUL	
	0.025	−0.001	−0.003	−0.008	−0.006	−0.007	0.000	NDB
		0.014	−0.002	−0.002	−0.002	−0.005	−0.003	SOT
NDB	**0.037**		**0.014**	−0.001	−0.004	0.003	−0.007	SWZ
SOT	−0.001	**0.022**		**0.019**	0.002	−0.002	−0.008	TSW
SWZ	−0.004	−0.003	**0.021**		**0.024**	−0.005	−0.009	VEN
TSW	−0.013	−0.003	−0.002	**0.030**		**0.021**	−0.005	XOS
VEN	−0.009	−0.003	−0.006	0.003	**0.037**		**0.031**	ZUL
XOS	−0.010	−0.007	0.004	−0.003	−0.008	**0.031**		
ZUL	0.000	−0.005	−0.010	−0.012	−0.013	−0.007	**0.047**	
	NDB	SOT	SWZ	TSW	VEN	XOS	ZUL	

Minimum $F_{st} = 0.0211$.
Estimated $F_{st} = 0.0320$.

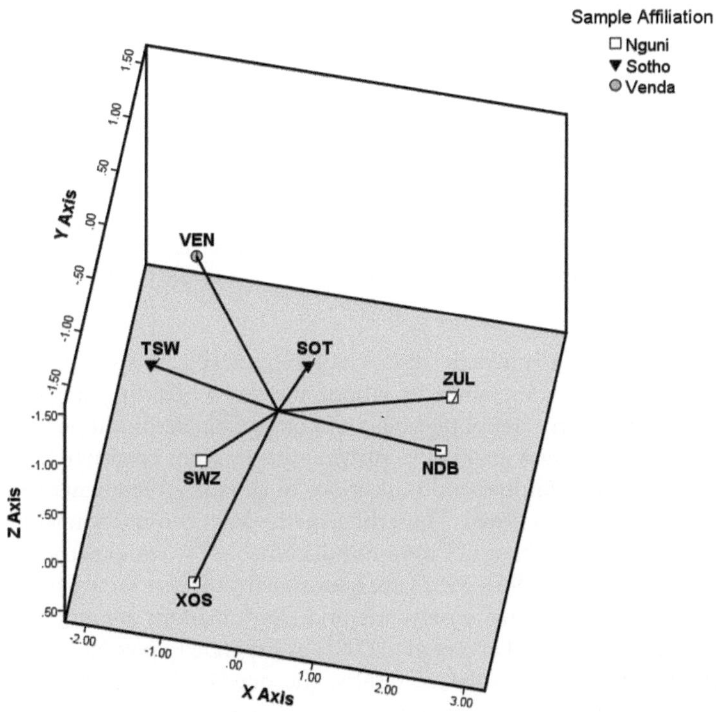

FIGURE 20.7

Three-dimensional MDS approximation of the MMD-based *R*-matrix for the seven "Bantu" samples. The three-letter sample abbreviations are defined in Table 20.1 and the text.

Modified from Irish, J.D., 2016. Who were they really? Model-free and model-bound dental nonmetric analyses to affirm "known" population affiliations of seven South African "Bantu" samples. American Journal of Physical Anthropology 159, 655–670.

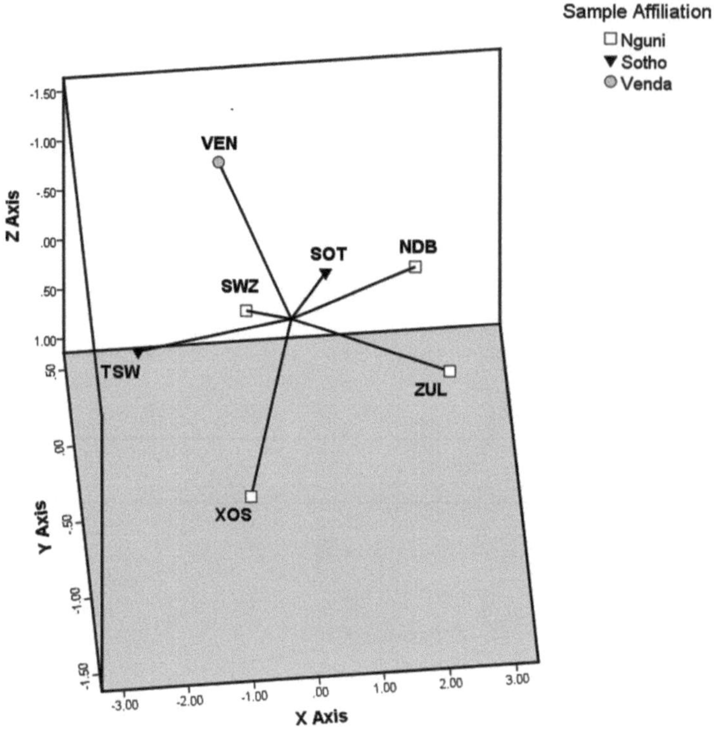

FIGURE 20.8

Three-dimensional MDS approximation of the D^2-based R-matrix for the seven "Bantu" samples. The three-letter sample abbreviations are defined in Table 20.1 and the text.

correlated with the MMD than D^2 phenetic distances (Irish, 2010), as also reported by Schillaci et al. (2009). And with regard to the results, similarity among the seven "Bantu" samples is evident; however, some recognizable trends or patterns are noticeable and comparable across all quantitative analyses, with both the model-free and model-bound analyses identifying this uniform variation. Such constancy suggests that the among-sample phenetic affinities and indications of genetic structure are real, and not statistical artifacts of the individual methods employed. Thus, these methods, in conjunction with the dental trait data, can apparently identify relationships that (1) were not discernable by craniometric (ie, De Villiers, 1968) and dental morphometric (Jacobson, 1967, 1982) analyses in many of these same Dart Collection crania, but (2) do parallel those based on autosomal serogenetic and DNA markers among most of the same, albeit contemporary, groups examined here (Lane et al., 2002), as expanded upon later.

Consequently, based on these quantitative results, the question is whether the original ethnic affiliations assigned to individuals in these samples, or at least most of them, seem valid based on the dental data. This question is comprehensively answered in light of the hypotheses/expectations in Irish (2016); an abridged version is presented in the following text, though with extra insight gained from the D^2 output.

Table 20.8 Geographic Straight-Line Distances in km Among the Seven South African "Bantu" Populations From the Approximated Centers of Their Historic Homelands

	NDB	SOT	SWZ	TSW	VEN	XOS	ZUL
NDB	0	473.83	294.14	599.72	314.36	875.28	474.00
SOT	473.83	0	453.94	650.86	766.41	403.53	430.36
SWZ	294.14	453.94	0	849.96	409.42	830.24	201.14
TSW	599.72	650.86	849.96	0	848.45	874.47	965.21
VEN	314.36	766.41	409.42	848.45	0	1169.58	605.61
XOS	875.28	403.53	830.24	874.47	1169.58	0	739.22
ZUL	474.00	430.36	201.14	965.21	605.61	739.22	0

NDB = *Ndebele;* SOT = *Sotho;* SWZ = *Swazi;* TSW = *Tswana;* VEN = *Venda;* XOS = *Xhosa;* ZUL = *Zulu (see text for sample details).*

First, it appears that ancestral relationships can still be discerned to some extent. That is, with exception (VEN) most do show much trait uniformity (Table 20.2), with low phenetic (Table 20.5) and genetic distances (Tables 20.6 and 20.7), and F_{st} estimates suggesting that only 2.1–3.8% of total genetic variation occurs among groups (paralleling statements of overall uniformity among these same samples by De Villiers, 1968; Jacobson, 1967, 1982; also Abbé et al., 2006). Nevertheless, all Nguni samples lie on the same general side of Fig. 20.6 (also Figs. 20.7 and 20.8), showing separation from TSW, SOT, and especially VEN. In Fig. 20.5 SWZ is farther from XOS and ZUL than expected (see later), but all other affinities are in the anticipated directions (ie, TSW and SOT somewhat similar; VEN divergent). Thus,

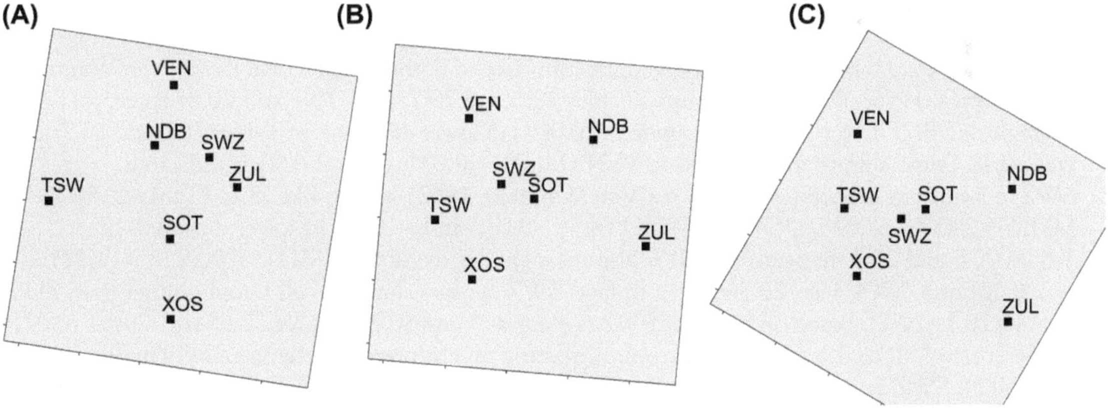

FIGURE 20.9

Two-dimensional MDS graphs of intersample (A) geographic distances in km, (B) 21-trait MMD distances, and (C) 21-trait D^2 distances among the seven "Bantu" samples. The three-letter sample abbreviations are defined in Table 20.1 and the text.

Modified from Irish, J.D., 2016. Who were they really? Model-free and model-bound dental nonmetric analyses to affirm "known" population affiliations of seven South African "Bantu" samples. American Journal of Physical Anthropology 159, 655–670.

historic events may obscure ancient relationships (eg, Relethford and Crawford, 1995; Relethford et al., 1997), but the D^2 and especially MMD results seemingly do identify linguistic and other ancestral ties (Greenberg, 1963; Nurse et al., 1985; Maylam, 1986; July, 1992), as also reported by Lane et al. (2002) in modern "Bantu" individuals.

Second, samples from populations in close geographic proximity do, for the most part, show greater numeric affinity. Figs. 20.2 and 20.4–20.8, as noted, appear qualitatively comparable to the population homelands in Fig. 20.1; the clear exceptions are SWZ and NDB. Again, Mantel correlations between D^2 and geographic distances are low, in accordance with previous findings (eg, Irish, 2010). So MMD distances are used to test the stepping-stone variant of the isolation-by-distance model (Irish, 2016). With straight-line distances it is assumed that an infinite number of subpopulations live along linear habitats and exchange migrants equivalently with contiguous subpopulations. Some gene flow may occur with other groups (eg, Khoesan) (see Kimura and Weiss, 1964; Konigsberg, 1990; Schillaci et al., 2009). The among-samples correlation is 0.195, which increases to 0.242 and 0.308 when SWZ and NDB are removed. Lane et al. (2002) note an r of 0.399 among many of these groups based on Y-chromosome haplotypes. As earlier, the SWZ phenetic distances (Table 20.5) are unexpected, so it may not be representative of the Swazi. The NDB incongruity likely has more to do with the Ndebele group's original genetic and geographic proximity to the Zulu (see discussion in Irish, 2016, and previously), that is not yet reflected by their documented 19th century population movement to their current location (Fig. 20.1). In any case, the correlation of 0.308 does provide moderate support for the isolation-by-distance model among five of the seven samples.

Finally, most of the seven expected scenarios concerning among-sample relationships are identified by the quantitative analyses. Each one is laid out as follows in reference to the MMD and D^2 results, with the overall interpretation presented at the end.

1. NDB is more distinct from XOS (MMD = 0.038, $D^2 = 2.508$) than ZUL (MMD = 0.033, $D^2 = 2.355$) from whom they may have diverged (Van Warmelo, 1962; Seligman, 1967), and SWZ (MMD = 0.000, $D^2 = 1.885$) (also Figs. 20.5 and 20.6). They appear similar to SOT (MMD = 0.000, $D^2 = 1.221$), likely given the influence of Sotho peoples near them (Van Warmelo, 1962; Byrnes, 1996). Genetic distances (Tables 20.6 and 20.7; Figs. 20.7 and 20.8) agree, for example, NDB/ZUL $r_{ij} = 0.00034$ (rounded to 0.000) in lower diagonals of Tables 20.6 and 20.7, and vice versa. Some affinity to neighboring VEN (MMD = 0.031, $D^2 = 2.622$) is indicated.
2. SWZ, contrary to expectations (also see Van Warmelo, 1962) is least like ZUL (Table 20.5, MMD = 0.037 $p > .025$, $D^2 = 2.465$) and ($r_{ij} = -0.010$ and -0.124 in lower diagonals of Tables 20.6 and 20.7, respectively). It is also most similar to XOS (MMD = 0.000, $D^2 = 1.221$; $r_{ij} = 0.001$ and 0.004; Figs. 20.5–20.8). In fact, SWZ appears similar to all samples other than ZUL (Tables 20.5–20.7). Based on r_{ii} values SWZ is second closest (0.023 Table 20.6) and closest (0.021 Table 20.7) of all to the regional centroid, suggesting much internal heterogeneity. Finally, other than NDB, SWZ is most divergent concerning phenetic versus geographic distances (Fig. 20.9).
3. ZUL, as shown earlier, shows a resemblance to NDB (MMD = 0.033, $D^2 = 2.355$, $r_{ij} = 0.00034$) (also Van Warmelo, 1962; Seligman, 1967), and are more distinct from XOS (MMD = 0.054 $p > .025$, $D^2 = 2.597$, $r_{ij} = -0.013$ and -0.007) (Tables 20.5–20.7 and Figs. 20.5–20.8), plus the ostensible SWZ outlier. It is divergent from TSW and VEN as expected, but like SOT (MMD = 0.013, $D^2 = 2.213$, MMD$r_{ij} = 0.001$) as discussed later. ZUL is farthest from the regional centroid ($r_{ii} = 0.061$ and 0.045 in Tables 20.6 and 20.7; Figs. 20.7 and 20.8), suggesting it is the most

homogeneous sample, perhaps from greater outside admixture (Konigsberg, 2006) and drift (Relethford et al., 1997); unfortunately, the latter cannot be quantified because of nonspecific census data that prevents estimation of relative population sizes.

4. XOS differs from NDB though not significantly (ie, MMD = 0.033 $p \leq .025$), and is more divergent from ZUL (Tables 20.5–20.7 and Figs. 20.5–20.8), in accordance with expectations. It is distinct from VEN (MMD = 0.044 $p > .025$, $D^2 = 2.395$, $r_{ij} = -0.017$ and -0.008). XOS shares an affinity with SOT [MMD = 0.008, $D^2 = 1.888$, though with negative (yet small) genetic measures (MMD$r_{ij} = -0.006$, $D^2 r_{ij} = -0.007$)], and TSW (MMD = 0.006, $D^2 = 1.886$, MMD$r_{ij} = 0.005$); perhaps the Khoesan gene flow played a role (Van Warmelo, 1962; Maylam, 1986; Byrnes, 1996) as suggested (Table 20.2) by the 31.58% presence of Bushman Canine that characterize Khoesan (Haeussler et al., 1989; Irish, 1993, 1997). Some phenetic and geographic correspondence (Fig. 20.9) is evident.
5. TSW is near SOT (eg, MMD = 0.001, $D^2 = 1.596$) (Tables 20.6 and 20.7; Figs. 20.5–20.8), as expected due to common ancestry and, perhaps, from gene flow with San (Van Warmelo, 1962; July, 1992) after reaching their homelands (Fig. 20.1). Khoesan influence is evident in TSW (Table 20.2). There is general phenetic/geographic correspondence (Fig. 20.9).
6. SOT is much like TSW. Based on its central location (Fig. 20.1), it is also comparable to the remaining samples (Table 20.5 and Figs. 20.5 and 20.6) including VEN. The latter affinity may be from Venda contact with Northern Sotho. The SOT resemblance to all samples is supported by *R*-matrices (Tables 20.6 and 20.7) that, despite mostly (small) negative r_{ij} values, show SOT as closest (0.021 in Table 20.6) and second closest (0.022 in Table 20.7) to the regional centroid (Figs. 20.7 and 20.8). Again, this proximity indicates heterogeneity from gene flow in a population positioned nearest to all others.
7. VEN, finally, is similar to NDB (earlier) but distinct from ZUL (MMD = 0.062 $p > .025$, $D^2 = 3.117$, $r_{ij} = -0.013$ and -0.018) and XOS (MMD = 0.044 $p > .025$, $D^2 = 2.395$, $r_{ij} = -0.008$ and -0.017) (Tables 20.5–20.7; Figs. 20.5–20.8), as expected (also Loubser, 1989). Otherwise, it is akin to SOT (MMD = 0.000, $D^2 = 1.810$, $r_{ij} = -0.003$ and -0.001) and TSW (MMD = 0.005, $D^2 = 1.732$, $r_{ij} = 0.003$ and 0.004), which may be explained by their association with Northern Sotho (Loubser, 1989). Again, phenetic/geographic correspondence is evident.

Taken together, these quantitative results suggest that ethnic/population identities assigned to individuals comprising the ZUL, XOS, TSW, SOT, and VEN cannot be rejected. The same may be said for the NDB sample; although there is a lack of correspondence between phenetic and geographic distances, it may be explained by the historic relocation of Ndebele peoples from their original far-eastern habitation to their current northeastern, KwaNdebele, homeland. Lastly, the findings imply that only the sample of SWZ individuals likely is not representative of the Swazi population, whether from recent changes obscuring ancient relationships (eg, Relethford and Crawford, 1995) or problems with the assigned ethnicity.

SUMMARY AND CONCLUSIONS

To sum up, this chapter describes and documents the use of the MMD and D^2 distance statistics with dental nonmetric data to further assess ethnic affiliations assigned to individuals comprising seven Dart

Collection samples: Ndebele, Sotho, Swazi, Tswana, Venda, Xosa, and Zulu (see Irish, 2016). Ethnic assignment of 20th century cadavers from which the skeletal remains were derived was often subjective so that, together with other curatorial issues, some questions of credibility arose. Phenetic distances from both statistics were produced, to which intersample geographic distances were compared to assess fit of the isolation-by-distance model, and from which genetic relationship or *R*-matrices and Sewall Wright's fixation index, or F_{st} were derived (see Irish, 2010). This output, in turn, was compared with documented population relationships in an attempt to provide support for, or evidence against, assigned affiliations.

In comparing the performance of the MMD and D^2 distances, the findings are in overall agreement with those presented elsewhere (Irish, 2010). That is, for model-free applications the former appears most robust, giving consistent results before and after the removal of problematic traits (ie, highly correlated trait pairs, many missing data, fixed frequencies; see also Nikita, 2015); after trait editing, both statistics generated comparable intersample results. With model-bound analyses, the MMD distances are most highly correlated with geographic distances for use in assessing fit of the isolation-by-distance model. The squared Euclidean-based D^2 distances can more easily be used to approximate an *R*-matrix and F_{st}, but nonlinear MMD distances can yield this output (Irish, 2010), and both sets of results are highly concordant.

From these model-free and model-bound results it appears that the SOT, TSW, VEN, XOS, and ZUL samples do largely consist of Sotho, Tswana, Venda, Xosa, and Zulu individuals, respectively. That is, most if not all of the cadaver-derived skeletal remains making up each of these samples were apparently given valid ethnic group/population affiliations. This statement is based on the finding that all yield expected intersample affinities based on (1) Nguni, Sotho, and Venda ancestry, (2) overall fit of the isolation-by-distance model, and (3) documented gene flow and migration during historic times. The NDB sample may also be, in total or part, comprised of Ndebele individuals. Its phenetic and geographic distances do not correspond as shown previously, possibly because Ndebele peoples have lived near their current homeland for a much shorter time than all others; however, the pairwise affinities do seem to mirror historic events known to have affected the population. It is only the SWZ sample results that clearly do not correspond with population history; as such it is suggested that either most or none of these individuals are representative of the Swazi ethnic group/population, either from misidentification or other curatorial issues. The takeaway message, then, is that "five (or six) out of seven ain't bad." The indications of credible identities, at least as seemingly demonstrated for most individuals in these samples, is, of course, critical for use of the Collection by researchers to address anthropological problems at regional and broader scales.

Acknowledgments

I would like to thank Marin Pilloud and Joseph Hefner for the invitation to their AAPA symposium and, now, this edited volume. Thanks also go to Brendan Billings, Curator of the Dart Collection at the University of the Witwatersrand, and everybody else there who helped me out. Funding was provided by the National Science Foundation (BCS-0840674).

References

Abbé, E.N., Ribot, I., Steyn, M., 2006. A craniometric study of the 20th century Venda. South African Archaeological Bulletin 61, 19–25.

Bermudez de Castro, J.M., 1989. The Carabelli trait in human prehistoric populations of the Canary Islands. Human Biology 61, 117–131.

Borg, I., Groenen, P., 1997. Modern Multidimensional Scaling. Springer-Verlag, New York.

Borgatti, S.P., 1997. Multidimensional Scaling. www.analytictech.com/borgatti/mds.htm.

Byrnes, R.M., 1996. South Africa: A Country Study. GPO for the Library of Congress, Washington.

Christopher, A.J., 2011. The Union of South Africa censuses 1911–1960: an incomplete record. Historia 56, 1–18.

Cohen, J., 1988. Statistical Power Analysis for the Behavioral Sciences, second ed. Erlbaum, Hillsdale.

Cox, T.F., Cox, M.A.A., 1994. Multidimensional Scaling. Chapman and Hall, London.

Davidson, B., 1974. Africa in History. Macmillan Publishing Company, New York.

Dayal, M.R., Kegley, A.D.T., Strkalj, G., Bidmos, M.A., Kuykendall, K.L., 2009. The history and composition of the Raymond A. Dart Collection of human skeletons at the University of the Witwatersrand, Johannesburg, South Africa. American Journal of Physical Anthropology 140, 324–335.

De Villiers, H., 1968. The Skull of the South African Negro. Witwatersrand University Press, Johannesburg.

Denbow, J.R., 1981. Broadhurst: a 14th century AD expression of the Early Iron Age in south-eastern Botswana. South African Archaeological Bulletin 66–74.

Ersts, P.J., 2014. [Internet] Geographic Distance Matrix Generator (Version 1.2.3). American Museum of Natural History, Center for Biodiversity and Conservation. Available from: http://biodiversityinformatics.amnh.org/open_source/gdmg.

Green, R., Suchey, J., 1976. The use of inverse sine transformation in the analysis of non-metrical data. American Journal of Physical Anthropology 45, 61–68.

Greenberg, J.H., 1963. The Languages of Africa. Mouton & Co., The Hague.

Greene, R., Suchey, J., Gokhale, D., 1979. The statistical treatment of correlated bilateral traits in the analysis of cranial material. American Journal of Physical Anthropology 50, 629–634.

Haeussler, A.M., Turner II, C.G., Irish, J.D., 1988. Concordance of American and Soviet methods in dental anthropology. American Journal of Physical Anthropology 75, 218.

Haeussler, A.M., Irish, J.D., Morris, D., Turner II, C.G., 1989. Morphological and metrical comparison of San and Central Sotho dentitions from southern Africa. American Journal of Physical Anthropology 78, 115–122.

Hall, S., 2010. Farming communities of the second millennium: internal frontiers, identity, continuity and change. In: Hamilton, C., Mbenga, B.K., Ross, R. (Eds.), Cambridge History of South Africa. Cambridge University Press, Cambidge, pp. 112–167.

Hanihara, T., 1992. Dental and cranial affinities among populations of East Asia and the Pacific: the basic populations in East Asia, IV. American Journal of Physical Anthropology 88, 163–182.

Harris, E.F., Sjøvold, T., 2004. Calculation of Smith's mean measure of divergence for intergroup comparisons using nonmetric data. Dental Anthropology 17, 83–93.

Hintze, J.L., 2007. NCSS Help System. NCSS, LLC, Kaysville, Utah.

Huffman, T.N., 1989. Ceramics, settlements and late Iron Age migrations. African Archaeological Review 7, 155–182.

Huffman, T.N., 2007. Handbook to the Iron Age: The Archaeology of Pre-Colonial Farming Societies in Southern Africa. University of Natal Press, Pietermaritzburg.

Hughes, T.E., Townsend, G.C., 2011. Twin studies of dental crown morphology: genetic and environmental determinants of the Cusp of Carabelli. In: Program 15th International Symposium on Dental Morphology, 37 (Newcastle, UK).

Irish, J.D., 1993. Biological Affinities of Late Pleistocene through Modern African Aboriginal Populations: The Dental Evidence (Ph.D. dissertation). Arizona State University, Tempe.

Irish, J.D., 1997. Characteristic high- and low-frequency dental traits in Sub-Saharan African populations. American Journal of Physical Anthropology 102, 455–467.

Irish, J.D., 2005. Population continuity versus discontinuity revisited: dental affinities among Late Paleolithic through Christian era Nubians. American Journal of Physical Anthropology 128, 520–535.

Irish, J.D., 2006. Who were the ancient Egyptians? Dental affinities among Neolithic through post-dynastic peoples. American Journal of Physical Anthropology 129, 529–543.

Irish, J.D., 2010. The mean measure of divergence (MMD): its utility in model-free and model-bound analyses relative to the Mahalanobis D^2 distance for nonmetric traits. American Journal of Human Biology 22, 378–395.

Irish, J.D., 2013. Afridonty: the "Sub-Saharan African Dental Complex" revisited. In: Scott, G.R., Irish, J.D. (Eds.), Anthropological Perspectives on Tooth Morphology: Genetics, Evolution, Variation. Cambridge University Press, Cambridge, pp. 278–295.
Irish, J.D., 2016. Who were they really? Model-free and model-bound dental nonmetric analyses to affirm "known" population affiliations of seven South African "Bantu" samples. American Journal of Physical Anthropology 159, 655–670.
Jacobson, A., 1967. The Bantu Dentition: A Morphological and Metrical Study of the Teeth, the Jaws and the Bony Palate of Several Large Groups of South African Bantu-Speaking Negroids (Ph.D. thesis). University of the Witwatersrand, Johannesburg.
Jacobson, A., 1982. The Dentition of the South African Negro. Higgenbotham, Inc., Anniston, AL.
July, R.W., 1992. A History of the African People. Waveland Press, Prospect Heights, IL.
Kimura, M., Weiss, G.H., 1964. The stepping-stone model of population structure and the decrease of genetic correlation with distance. Genetics 49, 561–576.
Konigsberg, L.W., Kohn, L.A.P., Cheverud, J.M., 1993. Cranial deformation and nonmetric trait variation. American Journal of Physical Anthropology 90, 35–48.
Konigsberg, L.W., 1990. Analysis of prehistoric biological variation under a model of isolation by geographic and temporal distance. Human Biology 62, 49–70.
Konigsberg, L.W., 2006. A post-Neumann history of biological and genetic distance studies in bioarchaeology. In: Buikstra, J.E., Beck, L.A. (Eds.), Bioarchaeology: The Contextual Analysis of Human Remains. Academic Press, New York, pp. 263–279.
Kruskal, J.B., Wish, M., 1978. Multidimensional Scaling. Sage Publications, Beverly Hills, CA.
Lane, A.B., Soodyall, H., Arndt, S., Ratshikhopha, M.E., Jonker, E., Freeman, C., Young, L., Morar, B., Toffie, L., 2002. Genetic substructure in South African Bantu-speakers: evidence from autosomal DNA and Y-chromosome studies. American Journal of Physical Anthropology 119, 175–185.
Larsen, C.S., 1997. Bioarchaeology. Cambridge University Press, Cambridge.
Leigh, S.R., Relethford, J.H., Park, P.B., Konigsberg, L.W., 2003. Morphological differentiation of Gorilla subspecies. In: Taylor, A.B., Goldsmith, M.L. (Eds.), Gorilla Biology: A Multidisciplinary Perspective. Cambridge University Press, Cambridge, pp. 104–131.
Loubser, J.H.N., 1989. Archaeology and early Venda history. South African Archaeological Society Goodwin Series 6, 54–61.
Martinon-Torres, M., Bermudez de Castro, J., Gomez-Robles, A., Arsuaga, J., Carbonell, E., Lordkipanidze, D., Manzi, G., Margvelashvili, A., 2007. Dental evidence on the hominin dispersals during the Pleistocene. Proceedings of the National Academy of Sciences 104, 13279–13282.
Maylam, P., 1986. A History of the African People of South Africa: From the Early Iron Age to the 1970s. St. Martin's Press, New York.
Monnig, H.O., 1967. The Pedi. JL Van Schaik Ltd., Pretoria.
Newman, J.L., 1995. The Peopling of Africa: A Geographic Interpretation. Yale University Press, New Haven.
Nikita, E., 2015. A critical review of the mean measure of divergence and Mahalanobis distances using artificial data and new approaches to the estimation of biodistances employing nonmetric traits. American Journal of Physical Anthropology 157, 284–294.
Nurse, G.T., Weiner, J.S., Jenkins, T., 1985. The Peoples of Southern Africa and Their Affinities. Clarendon Press, Oxford.
Parkington, J.E., 1981. Southern Africa: hunters and food-gatherers. In: Mokhtar, G. (Ed.), General History of Africa II: Ancient Civilizations of Africa. University of California Press, Berkeley, pp. 639–670.
Relethford, J., Blangero, J., 1990. Detection of differential gene flow from patterns of quantitative variation. Human Biology 62, 5–25.
Relethford, J.H., Crawford, M.H., 1995. Anthropometric variation and the population history of Ireland. American Journal of Physical Anthropology 96, 25–38.

Relethford, J.H., Harpending, H.C., 1994. Craniometric variation, genetic theory, and modern human origins. American Journal of Physical Anthropology 95, 249–270.

Relethford, J.H., Crawford, M.H., Blangero, J., 1997. Genetic drift and gene flow in post-famine Ireland. Human Biology 69, 443–465.

Relethford, J.H., 1994. Craniometric variation among modern human populations. American Journal of Physical Anthropology 95, 53–62.

Relethford, J., 2004. Global patterns of isolation by distance based on genetic and morphological data. Human Biology 76, 499–513.

Rightmire, G.P., 1999. Dental variation and human history. Archaeological Review 20, 1–3.

Ruhlen, M., 1994. The Origin of Language: Tracing the Evolution of the Mother Tongue. John Wiley & Sons, Inc., New York.

de Souza, P., Houghton, P., 1977. The mean measure of divergence and the use of non-metric data in the estimation of biological distances. Journal of Archaeological Science 4, 163–169.

Schillaci, M.A., Irish, J.D., Wood, C., 2009. Further analysis of the population history of ancient Egyptians. American Journal of Physical Anthropology 139, 235–243.

Scott, G.R., Turner II, C.G., 1997. The Anthropology of Modern Human Teeth: Dental Morphology and its Variation in Recent Human Populations. Cambridge University Press, Cambridge.

Scott, G.R., 1973. Dental Morphology: A Genetic Study of American White Families and Variation in Living Southwest Indians (Ph.D. dissertation). Arizona State University, Tempe, AZ.

Scott, G.R., 1980. Population variation of Carabelli's trait. Human Biology 52, 63–78.

Seligman, C.G., 1967. Races of Africa, fourth ed. Oxford University Press, Oxford.

Sjøvold, T., 1973. Occurrence of minor non-metrical variants in the skeleton and their quantitative treatment for population comparisons. HOMO 24, 204–233.

Sjøvold, T., 1977. Non-metrical divergence between skeletal populations: the theoretical foundation and biological importance of C.A.B. Smith's mean measure of divergence. Ossa 4 (Suppl. 1), 1–133.

Smith, P., Shegev, M., 1988. The dentition of Nubians from Wadi Halfa, Sudan: an evolutionary perspective. Journal of the Dental Association of South Africa 43, 539–541.

Smouse, P.E., Long, J.C., Sokal, R.R., 1986. Multiple regression and correlation extensions of the Mantel test of matrix correspondence. Systematic Zoology 35, 627–632.

Statistics South Africa, 2014. Mid-Year Population Estimates. Statistical release P0302. www.statssa.gov.za.

Sutton, J.E.G., 1981. East Africa before the seventh century. In: Mokhtar, G. (Ed.), General History of Africa II: Ancient Civilizations of Africa. University of California Press, Berkeley, pp. 568–592.

Tal, H., Tau, S., 1983. Statistical survey of the human skulls in the Raymond Dart Collection of skeletons. South African Journal of Science 79, 215–217.

Tobias, P.V., 1974. Biology of the South African Negro. University of the Witwatersrand, Capetown.

Turner II, C.G., Nichol, C.R., Scott, G.R., 1991. Scoring procedures for key morphological traits of the permanent dentition: the Arizona State University dental anthropology system. In: Kelley, M.A., Larsen, C.S. (Eds.), Advances in Dental Anthropology. Wiley-Liss, New York, pp. 13–32.

Van Warmelo, N.J., 1962. Grouping and ethnic history. In: Schapera, I. (Ed.), Bantu-Speaking Tribes of South Africa: An Ethnographical Survey. Routledge & Kegan Paul, Ltd., London, pp. 43–66.

Vogel, J.O., 1997. Bantu expansion. In: Vogel, J.O. (Ed.), Encyclopedia of Precolonial Africa: Archaeology, History, Languages, Cultures, and Environments. Alta Mira Press, Walnut Creek, pp. 435–438.

Warren, K.A., Hall, S., Ackermann, R.R., 2014. Craniodental continuity and change between Iron Age peoples and their descendants. South African Journal of Science 110. Art. #'2013-0275.

Williams-Blangero, S., Blangero, J., 1989. Anthropometric variation and the genetic structure of the Jirels of Nepal. Human Biology 61, 1–12.

Wright, S., 1943. Isolation by distance. Genetics 28, 114–138.

CHAPTER 21

Crossroads of the Old World: Dental Morphological Data and the Evidence for a Eurasian Cline

K. Heim, C. Maier, M.A. Pilloud, G.R. Scott
University of Nevada, Reno, Reno, NV, United States

CHAPTER OUTLINE HEAD

Materials 392
Methods 393
Results 396
Discussion 399
Conclusions 407
Acknowledgments 407
Endnote 407
References 407

The Eurasian landmass is unique in that it is made of two continents with no clear geographic separation. In fact, the distinction of Europe and Asia as two separate continents is largely a political and cultural distinction (Bassin, 1991). Throughout human prehistory and history, this landmass has served as a natural passage for migration, with Central Asia serving as an intersection for human movement (Martínez-Cruz et al., 2011).

Evidence of migration, and concomitant gene flow, has been identified in various genetic markers among living peoples in this region. A genetic cline for Eurasia was first identified in the distribution of the allele for blood type B. In Northeast Asia, this allele exists in some of the highest proportions in the world, and steadily decreases in frequency toward Western Europe (Candela, 1942). This pattern has also been seen with Y-chromosome haplotypes (Rosser et al., 2000) and nuclear DNA (Cavalli-Sforza et al., 1994).

The genetic cline across Eurasia has been attributed to various human migrations in the past. Candela (1942) argued the distribution of the B allele could be attributed to Mongol invasions between the 5th and 15th centuries. Recent work on the mtDNA of Mongolian populations confirms at least a maternal influence from Central Asian Mongols (Cheng et al., 2008). Other studies argue earlier migrations generated the cline. Yang et al. (2008) suggest the ancient Silk Road connecting Eastern and Central Asia beginning in the 2nd century BCE played a role in Eurasian admixture. Their argument is based on evidence for European and Eastern Asian haplogroups in the Gansu Corridor in China. Ashman (1950) argued for an even earlier origin of this cline, claiming that observed allele frequencies in Europe (focusing on the distribution of the B allele) would have taken more time to develop, proposing that gene flow began with Neolithic peoples from the east.

Modern populations show clear evidence of a Eurasian genetic cline, but researchers have had difficulty in establishing the exact timeline of population movements. The present study explores the existence of

Biological Distance Analysis. http://dx.doi.org/10.1016/B978-0-12-801966-5.00021-4

this cline and the timing of gene flow through an analysis of dental phenotypes using archaeological samples from across Eurasia spanning several time periods. Dental morphology is used as a proxy for genetic markers in this analysis as these traits show high levels of heritability and have been shown to reflect the underlying genetic makeup of a population (Hillson, 1996; Scott and Turner, 1997). Archaeological skeletal samples serve as a means to identify the existence of a cline through time and offer insights into the origins of modern population variation within Eurasia. This study focuses particularly on Central Asia as an intermediary in phenotypic expression to illustrate gene flow between European and East Asian populations.

MATERIALS

Archaeological sites were identified that spanned the Eurasian landmass and represented a broad range of time periods. Skeletal samples were then consolidated into broad geographic groups: Europe, Northeast Asia, Southeast Asia, South Asia, West Asia, and Central Asia. For the purposes of this study, European populations are those found geographically within the modern political entity of Europe and are known to express the Eurodont dental complex. Northeast Asia is defined as populations geographically within the area most commonly associated with the Sinodont dental pattern (ie, China, Mongolia, Japan, Northeast Siberia). Similarly, Southeast Asia refers to populations within the area known for Sundadonty (ie, Thailand, Taiwan, Malaysia, Indonesia, Borneo). See Table 21.1 for a list of dental morphological traits associated with each of these dental complexes. South Asian populations are politically within Southern Asia but are not Sundadonts (ie, India, Pakistan, Afghanistan). West Asian populations are within Asia politically, west of the Caspian Sea.

Finally, the boundaries of Central Asia are set by the Caspian Sea to the west, the Hindu Kush region of the Himalayan Mountains to the south, the Yenisei River to the east, and the 60th parallel to the north (Fig. 21.1). The area constituting Central Asia was drawn by hand using ArcMap (ESRI, 2014); therefore, a 50 km buffer was added to account for human error. The Yenesei sample was originally outside these defined bounds of the Central Asian region. As this sample is considered culturally Central Asian, the region was marginally expanded to include the Yenesei sample in this analysis. It is worth noting that the availability of data has created an eastern bias in the Central Asian sample composition. The absence of sites in the western half of Central Asia may affect the accuracy of the clines presented later.

Collapsing this large geographic region into culturally meaningful time periods is difficult, as each region has its own cultural progression. Therefore, general temporal categories were identified to incorporate extremely broad overall cultural changes. The Neolithic period begins with the adoption of agriculture, starting at roughly 10,000 BCE in the Middle East and extending to around 2000 BCE in parts of Europe. The Chalcolithic, Bronze, and Iron Ages follow the Neolithic and are broadly identified as the Early Metal Ages (2000–0 BCE), although the Chalcolithic can have a much earlier start in parts of the Middle East. The next time period is the Medieval time period, or the Middle Ages (CE 300–1500). The final period is the Historic/Recent period (CE 1700+). These time ranges incorporate all established dates for the sites in this study.

Each sample was grouped into one of these broad time periods based upon recorded dates. The sample from Tajikistan represents an exception to this norm as this site was occupied during both the Early Metal Ages and Medieval times; therefore, this sample was included in the analyses for both time periods. The samples and their broad geographic and temporal groups are listed in Table 21.2.

Table 21.1 Traits Associated With the Major Dental Complexes That Have Been Identified in Eurasia

Trait	Sinodont	Eurodont	Sundadont
Winging	High	Low	***
Shoveling	High	Low	***
Double shoveling	High	Low	***
Tuberculum dentale	High	High	High
Hypocone	Low	High	***
Cusp 5	Low	Low	***
Carabelli's cusp	Low	High	High
Parastyle	High	***	Low
Enamel extension	High	Low	***
Root number UP1	Low	High	***
Root number UM2	Low	High	***
Pegged-reduced-missing UM3	High	Low	Medium
Lingual cusp number LP2	High	High	High
Cusp 6	High	Low	High
4-Cusped LM2	Low	High	Medium
Deflecting wrinkle	Low	Lowest	***
Protostylid	High	Low	Medium
Root number LC	Low	High	***
3-Rooted LM1	High	Low	***

*Traits where population variation is not significant are indicated as ***.*
Based on Turner, C.G., 1985. The dental search for Native American origins. In: Kirk, R., Szathmary, E. (Eds.), Out of Asia, Peopling of the Americas and the Pacific Journal of Pacific Prehistory, Canberra, Australia, pp. 31–78; Turner, C.G., 1990. Major features of Sundadonty and Sinodonty, including suggestions about East Asian microevolution, population history, and late Pleistocene relationships with Australian aboriginals. American Journal of Physical Anthropology 82, 295–317; Scott, G.R., Turner, C.G., 1997. The Anthropology of Modern Human Teeth. Cambridge University Press, Cambridge; Scott, G.R., Anta, A., Schomberg, R., De La Rue, C., 2013. Basque dental morphology and the "Eurodont" dental pattern. In: Scott, G.R., Irish, J.D. (Eds.), Anthropological Perspectives on Tooth Morphology: Genetics, Evolution, Variation. Cambridge University Press, Cambridge, pp. 296–318; and Scott (personal communication).

METHODS

Data were collected by C.G. Turner II, G.R. Scott (Spanish Basques), and M.A. Pilloud (Çatalhöyük) following the guidelines established by the Arizona State University Dental Anthropology System (Turner et al., 1991). Males and females were pooled for analyses, as these traits do not exhibit sexual dimorphism (Scott and Turner, 1997); data presented here are for permanent teeth only. Only those variables with significant population variation and minimal missing data were included in the analysis. For example, a trait like the parastyle that has a frequency of less than 10% in all world groups was not included. Interregional variation in mean trait frequencies were typically 25% or more. To handle missing data, only traits that had been recorded in over 90% of the samples were analyzed. Focal teeth and breakpoints are listed for each trait in Table 21.3.

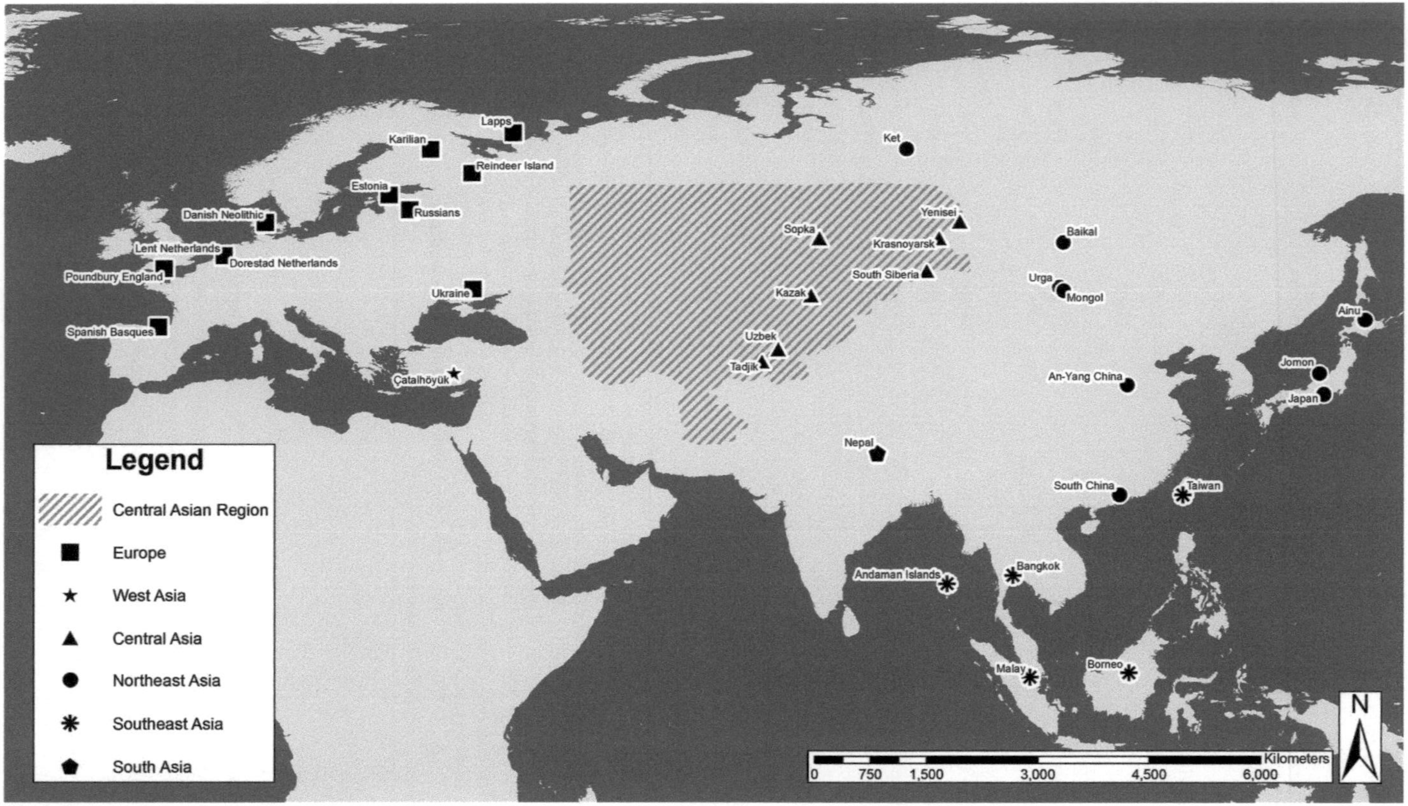

FIGURE 21.1

Map of sample locations based upon recorded proveniences. The geographic region of each sample is specified.

Dangol, B., 2013. Hindu Kush Himalayan Physiography. International Centre for Integrated Mountain Development; ESRI, 2011. World Water Bodies. DeLorme Publishing Company, Inc.; Law, M., Collins, A., 2013. Getting to Know ArcGIS for Desktop. ESRI Press, Redlands, CA.

Table 21.2 Geographic and Temporal Grouping of Skeletal Samples

Sample	Geographic Region	Time Period
Krasnoyarsk	Central Asia	Neolithic
Sopka	Central Asia	Early Metal Age
Tadjik	Central Asia	Early Metal Age/Medieval
Uzbek	Central Asia	Early Metal Age
Kazak	Central Asia	Recent/Historic
South Siberia	Central Asia	Recent/Historic
Yenisei	Central Asia	Recent/Historic
Baikal	NE Asia	Neolithic
An-Yang China	NE Asia	Early Metal Age
Jomon	NE Asia	Early Metal Age
Ainu	NE Asia	Recent/Historic
Japan	NE Asia	Recent/Historic
Ket	NE Asia	Recent/Historic
Mongol	NE Asia	Recent/Historic
South China	NE Asia	Recent/Historic
Urga	NE Asia	Recent/Historic
Danish Neolithic	Europe	Neolithic
Reindeer Island	Europe	Neolithic
Ukraine	Europe	Neolithic
Estonia	Europe	Early Metal Age
Dorestad Netherlands	Europe	Medieval
Lent Netherlands	Europe	Medieval
Poundbury England	Europe	Medieval
Spanish Basques	Europe	Medieval
Karilian	Europe	Recent/Historic
Lapps	Europe	Recent/Historic
Russians	Europe	Recent/Historic
Taiwan	SE Asia	Early Metal Age
Andaman Islands	SE Asia	Recent/Historic
Bangkok	SE Asia	Recent/Historic
Borneo	SE Asia	Recent/Historic
Malay	SE Asia	Recent/Historic
Nepal	South Asia	Recent/Historic
Çatalhöyük	West Asia	Neolithic

Population trait frequencies were explored with multivariate and univariate statistical methods using the R statistical package (R Core Team, 2013). Unrooted trees were created using Bray–Curtis polar ordination to illustrate population relationships (Bray and Curtis, 1957). The relative distance on the unrooted trees is a reflection of the biological distance between samples. The absolute distance is a product of the number of samples under analysis (ie, analyses with fewer samples will show absolutely greater

Table 21.3 Morphological Traits Used in This Study With Focal Teeth and Breakpoints Indicated for Each

Trait	Abbreviation	Score	Tooth[a]	Frequency Calculated
Winging	WING	1–4	UI1	1
Shoveling	SHOV	0–6	UI1	3–6
Double shoveling	DSHOV	0–6	UI1	2–6
Interruption groove	INT.GR	0–1	UI2	1
Tuberculum dentale	TD.UI2	0–6	UI2	1–6
Canine mesial ridge	BUSH.C	3	UC	2–3
Hypocone	HYP.UM2	0–5	UM2	0–1
Metaconule (cusp 5)	C5.UM1	0–5	UM1	1–5
Carabelli's cusp	CARA	0–7	UM1	3–7
Parastyle	PARA	0–6	UM3	1–6
Enamel extension	EN.EXT	0–3	UM1	2–3
Root number	RT.UP1	1–3	UP1	3 roots
Root number	RT.UM2	1–4	UM2	3 or 4 roots
Pegged-reduced-missing molar	PRM.M3	0–1	UM3	1
Lingual cusp number	LCN.LP2	A, 0–9	LP2	2–9
Groove pattern	GP.LM2	X, Y, +	LM2	Y-pattern
Cusp 6	C6.LM1	0–5	LM1	1–5
Hypoconulid (cusp 5)	X4C.LM2	0–5	LM2	0 (absence)
Protostylid	PROT	0–7	LM1	2–7
Cusp 7	C7.LM1	0–4	LM1	1–4
Tomes root	TOMES	0–5	LP3	4–5
Root number	RT.LC	1–2	LC	2 (two roots)
3-Rooted molar	X3RM1	1–3	LM1	3 (three roots)
Root number	RT.LM2	1–3	LM2	2 (two roots)
Odontome	ODONT	0–1	LP3/4	1

[a]*C, canine; I, incisor; L, lower; M, molar; P, premolar; U, upper; number indicates tooth position.*

distances between them). However, these distances are not indicative of the degree of similarity among samples. Chi-square and analysis of variance (ANOVA) were conducted for each of the morphological traits to identify significant differences between populations. Traits that were significantly different ($p < .0001$ in both analyses) were used as the basis of interpolation maps created using ArcMap (ESRI, 2014). The method chosen for interpolation was Kriging, to accommodate the sporadic distribution of samples across the landscape (Conolly and Lake, 2006).

RESULTS

The unrooted tree based on Bray–Curtis dissimilarity values (Fig. 21.2) illustrates a clear divide between European (Eurodont) and Northeast Asian (Sinodont) samples. Five of the seven samples categorized as geographically Central Asian (Sopka, Yenisei, Kazak, South Siberia, and Krasnoyarsk) cluster between

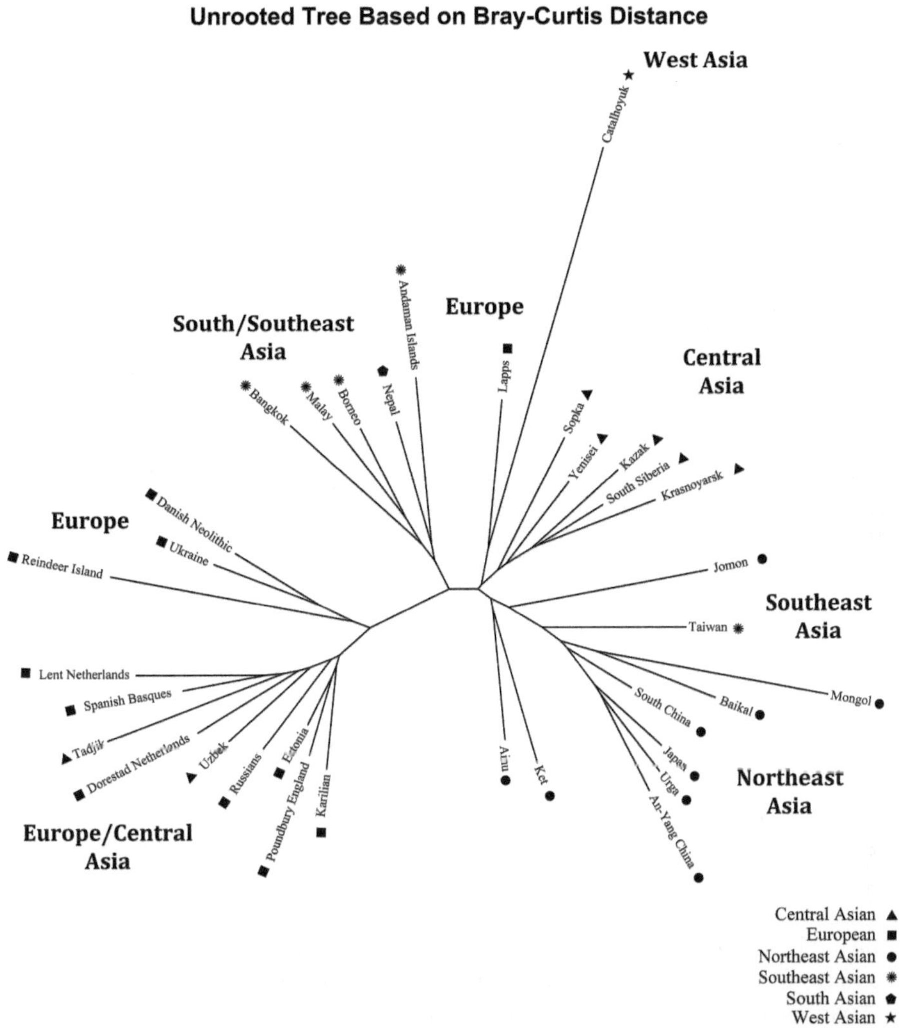

FIGURE 21.2

Unrooted tree based on Bray–Curtis distance for all samples. The geographic region of each sample is specified.

these two poles. The remaining two Central Asian samples, Tadjik and Uzbek, cluster with the European branch of the tree.

The analyses of temporal groups resulted in four additional unrooted trees. The tree for the Neolithic period (Fig. 21.3) illustrates the same polar patterning between the European samples and the Northeast Asian sample. Central (Krasnoyarsk) and West (Çatalhöyük) Asian samples are intermediate, but align more closely with Northeast Asia to form an Asian branch. During the Early Metal Ages, Central Asian and European samples occupy one end of the unrooted tree, whereas Northeast and Southeast Asian

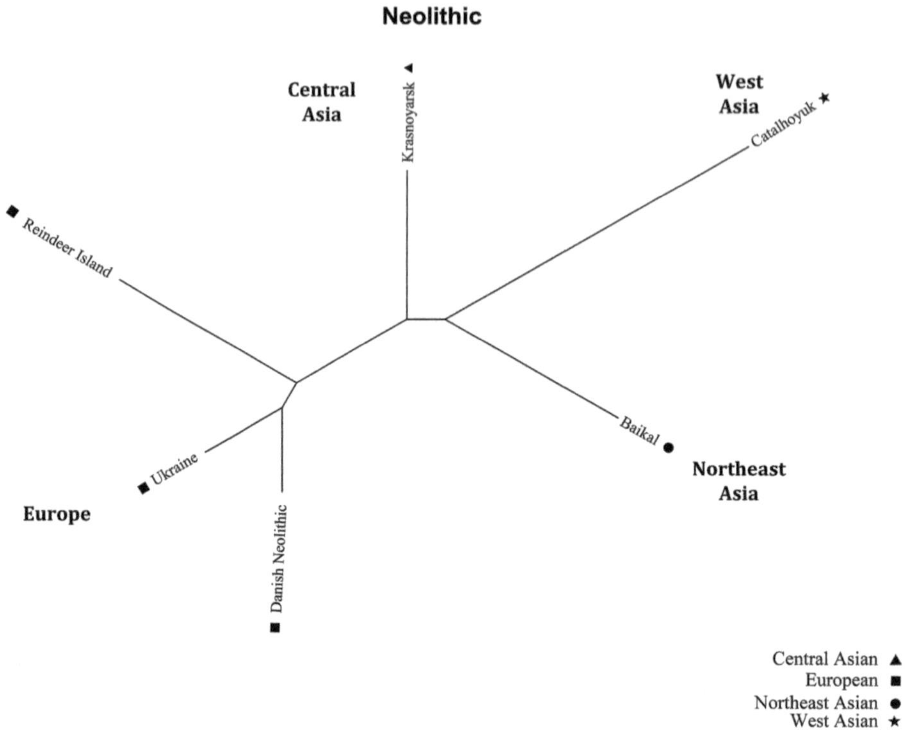

FIGURE 21.3

Unrooted tree based on Bray—Curtis distance for samples dated to the Neolithic period. The geographic region of each sample is specified.

samples are at the other end; however, Sopka, a Central Asian site, exhibits intermediacy between the two ends (Fig. 21.4). The majority of samples that date to the Medieval period are European (Fig. 21.5); therefore, the Bray—Curtis analysis is not informative, as the European samples cluster together with the one Central Asian sample to the side. Finally, during the Historic/Recent period (Fig. 21.6), three main clusters are identified: one with predominantly European and Central Asian samples, another with South and Southeast Asian groups, and a third with Northeast Asian samples. The only exception is the Ainu, a Northeast Asian sample that clusters with Central Asian and European samples.

To better understand the variation behind these unrooted trees, samples were compared by geographic region; this allowed for comparisons between larger groups rather than individual populations. Pairwise differences between European samples, Northeast Asian samples, and Central Asian samples, generated using ANOVA and Chi-square, suggest that the six traits exhibiting strong variation between samples ($p < .0001$ in both analyses) are UI1 shoveling, UM1 enamel extensions, LM1 cusp 6, four-cusped LM2, LM1 protostylid, and three-rooted LM1 (3RM1).[1] These traits were selected to demonstrate the geographic distribution of dental morphological features across Eurasia. The map illustrating UI1 shoveling (Fig. 21.7) shows a cline of this trait from East to West, with generally low frequencies in Europe and

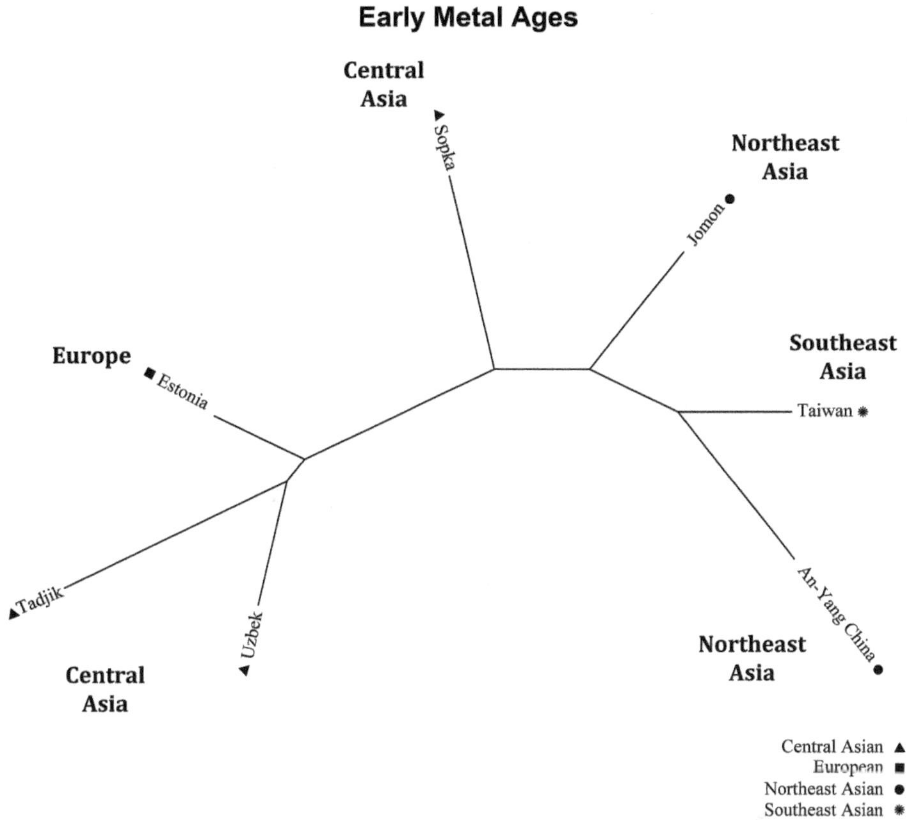

FIGURE 21.4

Unrooted tree based on Bray—Curtis distance for samples dated to the Early Metal Ages period. The geographic region of each sample is specified.

a slightly elevated frequency in Çatalhöyük. The frequencies of enamel extensions (Fig. 21.8), cusp 6 (Fig. 21.9), and 3RM1 (Fig. 21.10) show a similar pattern, with decreasing numbers moving from East to West. Conversely, four-cusped LM2 (Fig. 21.11) and the protostylid (Fig. 21.12) demonstrate a pattern previously observed in the Bray—Curtis unrooted trees. Two of the Central Asian samples (Tadjik and Uzbek) exhibit frequencies more consistent with the European samples than with the other samples categorized as geographically Central Asian.

DISCUSSION

This analysis of dental morphology identifies trait clines across Eurasia observed for a variety of genetic markers. As a result of this genetic cline, Central Asian populations often occupy an intermediate position. To explain this genetic intermediacy, two opposing theories have been proposed. The first theory

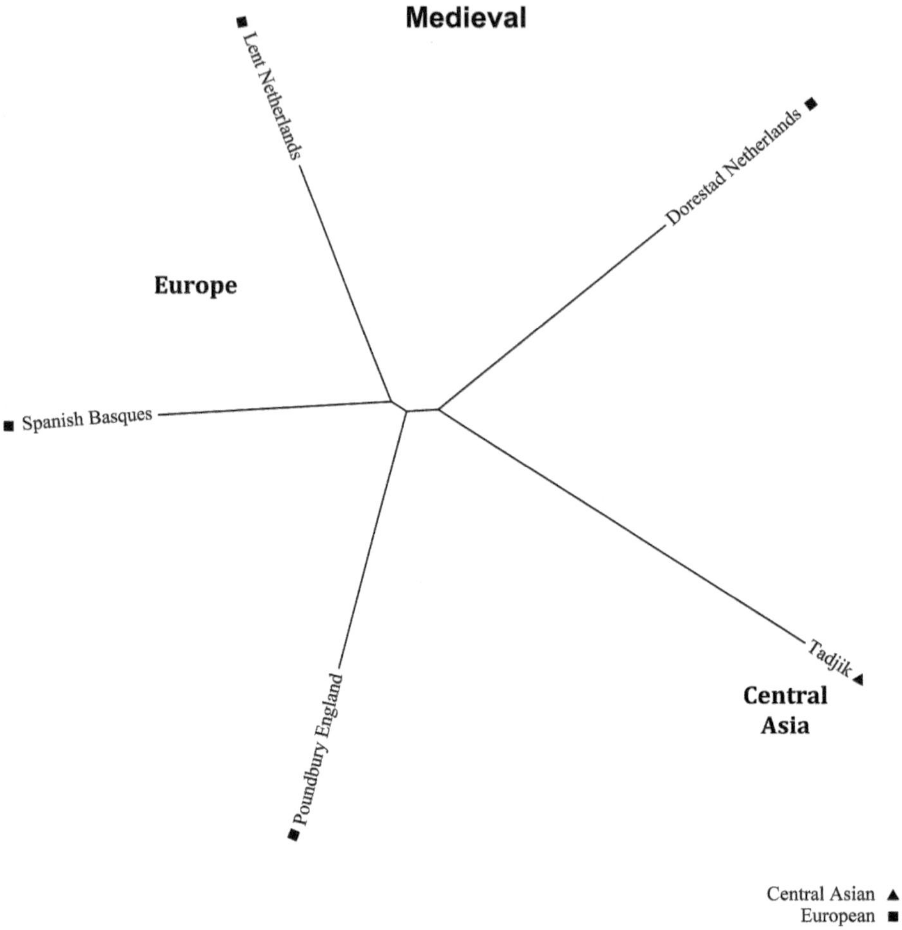

FIGURE 21.5

Unrooted tree based on Bray–Curtis distance for samples dated to the Medieval period. The geographic region of each sample is specified.

suggests Central Asia is genetically intermediate because it is the ancestral population for both European and East Asian populations (Bowles, 1977; Comas et al., 1998; Martínez-Cruz et al., 2011; Quintana-Murci et al., 2003; Wells et al., 2001). Under this model, populations of anatomically modern humans emerging from Africa underwent a maturation phase (Comas et al., 1998; Martínez-Cruz et al., 2011; Quintana-Murci et al., 2003) in Central Asia, later migrating both east into Asia and west into Europe. Y-chromosomal analyses support this hypothesis, suggesting that haplotypes seen in Central Asia are present across Eurasia and are among the oldest on the continent (Wells et al., 2001). The second theory posits that Central Asian intermediacy is the result of gene flow between differentiated populations in Europe and East Asia (Bowles, 1977; Comas et al., 1998; Martínez-Cruz et al., 2011; Quintana-Murci

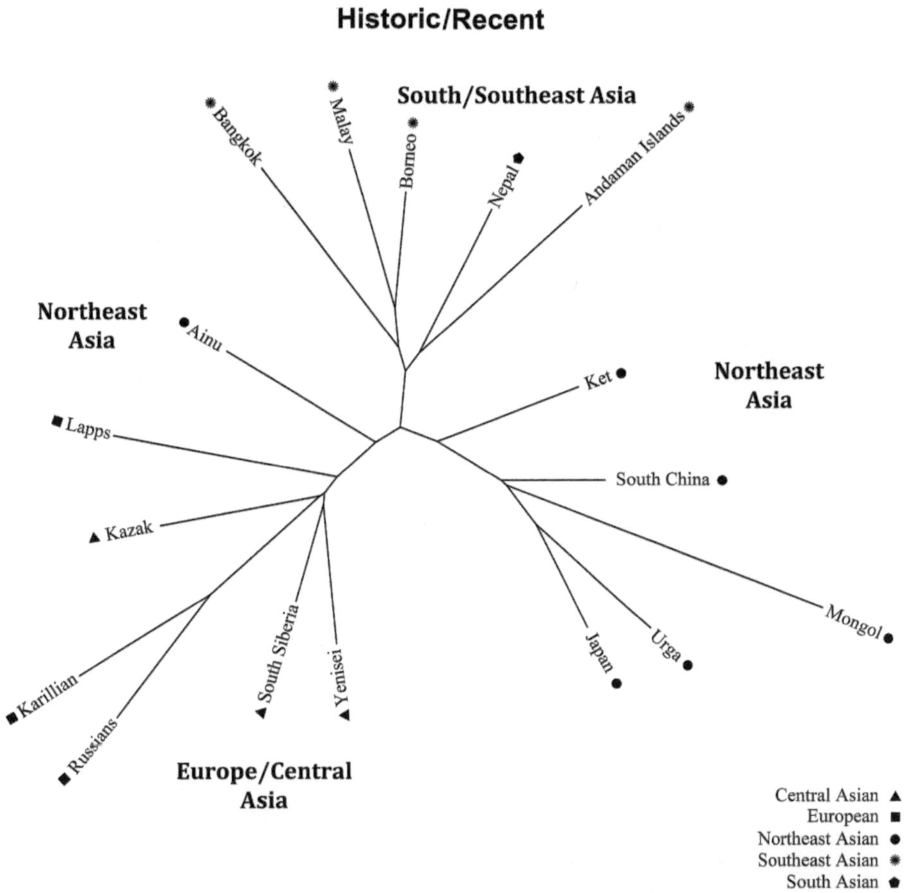

FIGURE 21.6

Unrooted tree based on Bray—Curtis distance for samples dated to the Historic/Recent period. The geographic region of each sample is specified.

et al., 2003; Zerjal et al., 2002). This position is supported by the analysis of mtDNA (Comas et al., 1998, 2004; Quintana-Murci et al., 2003), which suggests too few haplogroups are shared between European and Asian populations for common ancestry to be a feasible explanation. It is possible (perhaps even likely) that Y-chromosome and mtDNA analyses support alternate theories as a result of differential population movement. However, analysis of these movements is beyond the scope of this chapter.

With respect to dental morphology, this cline is evident in the interpolation maps based on six significantly different morphological traits. These traits are characteristic of either the Sinodont dental complex (UI1 shoveling, UM1 enamel extensions, LM1 cusp 6, LM1 protostylid, and three-rooted LM1) or the Eurodont dental complex (four-cusped LM2) (see Scott et al., 2013; Turner, 1985). The dichotomous nature of these dental complexes is likely why they are significantly different. The maps clearly show an East—West clinal distribution of Sinodont traits (UI1 shoveling, enamel extensions, three-rooted

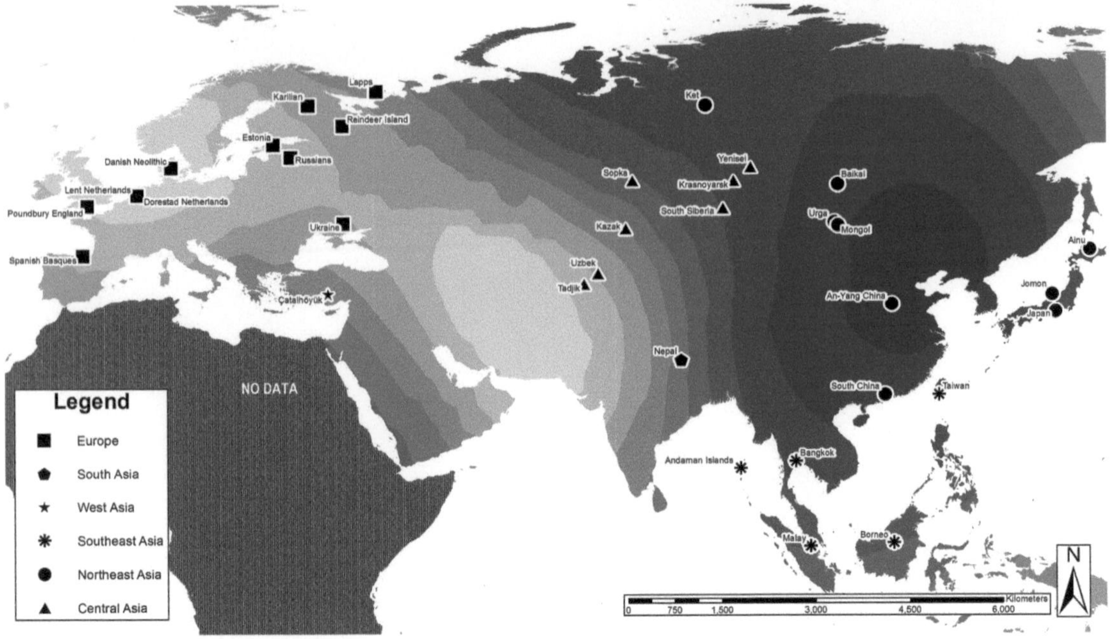

FIGURE 21.7

Interpolation map for frequency of upper first incisor shoveling in Eurasia, using Kriging interpolation technique. Darker bands represent areas expected to have high frequencies of UI1 shoveling, while lighter areas are expected to have low frequencies.

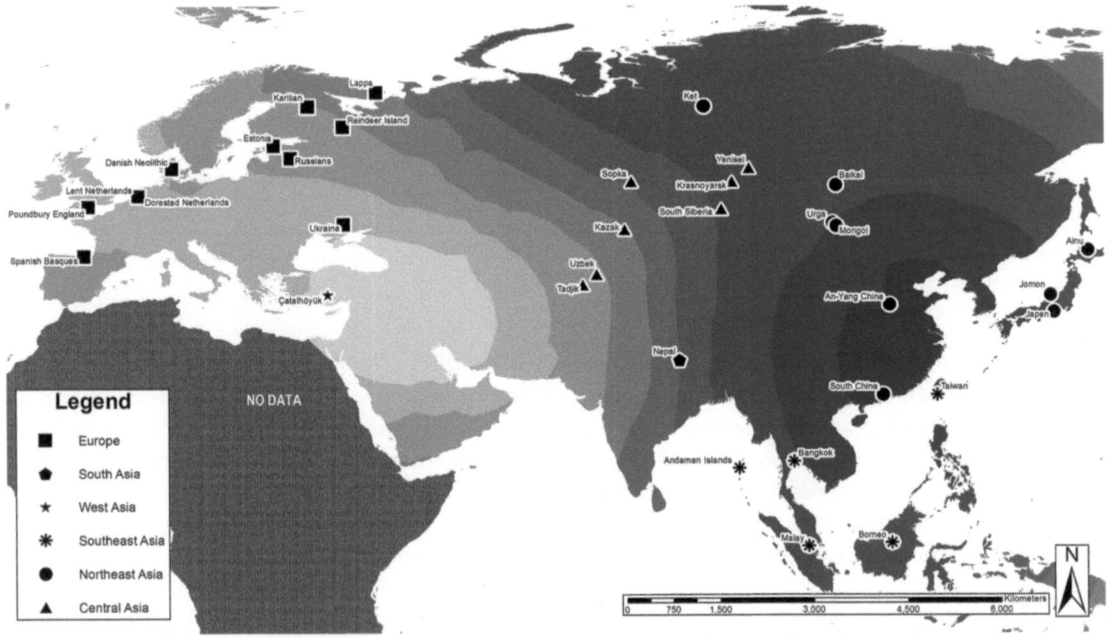

FIGURE 21.8

Interpolation map for frequency of upper first molar enamel extensions in Eurasia, using Kriging interpolation technique. Darker bands represent areas expected to have high frequencies of UM1 enamel extensions, while lighter areas are expected to have low frequencies.

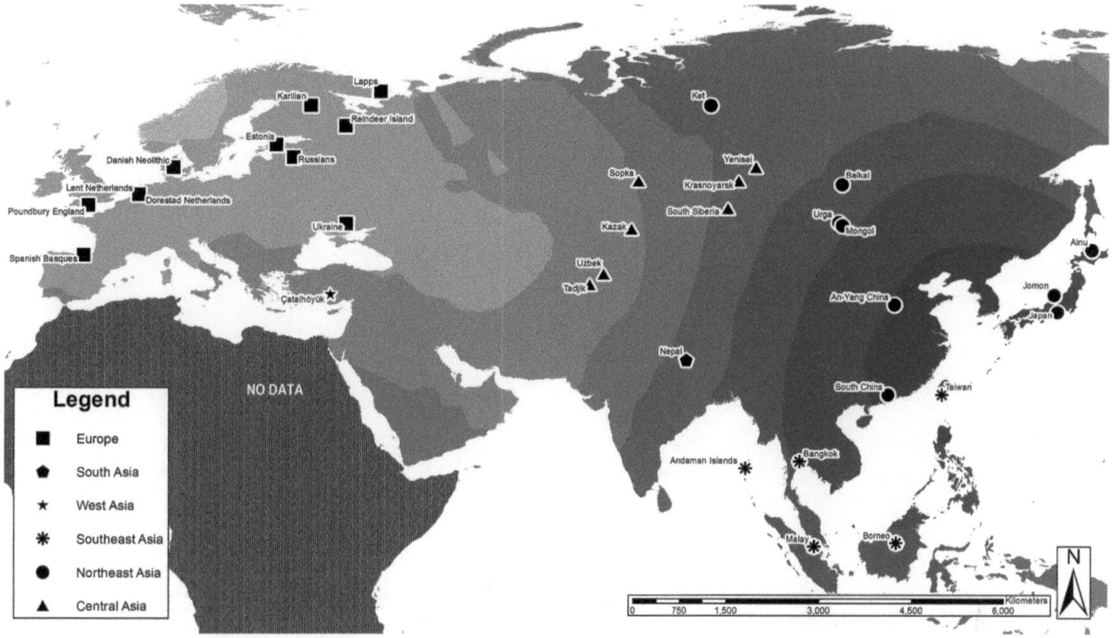

FIGURE 21.9

Interpolation map for frequency of lower first molar cusp 6 in Eurasia, using Kriging interpolation technique. Darker bands represent areas expected to have high frequencies of LM1 cusp 6, while lighter areas are expected to have low frequencies.

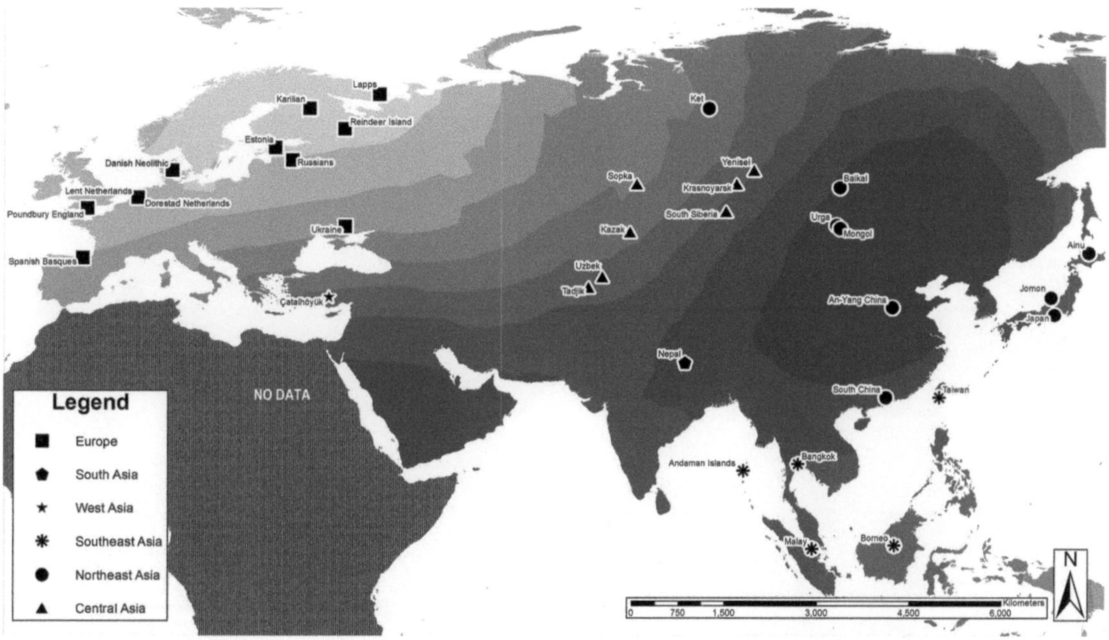

FIGURE 21.10

Interpolation map for frequency of three-rooted lower first molars in Eurasia, using Kriging interpolation technique. Darker bands represent areas expected to have high frequencies of three-rooted LM1, while lighter areas are expected to have low frequencies.

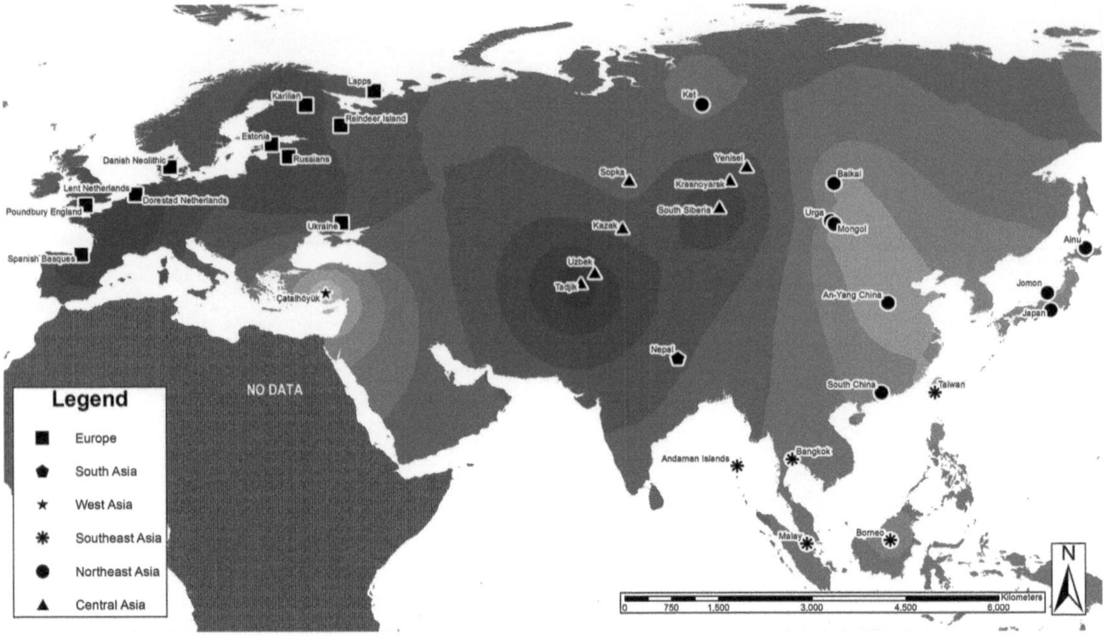

FIGURE 21.11

Interpolation map for frequency of four-cusped lower second molars in Eurasia, using Kriging interpolation technique. Darker bands represent areas expected to have high frequencies of four-cusped LM2, while lighter areas are expected to have low frequencies.

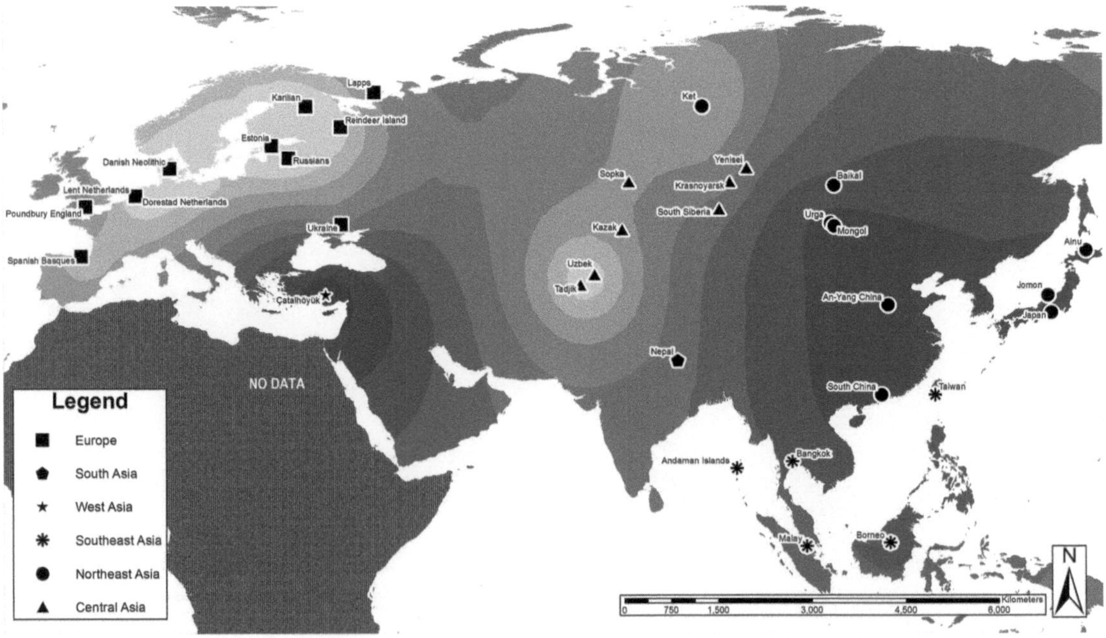

FIGURE 21.12

Interpolation map for frequency of lower first molar protostylid in Eurasia, using Kriging interpolation technique. Darker bands represent areas expected to have high frequencies of LM1 protostylid, while lighter areas are expected to have low frequencies.

LM1, and LM1 cusp 6). However, the protostylid does not show this same pattern; instead, Central Asia emerges as being more similar to European populations. This pattern is echoed by four-cusped LM2 (a Eurodont trait). This Central Asian tendency to show ties with Europe is most evident in the Uzbek and Tadjik samples. In the Bray—Curtis analyses (regardless of time period), Tadjik and Uzbek consistently cluster with European populations. In the large Bray—Curtis tree that includes all samples, the remainder of the Central Asian samples cluster on their own with one other European sample (Lapps) and Çatalhöyük. However, it is important to look at these biodistance analyses within each time period to adequately explore the depths of population affinity and migration. Therefore, the present data are best contextualized through the study of movements throughout the Eurasian landmass during the defined time periods.

Analyses during the Neolithic show Northeast Asia and Europe at opposite ends of the dental spectrum, with Central (Krasnoyarsk) and West Asia (Çatalhöyük) in an intermediate position. This finding suggests the genetic cline may date to this period, and may be related to the development of farming. Archaeological data suggest early plant domesticates centering on wheat, rye, and barley emerge in the Levant as early as 10,700 cal BP (Fuller et al., 2012; Wilcox, 2012). A separate complex, involving rice and millet, is seen in East Asia several thousand years later (Crawford, 2008; Crawford and Shen, 1998; Sweeney and McCouch, 2007). In Central Asia, the first agricultural populations emerge in the archaeological record between 6000 and 4000 BCE and utilize wheat-based domesticates (Cavalli-Sforza et al., 1994; Harris and Gosden, 1996; Miller, 1999a). The presence of these domesticates in Central Asian agricultural sites indicates a population dispersal out of West Asia. In fact, craniometric (Pinhasi and Pluciennik, 2004; Pinhasi and von Cramon-Taubadel, 2009) and mitochondrial DNA (Fernández et al., 2014; Hervella et al., 2015) data also support a movement of West Asians to the west toward Europe.

Further evidence for population movement during the Neolithic period is provided by linguistic analyses. The spread of Indo-European languages likely reflects the movement of populations, although the specifics of this spread are debated (eg, Gimbutas, 1956; Renfrew, 1987). One theory suggests Indo-European languages spread in tandem with agriculture out of West Asia, first moving northwest into Europe and then southeast through Central Asia into South and Southeast Asia (Renfrew, 1987), as supported by archaeological and craniometric data. Alternatively, Indo-European languages may have been spread by groups originating in Central Asia. These pastoralist groups were highly mobile and may have spread in both an easterly and westerly direction out of Central Asia (Anthony, 2007; Gimbutas, 1956, 1997; Haak et al., 2015). Regardless of the exact origin of Indo-European languages (West vs Central Asia), both areas play an intermediary role in Eurasia as early as the Neolithic.

In the Bray—Curtis analysis of the Early Metal Ages, Central Asian dental morphology aligns more closely with Europe, while Southeast and Northeast Asian samples cluster together. Such clustering is in line with proposed population movements during the Neolithic, such that Central and West Asia and Europe are experiencing gene flow associated with the demic diffusion of agriculture. Additionally, at the beginning of the Early Metal Ages, agriculture is still predominant in Central Asia (Hiebert, 1994; Miller, 1999a; Moore et al., 1994), with evidence for West Asian domesticates suggesting that the primary cultural, and by extension genetic, influence continues from the west (Miller, 1999b). However, it is during the Early Metal Ages that agriculture in Central Asia fails due to the harsh environmental conditions (Nesbitt and O'Hara, 2000; O'Hara, 2000). The effects of environmental change in an area as vast as Central Asia are unlikely to be uniform; as areas of Central Asia begin to experience a more arid climate, pastoral nomadism emerges as the favored subsistence pattern (Frank, 1992). Although occurring in separate isolated regions at different times, the trend in the later Early Metal Ages is toward this subsistence pattern, leading to greater mobility (Frank, 1992). This increase in movement may explain the shifts in population affinity that emerge in later time periods.

During the Early Metal Ages, around 1300 BCE, Aryan tribes from Central Asia first invade Iranian territory to the west (Martínez-Cruz et al., 2011). A branch of these Aryan tribes, the Scythians, are later mentioned both by Chinese texts in 700 BCE and then by the Greek historian Herodotus. In both accounts, the Scythians are described as possessing European traits and speaking Indo-Iranian languages (Comas et al., 1998; Martínez-Cruz et al., 2011). The description of these tribes as phenotypically European suggests the relationship between European and Central Asian populations must have been established at this time. In addition to Central Asian movements, there are many documented movements of European populations into Central Asia during this time period (eg, Darius I of Persia and Alexander the Great) (Frank, 1992; Grousset and Walford, 1970). The trend of European incursion into Central Asia during the Early Metal Ages may have further impacted the phenotypic relationships identified between European and Central Asian samples.

At the end of the Early Metal Ages, East Asian movement into Central Asia becomes more prevalent. Between 200 and 100 BCE, Hunnic groups enter Central Asia, bringing with them the East Asian phenotype (Martínez-Cruz et al., 2011). The Han Dynasty of China has a later period of expansion into Central Asia following the Han–Xiongnu Wars (Chang, 2007; Di Cosmo, 2002; Loewe, 1986). Perhaps the most important event in the final years of the Early Metal Ages is the establishment of the Silk Road in 200 BCE, stretching from the Mediterranean to East Asia (Comas et al., 1998). As the predominant land trade route for 1600 years, this corridor is critical to population movements between Europe and East Asia. Its route ensured that travelers from both extremes had to pass through Central Asia (Comas et al., 1998; Martínez-Cruz et al., 2011). For the entirety of the Medieval period, the majority of population movement in Central Asia occurs along the Silk Road. Historically attested movements during this time (eg, Bentley, 1998; Christian, 2000; Edwardes, 1971; Wood, 2002) indicate population movement was bidirectional, with both European and East Asian populations traversing Eurasia. Therefore, more pronounced intermediacy would be expected in the dental morphological evidence. However, in this study, no Northeast Asian samples date to this time period; consequently, the analysis presented for the Medieval time period cannot speak to these movements.

The trend where Central Asian samples align more closely with European samples on the basis of dental morphology continues into the Historic/Recent time period, suggesting broad contact between these populations. The beginning of this period is characterized by two major changes to the Central Asian way of life. First, the establishment of safer nautical trade routes between Europe and Asia leads to a decline in use of the Silk Road (Bentley, 1998; Liu, 2001; Whitfield, 1999; Wood, 2002). Dwindling use of the Silk Road translates into a decrease in population movement through Central Asia, thus eliminating a major corridor for transcontinental gene flow (eg, Comas et al., 1998). Second, the agrarian populations around the periphery of Central Asia adopt gunpowder weapons. This technological development provided an advantage over the steppe nomads and allowed European and East Asian populations to make permanent incursions into Central Asia (Hildinger, 1997; Perdue, 2005).

In CE 1758, China invades and takes over most of Mongolia (Cosmo, 1998; Perdue, 2005). While this is outside the defined Central Asian region in this study, the increase of East Asian individuals at the Central Asian border implies greater opportunity for gene flow between these two populations. The greatest source of European influence in this period comes from Russia. Around CE 1800, Russia takes over much of northern Central Asia (Allworth, 1994; Bacon, 1996). After taking political control of the area,

Russian policy opens up the plains of Central Asia for farming in the 1870s (Bacon, 1996; Becker, 1968; Clem and Lewis, 1992). Subsequently, many Russian farmers occupy the area, some reaching as far south as East Kazakhstan. In response to Russia's occupation of Central Asia, British colonial powers in India begin to move north. In CE 1887, the Russian and British fronts meet, together negotiating the northern border of Afghanistan (Hopkirk, 1990; Kazemzadeh, 1968; Siegel, 2002). At this point in the Historic/Recent period, the area defined as Central Asia is now almost entirely occupied by European colonial powers.

In the context of these population movements, the Bray–Curtis analysis of the Historic/Recent period can be readily explained. Two of the European samples (Karilian and Russian) are from Russia, while two of the three Central Asian samples (South Siberia and Yenisei) are within the political boundaries of Russia. The final Central Asian sample (Kazak) is in Kazakhstan, an area into which Russian farmers moved. Therefore, the European affinity of the Central Asian samples in the Historic/Recent period could be interpreted as a product of Russian migration into Central Asia.

CONCLUSIONS

The cline across Eurasia is well attested by genetic and blood group studies. Dental morphology provides another suite of traits that can be used to analyze this cline. Teeth also allow for the analysis of spatial and temporal relationships. Measures of biodistance show that Central Asian dental morphology is intermediate between that of European and Northeast Asian populations. Additionally, the analyses presented here demonstrate the need to use multiple lines of evidence, including an understanding of (pre)historical context, when conducting biodistance research. The population movements across Eurasia over the past 12,000 years are complex. The current genetic variation of modern peoples is a reflection of that complexity. Further research using ancient DNA will provide additional insights into past population movements and their effects on present populations.

Acknowledgments

The authors are indebted to the late Christy G. Turner II whose data formed the backbone of this analysis.

Endnote

1. UI1 stands for upper first incisor; UM1 stands for upper first molar; LM1 stands for lower first molar; and LM2 stands for lower second molar.

References

Allworth, E., 1994. Central Asia, 130 Years of Russian Dominance: A Historical Overview. Duke University Press, Durham, NC.

Anthony, D.W., 2007. The Horse, the Wheel, and Language: How Bronze Age Riders from the Eurasian Steppes Shaped the Modern World. Princeton University Press, Princeton, NJ.

Ashman, R., 1950. Origins of blood groups ABO, and the European Mongoloid problem. American Journal of Physical Anthropology 8 (4), 427–452.

Bacon, E.E., 1996. Central Asians Under Russian Rule: A Study in Culture Change. Cornell University Press, Ithaca, NY.

Bassin, M., 1991. Russia between Europe and Asia: the ideological construction of geographical space. Slavic Review 50, 1–17.
Becker, S., 1968. Russia's Protectorates in Central Asia: Bukhara and Khiva, 1865–1924. Harvard University Press, Cambridge, MA.
Bentley, J.H., 1998. Hemispheric integration, 500–1500 CE. Journal of World History 9 (2), 237–254.
Bowles, G.T., 1977. The People of Asia. Charles Scribner's Sons, New York.
Bray, J.R., Curtis, J.T., 1957. An ordination of upland forest communities of southern Wisconsin. Ecological Monographs 27, 325–349.
Candela, P.B., 1942. The introduction of the blood group B into Europe. Human Biology 14 (4), 413–443.
Cavalli-Sforza, L., Menozzi, P., Piazza, A., 1994. The History and Geography of Human Genes. Princeton University Press, Princeton.
Chang, C., 2007. The Rise of the Chinese Empire: Volume 2, Frontier, Immigration, and Empire in Han China, 130 B.C.–A.D. 157. The University of Michigan Press, Ann Arbor, MI.
Cheng, B., Tang, W., He, L., Dong, Y., Lu, J., Lei, Y., Yu, H., Zhang, J., Xiao, C., 2008. Genetic imprint of the Mongol: signal from phylogeographic analysis of mitochondrial DNA. Journal of Human Genetics 53 (10), 905–913.
Christian, D., 2000. Silk Roads or Steppe Roads? The Silk Roads in world history. Journal of World History 11, 1–26.
Clem, R.S., Lewis, R., 1992. The Frontier and Colonialism in Russian and Soviet Central Asia. In: Lewis, R. (Ed.), Geographic Perspectives on Soviet Central Asia. Routledge, New York, pp. 19–36.
Comas, D., Calafell, F., Mateu, E., Pérez-Lezaun, A., Bosch, E., Martínez-Arias, R., Clarimon, J., Facchini, F., Fiori, G., Luiselli, D., Pettener, D., Bertranpetit, J., 1998. Trading genes along the silk road: mtDNA sequences and the origin of central Asian populations. American Journal of Human Genetics 63 (6), 1824–1838.
Comas, D., Plaza, S., Wells, R.S., Yuldaseva, N., Lao, O., Calafell, F., Bertranpetit, J., 2004. Admixture, migrations, and dispersals in Central Asia: evidence from maternal DNA lineages. European Journal of Human Genetics 12 (6), 495–504.
Conolly, J., Lake, M., 2006. Geographical Information Systems in Archaeology. Cambridge University Press, Cambridge.
Cosmo, N.D., 1998. Qing colonial administration in Inner Asia. The International History Review 20 (2), 287–309.
Crawford, G.W., Shen, C., 1998. The origins of rice agriculture: recent progress in East Asia. Antiquity 78, 858–866.
Crawford, G.W., 2008. East Asian plant domestication. In: Stark, M.T. (Ed.), Archaeology of Asia. John Wiley and Sons, Inc., New York, pp. 77–95.
Dangol, B., 2013. Hindu Kush Himalayan Physiography. International Centre for Integrated Mountain Development.
Di Cosmo, N., 2002. Ancient China and Its Enemies: The Rise of Nomadic Power in East Asian History. Cambridge University Press, Cambridge.
Edwardes, M., 1971. East-West Passage: The Travel of Ideas, Arts, and Inventions between Asia and the Western World. Taplinger Publishing Company, New York.
ESRI, 2011. World Water Bodies. DeLorme Publishing Company, Inc.
ESRI, 2014. ArcGIS 10.2.2 for Desktop. Environmental Systems Research Institute, Redlands, California.
Fernández, E., Pérez-Pérez, A., Gamba, C., Prats, E., Cuesta, P., Anfruns, J., Molist, M., Arroyo-Pardo, E., Turbón, D., 2014. Ancient DNA analysis of 8000 B.C. Near Eastern farmers supports an early Neolithic pioneer maritime colonization of Mainland Europe through Cyprus and the Aegean Islands. PLoS Genetics 10 (6), e1004401.
Frank, A.G., 1992. The centrality of Central Asia. Studies in History 8 (1), 43–97.
Fuller, D.Q., Willcox, G., Allaby, R.G., 2012. Early agricultural pathways: moving outside the 'core area' hypothesis in Southwest Asia. Journal of Experimental Botany 63 (2), 617–633.
Gimbutas, M., 1956. The Prehistory of Eastern Europe: Part 1, Mesolithic, Neolithic, and Copper Age Cultures in Russia and the Baltic Area. The Peabody Museum, Cambridge, MA.
Gimbutas, M., 1997. The Kurgan culture and the Indo-Europeanization of Europe: selected articles from 1952 to 1993. In: Robbins Dexter, M., Jones-Bley, K. (Eds.), Journal of Indo-European Studies Monograph No. 19. Institute for the Study of Man, Washington, DC.

Grousset, R., Walford, N., 1970. The Empire of the Steppes: A History of Central Asia. Rutgers University Press, New Brunswick, NJ.

Haak, W., Lazaridis, I., Patterson, N., Rohland, N., Mallick, S., Llamas, B., Brandt, G., Nordenfelt, S., Harney, E., Stewardson, K., Fu, Q., Mittnik, A., Banffy, E., Economou, C., Francken, M., Friederich, S., Pena, R.G., Hallgren, F., Khartanovich, V., Khokhlov, A., Kunst, M., Kuznetsov, P., Meller, H., Mochalov, O., Moiseyev, V., Nicklisch, N., Pichler, S.L., Risch, R., Rojo Guerra, M.A., Roth, C., Szecsenyi-Nagy, A., Wahl, J., Meyer, M., Krause, J., Brown, D., Anthony, D., Cooper, A., Alt, K.W., Reich, D., 2015. Massive migration from the steppe was a source for Indo-European languages in Europe. Nature 522 (7555), 207–211.

Harris, D.R., Gosden, C., 1996. The beginnings of agriculture in western Central Asia. In: Harris, D.R. (Ed.), The Origins and Spread of Agriculture and Pastoralism in Eurasia. Routledge, New York, pp. 370–389.

Hervella, M., Rotea, M., Izagirre, N., Constantinescu, M., Alonso, S., Ioana, M., Lazăr, C., Ridiche, F., Soficaru, A.D., Netea, M.G., de-la-Rua, C., 2015. Ancient DNA from south-east Europe reveals different events during Early and Middle Neolithic influencing the European genetic heritage. PLoS One 10 (6), e0128810.

Hiebert, F.T., 1994. Origins of Bronze Age Oasis Civilization in Central Asia, No. 42. Harvard University Press, Cambridge, MA.

Hildinger, E., 1997. Warriors of the Steppe: A Military History of Central Asia, 500 BC to 1700 AD. Da Capo Press, Boston, MA.

Hillson, S., 1996. Dental Anthropology. Cambridge University Press, Cambridge.

Hopkirk, P., 1990. The Great Game: The Struggle for Empire in Central Asia. Kodansha International, New York.

Kazemzadeh, F., 1968. Russia and Britain in Persia. 1864–1914: A Study in Imperialism. Yale University Press, New Haven, CT.

Law, M., Collins, A., 2013. Getting to Know ArcGIS for Desktop. ESRI Press, Redlands, CA.

Liu, X., 2001. The Silk Road in World History. Oxford University Press, New York.

Loewe, M., 1986. The former Han dynasty. In: Twitchett, D., Loewe, M. (Eds.), The Cambridge History of China Volume 1: The Ch'in and Han Empires, 221 BC–AD 220. Cambridge University Press, New York, pp. 103–222.

Martínez-Cruz, B., Vitalis, R., Ségurel, L., Austerlitz, F., Georges, M., Théry, S., Quintana-Murci, L., Hegay, T., Aldashev, A., Nasyrova, F., Heyer, E., 2011. In the heartland of Eurasia: the multilocus genetic landscape of Central Asian populations. European Journal of Human Genetics 19 (2), 216–223.

Miller, N.F., 1999a. Agricultural development in western Central Asia in the Chalcolithic and Bronze Ages. Vegetation History and Archaeobotany 8, 13–19.

Miller, N.F., 1999b. Interpreting ancient environment and patterns of land use: seeds, charcoal and archaeological context. TUBA-AR II, 15–29.

Moore, K.M., Miller, N.F., Hiebert, F.T., Meadow, R.H., 1994. Agriculture and herding in the early oasis settlements of the Oxus Civilization. Antiquity 68 (259), 418–427.

Nesbitt, M., O'Hara, S., 2000. Irrigation agriculture in Central Asia: a long-term perspective from Turkmenistan. In: Barker, G., Gilbertson, D. (Eds.), The Archeology of Drylands. Living at the Margins. Routledge, London, pp. 103–122.

O'Hara, S.L., 2000. Lessons from the past: water management in Central Asia. Water Policy 2 (4), 365–384.

Perdue, P.C., 2005. China Marches West: The Qing Conquest of Central Eurasia. The Belknap Press of Harvard University Press, Cambridge, MA.

Pinhasi, R., Pluciennik, M., 2004. A regional biological approach to the spread of farming in Europe. Current Anthropology 45 (Suppl.), S59–S82.

Pinhasi, R., von Cramon-Taubadel, N., 2009. Craniometric data supports demic diffusion model for the spread of agriculture into Europe. PLoS One 4 (8).

Quintana-Murci, L., Veitia, R., Fellous, M., Semino, O., Poloni, E.S., 2003. Genetic structure of Mediterranean populations revealed by Y-chromosome haplotype analysis. American Journal of Physical Anthropology 121, 157–171.

R Core Team, 2013. R: A Language and Environment for Statistical Computing. R Foundation for Statistical Computing, Vienna, Austria, ISBN 3-900051-07-0. URL: http://www.R-project.org.

Renfrew, C., 1987. Archaeology and Language: The Puzzle of Indo-European Origins. Cambridge University Press, New York.

Rosser, Z.H., Zerjal, T., Hurles, M.E., Adojaan, M., Alavantic, D., Amorim, A., Amos, W., Armenteros, M., Arroyo, E., Barbujani, G., Beckman, G., Beckman, L., Bertranpetit, J., Bosch, E., Bradley, D.G., Brede, G., Cooper, G., Côrte-Real, H.B.S.M., de Knijff, P., Decorte, R., Dubrova, Y.E., Evgrafov, O., Gilissen, A., Glisic, S., Gölge, M., Hill, E.W., Jeziorowska, A., Kalaydjieva, L., Kayser, M., Kivisild, T., Kravchenko, S.A., Krumina, A., Kučinskas, V., Lavinha, J., Livshits, L.A., Malaspina, P., Maria, S., McElreavey, K., Meitinger, T.A., Mikelsaar, A.-V., Mitchell, R.J., Nafa, K., Nicholson, J., Nørby, S., Pandya, A., Parik, J., Patsalis, P.C., Pereira, L., Peterlin, B., Pielberg, G., Prata, M.J., Previderé, C., Roewer, L., Rootsi, S., Rubinsztein, D.C., Saillard, J., Santos, F.R., Stefanescu, G., Sykes, B.C., Tolun, A., Villems, R., Tyler-Smith, C., Jobling, M.A., 2000. Y-chromosomal diversity in Europe is clinal and influenced primarily by geography, rather than by language. The American Journal of Human Genetics 67 (6), 1526–1543.

Scott, G.R., Turner, C.G., 1997. The Anthropology of Modern Human Teeth. Cambridge University Press, Cambridge.

Scott, G.R., Anta, A., Schomberg, R., De La Rue, C., 2013. Basque dental morphology and the "Eurodont" dental pattern. In: Scott, G.R., Irish, J.D. (Eds.), Anthropological Perspectives on Tooth Morphology: Genetics, Evolution, Variation. Cambridge University Press, Cambridge, pp. 296–318.

Siegel, J., 2002. Endgame: Britain, Russia and the Final Struggle for Central Asia. I.B. Tauris Publishers, New York.

Sweeney, M., McCouch, S., 2007. The complex history of the domestication of rice. Annals of Botany 100, 951–957.

Turner, C.G., Nichol, C.R., Scott, G.R., 1991. Scoring procedures for key morphological traits of the permanent dentition: the Arizona State University dental anthropology system. In: Kelley, M.A., Larsen, C.S. (Eds.), Advances in Dental Anthropology. Wiley-Liss, New York, pp. 13–31.

Turner, C.G., 1985. The dental search for Native American origins. In: Kirk, R., Szathmary, E. (Eds.), Out of Asia, Peopling of the Americas and the Pacific. Journal of Pacific Prehistory, Canberra, Australia, pp. 31–78.

Turner, C.G., 1990. Major features of Sundadonty and Sinodonty, including suggestions about East Asian microevolution, population history, and late Pleistocene relationships with Australian aboriginals. American Journal of Physical Anthropology 82, 295–317.

Wells, R.S., Yuldasheva, N., Ruzibakiev, R., Underhill, P.A., Evseeva, I., Blue-Smith, J., Jin, L., Su, B., Pitchappan, R., Shanmugalakshmi, S., Balakrishnan, K., Read, M., Pearson, N.M., Zerjal, T., Webster, M.T., Zholoshvili, I., Jamarjashvili, E., Gambarov, S., Nikbin, B., Dostiev, A., Aknazarov, O., Zalloua, P., Tsoy, I., Kitaev, M., Mirrakhimov, M., Chariev, A., Bodmer, W.F., 2001. The Eurasian Heartland: a continental perspective on Y-chromosome diversity. Proceedings of the National Academy of Sciences of the United States of America 98 (18), 10244–10249.

Whitfield, S., 1999. Life along the Silk Road. University of California Press, Berkeley, CA.

Wilcox, G., 2012. The beginnings of cereal cultivation and domestication in Southwest Asia. In: Potts, D.T. (Ed.), A Companion to the Archaeology of the Ancient Near East. Blackwell, Malden, MA, pp. 163–180.

Wood, F., 2002. The Silk Road: Two Thousand Years in the Heart of Asia. University of California Press, Berkeley, CA.

Yang, L., Tan, S., Yu, H., Zheng, B., Qiao, E., Dong, Y., Zan, R., Xiao, C., 2008. Gene admixture in ethnic populations in upper part of Silk Road revealed by mtDNA polymorphism. Science in China. Series C, Life Sciences 51 (5), 435–444.

Zerjal, T., Wells, R.S., Yuldasheva, N., Ruzibakiev, R., Tyler-Smith, C., 2002. A genetic landscape reshaped by recent events: Y-chromosomal insights into Central Asia. The American Journal of Human Genetics 71 (3), 466–482.

CHAPTER

22

A Baffling Convergence: Tooth Crown and Root Traits in Europe and New Guinea

G.R. Scott, R. Schomberg
University of Nevada, Reno, Reno, NV, United States

CHAPTER OUTLINE HEAD

Introduction **411**
A Closer Look at the Baffling Convergence **412**
Traits 412
Methods 412
Results **415**
Analysis of Variance 415
New Guinea = Europe ≠ Australia 415
New Guinea = Australia ≠ Europe 416
Australia = Europe ≠ New Guinea 416
New Guinea = Australia = Europe 416
Correspondence Between Distance Values 416
Distance Values 417
Dendrograms 417
Discussion **421**
Conclusions **422**
Acknowledgments **423**
Endnote 423
References **423**

INTRODUCTION

All members of *Homo sapiens* share the same fundamental bauplan. That is why the medical community has long trained practitioners following normative standards. Only recently have doctors started paying more heed to variation in body size, gender, ethnicity, and so on when prescribing drugs and interpreting metabolic panels. In contrast to the medical arts, the roots of anthropology can be traced back to describing world and regional variation in stature, hair and eye color, hair and eye form, and nose form. These anthroposcopic variables were supplanted initially by precise measurements of the skeleton and body (osteometrics/anthropometrics) and these, in turn, were supplanted by variation in nuclear genetic markers and increasingly elaborate characterizations of the human genome (mtDNA and Y chromosome haplogroups, microsatellites, genomics, etc.).

Biological Distance Analysis. http://dx.doi.org/10.1016/B978-0-12-801966-5.00022-6

For most measures of variation, two particular geographic groupings, Europeans and New Guineans, are diametrically opposed. The former are medium- to tall-statured and light-skinned while the latter are short-statured and dark-skinned. They differ in marked ways for hair form and color, eye color, and countless genetic variables. Not surprisingly, biodistance studies of world populations place Europe and New Guinea on the opposite branches/quadrants of dendrograms and ordinations (cf. Cavalli-Sforza et al., 1994; Nei and Roychoudhury, 1982, 1993).

Until recently, teeth played no role in worldwide biodistance studies so little attention was paid to the similarities and differences in tooth crown and root morphology between Europe and New Guinea. The presumption was that they would show a contrast in dental characteristics parallel to their differences for other biological and/or genetic variables.

In 1997, Scott and Turner analyzed world variation in dental morphology. In one analysis that involved 23 crown and root traits in 21 major regional groups (Figure 7.5, page 289), they found one major discordant result. Their dendrogram showed that most groups clustered in a manner that conformed to the analyses of genetic markers and cranial dimensions. One group, however, was out of place. Rather than clustering with Australia, Melanesia, and other Southeast Asian/Pacific populations, New Guinea clustered with Western Eurasians (Western and Northern Europe, North Africa). The authors were aware of this oddity but multiple analyses yielded the same result so they were presented as found, not as hoped for.

In a review of *The Anthropology of Modern Human Teeth* (Scott and Turner, 1997), Stodder (1998, p. 73) noted the anomalous placement of New Guinea and added that "One hopes that they fill some data gaps—New Guinea, Melanesia, Australia—so that future analyses will avoid perplexing results like the grouping of New Guinea dentition with those of Western Eurasians." The goal of this paper is to do just that—fill some data gaps and evaluate the veracity of the bizarre linkage of New Guinea and Europe.

A CLOSER LOOK AT THE BAFFLING CONVERGENCE

To derive the dendrogram that clustered New Guinea with Western Eurasians, the senior author had access only to samples that were composites of many smaller samples. In 2013, it became possible to access a greater variety of samples, including multiple subsamples from New Guinea, Australia, Europe, Southeast Asia, East Asia, and the Pacific. With a much larger assemblage of samples from the Christy G. Turner II database, it is now possible to reassess biodistance on a finer scale to determine if the tree linking New Guinea to Europe was an artifact of the earlier analysis.

Traits

Eighteen crown and six root traits, scored on the basis of the Arizona State University Dental Anthropology System (ASUDAS) standards (Turner et al., 1991), were employed to reevaluate the puzzling New Guinea–European cluster. The traits are listed in Table 22.1 along with mean trait frequencies for New Guinean, Australian, European, Southeast Asian, Polynesian, and Melanesian samples. All numbers represent mean total trait frequencies unless noted by breakpoints.

Methods

Although our primary emphasis is on biodistance, Model I Analysis of Variance was first used to compute means and standard deviations for multiple samples from each of the following regions: New Guinea,

Table 22.1 Mean Trait Frequencies for Seven Regional Groupings With an Emphasis on New Guinea, Australia, and Europe

			New Guinea (4–8)		Australia (8–15)		Europe (9–11)		SE Asia (13–18)		East Asia (9–15)		Polynesia (4–7)		Melanesia (4–5)	
Trait	Tooth	BP	Mean	S.D.	Mean	S.D.	Mean	S.D.	Mean	S.D.	Mean	S.D.	Mean	S.D.	Mean	S.D.
NG = Europe ≠ Australia																
Shoveling	UI1	3+	0.000	0.0000	0.162	0.1497	0.040	0.0502	0.421	0.2083	0.531	0.2596	0.132	0.1002	0.170	0.0811
Distal accessory ridge	UC	2+	0.345	0.1920	0.601	0.2714	0.434	0.1499	0.623	0.2816	0.604	0.1568	0.413	0.1085	0.672	0.2740
Root number	UM2	3	0.550	0.1205	0.811	0.0478	0.596	0.0328	0.752	0.1026	0.645	0.1471	0.475	0.0936	0.735	0.0924
Lingual cusp number	LP2	2+	0.611	0.2538	0.745	0.1103	0.633	0.0860	0.783	0.0982	0.700	0.1461	0.836	0.0961	0.885	0.1133
Cusp 6	LM1	1+	0.133	0.1773	0.645	0.1494	0.077	0.0575	0.369	0.1273	0.367	0.1279	0.589	0.1092	0.463	0.0781
Cusp number	LM2	4	0.556	0.1517	0.096	0.0514	0.734	0.1558	0.311	0.1101	0.303	0.1696	0.331	0.0858	0.435	0.0774
Deflecting wrinkle	LM1	2+	0.104	0.1259	0.388	0.1193	0.137	0.0667	0.429	0.1665	0.363	0.2261	0.289	0.2180	0.298	0.1257
Tomes' root	LP1	1	0.038	0.0427	0.287	0.0640	0.108	0.0674	0.219	0.1118	0.158	0.1326	0.163	0.1273	0.230	0.1181
Root number	LM1	3	0.000	0.0000	0.055	0.0315	0.005	0.0070	0.111	0.0507	0.197	0.1332	0.090	0.0723	0.039	0.0128
NG = Australia ≠ Europe																
Winging	UI1	1	0.140	0.2190	0.104	0.0889	0.016	0.1553	0.230	0.1357	0.254	0.0688	0.225	0.1508	0.172	0.0783
Double shoveling	UI1	2+	0.045	0.1167	0.063	0.1293	0.240	0.2175	0.284	0.2595	0.350	0.2426	0.186	0.1163	0.204	0.1977
Interruption groove	UI2	1+	0.146	0.0770	0.200	0.1161	0.379	0.0875	0.322	0.1296	0.413	0.1375	0.272	0.1097	0.243	0.0885
Hypocone	UM2	0 + 1	0.049	0.0398	0.042	0.0605	0.243	0.0873	0.101	0.0699	0.146	0.0586	0.090	0.1014	0.070	0.0407
Cusp 5	UM1	1+	0.622	0.1046	0.613	0.1408	0.152	0.0941	0.246	0.1220	0.191	0.1148	0.344	0.1733	0.489	0.1159
Missing-pegged	UM3	1	0.068	0.0233	0.054	0.0295	0.165	0.0758	0.213	0.2343	0.397	0.2317	0.310	0.0454	0.088	0.0412
Root number	LC	2	0.004	0.0078	0.000	0.0000	0.059	0.0359	0.009	0.0134	0.012	0.0194	0.005	0.0093	0.000	0.0000

Continued

Table 22.1 *Mean Trait Frequencies for Seven Regional Groupings With an Emphasis on New Guinea, Australia, and Europe—Continued*

			New Guinea (4–8)		Australia (8–15)		Europe (9–11)		SE Asia (13–18)		East Asia (9–15)		Polynesia (4–7)		Melanesia (4–5)	
Trait	Tooth	BP	Mean	S.D.	Mean	S.D.	Mean	S.D.	Mean	S.D.	Mean	S.D.	Mean	S.D.	Mean	S.D.
Australia = Europe ≠ NG																
Root number	UP1	2	0.272	0.0530	0.448	0.0722	0.479	0.1524	0.373	0.1131	0.256	0.0900	0.338	0.0813	0.445	0.0627
Groove pattern	LM2	Y	0.389	0.1453	0.257	0.0954	0.261	0.0755	0.310	0.1113	0.250	0.0815	0.284	0.0296	0.356	0.1136
Distal trigonid crest	LM1	1	0.000	0.0000	0.048	0.0536	0.038	0.0367	0.074	0.0784	0.061	0.0705	0.072	0.0786	0.038	0.0403
Protostylid	LM1	2+	0.049	0.0798	0.015	0.0211	0.008	0.0169	0.046	0.0371	0.087	0.0503	0.083	0.0406	0.050	0.0700
Odontomes	All PM	1+	0.000	0.0000	0.035	0.0479	0.016	0.0378	0.024	0.0268	0.058	0.1467	0.015	0.0153	0.033	0.0300
NG = Australia = Europe																
Tuberculum dentale	UI2	2+	0.254	0.0900	0.309	0.1082	0.249	0.1271	0.297	0.1290	0.211	0.1086	0.248	0.1269	0.396	0.0614
Bushman canine	UC	2+	0.020	0.0500	0.008	0.0125	0.019	0.0198	0.030	0.0378	0.009	0.0105	0.010	0.0125	0.055	0.1091
Carabelli's cusp	UM1	3+	0.370	0.0940	0.342	0.0897	0.391	0.1455	0.310	0.1133	0.210	0.0893	0.270	0.0965	0.283	0.0899
Parastyle	UM1	1+	0.038	0.0420	0.059	0.0556	0.024	0.0285	0.042	0.0406	0.048	0.0413	0.050	0.0086	0.054	0.0253
Enamel extensions	UM1	2+	0.046	0.0272	0.083	0.0379	0.035	0.0482	0.325	0.1678	0.415	0.1797	0.204	0.0655	0.076	0.0635
Cusp 7	LM1	1+	0.045	0.0452	0.048	0.0315	0.040	0.0392	0.077	0.0582	0.055	0.0343	0.032	0.0170	0.115	0.0518
Root number	LM2	2	0.813	0.0792	0.932	0.0534	0.741	0.0802	0.751	0.1103	0.700	0.1426	0.692	0.0696	0.867	0.0853

Numbers in parentheses next to regional grouping refer to number of samples used to compute means (which varied by trait).

Australia, Europe, Southeast Asia, East Asia, Polynesia, and Melanesia. With few exceptions, the frequencies for these regions were drawn from the Christy G. Turner II database. The number of samples ranged from 4 to 17 relative to region and individual trait.

Biodistance was analyzed for three sets of data that differed in number of samples, geographic regions compared, and number of traits used. The first analysis was performed on a dataset that contained 45 samples from New Guinea, Australia, Southeast Asia, Oceania, East Asia, and Europe. This analysis used 24 nonmetric dental traits. The second analysis was performed on a more restricted set of samples from the same regions (ie, 29 samples and 24 dental traits). The third analysis expanded the geographic reach of the previous analyses with the addition of 14 South Asian samples and two sub-Saharan African samples from Hawkey (1998) and Irish (1993). For this analysis, we analyzed 23 nonmetric dental traits in 45 samples.

Four types of quantitative analysis were performed on the three datasets using R: A Language and Environment for Statistical Computing (R Core Team, 2013). The first method was to calculate biodistance statistics for each set of samples. The first statistic used was the mean measure of divergence (MMD) developed by C.A.B. Smith (Constandse-Westermann, 1972). This was conducted in the R environment using a script developed by Sołtysiak (2011). After the MMD values were calculated, Bray—Curtis measures of dissimilarity (Bray and Curtis, 1957) were computed. The final two measures of biodistance were the Mahalanobis (1936) and Euclidean distance functions found in the R package, ecodist (Goslee and Urban, 2007). The results for the MMD, Bray—Curtis, Mahalanobis, and Euclidean values were presented in the form of similarity/distance/dissimilarity matrices for each dataset. The Mantel test was performed in R using the ade4 package to derive correlations between each pair of matrices (Dray et al., 2007).

To create dendrograms, or trees, the hclust function in R was used to derive hierarchical clusters from each matrix generated in the first method of analysis. Trees were drawn from the clusters using the plot and as.phylo functions in R. The as.phylo function instructions are to draw clusters in the form of trees. This function is found in the APE package (Paradis et al., 2004).

RESULTS

Analysis of Variance

Table 22.1 shows the summary statistics from Model I ANOVAs for 28 crown and root traits. The analysis involved 12 regional groupings, but results are restricted to New Guinea, Australia, Europe, Southeast Asia, East Asia, Polynesia, and Melanesia. Although Asian and Pacific groupings are included in the table, our focus is on the differences and similarities between New Guinean, Australian, and European trait means (ie, NG = Eur ≠ Aus; NG = Aus ≠ Eur; Aus = Eur ≠ NG; Aus = NG = Eur).

New Guinea = Europe ≠ Australia

For 9 of 28 variables, New Guinea and Europe show similar mean frequencies and differ significantly from Australia. For eight of nine traits, the frequencies for Australia are significantly higher. The single exception is lower second molar (LM2)[1] cusp number. For that variable, we used the frequency of 4-cusped LM2. If we focused on the frequency of 5-cusped teeth, then all nine variables would be significantly higher in Australia. Noteworthy similarities between Europe and New Guinea include a very low frequency of UI1 shoveling, more UM2 root simplification, and the virtual absence of 3-rooted LM1. Cusp 6 is very low in Europe and New Guinea, a contrast to not only Australia but to all other Asian and Pacific groupings. Four-cusped LM2 frequencies in New Guinea are second only to Europeans, and this is a hallmark of the Eurodont dental pattern (Scott et al., 2013).

New Guinea = Australia ≠ Europe

Seven variables are similar in New Guinea and Australia and differ significantly from Europeans. Of note, Europeans have higher frequencies of UI2 interruption grooves, missing-pegged UM3, and 2-rooted LC (another element of the Eurodont dental pattern). In contrast to the cusp number reduction shown in the lower second molars, there is relatively little cusp reduction in the upper second molar (ie, hypocone) of New Guineans. One hallmark of the Australian dentition, UM1 cusp 5, has an almost identical frequency in New Guinea (61.3% and 62.2%, respectively). Bilateral incisor winging, a rare trait in Europeans, is around 10–15% in New Guinea and Australia, somewhat lower than the frequency range in Asian and Pacific populations (17–25%).

Australia = Europe ≠ New Guinea

Five variables distinguish Australia and Europe from New Guinea. Two-rooted UP1 is much lower in New Guinea while LM2 Y pattern is significantly higher. Although rare in all groups, odontomes were not observed in any New Guinea sample but attain low frequencies in Australia and Europe.

New Guinea = Australia = Europe

Seven traits fail to differ significantly between New Guinea, Australia, and Europe. The cusp form of Carabelli's trait (grades 5–7) is almost identical in the three groups (34–39%). New Guineans and Australians share with Europeans a low frequency of enamel extensions, which sets them apart from Asians and Polynesians but not Melanesians. Cusp 7, an Afridont trait (Irish, 2013), is in low frequency in all groups (3–7%), except for Melanesians where it is slightly higher (11%). UI2 *tuberculum dentale* is likewise similar for all groups falling generally in the 20–30% range.

When the surprising dental morphological linkage between New Guinea and Europe was first noted, the opportunity to examine this result was not available. Now that multiple samples from all geographic areas can be evaluated for a full suite of dental traits, the explanation for the finding is more apparent. Initially, it was thought that the high frequency of 4-cusped LM1 and LM2 played the major role in bringing New Guinea into the Western Eurasian sphere. A trait-by-trait breakdown shows 4-cusped lower molars are only part of the equation. Australians show significantly more shoveling, 3-rooted UM2, cusp 6, deflecting wrinkle, Tomes' root, and 3-rooted LM1 than New Guinea and Europe. Only 4-cusped LM2 is significantly more common in New Guinea and Europe but for the presence of the hypoconulid, Australia would again have the highest frequency. For all of these traits, Australia is more in line with Southeast Asia. Turner (1992) may have been correct in noting Australians as proto-Sundadont but this does not apply to New Guinea. For this group of traits, New Guinea is more in line with the simplified dentition of Europe.

Correspondence Between Distance Values

A Mantel test evaluated the level of correlation between the four biodistance methods: MMDs, Bray–Curtis, Mahalanobis, and Euclidean squared distance (Table 22.2). Distance methods should produce relatively congruent results with associated high levels of correlation between pairwise values in a distance

Table 22.2 Mantel Test for Correlation of Distance Matrices (45/29 Samples)				
	Mean Measure of Divergence (MMD)	**Bray–Curtis**	**Mahalanobis**	**Euclidean**
MMD	1			
Bray–Curtis	0.785/0.813	1		
Mahalanobis	0.204/0.144[a]	0.425/0.197[b]	1	
Euclidean	0.860/0.896	0.946/0.955	0.392/0.197[a]	1

[a]p = .03.
[b]p = .02.

matrix. In this instance, that was the case for MMDs, Bray–Curtis, and Euclidean distances, all of which showed correlations ranging from 0.80 to 0.95. The odd statistic out was Mahalanobis. The correlations between Mahalanobis and the other three distance measures varied between 0.20 and 0.40. For the distances based on 29 samples, the correlations between Mahalanobis and the other three distance matrices were significantly different.

Distance Values

Space precludes the inclusion of 12 large distance matrices (three datasets × four distance statistics). As focus is on the New Guinea–European similarity, Table 22.3 presents a summary pairwise matrix based on mean MMDs between nine regional groups (including India and Africa). In addition to the individual pairwise values, mean MMDs were computed for each region. At the bottom of the table, the rank order of regions relative to the regions noted along the top horizontal axis are listed from most to least similar.

In the summary matrix, the highest mean MMD values are associated with Africa, East Asia, India, and Australia, in that order. New Guinea has the lowest average MMD value compared to other regional groups followed by Melanesia, Southeast Asia, and Polynesia. Of the nine groups, Europe is exactly in the middle. Based on the distance rankings, Europe has the smallest MMD value with New Guinea (0.063). Melanesia is also close to New Guinea (0.071), but Australia is no closer to New Guinea (0.139) than Polynesia (0.133). For Europe, its closest distance is to New Guinea even with India included in the matrix. Interestingly, Australia is closer to Melanesia (0.091) than to New Guinea (0.139) and is quite divergent from Europe (0.312).

Dendrograms

Two tree diagrams are presented as Figs. 22.1 and 22.2. Both diagrams include 45 samples but Fig. 22.1 includes samples from Europe, Asia, and the Pacific while Fig. 22.2 includes those regions plus 14 Indian and 2 African samples.

In Fig. 22.1, the first division in the dendrogram is between East Asian groups and everyone else. These samples are representative of the highly specialized Sinodont dentition (Turner, 1990). The next major split in the tree diagram is between a top cluster that includes European and New Guinea samples and a bottom cluster that includes an Australian branch and a Southeast Asian/Pacific branch. In other words, even with multiple samples representing Europe and New Guinea, as well as other Asian and Pacific samples, Europe and New Guinea still cluster together. This is consistent with both the findings of trait-by-trait comparisons via analysis of variance and the mean MMD values shown in Table 22.3.

Table 22.3 ***Mean Measure of Divergence Values Between Nine Regional Groupings***

	NG	AUS	EUR	SEA	EA	MEL	POL	IND	AFR
New Guinea	0.000								
Australia	0.139	0.000							
Europe	0.063	0.312	0.000						
SE Asia	0.157	0.166	0.205	0.000					
East Asia	0.275	0.280	0.325	0.075	0.000				
Melanesia	0.071	0.091	0.172	0.075	0.182	0.000			
Polynesia	0.133	0.149	0.213	0.078	0.138	0.084	0.000		
India	0.149	0.409	0.121	0.257	0.408	0.252	0.272	0.000	
Africa	0.254	0.433	0.335	0.319	0.456	0.333	0.335	0.185	0.000
	Europe	Melanesia	New Guinea	East Asia	SE Asia	New Guinea	SE Asia	Europe	India
	Melanesia	New Guinea	India	Melanesia	Polynesia	SE Asia	Melanesia	New Guinea	Europe
MMD values	Polynesia	Polynesia	Melanesia	Polynesia	Melanesia	Polynesia	New Guinea	Africa	SE Asia
From smallest	Australia	SE Asia	SE Asia	New Guinea	New Guinea	Australia	East Asia	SE Asia	Melanesia
to largest:	India	East Asia	Polynesia	Australia	Australia	East Asia	Australia	Melanesia	Polynesia
	SE Asia	Europe	Australia	Europe	Europe	Europe	Europe	Polynesia	Europe
	Africa	India	East Asia	India	India	India	India	East Asia	Australia
	East Asia	Africa	Africa	Africa	Africa	Africa	Africa	Australia	East Asia

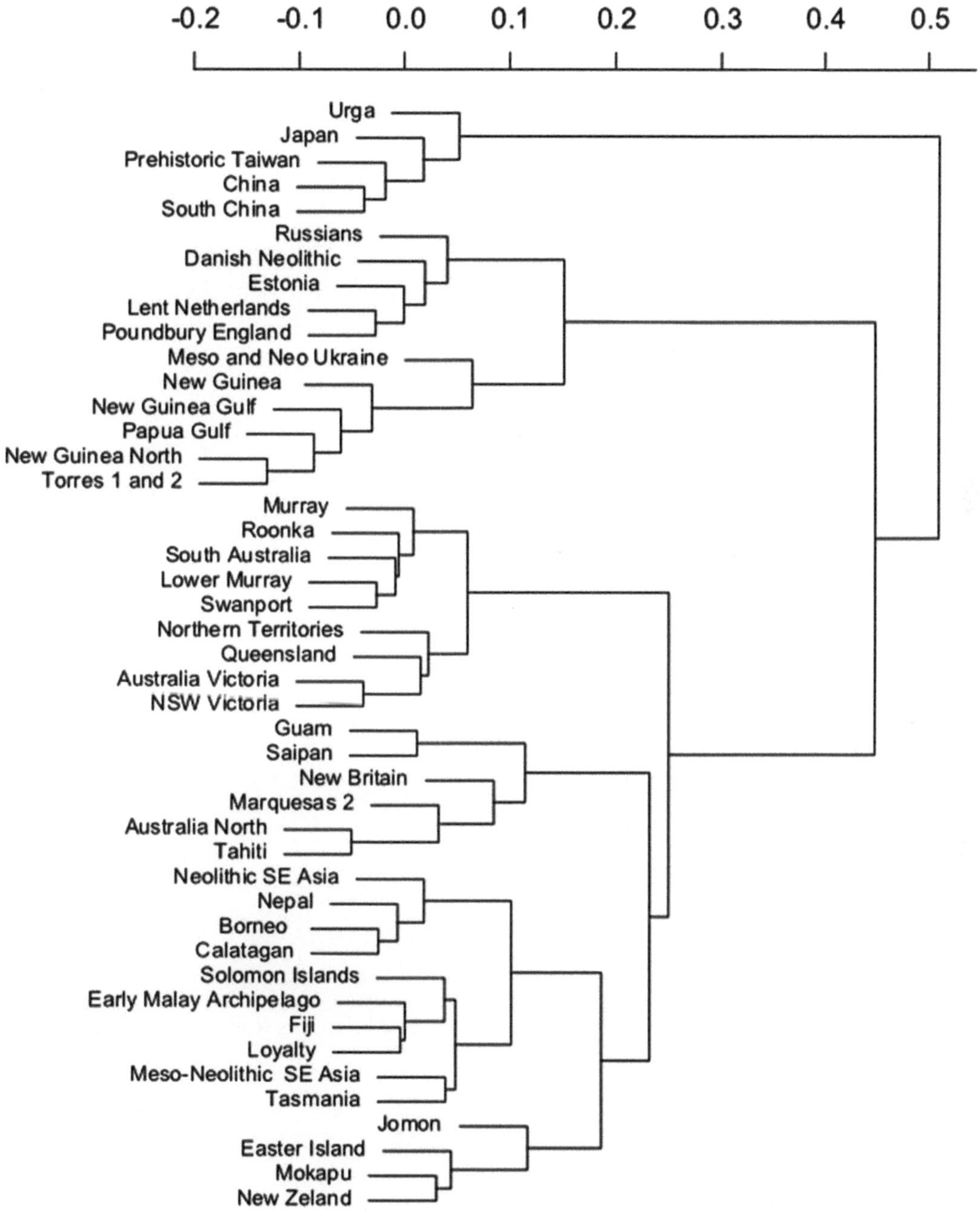

FIGURE 22.1

Complete linkage dendrogram based on Mean Measure of Divergence values for 45 samples from New Guinea, Australia, East Asia, Southeast Asia, Melanesia, Polynesia, and Europe.

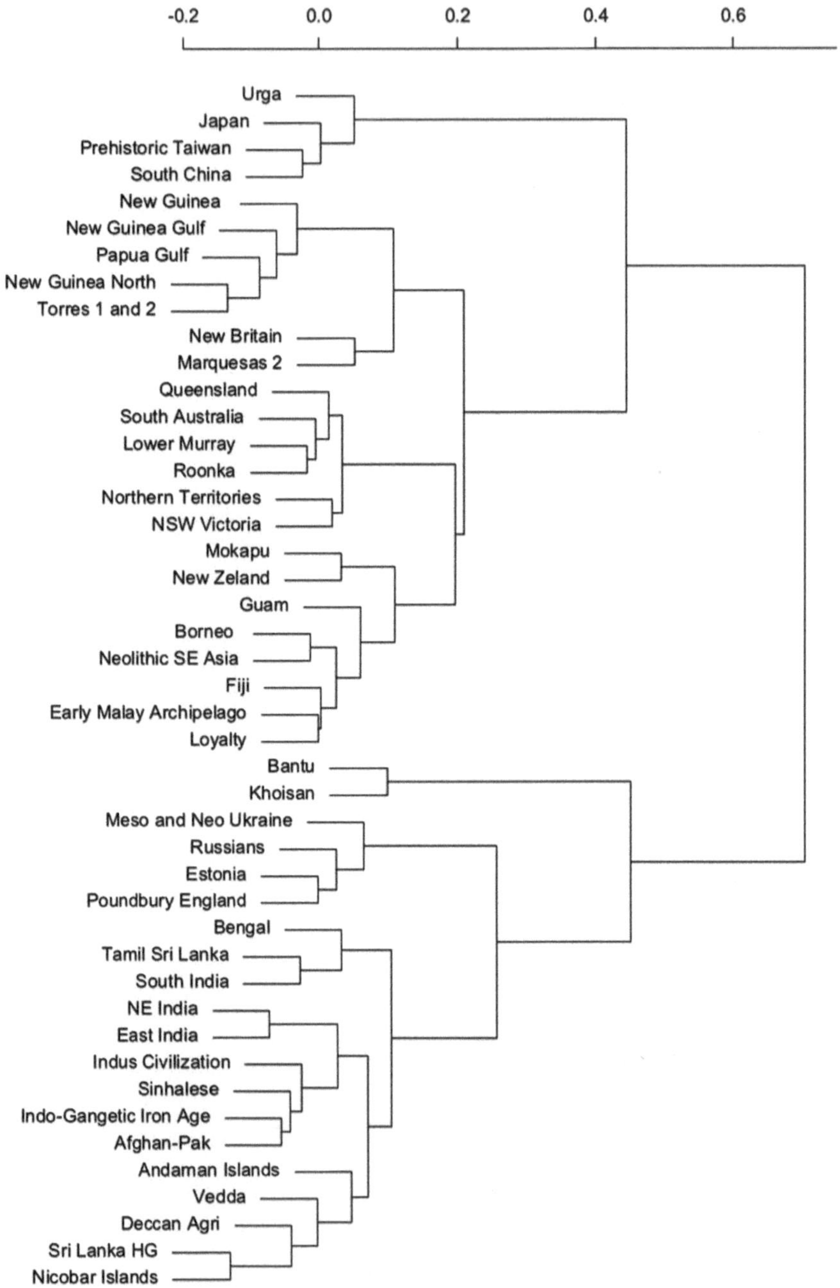

FIGURE 22.2

Complete linkage dendrogram based on Mean Measure of Divergence values for 45 samples from New Guinea, Australia, East Asia, Southeast Asia, Melanesia, Polynesia, Europe, Africa, and India.

The inclusion of Indian and African samples in Fig. 22.2 has a significant impact on how populations cluster. For this tree, there is a major dichotomy between the top and bottom clusters that are differentiated at the highest level. Within the top cluster, East Asia separates out from other Asian and Pacific groups. A second level division within the top cluster separates New Guinea from Australia and Pacific groups. As discussed in the section comparing trait frequencies among regions, Australia is closer to Southeast Asia and Pacific populations than to New Guinea. However, in this instance, New Guinea clusters with Australia/Pacific and not Europe. In the bottom segment of this tree, there are three clusters with the two African samples splitting off first. The remaining two major clusters show the linkage between Europe (four samples) and India (14 samples).

DISCUSSION

Genetic studies do not agree on whether or not the populations of Australia and New Guinea were derived from a single colonizing event 40 to 60 thousand years ago or if they were a product of two independent peopling events. Many agree that Australia and New Guinea are more closely related to one another than they are to any other group in Asia or the Pacific (cf. Bowcock et al., 1994; Hudjashov et al., 2007; Ingman and Gyllensten, 2003; Roberts-Thomson et al., 1996; Serjeantson et al., 1982). Despite the commonly held assumption that Australians and New Guineans, the long-time occupants of Sahulland, are related to one another, mtDNA suggests the two groups had very different histories, possibly reflecting two separate peopling events (Redd and Stoneking, 1999). Kayser et al. (2001) found a similar distinction between Australia and Melanesia (ie, Papua New Guinea) for Y chromosome haplotypes.

With relatively few exceptions, patterns of relationships indicated by dental morphology are congruent with genetic analyses. The convergence between Europe and New Guinea in crown and root morphology remains an enigma that is not easily reconciled with nuclear genetic markers or mtDNA and Y chromosome haplogroups. Nine traits show a close similarity between Europe and New Guinea and a significant difference from Australia. In every instance, the Australian frequencies are in the direction of East and Southeast Asian and Pacific populations. In other words, New Guinea frequencies are in the direction of the more simplified European dentition with less shoveling and more simplified lower molar cusp number (more 4-cusped LM2 and lower cusp 6 frequencies). Paradoxically, New Guinea shares with Australia more complex upper molars (ie, little hypocone reduction and the world's highest frequencies of cusp 5). For roots, New Guinea does not have the 2-rooted canine most common in Europeans nor the 3-rooted LM1 most common in Asians (and >5% in Australians). In other words, for some traits, New Guinea converged toward the simplified crown pattern of Europeans while in other instances, they retained the more complex crown traits common in Australians.

There are many genetic studies of New Guinea populations, but little attention has been paid to dental variation. In a broader study of the Eastern Highlands populations of New Guinea, Robert Littlewood collected over 200 dental impressions from four villages. Following Dahlberg's (1956) traditional set of crown traits, Barksdale (1972) characterized these highland samples and made intervillage comparisons. Although done at a time before much was known of New Guinea teeth, Barksdale (1972, p. 174) concluded that "The dental morphology of the Eastern Highlands native is suggestive of the Negroid pattern, although this pattern has not been defined specifically. It is similar to the West Africa Negro, the Melanesian, and the Australian Aboriginal dentitions. The Mongoloid influence on the dentition appears to be slight." We know much more today about world populations and the similarities to Africans, Melanesians, and Australians are overstated. However, we fully concur with Barksdale on the absence of influence from East Asian Sinodont populations.

In a more recent study, Itou and Matsuno (2011) observed 17 crown traits in 117 Kasi villagers from the New Guinea highlands. They followed the ASUDAS standards employed in this study to score traits. Their results are remarkably consistent with the New Guinea frequencies reported in Table 22.1. That is, they report very low frequencies of UI1 shoveling and double shoveling, the protostylid, deflecting wrinkle, cusp 6, and cusp 7. Also parallel to the present study, they found very high frequencies of 4-cusped LM2, LM2 Y-pattern, and UM1 cusp 5. The only notable disagreements were for Carabelli's trait and odontomes where they found lower and higher frequencies, respectively. In a two-dimensional ordination based on MMD values, their modern New Guinea sample was compared to 13 Sinodont and 17 Sundadont groups. Although in the same quadrant of some (though not all) Sundadont groups, their sample is a distinct outlier in this broader Asian/Pacific context. Although they did not include Australian samples in their comparisons, Itou and Matsuno (2011, p. 197) note in regard to New Guinea that "They are considered to be closely related to Aboriginal Australians on the basis of genetic and archaeological studies. However, their dental characters are distinctively different than to those of Australians."

Turner (1990, 1992) noted the differences and similarities between the Australian dentition and those of Southeast Asians and concluded that Australians exhibited a dental pattern that anticipated the Sundadont pattern of Southeast Asia. He referred to the Australian pattern as proto-Sundadont. In Table 22.1, this tendency was indicated for many traits. Australian frequencies differ from both Sinodont and Sundadont dental patterns, but the differences are quantitative rather than qualitative. The European dentition, by contrast, differs from both Asian patterns quantitatively and qualitatively. In many regards, the same could be said of New Guinea. Unlike the Australian dentition, the New Guinea dentition does not presage Sundadonty.

For most studies, the 28 traits listed in Table 22.1 are sufficient to discriminate among the major populations of the world in a manner consistent with other biological evidence. The addition of more traits to this list might rectify, to some degree, the New Guinea—Europe convergence. For example, a sample of casts from living New Guinea Highlanders shows a high frequency of labial convexity, a rare trait in modern European populations (but one very common in Neanderthals and *Homo heidelbergensis*). It is unknown at this time if there are other traits that show a similar contrast.

Understanding New Guinea population history, impacted by numerous remote mountain valleys and highly differentiated languages, remains a unique challenge. The discovery of a relatively high frequency of Denisovan DNA only adds to the puzzle (cf. Reich et al., 2011). As for the dentition, puzzled or not, we know more than we used to. This study has provided a few answers and generated even more questions on the baffling evolution of New Guinea crown and root morphology.

CONCLUSIONS

Stimulated in part by Ann Stodder's comment that our methods might be amiss given the linkage of New Guinea with Western Eurasian groups, a closer examination of a broader data set brings us full circle and to the same result. A few points on this finding:

- We are not suggesting Europeans and New Guineans are closely related in the sense of recent common ancestor. Their respective histories suggest a long period of geographic and reproductive isolation (perhaps as far back as 80—100 thousand years).
- Although Australia and New Guinea often cluster together in the analyses of simple genetic markers (Cavalli-Sforza et al., 1994; Nei and Roychoudhury, 1982, 1993), the linkage is not close and often

shows a very deep root (ie, they are closer to each other than to anyone else but are still not close). The genetic distinctions between Australia and New Guinea have been summarized by Kayser (2010).

- Similarity between Europe and New Guinea may reflect convergence through simplification. The traits where the two groups show parallels are found in much lower frequencies than in Australians. This conclusion is similar to that of Itou and Matsuno (2011, p. 197), who opine that the "unique set of dental characters in Papua New Guinea was acquired by morphological reduction from the original Australian type of dental characters and by admixture with south Asian and Pacific peoples." Although it is difficult to evaluate the role of admixture in the development of the distinct New Guinea dental pattern, we concur that the highland populations have evolved a more simplified dentition than their Australian, Southeast Asian, and Pacific neighbors.

Acknowledgments

We would like to thank our editors Joe Hefner and Marin Pilloud for the invitation to participate in their AAPA symposium on biodistance and to contribute a paper to this volume. The authors are wholly indebted to the late Christy G. Turner II whose data formed the basis of this analysis. A major goal of his life was to address anthropological problems through teeth. The New Guinea–Europe enigma is one of those problems.

Endnote

1. Within this text teeth are abbreviated in the following manner: U = upper, L = lower, I = incisor, C = canine, M = molar; and number indicates position in the tooth row.

References

Barksdale, J.T., 1972. Appendix III: a descriptive and comparative investigation of dental morphology. In: Littlewood, R.A. (Ed.), Physical Anthropology of the Eastern Highlands of New Guinea. University of Washington Press, Seattle, pp. 113–174.

Bowcock, A.M., Ruiz-Linares, A., Tomfohrde, J., Minch, E., Kidd, J.R., Cavalli-Sforza, L.L., 1994. High resolution of human evolutionary trees with polymorphic microsatellites. Nature 368, 455–457.

Bray, J.R., Curtis, J.T., 1957. An ordination of upland forest communities of Southern Wisconsin. Ecological Monographs 27, 325–349.

Cavalli-Sforza, L.L., Menozzi, P., Piazza, A., 1994. The History and Geography of Human Genes. Princeton University Press, Princeton, NJ.

Constandse-Westermann, T.S., 1972. Coefficients of Biological Distance. Anthropological Publications, Oosterhout.

Dahlberg, A.A., 1956. Materials for the Establishment of Standards for Classification of Tooth Characters, Attributes, and Techniques in Morphological Studies of the Dentition. Zollar Laboratory of Dental Anthropology, University of Chicago (mimeo).

Dray, S., Dufour, A.B., Chessel, D., 2007. The ade4 package: implementing the duality diagram for ecologists. Journal of Statistical Software 22 (7), 1–20.

Goslee, S.C., Urban, D.L., 2007. The ecodist package for dissimilarity-based analysis of ecological data. Journal of Statistical Software 22 (4), 1–19.

Hawkey, D.E., 1998. Out of Asia: Dental Evidence for Affinities and Microevolution of Early Populations from India/Sri Lanka (Ph.D. dissertation). Arizona State University, Tempe.

Hudjashov, G., Kivisild, T., Underhill, P.A., Endicott, P., Sanchez, J.J., Lin, A.A., Shen, P., Oefner, P., Renfrew, C., Villems, R., Forster, P., 2007. Revealing the prehistoric settlement of Australia by Y chromosome and mtDNA analysis. Proceedings of the National Academic of Sciences United States of America 104 (21), 8726–8730.

Ingman, M., Gyllensten, U., 2003. Mitochondrial genome variation and evolutionary history of Australian and New Guinea aborigines. Genome Research 13, 1600–1606.

Irish, J.D., 1993. Biological Affinities of Late Pleistocene Through Modern African Aboriginal Populations: The Dental Evidence (Ph.D. dissertation). Arizona State University, Tempe.

Irish, J.D., 2013. Afridonty: "the sub-Saharan African dental complex" revisited. In: Irish, J.D., Scott, G.R. (Eds.), Anthropological Perspectives on Tooth Morphology: Genetics, Evolution, Variation. Cambridge University Press, Cambridge, pp. 278–295.

Itou, Y., Matsuno, M., 2011. Non-metric dental characters in Papua New Guinea Highlanders with special reference to other Asia-Pacific populations. International Journal of Oral-Medical Sciences 9 (3), 197–205.

Kayser, M., Brauer, S., Weiss, G., Schiefenhövel, W., Underhill, P.A., Stoneking, M., 2001. Independent histories of human Y chromosomes from Melanesia and Australia. American Journal of Human Genetics 68, 173–190.

Kayser, M., 2010. The human genetic history of Oceania: near and remote views of dispersal. Current Biology 20, R194–R201.

Mahalanobis, P.C., 1936. On the generalized distance in statistics. Proceedings of the National Academy of Science, India B 1, 49–55.

Nei, M., Roychoudhury, A.K., 1982. Genetic relationship and evolution of human races. Evolutionary Biology 14, 1–59.

Nei, M., Roychoudhury, A.K., 1993. Evolutionary relationships of human populations on a global scale. Molecular Biology and Evolution 10, 927–943.

Paradis, E., Claude, J., Strimmer, K., 2004. APE: analyses of phylogenetics and evolution in R language. Bioinformatics Application Note 20, 289–290.

RCoreTeam, 2013. R: A Language and Environment for Statistical Computing. R Foundation for Statistical Computing, Vienna, Austria, ISBN 3-900051-07-0. http://www.R-project.org.

Redd, A.J., Stoneking, M., 1999. Peopling of Sahul: mtDNA variation in aboriginal Australian and Papua New Guinean populations. American Journal of Human Genetics 65, 808–828.

Reich, D., Patterson, M., Kircher, N., Delfin, F., Nandineni, M.R., Pugach, I., Ko, A.M.-S., Ko, Y.-C., Jinam, T.A., Phipps, M.E., Saitou, N., Wollstein, A., Kayser, M., Pääbo, S., Stoneking, M., 2011. Denisova admixture and the first modern dispersals into Southeast Asia and Oceania. American Journal of Human Genetics 89 (4), 516–528.

Roberts-Thomson, J.M., Martinson, J.J., Norwich, J.T., Harding, R.M., Clegg, J.B., Boettcher, B., 1996. An ancient common origin of Aboriginal Australians and New Guinea Highlanders is supported by α-globin haplotype analysis. American Journal of Human Genetics 58, 1017–1024.

Scott, G.R., Turner II, C.G., 1997. The Anthropology of Modern Human Teeth: Dental Morphology and Its Variation in Recent Human Populations. Cambridge University Press, Cambridge.

Scott, G.R., Anta, A., Schomberg, R.S., de la Rua, C., 2013. Basque dental morphology and the "Eurodont" dental pattern. In: Irish, J.D., Scott, G.R. (Eds.), Anthropological Perspectives on Tooth Morphology: Genetics, Evolution, Variation. Cambridge University Press, Cambridge, pp. 296–318.

Serjeantson, S.W., Ryan, D.P., Thompson, A.R., 1982. The colonization of the Pacific: the story according to human leucocyte antigens. American Journal of Human Genetics 34, 904–918.

Sołtysiak, A., 2011. Technical note: an R script for Smith's mean measure of divergence. Bioarchaeology of the Near East 5, 41–44.

Stodder, A., 1998. Review of "the anthropology of modern human teeth." Quarterly Review of Biology 73, 544.

Turner II, C.G., Nichol, C.R., Scott, G.R., 1991. Scoring procedures for key morphological traits of the permanent dentition: the Arizona State University dental anthropology system. In: Kelley, M.A., Larsen, C.S. (Eds.), Advances in Dental Anthropology. Wiley-Liss, New York, pp. 13–31.

Turner II, C.G., 1990. Major features of Sundadonty and Sinodonty, including suggestions about East Asian microevolution, population history, and late Pleistocene relationships with Australian aboriginals. American Journal of Physical Anthropology 82, 295–317.

Turner II, C.G., 1992. The dental bridge between Australia and Asia: following Macintosh into the East Asian hearth of humanity. Perspectives in Human Biology 2/Archaeology in Oceania 27, 143–152.

CHAPTER

23

Population Biodistance in Global Perspective: Assessing the Influence of Population History and Environmental Effects on Patterns of Craniomandibular Variation

N. von Cramon-Taubadel
University at Buffalo, Buffalo, NY, United States

CHAPTER OUTLINE HEAD

Introduction 425
Case Study 1: Do Global Patterns of Cranial Shape Variation Conform to the Predictions of a Neutral Model of Microevolutionary Expectation? 428
Materials 429
Methods 429
Results 432
Discussion 435
Case Study 2: To What Extent Can Global Patterns of Craniomandibular Variation Be Explained by Variation in Subsistence Strategy? 436
Materials 437
Methods 437
Results 437
Discussion 440
Conclusions 441
References 442

INTRODUCTION

Bioarchaeological and anthropological enquiries into the geographically mediated historical processes that lead to observed patterns of population biological variation often begin with a quantification of among-population biological distance (or biodistance). Conventionally, biodistance studies have focused on patterns of between-population differences based on multivariate skeletal metric and nonmetric traits under the basic premise that among-population phenotypic variation patterns reflect underlying genetic variation (eg, Buikstra et al., 1990; Larsen, 2015). The underlying principle is simple: Groups or

Biological Distance Analysis. http://dx.doi.org/10.1016/B978-0-12-801966-5.00023-8

populations that are closer to one another in a multivariate matrix of phenotypic distance (or dissimilarity) are presumed to be genetically more closely related, while those that are more distant are less genetically similar. As reviewed by Stojanowski and Schillaci (2006; Larsen, 2015) and in Chapter 1, this volume, analysis of biodistance matrices has a long history of usage in bioarchaeology and biological anthropology for testing key evolutionary and historical phenomena. It allows for the testing of specific hypotheses regarding extrinsic forces that may be responsible for observed biodistance patterns, such as the influence of external gene flow via migration, population history, or cultural contact between distantly related groups (eg, Stojanowski and Schillaci, 2006; González-José et al., 2007; Stynder et al., 2007; Kemp et al., 2010; Ricaut et al., 2010; von Cramon-Taubadel and Pinhasi, 2011; Hanihara et al., 2012; McIlvaine et al., 2014; Hubbard et al., 2015; Ragsdale and Edgar, 2015).

The specific goal of this chapter is to provide an overview, via two case studies, of the implementation of biodistance techniques in the microevolutionary assessment of global patterns of human craniomandibular variation. Such analyses are generally concerned with addressing broad microevolutionary questions regarding the prevailing causes of among-population craniomandibular shape covariation, when analyzed within a model-bound evolutionary framework (eg, Relethford, 1994, 2004; Roseman, 2004; Roseman and Weaver, 2007; von Cramon-Taubadel, 2014). For example, can global patterns of among-population cranial shape variation be explained on the basis of a neutral model of microevolutionary diversification (ie, due to the historical processes of mutation, migration, and genetic drift)? Alternatively, to what extent do extrinsic environmental factors such as global climatic variation or differences in subsistence economy play a role in determining global patterns of phenotypic variation?

As elucidated in further detail in the two case studies presented in the following section, there are generally three steps involved in such analysis. First, it is necessary to match relevant datasets for the sample of populations under investigation (eg, craniomandibular, genetic, geographic, and climatic datasets for the same groups). It is worth noting at this point that the nature of these population samples may differ from study to study, depending on the type of questions being asked. In some archaeological enquires populations may be skeletal samples from different burial sites distributed across the landscape and from different time periods (eg, Pinhasi and von Cramon-Taubadel, 2009). In formulating a biological distance matrix among such burial sites, it is assumed that they form biological populations in the sense of interbreeding demes that are, therefore, on average genetically more affine within-populations than they are between. Any biodistance analysis of these skeletal populations would need to account for their spatial distribution and also any temporal variation among them (eg, Konigsberg, 1990; Pinhasi and von Cramon-Taubadel, 2009). On a contemporary global scale, populations may comprise museum collections of crania from particular ethnographically, geographically, linguistically, or otherwise defined groups (eg, Basque, from France). As discussed in greater detail elsewhere (von Cramon-Taubadel, 2014), the notion of population is largely a conceptual tool linked with the theoretical and methodological developments of the Modern Synthesis in evolutionary biology (Huxley, 1942), and the need for taxonomic units of analysis below the biological species (*sensu* Mayr, 1942) level. While the concept of a deme or randomly mating population is a fundamental concept within evolutionary biology, it can be difficult to define in a consistent, operational sense (eg, Cavalli-Sforza et al., 1994). The concept of a randomly interbreeding human population is, therefore, operationalized according to practical, tangible criteria such as geographic location, ethnographic identity, and linguistic affiliation. In some cases, it may be preferable to avoid the term population due to its particular biological connotations, and resort instead to the more neutral term of operational taxonomic units

(OTUs) (eg, Pinhasi and von Cramon-Taubadel, 2009), which are explicit conceptual tools designed to facilitate taxonomic analyses (Sokal and Sneath, 1963).

Once the populations or OTUs of interest have been established, different forms of data for those same groups are collated such that they can be converted into pairwise among-group distance (dissimilarity) matrices. For example, it may be possible to generate a multivariate biodistance matrix for cranial measurements, a geographic distance matrix (in km) based on longitude and latitude coordinates for those same groups, and a Euclidean distance matrix based on some matched climatic variables such as a mean annual temperature and rainfall.

The next step may (but does not necessarily need to) involve some form of ordination technique, which allows us to decompose the different matched distance matrices into lower dimension factors or axes for visualization purposes. Some commonly used techniques include principal coordinates analysis (PCO) (Gower, 1966) and multidimensional scaling (MDS) (Kruskal and Wish, 1978). These ordination techniques have the advantage of reducing analogous distance matrices (eg, cranial distance, geographic distance, and climatic distance) into a smaller number of dimensions such that the relative affinities of the populations in question for each of the different types of data can be assessed.

Finally, the relative congruence of the population affinity patterns expressed by the different types of matched data can be assessed using a range of analytical techniques. The most commonly applied technique is that of Mantel tests (Mantel, 1967) and its derivatives. Mantel tests are extensions of basic correlation statistics designed for pairwise distance matrices. In this case the assessment of statistical significance is carried out via a permutation procedure (Smouse et al., 1986; Smouse and Long, 1992) as the off-diagonal elements of a matrix violate the assumptions of independence of traditional correlation statistics. Mantel tests are flexible in that multiple matrices can be correlated simultaneously (multiple correlation) and the effects of particular matrices on the congruence of any two matrices can also be assessed (partial correlation). However, Mantel tests have also been criticized on the basis of low statistical power and high rejection rates (elevated Type I errors), particularly when one or more of the matrices under investigation are spatially autocorrelated (Harmon and Glor, 2010; Legendre and Fortin, 2010; Guillot and Rousset, 2013). Given this, it may be prudent in some cases to employ a lower critical α-level than the standard $\alpha = 0.05$ and implementation of correction for multiple comparisons (eg, Bonferroni) may be required for certain analyses.

Another method employed by Relethford (2010) and Hererra et al. (2014) involves the use of Procrustes rotation (Mardia et al., 1979; Dryden and Mardia, 1998; Jackson, 1995; Peres-Neto and Jackson, 2001) between coefficients resulting from a reduced dimension ordination procedure such as MDS or PCO. Effectively, each group or population is rendered in a small number of dimensions (usually 2–4) for each datatype (eg, cranial distance, geography, and climate) such that a Procrustes rotation of two datatype ordination configurations minimizes the overall sum of squares distance among all populations. Statistical significance can be assigned to the congruence between rotated datatype ordinations (Jackson, 1995; Peres-Neto and Jackson, 2001) using a permutation test. The advantage of this latter methodology (referred to as Procrustes rotation congruence assessment (PROTEST)) over Mantel tests is that the residual differences between datatypes for individual populations can be explicitly quantified. Therefore, while Mantel tests provide a quantification of the overall congruence between two datatypes (eg, cranial distance and geographic distance), the residuals from a Procrustes rotation show whether all groups are approximately equally (in)congruous or whether a particular subset of the populations might be driving the overall congruence statistic. Peres-Neto and Jackson (2001) have shown that Jackson's (1995) permutation approach to quantifying statistical significance may be more powerful than Mantel tests for detecting associations between matrices. On the flip side, the major disadvantage of the PROTEST methods, relative to the Mantel tests, is the lack of control over the effects of a third matrix, which may actually be driving the (spurious) correlation between two matrices.

Each of these methodological steps and the two main analytical approaches of Mantel tests and PROTEST analyses mentioned earlier will be demonstrated in the following two case studies:

1. Test of neutral model for explaining global patterns of human cranial shape variation.
2. Test of the effects of subsistence strategy on global mandibular shape variation.

CASE STUDY 1: DO GLOBAL PATTERNS OF CRANIAL SHAPE VARIATION CONFORM TO THE PREDICTIONS OF A NEUTRAL MODEL OF MICROEVOLUTIONARY EXPECTATION?

When viewed from an evolutionary perspective, a particular among-population biodistance pattern potentially reflects the historical effects of genetic mutation, gene flow (migration), genetic drift, and selection. The neutral theory of evolution (Kimura, 1983) posits that the majority of genetic change at the molecular level is caused by the random fixation of selectively neutral alleles, rather than emphasizing the predominant role of natural selection in favoring or selecting against particular alleles. The importance of natural selection in shaping gene frequency patterns within and between populations is not denied completely, but the corollary of the neutral theory is that the majority of genetic polymorphisms within populations are maintained through a balance between mutation and genetic drift (Kimura, 1983). Quantitative genetics is the subdiscipline of evolutionary population genetics designed to model the (partial) inheritance and evolution of continuous phenotypic traits (eg, Falconer and Mackay, 1996). When analyzed in an explicitly quantitative genetic framework, continuous phenotypic traits (such as craniometric measurements) can be employed as a proxy for genetic data, under the assumptions of an equal and additive effects polygenic inheritance model (Relethford and Blangero, 1990). Hence, the neutral theory of evolution is equally applicable to phenotypic covariation patterns as it is to genetic diversity patterns.

As noted by Roseman and Weaver (2007), the neutral theory should not be viewed as a strict alternative hypothesis to any particular adaptive hypothesis, but rather as a null hypothesis that must be rejected before more tenuous and complex adaptive explanations are considered. The major advantage of the neutral theory of microevolution is not that it is expected to be the correct or most accurate explanation, but rather that it provides clear and readily testable empirical predictions that can be easily compared against observed patterns of among-population diversity (Roseman and Weaver, 2007). In contrast, adaptationist explanations for observed phenotypic covariation patterns are usually multiple, less parsimonious, and tend not to form mutually exclusive null hypotheses.

In the case of modern humans, global geography has largely mediated the historical processes of population divergence, migration, and gene flow that have shaped the genetic and phenotypic diversity structure of our species (eg, Prugnolle et al., 2005; Ramachandran et al., 2005; von Cramon-Taubadel and Lycett, 2008; Betti et al., 2009, 2012; Reyes-Centeno et al., 2014; von Cramon-Taubadel, 2014). Therefore, we would expect a significant correlation between geography and neutral genetic/phenotypic among-population diversity patterns (Howells, 1973; Relethford, 1994, 2004; Betti et al., 2010; von Cramon-Taubadel, 2009, 2011, 2014). However, many potentially adaptive explanations might also predict a link between geographic distance and phenotypic patterns given potential correlations between climate, local ecology, and global geography. In order to convincingly demonstrate that a correlation between an environmental factor (eg, climate) and phenotypic diversity is actually a causative relationship requires us to first control for the effects of shared population history (ancestry) (eg, Felsenstein, 1985), a phenomenon sometimes referred to as Galton's Problem (Naroll, 1961). The neutral theory of evolution provides a number of clear and simple empirical expectations regarding among-population variation/covariation patterns (ie, biodistance patterns) under the assumption that the main evolutionary forces at play are mutation, gene flow, and genetic drift. If these expectations can be rejected, then higher-level adaptationist explanations for the observed patterns should be invoked and tested (Roseman and Weaver, 2007). Here, using previously published data (von Cramon-Taubadel, 2009), the neutral theory is tested for global patterns of craniometric shape using a biodistance framework. Under a neutral model the null expectation is that among-population cranial distance will be strongly and significantly correlated with neutral genetic distance and also with geographic distance (Relethford, 2004; Roseman, 2004; Roseman and Weaver, 2007). Conversely if climatic variation has been largely responsible for shaping global patterns of cranial shape variation, then a strong and significant correlation between cranial and climatic distance is expected, even after the effects of neutral genetic distance (population history) are controlled for.

Materials

Data comprise matched cranial shape, classical genetic marker, and climatic variable datasets for 15 globally distributed populations previously analyzed in von Cramon-Taubadel (2009). In brief, the cranial distance matrix was based on 138 principal component (PC) scores required to explain 95% of the total cranial shape variation following a geometric morphometric analysis of 141 cranial landmarks (Fig. 23.1, this chapter; and Table 5 in von Cramon-Taubadel, 2009). D^2-matrices based on the PC scores were generated in RMET 5.0 following the quantitative genetic model of Relethford and Blangero (1990). Given the lack of reliable population-specific heritability values for overall cranial shape, the D^2-matrix was generated under the assumption of complete heritability (ie, $h^2 = 1$). An analogous genetic D^2-matrix was generated from 59 classical marker alleles (across 13 loci) matched for these 15 populations (Table 2 in von Cramon-Taubadel, 2009) taken from Cavalli-Sforza et al. (1994). The genetic D^2-matrix was generated in RMAT 1.2. (available from John Relethford) following the Harpending and Ward (1982) model. Squared Euclidean distances between populations were calculated in PAST v3.07 (Hammer et al., 2001) using 12 climatic variables collated for all 15 populations (Table 3 in von Cramon-Taubadel, 2009). These variables comprised annual mean, minimum, and maximum values for temperature, precipitation, cloud cover, and vapor pressure. In addition to these three matched datasets, a pairwise great-circle geographic distance matrix (km) was calculated using the Geographic Distance Matrix Generator v1.2.3 (Ersts, 2015) from the longitude and latitude coordinates presented in Table 23.1. In order to prevent unrealistic ocean and mountain range crossing between populations, a number of way-points were added to constrain the between-population distances (Table 23.1).

Methods

All four distance matrices (cranial, geographic, genetic, and climatic) were subject to three-dimensional nonmetric MDS (Kruskal, 1964) in PAST v3.07 implementing the algorithm of

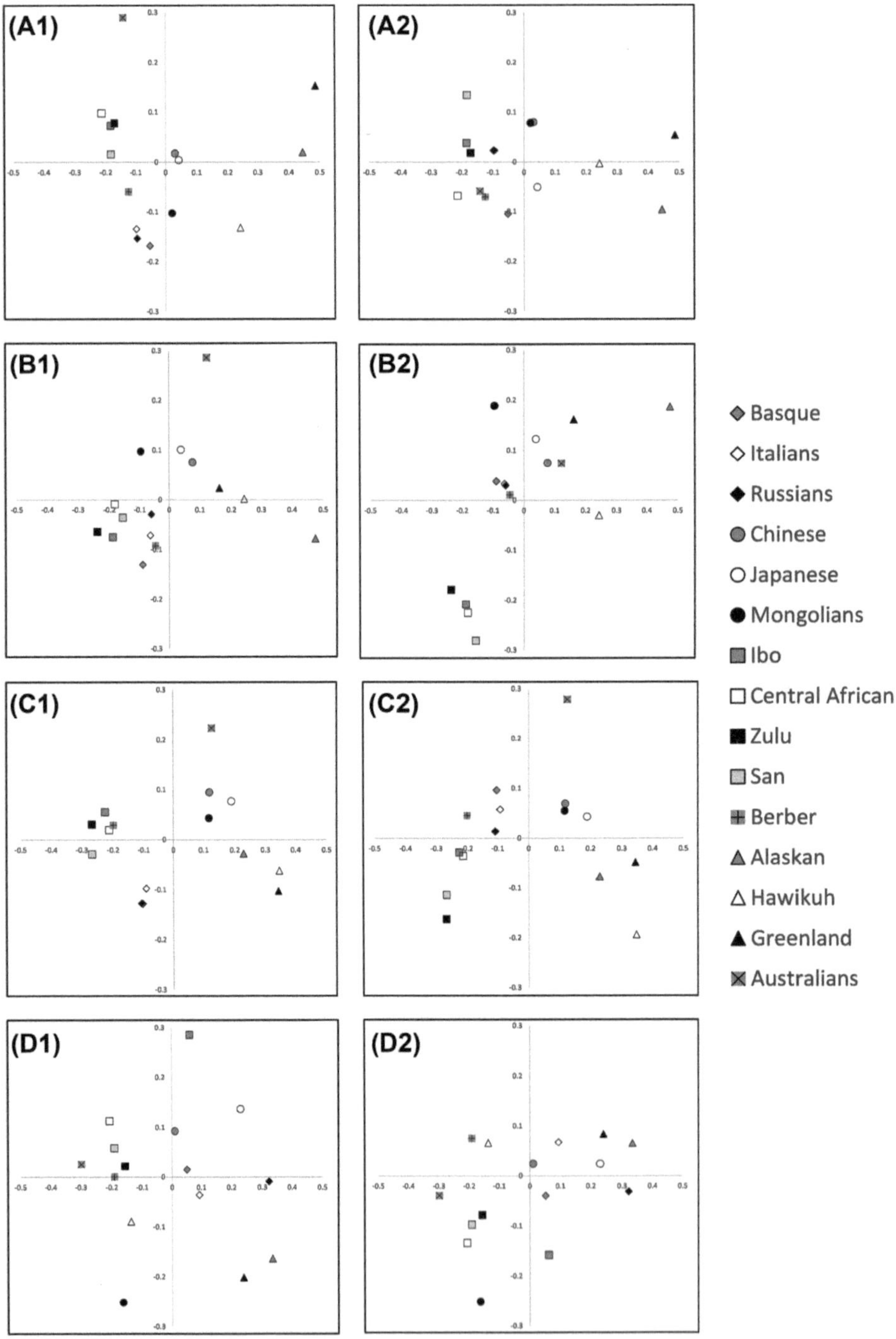

FIGURE 23.1 Case study 1: multidimensional scaling (MDS) plots.

(A) Craniometric distance. (B) Genetic distance. (C) Geographic distance. (D) Climatic distance. In each case the first plot (eg, A1) shows MDS axis 1 (*x*-axis) against MDS axis 2 (*y*-axis), and the second plot shows axis 1 against axis 3 (*y*-axis).

Table 23.1 Overview of Population Samples Employed in the Two Case Studies (Additional Geographic Locations Provided Were Used as Way-Points in the Calculation of Between-Population Geographic Distances)

Population/ Waypoint	Cranial (n)	Classical Genetic[a]	Latitude	Longitude	Mandibular (n)	Subsistence[b]
Basque (French)	30	French Basque	43.0	0.0	—	—
Italians	30	Italians	46.0	10.0	19	Intensive agriculture
Russians	30	Russians	61.0	40.0	—	—
Chinese (Han)	30	Han Chinese	32.5	114.0	27	Intensive agriculture
Japanese	30	Japanese	38.0	138.0	30	Intensive agriculture
Mongolians	30	Mongol	45.0	111.0	30	Mainly pastoralism
Ibo	30	Yoruba/Ibo	7.5	5.0	30	Extensive agriculture
Central African	21	Biaka Pygmy	4.0	17.0	19	Mainly hunting
Zulu	30	Zulu	−28.0	31.0	—	—
San	31	San	−21.0	20.0	23	Mainly gathering
Berber	30	Algerian Berber	32.0	3.0	—	—
Hawikuh	30	Pima	33.5	−109.0	30	Intensive agriculture
Alaskan Inuit	30	Alaskan Inuit	69.0	−158.0	30	Mainly hunting
Greenland Inuit	30	Greenland Inuit	70.5	−53.0	30	Mainly fishing
Australians	30	Austral Aborigine	−22.0	126.0	27	Mainly gathering
Cairo			30.0	31.0		
Istanbul			41.0	29.0		
Phnom Penh			11.0	104.0		
Anadyr			64.0	177.0		
Prince Rupert			54.0	−130.0		

[a]*Collated from Cavalli-Sforza et al. (1994).*
[b]*Predominant subsistence economy classification for each population based on Ethnographic Atlas (Gray, 1999).*

Taguchi and Oono (2005). Stress measures are provided in each case that quantify the discrepancy between the ranked differences among populations in the original distance matrix and the ranked differences among populations in the resultant MDS axes. The lower this stress measure, the better the extracted MDS axes capture the original structure of the inputted distance matrix. Generally speaking, stress levels will decrease as the numbers of dimensions (MDS axes) are increased, with $n-1$ axes (where n equals the number of groups or populations) representing the maximum number of axes possible.

However, for the purposes of both simple and directly comparable visualization of the four distance matrices here, three axes were extracted in each case. Stress levels for each of the four distance matrices were as follows: cranial = 0.0788, geographic = 0.0484, genetic = 0.0572, climatic = 0.0237. These low stress levels indicate that three dimensions capture the overall among-population variability of the four datasets very well and are all substantially below the acceptable threshold of 0.15 (Dugard et al., 2010).

Mantel and partial Mantel tests were implemented in *R* using the *mantel* and *mantel.partial* functions from the *vegan* package, with statistical significance based on 9999 permutations. Given the number of comparisons made and previous suggestions that Mantel tests are prone to Type I errors, the critical α-level was set to 0.0125 following Bonferroni correction. Cranial distance was correlated against geographic, genetic, and climatic distance, with a fourth test of congruence between cranial distance and climatic distance controlling for the effects of shared population history (genetic distance). In the case of the Mantel tests the input data were the original distance matrices prior to MDS ordination.

Thereafter, the three-dimensional MDS ordination data for each of the four datatypes were subject to Procrustes rotation and PROTEST analyses (eg, Relethford, 2010; Herrera et al., 2014). Procrustes rotation was carried out between the cranial MDS data configurations and each of the three data configurations (ie, genetics, geography, climate) using the *procrustes* function in *R*. In each case a symmetric linear transformation and rotation was employed, such that the resultant Procrustes variables (three dimensions per population) for each dataset were directly comparable. Procrustes rotation minimizes the residual sum of squares (m^2) with the relative correlation (r-value) between the two data configurations calculated as $r = \sqrt{1 - m^2}$ (Jackson, 1995; Peres-Neto and Jackson, 2001). Statistical significance ($\alpha = 0.017$) was assigned using the *protest* function in *R* (Jackson, 1995; Peres-Neto and Jackson, 2001), which applies a permutation test (9999 permutations) based on the probability of observing a fit between data configurations as low or lower than that observed by chance. Peres-Neto and Jackson (2001) show that this permutation test and Procrustes fit of ordination method may be more powerful than the Mantel test in detecting significant correlations between matrices (see also Relethford, 2010; Herrera et al., 2014). Moreover, in contrast with the Mantel test results, which only provide an assessment of overall congruence between data matrices, the Procrustes rotation method provides measures of residual deviations between the two data configurations for each individual population. Therefore, populations with a relatively larger residual distance between their position in cranial ordination space and either geographic or genetic ordination space are assumed to not fit a neutral model of evolution as well as those with smaller residuals (Relethford, 2010).

Results

Fig. 23.1 shows bivariate plots of the three MDS axes that result from the ordination of each of the four datasets (A: cranial, B: genetic, C: geographic, and D: climatic). In each case the first plot (eg, A1) represents the first (x-axis) and the second (y-axis) MDS axes, and the second plot (eg, A2) represents the first and third (y-axis) MDS axes. It is clear that all four datatypes share certain commonalities in terms of population (bio)distance patterns, with the first axes generally differentiating between African populations (negative end) and New World populations (positive end). In the case of the craniometric, genetic, and geographic plots (A—C), populations from similar geographic locations tend to cluster together (eg, three East Asian populations). However, in all four datatypes discrepancies in the relative positions of individual populations are also obvious. For example, in the genetic (B) and geographic (C) plots the Australian population is both quite distinct from the remainder of the populations and falls

Table 23.2 Case Study 1. Results of the Mantel Tests, Procrustes Rotation, and PROTEST Analyses of Congruence Between Cranial Biodistance, Genetic Biodistance, Geographic Distance, and Climatic Distance. Mantel Test α-Level = 0.0125 Following Bonferroni Correction; α = 0.017 for PROTEST Following Bonferroni Correction. Significant results are in bold.

	Mantel Tests		Procrustes/PROTEST		
	r-Value	*p*-Value	Sum of Squares	*r*-Value	*p*-Value
Genetics	**.631**	.001	0.486	**.717**	.001
Geography	**.642**	.001	0.431	**.754**	.001
Climate	**.386**	**.004**	0.706	.542	.024
Climate/genetics	.256	.034	—	—	—

closer to the Asian and New World populations, while in the craniometric (A) and the climatic (D) plots, the Australians share greater affinity with African populations.

Table 23.2 provides the results of the Mantel, partial Mantel, and PROTEST analyses of congruence between the four datatypes. Both the Mantel and PROTEST results show an overall strong ($r > .6$) congruence between cranial distance and both genetic and geographic distance, as expected under a neutral model of microevolutionary differentiation. In the case of the Mantel tests, there was also a significant, although much weaker ($r < .4$), correlation between cranial distance and climatic distance. However, this relationship was not significant once the effects of genetic distance were accounted for in a partial Mantel test.

Fig. 23.2 shows the residual distances for each population between cranial and genetic (Fig. 23.2A) and geographic ordination configurations (Fig. 23.2B), respectively. Only 4 of the 15 populations show a residual distance between craniometric and genetic configurations (Fig. 23.2A) greater than 0.15; Greenland Inuit, Australians, Hawikuh, and San. Comparing the relative positions of these populations in the cranial (A) and genetic (B) MDS ordinations in Fig. 23.1 helps to explain these findings. In the case of the Greenland Inuit, their cranial shape morphology is more divergent (ie, more distant from the centroid) than would be predicted based on the genetic data. Interestingly, while the Alaskan Inuit cranial shape is also very divergent, they also have a classical genetic allelic signature that is quite divergent, explaining why they do not share the same high residual distances as the Greenland Inuit. The findings for the Australians suggest that they are genetically more similar to Asian/New World populations yet are craniometrically more affine with the African populations. The Hawikuh appear to be more similar to mainland Asian populations genetically than they are craniometrically. The San are the most genetically divergent on the third MDS axis (Fig. 23.1, B2) yet are not particularly divergent in terms of cranial shape data. Therefore, this residual distance may be explained by the fact that the San are genetically diverse, even relative to other sub-Saharan populations, and have the highest genetic distances from other African and non-African populations (Tishkoff et al., 2009), yet craniometrically are not particularly distinctive relative to other sub-Saharan African populations.

The residual distances between cranial and geographic ordination configurations (Fig. 23.2B) also suggest that Inuit populations and Australians are relatively less similar in terms of their positions in three-dimensional MDS space. Comparing plots A1/A2 and C1/C2 in Fig. 23.1 suggests that in the case of the

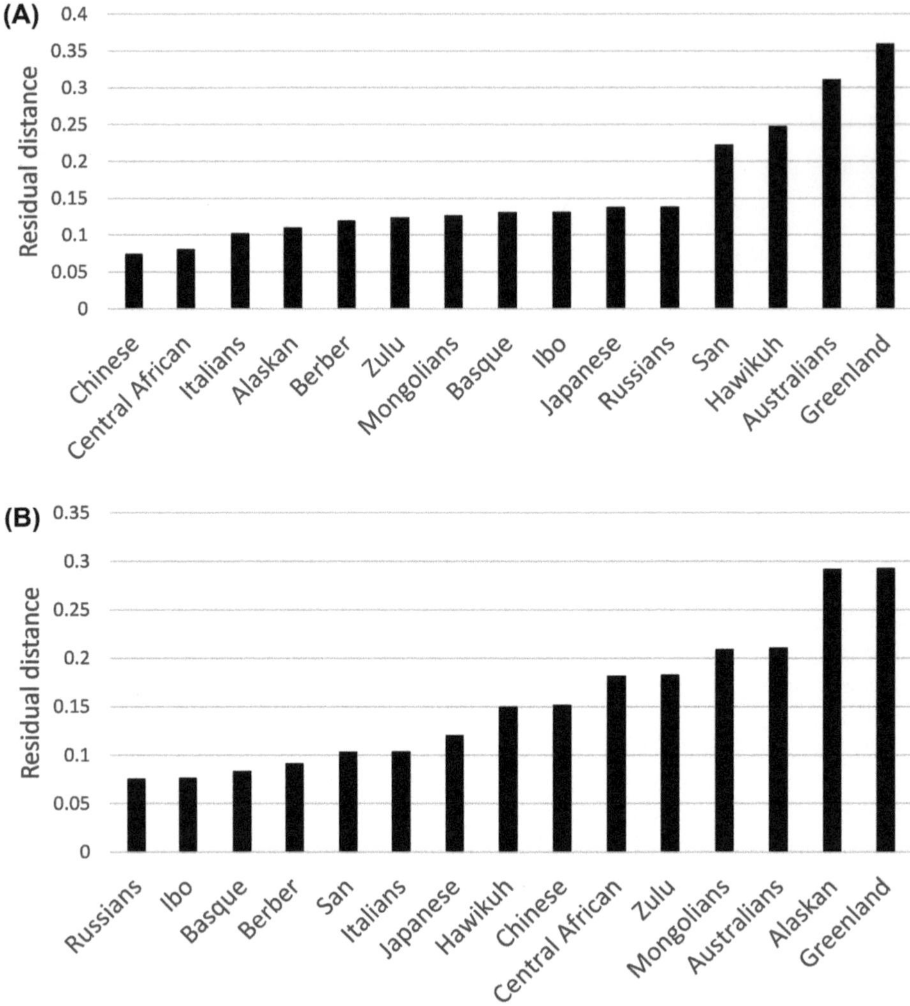

FIGURE 23.2 Population-specific residual distances.

(A) Craniometric versus genetic ordinations. (B) Craniometric versus geographic ordinations.

Australians this can be explained by their relatively closer geographic proximity with mainland Asian populations, while craniometrically they are closer to sub-Saharan Africans. The Inuit pattern can be explained via the fact that geographically they are not particularly distant relative to the other New World population (Hawikuh) or indeed the mainland Asian populations, while craniometrically they are quite distinctive on the first MDS axis from the remainder of the dataset. This divergence could be explained by climatically driven adaptation in these high-latitude populations (see also Roseman, 2004; Relethford, 2010). Both Inuit populations are relatively distinct on the first and second MDS axes (Fig. 23.1, D1) for climatic distance, which is consistent with the notion that they may have high divergence in overall cranial shape that is correlated with their more extreme (cold) climates. Hence, while climatically driven adaptation may not explain the overall craniometric affinity patterns among all populations on a global scale, it may be relevant when understanding patterns of cranial shape variation among extreme cold-dwelling populations (von Cramon-Taubadel, 2014).

Discussion

The results presented here confirm previous findings (Relethford, 1994, 2004, 2010; Roseman, 2004; Harvati and Weaver, 2006; Betti et al., 2009, 2010; Smith, 2009, 2011; von Cramon-Taubadel, 2009, 2011, 2014) that overall patterns of global craniometric shape variation largely conform to the expectations of the neutral null model of expectation. The Mantel and PROTEST results show that 50–60% of overall craniometric variation can be explained by classical genetic and/or geographic distance, while only ~15% of variation is explained by climatic distance using a full Mantel test. The results of the partial Mantel test suggest that much of this explained variance may be due to the effects of shared population history rather than climatic variation representing a true causative source of craniometric diversity. Moreover, the comparison of residual differences for each population between cranial and genetic/geographic configurations show that only a small number of populations show high residual differences between these datatypes.

Two major observations were made in terms of discrepancies between cranial distance and neutral expectation. First, the Australian population sample shows high residuals between craniometric and both genetic and geographic distance, with a genetic/geographic expectation that they show higher affinities with mainland Asian populations, but showing instead high craniometric affinity with sub-Saharan African populations. This observation is consistent with the hypothesis that contemporary indigenous Australians represent the descendants of an early migration out of Africa (most likely via a southern route around the Indian Ocean) leading to the early colonization of Australia and island Melanesia (eg, Reyes-Centeno et al., 2014). These Australasian populations remained relatively isolated but with some gene flow from subsequent migrations that led to the large-scale colonization of mainland Asia (Rasmussen et al., 2011; Reyes-Centeno et al., 2014). Second, in the case of the two Inuit populations, the most likely explanation for their relatively high residuals is climatically driven (ie, nonneutral) diversification in these high-latitude populations. This is consistent with the findings of Roseman (2004), who found that the Siberian Buriat population (taken from W.W. Howells' craniometric dataset) showed morphological differentiation from the remainder of the populations, representing a departure from the neutral model of expectation. This could also be explained on the basis of climatically driven diversification as removal of this single population from the sample resulted in no significant association between mean annual temperature and craniometric distance (Roseman, 2004). Relethford (2010) also found the Buriat population to exhibit high residual distances between cranial and geographic distances, relative to 21 other global populations.

In summary, the analyses conducted here within a biodistance framework show that overall global patterns of cranial shape variation fit a neutral model of divergence quite well, while climatic variation is generally a poor predictor of cranial affinity patterns. However, the Procrustes rotation approach also provides a more nuanced assessment of how individual populations differ in terms of their geographic, biological, and climatic affinity patterns. In particular, it is clear that Inuit populations show greater divergence in terms of the overall cranial shape than would be expected under a neutral model, and this is consistent with climatically driven adaptation in these groups. Specifically, it may be the cold temperatures sustained by these populations on an annual basis that is driving this nonneutral diversification. In this study climate was quantified using not only temperature, but also precipitation, cloud cover, and vapor pressure variables, the latter three of which may not play a pertinent role in causing Inuit cranial shape diversification. Therefore, it is possible that the potential causative link between climate and cranial diversification in Inuit populations may not be represented particularly well by the climatic distance matrix used here. Hence, further more detailed analysis of climatic adaptation in these cold-adapted populations is warranted (see, eg, Evteev et al., 2014).

CASE STUDY 2: TO WHAT EXTENT CAN GLOBAL PATTERNS OF CRANIOMANDIBULAR VARIATION BE EXPLAINED BY VARIATION IN SUBSISTENCE STRATEGY?

In contrast with other primate species, some human populations underwent a substantial shift in subsistence strategy from one based primarily on hunting and gathering to one based on extensive horticulture or animal husbandry (eg, Gignoux et al., 2011). The adoption of a more agriculture-based subsistence strategy also had an effect on paramasticatory behavior given concomitant changes in the intensification of food processing and the consumption of a softer diet overall (Larsen, 2015). On this basis, it has long been hypothesized that this shift in dietary behavior may also have affected craniomandibular growth and development (eg, Carlson and Van Gerven, 1977; Lieberman, 2008, 2011; Paschetta et al., 2010; Holmes and Ruff, 2011; von Cramon-Taubadel, 2011; Larsen, 2015). In particular, it might be expected that the mandible be particularly affected by such dietary shifts, given that it is a key biomechanical component of the masticatory apparatus (Lieberman, 2011) and yet is somewhat morphologically independent from the remainder of the cranial complex.

Several studies (Carlson and Van Gerven, 1977; González-José et al., 2005; Pinhasi et al., 2008; Paschetta et al., 2010; Holmes and Ruff, 2011) have suggested that a general decrease in biomechanical stress associated with mastication may affect the overall shape and size of the mandible via the mechanism of phenotypic plasticity (see also Holton et al., 2014). The basic idea being that as the mandible experiences less or different biomechanical forces during growth and development, its growth trajectory will change, leading ultimately to a different form in adults who grew up with an agricultural diet compared to those experiencing a (presumably) more biomechanically demanding hunting/gathering diet. If this were the case, then we would expect to see a departure from a global among-population biodistance pattern expected under neutral microevolutionary conditions for mandibular shape. In other words, in contrast with the pattern observed for the whole cranium, we would expect that the biodistance pattern for the mandible to not follow a model of neutral expectation, but instead match a global affinity pattern based on overall similarities and differences in diet and subsistence behavior.

In order to test these ideas using a biodistance framework, a similar approach as was adopted in the previous case study will also be employed here. As shown in Table 23.1, matched mandibular data were available for a subset ($n = 11$) of the 15 populations employed in the previous case study. In addition, as described in greater detail in von Cramon-Taubadel (2011), it was possible to match information regarding subsistence strategy for each of these 11 populations from the updated Ethnographic Atlas (Gray, 1999). Data comprised information on the average percentage of time each population spent gathering, hunting, fishing, conducting animal husbandry (pastoralism), and agriculture. These data were employed to construct dissimilarity matrices in four different ways (see von Cramon-Taubadel, 2011).

Here, just one of these (called subsistence matrix 3 in von Cramon-Taubadel, 2011) was employed, which does not distinguish, from a dietary point of view, between hunting and fishing as separate subsistence strategies.

First, the null hypothesis of neutrality was tested for the mandible and the cranium as in the previous case study. Thereafter, the congruence between mandibular shape and subsistence strategy was statistically compared to test the hypothesis that global mandibular shape biodistance can be explained by differences in dietary behavior.

Materials

Data comprise matched mandibular shape, cranial shape, classical genetic markers, and subsistence datasets for 11 globally distributed populations previously analyzed in von Cramon-Taubadel (2011). The mandibular distance matrix was based on 42 PC scores required to explain 95% of the total mandibular shape variation following a geometric morphometric analysis of 33 mandibular landmarks (Fig. 1 in von Cramon-Taubadel, 2011). The cranial distance matrix is similar to the one used in the previous case study, except that 123 PCs explained 95% of the total variance for the 11 populations. D^2 matrices for both cranial and mandibular data based on PC scores and an analogous classical genetic D^2 matrix were generated as described in the previous case study. Similarly, a pairwise great-circle geographic distance matrix (km) was calculated from the geographic coordinates presented in Table 23.1 using waypoints. Finally, a subsistence distance matrix was created based on the square root of the sum of the squared differences between frequency values for each of six quantitative subsistence variables collated from the Ethnographic Atlas (Gray, 1999). These six values were the relative percentage of time each population spends gathering, hunting, fishing, conducting animal husbandry (pastoralism) and agriculture, and whether milking was part of their subsistence economy (Table 2, von Cramon-Taubadel, 2011). The advantage of this method of subsistence quantification is that it avoids the artificial dichotomization between hunter-gatherers and farmers, but rather allows for an assessment of relative affinity among populations based on subsistence economy.

Methods

As in the previous case study, all distance matrices (mandibular, cranial, geographic, genetic, and dietary) were subject to three-dimensional nonmetric MDS in PAST v3.07. Stress measures for each distance matrix were as follows: mandibular = 0.0972, cranial = 0.0782, geographic = 0.0214, genetic = 0.0370, subsistence = 0.0290. As in the previous case study these stress levels were all well below the acceptable threshold of 0.15.

As before, Mantel and partial Mantel tests were implemented in *R* with statistical significance based on 9999 permutations, and critical α-level was set to 0.007 (Bonferroni correction). The 3D MDS ordination data for each of the datatypes were subject to Procrustes rotation and PROTEST analyses as described in the previous case study with $\alpha = 0.008$.

Results

Fig. 23.3 shows bivariate plots of the three MDS axes that result from the ordination of each of four datasets (A: mandibular, B: genetic, C: geographic, D: subsistence). The genetic and geographic datasets

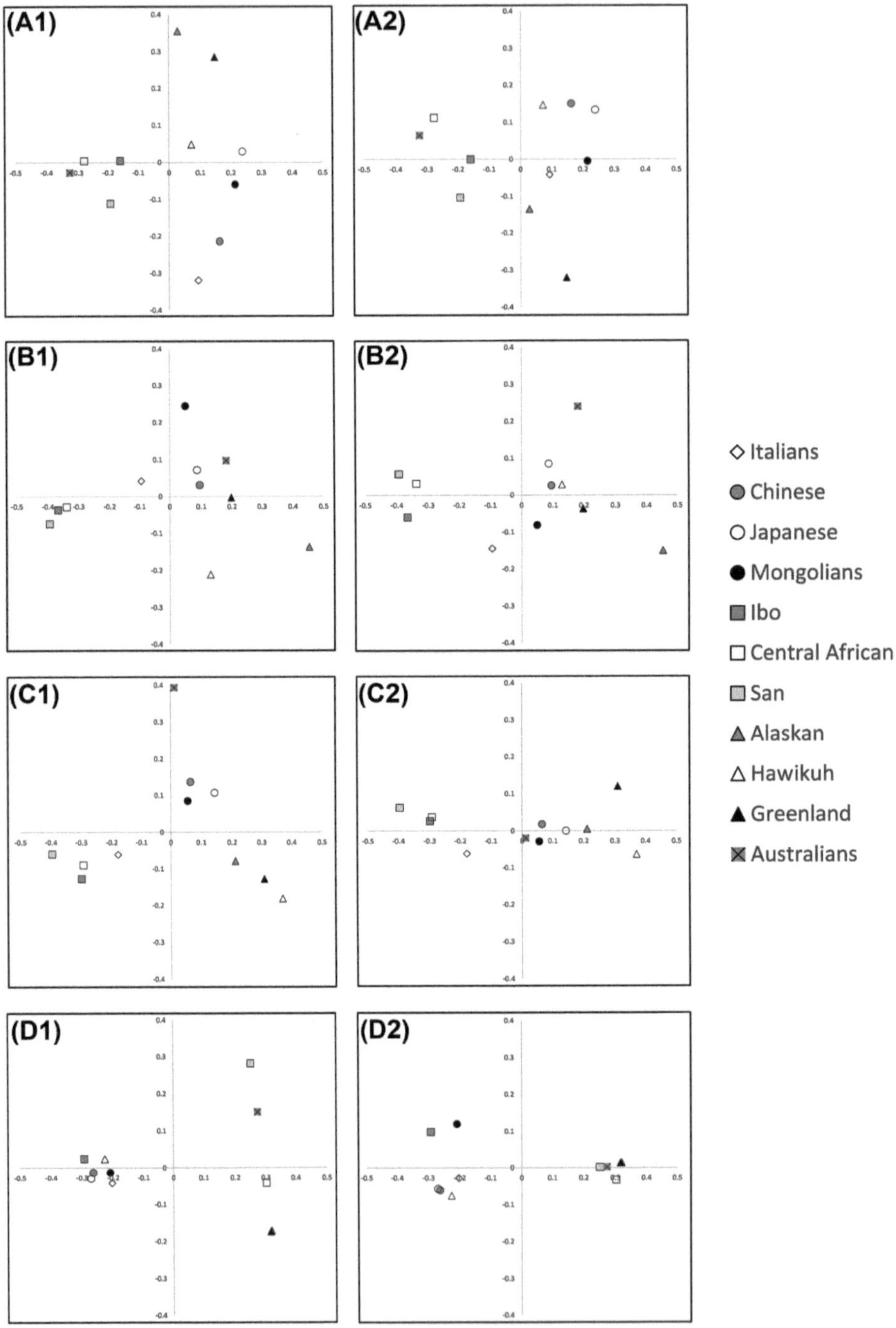

FIGURE 23.3 Case study 2: multidimensional scaling (MDS) plots.

(A) Mandibular distance. (B) Genetic distance. (C) Geographic distance. (D) Subsistence distance. In each case the first plot (eg, A1) shows MDS axis 1 (*x*-axis) against MDS axis 2 (*y*-axis), and the second plot shows axis 1 against axis 3 (*y*-axis).

(Fig. 23.3B and C) share the same common biodistance pattern observed in the previous case study, differentiating between African populations (negative end) and New World populations (positive end) on the first axis. In the case of genetic distance, the third axis (B2) differentiates among East Asian and New World populations, and separates the Australian population from the Asian/New World populations. In the case of geographic distance, the third axis (C2) adds little additional information, except for separating the Greenland Inuit from the other New World populations. In the mandibular ordination, a basic geographic pattern is clear on axis 1 (A1), separating the Australian and African populations from the remaining populations. Axis 2 distinguishes broadly between hunting-gathering populations on the positive end and mainly farming or pastoralist populations on the negative end. For example, it distinguishes between the mainly agricultural Ibo population and the remaining hunter-gatherer groups from sub-Saharan Africa. Axis 3 (A2) mainly distinguishes between the East Asian and farming New World population and the mainly hunter-gatherer Inuit populations. Finally, Fig. 23.3 (D1) shows the dichotomy between those populations who primarily conduct agriculture or pastoralism (see Table 23.1) on the negative end of axis 1, versus those that primarily hunt, fish, and gather on the positive end of axis 1. Axis 2 distinguishes among the gatherers (positive) and the hunter-fishers (negative), while axis 3 (Fig. 23.3, D2) distinguishes among those agriculturalists with more fishing (negative) versus those with less fishing (positive).

Table 23.3 provides the results of the Mantel, partial Mantel, and PROTEST analyses of congruence between all distance matrices. Both the Mantel and PROTEST results show a nonsignificant congruence between overall mandibular distance and both genetic and geographic distance, thereby rejecting the basic expectations of a neutral model of microevolutionary differentiation. As a point of reference, the results for cranial distance still conform to neutral expectations, even with the reduced number of populations (Table 23.3). Moreover, mandibular distance is significantly correlated with subsistence distance

Table 23.3 Case Study 2. Results of the Mantel Tests, Procrustes Rotation, and PROTEST Analyses of Congruence Between Mandibular/Cranial Biodistance, Genetic Biodistance, Geographic Distance, and Subsistence Strategy. Mantel Test α-Level = 0.007 Following Bonferroni Correction; α = 0.008 for PROTEST Following Bonferroni Correction. Significant results are in bold.

	Mantel Tests		Procrustes/PROTEST		
	r-Value	*p*-Value	Sum of Squares	*r*-Value	*p*-Value
Mandible vs					
Genetics	.229	.089	0.688	.559	.102
Geography	.316	.025	0.665	.579	.080
Subsistence	**.374**	**.008**	0.524	**.690**	**.007**
Subs/genetics	**.363**	**.005**	—	—	—
Cranium vs					
Genetics	**.614**	**.001**	0.389	**.782**	**.001**
Geography	**.665**	**.001**	0.397	**.777**	**.002**
Subsistence	.264	.052	0.750	.499	.172

in both the Mantel and PROTEST results, even when the effects of shared population history were accounted for via a partial Mantel test. In contrast, cranial shape distance is not significantly associated with subsistence in either the PROTEST or the Mantel test results.

Discussion

The results clearly show a difference between the cranial shape and mandibular shape biodistance patterns in terms of their fit with a neutral model of expectation. Mandibular biodistance does not fit a neutral model, but instead is consistent with broad among-population differences in subsistence behavior. This result is particularly forceful given that the cranial and mandibular data are matched for exactly the same biological specimens, and therefore, any discrepancy between cranial and mandibular biodistance patterns cannot be attributed to poorly matched datasets. Fig. 23.4 shows the biodistance affinities for all 11 populations in Procrustes rotated space based on the first two MDS axes for mandibular and cranial shape. Polygons in solid black (mandible) and gray (cranium) lines show the maximum distributions of hunter-gatherer populations, while dashed polygons delineate agricultural-pastoralist populations. While there is

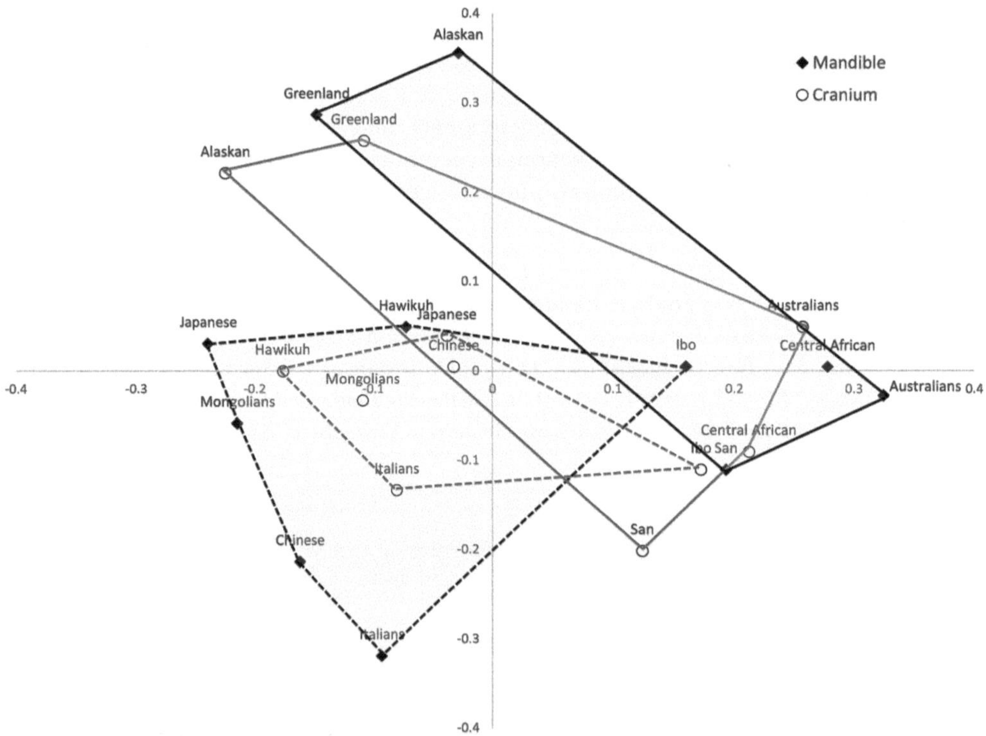

FIGURE 23.4 Procrustes rotated ordinations for cranial and mandibular distance.

x-axis = MDS 1, *y*-axis = MDS 2. *Black solid polygon* = hunter-gatherer mandibles. *Black dashed polygon* = agriculturalist mandibles. *Gray solid polygon* = hunter-gatherer crania. *Gray dashed polygon* = agriculturalist crania.

some correlation between population geography and subsistence type (eg, more agricultural populations in East Asia, more hunter-gatherer populations in Africa), it is clear that for the cranium there is considerable overlap between populations from the two major subsistence groups, and that the pattern is consistent with population history. However, the mandibular biodistance pattern is such that hunter-gatherer populations are displaced positively on axes 1 and 2 (upward and to the right) relative to their cranial positions, while farming/pastoralist populations are displaced negatively on axes 1 and 2 (downward and to the left). This has the effect of increasing the overall dispersion of all populations based on mandibular shape, relative to cranial shape, with the main axis of divergence corresponding to major differences in subsistence economy.

This biodistance pattern for mandibular shape is also consistent with the findings of Nicholson and Harvati (2006), who found a considerable congruence between global mandibular shape variation and geographic distance. In the case of the latter study, the samples were not separated according to subsistence type, and therefore, the authors were able to detect a weak signal of population history. Taken together with the results of von Cramon-Taubadel (2011), these results suggest that a global sample of hunter-gatherer mandibles might fit a neutral model relatively well, although this remains to be explicitly tested (von Cramon-Taubadel, 2014).

CONCLUSIONS

A biodistance framework for assessing the microevolutionary history of global patterns of among-population variation patterns was implemented via two craniomandibular case studies. By situating the analysis of biodistance patterns within an explicitly evolutionary theoretical framework, it is possible to establish null expectations for such patterns based on a neutral model of genetic/phenotypic differentiation. These null expectations are relatively easy to test, and potentially reject, such that more complex evolutionary scenarios involving nonneutral processes might be explored. These nonneutral processes might be environmentally driven diversification via natural selection or phenotypic plasticity, as suggested by the results for Inuit cranial diversification and global mandibular shape, respectively.

The advantage of the framework showcased here is that the overall statistical congruence between among-population patterns can be easily assessed, as can be the effects of individual populations on that overall congruence. While the PROTEST may be statistically more powerful than using Mantel tests (Jackson, 1995; Peres-Neto and Jackson, 2001), it has the disadvantage of not allowing us to control for the effects of a third (or multiple) matrix(ces). Moreover, the Procrustes rotation method requires a reduced dimension ordination of among-population distance matrices prior to congruence assessment, which may also introduce some bias, particularly if some matched datatypes are easily rendered in two or three dimensions, while others require a higher number of dimensions to accurately depict the original population distance structure. Mantel tests (and their derivatives) have the advantage of using the original distance matrices without ordination, and can handle multiple distance/dissimilarity measures incorporated into the same framework. It also allows for the flexible testing of single and multiple regressions, and partial correlations where the effects of certain matrices are held constant. However, it has been suggested that Mantel tests may be more prone to low statistical power and elevated Type I errors (eg, Guillot and Rousset, 2013), especially when matrices are spatially autocorrelated. Also, while Mantel tests allow for an assessment of overall congruence, it is not possible to assess the contribution of any individual population to the correlation via residual analyses, as is the case with the Procrustes rotation method. Given this, one or other method may be more appropriate, depending on the specific questions being asked of the data. The statistical results from the Mantel and PROTEST analyses were very comparable in the two case studies presented here, suggesting that it may be prudent to adopt both methods in studies that wish to simultaneously assess overall congruence, assess partial correlations, and gain insight into the residual differences between datatypes for individual groups.

Finally, one important type of data not considered here is that of temporal distance. In the case of the largely contemporaneous populations under consideration here, temporal distance was not of major concern. However, time could be a substantial source of biological variation in many bioarchaeological and paleoanthropological applications of biodistance matrix approach where considerable temporal variation exists among different groups (eg, Konigsberg, 1990; Stojanowski and Schillacci, 2006; Pinhasi and von Cramon-Taubadel, 2009; Hubbe et al., 2010; von Cramon-Taubadel and Pinhasi, 2011; Reyes-Centeno et al., 2014). Fortunately, the flexible analytical system showcased here allows for the integration of multiple datatypes and potential explanatory factors, such as time, space, environmental factors, and indeed arbitrary model distance matrices designed to quantify particular hypotheses regarding observed biodistance patterns (eg, Pinhasi and von Cramon-Taubadel, 2009; von Cramon-Taubadel and Pinhasi, 2011). Hence, it is likely that biodistance-based analyses will continue to play an important role in future studies of global human population history and adaptation.

References

Betti, L., Balloux, F., Amos, W., Hanihara, T., Manica, A., 2009. Distance from Africa, not climate, explains within-population phenotypic diversity in humans. Proceedings of the Royal Society, B 276, 809–814.

Betti, L., Balloux, F., Hanihara, T., Manica, A., 2010. The relative role of drift and selection in shaping the human skull. American Journal of Physical Anthropology 141, 76–82.

Betti, L., von Cramon-Taubadel, N., Lycett, S.J., 2012. Human pelvis and long bones reveal differential preservation of ancient population history and migration out of Africa. Human Biology 84, 139–152.

Buikstra, J.E., Frankenberg, S.R., Konigsberg, L.W., 1990. Skeletal biological distance studies in American physical anthropology: recent trends. American Journal of Physical Anthropology 82, 1–7.

Carlson, D.S., Van Gerven, D.P., 1977. Masticatory function and post-Pleistocene evolution in Nubia. American Journal of Physical Anthropology 46, 495–506.

Cavalli-Sforza, L.L., Menozzi, P., Piazza, A., 1994. The History and Geography of Human Genes. Princeton University Press, New Jersey.

Dryden, I.L., Mardia, K.V., 1998. Statistical Shape Analysis. Wiley, Chicester.

Dugard, P., Todman, J., Staines, H., 2010. Approaching Multivariate Analysis: A Practical Introduction. Routledge, New York.

Ersts, P.J., (Internet), 2015. Geographic Distance Matrix Generator v. 1.2.3. American Museum of Natural History, Center for Biodiversity and Conservation.

Evteev, A., Cardini, A.L., Morozova, I., O'Higgins, P., 2014. Extreme climate, rather than population history, explains mid-facial morphology of northern Asians. American Journal of Physical Anthropology 153, 449–462.

Falconer, D.S., Mackay, T.F.C., 1996. Introduction to Quantitative Genetics. Pearson Prentice Hall, London.

Felsenstein, J., 1985. Phylogenies and the comparative method. The American Naturalist 125, 1–15.

Gignoux, C.R., Henn, B.M., Mountain, J.L., 2011. Rapid, global demographic expansions after the origins of agriculture. Proceedings of the National Academy of Sciences, USA 108, 6044–6049.

González-José, R., Ramirez-Rozzi, F., Sardi, M., Martínez-Abadías, N., Hernandez, M., Pucciarelli, H., 2005. Functional-cranial approach to the influence of economic strategy on skull morphology. American Journal of Physical Anthropology 128, 757–771.

González-José, R., Martínez-Abadías, N., González-Martín, A., Baustista-Martínez, J., Gómez-Valdés, J., Quinto, M., et al., 2007. Detection of a population replacement at the Classic-Postclassic transition in Mexico. Proceedings of the Royal Society B 274, 681–688.

Gower, J.C., 1966. Some distance properties of latent root and vector methods used in multivariate analysis. Biometrika 53, 325–338.

Gray, J.P., 1999. A corrected ethnographic atlas. World Cultures 10, 24–85.

Guillot, G., Rousset, F., 2013. Dismantling the Mantel tests. Methods in Ecology and Evolution 4, 336–344.

Hammer, Ø., Harper, D.A.T., Ryan, P.D., 2001. Paleontological statistics software packagefor education and data analysis. Paleontologia Electronica 4, 1–9.

Hanihara, T., Matsumura, H., Kawakubo, Y., Nguyen, L.C., Nguyen, K.T., Dodo, Y., 2012. Population history of northern Vietnamese inferred from nonmetric cranial trait variation. Anthropological Science 120, 157–165.

Harmon, L.J., Glor, R.E., 2010. Poor statistical performance of the Mantel test in phylogenetic comparative analyses. Evolution 64, 2173–2178.

Harpending, H.C., Ward, R.H., 1982. Chemical systematics and human evolution. In: Nitecki, M. (Ed.), Biochemical Aspects of Evolutionary Biology. University of Chicago Press, Chicago, pp. 213–256.

Harvati, K., Weaver, T.D., 2006. Human cranial anatomy and the differential preservation of population history and climate signatures. The Anatomical Record Part A 288A, 1225–1233.

Herrera, B., Hanihara, T., Godde, K., 2014. Comparability of multiple data types from the Bering Strait region: cranial and dental metrics and nonmetrics, mtDNA, and y-chromosome DNA. American Journal of Physical Anthropology 154, 334–348.

Holmes, M.A., Ruff, C.B., 2011. Dietary effects on development of the human mandibular corpus. American Journal of Physical Anthropology 145, 615–628.

Holton, N.E., Franciscus, R.G., Ravosa, M.J., Southard, T.E., 2014. Functional and morphological correlates of mandibular symphyseal form in a living human sample. American Journal of Physical Anthropology 153, 387–396.

Howells, W.W., 1973. Cranial Variation in Man: A Study by Multivariate Analysis of Patterns of Difference Among Recent Human Populations. Peabody Museum of Archaeology and Ethnology, Harvard University, Cambridge, MA.

Hubbard, A.R., Guatelli-Steinberg, D., Irish, J.D., 2015. Do nuclear DNA and dental nonmetric data produce similar reconstructions of regional population history? An example from modern coastal Kenya. American Journal of Physical Anthropology 157, 295–304.

Hubbe, M., Neves, W.A., Harvati, K., 2010. Testing evolutionary and dispersion scenarios for the settlement of the New World. PLoS One 5, e11105.

Huxley, J., 1942. Evolution: The Modern Synthesis. George Allen and Unwin Ltd, London.

Jackson, D.A., 1995. PROTEST: a PROcrustean randomization TEST of community environment concordance. Ecoscience 2, 297–303.

Kemp, B.M., González-Oliver, A., Malhi, R.S., Monroe, C., Schroeder, K.B., McDonough, J., et al., 2010. Evaluating the farming/landguage dispersal hypothesis with genetic variation exhbitied by populations in the Southwest and Mesoamerica. Proceedings of the National Academy of Sciences, USA 107, 6759–6764.

Kimura, M., 1983. The Neutral Theory of Molecular Evolution. Cambridge University Press, Cambridge.

Konigsberg, L.W., 1990. Analysis of prehistoric biological variation under a model of isolation by geographic and temporal distance. Human Biology 62, 49–70.

Kruskal, J.B., Wish, M., 1978. Multidimensional Scaling. Sage University Series on Quantitative Applications in the Social Sciences. Sage Publications, Beverly Hills.

Kruskal, J.B., 1964. Nonmetric multidimensional scaling: a numerical method. Psychometrika 29, 115–129.

Larsen, C.S., 2015. Bioarchaeology: Interpreting Behavior from the Human Skeleton. Cambridge University Press, Cambridge.
Legendre, P., Fortin, M.-J., 2010. Comparison of the Mantel test and alternative approaches for detecting complex multivariate relationships in the spatial analysis of genetic data. Molecular Ecology Resources 10, 831–844.
Lieberman, D.E., 2008. Speculations about the selective basis for the modern human craniofacial form. Evolutionary Anthropology 17, 55–68.
Lieberman, D.E., 2011. The Evolution of the Human Head. Harvard University Press, Cambridge, MA.
Mantel, N.A., 1967. The detection of disease clustering and a generalized regression approach. Cancer Research 27, 209–220.
Mardia, K.V., Kent, J.T., Bibby, J.M., 1979. Multivariate Analysis. Academic Press, London.
Mayr, E., 1942. Systematics and the Origin of Species. Columbia University Press, New York.
McIlvaine, B.K., Schepartz, L.A., Larsen, C.S., Sciulli, P.W., 2014. Evidence for long-term migration on the Balkan peninsula using dental and cranial nonmetric data: early interaction between Corinth (Greece) and its colony in Apollonia (Albania). American Journal of Physical Anthropology 153, 236–248.
Naroll, R., 1961. Two solutions to Galton's problem. Philosophy of Science 28, 15–39.
Nicholson, E., Harvati, K., 2006. Quantitative analysis of human mandibular shape using three-dimensional geometric morphometrics. American Journal of Physical Anthropology 131, 368–383.
Paschetta, C., de Azevedo, S., Castillo, L., Martínez-Abadías, N., Hernández, M., Lieberman, D.E., et al., 2010. The influence of masticatory loading on craniofacial morphology: a test case across technological transitions in the Ohio valley. American Journal of Physical Anthropology 141, 297–314.
Peres-Neto, P.R., Jackson, D.A., 2001. How well do multivariate datasets match? The advantages of a Procrustean superimposition approach over the Mantel test. Oecologia 129, 169–178.
Pinhasi, R., von Cramon-Taubadel, N., 2009. Craniometric data supports demic diffusion model for the spread of agriculture into Europe. PLoS One 4, e6747.
Pinhasi, R., Eshed, V., Shaw, P., 2008. Evolutionary changes in the masticatory complex following the transition to farming in the southern Levant. American Journal of Physical Anthropology 135, 136–148.
Prugnolle, F., Manica, A., Balloux, F., 2005. Geography predicts neutral genetic diversity of human populations. Current Biology R129.
Ragsdale, C.S., Edgar, H.J.H., 2015. Cultural interaction and biological distance in postclassic period Mexico. American Journal of Physical Anthropology 157, 121–133.
Ramachandran, S., Deshpande, O., Roseman, C.C., Rosenberg, N.A., Feldman, M.W., Cavalli-Sforza, L.L., 2005. Support from the relationship of genetic and geographic distance in human populations for the serial founder effect originating in Africa. Proceedings of National Academy Science, USA 102, 15942–15947.
Rasmussen, M., Guo, X., Wang, Y., Lohmueller, K.E., Rasmussen, S., Albrechtsen, A., et al., 2011. An aboriginal Australian genome reveals separate human dispersals into Asia. Nature 334, 94–98.
Relethford, J.H., Blangero, J., 1990. Detection of differential gene flow from patterns of quantitative variation. Human Biology 62, 5–25.
Relethford, J.H., 1994. Craniometric variation among modern human populations. American Journal of Physical Anthropology 95, 53–62.
Relethford, J.H., 2004. Global patterns of isolation by distance based on genetic and morphological data. Human Biology 76, 499–513.
Relethford, J.H., 2010. Population-specific deviations of global human craniometric variation from a neutral model. American Journal of Physical Anthropology 142, 105–111.
Reyes-Centeno, H., Ghirotto, S., Détroit, F., Grimaud-Hervé, D., Barbujani, G., Harvati, K., 2014. Genomic and cranial phenotype data support multiple modern human dispersals from Africa and a southern route into Asia. Proceedings of the National Academy of Sciences, USA 111, 7248–7253.

Ricaut, F.-X., Auriol, V., von Cramon-Taubadel, N., Keyser, C., Murail, P., Ludea, B., et al., 2010. Comparison between morphological and genetic data to estimate biological relationships: the case of the Egyin Gol necropolis (Mongolia). American Journal of Physical Anthropology 143, 355–364.

Roseman, C.C., Weaver, T.D., 2007. Molecules versus morphology? Not for the human cranium. BioEssays 29, 1185–1188.

Roseman, C.C., 2004. Detecting interregionally diversifying natural selection on modern human cranial form by using matched molecular and morphometric data. Proceedings of the National Academy of Sciences of the United States of America 101, 12824–12829.

Smith, H.F., 2009. Which cranial regions reflect molecular distances reliably in humans? Evidence from three-dimensional morphology. American Journal of Human Biology 21, 36–47.

Smith, H.F., 2011. The role of genetic drift in shaping modern human cranial evolution: a test using microevolutionary modeling. International Journal of Evolutionary Biology 2011, 1–11, 145262.

Smouse, P.E., Long, J.C., 1992. Matrix correlation analysis in anthropology and genetics. Yearbook of Physical Anthropology 35, 187–213.

Smouse, P.E., Long, J.C., Sokal, R.R., 1986. Multiple regression and correlation extensions of the Mantel test of matrix correspondence. Systematic Zoology 35, 627–632.

Sokal, P.H.A., Sneath, R.R., 1963. Principles of Numerical Taxonomy. W.H. Freeman, San Francisco.

Stojanowski, C.M., Schillaci, M.A., 2006. Phenotypic approaches for understanding patterns of intracemetery biological variation. Yearbook of Physical Anthropology 49, 49–88.

Stynder, D.D., Ackermann, R.R., Sealy, J.C., 2007. Craniofacial variation and population continuity during the South African holocene. American Journal of Physical Anthropology 134, 489–500.

Taguchi, Y-h., Oono, Y., 2005. Relational patterns of gene expression via non-metric multidimensional scaling analysis. Bioinformatics 21, 730–740.

Tishkoff, S.A., Reed, F.A., Friedlaender, F.R., Ehret, C., Ranciaro, A., Froment, A., et al., 2009. The genetic structure and history of Africans and African Americans. Science 324, 1035–1044.

von Cramon-Taubadel, N., Lycett, S.J., 2008. Brief Communication: human cranial variation fits iterative founder effect model with African origin. American Journal of Physical Anthropology 136, 108–113.

von Cramon-Taubadel, N., Pinhasi, R., 2011. Craniometric data support a mosaic model of demic and cultural Neolithic diffusion to outlying regions of Europe. Proceedings of the Royal Society, B 278, 2874–2880.

von Cramon-Taubadel, N., 2009. Congruence of individual cranial bone morphology and neutral molecular affinity patterns in modern humans. American Journal of Physical Anthropology 140, 205–215.

von Cramon-Taubadel, N., 2011. Global human mandibular variation reflects differences in agricultural and hunter-gatherer subsistence strategies. Proceedings of the National Academy of Sciences, USA 108, 19546–19551.

von Cramon-Taubadel, N., 2014. Evolutionary insights into global patterns of human cranial diversity: population history, climatic and dietary effects. Journal of Anthropological Sciences 92, 43–77.

CHAPTER

A Biodistance Analysis of Mandibles From Taiwan, Asia, and the Pacific: A Search for Polynesian Origins

24

M. Pietrusewsky[1], A. Lauer[2], C.-H. Tsang[3], K.-T. Li[3], M.T. Douglas[1]
University of Hawaii at Manoa, Honolulu, HI, United States[1]; International Archaeological Research Institute, Inc., Honolulu, HI, United States[2]; Academia Sinica, Taipei, Taiwan, Republic of China[3]

CHAPTER OUTLINE HEAD

Introduction 447
Biological Distance Studies 448
Material and Methods 449
  The Nankuanli East (南關里東) Site: Early Neolithic 449
  Shihsanhang Site, Northwestern Taiwan: Iron Age 449
  Comparative Skeletal Assemblages 449
  Mandible Measurements and Multivariate Statistics 449
Results 453
  Stepwise Discriminant Function Analysis 453
  Mahalanobis' Generalized Distance 454
Discussion 456
Conclusions 458
Acknowledgments 459
Endnote 459
References 459

INTRODUCTION

Although challenged as too simplistic (eg, Barker and Richards, 2013), linguistic, archaeological, and genetic data have been used to support narratives that champion Taiwan as the homeland of a Neolithic expansion of Austronesian-speaking farmers, an expansion that ultimately extended from Madagascar to Easter Island. The Taiwan Neolithic [Tapenkeng (TPK)] or Dabenkeng culture has been linked to the farming/language dispersals that would ultimately lead to the peopling of previously uninhabited regions of the Pacific such as Remote Oceania and Polynesia, beginning approximately 5000 years BP (Bellwood, 2005; Chang, 1995; Li, 2013; Tsang, 2005). Alternative models, such as those that focus on cultural diffusion rather than large-scale migration have also been proposed.

The Taiwanese Neolithic is believed to have originated from pre-TPK cultures in the Pearl River Delta and southeastern coastal regions of China between 6000 and 4000 BC[1] (Bellwood, 2005; Hung

Biological Distance Analysis. http://dx.doi.org/10.1016/B978-0-12-801966-5.00024-X

and Carson, 2014; Jiao, 2007; Tsang, 2010). The Taiwanese Neolithic is characterized by the emergence of pottery production, polished stone tools, fishing and foraging, tuber horticulture, and cereal agriculture involving rice and millet (Hung and Carson, 2014). There is broad consensus (eg, Chang and Goodenough, 1996) that Taiwan's historic Austronesian-speaking peoples, the Indigenous Taiwanese, are the descendants of these early Neolithic cultures.

Given Taiwan's central role in the Neolithic expansion eastward to Island Southeast Asia and the Pacific, human skeletons associated with the earliest Neolithic of Taiwan should inform on the biological origins of the first inhabitants of Remote Oceania, including the origins of the Polynesians. Further, because the Lapita Culture Complex is tied to the initial human colonization of Remote Oceania, skeletons associated with Lapita culture should show biological relationships to those associated with the Neolithic of Taiwan. Unlike molecular genetic studies, human skeletons provide direct evidence for identifying the biological ancestors of Polynesians.

In this chapter, multivariate statistical procedures are applied to measurements recorded in mandibles from Taiwan, including those from one of the earliest Neolithic sites in Taiwan, Nankuanli East, for comparison with mandibular samples from Taiwan, East Asia, Southeast Asia, and the Pacific. These comparisons provide a basis for assessing the biological relationships and population history of Taiwan and their relationship to the surrounding regions, and whether Taiwan's earliest inhabitants are the ancestors of the earliest inhabitants of Remote Oceania, including Polynesia.

BIOLOGICAL DISTANCE STUDIES

The reconstruction of population history, including ancestry determination, has played a central role in physical anthropology since its inception. While earlier attempts to understand human variation and biological relationships among human groups was flawed and mired in typological racial classification, advances in evolutionary theory, population genetics, and quantitative methods beginning in the mid-20th century have put biological distance (or biodistance) studies on a more sound foundation (see Chapter 1, this volume). The demonstrated correlation between phenotypic and genotypic similarities and the heritability component of phenotypic traits, such as cranial measurements, have further strengthened attempts to assess biological relatedness among past populations.

While some aspects of cranial morphology may be susceptible to climatic adaptation (see, eg, Hubbe et al., 2009), craniometric variation, on average, correlates with a neutral model of evolution (ie, genetic drift, gene flow, and mutation) rather than selection (eg, Betti et al., 2010; Harvati and Weaver, 2006; Relethford, 2004, 2009; Roseman, 2004; von Cramon-Taubadel, 2009). As such, craniometric data are now used as a proxy for genetic data, increasing the popularity of this category of variation in biodistance studies (von Cramon-Taubadel, 2009).

Because of their stronger correlation with neutral genetic data, bones of the cranium, such as the temporal bone, may be more reliable for reconstructing human population history than other bones of the skull (eg, Smith, 2011; von Cramon-Taubadel, 2009). However, while mandibular shape has been shown to reflect subsistence strategy rather than neutral genetic patterns, geometric morphometric studies demonstrate that even human mandibular shape exhibits considerable geographic patterning (Nicholson and Harvati, 2006; von Cramon-Taubadel, 2011). The mandible, because of its compactness, is often the only part of the skull that remains intact. In addition to the strong geographic patterning and selective neutrality of craniometric variation, the amenability of continuous variation to multivariate statistical analysis has insured the continued use of this category of variation in biodistance analyses.

MATERIAL AND METHODS

The Nankuanli East (南關里東) Site: Early Neolithic

The Nankuanli East (NKLE) site is located approximately 500 m east of the Nankuanli (南關里) (Nanguanli in Pinyin) site on the flood plains of Shanhua district, Tainan City, in southwestern Taiwan. The sites represent two of the oldest sites associated with the TPK culture excavated in the Tainan Science Park (TSP), which includes at least 80 sites that span the time period from approximately 5000 years BP to the first Han Chinese settlements beginning a few 100 years BP. Thus far, the skeletons of approximately 2000 individuals have been excavated from the TSP.

An estimated 82 extended supine burials were excavated at the NKLE site in 2002 and 2003. The NKLE burials were associated with polished stone adzes, pottery, ornaments, shell-bracelet funerary objects, and the remains of domesticated and wild animals. In addition to ceramic ware (ie, jars and bowls), the archaeological record includes the presence of foxtail millet (*Setaria italica* L.), dogs, deer, wild boars, fish, shellfish, reaping knives made of shell, fishing sinkers, ground adzes, and projectile points (Li, 2013; Tsang, 2005). Although terrestrial mammals, especially dog, deer, and wild boar, were important, fish represent the most abundant potential food source to the inhabitants of NKLE (Li, 2013).

Given the extensive postmortem damage due to 7–8 m of overlying sediment and the manner in which these burials were excavated, only 23 of the most complete and best-preserved adult skulls from the NKLE have been examined in detail (Pietrusewsky et al., 2013). Of these, only seven complete, or nearly complete, male mandibles were available for this study.

Shihsanhang Site, Northwestern Taiwan: Iron Age

The Shihsanhang (SSH) is an Iron Age site located on the northwestern coast of Taiwan. More than 200 well-preserved human skeletons, many in the flexed position, were excavated from the SSH site, which dates from approximately 1800–500 years BP (Tsang, 2000). Ten of the most complete and best-preserved male mandibles are used in the present analysis.

Comparative Skeletal Assemblages

The comparative mandibular samples (Table 24.1) used in this analysis include a Late Lapita (c.2750–2500 BP) sample of mandibles from the Reber-Rakival (SAC) site on Watom Island, located off the northern coast of New Britain in the Bismarck Archipelago, Papua New Guinea. The remaining samples include modern or near modern mandibles from Polynesia, Micronesia, Melanesia, Southeast Asia, and East Asia. The approximate location of these series and those from Taiwan are shown in the map (Fig. 24.1).

Mandible Measurements and Multivariate Statistics

In this analysis two multivariate statistical procedures, stepwise discriminant function (canonical) analysis and Mahalanobis' generalized distance, are applied to nine mandibular measurements (Table 24.2) recorded in 22 samples from East Asia, Southeast Asia, and the Pacific. This was the largest number of measurements common to the series.

Table 24.1 Male Mandibular Samples

Name (Abbrev.)	Sample Size	Location and Year Examined[a]	Remarks
1. Nankuanli East (NKLE)	7	TSP-2008	Burial nos. F3B3, E4B4, E3B2, D3B2, F5B26, F5B27, and F5B40.
2. Shihsanhang (SSH)	10	TPE-2000	Burial nos. BM18, BM72, BM76, CM1, CM11, CM40, EM17, HM36, HM41, and HM47.
3. Watom Island, New Britain, Papua New Guinea (WAT)	5	DUN-1987/ 2012	Five of the most complete mandibles from the SAC site on Watom Island, East New Britain Province, Papua New Guinea: Cat. nos. 3, 6, 8, 15, and M2.
4. New Zealand(NZ)	15	DUN-1984	The majority of the skulls in this sample were collected in the late 19th century from known locations in the Otago region of the South Island of New Zealand. The following Cat. nos. are included: B68, B139, B151, B168, B173, B174, B214, B342, B399, E21, E23, E41, E72, 202, and 319.
5. Tonga—Samoa (TOG)	7	BPB-1992	This series includes 5 Tongan skulls (Cat. nos. 430, 431, 433, 436, 440) excavated by W. C. McKern during excavations on Tongatapu Island in 1920—21 as part of the Bayard-Dominick Expedition to Polynesia for the B. P. Bishop Museum. One more mandible from Tongatapu was examined in the B. P. Bishop Museum (Cat. no. 2930). One mandible is from Samoa (Cat. no. 2946).
6. Hawaiian Islands (HAW)	15	SIM-1990	The skulls were collected from Kauai Island. All specimens are presumed to be prehistoric.
7. Marquesas Islands (MRQ)	8	BPB-1992	All mandibles are from the island of Ua Huka in the northern group, six are from the Hane Dune site (Cat. nos. 2843, 2845, 2848, 2851, 2896, 2897) and the origin of two more (Cat. nos. 355 and 358) is identified as Ua Huka.
8. Society Islands (SOC)	11	BPB-1992	Mandibles are from Tahiti Island (Cat. nos. 927, 940A, 940B, 940C, 940D); Moorea Island (Cat. nos. 924 and M5-3-Sk-4-4); Maupiti Island (Cat. no. 2829); Bora Bora Island (Cat. no. 3183A), and Society Islands (Cat. nos. 219 and 220).
9. Pohnpei (Ponape) (PON)	9	TKO-1988	Eight burials are from Ponape (Cat. nos. 2512—2526: 1, 2, 3, 4, 10, 12, 14, 15) and one is from Malem, Kosrae.
10. Northern Mariana Islands (MAR)	10	BPB-1987	Five skulls are from the House of Taga site on Tinian excavated by H. G. Hornbostel in 1925 (Cat. nos. 874, 875, 878A, 881, 907); three more, also attributed to Hornbostel, are associated with latte structures on Tinian (Cat. nos. 879, 889, and 905); two skulls are from Saipan (Cat. nos. 890 and 904).

Table 24.1 Male Mandibular Samples—Continued

Name (Abbrev.)	Sample Size	Location and Year Examined[a]	Remarks
11. Sigatoka, Fiji (SIG)	15	DUN-1992	The burials from the Sigatoka sand dune site VL 16/1 on Viti Levu, Fiji, are generally assumed to belong to the Navatu phase (level 2) that dates from 1700 to 1300 calBP (Anderson et al., 2006, pp. 146–147). Measurements were recorded in the some of the most complete mandibles from this site: Cat. nos. 4C, 1/1, 1A, 1B, 1C, 2A, 10A, 10B, 10C, 13A, 16, 17A, 17B, 19, and 20.
12. Namu, Taumako Island, (Duff Island), Santa Cruz, Solomon Islands (NAM)	16	DUN-1984	The burials are from the Namu site on Taumako Island, an island in the Duff (Taumako) Islands of the Santa Cruz Islands in Temotu Province of Solomon Islands. Human bone radiocarbon dates indicate the Namu burials range between 200 and 800 calBP (Leach and Davidson, 2008, p. 146). Measurements were recorded in 16 mandibles for burial nos.: 1, 13, 21, 34, 36, 73, 104, 126, 155, 164, 169, 179, 183, 184, 185, and 198.
13. Vietnam (VTN)	15	HCM-1989	Eight skulls are from north Vietnam (most are coffin burials from the Van Dien Cemetery approximately 10 km from Hanoi) and seven come from dissecting room collection in Ho Chi Minh City in the south.
14. Thailand (THI)	15	SIR-1989	The skeletons are identified as male Thai whose corpses were donated to the Department of Anatomy of the Siriraj Hospital for teaching purposes. The age at death is known for these skeletons.
15. Kanto (KAN)	15	CHB-1990	A dissecting room sample of modern Japanese from the Kanto district of eastern Honshu Island. The majority of the individuals in this collection were born during the Meiji period (1868–1911) and died well before 1940.
16. Ryukyu Islands (RYU)	9	KYO-1990	Cat. nos. 991, 994, 130, 995, 996, 997, 060, 258, 285.
17. Manchuria (MAN)	15	TKO-1990	The skulls in this sample are from northeastern China, a region formerly referred to as Manchuria, which today includes Heilongjiang and Jilin Provinces and adjacent northern Korea. Many of the crania were identified as soldiers or cavalrymen who died in battle in the late 19th century.
18. Hong Kong (HK)	15	HKU-1988	The skulls are from skeletons of known individuals who died in Hong Kong between 1978 and 1979 that were exhumed from the Wo Hop Sek cemetery in Hong Kong and donated to the Prince Philip Dental Hospital. The majority of individuals in this sample, who were unclaimed after exhumation, are from southern China (Guangdong and Fujian provinces).

Continued

Table 24.1 Male Mandibular Samples—Continued

Name (Abbrev.)	Sample Size	Location and Year Examined[a]	Remarks
19. Shanghai, China (SHA)	15	SHA-1988; CGQ-1988	The skulls in the collections of Fudan University are mostly from post-Qing cemeteries in Shanghai. The skulls in Chongqing are from unmarked graves encountered during the construction of the Shanghai Airport in 1949–50. The latter are presumed to represent individuals who were buried in a pauper's cemetery.
20. Korea (KOR)	14	TKO-1990 KYO-1990 KYU-1990 SEN-1990	Exact location of the skulls from Korea is unknown; some may be from dissecting room collections while others are from excavations in Korea.
21. Mongolia (MOG)	15	SIM-1990	The skulls, purchased by Aleš Hrdlička on a trip to Mongolia and Siberia in 1912, are from Ulaanbaatar (Urga), Mongolia (Hrdlička, 1924).
22. Siberia (SIB)	12	SIM-1990	Buriat skulls, purchased by Aleš Hrdlička while on a trip to Mongolia and Siberia in 1912 (Hrdlička, 1924).

[a]BPB, *B. P. Bishop Museum, Honolulu, US;* CGQ, *Anatomy Department, Chongqing Medical University, Chongqing, People's Republic of China;* CHB, *Chiba University School of Medicine, Chiba, Japan;* DUN, *Department of Anatomy, University of Otago, Dunedin, New Zealand;* HCM, *Faculty of Medicine, Ho Chi Minh City, Vietnam;* HKU, *Prince Philip Dental Hospital, University of Hong Kong, Hong Kong;* KYU, *Department of Anatomy, Faculty of Medicine, Kyushu University, Fukuoka, Japan;* KYO, *Physical Anthropology Laboratory, Faculty of Science, Kyoto University, Kyoto, Japan;* SEN, *Department of Anatomy, School of Medicine, Tohoku University, Sendai, Japan;* SHA, *Institute of Anthropology, College of Life Sciences, Fudan University, Shanghai, People's Republic of China;* SIM, *National Museum of Natural History, Smithsonian Institution, Washington, DC, USA;* SIR, *Department of Anatomy, Siriraj Hospital, Bangkok, Thailand;* TKO, *University Museum, University of Tokyo, Tokyo, Japan;* TPE, *Institute of History and Philology, Academia Sinica, Taipei, Taiwan, Republic of China;* TSP, *Tainan Science Park, Tainan, Taiwan, Republic of China.*

The major purpose of discriminant function, or canonical analysis is to maximize differences between groups by producing weighted variables, referred to as discriminant functions or canonical variates (Pietrusewsky, 2008). Typically, the first few functions, or canonical variates, account for most of the variation present. The computer program, BMDP-7M (Dixon, 1992) was used to perform the stepwise discriminant function analysis selecting those measurements that contribute the most to the separation of the groups in advance of the remaining variables (Dixon, 1992). At the end of the stepping process, each individual is classified into one of the original groups based on the discriminant scores it receives through the calculation of posterior (regular classification) and/or typicality (jackknifed classification) probabilities. The correct and incorrect classification results allow an assessment of the homogeneity or heterogeneity of the original series. The computer program, NTSYS-pc (Rohlf, 1993) was used to generate the plots of the group means, or centroids, on the first few canonical variates, for a visualization of group relationships.

Mahalanobis generalized distance provides a single quantitative measure of dissimilarity (distance) between individual groups using multiple variables while taking into account the intercorrelation between the variables (Mahalanobis, 1936). The computer program, NTSYS-pc (Rohlf, 1993), was used to

FIGURE 24.1

Map showing the approximate locations of 22 samples used in this study.

generate the dendrogram using the Unweighted Pair Group Method Algorithm (UPGMA). Further explanation of these methods is given in Pietrusewsky (2008, 2014).

RESULTS

Stepwise Discriminant Function Analysis

Applying stepwise discriminant function analysis to nine measurements recorded in 267 male mandibles indicates that mandibular length, bigonial breadth, and bicanine breadth contribute most to the discrimination in this analysis.

Eigenvalues (values not shown), which represent the amount of variance accounted for by each function or variate, expressed as the percentage of total dispersion, provide an indication of the proportion of dispersion accounted for by each canonical variate. In this analysis, the first three canonical variates

Table 24.2 Mandibular Measurements Used in the Present Study[a]
Mandibular length (O) (Olivier, 1969)
Bigonial breadth (M-66)(Martin and Saller, 1957)
Bicanine breadth (T-CEB) (Trinkaus, 1978)
Symphyseal height (M-69)
Mental foramen height [M-69(1)]
Symphyseal breadth (O)
Mental foramen breadth [M-69(3)]
Ramus breadth (M-71)
Molar 1 to molar 2 length (S-32) (Stewart, 1979)

[a]*Definitions of the measurements:* M, *Martin and Saller (1957);* O, *Olivier (1969);* S, *Stewart (1979); and* T, *Trinkaus (1978). The numeric and alphabetical abbreviations (in parentheses), if available, follow those used by the authors.*

account for 70% of the total variation. The first five eigenvalues are significant at the 1% level, indicating significant heterogeneity for these canonical variates.

The jackknifed classification results (not shown) indicate that the Namu, Watom Island, New Zealand, and Sigatoka are among the series with the best classification results, with more than 45% of the cases correctly assigned to their original group. None of the seven mandibles from NKLE is correctly classified; two are reclassified as Korea and one each is classified as Pohnpei, Namu, Ryukyu, Kanto, and Siberia. The majority of the misclassifications of NKLE are to Asian mandibular series. Overall, six mandibles from Asia and two from Micronesia are reclassified as NKLE. Surprisingly, four of the SSH mandibles are reclassified to Hawaii, two are assigned to New Zealand, and one each to Northern Mariana and Namu series representing the Pacific Islands. Three of the Late Lapita mandibles from Watom are correctly classified to Watom and the remaining two are reclassified to the Northern Marianas.

Some general associations emerge when the group means are plotted on the first two canonical variates (Fig. 24.2). With the exception of New Zealand Maori, the Polynesian series form a loose cluster with the Northern Marianas mandibular series in this diagram. NKLE clusters with the series from East and Southeast Asia while Shihsanhang is closest to Pohnpei, a series from Micronesia. NKLE is closest to Mongolia, Siberia, and the Ryukyu Island mandibular series. Shihsanhang is moderately close to Pohnpei. The Late Lapita mandibular series from Watom Island (New Britain), Namu (in eastern Solomon Islands), and New Zealand occupy marginal positions in this plot.

When the group means are plotted on the first three canonical variates (Fig. 24.3), NKLE again is closest to the mandibular series from Siberia, Manchuria, Hong Kong, and Mongolia. Shihsanhang, Shanghai, and the Northern Marianas form a relatively tight association. Again, Watom, Namu, and New Zealand occupy marginal positions in this plot.

Mahalanobis' Generalized Distance

Applying the UPGMA clustering algorithm to the distances for 22 groups results in the dendrogram shown in Fig. 24.4. A major clustering of the mandibular series from North, East, and Southeast Asia, including Neolithic and Iron Age series from Taiwan, is evident in this diagram of relationship. NKLE

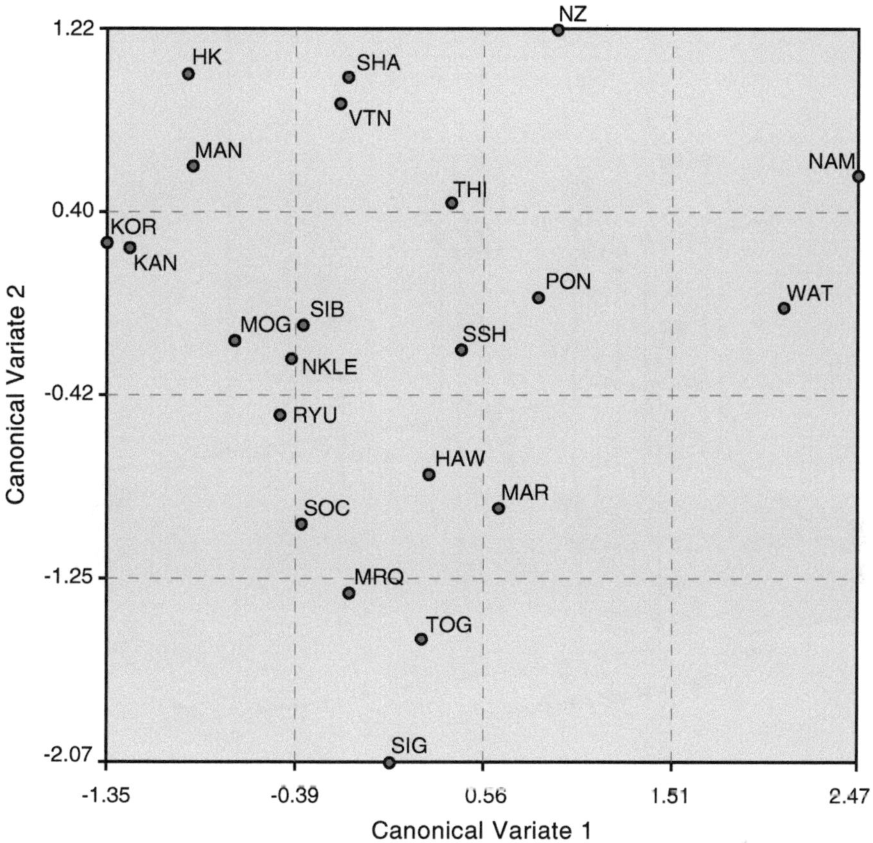

FIGURE 24.2

Plot of 22 group means on the first two canonical variates resulting from the application of stepwise discriminant function analysis to nine mandibular measurements. Abbreviations of the cranial samples are explained in Table 24.1.

clusters with the Ryukyu Islands. Shihsanhang clusters closely with the series from Mongolia (East Central Asia) and Siberia (North Asia). The remaining series, representing the Pacific, fall well outside this major Asiatic constellation. The late Lapita mandibular series from Watom Island loosely clusters with two other peripheral series, New Zealand and Namu.

An examination of the distances (table not shown) provides information on biological relatedness not immediately apparent in the dendrogram. Using smaller distances as measures of greater similarity, the groups from eastern and northern Asia are most similar to NKLE. Siberia and Mongolia, followed by Hawaii and Thailand, are most similar to the SSH series. Although the distances are relatively large, further inspection reveals that Northern Mariana Islands and Pohnpei, two series from Micronesia, are closest to NKLE and SSH. The distances involving Watom Island, Namu, and New Zealand are some of the largest, underscoring the relatively dissimilarity of these series. Watom and New Zealand are closest to the Taiwan Iron Age series from SSH.

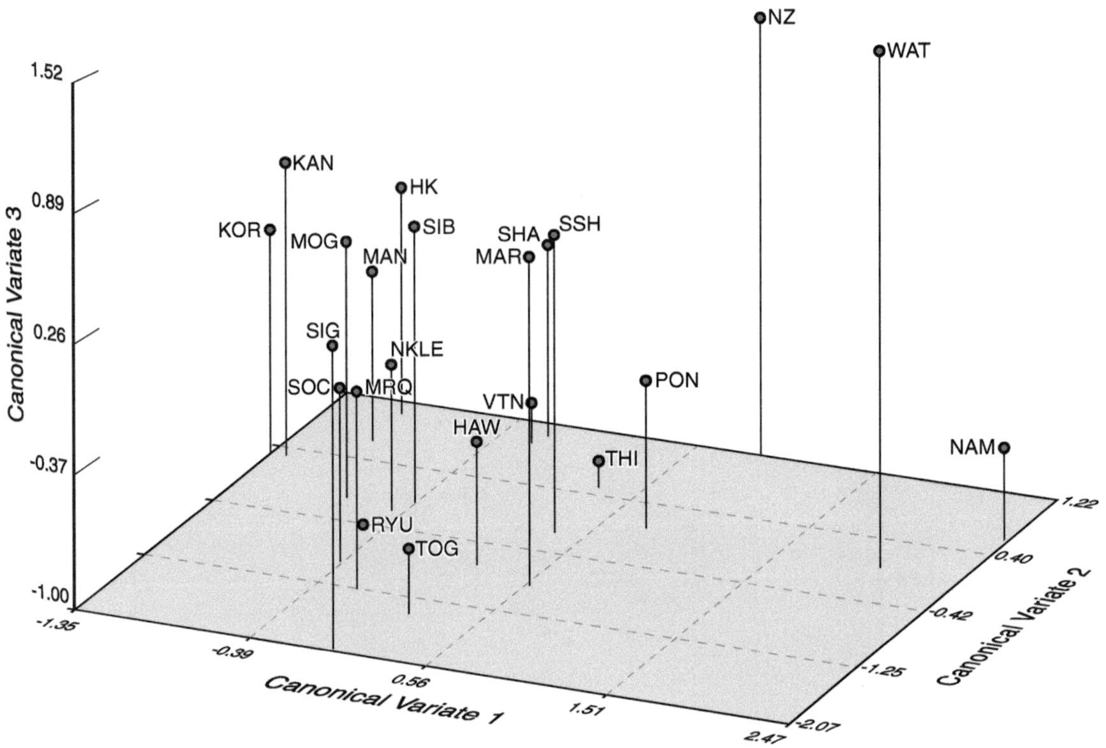

FIGURE 24.3

Plot of 22 group means on the first three canonical variates resulting from the application of stepwise discriminant function analysis to nine mandibular measurements. Abbreviations of the cranial samples are explained in Table 24.1.

DISCUSSION

Earlier biodistance studies that utilize craniometric data from Taiwan (eg, Pietrusewsky, 1995, 2008) were restricted to a single Indigenous Taiwanese group, the Atayal. These previous multivariate analyses indicated that the Atayal were not related to any of the Pacific series, including those from Polynesia. Rather, the Atayal demonstrated affinities with several of the series from East and North Asia (eg, Korea, Japan, China, Taiwan), suggesting possible admixture. Another analysis of craniometric data (Pietrusewsky and Chang, 2003) indicated that recent Indigenous Taiwanese groups (Atayal, Bunun, Babuza, Pazeh), while being related to East/North Asian and Southeast Asian series, were among the most differentiated groups, a finding echoed in most genetic studies. In the same study, only Iron Age Shihsanhang showed a relationship, albeit not strong, with cranial series from Polynesia and Guam.

In this study, results of stepwise discriminant function analysis of mandibular measurements, suggest Neolithic Taiwan (NKLE) is more closely related to groups from northern and eastern Asia than Southeast Asia and the Pacific. Inspection of the distances reiterates these associations and further indicates a close relationship with the Ryukyu Islands, an island group to the northeast of Taiwan.

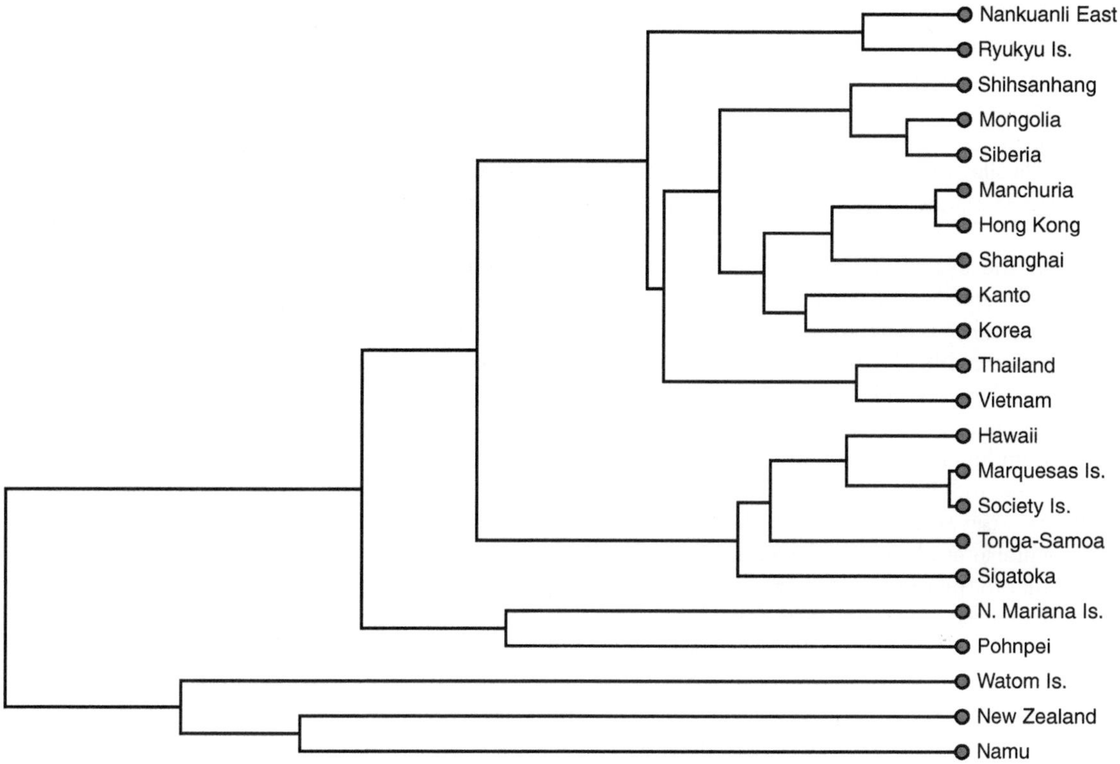

FIGURE 24.4

Dendrogram resulting from applying the UPGMA clustering algorithm to Mahalanobis' distances using nine mandibular measurements recorded in 22 male groups.

Inspection of the smallest distances indicates that two groups from Micronesia (Northern Mariana Islands and Pohnpei) are more similar to NKLE than to any other group included in this analysis. Unfortunately, with the exception of the SSH series, no mandibles were available for Atayal or any other Indigenous Taiwanese group in the present analysis.

Shihsanhang's relationship in the present analysis, based on mandible measurements, remains somewhat equivocal. Inspection of the jackknifed classification results and canonical plots indicates relatively close connections with several Polynesian (Hawaii and New Zealand) and the two Micronesian series. However, the results of distance analysis reveal Shihsanhang is closest to Siberia and Mongolia from northern Asia, while inspection of the smallest distances indicates Hawaii and New Zealand, two series from Polynesia, are among the groups closest to the Iron Age series from Taiwan.

The early Neolithic and later Iron Age series from Taiwan, separated by nearly 4500 years, are not closely related to each other. Mongolia and Shanghai are the closest to NKLE and SSH. While the groups closest to NKLE are from the Ryukyu Islands and Asian mainland, the groups closest to SSH include these and groups from Southeast Asia and the Pacific, suggesting wider contact with surrounding groups in the later time period.

A biodistance analysis of mandibles (Pietrusewsky et al., 2014) suggested the skeletons from the Lapita burial ground on Watom Island in New Britain Province, Papua New Guinea, were phenotypically more similar to other series from western Remote Oceania (eg, Vanuatu, Loyalty Islands, New Caledonia) than they were to Polynesians. In the present analysis, Watom, New Zealand, and Namu are among the most differentiated groups investigated. Watom is moderately close to New Zealand and Namu. In the jack-knifed classification results, two of the mandibles originally assigned to Watom were reclassified as Northern Marianas. Overall, the Watom series is unrelated to early Neolithic or Iron Age mandibles from Taiwan.

With the exception of New Zealand, the series representative of Polynesia (Hawaii, Marquesas, Society, Tonga—Samoa) and Fiji (Sigatoka) are most closely related to other Polynesian and Fijian series. This relationship is most apparent in the diagram of distances. However, some of the smallest distances are those between NKLE and series from Micronesia and Polynesia, implying some degree of biological relatedness between these groups.

Although not unequivocal (see, eg, Soares et al., 2011), and despite various degrees of admixture from the surrounding regions, genetic studies of living peoples generally support the Out of Taiwan model that depicts the indigenous Taiwanese as the ancestors of Polynesians and other inhabitants of Island Southeast Asia and Oceania (Friedlaender et al., 2008; Ko et al., 2014; Lipson et al., 2014; Melton et al., 1998; Mirabal et al., 2013; Trejaut et al., 2005; Zeng et al., 2014).

Similar to the results of genetic studies, the Neolithic Taiwanese in the present analysis are among the most differentiated groups, suggesting high levels of isolation, endemism, and/or drift. Unlike the genetic evidence, however, there is little support for the Neolithic farming/language dispersal model given the lack of close biological relatedness between Neolithic Taiwan, Polynesia, or Late Lapita-associated mandibles from Watom Island in the Bismarck Archipelago. However, by the Iron Age, connections between Taiwan and Pacific are more apparent, although the inhabitants of the Late Lapita site on Watom Island in the Bismarck Archipelago and the first settlers of Remote Oceania postdate the Iron Age site on Taiwan.

CONCLUSIONS

While the sample sizes for NKLE and Shihsanhang are small, this new biological distance analysis allows a few tentative conclusions regarding biological relationships of the earliest Neolithic skeletons and the origins of Polynesians.

- The Neolithic NKLE mandibles are closest to Ryukyu Islands, and other mandibular series from East and North Asia. There is no evidence in this analysis of a biological relationship between the earliest Neolithic inhabitants of Taiwan, Pacific Islanders, or Polynesians.
- The mandibles associated with the Iron Age Shihsanhang series, while generally related to Northern Asian series (eg, Siberia, Mongolia), also show connections with some of the Pacific Island series (eg, Hawaii, New Zealand, and the Northern Marianas Islands).
- Neolithic and Iron Age Taiwanese are more closely related to several North Asian groups than they are to each other.
- In addition to New Zealand (Polynesia) and Namu (eastern Solomon Islands), the Late Lapita series from Watom Island is one of the most biologically differentiated groups in these comparisons.
- The earliest Neolithic inhabitants of Taiwan are not the ancestors of Polynesians.

In addition to small sample sizes, this study is complicated by the absence of several key groups such as modern Indigenous Taiwanese, and more mandibular series from geographical Melanesia and Island Southeast Asia are needed. Augmentation of the existing samples and additional series from Pacific and Asia will improve our understanding of Taiwan's role in understanding the origins of Polynesians.

Acknowledgments

We gratefully acknowledge Mr. Marween Yagin, Instructional Resource Center of the University of Hawai'i-Manoa, for his assistance with the figures that accompany this paper. Ms. I-Ping Chan, Ms. Yu-hsuan Tseng, Ms. Ivy Yeh, and Mr. Albert Liu assisted with the study of the Nankuanli East skeletons in July 2008. The National Science Council of the Republic of China supported this research.

Endnote

1. International Archaeological Research Institute, Inc. Honolulu, HI, United States

References

Anderson, A., Roberts, R., Dickinson, W., Clark, G., Burley, D., de Biran, A., Hope, G., Nunn, P., 2006. Times of sand: sedimentary history and archaeology at the Sigatoka dunes. Fiji. Geoarchaeology 21 (2), 131–154.

Barker, G., Richards, M.B., 2013. Foraging-farming transitions in Island Southeast Asia. Journal of Archaeological Method and Theory 20, 256–280.

Bellwood, P., 2005. First Farmers: The Origins of Agricultural Societies. Blackwell Publishing, Malden, Massachusetts.

Betti, L., Balloux, F., Hanihara, T., Manica, A., 2010. The relative role of drift and selection in shaping the human skull. American Journal of Physical Anthropology 141 (1), 76–82.

Chang, K.C., Goodenough, W.H., 1996. Archaeology of southeastern coastal China and its bearing on the Austronesian homeland. In: Goodenough, W.H. (Ed.), Prehistoric Settlement of the Pacific. Transactions of the American Philosophical Society, New Series, vol. 86 (5). American Philosophical Society, Philadelphia, pp. 36–56.

Chang, K.C., 1995. Taiwan Strait archaeology and proto-Austronesian. In: Li, P.J.-K., Tsang, C.-H., Huang, Y.-K., Ho, D.A., Tseng, C.-Y. (Eds.), Austronesian Studies Relating to Taiwan. Symposium Series of the Institute of History and Philology, No. 3. Academia Sinica, Taipei, Taiwan, pp. 161–183.

Dixon, W.J., 1992. Version 7.0 Manual. BMDP Statistical Software, vols. 1 and 2. University of Cailfornia Press, Berkeley, CA.

Friedlaender, J.S., Friedlaender, F.R., Reed, F.A., Kidd, K.K., Kidd, J.R., Chambers, G.K., Lea, R.A., Loo, J.-H., Koki, G., Hodgson, J.A., 2008. Correction: the genetic structure of Pacific Islanders. PLoS Genetics 4 (3). http://dx.doi.org/10.1371/annotation/cbdd1311a1370-1374a1329-1374e1377c-1379e1374e-c1300a1184c7777.

Harvati, K., Weaver, T.D., 2006. Human cranial anatomy and the differential preservation of population history and climate signatures. The Anatomical Record Part A: Discoveries in Molecular, Cellular, and Evolutionary Biology 288 (12), 1225–1233.

Hrdlička, A., 1924. Catalogue of human crania in the United States National Museum collections. The Eskimo, Alaska and related Indians, northeastern Asiatics. In: Proceedings of the United States National Museum, 63. Smithsonian Institution, Washington, DC.

Hubbe, M., Hanihara, T., Harvati, K., 2009. Climate signatures in the morphological differentiation of worldwide modern human populations. The Anatomical Record 292 (11), 1720–1733.

Hung, H.C., Carson, M.T., 2014. Foragers, fishers and farmers: origins of the Taiwanese Neolithic. Antiquity 88 (342), 1115–1131.

Jiao, T., 2007. The Neolithic of Southeast China: Cultural Transformation and Regional Interaction on the Coast. Cambria Press, Youngstown, New York.

Ko, A.M.S., Chen, C.-Y., Fu, Q., Delfin, F., Li, M., Chiu, H.L., Stoneking, M., Ko, Y.C., 2014. Early Austronesians: into and out of Taiwan. American Journal of Human Genetics 94 (3), 426–436.

Leach, F., Davidson, J., 2008. The Archaeology of Taumako: A Polynesian Outlier in the Eastern Solomon Islands. Dunedin, New Zealand Journal of Archaeology Special Publication.

Li, K.-T., 2013. First farmers and their coastal adaptation in prehistoric Taiwan. In: Underhill, A.P. (Ed.), A Companion to Chinese Archaeology. Blackwell Publishing, Ltd., Oxford, pp. 612–633.

Lipson, M., Loh, P.R., Patterson, N., Moorjani, P., Ko, Y.C., Stoneking, M., Berger, B., Reich, D., 2014. Reconstructing Austronesian population history in Island Southeast Asia. Nature Communications 5 (5), 4689. http://dx.doi.org/10.1038/ncomms5689.

Mahalanobis, P.C., 1936. On the generalized distance in statistics. Proceedings of the National Institute of Science, India 2, 49–55.

Martin, R., Saller, K., 1957. Lehrbuch der Anthropologie. Gustav Fischer Verlag, Stuttgart.

Melton, T., Clifford, S., Martinson, J., Batzer, M., Stoneking, M., 1998. Genetic evidence for the proto-Austronesian homeland in Asia: mtDNA and nuclear DNA variation in Taiwanese aboriginal tribes. American Journal of Human Genetics 63 (6), 1807–1823.

Mirabal, S., Cadenas, A.M., Garcia-Bertrand, R., Herrera, R.J., 2013. Ascertaining the role of Taiwan as a source for the Austronesian expansion. American Journal of Physical Anthropology 150 (4), 551–564.

Nicholson, E., Harvati, K., 2006. Quantitative analysis of human mandibular shape using three-dimensional geometric morphometrics. American Journal of Physical Anthropology 131 (3), 368–383.

Olivier, G., 1969. In: Thomas, Charles C. (Ed.), Practical Anthropology. Springfield.

Pietrusewsky, M., Chang, C.-F., 2003. Taiwan Aboriginals and peoples of the Pacific-Asia region: multivariate craniometric comparisons. Anthropological Science 111 (3), 293–332.

Pietrusewsky, M., Lauer, A., Tsang, C.-H., Li, K.-T., Douglas, M.T., 2013. Dental indicators of health in early Neolithic and Iron Age skeletons from Taiwan. Journal of Austronesian Studies 4 (2), 1–33.

Pietrusewsky, M., Buckley, H., Anson, D., Douglas, M.T., 2014. Polynesian origins: a biodistance study of mandibles from the Late Lapita site of Reber-Rakival (SAC), Watom Island, Bismarck Archipelago. Journal of Pacific Archaeology 5 (1), 1–20.

Pietrusewsky, M., 1995. Taiwan Aboriginals, Asians, and Pacific Islanders: A Multivariate Investigation of Skulls. Austronesian Studies Relating to Taiwan. Taipei: Symposium Series of the Institute of History and Philology, vol. 3, pp. 487–532.

Pietrusewsky, M., 2008. Metric analysis of skeletal remains: methods and applications. In: Katzenberg, M.A., Saunders, S.R. (Eds.), Biological Anthropology of the Human Skeleton, second ed. John Wiley and Sons, Inc., New York, pp. 487–532.

Pietrusewsky, M., 2014. Biological distance in bioarchaeology and human osteology. In: Smith, C. (Ed.), Encyclopedia of Global Archaeology. Springer, New York, pp. 889–902.

Relethford, J.H., 2004. Global patterns of isolation by distance based on genetic and morphological data. Human Biology 76 (4), 499–513.

Relethford, J.H., 2009. Race and global patterns of phenotypic variation. American Journal of Physical Anthropology 139, 16–22.

Rohlf, F.J., 1993. NTSYS-pc. Numerical Taxonomy and Multivariate Analysis System. Version 1.80. Setauket. Exeter Software, New York.

Roseman, C.C., 2004. Detecting interregionally diversifying natural selection on modern human cranial form by using matched molecular and morphometric data. Proceedings of the National Academy of Sciences of the United States of America 101 (35), 12824–12829.

Smith, H.F., 2011. The role of genetic drift in shaping modern human cranial evolution: a test using microevolutionary modeling. International Journal of Evolutionary Biology 2011. http://dx.doi.org/10.4061/2011/14526.

Soares, P., Rito, T., Trejaut, J., Mormina, M., Hill, C., Tinkler-Hundal, E., Braid, M., Clarke, D.J., Loo, J.-H., Thomson, N., 2011. Ancient voyaging and Polynesian origins. American Journal of Human Genetics 88 (2), 239–247.

Stewart, T.D., 1979. In: Thomas, Charles C. (Ed.), Essentials of Forensic Anthropology. Springfield.

Trejaut, J.A., Kivisild, T., Loo, J.H., Lee, C.L., He, C.L., Hsu, C.J., Li, Z.Y., Lin, M., 2005. Traces of archaic mitochondrial lineages persist in Austronesian-speaking Formosan populations. PLoS Biology 3, e247.

Trinkaus, E., 1978. Human Skeletal Measurements. Department of Anthropology. Peabody Museum, Harvard University, Cambridge, MA.

Tsang, C.-H., 2000. Recent advances in the Iron Age archaeology of Taiwan. Bulletin of the Indo-Pacific Prehistory Association 20, 153–158.

Tsang, C.-H., 2005. Recent discoveries at the Tapenkeng culture sites in Taiwan – implications for the problem of Austronesian origins. In: Sagart, L., Blench, R., Sanchez-Mazas, A. (Eds.), The Peopling of East Asia: Putting Together Archaeology, Linguistics, and Genetics. Routledge, London, pp. 63–71.

Tsang, C.-H., 2010. Neolithic interaction across the Taiwan Strait – implications for the issue of Austronesian origins and dispersal. In: Gadu, M., Lin, H. (Eds.), 2009 International Symposium on Austronesian Studies. National Museum of Prehistory, Taitung, Taiwan, pp. 1–10.

von Cramon-Taubadel, N., 2009. Congruence of individual cranial bone morphology and neutral molecular affinity patterns in modern humans. American Journal of Physical Anthropology 140 (2), 205–215.

von Cramon-Taubadel, N., 2011. Global human mandibular variation reflects differences in agricultural and hunter-gatherer subsistence strategies. Proceedings of the National Academy of Sciences of the United States of America 108 (49), 19546–19551.

Zeng, Z., Rowold, D.J., Garcia-Bertrand, R., Calderon, S., Regueiro, M., Li, L., Zhong, M., Herrera, R.J., 2014. Taiwanese aborigines: genetic heterogeneity and paternal contribution to Oceania. Gene 542 (2), 240–247.

CHAPTER

The Biocultural Evolution in the Osmore Valley: Morphological Dental Traits in Pre-Inca Populations

25

A. Cucina[1,2], C. Arganini[3], A. Coppa[4,5], F. Candilio[4,6]

Universidad Autónoma de Yucatán, Mérida, Yucatán, Mexico[1]; UC-MEXUS, University of California Riverside, Riverside, CA, United States[2]; Council for Agricultural Research and Economics, Research Center on Food and Nutrition (CRA-NUT), Rome, Italy[3]; "Sapienza" University of Rome, Rome, Italy[4]; MNHN, Paris, France[5]; University of Pennsylvania Museum of Archaeology and Anthropology, Philadelphia, PA, United States[6]

CHAPTER OUTLINE HEAD

Introduction 463
Materials and Methods 464
Results 466
Discussion 473
Acknowledgments 475
References 475

INTRODUCTION

The Osmore (Moquegua) Valley, in the South Central Andes, has an extremely varied history of human occupation that goes back at least 12,000 years (Rice, 1989). The discovery, over the past decades, of a considerable number of Chinchorro, Tiwanaku, and Chiribaya mummies has triggered an extensive investigation of the cultural and genetic changes that took place in the valley in pre-Inca times (Blom, 2005; Blom et al., 1998; Lozada, 1998; Moraga et al., 2005; Sutter, 1997, 2000, 2005; Sutter and Mertz, 2004). These studies resulted in the formulation of different hypotheses that were aimed at accounting for the diversity and diffusion of the material culture throughout the region (Rostworowsky, 1977; Browman, 1980, 1984; Dillehay and Nuñez, 1988; Sutter, 2000). The most widely accepted hypothesis is the spread of ethnically diverse colonists from the Tiwanaku Empire, which occupied many areas of the Upper Osmore Valley, establishing permanent settlements like Chen Chen and Omo (Goldstein, 2013; Sutter and Sarrat, 2010). Archaeological evidence seems to indicate that the culturally and ethnically diverse Tiwanaku colonists had established relationships with the valley's indigenous populations (Goldstein, 2013). Conversely, the fewer Wari outposts in the valley, such as Cerro Baul (Nash and Williams, 2005; Williams, 2001), seem not to have instituted cultural relationships with their neighboring communities (Goldstein, 2013).

Biological Distance Analysis. http://dx.doi.org/10.1016/B978-0-12-801966-5.00025-1

To this day, most bioarchaeological research has focused on context-specific questions, like those applying to the Osmore or the Azapa Valleys (Blom, 2005; Blom et al., 1998; Sutter, 2000; Sutter and Mertz, 2004; Sutter and Sarrat, 2010), as well as the Wari region (Kemp et al., 2009; Knudson and Tung, 2011; Slovak et al., 2009; Tung and Knudson, 2011). However, much still must be understood regarding the different populations that inhabited the Osmore Valley and their interrelations and ties with the surrounding contemporaneous Andean populations (Rothhammer and Silva, 1989). More specifically, bioarchaeological research still needs to address several points: first, it must assess whether the expansion of Tiwanaku advanced to the coast; whether the Late Intermediate Chiribaya represented a continuity of the Tiwanaku or, instead, was part of a coastal tradition rather than an altiplanic one (Blom, 1999; Buikstra et al., 1998; Burgess, 1999; Lozada, 1998); and third, reconstruct the interaction between the two main polities attested to in the area during the Middle Horizon, the Wari and the Tiwanaku, an issue that has also been hampered by the paucity of Wari skeletal remains from the Osmore Valley.

The present chapter rests on the morphological analysis of human dental collections, dating from the Archaic (approximately 800 BC) to the Late Intermediate (AD 1100–1450) periods and unearthed in the Osmore Valley, as well as along the Central Coast and the South Central Highlands. It addresses the debates regarding continuity versus replacement, in situ biological change versus migration of pre-Inca societies within a wider regional and chronological frame.

MATERIALS AND METHODS

Dental morphology was analyzed on seven Peruvian samples that span chronologically from the Formative to the Late Intermediate periods and that geographically represent the Central and Southern Peruvian Andes (Table 25.1; Fig. 25.1). With the exception of the Late Intermediate Yaral and Chiribaya, whose data have been extrapolated from Sutter (1997), all the groups were studied directly by the authors, for a total number of 1005 individuals and 7287 permanent teeth (Table 25.2).

Dental traits were scored on all individuals' permanent teeth following the Arizona State University Dental Anthropology System (Turner et al., 1991). In those cases in which both antimeres were available, traits were scored on both left and right teeth. However, only the tooth showing the highest degree of expression was selected for further analysis given that it represents the highest genetic expression for that particular trait in the individual considered (Scott and Turner, 1997).

Seventy-nine morphological root and crown traits of the permanent dentition were initially recorded. Each trait was scored according to its own degree of expression; it was subsequently categorized into

Table 25.1 General Chart of the Pre-Inca Andean Cultures Included in the Present Study (Chronological Periods After Sutter and Mertz, 2004)

Geographical Location		Formative 1000 BC–AD 750	Middle Horizon AD 750–1100	Late Intermediate AD 1100–1450
South Central Coast (SCC)	Osmore Valley		Tiwanaku Wari	Chiribaya
South Central Highlands (SCH)			Tiwanaku	Altipiano Lake Kingdoms
Central Coast (CC)			Wari	Chancay
Central Highlands (CH)		Moche	Wari	

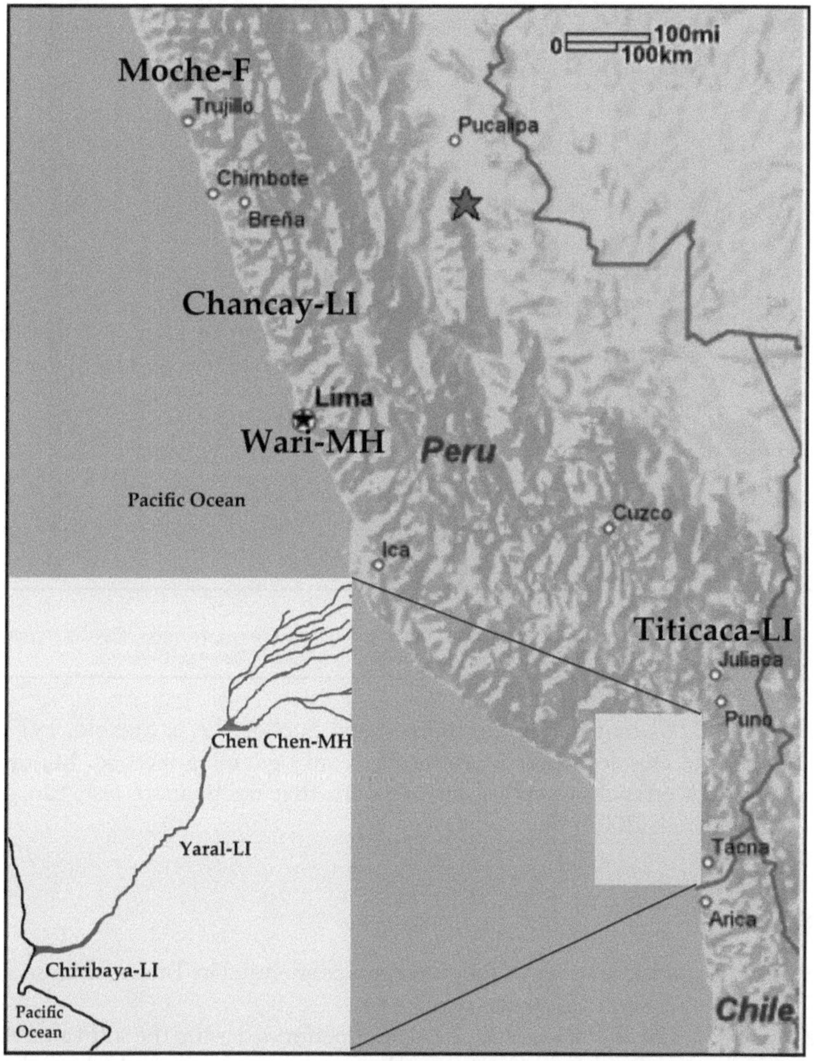

FIGURE 25.1

Overview of the geographic distribution of the samples.

presence/absence groups by selecting, for each trait, the breakpoint that best enabled the comparison with the data available in the literature (Tables 25.3a and b). Sexes were pooled given the absence of marked sexual dimorphism in the expression of dental morphological traits (Coppa et al., 1998, 2007; Scott, 1980). Statistical elaborations were then performed on 46 traits, out of the 79 initially scored, which were selected to match those published by Sutter (1997).

The biological affinities between samples were then evaluated by applying a principal component analysis (PCA), mean measure of divergence (MMD) with the Freeman-Tukey angular transformation for

Table 25.2 Samples Included in the Study and Number of Individuals and Teeth Analyzed

Samples[a]	Sites Analyzed	Individuals (N)	Teeth (N)
Moche-F (CH)	Sol y Luna	166	850
	Pasamayo		
	Paracas		
Chen Chen-MH (SCH)	Chen–Chen	119	1154
Wari-MH (CC)	Pachacamac	59	431
Chiribaya-LI[b] (SCC)	Chiribaya Alta	243	2140
	San Geronimo		
Yaral-LI[b] (SCH)	El Yaral	52	531
Titicaca-LI (SCH)	Molino Chilacachi	129	669
	Nunumarka		
	Salcedo		
	Rio llave46		
	Pucara Juli		
Chancay-LI (CC)	Ancon	237	1512
	Chancay		

[a]*See geographical abbreviations in Table 25.1.*
[b]*Morphological data from Sutter, R.C., 1997. Dental Variation and Biocultural Affinities among Prehistoric Populations from the Coastal Valleys of Moquegua, Perú, and Azapa, Chile (Ph.D. dissertation). University of Missouri-Columbia, Columbia.*

high (>0.95) or low (<0.05) trait frequencies (Green and Suchey, 1976; Sjøvold, 1977), multidimensional scaling (MDS), and cluster analysis (CA) using Ward's grouping method. Multiple quantitative techniques were used as a precaution, taking into account that multivariate tests can produce slightly different results (Coppa et al., 2007).

RESULTS

The frequencies observed for the 46 traits in the seven groups are listed in Tables 25.3a and b, respectively, for the upper (26 traits) and lower (20 traits) dentitions.

PCA (Hotelling, 1933; Cavalli Sforza et al., 1994) was performed using the software PAST 5. Fig. 25.2 shows the scatterplot extrapolated from the first and second components, which explains 63% of the overall variance (40.9% the first and 22.1% the second).

On the positive axis of the first component, Chen Chen gathers with its Wari coeval and the more ancient (Formative) Moche groups, alongside the Late Intermediate Chancay group. On the negative side of the component, we can appreciate all the Late Intermediate Chiribaya, Yaral, and Titicaca groups. The latter separates from the rest by lying on the uppermost positive side of the second component, while Chiribaya-LI gathers (along with the second component) with the Wari group.

The MMD was then employed to assess the pairwise morphological distances between the samples. This multivariate technique provides a quantitative estimate of biological divergence among samples based on the degree of phenetic similarity for all traits. The MMD statistic was performed on Excel based on Sjøvold's algorithm (1977) on dichotomized trait frequencies using the Freeman-Tukey transformation

Table 25.3a Sample Size and Frequencies of Traits Used for the Maxillary Dentition

Traits	Dichotomy		Chiribaya-LI	Yaral-LI	Titicaca-LI	Chancay-LI	Moche-F	Chen Chen-MH	Wari-MH
I2 Shoveling	0–7/3–7	%	60.5	71	0	66.7	100	100	100
		N	114	31	11	6	3	12	3
I1′ Double shoveling	0–6/2–6	%	72	72	8.3	88.9	75	100	100
		N	107	25	12	9	4	14	3
I2′ Double shoveling	0–6/2–6	%	69.2	56.2	36.4	85.7	100	100	80
		N	130	32	11	7	3	11	5
I2′ Interr. groove	0–1/1–1	%	47.8	56	0	60	60	87.5	83.3
		N	115	25	11	10	5	16	6
P3′ Cusp number	0–8/1–8	%	4.1	7.1	16.7	0	0	6.7	0
		N	97	28	12	19	12	30	10
P4′ Cusp number	0–8/1–8	%	3.3	7.7	0	0	0	7.1	0
		N	91	26	6	23	10	28	11
M1′ Metacone	0–5/4–5	%	98.2	100	100	98.3	100	90.6	100
		N	168	44	41	60	37	53	19
M2′ Metacone	0–5/3.5–5	%	91.2	84.6	97.7	92.9	87.8	84.4	90.9
		N	148	39	43	56	41	45	22
M3′ Metacone	0–5/3.5–5	%	82.8	79.4	64.3	82.6	86.4	82.4	90.9
		N	93	34	28	23	22	17	11
M1′ Hypocone	0–5/4–5	%	98.8	100	100	100	100	98.2	100
		N	164	44	29	56	39	55	18
M2′ Hypocone	0–5/3.5–5	%	73.2	78.9	87.5	71.7	82.1	90.5	57.9
		N	142	38	32	46	39	42	19
M3′ Hypocone	0–5/3.5–5	%	29.6	26.7	5.6	6.1	16.2	0	4.8
		N	115	30	18	49	37	53	21
M1′ Cusp 5	0–5/1–5	%	8.1	25.8	12.1	7.8	10	2.3	9.5
		N	124	31	33	51	40	43	21
M2′ Cusp 5	0–5/1–5	%	11.5	21.2	38.1	18.2	26.3	5.6	9.1
		N	87	33	21	22	19	18	11
M3′ Cusp 5	0–5/1–5	%	22.1	25	56.2	34.5	27.3	37.3	18.2
		N	149	40	16	29	22	51	11

Continued

Table 25.3a ***Sample Size and Frequencies of Traits Used for the Maxillary Dentition—Continued***

Traits	Dichotomy		Chiribaya-LI	Yaral-LI	Titicaca-LI	Chancay-LI	Moche-F	Chen Chen-MH	Wari-MH
M1′ Carabelli's cusp	0–7/2–7	%	2.1	2.7	4.8	6.5	10.3	7.5	0
		N	143	37	21	31	29	40	14
M2′ Carabelli's cusp	0–7/2–7	%	5.6	0	13	5.9	7.1	0	0
		N	90	33	23	17	14	18	9
M3′ Carabelli's cusp	0–7/2–7	%	5.6	11.6	3.3	6.7	28.6	4.1	9.1
		N	162	43	30	60	49	49	22
M1′ Parastyle	0–5/1–5	%	2.1	2.4	2.6	3.9	17.8	2.4	9.1
		N	143	41	38	51	45	42	22
M2′ Parastyle	0–5/1–5	%	5.6	2.9	19.2	10	17.6	17.6	10
		N	90	34	26	20	17	17	10
M3′ Parastyle	0–5/1–5	%	26.7	21.4	28.9	19.1	43.9	15.5	20.8
		N	150	42	45	68	41	58	24
P3′ Root number	1–3/1–1	%	47.4	43.2	70.6	26.8	48.8	35.7	29.2
		N	133	37	34	56	41	42	24
P4′ Root number	1–3/1–1	%	25	31	29.2	26.3	47.1	31.2	18.2
		N	84	29	24	19	17	16	11
M1′ Enamel extension	1–3/2–3	%	85.3	70	84.6	87.2	83.5	97.7	93.8
		N	163	40	52	86	91	86	32
M2′ Enamel extension	1–3/2–3	%	96.9	94.9	100	96.6	100	94	100
		N	159	39	41	87	83	84	40
M3′ Enamel extension	1–3/2–3	%	1.6	0	1.8	0	0	0	6.2
		N	126	36	55	41	21	12	16

Dichotomy shows the ASUDAS breaking points applied.

Table 25.3b *Sample Size and Frequencies of Traits Used for the Mandibular Dentition*

Traits	Dichotomy		Chiribaya-LI	Yaral-LI	Titicaca-LI	Chancay-LI	Moche-F	Chen Chen-MH	Wari-MH
M2. Groove pattern	Y/Y.X.+	%	34.5	30	0	27.8	40	19.1	25
		N	139	30	10	18	5	47	12
M3. Groove pattern	Y/Y.X.+	%	16.8	12.5	10	33.3	44.4	28.6	12.5
		N	107	32	20	12	9	35	8
M1. Cusp number	6/4–6	%	37.6	39.3	50	9.5	16.7	2	0
		N	133	28	4	21	6	50	16
M2. Cusp number	4/4–6	%	2.8	0	10	36.4	42.9	51	66.7
		N	108	24	10	22	7	49	15
M3. Cusp number	4/3–6	%	8.5	4.2	21	17.6	0	50	40
		N	94	24	19	17	10	48	10
M1. Protostylid	1–7/0–7	%	57.1	60.5	33.3	15.4	33.3	2.4	11.1
		N	156	38	3	13	3	41	9
M2. Protostylid	1–7/0–7	%	58.9	60	100	28.6	0	4.8	14.3
		N	141	35	3	14	4	42	7
M1. Cusp 5	3–5/0–5	%	97	93.1	100	93.8	75	85.4	85.7
		N	135	29	4	16	4	48	14
M2. Cusp 5	3–5/0–5	%	82.9	96.2	85.7	52.6	42.9	44	18.2
		N	111	26	7	19	7	50	11
M3. Cusp 5	3–5/0–5	%	74.7	68	61.1	40	55.6	36.2	40
		N	91	25	18	15	9	47	10
M1. Cusp 6	2–5/0–5	%	33.3	34.5	50	3.4	16.7	4.3	0
		N	135	29	4	29	6	47	17
M2. Cusp 6	2–5/0–5	%	29.7	30.8	28.6	3.8	11.1	3.9	0
		N	111	26	7	26	9	51	16
M3. Cusp 6	2–5/0–5	%	33	52	27.8	15.8	16.7	6.4	7.1
		N	94	25	18	19	12	47	14
M1. Cusp 7	1–4/0–4	%	15.7	48.4	0	0	0	2.1	0
		N	153	31	9	30	6	47	18

Continued

Table 25.3b *Sample Size and Frequencies of Traits Used for the Mandibular Dentition—Continued*

Traits	Dichotomy		Chiribaya-LI	Yaral-LI	Titicaca-LI	Chancay-LI	Moche-F	Chen Chen-MH	Wari-MH
M2. Cusp 7	1–4/0–4	%	2.9	9.7	0	0	0	0	0
		N	140	31	12	27	9	49	16
M3. Cusp 7	1–4/0–4	%	6	16.7	0	5.9	0	0	7.1
		N	117	30	17	17	12	46	14
C. Root number	1/1–2	%	100	97.6	100	100	100	100	100
		N	165	41	33	57	27	107	22
M1. Root number	3/1–3	%	2.9	7.7	16.7	2.4	15	2.1	0
		N	172	39	24	42	20	96	15
M2. Root number	1/1–3	%	23.3	37.8	44.4	14.3	23.1	29.8	33.3
		N	150	37	18	28	13	84	12
M3. Root number	1/1–3	%	33	22.6	37.5	64.3	50	56.7	50
		N	112	31	16	14	8	60	10

Dichotomy shows the ASUDAS breaking points applied.

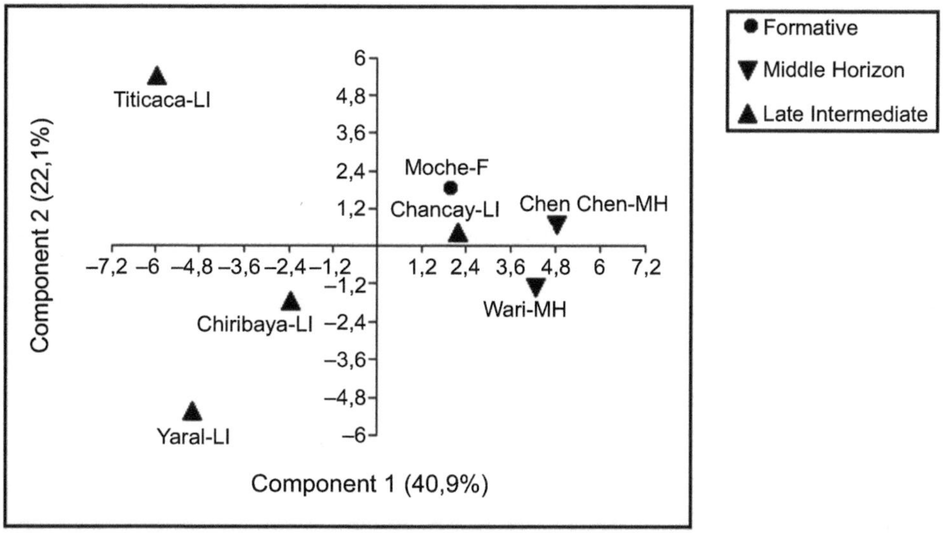

FIGURE 25.2

Principal component analysis; scatterplot of the first and second components.

recommended by Green and Suchey (1976). An MMD calculated between sample pairs is a dissimilarity measure; thus lower values indicate greater affinity (Irish, 2010). Samples significantly differ from one another when the MMD value is twice or more its standard deviation (Sjøvold, 1977).

The MMD values (and their relative standard deviation) are listed for each sample in Table 25.4. The matrix shows morphological distances that denote chronological patterns of continuity in both the Central Coast and the South Central one. Similar to the PCA plot, Chen Chen shows greater similarity with the Wari and Moche groups, while greater distance can be appreciated with Late Intermediate Titicaca and Yaral groups.

***Table 25.4** Mean Measure of Divergence Matrix*

	Moche-F	Chancay-LI	Chiribaya-LI	Chen Chen-MH	Wari-MH	Titicaca-LI	El Yaral-LI
Moche-F	0	0.0486	**0.0421**	**0.0434**	0.0579	**0.0554**	**0.0448**
Chancay-LI	0.0109	0	**0.0244**	**0.0236**	0.0386	**0.0359**	**0.0249**
Chiribaya-LI	0.1299	0.069	0	**0.0191**	**0.0316**	**0.0308**	0.0219
Chen Chen-MH	0.0169	0.0687	0.328	0	0.034	0.0304	**0.0201**
Wari-MH	−0.0544	−0.0172	0.228	−0.0588	0	**0.0444**	**0.0341**
Titicaca-LI	0.3209	0.2695	0.1485	0.6475	0.5033	0	**0.0318**
El Yaral-LI	0.1579	0.1821	0.0076	0.4167	0.3088	0.2199	0

MMDs are listed in the lower left triangle, standard deviation (s.d.) values are set in the upper right. Statistically significant distances are represented by values in bold.

The application of MDS to the standardized matrix of divergence permitted a two-dimensional visual representation of the in-between sample affinities quantified through the MMD (Fig. 25.3) using the software PAST 5. The MDS employs each of the MMD values as Euclidean distances; the samples showing the greatest similarities are plotted closer to each other on the resulting scatterplot. The goodness of fit of the scaled data compared to the unscaled data in a reduced space was then quantified using the stress value; the lower the stress, the better the fit. In the present case a stress value of 0.0001 indicates a good representation of the data.

The resulting plot (Fig. 25.3) once again confirms the scenario observed in both the PCA and MMD. Moche and Wari groups manifest closer relationships with Chen Chen, with Wari directly connected to the latter. On the other side, and farther from this group, we find the three other Late Intermediate groups, interconnected to one another. A closer inspection of the first cluster again shows that the Titicaca Late Intermediate sample has some peculiarities and tends to separate somewhat from all other samples. The Yaral sample from an inland site plots close to the coastal valley South Central Andean samples but, once again, slightly detached from the other samples comprising the cluster.

Whereas PCA and MDS procedures categorize the data based upon a predetermined number of dimensions, the Hierarchical CA creates natural groupings in the data. This analysis was employed to further investigate the biological relations among the samples. The diagram produced using Ward's grouping method is shown in Fig. 25.4.

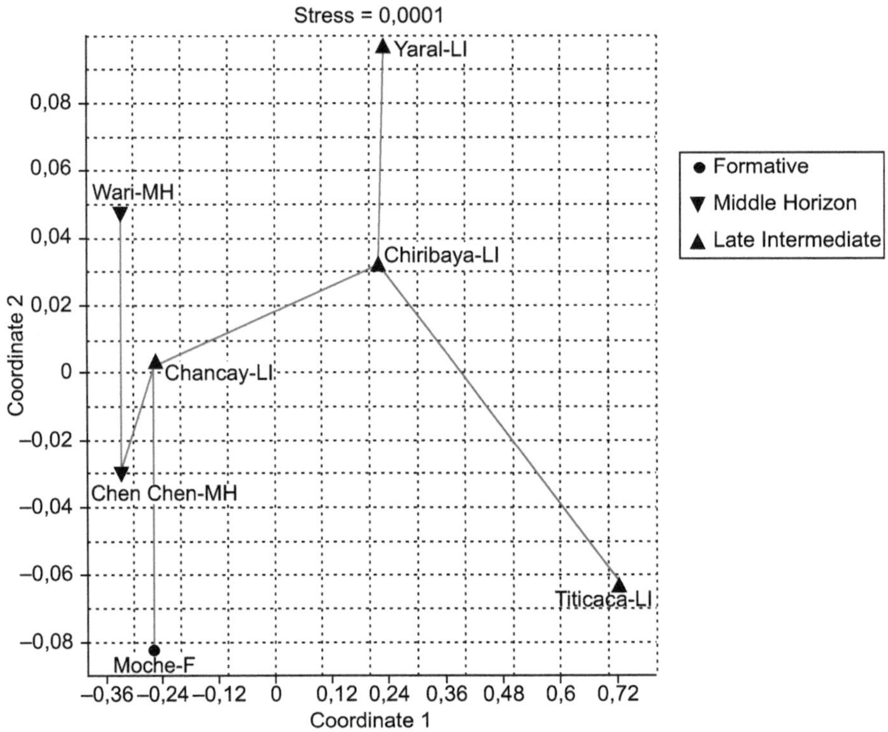

FIGURE 25.3

Bidimensional distribution of multidimensional scalings.

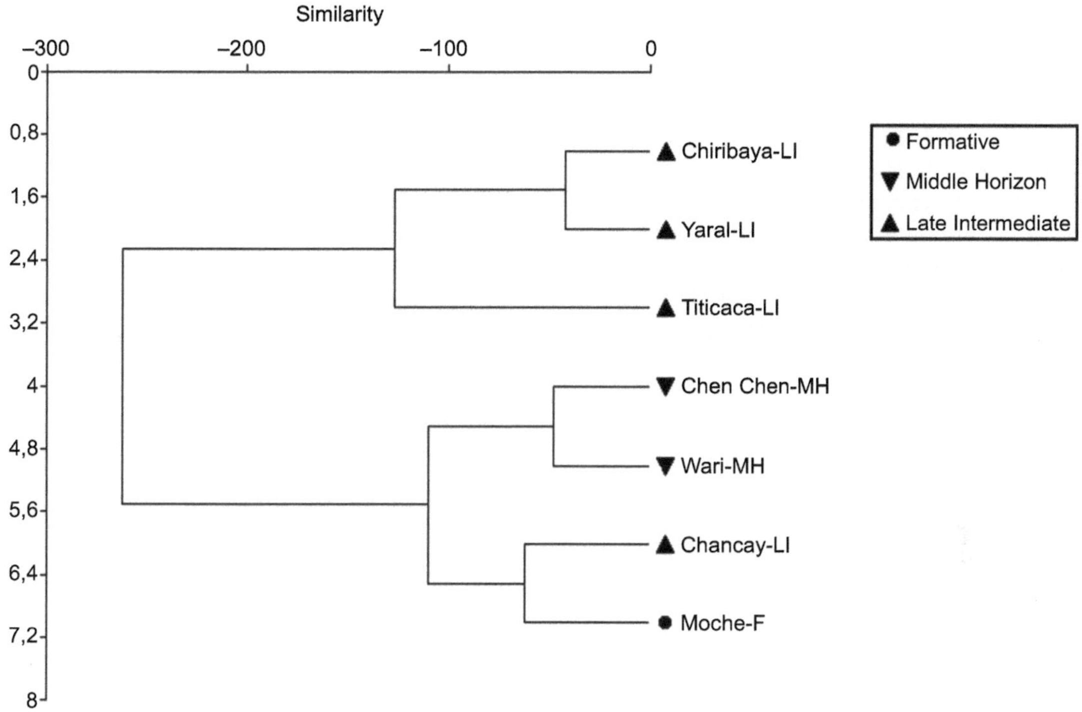

FIGURE 25.4

Ward's linkage hierarchical dendrogram.

The dendrogram separates the samples into two large clusters, which are consistent with the ones previously identified through the other multivariate statistics. Consequently, Moche, Wari, Chancay, and Chen Chen samples are separated from all the other samples observed.

In particular, a closer observation of the first of these main clusters indicates that Chen Chen not only clusters with the Moche, Wari, and Chancay, but it shows the greatest affinity with the contemporaneous Wari sample, clustering directly with it. Similarly, a closer inspection of the second cluster shows that the Titicaca Late Intermediate sample sets apart from the subcluster formed by the other South Central Andean samples.

DISCUSSION

In the last decades, various bioarchaeological investigations have focused on the cultural and genetic changes that took place in the Osmore Valley in pre-Inca times (Blom et al., 1998; Lozada, 1998; Moraga et al., 2005; Sutter, 1997, 2000, 2005; Sutter and Mertz, 2004; Sutter and Sarrat, 2010). Still, many issues and contrasting hypotheses concerning the biological relationships among Andean populations are far from resolved (Rothhammer and Silva, 1989).

Bioarchaeological studies of cranial deformation and biological affinities (Blom, 1999, 2005; Blom et al., 1998) suggest close relationships between the Tiwanaku colonists in the Osmore Valley (ie, Chen Chen) and highland populations. Recently, strontium and oxygen isotope analyses also indicate migratory movement of people from the southern Titicaca basin into the Tiwanaku colonies in the valley (Goldstein, 2013; Knudson et al., 2004). However, these biodistance studies did not take into consideration samples from other regions.

Contrary to expectations, the present study shows that the skeletal remains from Chen Chen are biologically distant from all the other samples in the Osmore Valley, showing no relation with the earlier or later samples of the Coastal Valleys, or even with the Titicaca samples. From this perspective, we would have expected a similarity to the Late Intermediate groups from the Lake Titicaca basin; yet the Titicaca sample, formed by individuals from archaeological sites located on the western shores of the Titicaca basin, never clusters close, or in some relation to, Chen Chen.

On the contrary, the multivariate analyses clearly show a direct link between Chen Chen and Wari, and to a lesser extent with the Moche. These culturally affiliated samples consist of skeletal remains from sites located south and north of Lima. Despite the fact that archaeological evidence proposes different scenarios (Goldstein, 2013), these results could be interpreted in light of archaeological data (Moseley et al., 1991, 2005; Owen, 1994, 2005) that suggest a face-to-face contact between Tiwanaku and Wari colonists in the Middle Osmore Valley, also in light of the geographical proximity between Chen Chen and Cerro Baul, the Wari outpost located some 20 km away from Chen Chen (Williams, 2001). Such a discrepancy may also rest on the heterogeneity within the Tiwanaku colonists, a diversity that has not yet been investigated through the lens of bioarchaeology.

As Goldstein (2013, p. 51) stated, Omo-style and Chen Chen-style represent two distinct Tiwanaku diasporas that coexisted in time and space, yet remained separate, perhaps representing independent action by two Tiwanaku "moieties, ethnic groups, or maximal ayllus" (2013). The availability of skeletal remains from the diverse groups would help us to understand such differences; unfortunately there is a generalized lack of materials that limits a clearer understanding of the complex population dynamics.

Similarly, the present study also lacks direct comparisons with original Tiwanaku skeletal samples; in fact, contrary to Sutter (1997), Blom's study (1999) did not publish dental nonmetric frequencies that would have constituted important comparative materials. Given this, we must of necessity maintain caution in any interpretation of the results.

The second set of evidence obtained from this study concerns the relationships between Tiwanaku and the Osmore Valley coast. It has long been thought that the collapse of Tiwanaku was followed by a second diaspora of Tiwanaku colonists toward the valley's coastal fringes (Owen, 2005). While continuity is chronologically possible, as suggested by various scholars (Owen, 1993; Stanish, 1992; Sutter, 2000, 2005), other studies (Lozada, 1998; Lozada and Buikstra, 2002) suggest that the Chiribaya groups were biologically distant from the Middle Osmore Tiwanaku colonists. Indeed, our results show no ties between the supposed Middle Horizon Tiwanaku colony of Chen Chen and the later coastal Chiribaya inhabitants, and are therefore consistent with Lozada's hypothesis and contrast with the idea of an intrusive highland population in the Coastal Osmore Valley.

Furthermore, the similarity between the supposed Tiwanaku colony of Chen Chen and the contemporaneous Wari inhabitants forces us to reconsider the very attribution and interpretation of Chen Chen, as well as the possible relations between the different populations settled in the Osmore Valley during the Middle Horizon.

The clear separation between coastal and highland samples seems to indicate a geographic or cultural barrier to the gene flow within the Coastal and Middle Osmore Valley. The Late Intermediate Yaral sample comes from a site (see Fig. 25.1) close to the junction between the Middle Osmore Valley and the dry, inhospitable region before the coastline. The fact that Yaral clusters with the coastal groups and is found farther from the Tiwanaku colony of Chen Chen seems to confirm the fact that Tiwanaku did not establish outposts all the way to the Pacific coast. It is, however, fundamental to stress that the present study could not use any true Tiwanaku samples.

Therefore, if the morphological distinction between the Chiribaya and Tiwanaku outpost of Chen Chen dismisses the hypothesis of a Tiwanaku origin for the former group, by itself it does not provide any information on the origins of the Chiribaya population. From this perspective, the strong morphological affinity encountered in this study suggests an ancestor—descendent relationship between the Chiribaya and the cultures that flourished in the Coastal Osmore Valley prior to their development, and at the same time supports the hypothesis of biocultural homogeneity among the Chiribayas (Lozada, 1998; Lozada and Buikstra, 2002; Sutter, 1997, 2000, 2005).

Lastly, the Late Intermediate Titicaca group does not fit into any of the models described in this study. This sample comes from the northwestern side of the Titicaca basin, far from the Tiwanaku territories. Its location away from Wari, Tiwanaku, and Chiribaya groups seems to indicate a community potentially characterized by isolation by distance. From this perspective it is not surprising that this sample shows unusual frequencies of some dental traits, suggesting genetic drift and founder effects.

In conclusion, the present study has shed further light on the complex dynamics that characterized the region before the conquest and that go beyond the valley's natural and political borders, and at the same time generates further questions for future research. The results once again confirm the absence of a single, general model capable of accounting for the great complexity and the regional differences observed in the biological and cultural history of the pre-Inca populations of the Osmore Valley.

The different dental anthropological studies conducted on remains from the area have all been very informative; however, one great obstacle must be overcome before they can also contribute to a reliable interpretation of the human dynamics in the area during prehistoric times. An effort needs to be made in order to allow the comprehensive study of all populations with homogeneous methodologies to allow the definitive placement of each population. This would require the authors to pool raw data, or at the very least, publish the trait frequencies for each of the populations studied, to finally allow a true synthesis.

Acknowledgments

We acknowledge the Italian Ministry of Education, University and Scientific Research (AOODGSINFS), Rome, for funding the data collection in Peru. We are grateful to Edmundo Moreno Terraza and Edmundo de la Vega, Universidad Nacional del Altiplano, Puno, Peru for granting access to the materials from the Lake Titicaca. The present publication was made possible by CONACyT grants CB-2010-154750 and I0010-2014-02-232831, and by UC-MEXUS Program (University of California Riverside) to A.C.

References

Blom, D.E., Hallgrimsson, B., Keng, L., Lozada, M.C., Buikstra, J.E., 1998. Tiwanaku state colonization: bioarchaeological implications for migration in the Moquegua Valley, Perù. World Archaeology 30 (2), 238–261.

Blom, D.E., 1999. Tiwanaku Regional Interaction and Social Identity: A Bioarchaeological Approach (Ph.D. dissertation). University of Chicago, Chicago.

Blom, D.E., 2005. Embodying borders: human body modification and diversity in Tiwanaku society. Journal of Anthropological Archaeology 24, 1–24.

Browman, D.L., 1980. Tiwanaku expansion and altipiano economic patterns. Estudios Arqueológicos 5, 107–120.
Browman, D.L., 1984. Tiwanaku development of interzonal trade and economic expansion in the altiplano. In: Browman, D.L., Burger, L., Rivera, M.A. (Eds.), Social and Economic Organization in the Prehispanic Andes. BAR International Series, vol. 194. British Archaeological Reports, Oxford, pp. 117–142.
Buikstra, J.E., Lozada, M.C., Rakita, G., Tomczak, P., 1998. Fechados radiocarbonico de sitios Chiribaya en la cuenca del Rio Osmore. In: Paper Presented at Seminario Sobre Archaeologia de Ilo. Pontificia Universidad Catolica del Peru, Lima.
Burgess, S.D., 1999. Chiribayan Skeletal Pathology on the South Coast of Perú: Patterns of Production and Consumption (Ph.D. dissertation). University of Chicago, Chicago.
Cavalli Sforza, L.L., Menozzi, P., Piazza, A., 1994. The History and Geography of Human Genes. Princetown University Press, Princetown.
Coppa, A., Cucina, A., Mancinelli, D., Vargiu, R., Calcagno, J., 1998. Dental anthropology of central-southern Iron Age Italy: the evidence of metric versus non-metric traits. American Journal of Physical Anthropology 107, 371–386.
Coppa, A., Cucina, A., Lucci, M., Mancinelli, D., Vargiu, R., 2007. Origins and spread of agriculture in Italy: a nonmetric dental analysis. American Journal of Physical Anthropology 133, 918–930.
Dillehay, T.D., Nuñez, L., 1988. Camelids, caravans and complex societies in the South-Central Andes. In: Saunders, N.J., de Montmollin, O. (Eds.), Recent Studies in Precolumbian Archaeology. BAR International Series, vol. 421. British Archaeological Reports, Oxford, pp. 603–634.
Goldstein, P.S., 2013. Tiwanaku and Wari state expansion: demographic and outpost colonization compared. In: Vranich, A., Stanish, C. (Eds.), Visions of Tiwanaku. Cotsen Institute of Archaeology, Los Angeles, pp. 41–63.
Green, R.F., Suchey, J.M., 1976. The use of inverse sine transformations in the analysis of non-metric cranial data. American Journal of Physical Anthropology 45, 61–68.
Hotelling, H., 1933. Analysis of complex statistical variables into principal components. Journal of Educational Psychology 24, 417–441.
Irish, J.D., 2010. The mean measure of divergence: its utility in model-free and model-bound analyses relative to the Mahalanobis D^2 distance for nonmetric traits. American Journal of Human Biology 22, 378–395.
Kemp, B.M., Tung, T.A., Summar, M.L., 2009. Genetic continuity after the collapse of the Wari empire: mitochondrial DNA profiles from Wari and post-Wari populations in the ancient Andes. American Journal of Physical Anthropology 140, 80–91.
Knudson, K.J., Tung, T.A., 2011. Investigating regional mobility in the southern hinterland of the Wari Empire: biogeochemistry at the site of Beringa, Peru. American Journal of Physical Anthropology 145, 299–310.
Knudson, K.J., Price, T.D., Buikstra, J.E., Blom, D.E., 2004. The use of strontium isotope analysis to investigate Tiwanaku migration and mortuary ritual in Bolivia and Peru. Archaeometry 46, 5–18.
Lozada, M.C., Buikstra, J., 2002. El Señorio de Chiribaya en la Costa Sur del Perú. IED Edition, Lima.
Lozada, M.C., 1998. The Senorío of Chiribaya: A Bioarchaeological Study in the Osmore Drainage of Southern Perú (Ph.D. dissertation). University of Chicago, Chicago.
Moraga, M., Santoro, C.M., Standen, V.G., Carvallo, P., Rothhammer, F., 2005. Microevolution in prehistoric Andean populations: chronological mtDNA variation in the desert valleys of northern Chile. American Journal of Physical Anthropology 127 (2), 170–181.
Moseley, M.E., Feldman, R.A., Goldstein, P.S., Watanabe, L., 1991. Colonies and conquest: Tiahuanaco and Huari in Moquegua. In: Isbell, W.H., McEwan, G.F. (Eds.), Huari Administrative Structure: Prehistoric Monumental Architecture and State Government. Dumbarton Oaks, Washington, DC, pp. 121–140.
Moseley, M.E., Nash, D.J., Williams, P.R., de France, S., Miranda, A., Ruales, M., 2005. Burning down the brewery: establishing and evacuating an ancient imperial colony at Cerro Baul, Peru. Proceedings of the National Academy of Sciences of the United States of America 102 (48), 17264–17271.
Nash, D.J., Williams, P.R., 2005. Architecture and power on the Wari–Tiwanaku frontier. Archaeological Papers of the American Anthropological Association 14, 151–174.

Owen, B., 1993. A Model of Multiethnicity: State Collapse, Competition and Social Complexity from Tiwanaku to Chiribaya in the Osmore Valley, Peru. Department of Anthropology, University of California, Los Angeles.
Owen, B., 1994. Were Wari and Tiwanaku in conflict, competition, or complementary coexistence? Survey evidence from the upper Osmore drainage, Perú. In: Paper Presented at the Society for American Archaeology 59th Annual Meeting.
Owen, B., 2005. Distant colonies and explosive collapse: the two stages of the Tiwanaku diaspora in the Osmore drainage. Latin American Antiquity 16 (1), 45–80.
Rice, D.S., 1989. Osmore drainage, Perú: the ecological setting. In: Rice, D.S., Stanish, C., Scarr, P.R. (Eds.), Ecology. Settlement and History in the Osmore Drainage, Perú, vol. 545. BAR, International Series, Oxford, pp. 17–34.
Rostworowsky, M., 1977. Coastal fishermen, merchants and artisans in prehispanic Peru. In: Benson, E. (Ed.), The Sea in the Pre-columbian World. Dumbarton Oaks, Washington, DC, pp. 167–186.
Rothhammer, F., Silva, C., 1989. Peopling of Andean South America. American Journal of Physical Anthropology 78, 403–410.
Scott, G.R., Turner, C.G., 1997. The Anthropology of Modern Human Teeth: Dental Morphology and Its Variation in Recent Human Populations. Cambridge University Press, Cambridge.
Scott, G.R., 1980. Population variation of Carabelli's trait. Human Biology 52, 63–78.
Sjøvold, T., 1977. Non-metrical divergence between skeletal populations. Ossa 4, 1–33.
Slovak, N.M., Paytan, A., Wiegand, B.A., 2009. Reconstructing Middle Horizon mobility patterns on the coast of Peru through strontium isotope analysis. Journal of Archaeological Science 36, 157–165.
Stanish, C., 1992. Ancient Andean Political Economy. University of Texas Press, Austin.
Sutter, R.C., Mertz, L., 2004. Nonmetric cranial trait variation and prehistoric biocultural change in the Azapa Valley, Chile. American Journal of Physical Anthropology 123 (2), 130–145.
Sutter, R.C., Sarrat, N., 2010. Continuity and transformation during the terminal Middle Horizon (AD 950–1150): a bioarchaeological assessment of Tumilaca origins within the Middle Moquegua Valley, Peru. Latin American Antiquity 21 (1), 67–86.
Sutter, R.C., 1997. Dental Variation and Biocultural Affinities among Prehistoric Populations from the Coastal Valleys of Moquegua, Perú, and Azapa, Chile (Ph.D. dissertation). University of Missouri-Columbia, Columbia.
Sutter, R.C., 2000. Prehistoric genetic and culture change: a bioarchaeological search for pre-Inca altipiano colonies in the coastal valleys of Moquegua, Peru, and Azapa, Chile. Latin American Antiquity 11 (1), 43–70.
Sutter, R.C., 2005. The prehistoric peopling of South America as inferred from genetically controlled dental traits. Andean Past 7, 183–217.
Tung, T.A., Knudson, K.J., 2011. Identifying locals, migrants, and captives in the Wari Heartland: a bioarchaeological and biogeochemical study of human remains from Conchopata, Peru. Journal of Anthropological Archaeology 30, 247–261.
Turner II, C.G., Nichol, C.R., Scott, G.R., 1991. Scoring procedures for key morphological traits of the permanent dentition: the Arizona State University dental anthropology system. In: Kelley, M.A., Larsen, C.S. (Eds.), Advances in Dental Anthropology. Wiley Sons, New York, pp. 13–31.
Williams, P.R., 2001. Cerro Baul: a Wari center on the Tiwanaku frontier. Latin American Antiquity 12, 67–83.

Appendix: Biodistance Resources

DATASETS

Howells Dataset

William W. Howells Craniometric Data Set, made available by Dr. Benjamin M. Auerbach at the following website: http://web.utk.edu/~auerbach/HOWL.htm (accessed May 2016).

Ossenberg Dataset

Nancy S. Ossenberg cranial nonmetric data, made available by Queen's University at the following website: http://library.queensu.ca/data/cntd (accessed May 2016).

Dental Metrics

A compilation of raw data from several sources and time periods. Also includes Neanderthals and nonhuman primates, at http://anthropologicaldata.free.fr/webteeth/index.html (accessed May 2016).

Konigsberg Ancient Dataset

A self-extracting *.exe file that contains nonmetric trait data from prehistoric sites in West Central Illinois (see http://konig.la.utk.edu/Traits.pdf for trait list), at http://konig.la.utk.edu/illnonm.exe (accessed May 2016).

Goldman Postcranial Dataset

Prehistoric postcranial dataset compiled by Dr. Benjamin Auerbach from skeletal collections housed around the world, at http://web.utk.edu/~auerbach/GOLD.htm (accessed May 2016).

FREE STATISTICAL PROGRAMS

PopTools

PopTools is an add-in for Microsoft Excel that aids in the analysis of matrix population models, at http://www.poptools.org/ (accessed May 2016).

RMet

Computer program used to calculate the R matrix from skeletal measurements. The program is made available by John Relethford and the State University of New York at Oneonta at the following website: http://employees.oneonta.edu/relethjh/programs/ (accessed May 2016).

R

Open-source system for statistical computation and graphics. Available from the Comprehensive R Archive Network (CRAN) at the following website: https://cran.r-project.org/bin/windows/base/ (accessed May 2016).

3D-ID

Java program that uses 3D coordinate data on cranial remains to aid in the estimation of ancestry and sex within a forensic context, at http://www.3d-id.org/ (accessed May 2016).

CranID

Freeware program that employs 29 measurements of the skull to aid in assessing biological ancestry. The program has been employed in archaeological and forensic contexts, at http://osteoware.si.edu/forum/osteoware-communityannouncements/cranid-richard-wright-0 (accessed May 2016).

COLIPR

Coordinate-based Legal Investigation Program (COLIPR) is a computer program that employs cranial measurements to aid in sex estimations of skeletal remains, at https://is.muni.cz/publication/764216?lang=en (accessed May 2016).

Morphologika

At https://sites.google.com/site/hymsfme/downloadmorphologica (accessed May 2016).

EVAN Toolbox

Software package developed by the European Virtual Anthropology Network (EVAN) and the EVAN Society to conduct form and shape analyses. The package uses geometric morphometrics and methods such as Principal Components Analysis, General Procurstes Analysis, and Thin-Plate Spline Warping, at http://www.evan-society.org/node/23 (accessed May 2016).

MorphoJ

A Java-based software program for geometric morphometric analysis, at http://www.flywings.org.uk/MorphoJ_page.htm (accessed May 2016).

Morpheus et al.

Comprehensive, cross-platform package for the acquisition, processing, and analysis of morphometric data. Versions for AIX, DOS/WIN, LINUX, and SGI, at http://morphlab.sc.fsu.edu/software.html (accessed May 2016).

Geoda

Open-source, cross-platform program for spatial data analysis, at https://geodacenter.asu.edu/projects/opengeoda (accessed May 2016).

PAST (3.x—the Past of the Future)

PAST is software for scientific data analysis, with functions for data manipulation, plotting, univariate and multivariate statistics, ecological analysis, time series and spatial analysis, morphometrics, and stratigraphy, at http://folk.uio.no/ohammer/past/ (accessed May 2016).

Landmark Editor

This program aids in the analysis of landmark and semilandmark data, at http://graphics.idav.ucdavis.edu/research/EvoMorph (accessed May 2016).

OTHER FREE PROGRAMS

Osteoware

Software program designed to aid in the standardized collection of skeletal data, at http://osteoware.si.edu/ (accessed May 2016).

3Skull

Software program that works with three-dimensional coordinate landmark data, at http://math.mercyhurst.edu/~sousley/Software/3Skull/contact.php (accessed May 2016).

R RESOURCES

R script to calculate Mahalanobis distance using binary traits.

Instructions and script made available by Lyle Konigsberg at the following website: https://50fc25581bb4561d048337efb1525036fe6ae84e.googledrive.com/host/0B-YNQGBRIWzxfmtwSUZreXpWTk1kVDA1TDVpVEZkd2ZhZnUzbEt6WjJDTTRlNEsyWU1ST0E/ (accessed May 2016).

AnthropMMD

A GUI for mean measure of divergence, at https://cran.r-project.org/web/packages/AnthropMMD/index.html (accessed May 2016).

R Studio Resource List

At https://support.rstudio.com/hc/en-us/articles/200552336-Getting-Help-with-R (accessed May 2016).

R for Beginners

At https://cran.r-project.org/doc/contrib/Paradis-rdebuts_en.pdf (accessed May 2016).

Quick R

Website with many R shortcuts and codes, at http://www.statmethods.net/ (accessed May 2016).

OTHER PROGRAMS FOR PURCHASE

FORDISC

Statistical program used to estimate ancestry based on a large sample population using any combination of standard cranial measurements. The program may be purchased at the following website: https://secure.touchnet.com/C21610_ustores/web/store_main.jsp?STOREID=15&SINGLESTORE=true (accessed May 2016).

Surfer

3D surface plotting and contouring program, at http://www.ssg-surfer.com/ (accessed May 2016).

Clustan

Statistical program that specializes in data mining and cluster analysis, at http://www.clustan.com/ (accessed May 2016).

Index

'*Note:* Page numbers followed by "f" indicate figures and "t" indicate tables.'

A

Afridont, 119, 119f
Anatomical landmarks, 37–38
Ancestry, 3–4, 12–13, 66–68, 75, 213–230, 268, 274, 285–299, 301–315, 318, 323, 370, 399–401, 448
Ancient DNA (aDNA), 12
Anterior teeth, 112–113
Arizona State University Dental Anthropology System (ASUDAS), 110

B

Bagging, 204–205
Bantu groups, 245
  dental trait recording, 366–367
  history, 365
  materials, 364–365, 364t, 371t–373t
  model-bound quantitative analyses, 368–370
  model-free quantitative analyses, 367–368
  population hypotheses/expectations, 370
  results, 370–379
    model-bound quantitative analyses, 375–379, 380t–381t, 383f, 383t
    model-free quantitative analyses, 374–375, 375f, 377t–378t
  samples and context, 365
Bioarchaeological applications, 148
Bioarchaeological/forensic approaches, 52–55
Boosting, 204–205
Bootstrapped cross-validation (BSCV), 203–204
Box measurements, 37
Bracero program, 233
Bregma–lambda chord, 39–40
Buccolingual diameter, 137

C

Canines, 111–113
Canonical analysis of principal (CAP) coordinates, 302, 304–306
Canonical discriminant analysis (CANDISC), 236
Caucasoid dental complex, 120
Chi-square metrics, 305
Clone theory, 136
Coefficient of racial likeness (CRL), 10
Comparative skeletal assemblages, 449, 450t–452t, 453f
Cranial measurements, 38
Cranial modification, 93–94
Cranial nonmetric trait data
  defined, 213–214
  materials and methods, 215–219
    decision tree, 218
    machine learning, 215–218
    random forest, 218–219
    statistical models, 215
    support vector machines (SVM), 219
    variable selection, 215, 216t–217t
  results, 219–221, 219t, 220f–221f, 222t
    biological distance, 225–226
    phenotypic variation, 223–225
    SVM models, 223
Cranial shape variation, global patterns
  materials, 429
  methods, 429–432, 430f, 431t
  results, 432–435, 433t, 434f, 439t
Craniomandibular variation, 436–441
  materials, 437
  methods, 437
  results, 437–440, 438f, 439t
Craniometric analysis, 4–6
Craniometric data analysis
  bioarchaeological and forensic approaches, 52–55
    common statistical methods, 53–55, 54f
  data collection protocols, 37–49
    error, 46–48
    instrumentation, 41–45, 42f–45f
    measurements types, 37–40, 38t–39t, 40f
    procedures, 48–49
    recording measurements options, 46
    selecting measurements, 40–41
  heritability, 49–52
  history, 36–37
Crown height, 137–139
Cusp number, 319

D

Data sets
  biological distance measures, 98–102
    bioarchaeology, 99–101
    forensic anthropology, 101–102
  cranial nonmetric data sets, 93–96
    data collection protocols, 94–95

Data sets (*Continued*)
heritability and cranial nonmetric traits, 95–96
morphoscopic data, 97–98
data collection protocols, 97, 98t
morphoscopic traits heritability, 98
3-D craniofacial morphological analysis
Brazilian groups, morphological affinity of, 79–80
African Brazilians/African Americans and Native Africans, 80, 82f–83f, 83t
European/Brazilians and Iberian populations, 79, 79t
Japanese Brazilians/Asians/Mesoamericans and South Americans, 80, 80t, 81f
computer-aided landmark processing, 66–68, 67f–68f
materials
ancestry assessment, 75, 76t
Brazilian data sets, 71, 71t
central European data sets, diachronic changes in, 72–73, 74f
3D-ID database, 68–69
European data sets, 69–71
European samples validation, 74–75
forensic 3-D database—European data sets, 76, 77t
methods, 72, 72t
morphological variation, brazilian groups, 76–79
Portuguese sample, intrapopulation variation for, 73
sex estimation, 74–75, 74t, 75f
reference data sets, 65–66
sex and ancestry assessment, 66–68
Decision tree, 218
Dental development, 136
Dental metrics, 9
alternative measurements, 139–140
bioarchaeological applications, 148
biological considerations
age, 142
sex, 141–142
stress, 143
buccolingual diameter, 137
crown height, 137–139
data, 136–140
dental development, 136
forensic applications, 147–148
heritability, 140
mesiodistal diameter, 137
population variation and evolution, 146–147
statistical analysis
negate multicollinearity methods, 144–146
observer error, 143–144
sexual dimorphism, 144
Dental morphological traits, 8–9
background, 318–322
developmental influences, 319
genes influencing, 319–320
genetic effects, quantitative analyses of, 320–321
statistical issues, 321–322
bioarchaeological application, 122–123
intracemetery, 123
population level, 123
data collection and treatment, 116–118, 117t
defined, 109
dental development, 114–115
evolution, 123–125
anatomically modern humans, 124–125
hominins, 124
forensic application, 117t, 120–122
heritability, 113–114
materials, 322, 322t
methods, 323–324, 323t
population variation, 118–120
Afridont, 119, 119f
Eurodont, 120, 120f
Sinodont/Sundadont, 118–119, 119f
results, 324–326, 324t–325t, 327t, 328f
terminology, 111–113, 112t
threshold traits, 115
Dichotomous traits, 92
Differential long-range gene flow, 29–30
Discontinuous traits, 92
Discriminant function analysis (DFA), 51, 238–241, 240f, 241t, 285–286

E

EDARV370A, 320
Eigenvalues, 453–454
Electronic data, 46
Elliptical Fourier analysis (EFA), 139
Epigenetic traits, 92
Equal-and-additive-effects model, 27
Euclidean distance, 24
Eurasian landmass
defined, 391–392
materials, 392, 393t, 394f, 395t
methods, 393–396, 396t
results, 396–399, 397f–403f
Bray-Curtis dissimilarity values, 396–397, 401–407
mtDNA analyses, 399–401
Neolithic period trees, 397–398
three-rooted LM1 (3RM1), 398–399
Eurodont, 120, 120f
Extreme curvature measurements, 37

F

FACTS. *See* Forensic Anthropology Center at Texas State (FACTS)
FORDISC 3.0, 287–288, 293–295
Forensic anthropology, 12–13
  Arizona/Texas migrants, 236
    forensic reference groups, 236
  background, 233–234
  canonical analysis of principal (CAP) coordinates, 302, 304–306
  materials and methods, 302–306, 303t
  model-bound methods, 232
  morphoscopic trait analysis, 301–302
  population groups
    craniometric data, 235–236, 236t
    forensic reference groups, 235, 235t
    migrant groups, 234–235, 235t
  results, 306–313, 307t–308t, 308f–312f, 310t–312t
    Arizona/Texas migrants, 236–238, 237f, 237t
    discriminant function analysis, 238–241, 240f, 241t
    forensic reference groups, 238, 238t–240t
  sample descriptions, 303, 303t
  US Border Patrol (USBP), 232
Forensic Anthropology Center at Texas State (FACTS), 234–235
Formal instrument calibration, 45
Formal observer error, 47
Freeman-Tukey angular transformation, 465–466
Frontal subtense (FRS), 37, 236–237
F-statistic (*F*ST)/inbreeding coefficient, 100–101

G

Genetic data collection
  global population samples, 167
  Norris Farms #36, 165–167
Genetic distances
  background, 158–161
  genetic *vs*. morphological comparisons, 168
  local interindividual analyses
    cranial *vs*. genetic distances, 169
    Norris Farms #36, 169
  methods, 161–168
    cranial landmark data, 167–168
    genetic data, 168
    genetic data collection. *See* Genetic data collection
    linear cranial data, 167
    morphological data collection. *See* Morphological data collection
    samples, 161
Genetic drift impact, 29

H

Hardy–Weinberg equilibrium, 49–50
Harpending–Ward model, 30
Heritability, 49–52
Hierarchical cluster analysis (HCA), 251–252
Hispanic samples, 306–309
Howells's Definitions, 36
Human variation, 12–13

I

Imputation methods
  defined, 183–186
  hot deck, 183
  iterative robust model-based imputations, 183–184
  k-Nearest Neighbor, 184–185
  materials, 182
  methods, 183–186
  variable mean, 185–186
Incisors, 111–113
Instrumentation, 44–45
Intercuspal dimensions, 139–140
Inter/intraobserver error, 7, 47, 81–82, 118, 143–144, 161–165
Interorbital breadth, 37
Intraobserver error, 47
IRMI. *See* Iterative robust model-based imputation (IRMI)
Iterative robust model-based imputation (IRMI), 183–184

J

Jackknifing residual variances, 30

K

Kernel probability density (KPD) classification, 202
Khoe-San contribution, 248
K-nearest neighbor analysis (kNN), 202

L

Leave-one-out cross-validation (LOOCV), 199, 206, 208–209
Linear discriminant function analysis (LDFA), 183
  defined, 197
  estimating classification accuracy, 198–199
  machine learning, 204–205
  materials and methods, 206
  measurements, 200–201
  overfitting, 199–200
  resampling, 202–204
  results and discussion, 206–210, 207t, 208f
  traditional classification methods, 201–202
  variance–covariance matrix (VCM), 197–198
Logistic regression (LR), 202

M

Machine learning (ML) methods, 204–205, 215–218
Macromorphoscopic Databank (MaMD), 97
Mahalanobis D^2, 100
Mahalanobis distance, 25
Mandibles
  biological distance studies, 448
  material and methods
    comparative skeletal assemblages, 449, 450t–452t, 453f
    measurements and multivariate statistics, 449–453, 454t
    Nankuanli East (NKLE) site, 449
    Shihsanhang site, Northwestern Taiwan, 449
  results
    Mahalanobis' generalized distance, 454–455, 457f
    stepwise discriminant function analysis, 453–454, 456f
Mass additive traits, 118–119
Maxillary observations, 324
Maxillo-alveolar breadth, 37
Maximum-likelihood variance components analysis, 96
Mean measure of divergence (MMD), 99–100, 122, 321–322, 465–471, 471t
Mesiodistal diameters, 116–117, 137
Mississippi State Asylum (MSA)
  defined, 286
  history, 286
  materials and methods, 287–289
    data collection/analysis, 288–289
    data collection and analysis, 288–289
    reference datasets. *See* Reference datasets
  results, 289–297, 290t–291t, 292f, 294f–296f
Moche collapses
  background, 351–352, 352f
  biodistance and population structure analyses, 353–356
  materials and methods, 352–356, 353f
  results
    biodistances and population structure, 356–358, 356t–357t
  R-matrix, 354–356
Molars, 111–113
Mongoloid Dental Complex, 118–119
Mongoloids, 121
Morphological data collection, 63, 81, 111, 114, 116, 123, 318, 322, 391–410
  global population samples, 165
  Norris Farms #36, 161–165, 163t–165t
Multivariate methods, 25

N

Nankuanli East (NKLE) site, 449
Natural philosophy, 4
k-Nearest Neighbor (kNN), 184–185
Negate multicollinearity methods, 144–146
Nonmetric trait analysis, 6–8
Normal mixtures clustering analysis (NMCA), 252, 257f, 259f

O

Observer error, 47–48, 143–144
  inter/intraobserver error, 7, 47, 81–82, 118, 143–144, 161–165
Optimized summed scored attribute (OSSA), 102, 285–286
Osmore Valley
  defined, 463
  materials and methods, 464–466, 464t, 465f, 466t
  results, 464–466, 464t, 465f, 466t–468t, 471t
Osteoware, 46
Ousley's analysis, 205

P

Patterning cascade model, 115
PCOME. *See* Pima County Office of the Medical Examiner (PCOME)
Phenotypic variation, 223–225
Pima County Office of the Medical Examiner (PCOME), 233–235
Polar teeth, 136
Population, 10–11, 165, 167–169, 234–236, 245–263, 307t–308t, 349–361, 370, 425–445
  analysis of variance, 415–416
  Australia = Europe ≠ New Guinea, 416
  Baffling convergence, 412–415
  biological distance measures, 98–102
    bioarchaeology, 99–101
    forensic anthropology, 101–102
  cranial nonmetric data sets, 93–96
    data collection protocols, 94–95
    heritability and cranial nonmetric traits, 95–96
  craniometric data analysis. *See* Craniometric data analysis
  defined, 245
  dendrograms, 417–421, 418t, 419f–420f
  differential long-range gene flow, 29–30
  distance values, 417, 418t
    correspondence between, 416–417, 417t
  Euclidean distance, 24
  genetic drift impact, 29
  Mahalanobis distance, 25
  methods, 412–415
  morphoscopic data, 97–98
    data collection protocols, 97, 98t
    morphoscopic traits heritability, 98
  New Guinea = Australia = Europe, 416
  New Guinea = Australia ≠ Europe, 416
  New Guinea = Europe ≠ Australia, 415–416

R-matrix theory, 25–26
quantitative traits, 26–28
in South Africa, 246–248
females, 253, 255t, 256f
genetic composition, 248
groups pooled sexes, 252–253, 253t, 254f
males, 253–255, 257t, 258f–259f
materials, 248–250, 249t, 250f
methods, 251–252, 251t
traits, 412, 413t–414t
variation, 118–120, 146–147
Population genetic theory, 11
Posterior teeth, 112–113
Postmarital residence analysis
defined, 335–336
quantitative trait phenotypic variability assessment, 337
dichotomous traits, 339–344, 340f–341f, 341t, 342f, 344f
prehistoric West Central Illinois, 338
within-site haplotypic diversity, 338–339, 339f
Premolars, 111–113
Principal components analysis (PCA), 141, 465–466

Q

Quadratic discriminant function analysis (QDFA), 201–202
Quantitative trait phenotypic variability assessment, 337
dichotomous traits, 339–344, 340f–341f, 341t, 342f, 344f
prehistoric West Central Illinois, 338
within-site haplotypic diversity, 338–339, 339f
Quantitative traits, 26–28
Quasi-continuous variables, 92

R

Race, 12–13, 36, 120–121, 146, 287, 295–297
Random forests method, 204–205, 218–219
Reference datasets
cranial macromorphoscopic traits, 288
dental metrics, 287
dental morphology, 287–288
Relethford–Blangero method, 30–31
Resampling methods, 204
R-matrix analysis, 354–356
R-matrix theory, 25–26

S

Sexual dimorphism, 144
Sharp/blunt teeth, 115
Short tandem repeats (STRs), 241
Shihsanhang site, Northwestern Taiwan, 449
Sinodont, 118–119, 119f
Sliding calipers, 41–42
Spreading calipers, 41–42
Squared distance, 24
Statistical approaches, 10–11
Structured query language (SQL), 46
Sundadont, 118–119, 119f
Support vector machines (SVM), 219
models, 223
Supraorbital projection, 39–40
Sutural measurements, 37

T

ThreeSkull, 46
Tooth size apportionment (TSA), 145–146

U

Unidentified decedent (UID)
Arizona/North Carolina, 268
deceased undocumented latinos, 267
foreign-born latinos, demographic profiles of, 266–267
geometric morphometrics, 269–271, 269t, 270f
isotopes, 274–275
isotope methods, 277
medical examiner/coroner's offices' casework issues, 268
results, 271–274, 271f–272f, 272t, 273f–274f, 277–278
sample, 269, 269t
two-pronged approach, 274–277, 276f
United States, 266
Unweighted Pair Group Method Algorithm (UPGMA), 452–455, 457f

V

Variable mean, 185–186
Variable selection, 215, 216t–217t
Variance–covariance matrix (VCM), 197–200
Variation measurement
analysis of variance, 415–416
Australia = Europe ≠ New Guinea, 416
Baffling convergence, 412–415
dendrograms, 417–421, 418t, 419f–420f
distance values, 417, 418t
correspondence between, 416–417, 417t
methods, 412–415
New Guinea = Australia = Europe, 416
New Guinea = Australia ≠ Europe, 416
New Guinea = Europe ≠ Australia, 415–416
traits, 412, 413t–414t

W

Wilks's lambda, 208–209, 208f

Z

Zygomaxillare radius, 40

FSC
www.fsc.org
MIX
Papier | Fördert gute Waldnutzung
FSC® C083411

Kolibri 360 GmbH
Ferdinand-Jühlke-Straße 7
99095 Erfurt, Deutschland
produktsicherheit@kolibri360.de